Macworld
Photoshop 2.5 Bible

Macworld
Photoshop 2.5 Bible

by Deke McClelland

IDG Books Worldwide, Inc.
An International Data Group Company

San Mateo, California ✦ Indianapolis, Indiana ✦ Boston, Massachusetts

Macworld Photoshop 2.5 Bible

Published by
IDG Books Worldwide, Inc.
An International Data Group Company
155 Bovet Road, Suite 310
San Mateo, CA 94402

Library of Congress Catalog Card No.: 93-78446

ISBN 1-56884-022-5

Printed in the United States of America

10 9 8 7 6 5 4

Distributed in the United States by IDG Books Worldwide, Inc.

Distributed in Canada by Macmillan of Canada, a Division of Canada Publishing Corporation; by Computer and Technical Books in Miami, Florida, for South America and the Caribbean; by Longman Singapore in Singapore, Malaysia, Thailand, and Korea; by Toppan Co. Ltd. in Japan; by Asia Computerworld in Hong Kong; by Woodslane Pty. Ltd. in Australia and New Zealand; and by Transworld Publishers Ltd. in the U.K. and Europe.

For information on where to purchase IDG Books outside the U.S., call Christina Turner at 415-312-0633.

For information on translations, contact Marc Jeffrey Mikulich, Foreign Rights Manager, at IDG Books Worldwide; FAX NUMBER 415-358-1260.

For sales inquiries and special prices for bulk quantities, write to the address above or call IDG Books Worldwide at 415-312-0650.

Dedication

To Elizabeth, whose companionship is a source of continual strength, and to Mom, whom I love dearly.

About the Author

A contributing editor to Macworld magazine, Deke McClelland also writes for PC World and Publish. He has authored nearly 30 books on desktop publishing and the Macintosh computer. He started out as artistic director at the first service bureau in the U.S. McClelland's awards include the Ben Franklin Award for the Best Computer Book, 1989; Computer Press Association, Best Product-Specific Book, 1990; Computer Press Association, Best Software Product Review, 1992.

Credits

Publisher
David Solomon

Acquisitions Editor
Janna Custer

Managing Editor
Mary Bednarek

Project Editors
Julie King
Diane Graves Steele

Editorial Assistant
Patricia R. Reynolds

Technical Reviewer
Ben Barbante

Production Manager
Beth Jenkins

Production Coordinator
Cindy L. Phipps

Production Staff
Mary Breidenbach
Drew Moore
Tony Augsburger

Proofreader
Sandy Grieshop

Indexer
Sherry Massey

Book Design
Beth Jenkins

About IDG Books Worldwide

Welcome to the world of IDG Books Worldwide.

IDG Books Worldwide, Inc., is a division of International Data Group, the world's largest publisher of computer-related information and the leading global provider of information services on information technology. IDG publishes over 194 computer publications in 62 countries. Forty million people read one or more IDG publications each month.

If you use personal computers, IDG Books is committed to publishing quality books that meet your needs. We rely on our extensive network of publications, including such leading periodicals as *Macworld*, *InfoWorld*, *PC World*, *Computerworld*, *Publish*, *Network World*, and *SunWorld*, to help us make informed and timely decisions in creating useful computer books that meet your needs.

Every IDG book strives to bring extra value and skill-building instruction to the reader. Our books are written by experts, with the backing of IDG periodicals, and with careful thought devoted to issues such as audience, interior design, use of icons, and illustrations. Our editorial staff is a careful mix of high-tech journalists and experienced book people. Our close contact with the makers of computer products helps ensure accuracy and thorough coverage. Our heavy use of personal computers at every step in production means we can deliver books in the most timely manner.

We are delivering books of high quality at competitive prices on topics customers want. At IDG, we believe in quality, and we have been delivering quality for over 25 years. You'll find no better book on a subject than an IDG book.

John Kilcullen
President and C.E.O.
IDG Books Worldwide, Inc.

IDG Books Worldwide, Inc. is a division of International Data Group. The officers are Patrick J. McGovern, Founder and Board Chairman; Walter Boyd, President. International Data Group's publications include: **ARGENTINA's** Computerworld Argentina, InfoWorld Argentina; **ASIA's** Computerworld Hong Kong, PC World Hong Kong, Computerworld Southeast Asia, PC World Singapore, Computerworld Malaysia, PC World Malaysia; **AUSTRALIA's** Computerworld Australia, Australian PC World, Australian Macworld, Network World, Reseller, IDG Sources; **AUSTRIA's** Computerwelt Oesterreich, PC Test; **BRAZIL's** Computerworld, Mundo IBM, Mundo Unix, PC World, Publish; **BULGARIA's** Computerworld Bulgaria, Ediworld, PC & Mac World Bulgaria; **CANADA's** Direct Access, Graduate Computerworld, InfoCanada, Network World Canada; **CHILE's** Computerworld, Informatica; **COLOMBIA's** Computerworld Colombia; **CZECH REPUBLIC's** Computerworld, Elektronika, PC World; **DENMARK's** CAD/CAM WORLD, Communications World, Computerworld Danmark, LOTUS World, Macintosh Produktkatalog, Macworld Danmark, PC World Danmark, PC World Produktguide, Windows World; **EQUADOR's** PC World; **EGYPT's** Computerworld (CW) Middle East, PC World Middle East; **FINLAND's** MikroPC, Tietoviikko, Tietoverkko; **FRANCE's** Distributique, GOLDEN MAC, InfoPC, Languages & Systems, Le Guide du Monde Informatique, Le Monde Informatique, Telecoms & Reseaux; **GERMANY's** Computerwoche, Computerwoche Focus, Computerwoche Extra, Computerwoche Karriere, Information Management, Macwelt, Netzwelt, PC Welt, PC Woche, Publish, Unit; **HUNGARY's** Alaplap, Computerworld SZT, PC World, ; **INDIA's** Computers & Communications; **ISRAEL's** Computerworld Israel, PC World Israel; **ITALY's** Computerworld Italia, Lotus Magazine, Macworld Italia, Networking Italia, PC World Italia; **JAPAN's** Computerworld Japan, Macworld Japan, SunWorld Japan, Windows World; **KENYA's** East African Computer News; **KOREA's** Computerworld Korea, Macworld Korea, PC World Korea; **MEXICO's** Compu Edicion, Compu Manufactura, Computacion/Punto de Venta, Computerworld Mexico, MacWorld, Mundo Unix, PC World, Windows; **THE NETHERLAND'S** Computer! Totaal, LAN Magazine, MacWorld; **NEW ZEALAND's** Computer Listings, Computerworld New Zealand, New Zealand PC World; **NIGERIA's** PC World Africa; **NORWAY's** Computerworld Norge, C/World, Lotusworld Norge, Macworld Norge, Networld, PC World Ekspress, PC World Norge, PC World's Product Guide, Publish World, Student Data, Unix World, Windowsworld, IDG Direct Response; **PANAMA's** PC World; **PERU's** Computerworld Peru, PC World; **PEOPLES REPUBLIC OF CHINA's** China Computerworld, PC World China, Electronics International, China Network World; **IDG HIGH TECH BEIJING's** New Product World; **IDG SHENZHEN's** Computer News Digest; **PHILLIPPINES'** Computerworld, PC World; **POLAND's** Computerworld Poland, PC World/Komputer; **PORTUGAL's** Cerebro/PC World, Correio Informatico/Computerworld, MacIn; **ROMANIA's** PC World; **RUSSIA's** Computerworld-Moscow, Mir-PC, Sety; **SLOVENIA's** Monitor Magazine; **SOUTH AFRICA's** Computing S.A.; **SPAIN's** Amiga World, Computerworld Espana, Communicaciones World, Macworld Espana, NeXTWORLD, PC World Espana, Publish, Sunworld; **SWEDEN's** Attack, ComputerSweden, Corporate Computing, Lokala Natverk/LAN, Lotus World, MAC&PC, Macworld, Mikrodatorn, PC World, Publishing & Design (CAP), Datalngenjoren, Maxi Data, Windows World; **SWITZERLAND's** Computerworld Schweiz, Macworld Schweiz, PC & Workstation; **TAIWAN's** Computerworld Taiwan, Global Computer Express, PC World Taiwan; **THAILAND's** Thai Computerworld; **TURKEY's** Computerworld Monitor, Macworld Turkiye, PC World Turkiye; **UNITED KINGDOM's** Lotus Magazine, Macworld, Sunworld; **UNITED STATES'** AmigaWorld, Cable in the Classroom, CD Review, CIO, Computerworld, Desktop Video World, DOS Resource Guide, Electronic News, Federal Computer Week, Federal Integrator, GamePro, IDG Books, InfoWorld, InfoWorld Direct, Laser Event, Macworld, Multimedia World, Network World, NeXTWORLD, PC Games, PC Letter, PC World Publish, Sumeria, SunWorld, SWATPro, Video Event; **VENEZUELA's** Computerworld Venezuela, MicroComputerworld Venezuela; **VIETNAM's** PC World Vietnam

 The text in this book is printed on recycled paper.

Acknowledgments

Thank you to the following people and companies for their aid in providing me with the information and product loans I needed to complete this book.

Rita Amladi, Matt Brown, LaVon Peck, and Jeff Parker at Adobe Systems
Laurie McLean and Dana Lipsky at McLean Public Relations
SuperMac Technologies
Roger Kasten at Newer Technology
David Glickman and Kevin Fischer at Lapis Technologies
Burton Holmes at Burton Holmes Associates
Dennis Deerborne at Wacom
Danny Shapiro and Ramin Evans at Storm Technology
Steve Abramson at Trumatch
Joanne Sperans at A&R Partners
Mike Jurs and Bob Monzell at Golin/Harris
Karen Allen and Sari Barnhard at Toshiba
Kai Krause and Susan Kitchens at HSC Software
Julie Speigler at Xaos Tools
Jan Sanfrod at Pixar
Melody Haller and Lynn Rocha at Light Source
Mike Micheletti at FWB
Karen Wilson at 21st Century Media
Michael Zak at ColorBytes
Don Kent at PressLink
Tony Graham at Allsport
Mitch Koppelman at Reuters
Peter Rohowsky at Bettmann
Warren Vollmar at 3M
Andrei Lloyd at The Stock Market
Marjorie Baer, Galen Gruman, and Jim Martin at *Macworld* magazine

Thanks also to Mark Collen, Russell McDougal, Denise McClelland, Diane Steele, Julie King, Beth Jenkins, Bill Gladstone, John Kilcullen, and everyone else who was instrumental in creating and producing this book.

(The publisher would like to give special thanks to Patrick J. McGovern, without whom this book would not have been possible.)

Contents at a Glance

Full Color Instructional Gallery .... Follows page 354

Introduction 1

Part I: Photoshop Fundamentals 11

Chapter 1: Getting to Know Photoshop 13
Chapter 2: Welcome to Macintosh 23
Chapter 3: Preparing the Soil 65
Chapter 4: Inside Photoshop 89

Part II: Exploring Digital Imagery 123

Chapter 5: Image Fundamentals 125
Chapter 6: Acquiring the Raw Materials 167
Chapter 7: Printing Images 195

Part III: Retouching Techniques 225

Chapter 8: Painting and Editing 227
Chapter 9: Selections and Masks 261
Chapter 10: Duplication and Reversion Techniques 339

Part IV: Special Effects 367

Chapter 11: Text Effects 369
Chapter 12: Filtering Techniques 393
Chapter 13: Constructing Homemade Effects 475

Part V: The Wonderful World of Color 513

Chapter 14: Defining Colors 515
Chapter 15: Coloring Selections 545
Chapter 16: Mapping and Adjusting Colors 587
Chapter 17: Manipulating Channels 617

Part VI: Appendixes 643

Appendix A: Photograph Credits 645
Appendix B: Products and Vendors 649

Index 653

Reader Response Survey .... Back of Book

Table of Contents

Full Color Instructional Gallery ....follows page 354

Foreword xxix

Introduction 1

What Is Photoshop? 1
About This Book..2
How This Book Is Organized..2
  Part I: Photoshop Fundamentals 3
  Part II: Exploring Digital Imagery 3
  Part III: Retouching Images..4
  Part IV: Special Effects 4
  Part V: The Wonderful World of Color 5
  Part VI: Appendixes 6
Conventions..6
  Vocabulary..6
  Select versus choose 6
  Commands and options 7
  Version numbers 7
  Icons 8
How to Bug Me 9

Part I: Photoshop Fundamentals 11

Chapter 1: Getting to Know Photoshop...............13

In This Chapter 13
What Is Photoshop? 13
Image Editing Theory 14
  Bitmaps versus objects 14
  The ups and downs of painting..15
  The downs and ups of drawing..16
  When to use Photoshop 17
  When to use a drawing program..18
The Macintosh Design Scheme..18
Photoshop Scenarios 19
Summary..21

Chapter 2: Welcome to Macintosh 23
In This Chapter 23
Computers: Modern-Day Robots 23
Computer brains 24
The CPU 25
Memory 25
Disk space 25
Disk space is not memory 26
How digital space is measured 26
Computer sensory organs 27
Keyboard techniques 27
Mouse techniques 27
Keyboard and mouse, together at last 28
Using Your System Software 29
How system software is organized 29
Powering up 30
Anatomy of the system software 30
Meet the Finder desktop 32
Parts of the window 35
Reviewing System Software Elements 36
Menus and submenus 37
Dialog boxes and options 37
How to navigate via dialog boxes 39
The folder bar 39
The scrolling list 39
The navigation buttons 40
The Preview and Find options 41
Variations on the save 42
Working with Programs 43
Starting an application 44
Assigning application RAM 45
Using the Get Info command 45
Understanding memory fragmentation 47
Managing multiple applications 48
Switching between running applications 49
Background processing 50
Printing in the background 51
Using the Clipboard 52
Application Clipboards 53
The Scrapbook 54

Using Fonts 55
Installing PostScript screen fonts 56
Installing PostScript printer fonts 57
Using Adobe Type Manager 58
Making the leap to SuperATM 60
Installing TrueType fonts 60
Working with QuickTime 61
The state of QuickTime 61
QuickTime and still images 62
QuickTime image compression...62
QuickTime and Photo CD 62
Summary..64

Chapter 3: Preparing the Soil 65

In This Chapter 65
Hardware and Software Requirements 65
Hardware issues 65
Hard disk space 66
The CPU...66
RAM requirements...66
Video display requirements 66
Shopping for a computer 67
Software issues 70
How to Install Photoshop..71
Contents of the Photoshop disks 71
Installing Photoshop 2.5 75
Installing Photoshop 2.0 78
Memory Needs 79
When to buy additional RAM 79
How to allocate RAM to Photoshop...81
Virtual memory..81
How virtual memory works 81
The scratch disk 82
Video Capabilities...83
Video card technology 83
Third-party video boards 85
Monitor resolution..87
Summary..88

Chapter 4: Inside Photoshop 89

In This Chapter 89
A First Look at Photoshop 89
The Photoshop desktop 89
Tools 92
Cursors 94
Toolbox controls 97
The floating palettes 100
How to get around 102
The zoom ratio 102
The zoom tool 103
Creating a reference window 104
Scrolling inside the window 105
Shortcuts 105
Establishing function key shortcuts 108
Using a macro utility 109
Shortcut suggestions 110
Shortcuts in the absolute full screen mode 112
How to Customize the Interface 114
The File ⇨ Preferences commands 115
General environmental preferences 116
Summary 122

Part II: Exploring Digital Imagery 123

Chapter 5: Image Fundamentals 125

In This Chapter 125
How Images Work 125
Size and resolution 126
Printing versus screen display 127
Printed resolution 127
Moiré patterns 128
Screen resolution 129
How to Open and Save Images 130
Creating a new image 131
Column width 132
On-screen image size 132
Color mode and background 132

Opening an existing image 133
Saving an image to disk 133
Image File Formats 135
The native formats 135
Cross-platform formats 135
Amiga's IFF and HAM 135
Windows Paint's BMP 136
CompuServe's GIF 136
PC Paintbrush's PCX 137
PIXAR workstations 137
Scitex image-processors 137
TrueVision's TGA 137
Interapplication formats 138
Rendering an EPS illustration 138
Saving an EPS document 139
QuarkXPress DCS 140
Premier Filmstrip 141
MacPaint 143
PixelPaint 143
The mainstream formats 143
JPEG 143
PICT 146
TIFF 147
The oddball formats 148
Photo CD YCC images 148
Kodak CMS support 150
PICT resource (startup screen) 150
Opening a raw document 151
Saving a raw document 152
How to import PICT elements 154
Rendering a PICT drawing 154
Lifting PICT resources 155
Storm JPEG 156
PicturePress 157
ThunderStorm 157
Resampling and Cropping Methods 159
Resizing versus resampling 159
Resizing an image 159
Resampling an image 159

Cropping 161
Changing the canvas size 162
Using the crop tool 163
Rotating a crop marquee 163
Cropping a selection 164
Summary 165

Chapter 6: Acquiring the Raw Materials 167

In This Chapter 167
Turning Photographs into Computer Images 167
Scanning 168
Color options 168
Scanner models 169
Resolutions 170
Scanning software 171
Plug-in modules 171
TWAIN 173
Ofoto 175
Shooting Photos to Disk 176
Video capture 177
Video-input devices 177
Deinterlacing 177
The video source 178
Digital cameras 180
Using Images on CD-ROM 180
Kodak Photo CD 181
Hardware requirements 182
Software requirements 183
Commercial image collections 184
Collections offering unlimited reproduction rights 185
Stock photo agencies 186
Using On-Line Image Libraries 189
Summary 193

Chapter 7: Printing Images 195

In This Chapter 195
Welcome to Printing 195
Understanding Printing Terminology 196

Printing Composites 199
- Choosing a printer 200
- Setting up the page 202
- Changing the halftone screen 205
- Specifying a transfer function 209
- Printing pages 210

Creating Color Separations 212
- Monitor calibration 214
- Printer calibration 216
- How to prepare CMYK conversions 217
- Color trapping 219

Printing Duotones 220
- Creating a duotone 220
- Reproducing a duotone 222

Summary 223

Part III: Retouching Images 225

Chapter 8: Painting and Editing 227

In This Chapter 227

Paint and Edit Tool Basics 227
- Meet your tools 228
  - The paint tools 229
  - The edit tools 230
- Basic techniques 232
  - Drawing a straight line 232
  - Drawing a perpendicular line 234
  - Painting with the smudge tool 236

Brush Shape and Opacity 239
- The Brushes palette 239
  - Editing a brush shape 240
  - Creating and using custom brushes 244
- Opacity, pressure, and exposure 247

Tapered Lines 248
- Fade-out 248
  - Fading and spacing 249
  - Creating sparkles and comets 250

Lines created with pressure-sensitive tablets 252
How to undo pressure-sensitive lines 253
Pressure-sensitive options 254
The size disparity 255
Brush Modes 256
Summary 260

Chapter 9: Selections and Masks 261

In This Chapter 261
Selection Fundamentals 261
How selections work 262
Selection tools in depth 263
Geometric selection outlines 263
Free-form outlines 265
Magic wand tolerance 267
Ways to change existing selection outlines 269
Making automated adjustments 269
Manually adding and subtracting 270
Adding to a selection by command 271
Saving selections 274
How to move and duplicate selections 277
Making precision movements 278
Cloning a selection 278
Moving a selection outline 280
Floating a selection 281
Removing halos 282
How to soften selection outlines 283
How to Draw and Edit Paths 288
A first look at paths 288
How paths work 289
Using the Paths palette tools 290
Drawing with the pen tool 291
Defining points and segments 292
Test-driving the pen tool 294
Drawing curved segments 296
Creating cusps 298
Reshaping existing paths 302
Using the arrow tool 303
Adding and deleting points 305
Converting points 306

Transforming a path 307
Flipping, scaling, and rotating by degree 307
Applying free rotation and other transformations 310
Painting along a path 312
Using the Stroke Path command 312
Creating painted paths 313
Converting and saving paths 315
Converting paths to selections 316
Converting selections to paths 316
Saving paths with an image 317
Swapping paths with Illustrator 317
Exporting to Illustrator 318
Masking an image 318
Selection Masks 321
Painting inside a selection outline 321
Using the quick mask mode 324
Changing the red coating 328
Using a mask channel 329
Viewing mask and image 330
Deriving selections from images 332
Summary 337

Chapter 10: Duplication and Reversion Techniques 339

In This Chapter 339
Introducing the Amalgamated Rubber Stamp 339
Cloning Image Elements 341
The cloning process 342
Aligned and nonaligned cloning 343
Stamp differences 344
Touching up blemishes 345
Eliminating distracting background elements 347
Applying Repeating Patterns 352
Pattern options 352
How to create patterns 354
Selectively Undoing Changes 360
Using the traditional undo functions 360
Reverting to the last saved image 361
Reverting with the rubber stamp tool 363
Reverting from a snapshot 363
Reversion limitations 363
Summary 366

Part IV: Special Effects 367

Chpater 11: Text Effects 369

In This Chapter 369
Type Basics 369
Qualities of bitmapped type 370
The type tool 372
Entering and editing type 373
Formatting type..374
Manipulating type in the image window 378
Character Masks 380
Filling type with an image 380
Painting raised type 383
Feathering effects 384
Creating drop shadows 387
Converting characters to paths 389
Summary 392

Chapter 12: Filtering Techniques 393

In This Chapter 393
Filter Basics 393
A first look at filters 394
General filtering techniques 396
Previewing filters 397
Dissipating filtering effects 398
Ways to Adjust Focus 402
Sharpening an image using Unsharp Mask 402
Specifying the amount of sharpening 403
Distributing the effect 405
Recognizing edges 407
Using the preset sharpening filters 409
Using the High Pass filter 409
Blurring an image 413
Gaussian blur 413
The preset blurring filters 416
Directional blurring 417
Motion blurring 417
Using the Wind filter 418

Directional smudging 420
Radial blurring 422
Combining sharpening and blurring 424
Softening a selection 427
Minimum and Maximum 427
How to feather outward from a selection 427
Noise Factors 430
Adding noise 430
Noise variations 432
Randomizing selections 433
Chunky noise 434
Removing noise 435
Destructive Filters 437
The block filters 438
The Emboss filter 440
Distortion filters 444
Reflecting an image in a spoon 445
Twirling spirals 447
Creating concentric pond ripples 451
Creating parallel ripples and waves 453
Changing to polar coordinates 458
Distorting an image inside out 460
Third-Party Filtering Tools 465
Filter collections 465
DSP boards 468
How DSP acceleration works 469
Who needs DSP? 470
Changing the Location of a Filter Command 471
Summary 473

Chapter 13: Constructing Homemade Effects 475

In This Chapter 475
Creating a Custom Effect 475
The Custom filter 476
Custom filter advice 478
Applying Custom Values 481
Symmetrical effects 481
Sharpening 482
Blurring 485
Edge-detection 487

Non-1 variations 488
Lightening overly dark effects 488
Darkening overly light effects 490
Using extreme offsets 490
Other custom effects 493
Directional blurs 493
Directional sharpening 494
Embossing 495
Displacing Pixels in an Image 498
Displacement theory 500
Direction of displacement 500
Brightness value transitions 502
The Displace dialog box 503
Using Displacement Maps 506
Creating texture effects 506
Displacing an image onto itself 509
Summary 512

Part V: The Wonderful World of Color 513

Chapter 14: Defining Colors 515

In This Chapter 515
Selecting and Editing Colors 515
Specifying colors 516
Using the Color Picker 517
Entering numeric color values 521
Working in Different Color Modes 521
RGB 522
HSB and HSL 523
CMYK 525
Commercial subtractive primaries 525
Editing in CMYK 526
CIE's Lab 526
Understanding Lab anatomy 527
Using Lab 528
Indexed colors 528
Using the Indexed Color command 528
Creating images for the screen 530
Editing indexed colors 531

Grayscale 533
Black and white (bitmap) 534
Using Photoshop's Other Color Selection Methods 538
Predefined colors 538
Focoltone and Toyo 539
Newspaper Association of America 540
Trumatch 540
Pantone 540
The Colors palette 541
The eyedropper tool 542
Summary 544

Chapter 15: Coloring Selections 545

In This Chapter 545
Filling Portions of an Image 545
Filling an area with color 546
The paint bucket tool 546
The Fill command 549
How to fill paths 550
Delete-key techniques 550
Creating special fill effects 551
Applying Gradient Fills 553
The gradient tool 553
Gradient tool options 554
How to eliminate banding 557
Gradations and brush modes 558
Randomized gradations 559
Amorphous gradient bubbles 561
Sharpened amorphous bubbles 562
Gradations as masks 565
Fading an image 565
Applying special effects gradually 567
Applying Strokes and Arrowheads 568
Stroking a selection outline 569
Applying arrowheads 570
Overlaying Floating Selections 573
Overlay modes 575
Color exclusion sliders 581
Fuzziness 582
Color channel options 585
Summary 586

Chapter 16: Mapping and Adjusting Colors 587

In This Chapter 587
Mapping Colors 587
Color effects and corrections 587
Color mapping commands 589
Invert 589
Equalize 590
Threshold 591
Posterize 593
Hue Shifting and Colorizing 595
Using the Hue/Saturation command 595
Adjusting hue and saturation 598
Changing hues 598
Changing saturation levels 599
Colorizing images 600
Making Custom Brightness Adjustments 600
The Levels command 601
The Curves command 606
Continuous curves 610
Arbitrary curves 612
Summary 615

Chapter 17: Manipulating Channels 617

In This Chapter 617
Editing Color Channels 617
How to view channels 618
RGB channels 619
CMYK channels 620
Lab channels 620
HSB channels 622
Other channel functions 623
Color channel effects 625
Improving the appearance of color scans 625
Using multichannel techniques 626
Replacing and swapping color channels 627
Using Channel Operation Commands 628
Source and destination options 628
Calculate commands 630

Duplicate 631
Add and Subtract 632
Applying the Add command 632
Applying the Subtract command 635
Difference 635
Composite 637
More channel madness 640
Summary 641

Part VI: Appendixes 643

Appendix A: Photograph Credits 645

Appendix B: Products and Vendors 649

Index 653

Reader Response Survey ...... Back of Book

Foreword

In the tradition of Adobe Photoshop, the *Macworld Photoshop 2.5 Bible* book "raises the bar" in providing you with the tools you need to do your work. This book explores the new features and traditional functions of Adobe Photoshop with a uniquely engaging focus on you and your information needs — whether you are the expert, intermediate, or new user.

Deke makes great use of the visual world of graphics, icons, and illustrations, which he has gleaned from his own talents and his rich network of graphics resources, to create the blend of text and art that best presents the world of Adobe Photoshop to any user.

If you are new to Adobe Photoshop, only several pages into the book you'll begin to feel comfortable with the program. If you have been productive with Photoshop for awhile but need to learn Version 2.5, you'll find easy access to the program's new features in Deke's practical presentation. If you are looking for a definitive primary reference for Adobe Photoshop, you can rely on the *Macworld Photoshop 2.5 Bible* for its excellent depth and breadth of coverage. In addition, the new capabilities of Version 2.5.1 are covered in this printing of IDG's *Macworld Photoshop 2.5 Bible.*

Adobe has been an industry leader in moving beyond the world as it was before computer graphics, and Adobe Photoshop Version 2.5 is on the leading edge of the new graphics universe. You will be well served in your Photoshop adventures if you take along the gospel according to Deke McClelland, the *Macworld Photoshop 2.5 Bible.*

John Kunze
Director of Product Marketing
Adobe Systems Incorporated
November, 1993

Introduction

God bless Adobe. What other company could manage to produce such incredibly excellent software. But you've got to admit, they do a pretty inadequate job of documenting it. The manual is slim, most descriptions of complicated functions are glib (the rest are nonexistent), and the index is not terribly helpful. It's the perfect opportunity for yours truly, Mr. Seize the Day.

In fact, I'd be lying in a hammock dreaming about thousand dollar bills dancing freely into my wallet if it weren't for one little problem: adequately documenting Adobe Photoshop in a book of this size is like trying to explain quantum physics in a haiku. The program may seem fairly straightforward on the face of it, but lurking below the surface is an expanse of functions and features that extend so far down they would give even Jules Verne pause. Welcome to the center of the earth (or at least to a very convincing scan of it).

So instead of taking that much-needed vacation to Bora Bora, I spent many sleepless nights, ignoring my wife and no kids, to bring you every smidgen of Photoshop knowledge I could beg, borrow, or check out from the library. It's a quick read, but I warn you, ingesting it all in one sitting can melt your brain (or at least singe it around the edges). This is intense stuff.

What Is Photoshop?

Photoshop is software for the Macintosh computer that enables you to edit photos and artwork scanned to disk and print out your results. Here's an example: Your job is to take a picture of Mr. High-and-Mighty CEO, touch up his crow's feet, and publish his smiling face on the cover of the annual report. No problem. Just shoot the photo, have it digitized to a Photo CD or some other high-tech gizmo, open Mr. H & M inside Photoshop, dab on the digital wrinkle cream, fix his toupee (and for heaven's sake, do *something* about those jowls), and there you go. The man looks presentable no matter how badly the company is doing.

Photoshop, then, is about changing reality. And it goes beyond just reducing the distance between two Giza pyramids on the cover of *National Geographic* or plopping a leaning Tom Cruise, photographed in Hawaii, onto the supportive shoulder of Dustin

applications of photo-editing software). Photoshop brings you full-tilt creativity. Picture a diver leaping from the summit of Mount Everest, or a bright violet zebra galloping toward a hazel-green sunset, or an architectural rendering with wallpaper that looks exactly like the surface of the moon. Photoshop lets you paint snapshots from your dreams. The sky's the limit.

About This Book

I wrote *Macworld Photoshop 2.5 Bible* to serve as the ultimate guide to retouching and enhancing scanned images in Adobe Photoshop. After you finish reading this book, it is my sincere hope not only that you will understand virtually every nook and cranny of Photoshop, but also that you will know how to apply your vast expanse of knowledge to real-world design situations.

Moderately experienced Macintosh artists and designers are likely to benefit the most from this book. However, even snooty power users will learn gallons of stuff that they never imagined they could from a book with such a chatty introduction.

Artists and designers? Snooty power users? Does this mean you have to dye your hair black and hang out at espresso bars to understand what's going on? At your age, no way. In fact, *Macworld Photoshop 2.5 Bible* is designed to appeal to all sexes, income brackets, and experience levels.

If you're a free-lance designer cutting your first teeth on the Mac or an intermediate user with dreams of joining the artistic elite, begin by reading the first four chapters of this book, which are devoted to fundamental image editing issues. You'll get an introduction to the Photoshop program, learn how to negotiate with your Macintosh computer, tour Photoshop's amazing environment, and explore important hardware and software issues. In a few hours, you'll be a Photoshop virtuoso. (Hang in there, you can do it. Honest.)

How This Book Is Organized

Before I proceed so much as one step farther, I should take a moment to credit the folks who contributed the photos that appear on the following 700 or so pages. For the most part, the artistic embellishments are my own, but the original images derive from a variety of sources, including PhotoDisc, ColorBytes, Reuters, and the Bettmann Archive, as well as independents Russell McDougal, Mark Collen, and Denise McClelland. (In case you're wondering whether there's some kind of nepotism going on here, the answer is bingo. Denise is my sister.) Rather than clutter every single figure with credits and copyright statements, I provide this information in an appendix near the end of the book. You'll also find addresses and phone numbers in case you want to purchase one or more collections.

To enhance your enjoyment of Photoshop's mouth-watering capabilities, I sliced the task into five tasty parts and then diced those parts into a total of 17 digestible chapters. Bon appetite.

Part I: Photoshop Fundamentals

If you know nothing about Photoshop and next to nothing about the Mac, here's your chance to get acquainted. Even though each chapter assumes no previous knowledge, you'll find some pretty heavy-duty information throughout Chapters 3 and 4.

Chapter 1, Getting to Know Photoshop, explains how Photoshop fits into the larger experience of using the Mac to produce printed pages and on-screen presentations.

Chapter 2, Welcome to Macintosh, explores a range of topics that are fundamental to using a Macintosh computer. Get ready to familiarize yourself with CPUs, system software, random-access memory, fonts, QuickTime, and a whole bunch of other mystifying topics.

Chapter 3, Preparing the Soil, explains how to install the Photoshop application, as well as how to prepare your computer to sustain Photoshop. RAM, virtual memory, and video display are all covered in this chapter.

Chapter 4, Inside Photoshop, introduces you to the program's working environment and examines Photoshop's generous supply of tools, palettes, and preference settings.

Part II: Exploring Digital Imagery

Images represent a unique variety of computer graphics. These chapters show how you can exploit the inherent qualities of digital imagery, enhance scanned photographs, and print full-color artwork.

Chapter 5, Image Fundamentals, describes what digitized image means and how file formats such as TIFF and JPEG affect the content of an image and its size on disk. You also learn how to resample and crop images within Photoshop.

Chapter 6, Acquiring the Raw Materials, examines the many sources for digitized images, including scanners, video capture boards, on-line photographic libraries, and Kodak's Photo CD technology. Unlike the previous sections, this chapter is required reading not only for novices, but for experienced image editors as well.

Chapter 7, Printing Images, starts off with a glossary of printing terms that will help you better communicate with the folks at your service bureau or commercial print house. Following that, I explain how to print grayscale and color composites, four-color separations, and duotones, tritones, or quadtones.

Part III: Retouching Images

Every month or so, some fraudulent photo sparks a new flame of public scorn and scrutiny. Now it's your chance to give people something to talk about. These chapters show you how to exchange fact with a modicum of fantasy.

Chapter 8, Painting and Editing, shows you how to use Photoshop's brush tools to enhance and augment photographic images. I also explore ways to paint images from scratch using pressure-sensitive tablets.

Chapter 9, Selections and Masks, covers absolutely everything you ever wanted to know about the magic wand and the path tools, antialiasing and feathering, painting inside selection outlines, and using the quick mask mode and independent mask channels. If you're an intermediate user, this chapter alone will likely double your understanding of Photoshop.

Chapter 10, Duplication and Reversion Techniques, details the operation of the rubber stamp tool, the most versatile and possibly the most frequently overlooked editing tool available to Photoshop users. In addition, you learn how to create seamlessly repeating patterns and textures in Photoshop for use with the rubber stamp and other tools.

Part IV: Special Effects

Manual artistic enhancements are all very well and good, but it's easier to make your computer do the work. These chapters show ways to produce highly entertaining and effective results using fully automated operations.

Chapter 11, Text Effects, tells you how to create word art, including gradient text, characters with tiger stripes, raised letters, custom logos, and a whole mess of other effects guaranteed to make jaws drop and eyes boggle.

Chapter 12, Filtering Techniques, describes specific applications for Photoshop's abundant supply of built-in and plug-in filters, well beyond the usual sharpening of photographic detail and proliferation of gritty noise. I also briefly examine commercial filter collections available from four independent vendors.

Chapter 13, Constructing Homemade Effects, investigates the exact workings of the Custom and Displace filters, which multiply and shift pixels to create user-definable effects. Even folks who can't solve fractions will learn ways to create way-cool effects.

Part V: The Wonderful World of Color

In this section, you and I dive headfirst into the wonderful world of color. Not only can you use Photoshop to edit images containing upwards of 16 million hues and shades, but you can also add colors to images where once there were none. The publisher has concentrated all color figures within one insert. These pages serve not solely as image galleries, as in so many other books, but as essential learning tools.

Chapter 14, Defining Colors, covers the fundamentals of editing colors on a computer screen. I explain how you can manipulate common color models to display predictable results. I also examine the differences and similarities between the commercial printing standards Pantone and Trumatch.

Chapter 15, Coloring Selections, shows how to paint the interiors and outlines of images with solid colors and gradations. This chapter also covers overlay modes, which control the manner in which a floating image blends with its background.

Chapter 16, Mapping and Adjusting Colors, explores ways to change the color balance in scanned photographs to more accurately represent real life — or more radically depart from it. You learn how to make use of Photoshop's straightforward Variations options as well as more complex and rewarding features, such as histograms and arbitrary color maps.

Chapter 17, Manipulating Channels, looks at color channels, which are the building blocks of color images, and examines ways of editing them. I also detail Photoshop's Calculate commands, which enable you to create spectacular effects by impacting the pixels from one channel onto the pixels of another.

Part VI: Appendixes

Appendix A, Photograph Credits, contains complete information on the photographers, image collections, and news services that contributed images to this book.

Appendix B, Products and Vendors, provides a list of vendors whose products I covered in the book, complete with addresses, phone numbers, and retail prices.

Conventions

Every computer book seems to conform to a logic all its own, and this one's no exception. Although I try to avoid pig latin — ellway, orfay hetay ostmay artpay — I do subscribe to a handful of conventions that you may not immediately recognize.

Vocabulary

Call it computerese, call it technobabble, call it the synthetic jargon of propeller heads. The fact is, I can't explain the Mac or Photoshop in graphic and gruesome detail without reverting to the specialized language of the trade. However, to help you keep up, I can and have italicized vocabulary words (as in *random-access memory*) with which you may not be familiar or which I use in an unusual context. An italicized term is followed by a definition.

If you come across a strange word that is *not* italicized (that bit of italics was for emphasis), look it up in the index to find the first reference to the word in the book.

Select versus choose

Roget's Thesaurus lists the words *select* and *choose* — along with *cull, winnow,* and a few other gems that have escaped my notice these many years — as very close kin. When shopping, for example, you can select a dress, you can choose a dress, or you can wrap it around your head and do a little dance. I don't much care what you do on your own time. But in this book, select and choose have separate meanings.

If you select something, it stays selected so you can use it again and again. When you choose something, it performs its duty immediately and only once. Therefore, you select images, you select tools, and you select options in a dialog box, but you choose menu commands.

For an introduction to menu commands and the like, check out the "Reviewing System Software Elements" section in Chapter 2. For an introduction to Photoshop's tools, see "The Photoshop desktop" section in Chapter 4.

Commands and options

To distinguish the literal names of commands, dialog boxes, buttons, and so on, I capitalize the first letter in each word (for example, *click on the Cancel button*). The only exceptions are option names, which can be six or seven words long and filled with prepositions like *to* and *of*. Traditionally, prepositions and articles (*a, an, the*) don't appear in initial caps, and this book follows that time-honored rule, too.

When discussing menus and commands, I use an arrow symbol to indicate hierarchy. For example, *Choose File ⇨ Open* means to choose the Open command from the File menu. If you have to display a submenu to reach a command, I list the command used to display the submenu between the menu name and the final command. *Choose Image ⇨ Map ⇨ Invert* means to choose the Map command from the Image menu and then choose the Invert command from the Map submenu. (If this doesn't quite make sense to you now, don't worry. Future chapters will make it abundantly clear.)

Version numbers

A new piece of software comes out every 15 minutes. That's not a real statistic, mind you, but I bet I'm not far off. Only a few months after Adobe released Version 2.5, for example, they came out with Version 2.5.1. And there's always the chance that more updates and bug fixes will have come out by time you read this. So know that when I write *Photoshop 2.5,* I mean any version of Photoshop short of 3.0.

Similarly, when I write *Photoshop 2.0,* I mean both Version 2.0 and the more common 2.0.1.

The term *System 7* includes Versions 7.0, 7.01, 7.1, and any other version that begins with a 7. Illustrator 3.0 incorporates all versions up to and including 3.2.3 or whatever they're up to these days. Illustrator 5.0 includes every version of Illustrator short of 6.0 (if that ever occurs).

I'm sure that there are other examples, but you get the idea. Rather than clutter the book with a lot of references to Photoshop 2.5 and 2.5.1 or, worse yet, *Photoshop 2.5.x,* I tried to keep things as simple as possible by referring to the significant version only. In those few instances that I cite a specific minor update, such as Photoshop 2.5.1 or System 7.1, I am talking about that specific version only.

Icons

Like just about every computer book currently available on your green grocer's shelves, this one includes alluring icons that focus your eyeballs smack dab on important information. The icons make it easy for folks who just like to skim books to figure out what the heck's going on. Icons serve as little insurance policies against short attention spans. On the whole, the icons are self-explanatory, but I'll explain them anyway.

The Caution icon warns you that a step you're about to take may produce disastrous results. Well, perhaps "disastrous" is an exaggeration. Inconvenient, then. Uncomfortable. For heaven's sake, use caution.

The Note icon highlights some little tidbit of information I've decided to share with you that seemed at the time to be remotely related to the topic at hand. Then again, if its not even remotely related, it's still good info! Life's a grab bag.

The Background icon is like the Note icon, except that it includes a modicum of history. I tell you how an option came into existence, why a feature is implemented the way it is, or how things used to be better back in the old days. It's a perfect opportunity to gripe and moan.

The Photoshop 2.0 icon explains an option, command, or other feature that works differently in Photoshop 2.0 than it does in Photoshop 2.5. This way, if you can't afford to upgrade to Version 2.5 or you simply prefer the way certain functions work in the older program, you can easily follow along with the book.

Photoshop 2.5 is the first version of this remarkable program available on both the Macintosh and Windows platforms. (You should see what those poor Windows users had to put up with until now!) The Windows icon highlights Photoshop features that work differently under Windows.

This book is bursting with tips and techniques. If I were to highlight every one of them, whole pages would be gray with triangles popping out all over the place. The Operations Tip icon calls attention to shortcuts that are specifically applicable to the Photoshop application. For the bigger, more useful power tips, I'm afraid you'll have to actually read the text.

If your machine can't handle System 7, quietly and discreetly set this book down — you won't want anyone to suspect what you're up to — and then go home, throw your computer in the trash, and buy a new one. Really, truly, I hope you're using Photoshop with System 7. But if you aren't, the System 7 icon tells you what you're missing.

The Cross-Reference icon tells you where to go for information related to the current topic. I included one a few pages back and you probably read it without thinking twice. That means you're either sharp as a tack or an experienced computer-book user. Either way, you won't have any trouble with this icon.

How to Bug Me

This is my 30th book, or very close to it. But even with all that practice, I find that intrepid readers still manage to locate errors and oversights. If you notice those kinds of things and you have a few spare moments, please let me know what you think. I always appreciate readers' comments, especially the nice ones. (The mean ones make me sob with relentless grief, but by all means, don't let that stop you.)

If you want to share your insights, comments, or corrections, please write to me at the following address:

Deke McClelland
1911 11th Street, Suite 210
Boulder, CO 80302

If you're on America Online, drop me a message at DekeMc. You can also reach me via CompuServe at 70640,670. Don't fret if you don't hear from me for a few days, or months, or ever. I read every letter and try to implement nearly every idea anyone bothers to send me.

Now that you know everything you need to know to use this book and you realize just how much stuff there is to learn, you have my blessings to turn the page and dive right into the wealth of nonstop, exciting, information-packed pages. You'll learn how to create dazzling, professional-quality images — but only if you go ahead and turn the page. Astound your friends, amaze your clients, wake up your neighbors, but whatever you do, urntay hetay agepay. (There goes that pig latin again.)

Part I

Photoshop Fundamentals

Chapter 1:
Getting to Know Photoshop

Chapter 2:
Welcome to Macintosh

Chapter 3:
Preparing the Soil

Chapter 4:
Inside Photoshop

If you're new to the Mac, you've never used Photoshop, or you don't know the first thing about digital imagery, this section is for you. By the time you finish reading the following four chapters, you'll be prepared not only to begin using Photoshop in earnest, but also to engage in witty repartee with friends, neighbors, and business associates who claim to know everything about the Mac. You may even be able to one-up a couple of them. Now come on, that's got to be worth a little effort.

As for you knowledgeable types, you might be surprised at how much you'll benefit from spending a few moments glossing over the fundamentals. For example, if you think Photoshop is roughly equivalent to Illustrator or FreeHand, you should read *all* of Chapter 1; you have a few serious misconceptions to unlearn. If you're confident of your command over graphics software and Macintosh hardware, you probably will want to at least comb through Chapters 2 and 3 for the occasional icon notes. And even experienced users should read the last half of Chapter 4, which explains how to assign custom keyboard equivalents and change preference settings.

Regardless who you are, keep in mind that mastering any piece of software requires concerted effort. That goes for learning a new program from scratch or becoming more proficient with a familiar program. Some people thrive on gobbling up new information, but most of us hold back and even ridicule things we don't understand. I myself was once terrified of computers. But the fact is, you don't broaden your horizons without facing obstacles and applying yourself to their unqualified defeat. So take a deep breath and let me show you the ropes. I promise not to leave you behind.

Getting to Know Photoshop

CHAPTER 1

In This Chapter

- An introduction to Photoshop
- The difference between painting and drawing programs
- How Photoshop fits in the bigger Macintosh design scheme
- The many uses for Photoshop

What Is Photoshop?

Adobe Photoshop is the most powerful image editing application available for use on a personal computer — or so goes the tide of popular opinion. Fractal Design's ColorStudio is indisputably a powerful tool for the Mac, and image editors for the Microsoft Windows environment, such as Micrografx Picture Publisher, Aldus Photostyler, and Ventura PicturePro, are abundant. But none of these programs is nearly so popular as Photoshop. By some estimates, Adobe sells upwards of four times as many copies of Photoshop as any competing image editor. Other estimates say that Photoshop sales exceed those of all its competitors combined.

The term *application* — as in *image editing application* — is just another word for *computer program.* Photoshop satisfies a specific purpose, so programmers abuse the language by calling it an application. I also use the word in the conventional sense throughout the book, as in *Photoshop has many applications.* Hopefully, my meaning will remain clear.

The result of Photoshop's amazingly lopsided sales advantage is that Adobe has the capital to reinvest in Photoshop and regularly enhance its capabilities. Meanwhile, other vendors spin their wheels or let their products die on the vine. Therefore, the legacy of this program reads like a self-perpetuating fantasy. Photoshop hasn't always been the best image editor, but it's long been perceived as such. So now — thanks to substantial capital injections and highly creative programming on the part of Adobe's staff and Photoshop originators Thomas and John Knoll — it has evolved into the best program of its kind.

Image editing software for the Mac went through its infancy in the late 1980s. The first image editor for the Mac was ImageStudio, a gray scale program from Fractal Design, creators of ColorStudio and Painter. The first Macintosh image editor to feature color was an Avalon Development Group entry called PhotoMac, which is now all but forgotten. But rumor had it that the *best* photo editor during this time was Lumena from Time Arts, a DOS-based program that ran on IBM PCs and compatibles. Meanwhile, Photoshop was a custom program, used within the hallowed walls of George Lucas's Industrial Light and Magic, that converted file formats and combined images from different sources. We were almost into a new decade before Adobe purchased the product and set it on its current path.

Image Editing Theory

Having used mirrors, dry ice, and some rather titillating industry analysis to convince you of Photoshop's prowess, I now should answer that burning question: What the heck does Photoshop do?

Like any *image editor,* Photoshop enables you to alter photographs and other scanned artwork. You can retouch an image, apply special effects, swap details between photos, introduce text and logos, adjust color balance, and even add color to a gray scale scan. Photoshop also provides the tools you need to create images from scratch. These tools are fully compatible with pressure-sensitive tablets, so you can create naturalistic images that look for all the world like watercolors and oils.

Bitmaps versus objects

Image editors fall into the larger software category of *painting programs.* In a painting program, you draw a line, and the application converts it to tiny square dots called *pixels.* The painting itself is called a *bitmapped image,* but *bitmap* and *image* are equally acceptable terms. Every program I've discussed so far is a painting program. Other examples include PixelPaint, Color It, Sketcher, and the Mac's first program, MacPaint.

Photoshop uses the term *bitmap* exclusively to mean a black-and-white image, the logic being that each pixel conforms to one *bit* of data, 0 or 1 (off or on). In order to avoid ad hoc syllabic mergers like *pix-map* — and because forcing a distinction between a painting with exactly two colors and one with anywhere from four to 16 million colors is entirely arbitrary — I use the term bitmap more broadly to mean any image composed of a fixed number of pixels, regardless of the number of colors involved.

What about other graphics applications, such as Adobe Illustrator and Aldus FreeHand? Illustrator, FreeHand, Canvas, MacDraw Pro, and others fall into a different category of software called *drawing programs.* Drawings comprise *objects,* which are independent, mathematically defined lines and shapes. For this reason, drawing programs are sometimes said to be *object-oriented.* Some folks prefer the term *vector-based,* but I really hate that one because *vector* implies the physical components, direction and magnitude, that generally are associated with straight lines. Besides, my preference suggests an air of romance, as in, "Honey, I'm bound now for the Object Orient."

Illustrator and FreeHand are sometimes called *illustration programs,* though this is more a marketing gimmick — you know, like Father's Day — than a legitimate software category. The idea is that Illustrator and FreeHand provide a unique variety of features unto themselves. In reality, their uniqueness extends little beyond more reliable printing capabilities and higher prices.

The ups and downs of painting

Painting programs and drawing programs each have their strengths and weaknesses. The strength of a painting program is that it offers an extremely straightforward approach to creating images. For example, although many of Photoshop's features are complex — *exceedingly* complex on occasion — its core painting tools are as easy to use as a pencil. You alternately draw and erase until you reach a desired effect, just as you've been doing since grade school. (Of course, for all I know, you've been using computers since grade school. If you're pushing 20, you probably managed to log in many happy hours on paint programs in your formative years. Then again, if you're under 20, you're still in your formative years. Shucks, we're *all* in our formative years. Wrinkles, expanding tummies, receding hairlines . . . if that's not a new form, I don't know what is.)

In addition to being simple to use, each of Photoshop's core painting tools is fully customizable. It's as if you have access to an infinite variety of crayons, colored pencils, pastels, airbrushes, watercolors, and so on, all of which are entirely erasable. Doodling on the phone book was never so much fun.

The downside of a painting program is that it limits your *resolution* options. Because bitmaps contain a fixed number of pixels, the resolution of an image — the number of pixels per inch — is dependent upon the size at which the image is printed, as demonstrated in Figure 1-1. Print the image small, and the pixels become tiny, which increases resolution; print the image large, and the pixels grow, which decreases resolution. An image that fills up a standard 13-inch screen (640 × 480 pixels) prints with smooth color transitions when reduced to, say, half the size of a postcard. But if you print that same image without reducing it, you may be able to distinguish individual pixels, which means that you can see jagged edges and blocky transitions. The only way to remedy this problem is to increase the number of pixels in the image, which dramatically increases the size of the file on disk.

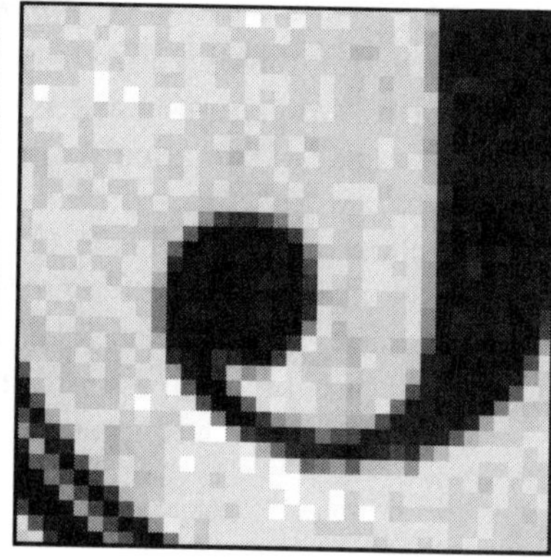

Figure 1-1: When printed small, paintings appear smooth (left). When printed large, they appear jagged (right).

Bear in mind that this is a very simplified explanation of how images work. For a more complete description that includes techniques for maximizing image performance, refer to the "How Images Work" section of Chapter 5.

The downs and ups of drawing

Painting programs provide tools reminiscent of traditional art tools. A drawing program, on the other hand, features tools that have no real-world counterparts. The process of drawing might more aptly be termed *constructing,* because you actually build lines and shapes point by point and stack them on top of each other to create a finished image. Each object is independently editable — one of the few structural advantages of an object-oriented approach — but you're still faced with the task of building your artwork one chunk at a time.

Nevertheless, because a drawing program defines lines, shapes, and text as mathematical equations, these objects automatically conform to the full resolution of the *output*

Figure 1-2: Small or large, drawings print smooth, but are a pain to create. This one took more than an hour out of my day, and as you can see, I didn't even bother with the letters around the perimeter of the design.

device, whether it's a laser printer, imagesetter, or film recorder. The drawing program sends the math to the printer and the printer *renders* the math to paper or film. In other words, the printer converts the drawing program's equations to printer pixels. Because your printer offers far more pixels than your screen — a 300 dots-per-inch (dpi) laser printer, for example, offers 300 pixels per inch (dots equal pixels), whereas most screens offer 72 pixels per inch — the printed drawing appears smooth and sharply focused regardless of the size at which you print it, as shown in Figure 1-2.

Another advantage of drawings is that they take up relatively little room on disk. The file size of a drawing depends on the quantity and complexity of the objects the drawing contains. Thus, the file size has almost nothing to do with the size of the printed image, which is just the opposite of the way bitmapped images work. A thumbnail drawing of a garden that contains hundreds of leaves and petals consumes several times more disk space than a poster-sized drawing that contains three rectangles.

When to use Photoshop

Thanks to their specialized methods, painting programs and drawing programs fulfill distinct and divergent purposes. Photoshop and other painting programs are best suited to creating and editing the following kinds of artwork:

- Scanned photos, including photographic collages and embellishments that originate from scans
- Realistic artwork that relies on the play between naturalistic highlights, midranges, and shadows
- Impressionistic-type artwork and other images created for purely personal or aesthetic purposes

- Logos and other display type that feature soft edges, reflections, or tapering shadows
- Special effects that require the use of filters and color enhancements you simply can't achieve in a drawing program

When to use a drawing program

You're probably better off using Illustrator, Canvas, FreeHand, or some other drawing program if you're interested in creating more stylized artwork, such as the items in the following list:

- Poster art and other high-contrast graphics that heighten the appearance of reality
- Architectural plans, product designs, or other precise line drawings
- Business graphics, such as charts and other "infographics" that reflect data or show how things work
- Traditional logos and text effects that require crisp, ultrasmooth edges. (Drawing programs are unique in that they enable you to edit character outlines to create custom letters and symbols.)
- Brochures, flyers, and other single-page documents that mingle artwork, logos, and standard-sized text (such as the text you're reading now)

If you're serious about computer graphics, you should own at least one painting program and one drawing program. If I had to rely exclusively on two graphics applications, I would probably choose Photoshop and Illustrator. Both are Adobe products, and the two function together almost without a hitch. Photoshop also works well in combination with Canvas and FreeHand.

The Macintosh Design Scheme

If your aspirations go beyond image editing into the larger world of Macintosh design, you'll soon learn that Photoshop is just one cog in a mighty wheel of programs used to create artwork, printed documents, and presentations. A dedicated scanning software, such as Light Source's Ofoto, can match colors in a photograph to their closest equivalents on-screen and remove moiré patterns that occur when scanning published photos. EFI's Cachet provides color-correction and printing capabilities that exceed those of Photoshop and dramatically improve your ability to match colors between original and printed photographs without losing any image data. These two products go a long way toward turning Photoshop into a professional-quality image production studio.

The natural-media paint program Fractal Design Painter emulates real-world tools, such as charcoal, chalk, felt-tip markers, calligraphic pen nibs, and camel-hair brushes, as deftly as a synthesizer mimics a thunderstorm. Three-dimensional drawing applications, such as Swivel 3D, Alias Sketch, and Ray Dream Designer, enable you to create hyper-realistic objects with depth, lighting, shadows, surface textures, reflections, refractions — you name it. If you're rich as Midas, the $7,000 ElectricImage goes one step further and throws animation into the equation. All these applications can import images created in Photoshop as well as export images you can then enhance and adjust with Photoshop.

Page-layout programs, such as Aldus PageMaker and QuarkXPress, let you integrate images into newsletters, reports, books (such as this one), and just about any other kind of document you can imagine. If you prefer to transfer your message to slides, you can use Microsoft PowerPoint or Aldus Persuasion to add impact to your images through the use of charts and diagrams. With Adobe Premier, you can merge images with video sequences recorded in the QuickTime format. You even can edit individual frames in Premier movies with Photoshop. MacroMind Director, Passport Producer, and others make it possible to combine images with animation, QuickTime movies, and sound to create multimedia presentations you can show on a screen or record on videotape. MacroMind MediaMaker is one of a handful of products that enable you to overlay images, text, and animation onto live video.

Photoshop Scenarios

All the programs just described run on the Macintosh computer, which is one of the primary reasons the Mac is regarded as such an amazing and essential design tool. But the number of programs you decide to purchase and how you use them is up to you. The following list outlines a few specific ways to use Photoshop alone and in tandem with other products:

- Scan a photograph into Ofoto or directly into Photoshop. Retouch and adjust the image as desired and then print the final image as a black-and-white composite (like the images in this book) or as color separations using Photoshop or Cachet.
- After scanning and adjusting an image inside Photoshop, use PageMaker or QuarkXPress to place the image into your monthly newsletter and then print the document from the page-layout program.
- After putting the finishing touches on a lovely tropical vista inside Photoshop, import the image for use as an eye-catching background inside PowerPoint or Persuasion. Then save the document as a self-running screen presentation or print it to overhead transparencies or slides from the presentation program.

- Capture a Macintosh screen by pressing Command-Shift-3 and then open the screen shot and edit it in Photoshop. Place the corrected image into Illustrator or Canvas, annotate the screen shot using arrows and labels, and print the finished figure from the drawing program.
- Paint an original image inside Photoshop, using a Wacom pressure-sensitive tablet. Use the image as artwork in a document created in a page-layout program or print it directly from Photoshop.
- Scan a surface texture, such as wood or marble, into Photoshop and edit it to create a fluid repeating pattern (as explained in Chapter 10). Import the image for use as a texture map in a three-dimensional drawing program. Render the 3-D graphic to an image file, open the image inside Photoshop, and retouch as needed.
- Create a repeating pattern, convert it to the system software's built-in 256-color palette inside Photoshop, and apply it as a desktop pattern at Finder level, using a utility such as ResEdit or Wallpaper.
- Take a problematic Illustrator EPS file that keeps generating errors when you try to print it, open it inside Photoshop, and render it as a high-resolution bitmap. Then place the image in a document created in a page-layout program or print it directly from Photoshop.
- Start an illustration in Adobe Illustrator and save it as an EPS file. Open the file in Photoshop and use the program's unique tools to add textures and tones that are difficult or impossible to create in a vector-based drawing program.
- Record a QuickTime movie in Premier and export it to the FilmStrip format. Open the file inside Photoshop and edit it one frame at a time by drawing on the frame or applying filters. Finally, open the altered FilmStrip file in Premier and convert it back to the QuickTime format.

Obviously, few folks have the money to buy all these products and even fewer have the energy or inclination to implement every one of these ideas. But quite honestly, these are just a handful of projects I can list off the top of my head. There must be hundreds of uses for Photoshop that involve no outside applications whatsoever. In fact, so far as I've been able to figure, there's no end to the number of design jobs you can handle in whole or in part using Photoshop.

Simply put, this is a versatile and essential product for any designer or artist who currently uses or plans to purchase a Macintosh computer. I, for one, wouldn't remove Photoshop from my hard drive for a thousand bucks. (Of course, that's not to say I'm not willing to consider higher offers. For $1,500, I'd gladly swap it to a Syquest cartridge.)

Summary

- Image editors such as Photoshop are painting programs that are designed specifically to facilitate the editing of photographs and artwork scanned to disk.
- To fully understand Photoshop, you need to understand how bitmapped images differ from other kinds of computer graphics.
- Use a drawing program such as Illustrator or FreeHand to create high-contrast or stylized graphics; use Photoshop to edit scanned images or to paint free-form artwork that features transitional colors.

Welcome to Macintosh

CHAPTER 2

In This Chapter

- The anatomy of a Macintosh computer
- How the system software lets you communicate with your Mac
- A first look at the Finder desktop
- An introduction to menus, dialog boxes, and options
- How to start programs and assign RAM space
- How to install PostScript and TrueType fonts
- The benefits and applications of QuickTime

Computers: Modern-Day Robots

There's this 1950s public-service film called *Housewife's Dream* or *Helping Out Mother* or … heck, I don't know what it's called. The point is, the film features a thoroughly contented homemaker of the future who owns a robot that looks for all the world like a bunch of tin plating with a union guy inside it. Of course, all the visiting service men and mail carriers totally freak out when they see Robbie, or Rusty, or Rubbish, or whatever his name is, but it turns out he's a gentle soul who enjoys helping around the house. He vacuums with his feet, he's equipped with a little saw for cutting ribbons on boxes of flowers (though the Mrs. has to hold the ribbon for him and even rub it against the saw to cut the darn thing), and he scares the living daylights out of the delivery guys so she doesn't have to worry about tipping. He even comes with a built-in church key that he uses to abuse cans of lima beans. The guy's a miracle.

In retrospect, that film represents one of the most insipid views of the future ever forced upon a hapless viewer. (These things must have been shown to elementary-school kids during snow days. Who else would put up with them?) But even the most insightful, provocative science fiction of the time doesn't tell the story of a person — regardless of gender — sitting down in front of the modern equivalent of a household robot, the personal computer. Can you imagine the reaction to a film like that? The housewife sits in front of the machine, boots it up, writes a letter to Grandma, balances the checkbook, downloads electronic mail from an on-line bulletin board, and plays a few arcade games. The audience would riot. "You mean this woman still has to vacuum for herself?" "Where's the little saw for cutting ribbons?" "We want tin plating!"

Because computers function on a level unparalleled by previous technology, many people have problems adapting to them. While the rest of us were dreaming of robots, a bunch of clever scientists, engineers, and other folks who didn't get out enough — otherwise they would have known they were *supposed* to be working on robots — were dabbling in something that turned out to be ten times as useful and could assume tasks previously performed by literally thousands of tools. And unlike Rubbish, who I wouldn't trust to open a can of creamed corn, computers outperform their predecessors on almost every level. They're so amazing, in fact, that millions of people still haven't figured out how they work or even come to terms with why they should be used.

You're lucky, because you already know the answer to half of that puzzle. Stop me if I'm wrong, but I'm guessing that because you're reading this book, you want a computer so you can retouch photos and edit digital images. Any information you can glean about the inner workings of your computer not only will help you as you learn to use Photoshop, but also when you decide to venture beyond Photoshop and start using your Mac to balance your checkbook and write letters to Grandma. (I'm afraid they're still grappling with that vacuuming software.) To that end, this chapter provides an overview of how the modern-day robot called the Macintosh operates.

Computer brains

Imagine your Macintosh computer as a person equipped with only a brain and sensory organs. No heart, no lungs. No hands or feet, either — which prevents the Mac from throttling you when you curse it and eliminates any potential for it to wander away just when you need it most. (You may think of the power supply as the entrails because it takes in the computer nutrients, but we'll skip that for now.)

To understand how the Mac works, you need to take a closer look at how its innards function. Don't worry, no blood or anything else gruesome is involved.

The CPU

I sense you're not all that interested in this topic, so I'll make it fast. The Mac's brain is the *motherboard* (also called the *logic board*), which is a big, green circuit board that contains a bunch of chips and rests on the bottom of the computer's housing. The main chip is the *central processing unit* (CPU). It does all the math and makes all the decisions required to create the images and noises that your computer produces. It also decides when and how to use memory and disk space — with your help, of course. Humans aren't completely out of the loop yet.

Memory

Like the CPU, *memory* is part of the motherboard, but it comprises many chips instead of just one. The first kind of memory is *read-only memory,* or ROM, which can never be altered. ROM is like an animal's instinct; your computer was born with this memory. It is *hard-wired* memory — meaning that it can only be changed by replacing the chips — and contains portions of the system software, which I explain in the upcoming section called "Using Your System Software" (uncanny naming convention).

The second kind of memory is *random-access memory,* or RAM, which you can alter at will. When you open a program, the CPU copies it to RAM in order to access it more quickly. When you quit the program, the CPU deletes it from RAM. When you restart or turn off your machine, all data stored in RAM is lost. So RAM data is entirely temporary in nature.

I hate pretentious, know-it-all computer dweebs, and the best way to recognize them is to listen to how they pronounce ROM or RAM. If they spell it out — as in NFL or UPS — cringe with disgust and disregard everything they say. If they say it like it looks — *rom* and *ram* — bringing to mind the mythical founders of Rome, listen to them with keen interest and secretly admire their wisdom. Needless to say, you should also follow their example.

Disk space

Disk space is separate from the motherboard. It acts as a collection of satellite brains that includes hard drives, floppy disks, and other *removable media devices,* such as SyQuest cartridges, optical drives, and tape-backup systems. Incidentally, *floppy disk* is just an informal name for those hard plastic disks you insert into the front of your computer. Beneath their hard plastic exteriors are flexible round disks, hence the term *floppy.*

Disk space is not memory

Some people incorrectly refer to disk space as memory, but the two are very separate concepts. You can't store data permanently in RAM, but you can store data permanently on disks. You can't change the data stored in ROM, but you can change the data on disks. (The one exception is when you work with CD-ROMs.)

The main difference between memory and disk space, however, is that the CPU controls the contents of memory and *you* control the contents of a disk. Although you can specify how RAM is divvied up among programs, you can't specify how a program makes use of that memory.

A CD-ROM is disk space, but you can't alter or delete data on it. It's just like a standard music CD. You can copy data to a CD-ROM only once, just as you can record music to a CD only once, and you need a special piece of professionally priced hardware (meaning that it's mondo expensive) to do the job. Consumer CD-ROM drives only let you read data, just as stereo CD decks only play.

For specific information on assigning RAM space to Photoshop, see "Assigning application RAM," later in this chapter. For information on how Photoshop can exploit virtual memory — disk space that acts like RAM — see Chapter 3.

How digital space is measured

Whether in memory or on disk, you measure digital space in terms of *bits* and *bytes.* As I discussed in the "Bitmaps versus objects" section of the preceding chapter, a bit is either 0 or 1, off or on. The bit is the absolute smallest unit of measurement. A byte is equal to eight bits.

To give you an idea of how small this is, every letter in a word processor consumes exactly one byte of disk or memory space. A *kilobyte* (K) is 1,000 bytes, and a *megabyte* (MB) is one million bytes or 1,000K. Typically, disk space and memory are measured in megabytes. For example, if you see an ad for an 8/230 Macintosh Centris, the computer is equipped with 8MB of RAM and 230MB of hard disk space. The next unit up is a *gigabyte,* which equals one billion bytes, one million K, or 1,000MB. No Mac user has this much RAM, and folks who have this much space on a single disk aren't likely to take time out to read this chapter. We're talking big bucks.

All computers rely on a *binary counting system,* in which there are only two digits, 0 and 1. This means your computer counts 0, 1, 10, 11, 100, 101, 110, 111, 1000, 1001, and so on. A bit is one digit long. A byte is eight digits long, meaning that it can accommodate up to 256 variations. How did I figure this out? Simple. Take the number 2 — as in 2 digits — and raise it to a power equal to the number of digits in the unit. In a byte, you have 2^8, which equals 256.

By no coincidence, the Macintosh alphabet contains 256 characters — including letters, numbers, foreign characters, and symbols — so one byte is enough to express one character of type. In countries such as Japan, where alphabets contain thousands of characters, the system software permits two bytes per each character. Each two-byte unit is 16 digits long, thus accommodating up to 2^{16} or 65,536 variations.

Computer sensory organs

With the exception of hard drives and removable media devices, everything that lies outside your computer's casing qualifies as a sensory organ. You communicate with your computer by typing on the keyboard and by moving the mouse. It responds to you by displaying images on screen, printing images on paper, and producing beeps and other noises from its speaker. (OK, the speaker is inside the casing, and so is the monitor on machines like the Color Classic, but you get the idea.) Your computer can even communicate with other computers by sending and receiving data over a modem or network.

Keyboard techniques

You can use the keyboard to produce text on-screen or to call up commands and options. For example, pressing Command-C implements the Copy command in all Macintosh programs. Such key combinations are called *keyboard equivalents* or simply *shortcuts*.

Mouse techniques

Moving the mouse changes the location of the on-screen *cursor,* which typically is an arrow that points up and to the left. (It's just another example of right-handers dominating the earth. As if we left-handers don't have a hard enough time trying to find a decent pair of scissors, now we have to put up with this.) The typical mouse features a single button on top that registers clicks and a trackball underneath that registers movement. If your mouse offers more than one button — very rare — you'll quickly discover that only the left button works with Macintosh programs. (More right-handed domination.)

In Photoshop, the cursor changes appearance based on its function. For example, when you select the paintbrush tool, the cursor becomes a little paintbrush. (Funny how that works.) For a complete guide to Photoshop cursors and their meanings, check out Chapter 4, "Inside Photoshop."

Here's a quick look at the terminology associated with using your mouse:

- To *move* your mouse is to move it without pressing the button.
- To *click* is to press the button and immediately release it without moving the mouse. Sometimes, you are instructed to *click on* an item on-screen. This instruction means to position the cursor over the item and then click the mouse button. In Photoshop, you sometimes are instructed to *click with* a tool, as in *click with the paintbrush tool.* This instruction means to select the tool, position its cursor in the image window, and then click the mouse button.
- To *double-click* is to press and release the button twice in rapid succession without moving the mouse. For example, in the case of many Photoshop tools, you can double-click on the tool icon to change its preference settings. Some programs even accept *triple-clicks* and *quadruple-clicks.* Photoshop does not go to such extremes.
- To *press and hold* is to press the button and hold it down for a moment. I refer to this operation when an item remains on-screen only while the mouse button is pressed. For example, you press and hold on a menu name to display a list of commands.
- To *drag* is to press the button and hold it down as you move the mouse. You then release the button to complete the operation. Sometimes, I instruct you to drag a screen element, as in *drag the title bar.* This instruction means to place the cursor on the title bar, press the mouse button and hold it down while dragging the bar. At other times, I tell you to *drag with* a tool — for example, *drag with the paintbrush tool.* This instruction means that you should select the paintbrush tool, position its cursor, and then drag the mouse.

Keyboard and mouse, together at last

You also can use the keyboard and mouse in tandem. In Photoshop, for example, you can press the Shift key while dragging with a selection tool to expand the selected area. To reduce the size of the image in the window, you can press Option while clicking with the zoom tool. Such actions are so common that key and mouse combinations sometimes are joined into compound verbs, such as *Shift-dragging* or *Option-clicking* (still more abuse of the language).

Using Your System Software

If the CPU, memory, and disk space represent the brain, and the mouse, keyboard, monitor, and so on are the sensory organs, then software represents knowledge. Software enables your computer to expand its range of capabilities. Adding a new piece of software to your hard drive is like enrolling your computer in night school. A single installation makes your computer smarter and more capable than its was before.

The *system software,* also referred to as the *operating system* or by its product name (System 6, System 7, and so on), provides your Mac with its most fundamental knowledge, which represents — in anthropomorphic terms — language and the capacity for learning. Other programs conform to the rules and regulations established by the system software and then go on to formulate their own.

How system software is organized

Some of the Mac's system software is stored in ROM. In effect, it is the core of the operating system, handling the most fundamental operations of the Macintosh computer, such as managing memory, disk drives, screen display, and other internal and external hardware. The *Toolbox,* a special portion of the ROM-based operating system, offers a collection of graphic routines that enables any piece of software — including the system software itself — to quickly draw windows, create dialog boxes, handle fonts, and perform basic text editing functions.

Because you can't manipulate ROM-based data, the only way to update this portion of the system software is to physically replace the ROM chips on your computer's motherboard, an expensive and intricate proposition. For this reason, the majority of the system software is located on your hard drive, inside the aptly named *System Folder.* This setup enables Apple to easily distribute updates — System 7.0, System 7.01, System 7.1, and so on — until they're blue in the face.

In case you ever wondered why zillions of manufacturers create IBM PC-compatible computers but Apple has a monopoly on the Mac, the ROM software is your answer. Apple refuses to license the ROM-based portion of its operating system to other vendors. By contrast, IBM's system software, whether it's DOS, OS/2, or Windows, is engineered and owned by Microsoft, which licenses it freely to Dell, NEC, Compaq, Zeos, AST, Gateway, Texas Instruments, Leading Edge, Zenith, Austin, Epson, Toshiba, Northgate, Hyundai (yes, it's the same Hyundai), and anyone else who has a few bucks and a hand to shake.

Powering up

When you turn on your computer, the CPU inspects the ROM for the first few tidbits of system software. It then loads that data and the remaining disk-based portion of the system software into RAM. The entire system software remains in RAM, available for use by other applications, until you turn off or restart your computer, at which point the motherboard interrupts the power supply to the RAM. That split-second suspension of electricity erases the RAM, deleting the system software and all the weird little artifacts left over by other programs. This situation explains why restarting your computer can take care of so many problems. It makes a clean sweep of things, getting rid of the garbage that amassed in RAM and made a mess of the operating system. Next time you turn on your computer, the system software loading sequence begins anew.

You'll know when your Mac switches from ROM-based to disk-based system software by the appearance of the happy Mac icon, that grinning cherub that makes so many people think of the Mac as a hopelessly goofy toy. If a Mac with an inset question mark appears instead, the CPU can't find the system software on the hard drive. In that case you need to insert a floppy disk that contains the software. You then should use the Startup Disk control panel to select the icon for the hard drive that contains the system software, as illustrated in Figure 2-1; doing so enables you to boot from the hard drive the next time you start your computer.

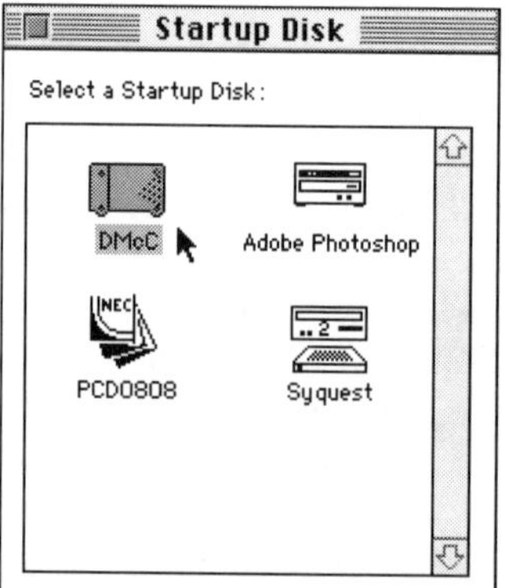

Figure 2-1: The Startup Disk control panel.

Anatomy of the system software

The disk-based portion of the Macintosh operating system is more than a single file. In fact, it comprises an entire folder of files working in tandem. You can customize the performance of your system by adding, deleting, and altering specific files inside the System Folder. These files include the following:

- **System:** The *System* file is the first of the two key players that make up the disk-based portion of the Macintosh operating system. It contains the fundamental data required by other applications. It also contains various kinds of *resources,* most notably fonts and sounds. You can add and delete resources from your system to increase the number of options available to other applications or to save space on disk and in RAM.
- **Finder:** On its own, the System file communicates with applications and hardware, but it can't communicate with the user. That is the job of the system's mouthpiece, the *Finder,* which actually is an independent application, just like Photoshop. The *Finder desktop* is displayed immediately after your Mac finishes loading the system software. It acts as a home base from which you can launch applications, view the contents of disks and hard drives, and rename, organize, duplicate, and delete files. The upcoming section "Meet the Finder desktop" explains the Finder desktop in detail.

Both the System and Finder files are essential to using a Macintosh computer. The following files represent optional elements of the system software:

- **System extensions:** Also known as *INITs, system extensions* expand or modify the performance of the system software. They also may control some aspect of an external piece of hardware. The CPU loads system extensions into RAM along with the System and Finder files during the start-up procedure. Many extensions display icons along the bottom of your screen as they load.
- **Control panels:** Like system extensions, *control panels* — also called *control panel devices,* or *cdevs* for short — slightly augment the capabilities of the System and Finder files. Many control panels load into memory during the start-up procedure. You can open a control panel to display a window of options that govern the performance of a feature or piece of hardware. For example, the General Controls cdev enables you to change the time, date, and desktop pattern. To access a control panel, choose the Control Panels command — Control Panel (singular) under System 6 — from the Apple menu at the Finder desktop.
- **Desk accessories:** *Desk accessories* (DAs) are mini-applications — or *utilities* — that reside under the Apple menu at the Finder desktop. Under System 7, the only indispensable desk accessory is the Chooser, which provides access to printer and network drivers. Under System 6, the Control Panel DA also is essential, because it provides access to cdevs. This DA was demoted to a folder under System 7. Unessential but equally common DAs include the Alarm Clock, Calculator, Key Caps (which shows the keyboard locations of characters in a specified font), and Scrapbook (which allows you to store copied text and images for easy retrieval).

- **Drivers:** *Drivers,* also called *Chooser extensions,* act as interpreters that enable your computer to communicate accurately with printers, networking systems like AppleTalk and Ethernet, and other devices that require specialized communications. For example, the LaserWriter file is a printer driver that translates instructions from the QuickDraw screen format to the PostScript printer language. To access a driver, choose the Chooser command from the Apple menu at the Finder desktop.
- **Support files:** This catch-all term refers to any files that may be required to successfully operate a system extension, control panel, or desk accessory. These files may contain preference settings or essential data. The most common example of a support file is the *Clipboard,* which offers access to text or images you copy using the Cut or Copy command.

Under System 7, optional system files are organized into one of several predefined subfolders within the System Folder. The Control Panels folder contains — you guessed it — control panels. The Extensions folder contains system extensions and drivers. The Apple Menu Items folder contains desk accessories, and the Preferences folder contains many, if not all, of the support files.

Meet the Finder desktop

The primary function of the Finder is to display and organize the contents of disks, whether they're floppy disks, hard drives, cartridges, CD-ROMs, tapes, optical drives, or volumes shared over a network. The Finder desktop facilitates this function by providing the elements shown in Figure 2-2.

If you're still using System 6, now's a great time to upgrade. Really. Get on the phone, call your local computer guy, and ask for System 7. I'll wait . . . you didn't do it, did you? You're still using System 6. I'm very disappointed. Maybe tomorrow you'll see the light. In the meantime, the Help menu, the Applications menu, and the Alias and Edition icons shown in Figure 2-2 will not appear on your desktop.

The elements of the Finder desktop work as follows:

- **Menu bar:** A single *menu bar* appears along the top of the desktop, a trait shared with all other Macintosh applications. Each word in the menu bar represents a menu that contains a list of *commands* you can use to manipulate selected files, change the way files are displayed in windows, and initiate other disk-management operations.

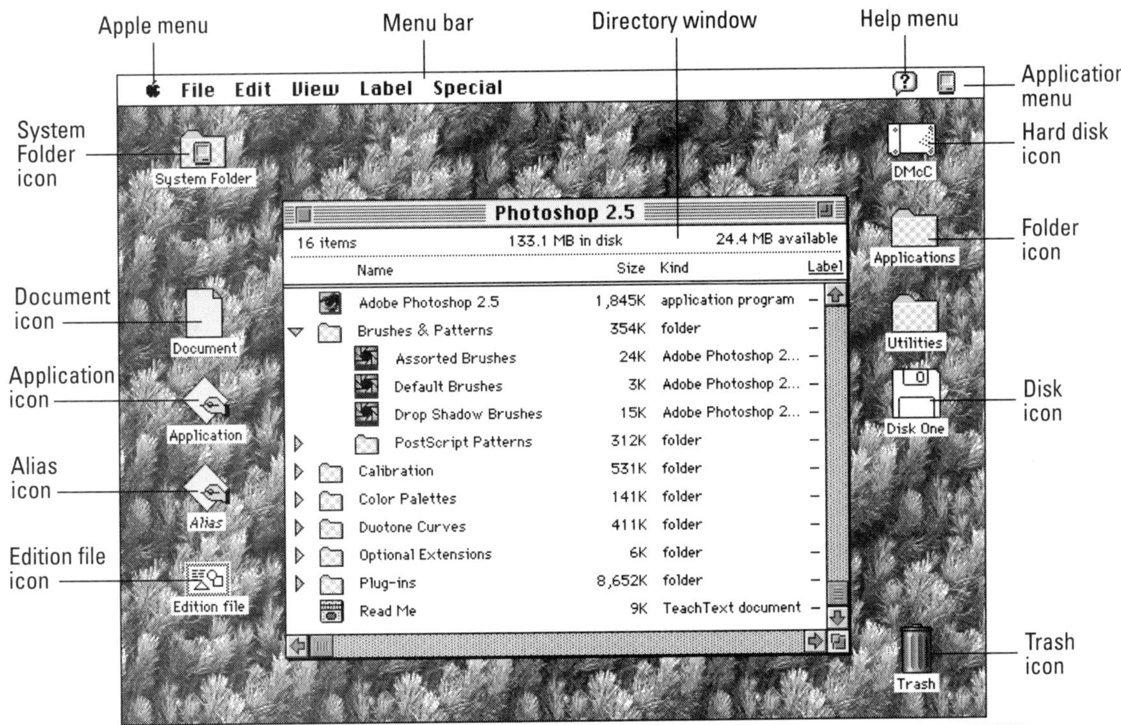

Figure 2-2: The Finder desktop as it might appear under System 7.

- **Apple menu:** The *Apple menu* contains a list of desk accessories. Under System 7, you can control the items that appear in the Apple menu by manipulating the contents of the Apple Menu Items folder in the System Folder.
- **Help menu:** Use the *Help menu* to activate System 7's *balloon help* feature, which displays a little text balloon filled with information about any desktop element you point to with your cursor. Just move your cursor around to find help on a range of topics. If you're new to the Mac, balloon help is a great way to get acquainted with your system software.
- **Applications menu:** Specific to System 7, the *Applications menu* lists all applications that are currently running, including the Finder. You can switch from one running application to another by choosing the application name from the menu. You also can hide windows from certain applications to eliminate screen clutter.
- **Hard disk icon:** An *icon* is a tiny picture that represents a disk, folder, file, or other desktop element. The icon in the upper right corner of the screen represents the hard drive that contains the current system software. Double-click on the hard drive icon to display its contents inside a directory window. (I explain the directory window in the next section.)

- **Folder icon:** *Folders* are optional organizational tools. You can create as many folders as you like and locate an indefinite number of files inside each folder. To create a folder, choose File ⇨ New Folder or press Command-N. You can create a folder directly at the desktop, as in the figure, or inside a directory window. You even can create folders within folders within folders, *ad infinitum.*
- **Disk icon:** A *disk icon* appears for each *mounted* floppy disk, SyQuest cartridge, CD-ROM, and so on. The Finder automatically mounts all available disks at the end of the start-up procedure so that you can access their contents. The Finder also mounts a disk any time you insert one in its drive. (You generally need special system extensions to mount removable media devices.) To dismount a disk and eject it from the drive, drag the disk icon to the Trash or select the icon and choose File ⇨ Put Away (Command-Y).
- **Trash icon:** Under System 7, deleting files is a two-step process. First, you drag the files to the *Trash icon,* and then you choose Special ⇨ Empty Trash. To bypass warnings and delete locked files, press the Option key while choosing the Empty Trash command. You can leave files in the Trash for as long as you like without emptying it. This option gives you the chance to rescue them if you change your mind. However, after you choose the Empty Trash command, the files are gone for good. (Actually, some commercial utilities, such as Norton Utilities for Macintosh, enable you to rescue files even after you choose Empty Trash, but these utilities aren't 100 percent foolproof. When in doubt, don't choose this command!)
- **System Folder icon:** The *System Folder* contains all the files necessary to run your computer. I think you've heard about as much on this topic as any human should have to withstand in one sitting.
- **Document icon:** A *document* is a file created with an application. Unlike applications, which can be executed independently of other programs (see the following paragraph), you have to use an application to open a document. The icon shown in Figure 2-2 is a generic document icon. Most applications assign special icons to their documents to provide a visual clue to their origin. You can open many document *formats* using a variety of applications, but some formats — called *native formats* — are exclusive to one brand of application only.
- **Application icon:** An *application icon* represents an *executable program;* that is, a file that runs and performs operations, offers its own desktop, opens other files, and so on. Under System 7, control panels and desk accessories also qualify as applications. To run an application, double-click on its icon. As with the document icon, the application icon shown in Figure 2-2 is a generic. Commercial programs such as Photoshop offer personalized icons to separate them from the crowd.
- **Alias icon:** Specific to System 7, an *alias* is a dummy file that references another file on disk. For example, if you create an alias for the Photoshop application, double-clicking on that alias icon runs Photoshop. Aliases are convenience tools,

great for tossing into the Apple Menu Items folder and positioning at the desktop. The file name of an alias is italicized to distinguish it from other kinds of files. To create an alias, select the original document and choose File ⇨ Make Alias.

- **Edition file icon:** System 7's *publish and subscribe* feature permits you to save a portion of a document to disk as an *edition file.* When you import the edition into a different document, the application creates a live link between the imported element and the edition file on disk. Whenever you update the edition file, the application updates the imported element automatically.
- **Directory window:** Double-click on a disk or folder icon to display the contents of the disk or folder in a *directory window.* You can change the manner and order in which files appear in a window using commands from the View menu.

Parts of the window

The window is an especially important part of the Macintosh interface. At the Finder desktop, a window displays the contents of an open disk or folder. In other applications, a window displays the contents of a file. Whether displayed at the Finder desktop, within Photoshop, or in some other application, a window includes the following basic elements, as labeled in Figure 2-3:

- **Title bar:** The *title bar* along the top of a directory window lists the name of the disk, folder, or file to which the window belongs. Inside other applications, the title bar lists the name of the open document. The *active* window is distinguished by the appearance of horizontal lines across the title bar. If you select an icon outside this window, you *deactivate* the window, making the close box, zoom box, size box, and scroll bars invisible. Drag the title bar to move an active window. To move a background window without making it active, press the Command key and drag the title bar.
- **Close box:** Click on the *close box* in the upper left corner of the title bar to close the active window. (Finally, some consideration for left-handers.) Press the Option key and click on the close box to close *all* directory windows at the desktop.
- **Zoom box:** Click on the *zoom box* in the upper right corner of the title bar to resize the active window to display as much of its contents as will fit on-screen. Click on the zoom box a second time to return the window to its previous size. Option-click on the zoom box to enlarge the window to full-screen size, regardless of its contents.
- **Size box:** Drag the *size box* in the lower right corner of the active window to resize the window manually.

- **Scroll bars:** Use the *scroll bars* along the right and bottom sides of the active window to display hidden contents of the window. If you click on a *scroll arrow,* you nudge the window slightly in that direction. Click on the gray area of a scroll bar to scroll the window more dramatically. Drag a *scroll box* to manually specify the distance scrolled. If all contents of a window are displayed, the scroll bars appear empty.

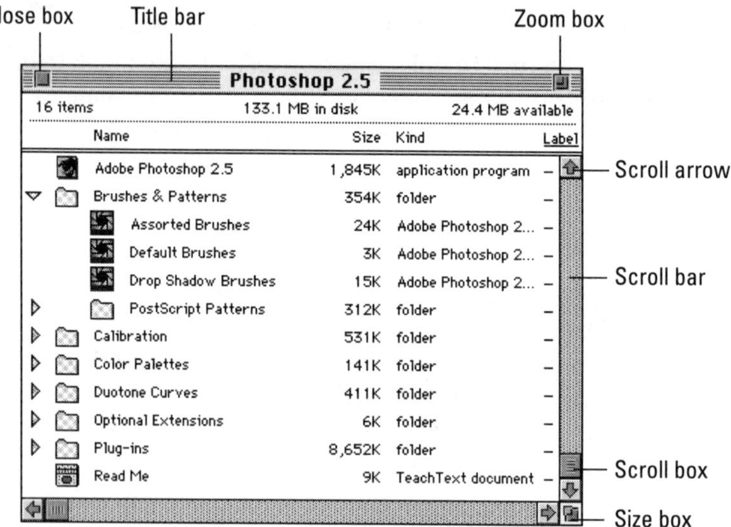

Figure 2-3: Basic elements in the Macintosh window.

If you use an *extended keyboard* — one that includes function keys along the top row — you can scroll the active window from the keyboard. Pressing the Page Down key scrolls down one screen, as if you had clicked on the gray area in the vertical scroll bar below the scroll box. Pressing Page Up scrolls up one screen. Pressing the End key scrolls all the way to the bottom of the active window, and pressing Home scrolls all the way to the top.

Reviewing System Software Elements

Next, I need to brief you on a few system software elements you'll use inside Photoshop and every other Macintosh application you care to take up. These elements make up the basic visual and logical composition of the Macintosh interface. They're so straightforward that explaining them is almost a waste of your time, but each element provides a few clues you may have overlooked. Hopefully, my explanations will help you predict the effect of unfamiliar functions throughout your future dealings with Macintosh software.

Menus and submenus

With the exception of a few applications that hide their menu bars, every Macintosh program features a series of menus across the top of the screen. Drag on a menu name to display a list of commands, each of which performs a specific function. If you choose a command followed by a right-pointing arrowhead, a *hierarchical submenu* (or just plain *submenu*) of related commands appears, as shown in Figure 2-4. Drag onto the submenu to choose the desired command.

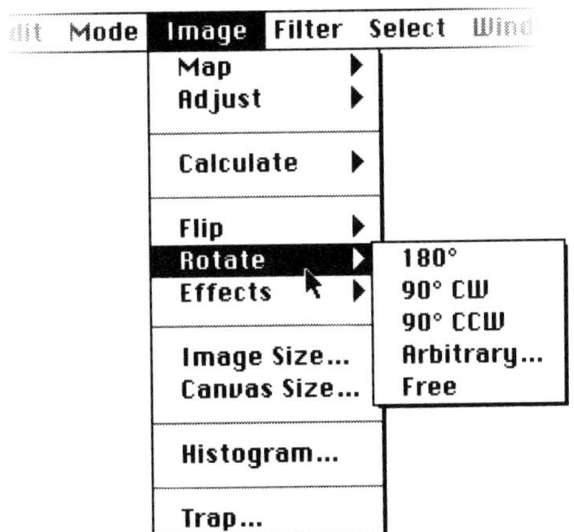

Figure 2-4: The Rotate command and its submenu.

Dialog boxes and options

If a command is followed by an ellipsis (...), as in Page Setup..., choosing the command displays a *dialog box*, as shown in Figure 2-5. The dialog box is a way for the application or system software to request additional information from you before executing the command. It's not much of a dialog in the traditional sense — the computer asks you questions, you respond, and that's the end — but it's about as sophisticated as computers get these days.

Dialog boxes request information by presenting a variety of *options*. Your response to each option determines the manner in which the command eventually executes. Figure 2-5 shows the five kinds of options that can appear in a dialog box:

- **Radio button:** You can select only one round *radio button* from a set of radio buttons. To select a radio button, click on the button or on the option name that follows it. The selected radio button is filled with a black dot; all deselected radio buttons are hollow.
- **Option box:** An option that allows you to enter a value or text is called an *option box*. Double-clicking on an option box *highlights* its contents. When the contents

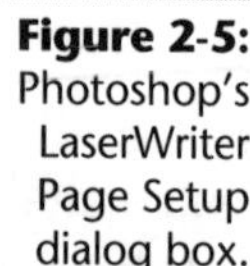

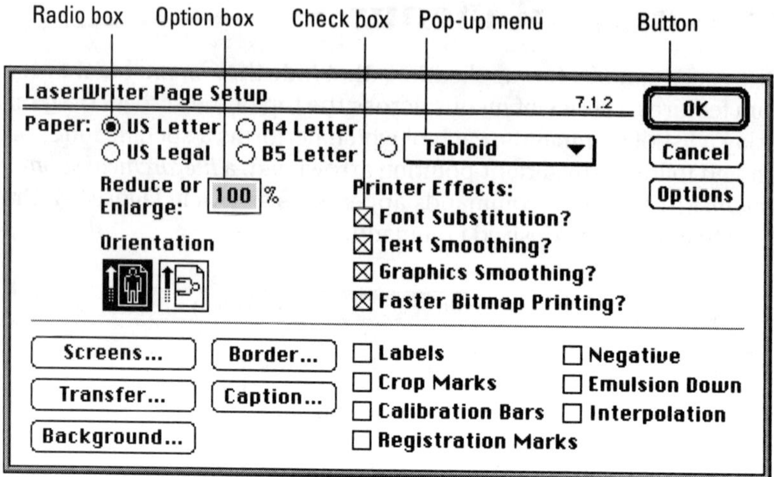

Figure 2-5: Photoshop's LaserWriter Page Setup dialog box.

of an option box are highlighted, you can replace them by entering new characters from the keyboard. If a dialog box contains multiple option boxes, press the Tab key to advance from one option box to the next.

- **Check box:** Although you can select only one radio button in a set of radio buttons, you can select any number of *check boxes* within a set of check boxes. To select a check box, click on the box or on the option name that follows it. Clicking on a selected check box deselects the option. A selected check box is filled with an X; a deselected check box is empty.
- **Pop-up menu:** To conserve space, some multiple-choice options appear as *pop-up menus.* Click and hold on the shadowed box to display a menu of option choices. Drag your mouse to highlight the desired option and release your mouse button to select it, just as if you were choosing a command from a standard menu.
- **Button:** Not to be confused with the radio button, a *button* allows you to close the current dialog box or display others. For example, click on the Cancel button to close the dialog box and cancel the current command. Click on the OK button to close the dialog box and execute the command according to the current settings. Click on the Options button to display another dialog box. When a button is surrounded by a heavy outline, you also can press the Return or Enter key to execute it.

The *alert box,* a variation on the dialog box, displays an error message or warning. Most alert boxes include only buttons — OK, No, Cancel, I Hear Ya, Get Off My Case, whatever. The classic example is the alert box that appears when you try to close a document that you haven't yet saved. Figure 2-6 shows two variations on the standard Save changes alert box, one as defined by the system software and the other as customized by Photoshop.

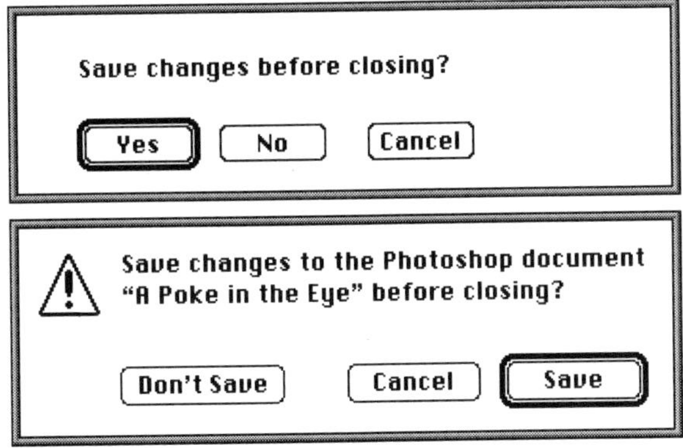

Figure 2-6: Examples of alert boxes.

How to navigate via dialog boxes

Two operations — the opening and saving of documents — are standardized across all Macintosh programs. They provide a first look at the practical application of menu commands and dialog boxes. But more importantly, they enable you to navigate through disks and folders in ways that the Finder doesn't make possible.

I've written the following discussions specifically with System 7 users in mind. Some features work slightly differently under System 6. For example, the Desktop button offered by System 7 is a Drive button under System 6.

The folder bar

Inside most programs, you choose File ⇨ Open (Command-O) to display the Open dialog box, shown in Figure 2-7. The open dialog box requests that you locate and select the document you want to open. The upper left corner of the dialog box features a *folder bar,* which tells you where you are inside the folder hierarchy. The name that appears in the bar reflects the current folder. Drag from the folder bar to relocate to a *parent folder,* that is, one of the folders that contains the current folder.

The scrolling list

Below the folder bar, the Open dialog box provides a scrolling list that contains the names of all folders inside the current folder as well as all documents you can open in the current application. Alias names appear italicized. You can use the scrolling list as follows:

- **Select a document or folder:** Select a document or folder by clicking on its name.
- **Select by key entry:** To quickly locate a specific document or folder name, enter the first few letters of its name from the keyboard. The first item in alphabetical order whose name begins with these letters becomes selected.

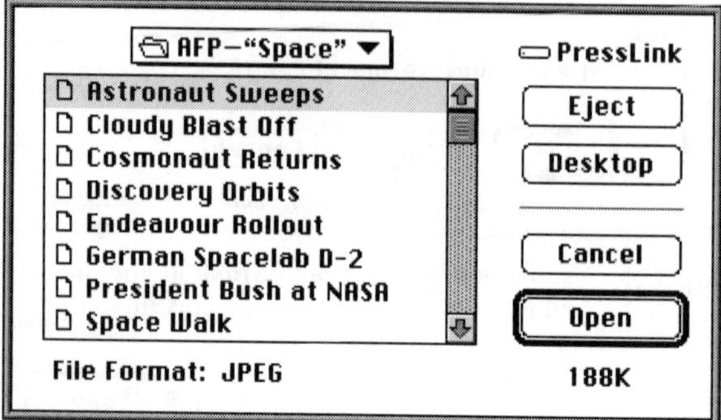

Figure 2-7: The Open dialog box lets you open a document in the current application.

- **Scroll through the list:** Press the up-arrow or down-arrow key to advance one name at a time through the scrolling list. On an extended keyboard, press the Page Up or Page Down key to scroll up or down several names at a time. Press the Home key to scroll all the way to the top of the list; press the End key to scroll all the way to the bottom.
- **Open an item:** Open a file or folder by double-clicking on its name or by selecting it and pressing the Return key.
- **Open a folder:** If a folder name is selected, press Command-down arrow to open that folder and display its contents.
- **Exit a folder:** To exit the current folder and display the contents of its parent folder, press Command-up arrow. You also can close the current folder by clicking on the disk icon above the Eject button.

The navigation buttons

To the right of the scrolling list is the name of the current disk. Below the disk name are four buttons. Each button has a keyboard equivalent, indicated in parentheses in the following list:

- **Eject (Command-E):** Ejects the current disk from the disk drive. The disk remains mounted, enabling you to access it later. If the current disk is a hard drive, the Eject button appears dimmed.
- **Desktop (Command-D):** Exits the current folder and displays all documents and folders located at the Finder desktop.
- **Cancel (Command-period):** Cancels the Open command and returns to the application desktop.
- **Open (Command-O):** Opens the selected document or folder. The fact that the Open button is surrounded by a heavy outline shows that you also can activate it by pressing the Return or Enter key.

Though the Desktop button replaces the System 6 Drive button, the functionality of the Drive button is not lost. Under System 7, you can switch from one drive to another from the keyboard. Press Command-right arrow to display the contents of the next disk; press Command-left arrow to display the contents of the previous disk.

The Preview and Find options

Photoshop 2.5.1 supplies the revised Open dialog box shown in Figure 2-8, which sports a thumbnail preview of the selected image on the left side of the scrolling list and two Find buttons on the right.

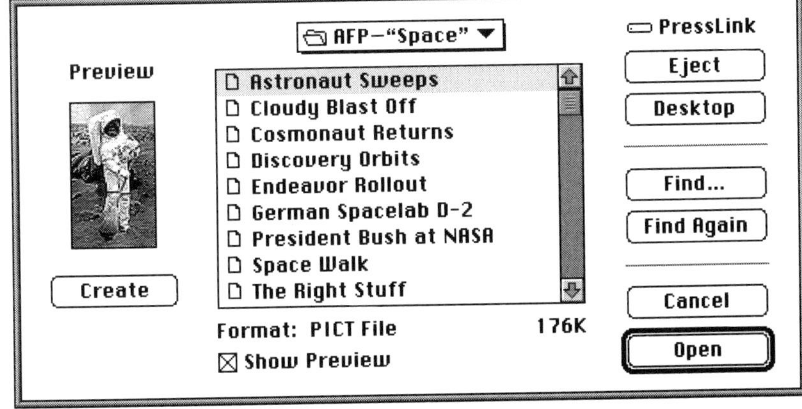

Figure 2-8: In Version 2.5.1, you can view a preview of an image on disk and search for a file by name.

Here's how the new options work:

- **Show Preview:** When selected, this check box instructs Photoshop to display the thumbnail preview image on the left side of the dialog box. If you deselect the option, the preview disappears and the Open dialog box collapses to save screen space.
- **Create:** A preview appears only if the Save Previews check box in the General Preferences dialog box was selected when you saved the image to disk. (See the "General environmental preferences" section near the end of Chapter 4 for complete information.) If no preview appears, you may be able to create a preview on the fly by clicking on the Create button. However, QuickTime must be running for this button to function, and even then, the button only applies to PICT images. If the image is saved in any other file format — TIFF, JPEG, EPS, and so on — you can generate a preview only by opening the image, selecting the Save Previews option in the General Preferences dialog box, and resaving the image to disk. So much for convenience, eh?
- **Find (Command-F):** Suppose that you know the name of a file — or at least part of the name — but you can't remember where you put it. Not to worry. Now you can search through the names of files using the Find button. Just click on the

button, enter some text in the resulting option box, and press the Return key. Photoshop searches the disk in a fairly random fashion and takes you to the first filename that contains the exact characters you entered.

- **Find Again (Command-G):** If the first filename isn't the one you're looking for, click on the Find Again button to find the next filename that contains your text. If you want to search for a different string of characters, click on the Find button and enter some different text.

Variations on the save

Choosing File ➪ Save (Command-S) or File ➪ Save As displays the Save dialog box (shown in Figure 2-9), which requires that you name the foreground document and specify its location. In many respects, the Save dialog box is identical to the Open dialog box, with a few interesting exceptions. For example, when you first display the Save dialog box, the Save This Document As option box in the lower left corner is active so that you can enter the name under which you want to store the document.

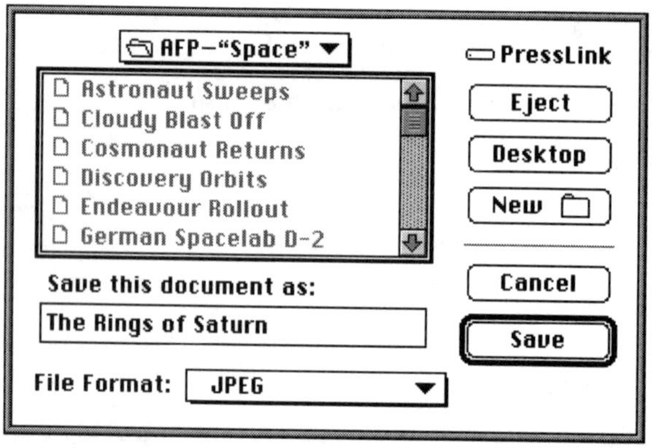

Figure 2-9: The Save dialog box lets you save a document from the current application.

If you click on the scrolling list or press the Tab key, you activate the scrolling list and deactivate the option box. A heavy line surrounds the scrolling list when it is active. You then can scroll through document and folder names by pressing keys from the keyboard, as described for the Open dialog box. To reactivate the Save This Document As option box, press Tab again.

The navigation buttons — Eject, Desktop, and Cancel — work identically to their counterparts in the Open dialog box. But two buttons are unique to the Save dialog box:

- **New Folder (Command-N):** Choosing this button creates a new folder inside the current folder. The system software displays an alert box that asks you to name the prospective folder.
- **Save (Command-S):** This button saves the current document under the name specified in the Save This Document As option box. If the option box is empty, the Save button appears dimmed. If you activate the scrolling list and select a

folder, the Save button temporarily changes to an Open button (which is why the button also reacts to pressing Command-O, even when it's labeled Save). To return to the Save This Document As option box and access the Save button, press Tab. You then can activate the Save button by clicking on it or by pressing the Return or Enter key.

Working with Programs

Though everyone's had years to mull it over, the jury remains split on the most important breakthrough achieved by the Mac when it debuted back in the mid-1980s. (I won't give away the exact year, but it had something to do with George Orwell and too many "Thriller" videos.) Many point to the machine's graphical interface, but I think it was the system software's ability to share information between applications.

A running application could access any system element, most notably fonts, which is why the Mac quickly became synonymous with desktop publishing. But you also could trade data between documents or programs by using the system's built-in Clipboard. To transfer text or images from Document 1 to Document 2, for example, you simply copied the items from Document 1, opened Document 2, and chose Edit ⇨ Paste. To transfer items between different programs, you had to quit one program before you launched the other one, but the system retained the contents of the Clipboard throughout.

Application management continues to be a hallmark of the Macintosh operating system. Only now, it's not limited to fonts and the Clipboard. You can run multiple programs at a time, assign chunks of RAM to each running program, and perform tasks in the background. Each of these options is explained in the upcoming pages.

System 7 enables you to run multiple programs simultaneously. Because the Finder remains available at all times, you can perform organizational tasks such as copying files to disk, renaming files, and so on without quitting any running application. Under System 6, you must activate a special file called the MultiFinder if you want to run more than one application at a time.

Like System 7, Windows 3.1 on the PC provides *cooperative multitasking,* in which all running programs are on their honor to amicably share the computer's time and attention. This means that if one program messes up, it can bring down the entire system. Windows NT (*New Technology*) will offer *protected-mode multitasking,* a better solution that prevents bad applications from crashing good ones. If an application goes down, it will bomb on its own and enable you to go about your business without restarting or losing important data.

Starting an application

Before you can use an application, you have to load it into RAM, thus making it available to the CPU. This is called *running, starting,* or *launching* a program. Of the three terms, I prefer the last because it's so active. I can just see the program zooming into RAM, jet streams of data flowing behind it. Unfortunately, whenever I say, "Go ahead and launch the program" (a phrase I utter constantly in day-to-day conversation), I get nothing but quizzical looks. "You want I should strap the disk to an Estes rocket and propel it into the stratosphere?" Well OK, no one's ever actually asked me that, but you can tell that's exactly what people are thinking. So I'll stick with *run.* Or maybe *start.* They're boring terms but at least they don't require a countdown.

You can run a program from the Finder desktop by using any of the following methods:

- **Open the application directly:** Double-click on the application icon or select the icon and choose the Open command from the File menu (Command-O).
- **Open a document belonging to the application:** Double-click on a document icon or select the document and choose File ⇨ Open (Command-O). The system software locates the application in which the document was last saved, runs that application, and opens the selected document.
- **Drag a document icon onto the application icon:** Suppose that you locate an old piece of bitmapped clip art. It was saved in the MacPaint format, but you want to open it in Photoshop, where you can colorize the image and apply special effects. Certainly, you can run Photoshop and then open the MacPaint file. But under System 7, you can eliminate the middleman. Just drag the MacPaint file icon onto the Photoshop application icon at the Finder desktop, as shown in Figure 2-10. This technique is called *drop-launching* (there's that word again). If the application supports the format of the document you drag onto it, the system software highlights the application icon, as shown in the figure. If the application does not support the format, the icon is not highlighted and the application does not launch.

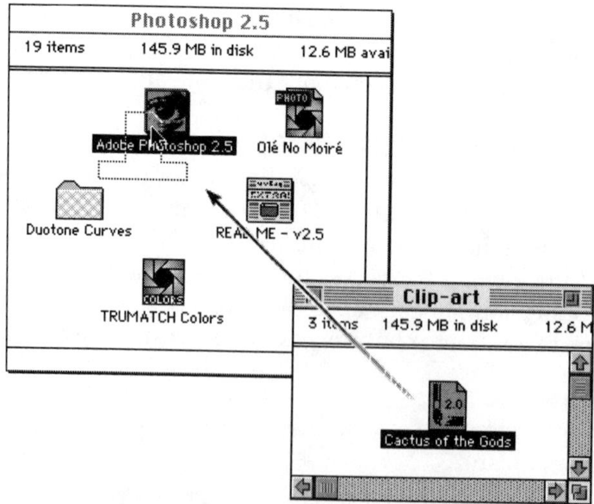

Figure 2-10: Drag a document icon onto an application icon to open the selected document inside the application.

Assigning application RAM

Before running a program, you may want to specify the amount of space it will consume in RAM. This technique can prove useful when you want to conserve RAM space or, alternatively, to use as much as physically possible.

Suppose that you're trying to create a document in QuarkXPress that involves images created in Photoshop and text created in Microsoft Word. You want to run all three programs at once, but your Mac is equipped with only 8MB of RAM. By curtailing the amount of RAM available to each program, you can get all three to run at the same time. The tradeoff is performance. When RAM is limited, a program may run slower, it may not be able to open large files, or both conditions exist.

The trade off is performance. When RAM is limited, a program may run slower, it may not be able to open large files, or both conditions exist.

On the flip side, suppose that you want to work in Photoshop exclusively. By increasing the amount of RAM available to Photoshop, you can significantly speed up its performance and permit the program to open large images.

Using the Get Info command

The amount of RAM set aside for use by a program is called the *application memory* or *application RAM.* You can adjust the amount of application memory the system software assigns to a program by choosing the Get Info command from the File menu (Command-I).

Again, I'll use Photoshop as an example. Before launching Photoshop, select its icon at the Finder desktop and choose File ⇨ Get Info to display the Info dialog box shown in Figure 2-11. System 7.1 provides three Memory Requirements values in the lower right corner of the dialog box:

- **Suggested Size:** The Suggested Size value indicates the minimum amount of RAM that the designers of the program recommend you use. You cannot change this value (nor would you want to do so; it's just a reference number).
- **Minimum Size:** The Minimum Size value represents the absolute minimum amount of RAM the program needs to remain stable. As long as this much RAM is available, the system software starts the program. Lower this value, and you're flirting with disaster. If you assign far too little RAM, the program won't be able to fit into the space you've assigned to it and will quit on its own. If you give the program just enough RAM to get by, it probably will crash after a few moments of use. You may even have to restart your machine. The only advisable use for this option is to raise the value. For example, if you want to increase the likelihood of a stable working environment inside Photoshop 2.5, raise the Minimum Size value from its default 3,072K to match the Suggested Size value of 5,120K.

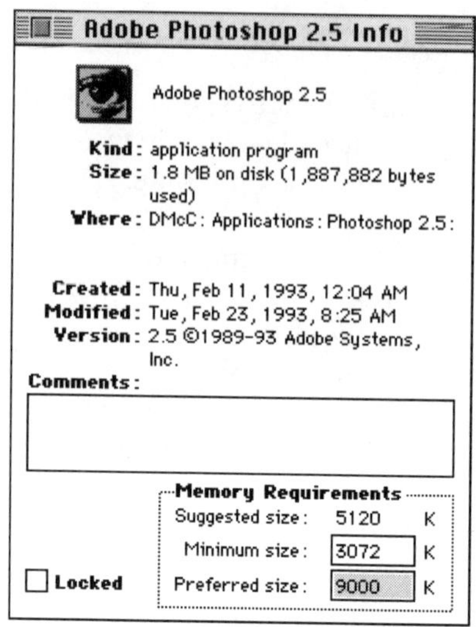

Figure 2-11: Adjust application memory assigned to the selected program by making changes in the Info dialog box.

- **Preferred Size:** Now we're talking. You can change this option all you want. The Preferred Size value determines the amount of application RAM that the program will use if sufficient RAM is available. The value must be larger than the Minimum Size value, but otherwise there are no constraints. If you go below the Suggested Size value but stay above the Minimum Size value, the program may perform sluggishly, but it should remain stable. If the amount of RAM available lies somewhere between the Minimum Size and Preferred Size values, the program ignores your recommendations and just consumes as much RAM as it can.

If you're using System 7.0, the Info dialog box offers only two memory values, Suggested Size and Current Size. The latter value serves the same purpose as the Preferred Size option provided by System 7.1.

The most important rule for managing digital space is to never completely fill it. Whether it's disk space or memory, try to leave no less than 10 percent of the space unused. This rule is particularly important when it comes to RAM, because your system software always needs room to expand. You can check how much RAM is available by choosing the About This Macintosh command from the Apple menu, as shown in Figure 2-12. The System Software value (last in list) includes the RAM space occupied by the Finder. If the Largest Unused Block value (upper right) reads `zero K`, as in Figure 2-12, you run an increased risk of encountering system problems. Symptoms include DAs and control panels quitting unexpectedly and the Finder refusing to open directory windows. To solve the problem, quit a running application, assign it a smaller Preferred Size value, and relaunch it. If problems persist, you may need to quit one or more running applications.

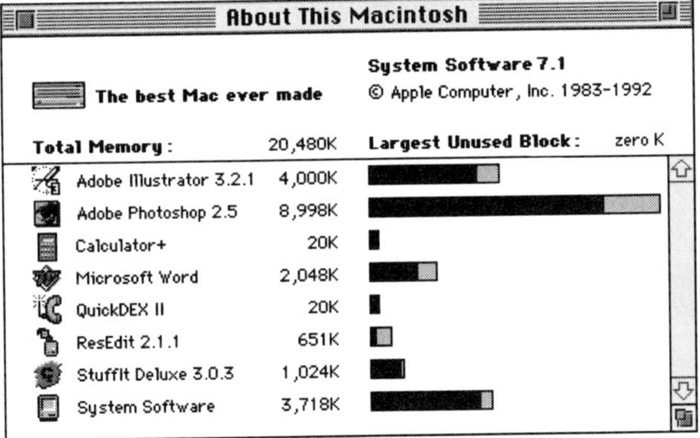

Figure 2-12: To view the way running applications make use of RAM, Choose Apple ⇨ About This Macintosh.

Understanding memory fragmentation

If your Mac does not have a sufficiently large uninterrupted block of RAM to accommodate an application you're trying to run, an error message appears and prevents you from continuing. The only solution — other than decreasing the Minimum Size value — is to free up some memory by quitting one or more of the applications that are currently running.

Notice that I wrote *uninterrupted* memory. Your machine may be equipped with 8MB of RAM and you're only running one application besides the Finder, but that doesn't mean you can also run Photoshop. Memory can become *fragmented* — that is, subdivided into blocks too small to launch other applications.

Consider the chart in Figure 2-13, which illustrates memory consumption on an 8MB machine. The white areas in the horizontal bars represent free RAM space. At start-up, no application other than the Finder is running. The system software is very small and consumes only 1MB of RAM, leaving 7MB free for additional application software. Suppose that after start-up, you run Microsoft Word, which requires at least 1MB of additional RAM. You then run the communications software America Online, which consumes another 1MB. Finally, you run Photoshop, which you've set to take up 4MB. Only 1MB of RAM remains free.

Now suppose that you want to launch PageMaker, which requires a minimum of 2MB to run. Before you can launch the program, you must quit one or more applications to free up enough RAM space. Because 1MB of RAM is currently free, you reason that you need to free up another 1MB, so you quit America Online. But when you try to launch PageMaker, you find that you still don't have enough memory. Although 2MB of free RAM is available, the memory is fragmented in 1MB chunks, as illustrated in the last bar on Figure 2-13. Like any Macintosh application, PageMaker requires uninterrupted RAM.

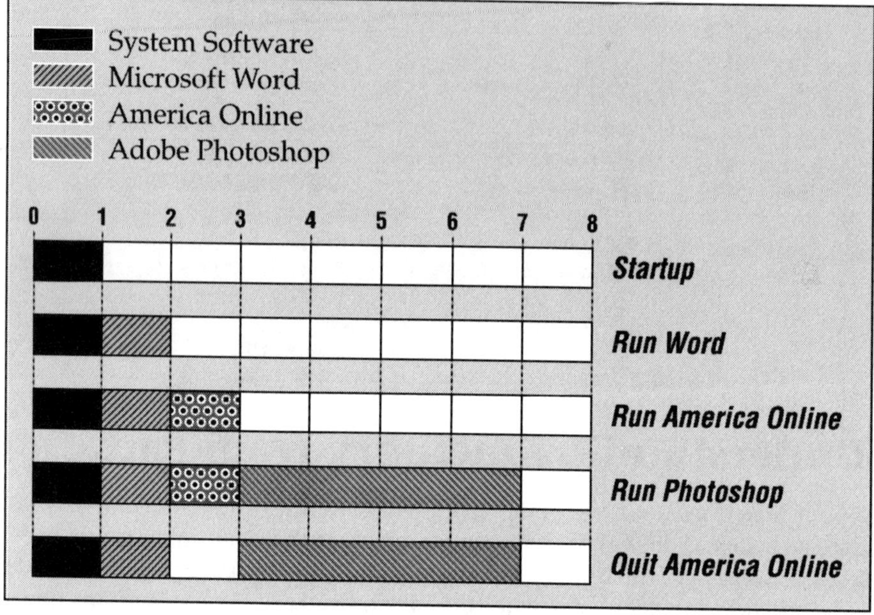

Figure 2-13: Running and quitting software can result in fragmentation of free RAM space (represented here by the white boxes).

Keep in mind that the 1MB figure for the system software suggested in Figure 2-13 is achievable, put pretty darn unrealistic. Your system will grow based on the number of control panels and extensions that load during start-up, the number of fonts and sounds you use, and a variety of other circumstances. My system tends to hover around 4MB, but I have all kinds of junk hooked up to this machine.

The only surefire way to avoid memory fragmentation is to quit applications in the *opposite* order in which you launched them. Because few of us work that systematically, you may prefer to completely free up your RAM by quitting *all* applications and then rerunning the desired software.

Managing multiple applications

Being able to run multiple applications simultaneously vastly increases the number of tasks you can perform and reduces the amount of time it takes to complete those tasks. But you need to know a few things in order to take advantage of this capability. First, you must learn how to switch quickly and accurately between running programs. Second, you need to understand when and how to instruct one program to carry out time-consuming tasks in the background while you remain productive using another program in the foreground. And third, you need to remember to clean up all that screen clutter periodically so that you can see what the heck you're doing.

Switching between running applications

At any one time, only one running application resides in the *foreground;* the others run in the *background.* You can access the capabilities of an application only when it runs in the foreground. To bring a program to the foreground and send the previous foreground application to the background, use a method called *switching.* Here are two different ways to switch to a new foreground application:

- **Choose the application from the Applications menu:** The Applications menu, located at the far right of the menu bar, provides access to every running application, including the Finder. Choose the desired application from the menu to bring that application to the foreground.
- **Click on a background window:** Like the Finder, every application offers its own desktop, including a menu bar, windows for open documents, and other elements (such as toolboxes, palettes, and floating rulers) that vary from application to application. You can click on an open window or other visible element to switch to the application where the element belongs. For example, when working in Photoshop, you can click on a directory window, a desktop icon, or the desktop pattern itself to bring the Finder to the foreground (shown in Figure 2-14). To switch back to Photoshop, click on the open image window, which brings Photoshop to the foreground, (shown in Figure 2-15).

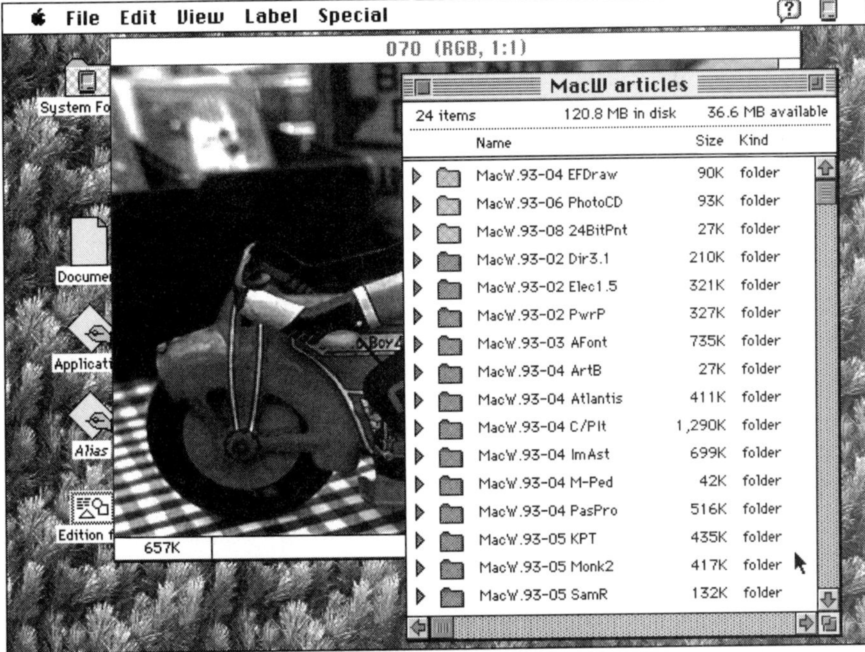

Figure 2-14: You can click on an open directory window to bring the Finder to the foreground.

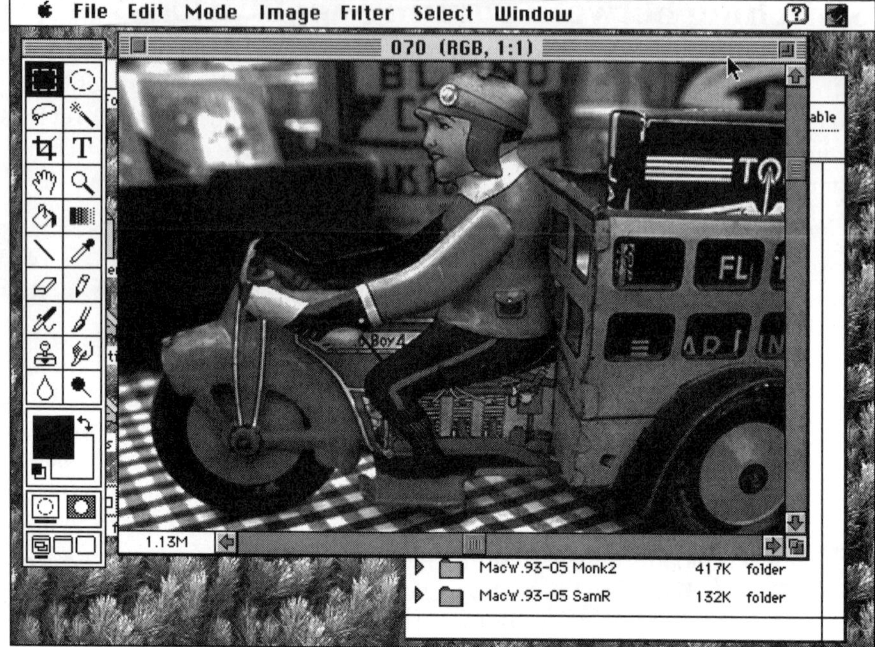

Figure 2-15: If you click on an open application window, you bring that application to the foreground. In this case, I've clicked on a Photoshop image. Note that the toolbox reappears; Photoshop hides the toolbox when it runs in the background.

Background processing

If you go away with nothing else from this chapter, at least ingrain these next few paragraphs in your mind. You won't believe how much time and waiting it will save you. You know how a watched pot never boils? Well, by the same token, a watched operation never finishes. But between System 7 and Photoshop, you'll never have to sit around staring at the screen again. You can always go off and do something productive.

Many applications permit *background processing;* that is, they perform time-consuming tasks in the background while you work in a different application in the foreground. But no program does it better than Photoshop. The only task that Photoshop won't perform in the background is launching. In fact, I am at this moment using Photoshop to open an enormous image from a Photo CD while I write this text in Microsoft Word. The word processor tracks my typing rather sporadically and even ignores some of what I type, so the experience is not altogether successful, but it's better than gawking at the screen like a hungry fish. Now I'm applying a complicated effect to the image using the Wave filter. Word tracks my typing much better this time around, not missing so much as a single character.

To background process, all you have to do is initiate a time-consuming operation in Photoshop or some other program and then click on a window belonging to a different application. Photoshop, specifically, is sophisticated enough to relinquish control to a different application whether you click on a window or use the Applications menu. (Many programs won't let you access the Applications menu while they're busy performing an operation, but you can usually get around this by clicking on a background window.) Photoshop even displays a Progress window, as shown in Figure 2-16, to keep you informed about how a background operation is coming along. When the Progress window disappears, you know the coast is clear and Photoshop is waiting for your next instruction.

If you don't like the way an operation is progressing, whether Photoshop is working in the background, foreground, or on some purely ethereal plane of digital existence (hey, you never know), you can stop it dead in its tracks by pressing Command-period, the universal Macintosh code for cancel.

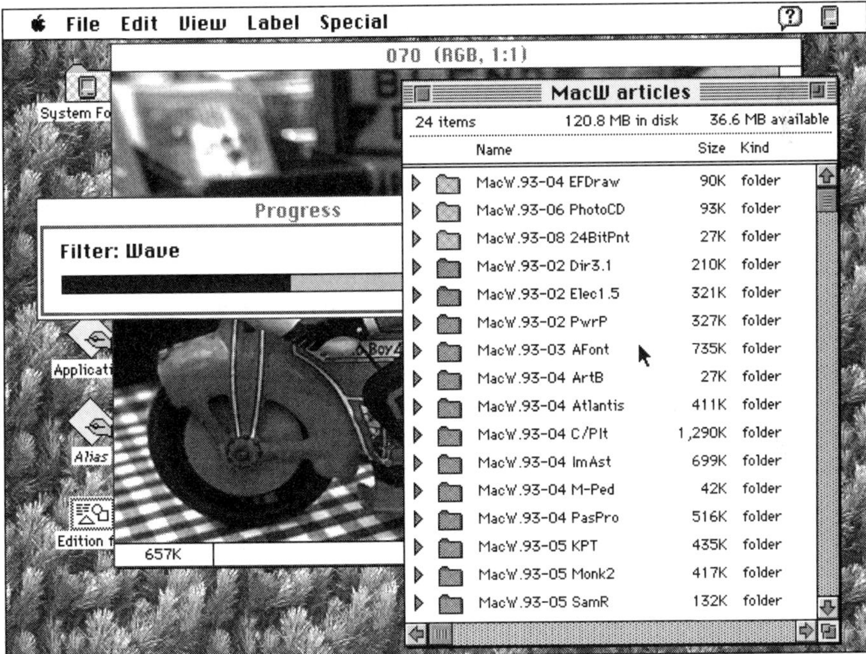

Figure 2-16: Photoshop displays a Progress window to let you know when an operation is completed.

Printing in the background

Depending on your output device, you also can print images from Photoshop in the background, but this operation requires the use of a special System 7 capability called *background printing*. Based on my own experience in a variety of situations, I don't recommend background printing because it so frequently results in printing errors. An image may print with several misplaced rows of pixels or it may not print at all. Nevertheless, I'll tell you how to turn on background printing so that you can try it out on your own. Keep in mind that this technique works only with the Personal LaserWriter LS, the StyleWriter, the LaserWriter SC series, and any model of printer equipped with PostScript.

Begin by choosing the Chooser from the list of desk accessories under the Apple menu. The Chooser window, shown in Figure 2-17, comes into view. From the scrolling list on the left, select the driver icon that corresponds to your printer model. If you own a PostScript printer, select the LaserWriter icon. Then select On from the Background Printing options. Close the Chooser window, and you're ready to go.

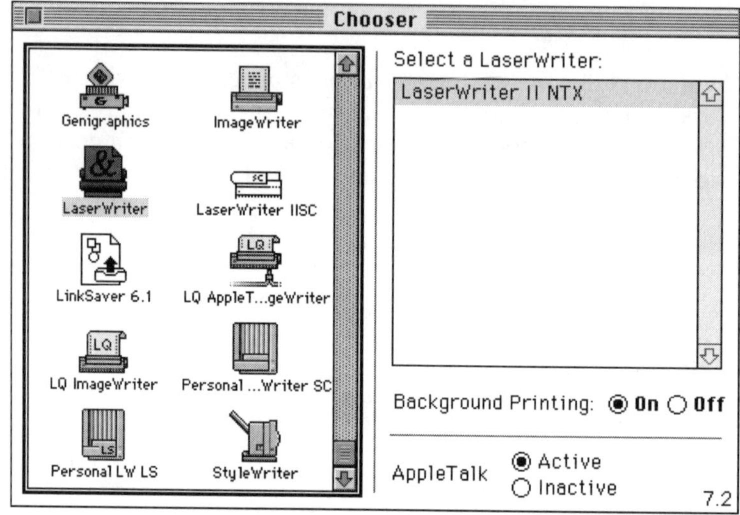

Figure 2-17: Turn on Background Printing inside the Chooser to instruct System 7 to print a document in the background while you continue to work in the foreground.

Using the Clipboard

Even before System 1, Macintosh users were able to swap data between documents and programs by using the *Clipboard,* a section of RAM (or *buffer*) set aside to hold a single collection of data. The Clipboard can hold three basic kinds of data: text, object-oriented graphics, and bitmapped images.

In case you thought all this system software numbering was just some kind of bizarre marketing scheme — not that it isn't — there indeed was a System 1. System 7 lets you take a peek at those days by holding down the Option key and choosing Apple ⇨ About The Finder. The splash screen that accompanied the very first system software appears in all its splendor. Actually, it's rather boring by modern Macintosh graphics standards, but it was a good indication of what the machine could do at the time.

You can manipulate the contents of the Clipboard from inside just about any program by choosing commands from the Edit menu:

- **Cut (Command-X):** This command removes the selected data from the foreground document and places it in the Clipboard, thus replacing the Clipboard's previous contents.
- **Copy (Command-C):** The Copy command makes a copy of the selected data in the foreground document and places that copy in the Clipboard, thus replacing the Clipboard's previous contents.

- **Paste (Command-V):** This command makes a copy of the contents of the Clipboard and places it in the foreground document. Unlike Cut and Copy, the Paste command leaves the contents of the Clipboard unaltered.

Many new users have trouble remembering the keyboard equivalents for the Clipboard commands. Command-C makes sense for Copy. Command-X is a stretch, but it sort of brings to mind Cut. But where did Command-V for Paste come from? The answer resides at the bottom left corner of your keyboard. The keys read Z, X, C, and V — that's Undo (the first command in the Edit menu), Cut, Copy, and Paste.

The most common way to use the Clipboard is to cut or copy text or graphics from one document and paste them into another. You also can cut, copy, and paste within a single document.

Application Clipboards

Many applications have their own internal Clipboards, and Photoshop is no exception. These *application Clipboards* are distinct from, but linked to, the operating system's Clipboard. For example, if you copy an image inside one Photoshop document and then paste it into a different document, Photoshop stores the image in a special buffer, separate from the buffer that holds the system's Clipboard. Only when you switch applications does Photoshop transfer the image from its Clipboard to the system's Clipboard. For this reason, you may get a slight delay when switching applications. If the Clipboard image is especially large, Photoshop displays a Progress window, as shown in Figure 2-18. The Cancel button is grayed out, or *dimmed,* because this is one operation you can't cancel, not even by pressing Command-Period.

You can copy Photoshop images and paste them into just about any other application. Copying data from another program and pasting it into Photoshop, however, is a different story. Normally, Photoshop recognizes the contents of the operating system's Clipboard only if the Clipboard contains bitmapped images. Therefore, you can't paste text or objects directly into the image window. If the Clipboard contains text, the only way to introduce it into Photoshop is to select the type tool, click on the image window to display the Type Tool dialog box (the Type dialog box in Version 2.0), and then choose Edit ⇨ Paste.

The only way to introduce an object into Photoshop is to open it from disk as described in Chapter 5, in the section "Rendering an EPS illustration." You can also copy paths from Illustrator 5.0 and paste them as selection paths in Photoshop, as described in "Swapping paths with Illustrator" in Chapter 9.

Figure 2-18: Photoshop displays a Progress window when transferring very large images from its Clipboard to the operating system Clipboard.

The Scrapbook

You can use the Scrapbook desk accessory — included with all versions of the Macintosh system software — to hold data copied from various documents and programs. Unlike the Clipboard, which can hold no more than one chunk of data at a time, the Scrapbook adds a new page every time you paste text or graphics into it. Also, whereas the Clipboard resides in RAM and thus is erased every time you restart or turn off your computer, the Scrapbook file resides on disk, ensuring that you can access it over and over again.

To transfer the contents of the Clipboard into the Scrapbook, choose the Scrapbook from the list of desk accessories under the Apple menu and then choose Edit ⇨ Paste (Command-V). A new page appears, showing the pasted text or graphic. If the graphic is too large to fit inside the window, the Scrapbook displays it at a reduced size, as shown in Figure 2-19. In this example, the Scrapbook displays the image at 65 percent of its actual size so you can see the entire image in the page window.

To retrieve data from the Scrapbook, open the Scrapbook window and scroll to the page that contains the desired text or graphic. If you want to delete the current page of data from the Scrapbook, choose Edit ⇨ Cut (Command-X). If you want to keep the data on hand for future use, choose Edit ⇨ Copy (Command-C).

Figure 2-19: An image copied from Photoshop and pasted into the Scrapbook.

Using Fonts

OK, so you won't be using Photoshop to type up the quarterly report. But it's a great program for creating outrageous text effects, the kind that professional designers always warn novices to use in moderation. I, for one, don't care if you turn out pages and pages of wacky type; as far as I'm concerned, the more the merrier. I just want you to feel as though your options are unlimited, and to do that, I first need to tell you how to install and use *fonts* on a computer.

In case you don't know what I'm talking about, fonts are electronic descriptions of typefaces such as Helvetica, Times, and Courier. Regardless of the system software you use, you can access a wide variety of fonts from inside any application.

Electronic typography took off with the advent of PostScript printing technology in 1985, one year after the introduction of the Mac. PostScript *outline fonts* offer mathematical, character-by-character outline definitions you can display on-screen or print to high-resolution output devices, including professional-quality typesetters. Today, almost a decade after it was born, PostScript is the accepted standard among typesetters, designers, and publishers.

If you use System 7, or System 6 with the TrueType system extension, you have access to two brands of outline font technology that can coexist harmoniously on your hard drive: PostScript and TrueType. You can scale outline fonts to absolutely any size, subject to the limitations of your software. Provided that you install Adobe Type Manager, included with Photoshop, your text will appear smooth and professional, regardless of size.

For specific information about how fonts work inside Photoshop and other painting programs, read the "Type Basics" section that begins Chapter 11.

Installing PostScript screen fonts

Every PostScript font includes two parts: a bitmapped *screen font* and a mathematically defined *printer font.* Technically, the screen font is designed to display characters on your monitor; the printer font contains the outline definitions used by the printer. However, if you use Adobe Type Manager, the printer font works with the screen font to smooth out the jagged edges once associated with on-screen type.

A screen font defines a single *type style* — plain, bold, italic, or other — when displayed at a single *type size,* measured in *points* — generally 9, 10, 12, 14, 18, or 24. (One point equals 1⁄72 inch.) Screen fonts are packaged inside a special file called a *suitcase,* shown in Figure 2-20. A suitcase file can contain multiple screen fonts. A printer font file, on the other hand, describes only one typeface and style.

Before you can access a PostScript font in an application, you must install its screen font in your system software. How you accomplish this installation depends on the system you are using.

- **System 6:** If you use System 6, you must copy screen fonts to the System file using Apple's Font/DA Mover utility. Upgrade to System 7 and you won't have to deal with this cumbersome, antiquated utility. (Sorry, but it's time you faced the tough facts.)
- **System 7.0:** Under System 7, you can open a suitcase at the Finder desktop by double-clicking on the suitcase icon as if it were a folder. (Doesn't that sound tempting, you System 6 users?) A directory window appears, displaying the contents of the suitcase, as shown in Figure 2-21. Each screen font icon looks like a folded page with a single letter *A* on it. Drag the screen font from the open suitcase window onto the System file icon to make it a part of the system software.
- **System 7.1:** The Version 7.1 of the system software, includes a Fonts folder, which provides increased convenience by enabling you to install and delete whole suitcase files. Rather than opening the suitcase file and copying individual fonts, you can simply drag the suitcase icon into the Fonts folder.

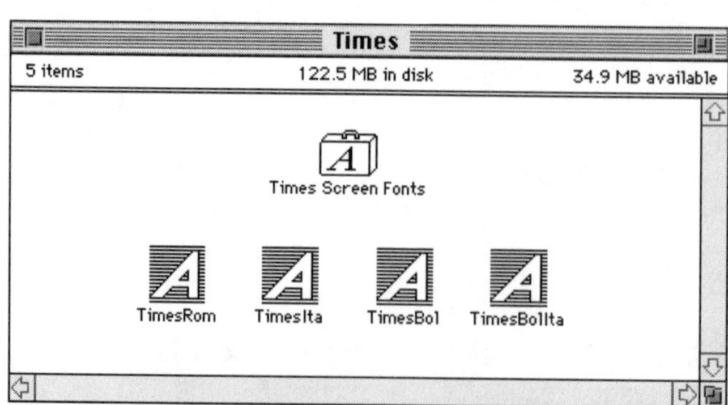

Figure 2-20: A single suitcase file (top) can contain many screen fonts, but each printer font file (bottom) defines just one typeface and style.

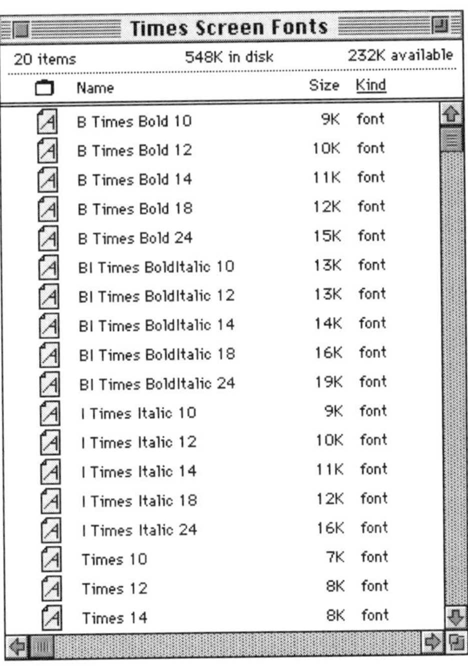

Figure 2-21: The contents of a suitcase file viewed at the Finder desktop using System 7.

System 7.1's Fonts folder can accommodate up to 128 suitcase files. (The number of screen fonts inside a suitcase has no limit.) If your enthusiasm for fonts knows no bounds, you may have to combine two or more suitcases into one by opening one suitcase and dragging its contents into another suitcase.

Do not add or delete screen fonts in the system software when any application but the Finder is open, because running applications cannot track the addition or deletion of fonts. To be safe, quit all applications before installing fonts.

Installing PostScript printer fonts

To get the most out of Photoshop, you should install Adobe Type Manager (ATM), which is included inside the Photoshop package. ATM displays PostScript fonts smoothly on-screen and renders them to non-PostScript printers. When using ATM, you need to install printer fonts for *all* typefaces you want to use with Photoshop — even if they're built into your printer. Use the following installation procedures:

- **System 6:** If you're still clinging to System 6, copy the printer fonts into the System Folder.
- **System 7.0:** Under System 7.0, you can copy the printer fonts either to the System Folder or to the Extensions folder inside the System Folder.

- **System 7.1 and Photoshop 2.0:** System 7.1 offers a Fonts folder and copies all fonts to that location by default. Unfortunately, Photoshop 2.0 ships with ATM 2.0.2, which requires that you copy the printer fonts into the Extensions folder. You must open the System Folder at the Finder desktop and drag the fonts onto the Extensions folder.
- **System 7.1 and Photoshop 2.5:** Photoshop 2.5 includes ATM 3.0, which permits you to copy printer fonts into the Fonts folder inside the System Folder. Drag the fonts onto the System Folder icon. Click on the OK button when the alert box appears requesting permission to put fonts into the Fonts folder.

For instructions on installing ATM, see Chapter 3, which details the entire Photoshop installation process.

To make newly installed printer fonts available to an application, you must restart your computer. ATM can only load printer fonts into RAM during the start-up procedure. After that, the printer fonts it makes available to applications are set in stone.

Using Adobe Type Manager

ATM works without much intervention from the user. However, you should be aware of a few options. By double-clicking on the ~ATM icon, you gain access to the Adobe Type Manager control panel, shown in Figure 2-22. The left side of the figure shows the control panel window for ATM 3.0, which is included with Photoshop 2.5; the right half shows the control panel window for ATM 3.5, which is part of SuperATM, sold separately.

Figure 2-22: The control panel windows for ATM 3.0 (left) and ATM 3.5 (right).

ATM 3.0 offers these three options:

- **On or Off:** OK, you didn't need my help on this one. You can figure out how to turn ATM on or off on your own. But leave it on when working with Photoshop.
- **Font Cache:** A *cache* is an allotment of RAM set aside to store the last few calculations made by a program. The reasoning is that computer users tend to repeat themselves, so if a program can store its most recent calculations, it can save time by recalling previous results from RAM as opposed to recalculating from scratch. Raising the Font Cache value allows ATM to store more calculations, but it also takes away RAM from other programs. As a general rule of thumb, you should set this value to roughly 1 percent of your total RAM and no lower than 96K when working with Photoshop.
- **Preserve:** This option compensates for text inside documents that were created without the use of ATM. You can select Line Spacing to retain the line breaks and page breaks in a document, or you can select the Character Shapes option, throwing breaks to the wind and concentrating on the quality of the individual letter outlines. Because ATM has been the established standard for a few years now, the possibility of opening non-ATM documents is becoming progressively less likely. That point is one of two in favor of Character Shapes. The other is that although line breaks and page breaks have absolutely nothing to do with Photoshop, the Line Spacing option can do a good deal of damage by clipping the bottoms of characters. Figure 2-23 illustrates the impact of the Preserve options on Palatino type. When the Preserve option is set to Line Spacing, clipping occurs (left). When it is set to Character Shapes, all is well in Photoshop (right).

Just in case you missed the gist of this section, I'll repeat myself in the form of a directive. Before using Photoshop, open the ATM control panel, select Character Shapes from the Preserve options, close the control panel, and restart your Mac to make the changes take effect.

Figure 2-23: Choosing Line Spacing can cause clipping (left); choosing Character Shapes resolves the problem (right).

Making the leap to SuperATM

Figure 2-22 shows two renditions of the ATM control panel, one for Version 3.0, which is included with Photoshop 2.5, and another for ATM 3.5, which is sold separately as part of SuperATM. As you can see, the difference between the control panels is a single option, Substitute for Missing Fonts. But when this option is turned on, the difference between the capabilities of Versions 3.0 and 3.5 is enormous.

ATM 3.5 — the heart of SuperATM — lets you view Adobe-brand PostScript fonts on-screen. It also enables you to output these fonts at high resolutions even when the corresponding printer fonts are unavailable. Here's how it works: If ATM 3.5 doesn't find a printer font, it consults a hefty 1.4MB database that contains *font metrics* (character size and spacing information) for 1,300 faces from the Adobe Type Library. After ATM locates the desired metrics, the program blends two *multiple master* fonts, one serif and the other sans serif, according to a recipe found inside the database. The result is a reasonable facsimile of the desired typeface. ATM 3.5 can display the result on-screen and print it at full resolution to a PostScript or non-PostScript printer.

Multiple master technology is another of Adobe's amazing inventions. An application consults two related fonts that represent extremes in weight, width, *optical size* (meaning the design of characters as they relate to legibility at small and large sizes), and/or style. The application then mixes the fonts to create a unique variation that lies somewhere in between the original two fonts. Literally thousands of variations are possible.

What good is SuperATM? With respect to Photoshop, the product enables you to test out typeface variations that a painting program simply can't address. After selecting a screen font from the immense collection that SuperATM bundles on CD-ROM, you can test out the font inside Photoshop. It's no substitute for the real printer font definition, but it opens whole new avenues for experimentation.

Installing TrueType fonts

We now leave the action-packed world of PostScript for the less interesting but more straightforward world of TrueType. A TrueType font is made up of a single *variable-size font* file, which is used both to display the font on-screen at any size and to describe the font to the output device. Like PostScript screen fonts, multiple TrueType fonts are generally packaged in a suitcase file. Font manufacturers sometimes include separate screen fonts that provide better legibility at small sizes. These fonts also are packaged in the suitcase file.

You install TrueType fonts in the exact same way that you install PostScript screen fonts. I've been through it once already, but to quickly recap:

- **System 6:** Use Apple's Font/DA Mover utility.
- **System 7.0:** Open a suitcase at the Finder desktop by double-clicking on the suitcase icon. Then drag the desired screen fonts from the open suitcase window onto the System file icon.
- **System 7.1:** Drag the suitcase icon into the Fonts folder.

Photoshop is 100 percent compatible with both PostScript and TrueType fonts. You gain no inherent advantage by using one font format over the other, except that PostScript fonts are more plentiful and, thanks to SuperATM and multiple master technology, PostScript fonts have a wider range of applications.

Working with QuickTime

If you follow the news in the Macintosh magazines and tabloids, you've no doubt read scads of hoopla about QuickTime, which is a system extension that enables you to edit *dynamic data* on the Mac. Dynamic data is any time-based media, including video, animation, and sound. With QuickTime, you can record a movie to disk, add and edit the soundtrack, compress the movie so that it consumes less space on disk, and even paste the movie inside that letter to Grandma that your robot keeps forgetting to mail. (That's assuming Grandma has a Mac, of course.)

QuickTime works with System 6.0.7 or later, but Apple didn't start bundling it with the system software until System 7.1. You also can find the QuickTime system extension on the Deluxe CD-ROM Edition of Photoshop, or you can purchase it directly from Apple.

The state of QuickTime

As QuickTime gradually gets up to speed, it will prove itself more and more indispensable. Just imagine the benefits of recording movies to disk. The recording is digital, so you won't have to worry about image and sound degradation no matter how many copies you make. You'll be able to create multiple backup copies to preserve your priceless home movies. The recording is 100 percent editable, which means you'll be able to mix sounds and add whiz-bang special effects that will make modern sci-fi flicks and music videos look tame by comparison. When you go to a video store, you'll be able to check out a disk with its own front-end navigation utility, enabling you to view details throughout the movie nonsequentially. What I'm saying is that whether it's QuickTime or some other dynamic data technology, digital film is sure to completely revise the way we view and exchange visual and aural information.

Unfortunately, the key word in the preceding paragraph is *imagine* (second sentence, second word). As things stand now, QuickTime is little more than a curiosity in the dynamic data department. Version 1.5 includes a Compact Video setting that lets you record frame sizes as large as 320 × 240 pixels at 24 frames per second on state-of-the-art computers. But that's still only 25 percent of the total screen area on a standard 13-inch monitor. To create full-screen movies, you need to purchase thousands of dollars of additional hardware. The technology is getting better, but it still has a long way to go.

QuickTime and still images

So QuickTime's a washout, right? No way. In reality, it's an essential tool for use with Photoshop because of the way it handles still images — a fact that tends to get overlooked in most QuickTime discussions. Any version of QuickTime can compress images on disk, and QuickTime 1.5 provides direct support for Kodak's Photo CD.

QuickTime image compression

QuickTime enables Photoshop and other painting programs to integrate the JPEG (pronounced *jay-peg*) compression scheme — named after its designers, the *Joint Photographic Experts Group* — into the standard Macintosh PICT format. JPEG *compresses* an image by deleting data that doesn't add to the appearance of the photo. The result is that the image consumes substantially less space on disk. Because QuickTime is an extension of the system software, it permits an application to open and save JPEG images without having to rely on specialized code that would increase the size and complexity of the application itself.

Chapter 5 provides a much more thorough explanation of the PICT and JPEG formats. The discussion assumes that you installed QuickTime on your machine.

QuickTime and Photo CD

Photo CD is new technology from Kodak that enables service bureaus and professional photo labs to scan photographic images onto CD-ROM disks. With the proper hardware, you then can view the images on a television or open and edit them on a computer. Of the two, I would venture that the latter is by far the more practical application (unless, of course, you feel some strange nostalgia for slide shows).

QuickTime 1.5 permits you to view the contents of a Photo CD in the form of a slide show, as demonstrated in Figure 2-24. (Every Photo CD disk has a Slide Show Viewer utility that works in conjunction with QuickTime 1.5 and later.) You can view thumbnails of each image in sequence. You also can decompress Photo CD images and view them on-screen as standard PICT files.

The section "Using Images on CD-ROM" in Chapter 6 explains how to create your own Photo CDs and what kind of hardware is required to view them. This technology is one you'll probably want to pursue in depth as you become more familiar with Photoshop.

Figure 2-24: An image from a Photo CD, viewed by using the Slide Show Viewer utility and QuickTime 1.5.

Summary

- Your computer's memory includes permanent data stored in ROM and temporary data stored in RAM. The CPU controls the contents of memory.
- You can use disk space to store system software, applications, and documents for later use. You can delete and update the contents of a disk at any time.
- A bit is one of two digits, 0 or 1. A byte comprises eight bits; 1,000 bytes is 1K; 1,000K equals 1MB.
- To get the most out of Photoshop, you use System 7.
- Some of your Mac's system software is included in ROM; the rest is provided on disk to make it easy to upgrade.
- The disk-based portion of the Macintosh operating system includes two main parts, the System and the Finder. The System defines the environment and offers up the resources required to run other programs; the Finder enables you to organize files on disk.
- Extensions and control panels increase the capabilities of your system software.
- The Open and Save dialog boxes allow you to navigate through disks and folders in ways that the Finder desktop does not.
- You can run an application by double-clicking on its icon at the Finder desktop or by dragging a document onto the application icon.
- Use the File ⇨ Get Info command to assign a minimum and maximum amount of application RAM to a program.
- If memory becomes fragmented to the point that you can't run a desired application, close all running applications and relaunch them.
- To switch between running programs, choose the desired program from the Applications menu or click on the program's window.
- Photoshop can open and save images, apply complex filtering effects, and carry out other time-consuming operations in the background while you work in a different application in the foreground.
- The Scrapbook desk accessory serves as a holding cell for Clipboard data you want to save for later use.
- Adobe Type Manager displays PostScript fonts on-screen and renders them to non-PostScript printers. The system software handles TrueType fonts internally.
- QuickTime allows you to shrink PICT images on disk using the JPEG compression scheme. QuickTime also facilitates the display of images stored on Photo CD.
- The century is almost over, and there's still no sign of robots.

Preparing the Soil

CHAPTER 3

In This Chapter

- Selecting the right machine
- Installing and deleting Photoshop files
- Understanding the relationship between RAM and virtual memory
- Upgrading color video

Hardware and Software Requirements

By now, your socks should be blown off and hanging from the rafters over the very idea of combining the inexhaustible power of Photoshop with the flexibility and innate graphics-handling prowess of the Mac. But you still have the problem of merging software and hardware together. In the next few pages, I explain what sort of hardware you need to run Photoshop and how to install Photoshop on your machine.

Hardware issues

Photoshop requires pretty sophisticated machinery, even by Macintosh standards. Not that the equipment is prohibitively expensive — you can get up and running for around $2,000 — but it does have to meet certain requirements.

When shopping for a computer to use with Photoshop or when trying to determine if Photoshop will work with your present machine, you must consider four main criteria: the hard disk, CPU, RAM, and video display.

Hard disk space

The computer must include a hard disk, as almost all computers do. Only the Mac Plus, SE, and earlier versions shipped without a hard disk, and Photoshop can't run on those machines anyway.

Plan on freeing up at least 10MB of disk space before installing Photoshop. Doing so creates room for the program and for a temporary virtual memory file (explained a little later in this chapter).

The CPU

Photoshop requires a 68020 CPU, but a 68030 or 040 CPU is preferable. Table 3-1 shows which models of Macintosh computers feature which kinds of CPU chips — the higher the number, the better. The table also lists *clock speed,* which you can think of as the CPU's heartbeat. A faster heartbeat enables the CPU to work faster. Clock speed is measured in *megahertz* (MHz), or millions of beats per second. (Kind of makes a rabbit drinking a Jolt cola look like a relaxed animal.)

Whereas Macs use Motorola CPU chips, PCs rely on the Intel variety. Intel chips feature a different numbering system, but they're roughly equivalent to the Motorola chips in terms of capability. The Intel 80286, found in the IBM AT, is comparable to the Motorola 68000, so it's not adequate for working with Photoshop. The 386SX is about equal to the 68020, meaning that it's barely enough to get by. The best alternatives are the 386 and 486, equivalent to the 030 and 040, respectively. In the future, expect to see an Intel Pentium duking it out with a Motorola 68060.

RAM requirements

Photoshop eats up RAM like, er, a voracious rabbit after too much Jolt cola. (I've never actually *seen* a rabbit drinking Jolt cola, mind you, but I sometimes feel like one after a few hours of basking in the color phosphors.) To run Photoshop, your Mac must be equipped with at least 4MB of RAM, and even then, you're pushing it. Get at least 8MB if you can. I currently have 20MB and yet I frequently feel constrained. Table 3-1 shows the maximum amount of RAM each Macintosh model can accommodate.

Video display requirements

Adobe claims Photoshop can run on a black-and-white machine. I've never tried Photoshop on a Classic II or a PowerBook 140, so I'll take Adobe's word for it. But what's the point? Without color, Photoshop is nothing. In fact, as far as I'm concerned, 32,000 colors is an absolute minimum; 16 million is best. If you're really in a pinch, you can get by with 256 colors, especially if you're just editing gray scale images.

Table 3-1 shows the maximum number of colors each Macintosh computer can display. To display 256 colors on most of the PowerBooks listed, you need an external monitor. The PowerBook 165c is an exception, but it offers a *passive matrix* LCD screen, which means you get a lot of ghosting and the colors don't hold up well to ambient light. (Future color PowerBooks will provide *active matrix* screens, which will result in richer and more distinct colors.)

To display 16 million colors on a desktop model, you need a separate 24-bit video card, which can range in price from $500 to $2,000, depending on its support for large screen sizes.

Shopping for a computer

Table 3-1 shows the clock speed, RAM, and color capabilities for each of the Macs marketed by Apple since the introduction of the Mac Plus back in 1986. I also took the liberty of rating each machine, on a five-star scale, with respect to how it handles Photoshop. Macs are listed according to speed — slowest to fastest — within CPU groupings. That's why the PowerBook 160 follows the 170 when you might think it would be the other way around. (Don't blame me, I didn't name the things.)

Machines marked with asterisks in the table were discontinued by Apple; others will be discontinued in time. But don't let that worry you. Frequently, some of the older models are the best buys. If you can find a used IIci for under $1,000, for example, snatch it up.

Ratings for some machines may be different if you add a PDS board. For more information, see "External video boards," near the end of this chapter.

To access the maximum RAM values shown in Table 3-1 for the SE/30, II, IIx, and IIcx, you must install the Mode/32 control panel from Connectix, distributed free of charge by Apple.

By the time you read this book, Apple no doubt will have released a few more machines. They're always doing that — I've tried to talk them out of it, but it's no use. Progress is job number-one and all that. Future PowerBooks will continue to rate two stars as long as they're limited to 256 colors. New desktop models with 040 CPU chips probably will rate at least four stars (provided they give you the option of 16 million colors).

In Table 3-1, I listed the maximum number of colors the machine can display on a 13-inch or larger monitor. For example, the LC II (same as the Performa 400) supports 32,000 colors on a 12-inch monitor, and the Color Classic manages the same number on

Table 3-1 Model Information and Photoshop Performance Ratings

Computer Model	*CPU Clock Speed*	*Maximum RAM*	*Maximum Colors*	*Photoshop Rating*
		68000 Series		
Plus*	8 MHz	4MB	2	incompatible
SE*	8 MHz	4MB	2	incompatible
Classic*	8 MHz	4MB	2	incompatible
Portable*	16 MHz	4MB	2	incompatible
PowerBook 100*	16 MHz	8MB	2	incompatible
		68020 Series		
LC*	16 MHz	10MB	256	★½
II*	16 MHz	68MB	16 million	★★½
		68030 Series		
PowerBook 140*	16 MHz	8MB	2	½
Classic II*	16 MHz	10MB	2	½
Performa 200*	16 MHz	10MB	2	½
LC II	16 MHz	10MB	256	★½
Performa 400*	16 MHz	10MB	256	★½
Performa 405	16 MHz	10MB	256	★½
Performa 410	16 MHz	10MB	256	★½
Performa 430	16 MHz	10MB	256	★½
Color Classic	16 MHz	10MB	256	★½
IIvi*	16 MHz	68MB	16 million	★★★
SE/30*	16 MHz	128MB	2	½
IIx*	16 MHz	128MB	16 million	★★★½
IIcx*	16 MHz	128MB	16 million	★★★½
IIsi*	20 MHz	65MB	16 million	★★★
PowerBook 145*	25 MHz	8MB	2	½
PowerBook 145B	25 MHz	8MB	2	★½
PowerBook 170*	25 MHz	8MB	2	½
Color Classic II	25 MHz	10MB	32,000	★★
PowerBook 160	25 MHz	14MB	256	★★
Duo 210	25 MHz	24MB	16	★
Duo 210 w/Dock	25 MHz	24MB	16 million	★★★

Table 3-1 (continued)

Computer Model	*CPU Clock Speed*	*Maximum RAM*	*Maximum Colors*	*Photoshop Rating*
LC III	25 MHz	36MB	32,000	★★½
Performa 450	25 MHz	36MB	32,000	★★½
LC 520	25 MHz	36MB	32,000	★★½
IIci*	25 MHz	128MB	16 million	★★★★
Performa 600*	32 MHz	64MB	16 million	★★★½
IIvx*	32 MHz	68MB	16 million	★★★½
PowerBook 165c	33 MHz	14MB	256	★★
PowerBook 180	33 MHz	14MB	256	★★
PowerBook 180c	33 MHz	14MB	256	★★
Duo 230	33 MHz	24MB	16	★
Duo 230 w/Dock	33 MHz	24MB	16 million	★★★
Duo 250	33 MHz	24MB	16	★
Duo 250 w/ Dock	33 MHz	24MB	16 million	★★★
Duo 270c	33 MHz	24MB	256	★★
Duo 270c w/ Dock	33 MHz	24MB	16 million	★★★
Performa 460	33 MHz	36MB	32,000	★★★
Performa 466	33 MHz	36MB	32,000	★★★
Performa 467	33 MHz	36MB	32,000	★★★
Performa 550	33 MHz	36MB	32,000	★★★
IIfx*	40 MHz	128MB	16 million	★★★★½
		68040 Series		
Centris 610*	20 MHz	68MB	32,000	★★★½
Quadra 605	25 MHz	36MB	16 million	★★★½
LC 475	25 MHz	36MB	16 million	★★★½
Performa 475	25 MHz	36MB	16 million	★★★½
Performa 476	25 MHz	36MB	16 million	★★★½
Quadra 610	25 MHz	68MB	16 million	★★★★
Quadra 660AV	25MHz	68MB	16 million	★★★★
Quadra 700	25 MHz	68MB	16 million	★★★★
Centris 650*	25 MHz	136MB	16 million	★★★★½

Table 3-1 *(continued)*

Computer Model	*CPU Clock Speed*	*Maximum RAM*	*Maximum Colors*	*Photoshop Rating*
Quadra 650	33 MHz	136MB	16 million	★★★★½
Quadra 900*	25 MHz	256MB	16 million	★★★★★
Quadra 800	33 MHz	136MB	16 million	★★★★★
Quadra 840AV	40 MHz	128MB	16 million	★★★★★
Quadra 950	33 MHz	256MB	16 million	★★★★★

* Discontinued Computer

its tiny 10-inch screen. But let's get real. Running Photoshop on anything less than the wide open 640 × 480 pixels is like sticking your head in a jelly jar; it's claustrophobic. (For a way to bolster the color capabilities of both machines, check out the "Video Capabilities" section later in this chapter.)

You may have noticed that Table 3-1 is missing a most important ingredient: machine price. But the way computer price wars are heating up lately, any retail price I write down today will change tomorrow. Also, you only can pick up the discontinued models used, in which case price becomes impossible to quantify, dependent as it is on the alignment of planets, the advice of channelers, and a bunch of other issues I haven't been able to figure out. (And I live in Boulder; you'd think I'd have a handle on this stuff.)

So instead, I've rated each model as if it cost the exact same amount. Sound crazy? Not at all. This way, if you see a brand new Performa 550 at the store for $1500, and your pal down the street is trying to con you into paying the same price for his four-year-old IIci, you know which one to buy right off the bat. Why, the IIci, of course! The IIci is slightly slower, but it offers a cache card slot for increased speed, it's expandable to 128K of RAM, and — here's the clincher — it gets four stars compared to the Performa 550's three on Deke's Amazing Photoshop Computer Rating Chart. No contest — the IIci is the clear winner.

Software issues

Photoshop requires System 6.0.7 or better, but System 7 is the recommended choice because it offers better application handling, RAM management options, background processing, and a more flexible working environment. System 7.1 presently is the best choice of all because it ships with and supports QuickTime 1.5, which offers more capabilities than Version 1.0. System 7.1 also introduces the Fonts folder, which simplifies the task of installing and removing PostScript and TrueType fonts. Quite frankly, the only reason to continue using System 6 is that it consumes less memory. But when using Photoshop — one of the greatest memory pigs of them all — you learn quickly that a RAM upgrade provides about the best return on your investment that money can buy. If you have enough memory to use Photoshop, you have enough to use System 7.

Chapter 2 explains the differences between Systems 6 and 7 in detail. If you're unfamiliar with such concepts as the Fonts folder, background processing, and QuickTime, and you skipped Chapter 2, I suggest you go back and read it.

If you insist on sticking with System 6 — in which case I can't help but admire your steadfastness in the face of my constant insistence to do otherwise — you should have 32-bit QuickDraw on hand. Included in the Photoshop package, this system extension enables Photoshop to display 16 million colors simultaneously on-screen. If your monitor can handle only 256 or 32,000 colors, 32-bit QuickDraw enables System 6 to mix differently colored pixels to mimic the colors in a full-color image. This effect is called *dithering*.

The functionality of 32-bit QuickDraw is built into System 7, another of its tremendous advantages. If you use System 7, you don't need to install the 32-bit QuickDraw extension.

How to Install Photoshop

The process of installing Photoshop is well documented in the user manual, and it's remarkably straightforward. So rather than wasting valuable pages slogging through a step-by-step discussion, I'll just touch on the few areas I think might prove helpful.

Contents of the Photoshop disks

Just as there's no good reason to go on using System 6 now that System 7 has arrived, you'll miss out if you keep using Photoshop 2.0 or 2.0.1 now that Version 2.5 is on the scene. That's easy for me to say; I received the software free for review purposes. But I know what it's like to buy software, and I can sympathize if you can't or don't want to spend the $200 or so necessary to upgrade from Version 2.0 to 2.5. For those of you in that category, I cover Version 2.0 in stride. (Sadly, Photoshop Versions 1.0 through 1.0.7 are too different from Versions 2.0 and later to specifically address them in the course of this book. I strongly advise that Photoshop 1 users upgrade their software.)

Table 3-2 lists the contents of the five disks that ship with Photoshop 2.0. Table 3-3 lists the contents of the five Photoshop 2.5 disks. And for those upwardly mobile types who own Photoshop Deluxe on CD-ROM, Table 3-4 lists the additional throngs of files available in that package. The tables also include brief descriptions of the files.

Table 3-2 Contents of Photoshop 2.0 Disks

Disk	*Filename*	*Description*
Program	Adobe Photoshop Installer	A utility that installs Photoshop when you double-click on it
Plug-ins	Color Toolkit — Read Me	A TeachText file explaining that you no longer need the Professional Color Toolkit (included with Photoshop 1.0) to access Pantone colors
	Gamma	A control panel enabling you to adjust the way colors appear on your monitor
	Photoshop Plug-ins	A folder containing 20 external filter and image-acquisition modules for use with Photoshop, as well as a collection of predefined displacement maps
	Third Party Software	A folder containing Switch-A-Roo, which enables you to change the number of colors displayed on-screen, and a sample plug-in module from Andromeda Software
Calibration	Custom brushes	A TIFF file filled with images you can use as specialized brushes
	Duo, Tri and Quadtones	A folder containing templates for printing duotones, tritones, and quadtones
	Olé No Moiré	A TIFF file designed to test color separations
Tutorial	Flowers	A color photograph of a vase of flowers that's referenced in the *Tutorial* manual included with Photoshop
	Still Life	A gray scale photograph of vegetables, also referenced in the *Tutorial* manual
ATM	~ATM™	Version 2.0.2 of the Adobe Type Manager control panel
	~ATM 68000	Support file for the ~ATM control panel, for use with the Mac Plus and other machines with 68000 CPUs
	~ATM 68020/030	Support file for use with more sophisticated Macintosh models
	Bitmapped Fonts	A folder containing screen fonts for the Courier and Brush Script typeface families
	BrushScr	Printer fonts for the Brush Script typeface family
	Couri, CouriBol, etc.	Printer fonts for the Courier typeface family
	~Font Porter 1.0™	A mediocre font-management program that you can feel free to ignore
	PostScript Patterns	A folder of Illustrator files that you can place into Photoshop and use as patterns
	Read Me Info	A TeachText file containing important information on ATM that's missing from the manual

Table 3-3 Contents of the Photoshop 2.5 Disks

Disk	*Filename*	*Description*
Disk 1	Adobe Photoshop Installer™	A utility that installs Photoshop when you double-click on it
	Adobe Type Manager™	Stuffed version of the ~ATM 3.0 control panel
	Adobe Type *f*	A StuffIt archive containing Courier and Brush Script fonts as well as Font Porter, a mediocre font-management program
	Brushes & Patterns *f*	Another StuffIt archive containing specialized brushes and patterns for use in Photoshop
	Install Script	Tells the Installer utility what to do
	Read Me	A TeachText file containing important information that's missing from the manual
	Read Me ˙ ATM 3.0	Late-breaking information on Adobe Type Manager
	TeachText	A small text editor that lets you view Read Me documents
	~ATM 68020/030	Support file for the ~ATM control panel
Disk 2	Adobe Photoshop™.1	The first half of a StuffIt archive containing the Photoshop application
Disk 3	Adobe Photoshop™.2	The second half of a StuffIt archive containing the Photoshop application
	Plug-ins *f*	A StuffIt file containing 33 external filter and image-acquisition modules for use with Photoshop
Disk 4	Tutorial *f*	A StuffIt archive containing the images, objects, and settings files that accompany the *Tutorial* manual included with Photoshop
Disk 5	32-bit QuickDraw	Stuffed version of the 32-bit QuickDraw extension needed to run Photoshop under System 6
	Calibration *f*	A StuffIt archive containing the Gamma control panel and three color-separation test files
	Color Palettes *f*	Stuffed color collections including standards from Pantone, Trumatch, and others
	Displacement Maps *f*	A stuffed collection of predefined displacement maps
	Duotone *f*	A StuffIt archive containing templates for printing duotones, tritones, and quadtones
	Optional *f*	A stuffed plug-in module called Dynamic Sliders, which updates the color of the sliders in the Colors palette to reflect their effect on the current color
	Third Party *f*	One last StuffIt archive containing sample plug-in modules from Aldus Consumer Division, Andromeda Software, and HSC Software

To save space on disk, Adobe compressed many of the files in the Photoshop 2.5 package using Aladdin's StuffIt, possibly the most popular compression utility for the Mac. Most of these files have florin characters (*ƒ*) in their names, as in *Adobe Type ƒ* (see Figure 3-1). If you own StuffIt 3.0 or later — whether it's StuffIt Deluxe, SpaceSaver, Lite, or any of the other spin-offs — you can open these files directly and decompress them. But if you do so, make sure that you know what you're doing. You'll be on your own to put each decompressed file where it belongs on your hard drive.

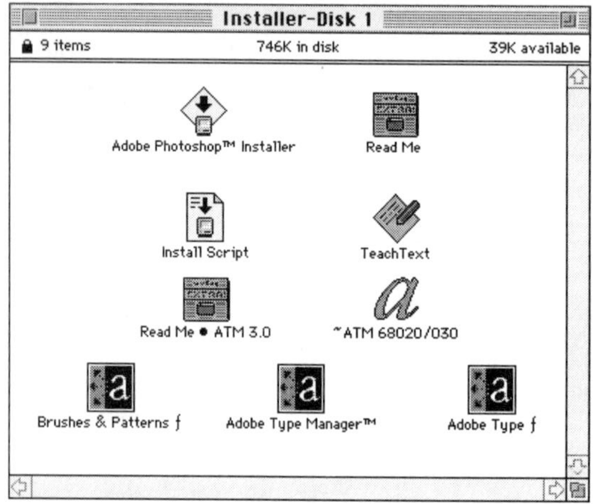

Figure 3-1: Disk 1 of the Photoshop 2.5 disks includes three StuffIt files with customized icons, shown here at the bottom of the directory window.

If you own the Deluxe CD-ROM version of Photoshop, be sure to open the Adobe Photoshop Deluxe file. An interactive screen presentation, it offers access to stock photos, sensational artwork, technical information, and all varieties of QuickTime-generated talking heads expounding their expertise. Figure 3-2 shows the file's table of contents and the director of Photoshop's technical support team — one of the folks who helped me formulate the contents of this book — explaining a mystifying new color mode. In case you want to build your own interactive screen presentation some day, this one was created using MacroMind Director.

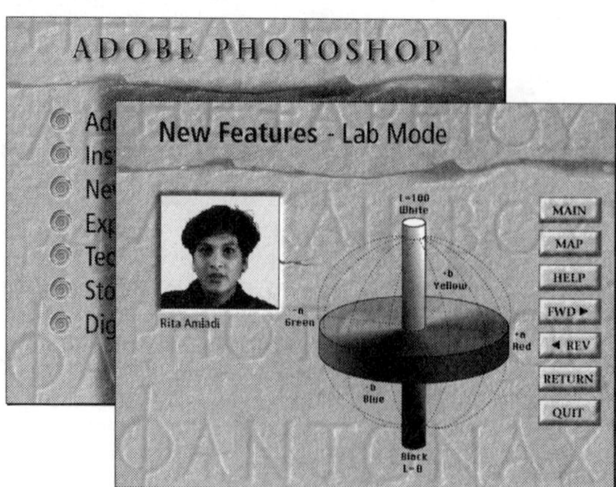

Figure 3-2: Part of the interactive screen presentation found in the Adobe Photoshop Deluxe file.

Table 3-4 Contents of the Photoshop 2.5 Deluxe CD-ROM

Filename	*Description*
Adobe Photoshop™ 2.5	A folder containing all the applications and documents provided on the five Photoshop 2.5 disks (see Table 3-3)
Adobe Photoshop™ Deluxe	An elegant interactive screen presentation that walks you through the contents of the disk and throws in a slew of tips and techniques (see Figure 3-2)
Adobe Products	Demonstration-only versions of three other Adobe graphics products: Dimensions, Illustrator, and Premier
Install Adobe Photoshop™	Double-click on this utility to install Photoshop
Puzzle	A larger version of the standard Puzzle desk accessory that came with your system software
QuickTime 1.5	The QuickTime system extension, required to run the Photoshop Deluxe presentation
Read Me First!	A TeachText file containing information about the contents of the disk
Stock Photography	A folder containing photographic scans in a variety of resolutions from ColorBytes, PhotoDisc, and Kodak — yours to modify and publish
Technical Library	A folder filled with technical support, tips, and advice documents in the MacWrite and Microsoft Word formats
Third Party Software	A folder containing sample plug-in modules from Aldus Consumer Division, Andromeda Software, HSC Software, and Xaos Tools, as well as a demo version of ScanMatch, which lets you precisely match scanned colors to your on-screen display

Installing Photoshop 2.5

You install Photoshop 2.5 by running the Installer utility, clicking on the Install button inside the Easy Install dialog box (Figure 3-3), and removing and inserting disks when asked. The Installer utility automatically installs everything required to use Photoshop and then some. Incidentally, the full installation of Photoshop 2.5 consumes nearly 6MB of disk space, so be sure that you have this much space available before beginning the installation process.

If you're the kind of person who always clicks on the Customize button to specify exactly what does and does not get installed, you're out of luck this time. In order for Photoshop to install correctly, you must click on the Install button and then delete and rearrange installed files as described in the upcoming section.

Figure 3-3: Installing Photoshop 2.5 is as easy as pressing the Return key and switching disks when prompted by the computer.

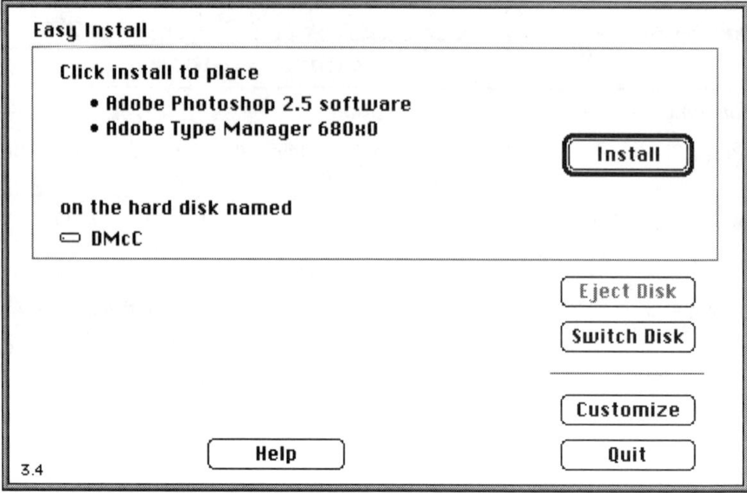

When the Photoshop 2.5 installation process is complete, the Installer displays an alert box with a single button, Restart. You must restart the machine to load Adobe Type Manager, which is also part of the installation process. But I recommend that instead of restarting your machine at this point, you change things around slightly by activating one file and deleting another, as described in the following steps. By doing this, you avoid the hassle of restarting the machine twice before using Photoshop. (If you already restarted, skip to step 2. If you're using System 6 or if step 1 is a little too scary for you, click on the Restart button and skip to step 2.)

STEPS: Fine-tuning the Photoshop 2.5 Installation

Step 1. Provided you're using System 7, you can press Command-Option-Esc to *force quit* the Installer. This technique usually is reserved for escaping a program when it crashes or locks up, but you also can use it to quit programs that offer you no option to quit. When the alert box shown in Figure 3-4 appears, click on the Force Quit button.

Step 2. Locate the Photoshop 2.5 folder. The Installer automatically creates a folder titled Adobe Photoshop 2.5 in the *root directory* — that is, outside any folder — of your hard drive. Move and rename the folder if desired.

Step 3. Open the Photoshop folder. It should contain 12 items, as shown in Figure 3-5, which is at least one too many. Like so many installation schemes, Photoshop's includes a copy of TeachText to ensure that you can open its Read Me documents. Most system software installers also include

TeachText, which means you probably have at least one other copy of this diminutive text editor on your hard drive. Under System 7, you can choose File ⇨ Find (Command-F) and File ⇨ Find Again (Command-G) to locate all occurrences of TeachText on your hard drive. If more than one TeachText is available, throw all but one in the Trash.

Step 4. Open the Calibration folder. It contains two items, the Separation Sources folder and the Gamma control panel. Drag Gamma onto your System Folder. When you do, System 7 displays an alert box that requests permission to place Gamma in the Control Panels folder automatically. Click on the OK button. Next, drag the Separation Sources folder out of the Calibration folder and place it anywhere in the Adobe Photoshop folder directory window. Then drag the empty Calibration folder to the Trash.

Step 5. Open the Third Party Filters folder. Inside it, you should find three folders, one each for Aldus Gallery Effects, Andromeda Software, and Kai's Power Tools. Before you can use these filters, you need to open each folder and drag its contents to the Plug-ins folder. Then drag the Thirds Party Filters folder to the Trash.

Step 6. The Optional Extensions folder contains the Dynamic Sliders module, which instructs Photoshop to preview color effects within the slider bars of the Colors palette. Adobe recommends that you use Dynamic Sliders only on a IIsi or better (see Table 3-1). If you want to use it (I find it to be a valuable tool), open the Optional Extensions folder and drag its contents into the Plug-ins folder. Then drag the empty Optional Extensions folder into the Trash.

Step 7. The contents of your Photoshop 2.5 folder should now look something like the one shown in Figure 3-6. Choose Special ⇨ Empty Trash to permanently delete the TeachText and the empty folders you threw away. Then choose Special ⇨ Restart to load the ATM and Gamma control panels into memory.

Figure 3-4: Press Command-Option-Esc to force quit a running application.

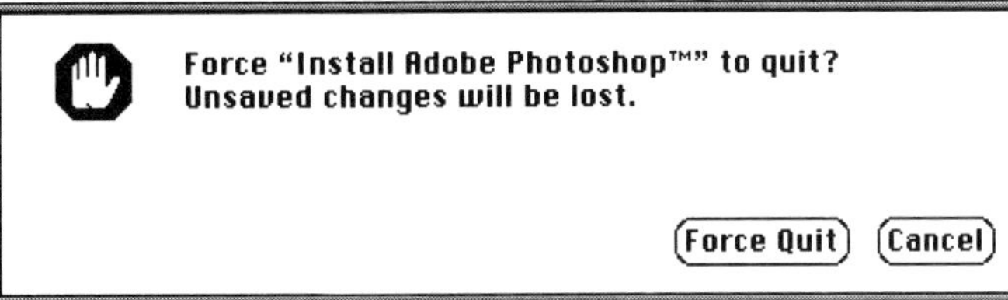
Force "Install Adobe Photoshop™" to quit?
Unsaved changes will be lost.
Force Quit
Cancel

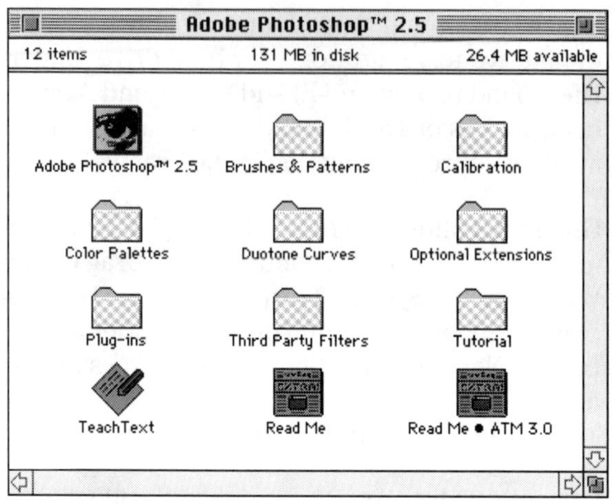

Figure 3-5: The contents of the Photoshop 2.5 folder that the Installer creates automatically. At least one file, TeachText, is extraneous.

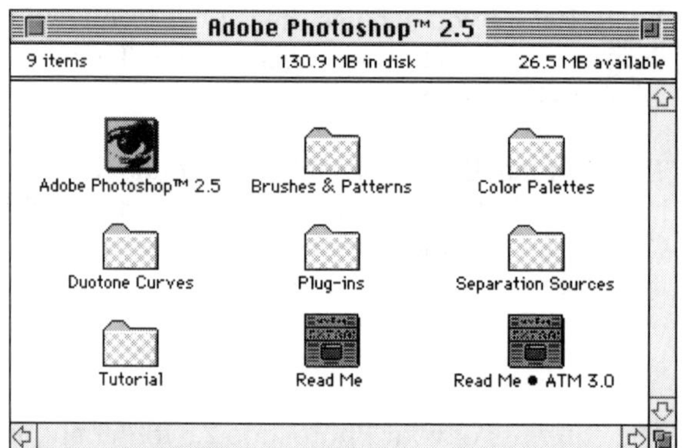

Figure 3-6: The Photoshop 2.5 folder as it appears after you relocate documents and delete folders as explained in the preceding steps.

Installing Photoshop 2.0

To install Photoshop 2.0, run the Adobe Photoshop Installer, which decompresses the Photoshop application, a Read Me file, and TeachText. You then must manually drag-copy the folders and files from the Plug-ins, Calibration, Tutorial, and ATM disks to complete the installation. Copy the Gamma file from the Plug-ins disk as well as the ~ATM(TM) and ~ATM 68020/030 files from the ATM disk to the System Folder. System 7 suggests that it moves Gamma and ~ATM(TM) to the Control Panels folder. Press Return to make it so.

Memory Needs

Just as the system software includes many elements — ROM-based code, System and Finder files, extensions, and all that other stuff I covered in Chapter 2 — Photoshop comprises several different elements. The Photoshop application works in tandem with satellite programs that reside in the Plug-ins folder. When you run Photoshop, it loads not only the application into memory, but also every one of these *plug-in modules* (or just *plug-ins* for short), which add functionality via the Filters menu and the File ⇨ Acquire submenu.

Plug-ins enhance Photoshop's range of capabilities, but they also eat up space inside Photoshop's allotment of application RAM. This is one reason why you'll probably want to raise the amount of RAM you assign to Photoshop right off the bat. By default, the system software assigns between 3,072 and 5,120K of RAM to Photoshop (as specified by the Minimum Size and Preferred Size values in the Info dialog box, discussed in the "Assigning application RAM" section of Chapter 2). The application and its plug-ins fill up roughly 3MB of that space, leaving little room for images.

When to buy additional RAM

Photoshop gobbles up RAM with an appetite unmatched by most varieties of programs. A few graphics programs are equally as gluttonous — multimedia and three-dimensional drawing and animation software top the list — but Photoshop is much more demanding and deserving than word processors, desktop publishing programs, spreadsheets, database managers, drawing programs, and whole slews of other software categories. So go ahead, feel free to give Photoshop as much RAM as you can.

Generally speaking, you can't have too much RAM, but we all live on budgets. I've seen folks who can't afford their rent buy $2,000 worth of RAM, only to decide later that they want to upgrade their machinery to a Centris 650 or some other model that requires completely different chips. So there they are, stuck with the old stuff, all on the basis of some bonehead advice delivered by a "power user."

Well, forget about power users for a moment, and particularly forget about trying to *be* a power user. The truth is, if you're new to this game, 8MB of RAM — but no less — is a good place to start. If you want to run one or more applications in tandem with Photoshop, you may want to start with 12MB or even 16MB. However, you must use System 7 to take advantage of more than 8MB RAM.

You can upgrade to higher quantities of RAM, but I would wait to do so until you're able to assess how well your original RAM suits your needs. Keep in mind, too, that although you expand your range of capabilities when you upgrade to 16MB RAM, when you go beyond 32MB you only gain speed and access to extremely large images.

System 7 lets you take advantage of more than 8MB of RAM by activating *32-bit addressing.* To do so, choose Apple ⇨ Control Panels at the Finder desktop and open the Memory control panel. Turn on the 32-Bit Addressing option, as shown in Figure 3-7. Then close the control panel and restart your computer to complete the operation.

If you decide to purchase more RAM, proceed deliberately. You're spending money, and RAM has absolutely *no* resale value. Unless you sell it off along with your machine, it's yours for life. I swear, we're all going to be trying to pass it off on our grandkids: "When I was your age, RAM didn't grow on trees, you know. The stuff used to be worth its weight in gold. The world might blow up tomorrow, and you'll have to go back to using a Mac Plus. Then you'll thank your lucky stars that Grandpa had a pocket full of RAM." The youngsters will just roll their eyes and return to their virtual reality chambers.

RAM is sold on little circuit boards called *SIMMs* (*single in-line memory modules,* for whatever that's worth). Most Macintosh models use *30-pin* SIMMs, which means each SIMM provides 30 tiny metal contacts that connect to the computer's RAM socket. The Quadra 800, Centris 610 and 650, LC III, and more recent desktop models require 72-pin SIMMs. The IIfx supports its own unique 64-pin SIMMs. The Portable and PowerBook series don't support SIMMs at all, but instead require the installation of special memory boards.

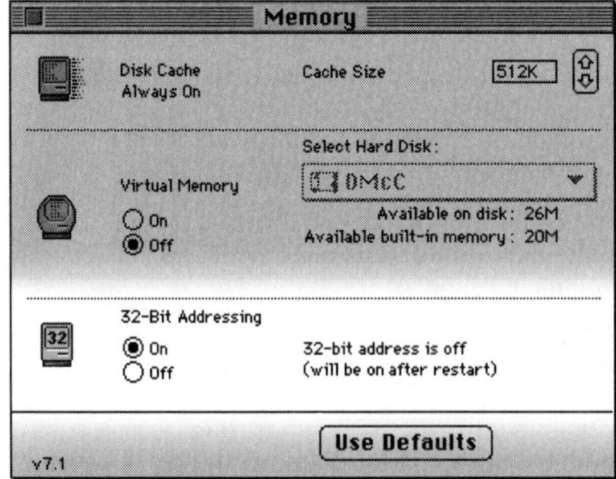

Figure 3-7: To access more than 8MB of RAM, turn on the 32-Bit Addressing option (available under System 7 only).

How to allocate RAM to Photoshop

After you purchase and install the desired amount of memory, you'll want to assign much of it to Photoshop. To determine the proper amount, choose the About This Macintosh command from the Apple menu right after you boot up your computer. The window that appears tells you how much free RAM you have after the system software loads. If you'll be using Photoshop exclusively, assign it about 80 percent of the free RAM (using File ⇨ Get Info). If you plan to use one or two other applications as well, subtract the RAM these programs consume from the free RAM value, and assign 80 percent of the remainder to Photoshop.

Here's a quick example. My awesome IIci (it really is a great machine) holds 20MB of RAM. My overburdened system software hovers around 4MB, leaving 16MB free. I use Microsoft Word daily, which takes up 1MB, and I set back about 4MB for one or two unknown applications that I might need to run on a moment's notice. This leaves 11MB free, and 80 percent of that is roughly 9MB. Sure, I wish I could assign more RAM to Photoshop, but I'm a paragon of virtue, so I live within my means.

Virtual memory

Even when you assign 9MB of RAM to Photoshop, memory can still be an issue when you work with large images. Photoshop offers a feature that helps you load such images into the available RAM space.

A typical 4 × 5-inch full-color image at 200 dots per inch, for example, consumes about 2.3MB of memory. Photoshop sets aside another 2.3MB to track the way the image looked prior to your most recent operation (in case you want to undo it), and it sometimes reserves yet another 2.3MB to compute intermediary images required to create a sophisticated effect. That's 7MB of RAM space for a single image, equal to nearly a million words of text. Yet you can open this image while Photoshop is set to its default 5MB of application RAM. Figure in the 3MB required by the application and plug-in modules, and the question becomes: How does Photoshop pack 10MB of data into half as much space?

How virtual memory works

It all boils down to Photoshop's ability to swap data back and forth quickly between RAM and disk space. When you open a 2.3MB image in Photoshop, the program looks to see if 7MB is available in RAM. If not, it creates a 7MB temporary file on your hard disk. This temporary file is called *virtual memory* because it's pretending to be RAM. Photoshop writes data to the virtual memory file and reads data back just as if it were reading and writing the data to RAM.

The only measurable differences are: 1) Photoshop requires more time — much more time — to read and write disk-bound data than data in RAM; and 2) so much reading and writing to disk theoretically can decrease the life of your hard drive. You can put up with the former, and you'll probably upgrade your hard drive before the latter becomes as issue. (My drive is in its forth year of Photoshop abuse and it spins like a top. Just the same, the hard drive is one of the few mechanical components in your computer, so it's one of the most likely to break down.)

In truth, virtual memory is a wonderful solution to a common photo editing problem. To ensure that it operates smoothly, keep at least 10MB of disk space free at all times. The only way to avoid virtual memory entirely is to go full throttle and upgrade your machine to upwards of 64MB or 80MB of RAM. If this is your ultimate goal, consult Table 3-1 to make sure you don't purchase a Performa 600, IIvx, Quadra 700, or some other machine that cuts you off at just over 60MB.

The scratch disk

If you own multiple hard drives or removable media devices, you can specify the *scratch disks* on which Photoshop stores its temporary virtual memory files by choosing File ⇨ Preferences ⇨ Scratch Disks inside the Photoshop application. In the Scratch Disk Preferences dialog box, shown in Figure 3-8, choose the desired temporary file destination from the Primary pop-up menu. If you're not sure that disk will provide enough room and you have a second drive available, choose a backup device from the Secondary pop-up menu. To implement your changes, quit the program and relaunch it.

If you can't afford to spare the room on your hard drive for the virtual memory files, an empty 44MB SyQuest cartridge or 21MB optical disk (the minimum size for each) does the trick just fine. Both offer the added advantage of sparing wear and tear on your hard drive. Wreck a SyQuest cartridge and you're out $70; wreck an optical disk and you're out $30. Just make sure that the removable media you select is available when you launch Photoshop.

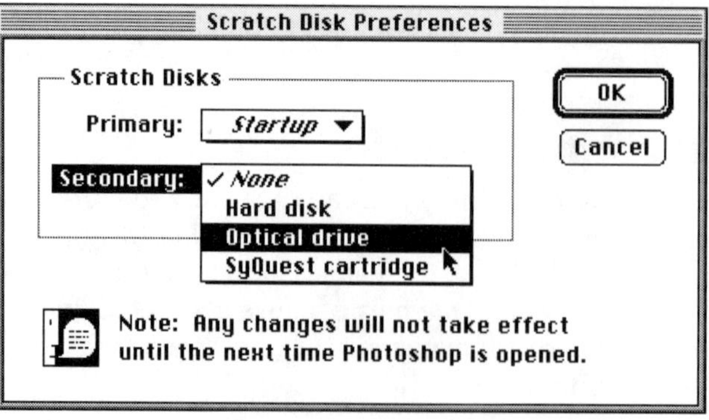

Figure 3-8: The Scratch Disk Preferences dialog box enables you to change the disks on which Photoshop creates its virtual memory files.

By default, Photoshop makes the *start-up disk* (the hard disk that contains the system software) the primary scratch disk and assigns no secondary scratch disk. If you change these settings and specify a removable cartridge as either the primary or secondary disk, the program reverts to its default settings if the cartridge is not mounted when you run Photoshop.

In Photoshop 2.0, choose File ⇨ Preferences ⇨ Virtual Memory to change the scratch disk. You can select a primary scratch disk only.

Video Capabilities

From your computer's point of view, delivering images to the user is a three-step process:

1. Via the system software and CPU, Photoshop conveys the image to the video card.
2. The video card explains the image to the monitor.
3. The monitor shows the image to the user.

Photoshop at all times can take advantage of the maximum 16 million colors made available by your Macintosh system software, but your video card and monitor may be hampered by limitations of their own.

In Photoshop, you also can define colors outside the Mac's 16 million color palette when you work in the print-standard CMYK color mode or the device-independent Lab color mode. For more information on both of these, read the "Selecting and Editing Colors" section of Chapter 14.

Video card technology

Let me back up for a moment. When I say *video card*, I mean any form of video output. It may be an internal video connector, like the one that goes directly to the built-in monitor on a Classic or PowerBook; a built-in video output port, like that found in just about every Mac manufactured in this decade (the exceptions being the first three PowerBooks — the 100, 140, and 170); or a separately purchased NuBus or PDS video board. (I explain NuBus and PDS in the upcoming "External video boards" section.)

But regardless of the variety, you can measure the capabilities of a video card in terms of the number of colors it can display at one time on the monitor. Like image editing, image display comes down to a question of memory. Your video card has its own supply of memory, called *VRAM* (video RAM). That memory enables it to devote a certain amount of data to each pixel on the monitor, as measured in bits (our old friends, 0 or 1). For this reason, the number of colors a video card can display is called its *bit depth.* The standard bit depths are as follows:

- **1-bit:** If a video card devotes only 1 bit per pixel, the result is a black-and-white screen display. Each pixel is either off or on, white or black.
- **4-bit:** PowerBook 160s and better provide 4-bit internal video capabilities. That's 2 to the 4th power, or 16 colors. Each color is a *gray value* — a shade of gray. In other words, you see only variations of gray, not blues, greens, reds, and so on. This display is appealing because you get smoother color transitions.
- **8-bit:** Any Mac with a built-in video port permits you to access at least 256 colors (2 to the 8th power). You can edit color images on an 8-bit (or 1-byte) screen in Photoshop, but you won't get an adequate impression of what your colors really look like. In my experience, 8-bit color is acceptable only if you plan to use Photoshop to edit gray scale images exclusively. An 8-bit display provides access to the entire range of Macintosh gray values.
- **16-bit:** Desktop Macs from the LC II on up offer 16-bit color output for small- and medium-sized monitors. You would think that 16-bit video translates to 2 to the 16th power, or 65,536 colors. But 16-bit and higher video signals must divide evenly into thirds — one each for the red, green, and blue color channels (hence *RGB video*). So the video card devotes 15 bits to color (5 bits per channel) and reserves the leftover bit for color overlay. Therefore, in practice, you get only 32,768 colors (2 to the 15th power).
- **24-bit:** Generally speaking, you need to purchase a separate 24-bit (or *full-color*) video board to access the Mac's full 16-million color range (2 to the 24th power equals 16,777,216 colors). Only the Quadras machines offer built-in 24-bit video ports.
- **32-bit:** When you hear someone talk about 32-bit color, nine out of ten times they mean 24-bit color. A 24-bit (or 3-byte) signal splits into 1 byte each for the primary colors red, green, and blue. Apple also reserves another byte of data for what it calls an *alpha channel,* but it has never specified a purpose for this data. The few video boards that offer 32-bit capabilities — TrueVision's NuVista+ and RasterOps' ProVideo32 among them — allocate one byte each for the primary colors and allocate the final byte of data for displaying analog images from videotape or laser disc. You then can layer 24-bit text and graphics over the video images to add titles and animation to news reports, movies, in-house presentations, and so on. Therefore, the final byte of data buys you more functionality, not more colors.

Images are measured in terms of bits as well, ranging from 1 bit to 24 bits. Regardless of your video card's color capabilities, Photoshop allows you to open and view 24-bit images. The system software automatically dithers the display to match the limitations of your video card. Figure 3-9 shows how Photoshop dithers an 8-bit image and displays it on a 4-bit monitor.

The dithering required to display a 24-bit image on an 8-bit screen is roughly equivalent to what you see in Figure 3-9. If you want my opinion, that much dithering is too intrusive to allow you to satisfactorily view an image; dithering a 24-bit image on a 16-bit screen is acceptable. But despite any perceived on-screen sacrifice, Photoshop enables you to edit and save the image to disk in full 24-bit color. Photoshop also prints the full range of colors found in the original image.

Third-party video boards

Full-color (24-bit) video boards come in two basic varieties, NuBus and PDS (*processor direct slot*). All the computers I listed way back in Table 3-1 as offering up to 16 million colors support NuBus boards. Full-color NuBus boards are available from a wide range of vendors, including Apple, SuperMac, RasterOps, E-Machines, and others.

The IIsi and Centris 610 require the addition of a NuBus adapter card. However, the Centris 610 can accept only 7-inch boards as opposed to the standard 12-inchers. Because no 7-inch full-color board was available at press time, I didn't credit the Centris 610 for 24-bit color in Table 3-1.

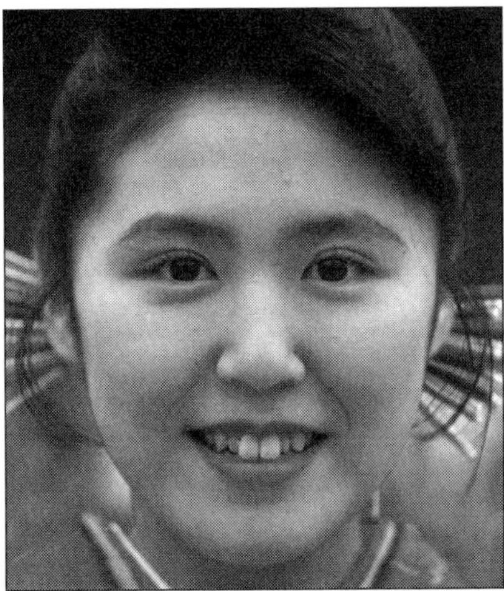

Figure 3-9: An 8-bit gray scale image (left) and the same image dithered on a 4-bit monitor (right).

All the machines in Table 3-1 that *aren't* listed as supporting 16 million colors are NuBus-incompatible. A few instead accept PDS boards. PDS boards are significantly less common, however, which is why I didn't take them into account when figuring the maximum colors and Photoshop rating in Table 3-1. In fact, the only vendor that provides PDS boards for the SE/30, all three kinds of LCs, *and* the Color Classic is Lapis Technologies. Another company, XCeed, also makes PDS boards but supports fewer Mac models. If you factor one of these boards with a 13-inch monitor into the equation, the landscape improves slightly (and the acceptability of one computer, the discontinued SE/30, improves dramatically, thanks to its hefty supply of RAM sockets). Table 3-5 contains revised star ratings that take Lapis PDS boards into consideration.

Considering the huge number of vendors with their hands in the PC-compatible pie, you'd expect 24-bit video to be a nightmare. But it's really not. First, 386 and 486 desktop PCs are better than Macs at providing expansion slots (akin to the NuBus and PDS slots built into Macintosh models). Second, inexpensive 24-bit video cards abound. However, you have to watch out, because many support only very low resolutions. The Diamond SpeedStar 24X is probably the best bargain — it currently lists for $250 — but the $800 ATI Graphics Ultra Pro displays images more quickly and supports higher resolutions.

Table 3-5 Revised Ratings Subject to Lapis PDS Boards

Computer Model	*CPU Clock Speed*	*Maximum RAM*	*Maximum Colors*	*Photoshop Rating*
		68020 Series		
LC	16 MHz	10MB	16 million	★★
		68030 Series		
SE/30	16 MHz	128MB	16 million	★★★½
LC II	16 MHz	10MB	16 million	★★
Performa 400	16 MHz	10MB	16 million	★★
Performa 405	16 MHz	10MB	16 million	★★
Performa 430	16 MHz	10MB	16 million	★★
Color Classic	16 MHz	10MB	16 million	★★
LC III	25 MHz	36MB	16 million	★★★

Monitor resolution

To understand the video picture clearly (no pun intended, trust me), you must consider not just the video board, but the resolution of your monitor as well. Because the board devotes a certain amount of data (measured in bits) to each pixel on the monitor, the number of screen pixels (referred to as the monitor's *resolution*) affects the number of colors a video card can display. Full-color video boards in the $500 to $1,000 range tend to top out at 640 ×480 pixels, the resolution of a 13-inch monitor. If you want to view 24-bit color on a larger screen, you'll have to shell out some more bucks and, in most cases, abandon your old 24-bit card.

Let's say you own a standard 13-inch monitor with a midpriced 24-bit video card. You decide to splurge and upgrade to a 20-inch SuperMatch monitor, which has a maximum resolution of 1152 × 870 pixels and a $3,000 retail price. But now you can't display more than 32,000 colors at a time, and even then, only when you set your system display to be lower than the monitor's maximum resolution. You're left with two choices: Accept things as they are, or upgrade your video card to something like the Thunder/24, which supports higher resolutions and also bundles Photoshop acceleration for another $3,000. It sort of makes a 64MB RAM upgrade look like a bargain.

So here's some advice:

- If you're used to 24-bit color and you're thinking of upgrading your monitor, keep in mind that you'll probably need to upgrade your video card as well.
- If you haven't yet discovered 24-bit color, you may want to invest in a video card that provides high-resolution options. If and when you outgrow your present monitor, the upgrade fee won't be quite so painful.
- If you're short on cash, you can survive on a 13-inch monitor and 16-bit color. Wait to leap into 24-bit color until you can afford a top-of-the-line video board.

The software drivers that accompany most video boards let you switch resolutions regardless of the monitor you're using. For example, the standard resolution of a 21-inch monitor is 1152 × 870 pixels, but you can lower it to 1024 × 768 pixels (the standard 19-inch setting) or 832 × 624 pixels (the 16-inch setting). Granted, you're compromising the amount of information you can display on screen, but it's a way to gain bit depth.

Summary

- The recommended minimum hardware configuration for using Photoshop is a desktop Mac with a 16 MHz 68030 CPU, 8MB of RAM, and a 16-bit video display.
- If you have your heart set on a PowerBook and you can afford only one computer, get a Duo 210 or 230 with a Duo Dock.
- After Installing Photoshop, you'll want to trash TeachText, which is probably already on your hard drive, and move the Gamma control panel into the System Folder.
- RAM is important, but it's not worth going to the poor house to purchase vast quantities. Upgrading to 16MB of RAM increases your range of capabilities; beyond 32MB, you only gain speed and access to very large images.
- Photoshop converts disk space to virtual memory so that you can open large images without a huge supply of RAM.
- NuBus video boards are common. Lapis Technologies makes 24-bit video boards for NuBus-incompatible machines, such as the SE/30, LC, and Color Classic.

CHAPTER 4

Inside Photoshop

In This Chapter

- A tour of the Photoshop desktop
- Brief introductions to Photoshop's tools, cursors, and control icons
- How to navigate using magnification and scrolling options
- Photoshop's hidden keyboard equivalents
- How to use a macro utility to create custom shortcuts
- Preference settings

A First Look at Photoshop

Four chapters into the book and we're finally ready to take a gander at the application itself. Just goes to show you, slow and steady really does win the race. Unlike all those other folks who dived right into the program, you have the foundation of knowledge you need to become a super-proficient Photoshop artist. Seriously, go ahead and test your knowledge: Ask the most knowledgeable Mac users you know why 16-bit video tops out at 32,000 colors. Ask them how you get 24-bit color out of an SE/30. What is memory fragmentation all about? Why do the bottoms of some letters get cut off when you use ATM? Why don't more rabbits drink Jolt cola? Those power users won't know, and they'll pretend they don't care, but deep down inside they'll be seething with envy.

OK, now that you're feeling superior (and rightfully so), it's time to put your newfound knowledge to work and begin exploring Photoshop in earnest.

The Photoshop desktop

Shortly after you launch Photoshop (using one of the methods described in the "Starting an application" section of Chapter 2), the Photoshop *splash screen* appears. Shown at the top of Figure 4-1, the splash screen explains the launching process by telling you which plug-in modules are loading. Any time while running Photoshop, you can re-access the splash screen by choosing the About Photoshop command from the Apple menu.

I know no one cares about the splash screen. In fact, the only reason I even mention it is because Photoshop 2.5 conceals two additional splash screens, also shown in Figure 4-1. If you press the Option key while choosing Apple ⇨ About Photoshop, you get the old Knoll Software screen that has been with Photoshop since Version 1.0. If you press Command and choose Apple ⇨ About Photoshop, you display the Double-secret About Box. It's like the toy surprise in a box of Cracker Jacks, only not so sticky. Purposeless but amusing secret features like these are called *Easter Eggs.* Now try to figure out what `OTKIN-ADAREB-UTAALK` means.

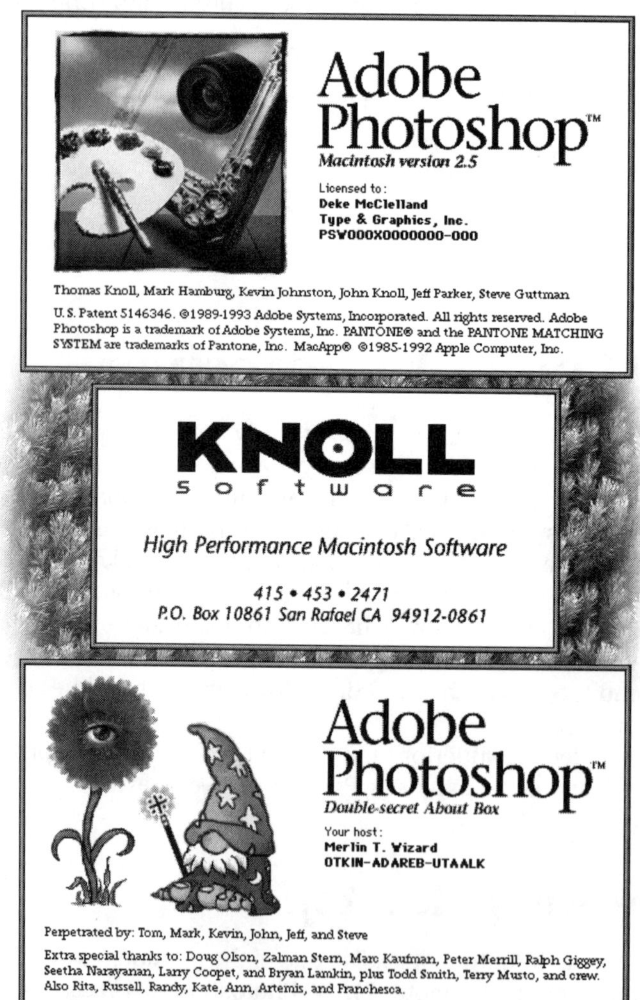

Figure 4-1: The splash screen from Photoshop 2.5 and its two hidden companions.

After the launch process is complete, the Photoshop desktop consumes the foreground. Figure 4-2 shows the Photoshop 2.5 desktop as it appears when an image is open and all palettes are visible. Photoshop 2.0 lacks palettes, mode controls, and a couple of color controls.

Figure 4-2: The Photoshop 2.5 desktop.

Many of the elements that make up the Photoshop desktop are old friends (if you're the kind of person who gets all choked up and teary-eyed recalling the contents of Chapter 2). They work just like the elements of the Finder desktop and the standard Macintosh application window. For example, the menu bar provides access to menus and commands, the title bar enables you to move the window around, and the scroll bars let you view the hidden portions of the image inside of the window. Other elements of the Photoshop desktop work as follows:

- **Image window:** You can open as many images in Photoshop as RAM and virtual memory allow. Each open image resides inside its own window. The lower left corner of the window features the *preview box*. Press and hold on the preview box to display a pop-up window that shows the placement of the image on the printed page.

- **Toolbox:** The *toolbox* offers 20 *tool icons,* each of which represents a selection, navigation, painting, or editing tool. To select a tool, click on its icon. Then use the tool by clicking or dragging with it inside the image window. The lower third of the toolbox features three sets of controls. The *color controls* let you change the colors with which you paint; the *mask controls* let you enter and exit the quick mask mode (exclusive to Version 2.5); and the *image window controls* enable you to change the state of the foreground window on the desktop.
- **Floating palettes:** Photoshop 2.5 offers five *floating palettes.* The term floating refers to the fact that each palette is independent of the image window and of other palettes. The floating palettes include Brushes, Channels, Paths, Colors, and Info. "The floating palettes" section, later in this chapter, provides a brief explanation of each of these palettes.

Tools

Photoshop 2.0 and 2.5 offer slightly different toolboxes, as shown in Figure 4-3. Version 2.5 introduces the mask controls and offers more color controls. Among the tools themselves, three differences exist. Version 2.5 sends the pen tool off to the Paths palette, moves the type tool to the old pen tool location, and introduces the dodge and burn tools.

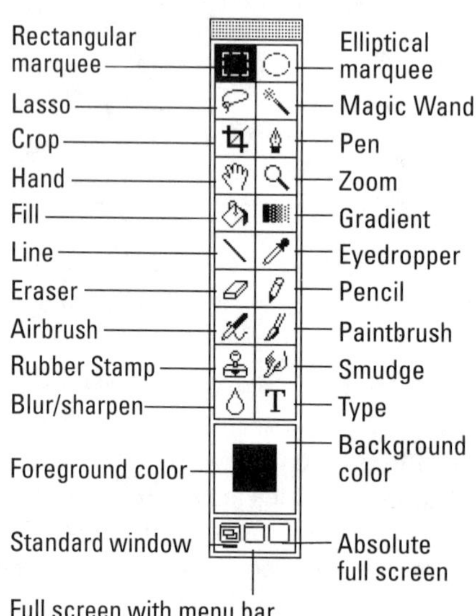

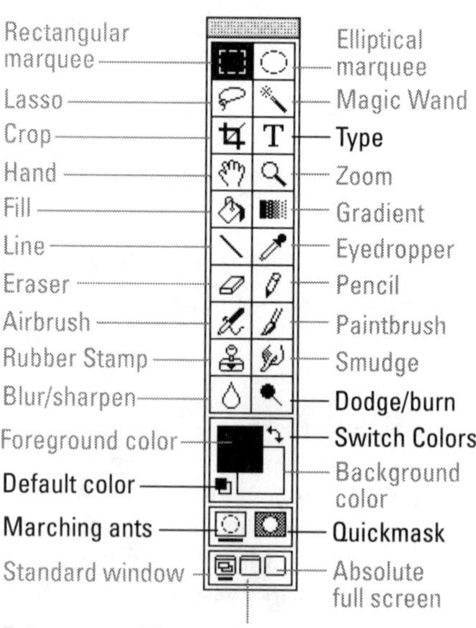

Figure 4-3: The toolboxes from Photoshop 2.0 (left) and 2.5 (right). Tools and controls that are new to Version 2.5 appear on the right in black.

The following paragraphs explain how to use each tool inside the image window. For example, if an item says *drag,* you drag in the image window, not on the tool icon itself. Keep in mind that these are merely the briefest of all possible introductions to Photoshop's tools. Future chapters reveal the details in their nitty-grittiest form.

- **Rectangular marquee:** Drag with this tool to enclose a portion of the image in a rectangular *marquee,* which is a pattern of moving dash marks that indicate the boundary of a selection. The dash marks are sometimes fondly called *marching ants* (hoorah, hoorah).
- **Elliptical marquee:** Drag with the elliptical marquee tool to enclose a portion of the window in an oval marquee.
- **Lasso:** Drag with the lasso tool to select a free-form portion of the image.
- **Magic wand:** Click with this tool to select a contiguous area of similarly colored pixels. To select discontiguous areas, you have to click in one area and then Shift-click in another.
- **Crop:** Drag with the crop tool to enclose within a rectangular marquee the portion of the image you want to retain. The crop marquee offers *corner handles* so you can resize the marquee after you create it. Click inside the marquee to crop away the portions of the image that lie outside it.
- **Type:** Click with the type tool to display the Type Tool dialog box, in which you can enter and format text. Note that you cannot use the type tool to edit existing text as you can in page-layout and drawing programs. (Like any other image, bitmapped type is just a bunch of colored dots. If you misspell a word, you must erase it and try again.)
- **Pen:** Whether accessed from the toolbox or the Paths palette, the pen tool lets you create *paths* one point at a time. In Photoshop, paths are free-form outlines that you can edit as objects and later convert to selections. When using the pen tool, you click to create a corner in a path and drag to create an arc.
- **Hand:** Drag an image with the hand tool to move the image inside the window. Double-click on the hand tool icon to magnify or reduce the image so it fits on-screen in its entirety (as when you first open the image).
- **Zoom:** Click with the zoom tool to magnify the image so that you can see individual pixels more clearly. Option-click to step back from the image and take in a broader view. Drag to enclose the specific portion of the image that you want to magnify. And finally, double-click on the zoom tool icon to restore the image to 100 percent view size.
- **Paint bucket:** Click with the paint bucket tool to fill a contiguous area of similarly colored pixels with the foreground color.
- **Gradient:** Drag with this tool to fill a selection with a gradual transition of colors (called a *gradient* or *gradation*) that begins with the foreground color and ends with the background color.

- **Line:** Drag with the line tool to create a straight line. Double-click on the tool icon to access arrowheads.
- **Eyedropper:** Click with the eyedropper tool on a color in the image window to make that color the foreground color. Option-click on a color in the image to make it the background color.
- **Eraser:** Drag with the eraser tool to paint in the background color, which in effect erases portions of the image. Option-drag to access the *magic eraser,* which changes portions of the image back to the way they appeared when last saved. Double-click on the eraser tool icon to erase the entire image.
- **Pencil:** Drag with the pencil tool to paint hard-edged lines.
- **Airbrush:** Drag with the airbrush tool to paint feathered lines that blend into the image — ideal for creating shadows and highlights.
- **Paintbrush:** Drag with the paintbrush tool to paint soft lines that are not as hard-edged as those created with the pencil, but not as soft as those created with the airbrush.
- **Rubber stamp:** Option-click with the tool to specify the area you want to reference. Then drag to *clone* that area to another portion of the image. This method enables you to hide defects in one portion of an image by duplicating another portion. You also can use the rubber stamp tool to change portions of an image to the way they looked when last saved (like a soft version of the magic eraser) and to paint with a pattern.
- **Smudge:** Drag with this tool to smear colors inside the image.
- **Blur/sharpen:** Drag with the blur/sharpen tool to decrease the contrast between neighboring pixels, which blurs the focus of the image. Option-drag to increase the contrast, which sharpens the focus.
- **Dodge/burn:** Drag with the dodge/burn tool to lighten pixels in the image; Option-drag to darken pixels. You won't find this tool in Photoshop 2.0.

You can adjust the performance of most tools by double-clicking on their icons in the toolbox. When you do this, a dialog box of individualized preference settings appears. The exceptions are the hand, zoom, and eraser tools (explained above); the type tool (double-clicking on the icon does nothing); and the eyedropper tool in Version 2.0 (double-clicking on the icon restores the default color settings).

Cursors

Together, Photoshop 2.0 and 2.5 provide 40 cursors. Most correspond to the selected tool, but a few have nothing to do with the tool you're using. All cursors, however, have unique meanings. Join me as we count down America's top 40 Photoshop cursors:

Arrow: The left-pointing arrow appears any time the cursor is outside the image window. You can select a tool, set palette options, or choose a command with this cursor.

Move: The right-pointing arrow appears when the cursor is inside a selected area and the rectangular marquee, elliptical marquee, lasso, magic wand, or type tool is selected. Drag the selected area to move it; Option-drag to clone it.

Marquee: The cross appears when the rectangular or elliptical marquee tool is selected and the cursor is outside a selected area. You can access the marquee cursor inside a selected area if you press the Shift or Command key. (Shift adds to the selection; Command subtracts.)

Lasso: The lasso cursor works the same way as the marquee cursor, except that it indicates that the lasso tool is selected.

Wand: Again, this cursor works the same as the lasso and marquee cursors, but it appears when you select the magic wand tool.

Gavel: The gavel cursor is exclusive to Photoshop 2.5. After you select an area and rotate it, stretch it, or apply some other transformation, you can accept the effect by clicking inside the selection with the gavel cursor. Until you click inside the selection, Photoshop remains in transformation mode, thus allowing you to test out multiple rotation angles, stretching percentages, and so on without diminishing the integrity of the selected image.

Cancel: The cancel cursor also is exclusive to Version 2.5. You can click outside a selection during a rotation or a stretch to cancel the transformation and return the selection to its original size and orientation. The cancel cursor warns you that if you click now, you lose your changes.

Crop: This cursor appears when the crop tool is selected and remains on-screen until you marquee the portion of the image that you want to retain.

Scissors: Click with the scissors cursor inside the crop marquee to cut away the portions of the image that lie outside the marquee. (If you move outside the marquee, the cancel cursor appears.)

Type: The common I-beam cursor indicates that the type tool is selected and ready to use. Click with this cursor to display the Type Tool dialog box. As I mentioned before, you can't use the type tool to edit text.

Pen: This cursor appears when the pen tool is selected, enabling you to add points to the path at hand.

Insert point: When a small plus sign accompanies the pen cursor, you can insert points into the current path.

Remove point: When this cursor is active, you can delete points from a path. A new segment joins the remaining points to prevent the path from breaking.

Convert point: Use this cursor to convert a corner to an arc or an arc to a corner. Just click on a point to change it to a corner; drag from a point to change it to an arc.

Close path: When you position your cursor over the first point in an open path — that is, a path that has a break in it — this symbol appears. Click with the cursor to close the path.

Select path: Here's one found only in Photoshop 2.0. After you draw a path and close it, click inside the path with this cursor to convert it to a selection. The solid path outline changes to marching ants. (You have to choose a command to convert a path in Version 2.5.)

Move path: When you move a point or whole path by Command-dragging with the pen tool, this cursor appears.

Clone path: Another Version 2.5 exclusive, the clone path cursor appears when you Command-Option-drag on a point or whole path. This technique enables you to make a duplicate of the path and store it separately or with the original path.

Hand: Number 19 on the Top 40 hit list is the hand cursor, which appears when you select the hand tool or when you press the spacebar with some other tool selected.

Zoom in: This cursor appears when you select the zoom tool or press Command-spacebar when some other tool is selected. Click to magnify the image on-screen.

Zoom out: The zoom out cursor appears when you press Option with the zoom tool selected or press Option-spacebar with some other tool selected. Click to reduce your view of the image.

Zoom limit: This cursor appears when you're at the end of your zoom rope. You can't zoom in beyond 1,600 percent or out beyond 6 percent (1⁄16).

Paint bucket: This cursor appears when the paint bucket tool is selected.

Line/gradient: This cursor appears when you select either the line or gradient tool. Drag with the cursor to determine the angle and length of a prospective straight line or gradient fill.

Eyedropper: This cursor appears when you select the eyedropper tool or when you press Option while using the type tool, paint bucket tool, gradient tool, or any painting tool other than the eraser. Click to lift a color from the image window.

Crosshair pickup: If the eyedropper cursor gets in the way, preventing you from seeing what you're doing, press the Caps Lock key to display a crosshair cursor, which hones in on an exact pixel. This specific crosshair appears when you use the eyedropper tool or press the Option key with the rubber stamp tool while Caps Lock is down.

Eraser: This cursor appears when you select the eraser tool.

Magic eraser: The magic eraser cursor appears when you press the Option key while using the eraser tool. You then can change portions of the image back to the way they looked when last saved to disk.

Pencil: This cursor appears when you select the pencil tool.

- **Crosshair:** You see this cursor when you press the Caps Lock key while using any painting or editing tool. I find it a particular blessing when I'm using the rubber stamp, smudge, and other editing tools that can sometimes prevent you from seeing what you're doing.
- **Airbrush:** You see this cursor when you paint with the airbrush.
- **Paintbrush:** When you select the paintbrush, this cursor appears.
- **Stamp:** This cursor denotes the selection of the rubber stamp tool.
- **Stamp pickup:** When you press the Option key while using the rubber stamp tool — and the Caps Lock key is up — you see this cursor. You then can specify which portion of an image you want to clone.
- **Smudge:** This cursor appears when the smudge tool is selected.
- **Blur:** When you use the blur tool, you see this cursor.
- **Sharpen:** This cursor appears when you press the Option key in combination with the blur tool or when you switch to the sharpen tool by double-clicking on the blur tool icon.
- **Dodge:** Exclusive to Version 2.5, this cursor appears when you select the dodge tool in order to lighten an image.
- **Burn:** If you prefer to darken portions of an image, press the Option key while using the dodge tool or double-click on the dodge tool icon to switch it to the burn tool. Either way, you get this cursor.
- **Watch:** The watch cursor is the universal Macintosh symbol for hurry up and wait. When you see the cursor inside Photoshop 2.5, you either can sit on your idle hands, waiting for the devil to start playing with them, or you can be industrious, switch to another application, and try to get some work done.

Toolbox controls

You have to love lists. They're fun to write and they're a joy to read. All right, so I'm lying. Making your way through lists of information is a monstrous chore, whether you're on the giving or receiving end. But these particular lists happen to contain essential reference information. So on we go with our newest and most astonishing list yet: the one that explains (gasp) the controls at the bottom of the toolbox. (By the way, in that last sentence, you're not supposed to read "gasp," you're supposed to actually gasp. Try again and see if it works better for you the second time.)

- **Foreground color:** Click on the foreground color icon to bring up the Color Picker dialog box. Select a color from Photoshop's immense palette and press Return to change the foreground color, which is used by all painting tools except the eraser. (I'm not sure why, but many users make the mistake of double-clicking on the foreground or background color icons when they first start using Photoshop. A single click is all that's needed.)

- **Background color:** Click on the background color icon to display the Color Picker and change the background color, which is used by the eraser and gradient tools. Photoshop also uses the background color to fill a selected area when you press the Delete key.
- **Default colors:** Click on this Photoshop 2.5 icon to automatically change the foreground color to black and the background color to white. In Photoshop 2.0, you can access this same function by double-clicking on the eyedropper tool icon.
- **Switch colors:** Click on the switch colors icon (also exclusive to Photoshop 2.5) to exchange the foreground and background colors. If you want a quick way to make the foreground color white, click on the default colors icon and then click on the switch colors icon.
- **Marching ants:** Click on this icon to exit the *quick mask mode,* which is a new function in Photoshop 2.5 that enables you to edit selection boundaries using painting tools. (I know this sounds strange, but it's an amazingly beneficial feature.) In the *marching ants mode,* Photoshop represents selection outlines as animated dotted lines that look like marching ants, hence the name. (Adobe calls this mode the *standard mode,* but I think *marching ants mode* better describes the function.)
- **Quick mask:** Click here to enter the quick mask mode. The marching ants vanish and the image appears half covered by a translucent layer of red, called a *rubylith* (after the traditional translucent red paste-up material). The rubylith covers the deselected — or *masked* — portions of the image. Paint with black to extend the areas covered by the rubylith, thereby subtracting from the selection. Paint with white to subtract from the rubylith, thereby adding to the selection.

The quick mask mode is too complex a topic to sum up in a few sentences. If you can't wait to find out what it's all about, refer to the "Selection Masks" section of Chapter 9.

You can change the color and translucency of the rubylith by double-clicking on the marching ants or quick mask icon. You also can change which portion of the image is covered by the color — that is, you can cover the selected area or the masked area.

- **Standard window:** Click on this icon to display the foreground image in a standard window, as shown earlier in Figure 4-2. By default, every image opens in the *standard window mode.*

- **Full screen with menu bar:** If you can't see enough of your image inside a standard window, click on this icon. The title bar and scroll bars disappear, as do all background windows, but you still can access the menu bar. A black-and-white dotted background fills any empty area around the image. Figure 4-4 shows this option applied to the image from Figure 4-2.
- **Absolute full screen:** Aesthetically speaking, the black-and-white dotted background that accompanies the full-screen with menu bar mode looks awful behind *any* image. I don't know why Adobe didn't just make the background solid gray, or better yet, paisley. But enough griping. To see your image set against a neutral black background — a thoroughly preferable alternative — click on the rightmost of the image window icons. The menu bar disappears, limiting your access to commands (you still can access commands via keyboard equivalents), but you can see as much of your image as can physically fit on-screen. Only the toolbox and palettes remain visible, as shown in Figure 4-5. Adobe calls this mode *Full screen without menu bar;* I call it the *absolute full screen mode,* which seems a bit more descriptive and less cumbersome.

Figure 4-4: Click on the full screen with menu bar icon to hide the title bar, scroll bars, and preview box.

Figure 4-5: Click on the absolute full screen icon to hide everything but the toolbox, floating palettes, and image.

If the toolbox gets in your way when you're viewing an image in full screen mode, you can hide it and all other open palettes by pressing the Tab key. To bring the toolbox back into view, press Tab again.

The floating palettes

Only Photoshop 2.5 offers floating palettes, so Version 2.0 users can leave the room for a few minutes now and get a beer or maybe some herbal tea. Skip to the section "How to get around" when you get back.

Every Photoshop palette offers a handful of standard elements, as shown in Figure 4-6. Most are shrunken versions of the elements associated with any window. For example, the close box, size box, and scroll bar work identically to their image-window counterparts. The title bar lacks a title, but you still can drag it to move the palette to another location on-screen. (Don't drag on the area that actually contains the palette title; it serves no operational purpose.)

Three elements are unique to floating palettes:

- **Palette options:** Each floating palette offers its own collection of options. These may include tools, icons, pop-up menus, slider bars, you name it.

- **Palette menu:** Drag from the right-pointing arrowhead icon to display a menu of commands specific to the palette. These commands enable you to manipulate the palette options and adjust preference settings.
- **Collapse box:** Click on the *collapse box* to decrease the on-screen space consumed by the palette. If you previously enlarged the palette by dragging the size box, your first click reduces the palette back to its default size. After that, clicking on the collapse box of the Channels and Info palettes eliminates all palette options.

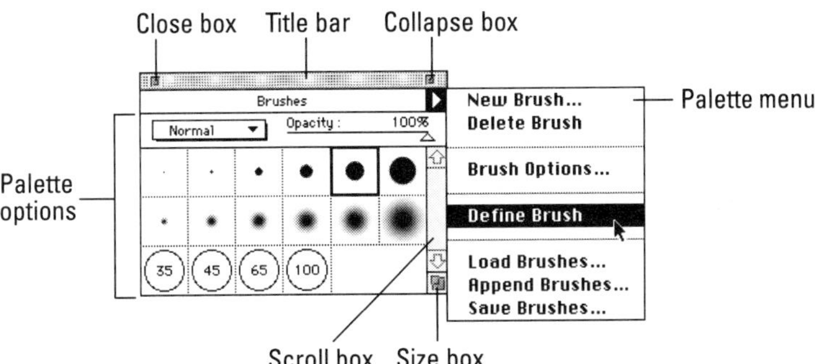

Figure 4-6: All Photoshop 2.5 palettes include the same basic elements as the Brushes palette, shown here.

Clicking on the collapse box of the Brushes, Paths, and Colors palettes chops off the bottom tier of palette options; to eliminate all options, Option-click on the collapse box. This technique works even if you have enlarged the palette by dragging the size box. Figure 4-7 shows how the different palettes appear when partially and fully collapsed.

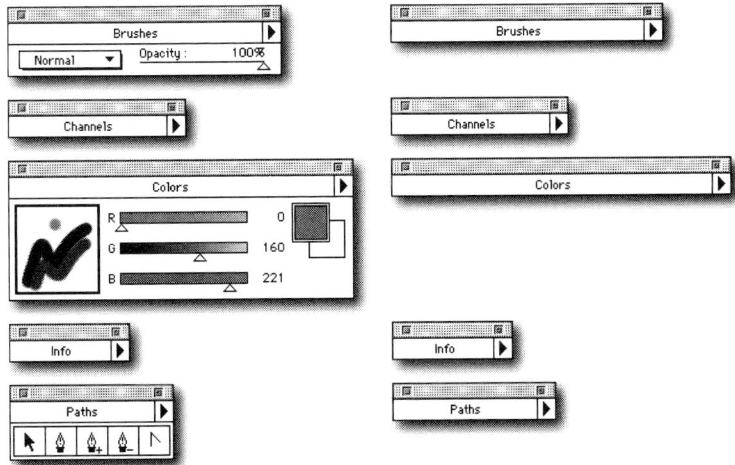

Figure 4-7: The five floating palettes when partially collapsed (left) and fully collapsed (right).

How to get around

All Macintosh programs provide a variety of navigational tools and functions that enable you to scoot around the program, visit the heartlands and nether regions, examine the fine details, and take in the big picture. Photoshop is no exception. In fact, it provides more navigational tricks per square pixel than just about any other graphics program.

The zoom ratio

In Photoshop, you can change the *view size* — the size at which an image appears on-screen — so that you can either see more of an image or concentrate on individual pixels. Each change in view size is expressed as a *zoom ratio,* which is the ratio between screen pixels and image pixels. A 1:1 zoom ratio means one screen pixel per each image pixel and is therefore equivalent to a 100 percent view size. A 1:2 zoom ratio equates to a 50 percent view size, as shown in Figure 4-8. A 2:1 zoom ratio is equivalent to a 200 percent view size, as shown in Figure 4-9. All told, Photoshop 2.5 provides 31 zoom ratios, ranging from 1:16 to 16:1 in single-digit increments (1:15, 1:14, 1:13, and so on).

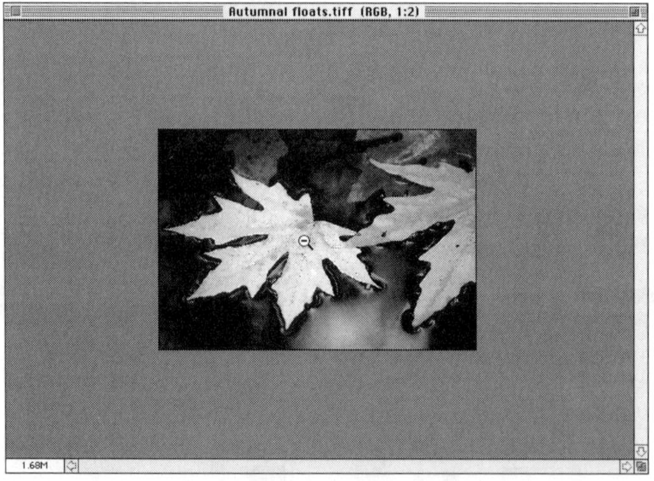

Figure 4-8: When viewed at the 1:2 zoom ratio, you see only a quarter of the total pixels in an image (half of the pixels vertically and half horizontally).

When you first open an image, Photoshop displays it on-screen at the largest zoom ratio (up to and including 1:1) that permits the entire image to fit on-screen in the standard window mode. Assuming that you don't change the size of the image, you can return to this view size — sometimes called the *fit-in-window view* — at any time during the editing cycle by double-clicking on the hand tool icon in the toolbox.

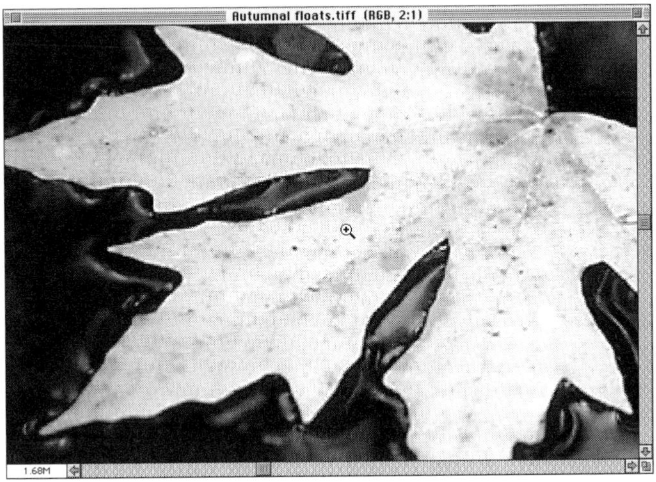

Figure 4-9: At the 2:1 zoom ratio, each pixel in the image measures 2 screen pixels tall and 2 screen pixels wide.

The zoom tool

The zoom tool enables you to change view sizes as follows:

- Click in the image window with the zoom tool to magnify the image to twice the previous zoom ratio.
- Option-click with the zoom tool to reduce the image to half its previous zoom ratio.
- Drag with the zoom tool to draw a rectangular marquee around the portion of the image you want to magnify. Photoshop magnifies the image so that the marqueed area fits just inside the image window. If the horizontal and vertical proportions of the marquee do not match those of the image window — for example, if you draw a tall, thin marquee or a short, wide one — Photoshop favors the smaller of the two possible zoom ratios to avoid hiding any detail inside the marquee.
- Double-click on the zoom tool icon in the toolbox to restore the foreground image to a 1:1 zoom ratio.

To temporarily access the zoom tool when some other tool is selected, press and hold the Command and spacebar keys. Release both keys to return control of the cursor to the selected tool. To access the zoom out cursor, press both Option and spacebar. These keyboard equivalents work from inside many dialog boxes, most notably those that provide preview options (like the Hue/Saturation, Levels, and Curves dialog boxes discussed in Chapter 16).

When you use the zoom tool, you magnify and reduce the image within the confines of a static image window. To change the dimensions of the window to fit those of the image, click on the zoom box in the upper right corner of the title bar.

To automatically resize the window along with the image, use the Zoom In (Command-plus) and Zoom Out (Command-minus) commands under the Window menu. Frequently, it's more convenient to use these commands than the zoom tool.

Creating a reference window

Many paint programs provide a small thumbnail view of your image at real size to serve as a reference when you work in a magnified zoom ratio; Photoshop does not. You can, however easily create a second view of your image by choosing Window ⇨ New Window. Use the new window to maintain a 100 percent view of your image while you zoom and edit inside the original window. Both windows track the changes to the image, as shown in Figure 4-10. The paintbrush strokes I applied to the leaves appear in both windows.

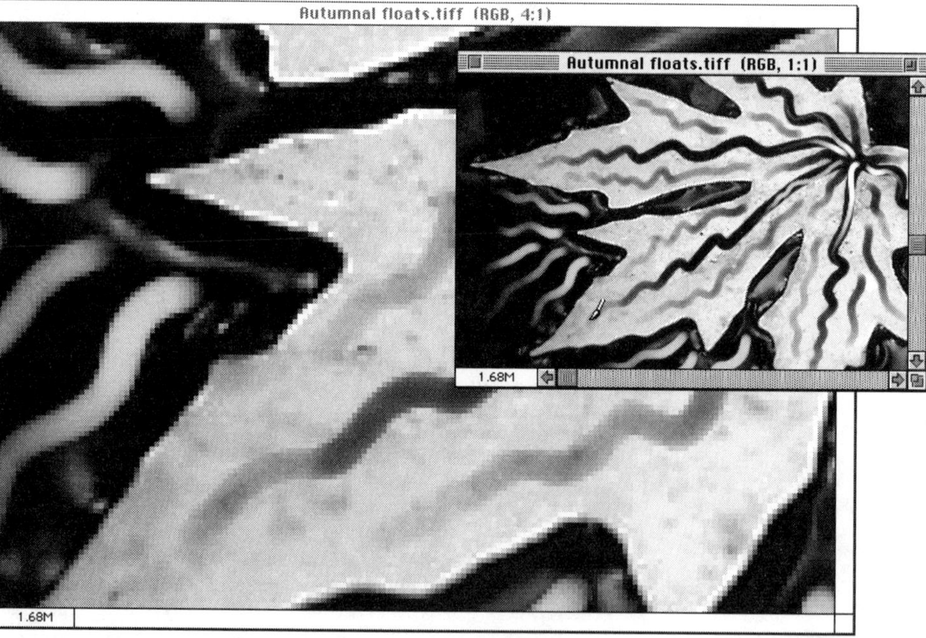

Figure 4-10: You can create multiple windows to track the changes made to a single image by choosing the New Window command from the Window menu.

Scrolling inside the window

In the standard window mode, you have access to scroll bars, just as you do in the Finder and other Macintosh applications. But as you become more proficient with Photoshop, you'll use the scroll bars less and less. One way to bypass the scroll bars is to use the keyboard equivalents listed in Table 4-1. Even folks who don't own extended keyboards have options — you just need a Control key.

Table 4-1 Scrolling from the Keyboard

Scrolling Action	*Extended Keyboard*	*Smaller Keyboard*
Up one screen	Page Up	Control-K
Up slightly	Shift-Page Up	Control-Shift-K
Down one screen	Page Down	Control-L
Down slightly	Shift-Page Down	Control-Shift-L
To upper left corner	Home	Control-A
To lower right corner	End	Control-D

Unfortunately, you can't scroll exclusively left or right from the keyboard. But who cares? You won't be scrolling from the keyboard that often anyway. Most of the time, you'll use the hand tool.

To temporarily access the hand tool when some other tool is selected, press and hold the spacebar. Releasing the spacebar returns the cursor to its original appearance. This keyboard equivalent even works from inside many dialog boxes.

Shortcuts

Shortcuts enable you to access commands and other functions without resorting to the laborious task of choosing commands from menus or clicking on some fool icon until your arm falls off. Many shortcuts are fairly obvious. For example, Photoshop lists keyboard equivalents for its commands next to the command in the menu. You can choose File ⇨ New by pressing Command-N, choose Edit ⇨ Undo by pressing Command-Z, choose Select ⇨ All by pressing Command-A, and so on. But a few of Photoshop's shortcuts are either hidden or can be overlooked easily.

Table 4-2 lists my favorite Photoshop shortcuts. I've already mentioned some of them, but they bear repeating. (Shortcuts marked with an asterisk are applicable only to Photoshop 2.5.)

Table 4-2 The Best Photoshop Shortcuts You'll Ever Learn

Operation	*Shortcut*
	Navigation tricks
Scroll image with hand tool	Press the spacebar and drag with any selected tool
Zoom in without changing window size	Command-spacebar-click
Zoom in and change window size to fit	Command-plus
Zoom out without changing window size	Option-spacebar-click
Zoom out and change window size to fit	Command-minus
Zoom to 100%	Double-click on the zoom tool icon
Fit image in window	Double-click on the hand tool icon
	Paint tool tricks
Lift foreground color with eyedropper (when any paint tool is selected)	Option-click
Lift background color	Option-click with the eyedropper tool
Erase entire image	Double-click on the eraser tool icon
Revert image with magic eraser	Option-drag with the eraser tool
Specify an area to clone	Option-click with the rubber stamp tool
Dip into the foreground color when smearing	Option-drag with the smudge tool
Sharpen with the blur tool or blur with the sharpen tool	Option-drag
Darken with the dodge tool or lighten with the burn tool	Option-drag
Paint or edit in a straight line	Click and then Shift-click with the painting or editing tool
Change opacity, pressure, or exposure of paint tools in 10% increments	Press 0 through 9 (1 is 10%, 9 is 90%, 0 is 100%)
Hide/show toolbox and other floating palettes	Tab (or Control-I, just in case your Tab key is on the fritz)
	Pen tool and path tricks (pen tool selected unless otherwise noted)
Move selected points	Command-drag on point
Select multiple points in path	Command-Shift-click on point
Convert corner to arc	Command-Control-drag on point
Convert arc to corner	Command-Control-click on point
Convert arc to cusp	Command-Control-drag the control handle

Table 4-2 (continued)

Operation	*Shortcut*
Insert point in path*	Command-Option-click on segment (when arrow tool is selected)
Remove point from path*	Command-Option-click on point (when arrow tool is selected)
Selection tricks	
Add to a selection	Shift-drag with selection tool (Shift-click with magic wand)
Subtract from a selection	Command-drag with selection tool (Command-click with magic wand)
Subtract all but intersected portion of a selection	Command-Shift-drag with selection tool (Command-Shift-click with magic wand)
Move selection	Drag inside selection with selection tool
Constrain movement vertically or horizontally	Shift after you begin to drag inside selection with selection tool
Move selection in 1-pixel increments	Any arrow key
Move selection in 10-pixel increments	Shift-any arrow key
Clone selection	Option-drag inside selection with selection tool
Clone selection in 1-pixel increments	Option-any arrow key
Clone selection in 10-pixel increments	Shift-Option-any arrow key
Move selection boundary independently of contents	Command-Option-drag inside selection with selection tool
Move selection boundary independently in 1-pixel increments	Command-Option-any arrow key
Fill selection with background color	Delete or Clear (or Control-H)
Fill selection with foreground color	Option-Delete (or Control-Option-H)
Float selection (separate it from the rest of the image)	Command-J
Change opacity of floating selection in 10% increments*	Press 0 through 9 when a selection tool is active (1 is 10%, 9 is 90%, 0 is 100%)
Hide/show marching ants	Command-H
Deselect everything	Command-D
Image and color adjustments	
Resize cropping boundary	Drag corner handle
Rotate cropping boundary	Option-drag corner handle
Reapply last filter used	Command-F
Display dialog box for last filter used	Command-Option-F

Table 4-2 (*continued*)

Operation	*Shortcut*
Bring up last settings used in Variations dialog box*	Option-choose Image ➪ Adjust ➪ Variations
Paste image and display Composite Controls dialog box	Command-Option-V
Replace color in Colors palette with foreground color	Option-click on color swatch
Delete color from Colors palette	Command-click on color swatch
	General
Switch between channels	Command-0 through Command-9 (0 is composite of color channels)
Change the preference settings	Command-K
Add previews and slider bars to Distortion filter dialog boxes	Option-choose Apple ➪ About Plug-in ➪ Displace, activate check box
Cancel the current operation	Command-period

* Applicable only to Version 2.5

Establishing function key shortcuts

Though pretty extensive, Table 4-2 doesn't include *every* shortcut, just the best ones. (I left out most of the keyboard equivalents you can see in the menus.)

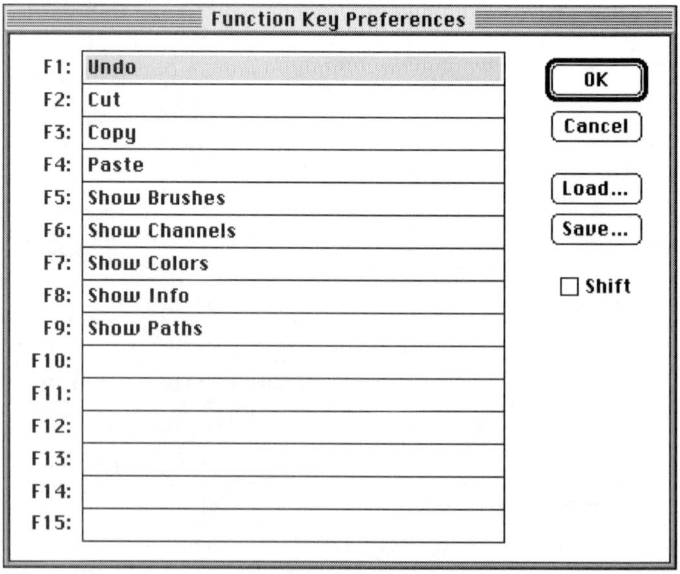

Figure 4-11: Assign commands to function keys by selecting an option box and choosing the command from the menu bar.

Function Key Preferences

F1: Undo
F2: Cut
F3: Copy
F4: Paste
F5: Show Brushes
F6: Show Channels
F7: Show Colors
F8: Show Info
F9: Show Paths
F10:
F11:
F12:
F13:
F14:
F15:

OK
Cancel
Load...
Save...
Shift

If you own an extended keyboard, you can specify additional keyboard equivalents inside Photoshop 2.5 by choosing File ⇨ Preferences ⇨ Function Keys. In the Function Key Preferences dialog box (Figure 4-11), you can assign any command to a function key or Shift-function key combination. Just position your cursor inside the desired option box and choose a command from the Photoshop menu bar. Select the Shift check box to access the Shift key combinations.

In case you folks with standard keyboards are filled with regret over your lack of function keys, rest assured that you're not missing out. In fact, this solution — assigning Photoshop keyboard equivalents to function keys — out and out stinks, for a number of reasons. First, most people who own extended keyboards have already assigned their function keys to universal operations using CE Software's QuicKeys, Affinity Microsystems' Tempo, or some other macro utility. Second, by limiting you to function keys, Photoshop unnecessarily constrains your range of options. For several years now, customizable programs such as Microsoft Word have permitted you to assign any key equivalent you can press, even if you have to bring your toes into the picture. Why does Photoshop stop at function keys? Why doesn't it offer the Command, Option, and Control keys as modifiers? I don't know — I thought maybe you knew.

If, despite my ravings, you decide to use function keys — I do, after all, end up recommending it myself in the upcoming "Shortcuts in the absolute full screen mode" section — be sure to save your settings to disk using the Save button. If your preferences file ever becomes corrupted or if someone goes and throws it away, you can retrieve the function keys by using the Load button.

Using a macro utility

To expand your range of shortcut options, you need to go outside of Photoshop and take advantage of a separate utility. Generally speaking, you have two software options. You can use Apple's ResEdit, which lets you assign keyboard equivalents that you save inside the Photoshop application, or you can choose one of two macro utility programs, QuicKeys or Tempo, which require that you store keyboard equivalents in a separate file. The advantages and disadvantages of each are as follows:

- **ResEdit advantages:** Because ResEdit makes keyboard equivalents part of the Photoshop application code, you can access commands when the menu bar is unavailable, as it is when you view an image in the absolute full screen mode. Also, ResEdit shortcuts appear in the menu, just like Photoshop's default shortcuts. You can even change the default shortcuts if you don't like them.

- **ResEdit disadvantages:** ResEdit enables you to assign Command-key equivalents only, and Photoshop already uses Command plus every key on the keyboard. Therefore, you must resort to special Option and Shift-Option symbols, which won't necessarily display correctly in the Photoshop menu. Also, with ResEdit, you are actually editing the Photoshop application code, and you can mess it up royally if you're not careful. Make sure to create a backup copy of Photoshop before you even *think* about using ResEdit.
- **QuicKeys/Tempo advantages:** The first advantage of a macro utility program is safety. Because you store the keyboard equivalents in a separate file, you can't harm the Photoshop application no matter how many mistakes you make. Second, it's easy to use. You can get up and running with QuicKeys, for example, in a matter of minutes. By contrast, ResEdit is one of those programs that takes years to grasp fully — and Apple distributes it without any documentation. (This is because ResEdit is designed with programmers, not end users, in mind.) Third, a macro utility provides access to any keystroke you care to press. Fourth, you can create shortcuts not only for commands but also for options, tools, control icons, and so on. And fifth, you can record *sequences,* which are shortcuts that perform many operations in response to a single keystroke.
- **QuicKeys/Tempo disadvantages:** Although macro utilities are inexpensive compared to other varieties of software, they do cost money — about $100 through mail-order vendors. ResEdit is distributed free of charge over electronic bulletin boards and the like. Another drawback is that you cannot choose a command unless the menu bar is available, which presents a potential problem when you work in the absolute full screen mode. Luckily, there is a way around this, as is explained in the upcoming section "Shortcuts in the absolute full screen mode."

Of the two macro utilities, QuicKeys is the more popular and the easier to use. But QuicKeys also is limited in its ability to perform conditional operations — "Do X if Y is true." Tempo is more difficult to use, but it is much more flexible. If you want to do more than launch programs and assign shortcuts to commands, Tempo is the better choice.

Shortcut suggestions

In the final analysis, macro utilities win out over ResEdit. Whether you ultimately select QuicKeys or Tempo, you can increase your speed and efficiency by creating shortcuts of your own. I don't have space in this book to document how to use a macro utility, but I can recommend keyboard equivalents you may want to explore. Table 4-3 contains a list of suggested shortcuts for commands and control icons. Keep in mind that these shortcuts represent only those commands I consider to be the most useful; I ignore all sorts of filters that are handy but on a less frequent basis.

All keystrokes employ the first letter of the function name when possible. When that keystroke is already taken, an alternate letter is selected. You may disagree with some of my reasoning, in which case I encourage you to experiment on your own and come up with shortcuts that work best for you.

As you can see in Table 4-3, I associate certain modifier keys with certain tasks, which helps me remember the shortcuts I've already assigned and their purposes. For example, I use Command-Control combinations exclusively to launch programs. Command-Control-A launches Adobe Photoshop. Similarly, I use Command-Shift combinations to edit selections, Command-Option combinations to edit an entire image, and Control-Option combinations to access icons.

Table 4-3 Potential Photoshop Shortcuts

Operation	*Shortcut*
Displaying palettes	
Windows ➪ Show Brushes	Command-Shift-1 (keypad)
Windows ➪ Show Channels	Command-Shift-2 (keypad)
Windows ➪ Show Colors	Command-Shift-3 (keypad)
Windows ➪ Show Info	Command-Shift-4 (keypad)
Windows ➪ Show Paths	Command-Shift-5 (keypad)
Editing selections	
Edit ➪ Fill	Command-Shift-F
Edit ➪ Stroke	Command-Shift-S
Edit ➪ Define Pattern	Command-Shift-P
Edit ➪ Composite Controls	Command-Shift-C
Image ➪ Rotate ➪ 90° CW	Command-Shift-right arrow
Image ➪ Rotate ➪ 90° CCW	Command-Shift-left arrow
Image ➪ Effects ➪ Scale	Command-Shift-Z
Filter ➪ Blur ➪ Gaussian Blur	Command-Shift-G
Filter ➪ Noise ➪ Add Noise	Command-Shift-N
Filter ➪ Sharpen ➪ Unsharp Mask	Command-Shift-U
Select ➪ Inverse	Command-Shift-I
Select ➪ Similar	Command-Shift-M
Select ➪ Feather	Command-Shift-T
Select ➪ Defringe	Command-Shift-D
Changing the image	
Image ➪ Canvas Size	Command-Option-C
Image ➪ Image Size	Command-Option-I
Mode ➪ Bitmap	Command-Option-B
Mode ➪ Grayscale	Command-Option-G
Mode ➪ Duotone	Command-Option-D

Table 4-3 (*continued*)

Operation	*Shortcut*
Mode ⇨ Indexed Color	Command-Option-X
Mode ⇨ RGB Color	Command-Option-R
Mode ⇨ CMYK Color	Command-Option-K
Mode ⇨ Lab Color	Command-Option-L
Control icons	
Foreground color	Control-Option-F
Background color	Control-Option-B
Default colors	Control-Option-D
Switch colors	Control-Option-S
Marching ants	Control-Option-M
Quick mask	Control-Option-Q
Standard window	Control-Option-W
Full screen with menu bar	Control-Option-Z
Absolute full screen	Control-Option-A

Assigning shortcuts for icons can be very tricky. Be sure to associate your click specifically with the toolbox window so that the macro utility doesn't click in the wrong place if you move the toolbox on-screen. In QuicKeys, for example, you instruct the macro to click inside the window named *Tools,* as demonstrated in Figure 4-12.

Shortcuts in the absolute full screen mode

You learned earlier that the menu bar disappears when you work in the absolute full screen mode. That means you can't access commands via the menu bar. The only way to choose commands is by using preset keyboard equivalents or custom shortcuts you assign to function keys. So what are you to do if you want to create custom shortcuts for Photoshop commands that will work even in the absolute full screen mode, but you already assigned away all or most of your function keys using a macro program? The answer is to use *keystroke aliases.*

First, you assign commands to function keys inside Photoshop. Then, inside the macro utility, you assign keystrokes to those Photoshop function keys. When you press the keystroke aliases, the macro sends the function key combination to Photoshop 2.5.

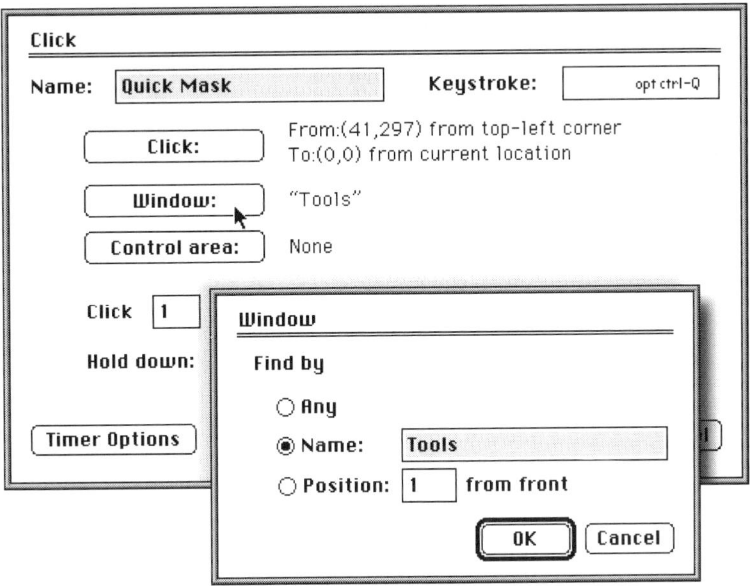

Figure 4-12: Tell QuicKeys to look for the Tools window when clicking on control icons.

This amazing technique works only in Version 2.5, because of the addition of the File ➪ Preferences ➪ Function Keys command, which Version 2.0 does not offer.

Here's an example. Suppose that you assigned the F5 key to open the Scrapbook. You've used this keyboard equivalent for years and you would sooner be tarred and feathered than change it just for the sake of Photoshop. By default, however, Photoshop 2.5 assigns F5 to open the Brushes palette. In absolute full screen mode, F5 provides the only access to the palette, because menu commands are unavailable. You want to continue using F5 to open the Scrapbook, but at the same time, you don't want to lose the ability to show and hide the Brushes palette in the absolute full screen mode. So what do you do? Create a keyboard alias for F5.

As illustrated in Figure 4-13, a macro utility intercepts all keystrokes before they go to the foreground application. If the utility doesn't recognize the keystrokes, it lets the keystroke pass. If the keystroke corresponds to one of its macros, it passes the macro on to the foreground application.

When you press F5, the macro utility intercepts the keystroke and converts it into the *Open Scrapbook* operation. F5 goes in, but F5 does not come out. You therefore can instruct the macro utility to convert a different keystroke to F5. In Table 4-3, I suggested assigning Command-Shift-1 to the Windows ➪ Show Brushes command. If you also establish Command-Shift-1 as a keystroke alias for F5, the macro not only fulfills the same purpose, it also works inside the absolute full screen mode.

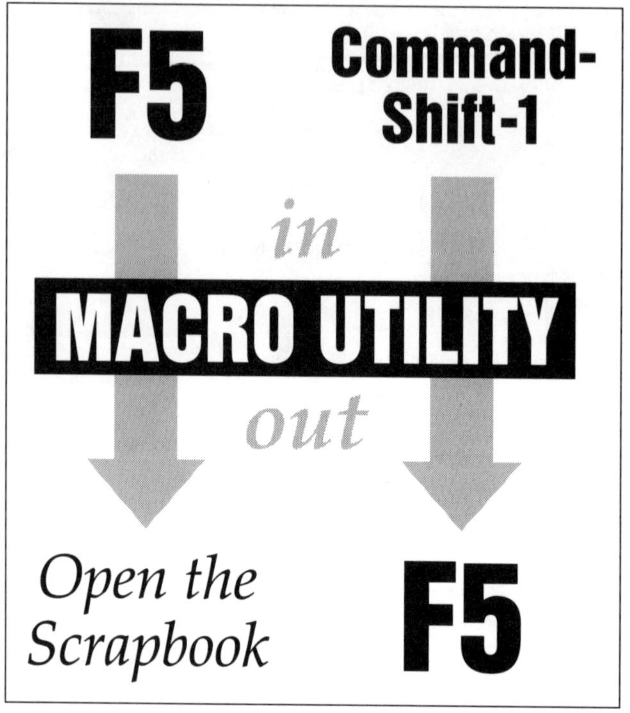

Figure 4-13: A macro utility can convert the F5 keystroke into an operation and convert another keystroke into F5.

The conclusion, therefore, is to use the Function Key Preferences dialog box to assign function and Shift-function keystrokes to your favorite 30 commands that don't already have preset keyboard equivalents. Then create keystroke aliases for the function keys using QuicKeys or Tempo. All 30 aliases will work in the absolute full screen mode.

How to Customize the Interface

In addition to adding your own keyboard equivalents, you can customize the Photoshop interface by changing the *preference settings.* Photoshop ships with certain preference settings already in force (these are called *factory default settings*), but you can change the settings to reflect your personal preferences.

You can change preference settings in two ways. You can make environmental adjustments using commands from the File ⇨ Preferences submenu, or you can change the operation of specific tools by double-clicking on a tool icon.

Photoshop 2.0 (or 2.0.1) remembers environmental preference settings by saving them to a file called *PS 2.0 Prefs* (or *PS 2.0.1 Prefs*) in the Plug-ins folder. Unfortunately, Versions 2.0 and 2.0.1 do not remember tool settings, so you must readjust the tools every time you run Photoshop. Version 2.5, on the other hand, remembers everything, including environmental preferences, tools settings, and even the file format under which you saved the last image. It stores this information in a file called *Photoshop Prefs* in the Preferences folder inside the System Folder (assuming you're using System 7).

To restore Photoshop's factory default settings, delete the PS 2.0 Prefs or Photoshop Prefs file when the application is *not* running. The next time you launch Photoshop, it creates a new preferences file automatically.

The File ➪ Preferences commands

Both Photoshops 2.0 and 2.5 offer File ➪ Preferences submenus, as shown in Figure 4-14. The submenu for Version 2.5, on the right side of the figure, differs from its counterpart in Version 2.0, shown on the left. Version 2.5 eliminates the Clipboard command and adds the Function Keys, Plug-ins, and Separation Tables commands. The new Scratch Disks command is an upgrade of the old Virtual Memory command.

Figure 4-14: The File ➪ Preferences submenus for Version 2.5 (right) and Version 2.0 (left).

Briefly stated, these commands work as follows:

- **General (Command-K):** This command provides access to the preference settings you'll need to adjust most often. I examine the General Preferences dialog box in the next section.
- **Function Keys:** I touched on this command a few pages ago. Exclusive to Version 2.5, it enables you to assign any command in Photoshop to a function key or Shift-function key combination.
- **Plug-ins:** Offered only by Photoshop 2.5, this command lets you change the folder in which Photoshop searches for the plug-in modules it loads during the launch cycle. This setting doesn't take effect until you relaunch the program.

- **Scratch Disks (Virtual Memory):** Discussed back in Chapter 3, "Preparing the Soil," this command lets you specify the hard drive or removable media device on which Photoshop stores its temporary virtual memory files. Again, this setting doesn't take effect until you relaunch the program.
- **Units:** This command enables you to change the units of measure that appear in every dialog box as well as the Info palette, in which you can specify the size of something. If you prefer picas to inches, for example, choose this command.
- **Clipboard:** Dropped from Photoshop 2.5, this command lets you specify the bit depth at which the program transfers cut or copied images to the system software's Clipboard. Lacking this command, Photoshop 2.5 transfers Clipboard images with all colors intact.

The lower portion of the File ⇨ Preferences submenu enables you to adjust the way colors appear on-screen (*monitor calibration*) and when printed (*color separation*). These options are explained in greater depth in Chapter 7, "Printing Images," but here is a quick rundown:

- **Monitor Setup:** This command enables you to change the way Photoshop displays colors on your monitor. You can specify the brand of monitor you use and the lighting conditions of the room in which you work. You also can adjust the *gamma,* which affects the brightness of the medium-range colors (or *midtones*) displayed on your monitor.
- **Printing Inks Setup:** Use this command to control the output of color proofs and CMYK (cyan, magenta, yellow, and black) separations for four-color offset reproduction. Together with the preceding command, Printing Inks Setup determines the way Photoshop converts colors between the RGB and CMYK modes.
- **Separation Setup:** This command lets you control the generation of four-color separations. You can adjust the black separation both independently and in tandem with the cyan, magenta, and yellow separations.
- **Separation Tables:** Exclusive to Photoshop 2.5, this command enables you to save the settings you selected in the Printing Inks Setup and Separation Setup dialog boxes to a special file for later use. Even though both of those dialog boxes provide save options of their own, only the Separation Tables dialog box lets you save both together.

General environmental preferences

Of all the Preferences commands, the General command is the most important. I touch on the other commands throughout the remainder of this book, but the General command deserves your immediate attention because it affects the widest range of Photoshop functions. Figure 4-15 shows the General Preferences dialog box as it appears in Versions 2.0 and 2.5.

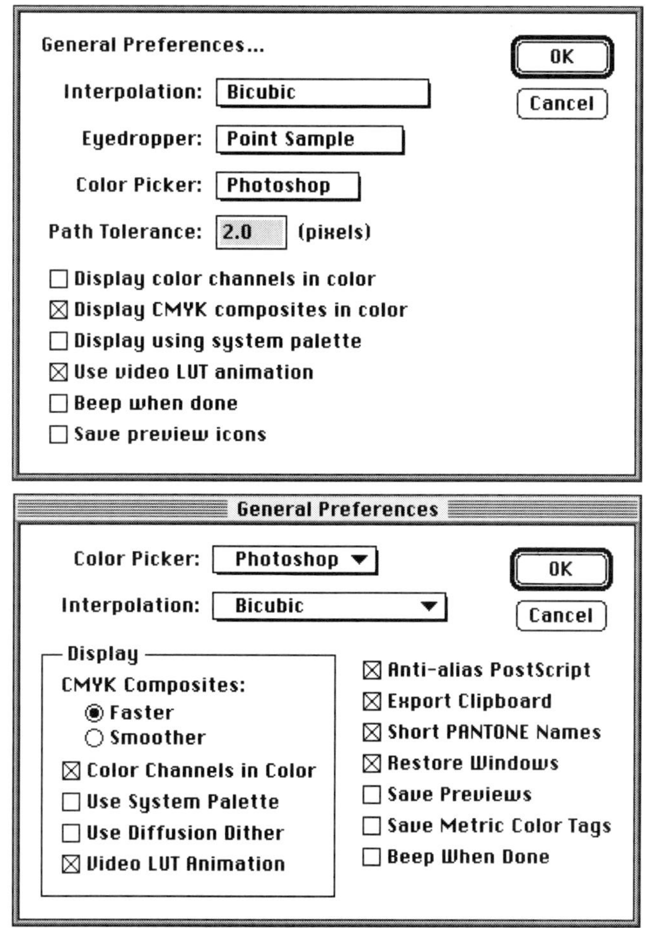

Figure 4-15: The General Preferences dialog box from Photoshop 2.0 (top) and Photoshop 2.5 (bottom).

In brief, the options inside these dialog boxes work as follows:

- **Color Picker:** When you click on the foreground or background color control icon in the toolbox, Photoshop displays one of two *color pickers,* its own or the one provided by the Apple system software. If you are familiar with other Macintosh graphics programs but new to Photoshop, the system software's Color Picker dialog box may be more familiar to you. However, Photoshop's color picker is more versatile.
- **Interpolation:** When you enlarge an image or transform it using one of the commands in the Image ⇨ Rotation or Image ⇨ Effects submenus, Photoshop has to make up — or *interpolate* — pixels to fill in the gaps. You can change how Photoshop calculates the interpolation by choosing one of the three options demonstrated in Figure 4-16.

If you choose Nearest Neighbor, Photoshop simply copies the next-door pixel when creating a new one. This is the fastest but least helpful setting. The Bilinear option smooths the transitions between pixels by creating intermediary shades. It takes more time, but typically, the softened effect is worth it. Still more time-intensive is the default setting, Bicubic, which boosts the amount of contrast between pixels in order to offset the blurring effect that generally accompanies interpolation.

Figure 4-16 shows how the Bicubic setting adds special dips and peaks in color transitions that the Bilinear setting leaves out. (The names *bilinear* and *bicubic* refer to the complexity of the polynomial used to calculate the interpolations. Better names might be *softened* and *softened with enhanced contrast.*) Figure 4-17 shows the gray boxes from the previous figure mapped onto bar graphs. Taller vertical graph lines indicate darker values. You can see that whereas bilinear interpolation simply rounds off the transition between neighboring colors, bicubic interpolation creates dips and peaks in color transitions that accentuate contrast and prevent overblurring.

- **Eyedropper:** In Photoshop 2.0, this pop-up menu lets you specify whether the eyedropper tool lifts the color from a single pixel or averages the colors of several neighboring pixels. In Photoshop 2.5, you access this option by double-clicking on the eyedropper tool icon.

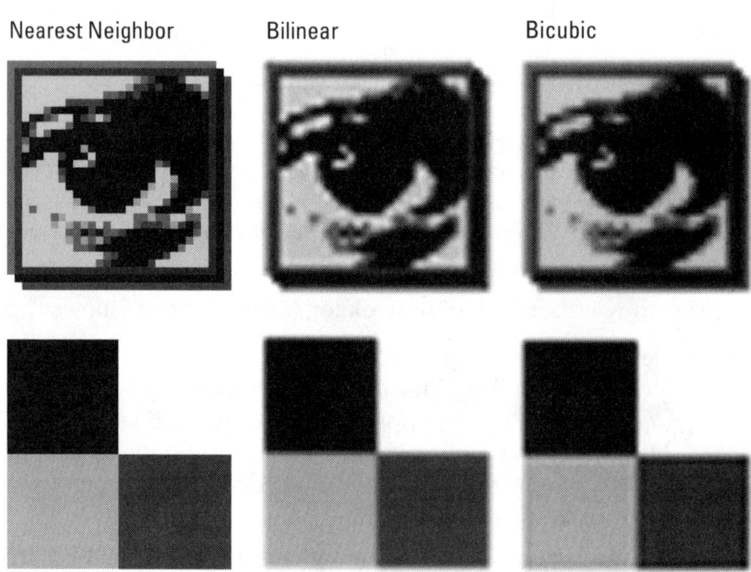

Figure 4-16: The Photoshop application icon and a simple box pattern shown as they appear when enlarged to 400 percent, subject to the three different types of interpolation.

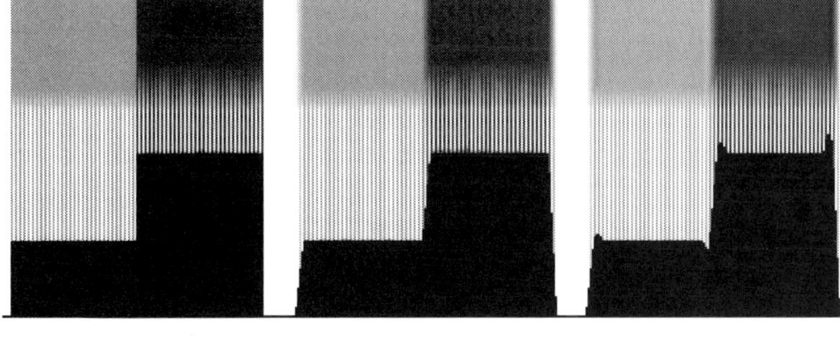

Figure 4-17: A cross-section of the gray boxes from the previous figure mapped onto a graph.

- **Path Tolerance:** When you convert a selection to a path using the Make Path command, Photoshop can either create an extremely complex path that retains all the little twists and turns in the selection boundary, or it can sacrifice some accuracy in the interest of creating a simplified path you can easily edit. A Path Tolerance value of 0.1 results in an extremely accurate, complex path; higher values result in more simplified paths. In Version 2.0, you specify a Path Tolerance value in the General Preferences dialog box. In Photoshop 2.5, the Path Tolerances option appears after you choose the Make Path command from the Paths palette menu.
- **Display CMYK Composites:** RGB is the color mode used to display images on a monitor; CMYK is the color mode used to print colors on paper. In effect, when you edit a CMYK image, you're trying to display images on-screen in the wrong color mode. Photoshop 2.5 provides two solutions: If you select the Smoother option, Photoshop preserves the actual CMYK color values in an image and converts them on the fly to your RGB display — a precise but excruciatingly slow process. If you specify the Faster option, Photoshop cheats by converting the colors in an image to their nearest RGB equivalents, which speeds up the screen display dramatically but sacrifices image quality.

  Photoshop 2.0 provides an even more drastic solution. By deselecting the Display CMYK Composites in Color option, you can abandon color display altogether. It's not an ideal solution, but you can edit the lightness values in an image without fear of harming the CMYK colors.

Of the Display options in Photoshop 2.5's General Preferences dialog box, only CMYK Composites can possibly affect the way the program prints an image or saves it to disk. The same holds true for the check box options provided by Photoshop 2.0 — only the Display CMYK Composites in Color option can affect the way the image is printed or saved to disk.

- **Display Color Channels in Color:** Individual color channels contain only 8 bits of information per pixel, which means they display grayscale images. Photoshop provides you with the option of colorizing the channel according to the primary color it represents. For example, when this option is turned on, the red color channel looks like a grayscale image viewed through red acetate. In my opinion, the effect isn't very helpful and does more to obscure your image than make it easier for you to see what's going on.
- **Display Using System Palette:** This option applies to using Photoshop on an 8-bit monitor. I advised you to use 16-bit video or better in Chapter 3, but in case you chose to ignore me, Photoshop lets you specify how you want it to dither colors on-screen. By default, Photoshop selects the 256 colors that are most suited to your image. In doing so, however, it must switch color palettes every time you bring a new document to the foreground. If you want all open documents to conform to the same color palette — the one built into the Macintosh system software — select this option.
- **Use Diffusion Dither:** 32-bit QuickDraw, built into System 7 and included as a system extension with System 6, automatically dithers colors using a grid-like dot pattern. Photoshop offers a more naturalistic *diffusion dither* that imitates colors slightly more accurately. But because the diffusion dither follows no specific pattern, you sometimes see distinct edges between selected and deselected portions of your image after applying a filter or some other effect. This option is not available in Photoshop 2.0.

To eliminate any visual disharmony that may occur when using the Use Diffusion Dither option, you can force Photoshop to redraw the entire image by double-clicking on the zoom tool icon or performing some other zoom function.

- **Use Video LUT Animation:** To speed display on 24-bit monitors, Photoshop uses a *color lookup table* (*CLUT,* or in this case, *LUT*). If you ever worked inside one of Photoshop's color manipulation dialog boxes with the Preview option turned off, you've seen *LUT animation* in progress. Photoshop changes the LUT on the fly according to your specifications and, in doing so, more or less previews the color change over the entire image. It's not a real preview, but it's the next best thing. If LUT animation causes a problem with your video board, you can turn it off using this option. Otherwise, leave it on.
- **Anti-alias PostScript:** Photoshop 2.5 can swap graphics with Adobe Illustrator 5.0 and Adobe Dimensions 1.0 via the Clipboard. The Anti-alias PostScript option smooths out the edges of PostScript paths pasted into Photoshop from the Clipboard. If you don't want antialiased (softened) edges, turn this option off.

- **Export Clipboard:** When selected, this option ensures that Photoshop 2.5 transfers a copied image from its internal Clipboard to the system's Clipboard when you switch applications. This capability enables you to paste the image into another running program, as discussed in the "Application Clipboards" section of Chapter 2. Turn this option off if you plan to use copied images only within Photoshop and you want to reduce the lag time that occurs when switching from Photoshop to another program. Even with this option off, you can paste images copied from other programs into Photoshop.
- **Short Pantone Names:** Photoshop 2.5 uses updated Pantone naming conventions. If you plan to import a Photoshop image that contains Pantone colors into a desktop publishing or drawing package, select this option to ensure that the receiving application recognizes the color names.
- **Restore Windows:** When this option is selected, Photoshop 2.5 remembers the location of the toolbox and floating palettes from one session to the next. If you deselect this check box, Photoshop displays only the toolbox in the upper left corner of the screen each time you run the program.

- **Save Previews:** Photoshop 2.5.1 now allows you to view a preview of an image from inside the Open dialog box. In fact, by selecting the Save Previews check box, you actually save two previews, one that you can view inside the Open dialog box and another than you can view from the Finder desktop under System 7. Thank you, Adobe, for finally offering us the best of both worlds.

- **Save Metric Color Tags:** If you use EFI's EfiColor for Photoshop to help in screen and printer calibration and you import and print most of your images inside QuarkXPress, turn this option on. Photoshop will then reference the active EfiColor separation table when saving an image in the TIFF or EPS file format, making the table available to XPress and thus maintaining consistent color between the two applications. If you don't use EfiColor, leave the option off. This check box is only available in Photoshop 2.5.1.

- **Beep When Done:** You can instruct Photoshop to beep at you whenever it finishes an operation that displays a Progress window. This option might be useful if you find yourself dozing off during particularly time-consuming operations. But I'm a firm believer that computers should be seen and not heard.

Out of context like this, Photoshop's preference settings can be a bit confusing. In future chapters, I'll try to shed some light on the settings you're likely to find most useful.

Summary

- In many cases, you can access options that let you change the way a tool works by double-clicking on the tool's icon in the toolbox.
- Photoshop's cursors show you what actions you can perform.
- The absolute full screen mode enables you to view as much of an image as will fit on-screen, minus title bar, menu bar, and scroll bars.
- To hide the toolbox and all floating palettes, press the Tab key. Press Tab again to bring them back.
- Click on the collapse box in a floating palette's title bar to hide most of its options so that it takes up less space on-screen.
- You can magnify an image at one of 31 zoom ratios without affecting the resolution or size of the image (much in the same way looking at an amoeba under a microscope doesn't change the size of the little critter).
- Photoshop lets you initiate many commands and other operations by pressing keystroke combinations.
- You can use QuicKeys or Tempo to automate additional Photoshop functions.
- Photoshop saves your preference settings to disk. You can delete this file to reinstate the factory default settings.

Part II

Exploring Digital Imagery

Chapter 5:
Image Fundamentals

Chapter 6:
Acquiring the Raw Materials

Chapter 7:
Printing Images

Because images comprise thousands or even millions of individually colored pixels, they are different from any other variety of computer graphics and require a special approach. The number of pixels in an image determines the size of the image on disk, the manageability of the image on-screen, and the clarity of the image when printed. As I examine at length in Chapter 5, size and resolution are steadfastly linked, from the moment you open an image or create a new one to the moment you present the finished artwork to a client or audience.

This section examines the core image editing process, taking you from input to output. You learn how to acquire an image, change its size and resolution, and print it to paper or film. I also examine more than 20 file formats that permit you to compress images on disk, trade images with other pieces of software, and export images for use on other computer platforms, such as DOS-based PCs, Microsoft Windows, or high-end imaging systems. Photoshop began life as a format-conversion program, so it's no wonder that file formats remain one of the fundamental themes of this vast and diverse application.

In addition to exploring the capabilities of Photoshop, these chapters apprise you of the larger world of image editing software and hardware. Photoshop is one of those rare applications that is so popular, an entire industry of supporting products has grown up around it. Compression utilities, plug-in modules, acceleration boards, scanners and scanning software, electronic image collections, and entirely new breeds of image technology are as important to image editing as Photoshop itself.

Chapters 5 through 7 are among the most important chapters in this book for developing a thorough understanding not only of Photoshop, but also of the image editing environment. Whether you are a beginner or expert, you will discover more information on acquiring and exploiting digital images than you could in any other single source. Certainly, writing these chapters was an eye-opening experience for me.

Image Fundamentals

5 CHAPTER

In This Chapter

- How to scale an image for the printer and for the screen
- Four ways to create an image in Photoshop
- Explanations of every image format supported by Photoshop
- The inner workings of the JPEG format
- How to render object-oriented PICT and EPS images
- How to use Storm Technology's PicturePress with a DSP board
- Ways to change the number of pixels in an image

How Images Work

Think of a bitmapped image as a mosaic made out of square tiles of various colors. When you view the mosaic up close, it looks like something you might use to decorate your bathroom. You see the individual tiles, not the image itself. But if you back a few feet away from the mosaic, the tiles lose their definition and merge together to create a recognizable work of art, presumably Medusa getting her head whacked off or some equally appetizing thematic classic.

Similarly, images are colored pixels pretending to be artwork. If you enlarge the pixels, they look like an unrelated collection of colored squares. Reduce the size of the pixels, and they blend together to form an image that looks for all the world like a standard photograph. Photoshop deceives the eye by borrowing from an artistic technique older than Mycenae or Pompeii.

Of course, there are differences between pixels and ancient mosaic tiles. Pixels come in 16 million distinct colors. Mosaic tiles of antiquity came in your basic granite and sandstone varieties, with an occasional chunk of lapis lazuli thrown in for good measure. Also, you can resample, color separate, and crop electronic images. We know from the time-worn scribblings of Dionysius of Halicarnassus that these processes were beyond the means of classical artisans.

But I'm getting ahead of myself. I won't be discussing resampling, cropping, or Halicarnassus for several pages. In the meantime, I'll address the inverse relationship between image size and resolution.

Size and resolution

If you haven't already guessed, the term *image size* describes the physical dimensions of an image. *Resolution* is the number of pixels per linear inch. I say linear because you measure pixels in a straight line. If the resolution of an image is 72 *ppi* — that is, *pixels per inch* — you get 5184 pixels per square inch (72 pixels wide × 72 pixels tall = 5184).

Assuming the number of pixels in an image is fixed, increasing the size of an image decreases its resolution and vice versa. Therefore, an image that looks good when printed on a postage stamp probably will look jagged when printed as an 11 × 17-inch poster.

Figure 5-1 shows a single image printed at three different sizes and resolutions. The smallest image is printed at twice the resolution of the medium-sized image, and the medium-sized image is printed at twice the resolution of the largest image. One inch in the smallest image includes twice as many pixels vertically and twice as many pixels horizontally as an inch in the medium-sized image, for a total of four times as many pixels per square inch. The result is an image that covers one-fourth of the area of the medium-sized image.

The same relationships exist between the medium-sized image and the largest image. An inch in the medium-sized image comprises four times as many pixels as an inch in the largest image. Consequently, the medium-sized image consumes one-fourth of the area of the largest image.

The number of pixels in an image doesn't grow or shrink automatically when you save the image or print it, but you can add or subtract pixels using one of the techniques discussed in the "Resampling and Cropping Methods" section later in this chapter. However, doing so may lead to a short-term sacrifice in the appearance of the image.

Figure 5-1: These three images contain the same number of pixels but are printed at different resolutions. Doubling the resolution of an image reduces it to 25 percent of its original size.

Printing versus screen display

You should select the resolution for an image based on what you want to do with the image. When printing an image, a higher resolution translates to a sharper image with greater clarity. If you plan to use the image in an on-screen presentation, the resolution of the image should correspond to the resolution of your monitor.

Printed resolution

When figuring the resolution of a printed image, Photoshop considers two factors:

- You can specify the working resolution of an image by choosing Image ⇨ Image Size and entering a value into the Resolution option box, either in pixels per inch or pixels per centimeter. The default resolution for a Macintosh screen image is 72 ppi. To avoid changing the number of pixels in the image, be sure the File Size check box is selected.
- You can instruct Photoshop to scale an image during the print cycle by choosing File ⇨ Page Setup and entering a percentage value into the Reduce or Enlarge option box.

To determine the printed resolution, Photoshop divides the Resolution value by the Reduce or Enlarge percentage. For example, if the image resolution is set to 72 ppi and you reduce the image during the print cycle to 48 percent, the printed image has a resolution of 150 ppi (72 divided by .48).

At the risk of boring some folks, I'll briefly remind the math haters in the audience that whenever you use a percentage in an equation, you first convert it to a decimal. For example, 100 percent is 1.0, 64 percent is .64, 5 percent is .05, and so on.

Both the Resolution and Reduce or Enlarge values are saved with an image. The Resolution setting determines the size and resolution at which an image imports into object-oriented applications, most notably desktop publishing programs such as PageMaker and QuarkXPress.

Moiré patterns

For best results, the resolution of the image should jibe with the resolution of your printer, which is measured in *dots per inch (dpi)*. For example, suppose you are printing a 72 ppi image to a 300 dpi laser printer. Assuming the Reduce or Enlarge option is set to 100 percent, each image pixel wants to take up 4⅙ printer dots (300 ÷ 72 = 4⅙). By definition, a printer dot can't be divvied up into pieces, so there is no such thing as a ⅙ printer dot. Each image pixel must be represented by a whole number of printer dots. But your laser printer can't simply round down every pixel in the image to four printer dots, or it would shrink the image. To maintain the size of the image, the printer assigns four dots to each of the first five pixels and five dots to the sixth. These occasionally larger pixels result in a throbbing appearance, called a *moiré pattern*. (In case you're wondering where this weird term came from, *moiré* — pronounced *moray* — is a French technique for pressing wavy patterns into fabric.)

To eliminate moiré patterns, set the resolution of the image so it divides evenly into the printer resolution. To avoid moiré patterns in the preceding example, you could set the Resolution value to 100 ppi, which divides evenly into 300 dpi (300 ÷ 100 = 3). Alternatively, you could set the Reduce or Enlarge value to 72 percent, which would effectively change the resolution of the printed image to 100 ppi (72 ÷ .72 = 100).

Use the Resolution option to account for the final output device resolution; use the Reduce or Enlarge option to account for the proof printer resolution. For example, suppose you want to print your final image to a 2540 dpi Linotronic 330 imagesetter and proof it to a 300 dpi LaserWriter. You can account for the imagesetter by setting the Resolution option to 127 ppi. However, although 127 divides evenly into 2540 dpi, it doesn't divide evenly into 300 dpi. To fudge the difference, set the Reduce or Enlarge option to 127 percent, which changes the image resolution to 100 ppi (127 ÷ 1.27 = 100).

If you use this technique, be sure to change the Reduce or Enlarge option back to 100 percent before printing the final image to the imagesetter.

Screen resolution

Regardless of the Resolution and Reduce or Enlarge values, Photoshop displays each pixel on-screen according to the zoom ratio. (The zoom ratio, displayed in the title bar, is discussed in Chapter 4.) If the zoom ratio is 1:1, for example, each image pixel takes up a single screen pixel. Zoom ratio and printer output are unrelated.

When creating an image for a screen presentation or display, you want the image size to fill every inch of the prospective monitor at a 1:1 zoom ratio. I say *prospective* monitor because although you may use a 16-inch monitor when you create the image, you may want to display the final image on a 13-inch monitor. In that case, you would set the image size to 640 × 480 pixels (the standard resolution of a 13-inch monitor), with no concern for resolution on your 16-inch monitor.

For your information, Table 5-1 lists common Macintosh and DOS-based PC screen sizes. Unless indicated otherwise, the monitors can handle color. On the Mac side, System 7 or System 6 equipped with the 32-bit QuickDraw extension automatically dithers 24-bit images to conform with an 8-bit display, so you don't necessarily need to worry about the number of colors in an image. Most PC systems don't provide access to more than 256 colors, and the system software provides no automatic dithering option.

Table 5-1 Macintosh and PC Monitor Standards

Monitor	*Pixels Wide*	*Pixels Tall*
	Macintosh	
9" (monochrome Plus, SE, Classic)	512	342
10" (Color Classic)	512	384
12"	512	384
PowerBook	640	400
PowerBook 180c	640	480
13" or 14"	640	480
15" (portrait)	640	870
16" or 17"	832	624
19" or 20"	1024	768
21" (two-page)	1152	870
	IBM compatibles	
Hercules (monochrome)	720	348
EGA (16 colors)	640	350
MCGA (4 colors)	640	480

Table 5-1 *(continued)*

Monitor	*Pixels Wide*	*Pixels Tall*
VGA or XGA	640	480
Video7 VGA	720	512
SuperVGA	800	600
8514/a or TIGA	1024	768

Monitors aren't quite as straightforward as Table 5-1 might suggest. On the Mac side, many 16-inch and larger monitors can handle resolutions from 640 × 480 pixels on up. On the PC, Video7 VGA can accommodate 640 × 480 pixels, 720 × 512 pixels, or 800 × 600 pixels, depending on VRAM. In addition to 640 × 480 pixels, the XGA adapter can go as high as 1024 × 768 pixels.

How to Open and Save Images

Before you can work on an image in Photoshop — whether you're creating a brand new document or opening an image from disk — you must first load the image into an image window. Here are the four basic ways to create an image window:

- **File ⇨ New:** Create a new window by choosing File ⇨ New (Command-N). After you fill out the desired size and resolution specifications in the New dialog box, Photoshop confronts you with a stark, white, empty canvas. You then face the ultimate test of your artistic capabilities — painting from scratch. Feel free to go nuts and cut off your ear.
- **File ⇨ Open:** Open an image saved to disk or CD-ROM by choosing File ⇨ Open (Command-O). Of the four ways to create an image window, you most likely will use this method most frequently. You can open images scanned in other applications, images purchased from stock photo agencies, slides and transparencies digitized to a Kodak Photo CD, or an image you previously edited in Photoshop.
- **Edit ⇨ Paste:** Photoshop automatically adapts a new image window to the contents of the Clipboard (provided those contents are bitmapped). So if you copy an image inside a different application or in Photoshop and then choose File ⇨ New, Photoshop enters the dimensions and resolution of the image into the New dialog box. All you have to do is accept the settings and choose Edit ⇨ Paste (Command-V) to introduce the image into a new window. This technique is useful for editing screen shots captured to the Clipboard and for testing out filtering effects on a sample of an image without harming the original.

- **File ⇨ Acquire ⇨ Scan:** If you own a scanner, it probably has a plug-in module that lets you scan directly into Photoshop. Just copy the module into Photoshop's Plug-ins folder and then run or relaunch the Photoshop application. To initiate a scan, choose the scanner driver from the File ⇨ Acquire submenu. For example, to scan from my Agfa Arcus scanner (alas, it's not really mine, it's just on loan), I choose File ⇨ Acquire ⇨ Agfa PhotoScan. A dialog box appears that enables me to scan the photograph or artwork under the scanner lid. When the scan is complete, the image appears in a new image window.

Scanning is by far the most complex method of loading an image into Photoshop. For a detailed discussion of the scanning process, read the "Scanning" section in Chapter 6.

Creating a new image

Whether you are creating an image from scratch or transferring the contents of the Clipboard to a new image window, choose File ⇨ New or press Command-N to bring up the New dialog box shown in Figure 5-2. If the Clipboard contains an image, the Width, Height, and Resolution option boxes show the size and resolution of that image. Otherwise, you can enter your own values in one of five units of measurement: pixels, inches, centimeters, picas, or points. (A pica, incidentally, is equal to roughly ⅙ inch, and a *point* is 1/12 pica, or roughly 1/72 inch.) If you're not sure exactly what size image you want to create, enter a rough approximation. You can always change your settings later.

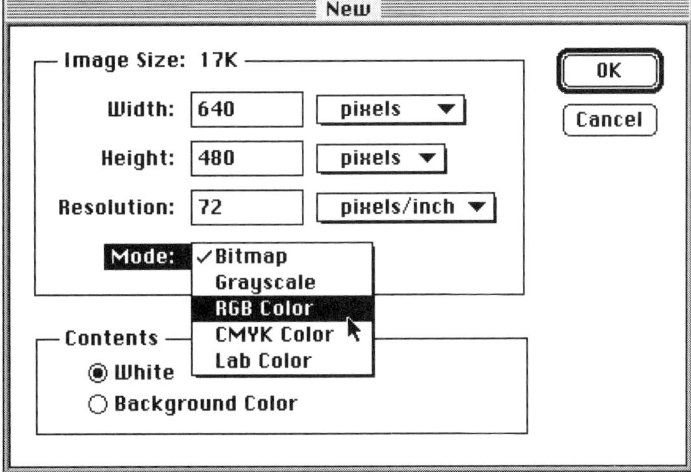

Figure 5-2: Use the New dialog box to specify the size, resolution, and color mode of your new image.

By default, Photoshop assigns *exactly* 72 points per inch and 6 picas per inch (which works out to be one point per screen pixel). Before the advent of computers, however, picas and points represented their own distinct measurement system. Although there are exactly 12 points in a pica, one inch really equals about 72.27 points, or 6.02 picas. If you prefer to use the traditional system — as when pasting up a page with an X-Acto knife and hot wax — choose File ⇨ Preferences ⇨ Units and select the Traditional (72.27 points/inch) radio button.

You can change the default unit of measure that appears in the Width and Height pop-up menus by choosing File ⇨ Preferences ⇨ Units and selecting a different option from the Ruler Units pop-up menu.

Column width

A sixth unit of measure, Column, is available from the Width pop-up menu. If you want to create an image that fits exactly within a certain number of columns when it's imported into a desktop publishing program, select the Column option. You can specify the width of a column and the gutter between columns by choosing File ⇨ Preferences ⇨ Units and entering values into the Column Size option boxes.

The Gutter value affects multiple-column images. Suppose that you accept the default setting of a 15-pica column width and a 1-pica gutter. If you specify a one-column image in the New dialog box, Photoshop makes it 15 picas wide. If you ask for a two-column image, Photoshop adds the width of the gutter to the width of the two columns and creates an image 31 picas wide.

The Height pop-up menu in the New dialog box lacks a Column option because vertical columns have nothing to do with an image's height.

On-screen image size

In most cases, the on-screen dimensions of an image depend on your entries in the Width, Height, and Resolution option boxes. If you set both the Width and Height values to 10 inches and the Resolution to 72 ppi, the new image will measure 720 × 720 pixels. The exception occurs if you choose pixels as your unit of measurement, as in Figure 5-2. In that case, the on-screen dimensions depend solely on the Width and Height options, and the Resolution value determines the size at which the image prints.

Color mode and background

Use the Mode pop-up menu to specify the number of colors that can appear in your image. Choose Bitmap to create a black-and-white image and choose Grayscale to access only gray values. RGB Color, CMYK Color, and Lab Color all provide access to the full range of 16 million colors, although their methods of doing so differ.

RBG stands for *red-green-blue; CMYK* for *cyan-magenta-yellow-black;* and *Lab* for *luminosity* and two abstract color variables, *a* and *b.* To learn how each of these color modes works, read the "Working in Different Color Modes" section of Chapter 14.

In Photoshop 2.5.1, the New dialog box provides two Contents radio buttons that allow you to select whether to fill the new image with white or with the current background color — assuming, of course, that the background color is something other than white. White is the default setting.

Opening an existing image

If you want to open an image stored on disk, choose File ⇨ Open or press Command-O to display the Open dialog box (introduced in the "How to navigate dialog boxes" section of Chapter 2.) The scrolling list contains the names of documents Photoshop recognizes that it can open. If you cannot find a desired document, it may be because Photoshop does not recognize the document's four-character *type code.* The type code for a document created or last edited on a Macintosh computer corresponds to the file format under which the image was saved (as explained in the upcoming "Image File Formats" section).

For example, TIFF is the type code for a TIFF image, PICT is the type code for a PICT image, and so on. However, if you transferred a document from another platform, such as the IBM PC or Commodore Amiga, it probably lacks a type code. In the absence of a type code, the Macintosh system software assigns a PC document the default type code TEXT, which indicates a text-only document. Photoshop does not recognize the TEXT code, so it does not list the corresponding document in the Open dialog box.

To see *all* documents regardless of type code, choose File ⇨ Open As. Then select the file format under which the image was saved from the File Format pop-up menu, as demonstrated in Figure 5-3. If the desired document conforms to the selected format option, Photoshop opens the image after you click on the Open button or press Return. If Photoshop displays an error message instead, you need to either select a different format option or try to open the document in a different application.

Incidentally, you can view and alter the type code for a document using CE Software's DiskTop or Apple's ResEdit, which are distributed separately.

Saving an image to disk

The first rule of storing an image on disk is to save it frequently. If the foreground image is untitled, as it is when you work on a new image, choosing File ⇨ Save displays the Save dialog box, enabling you to name the image, specify its location on disk, and select a file format. After you save the image once, choosing the Save command updates the file on disk without bringing up the Save dialog box.

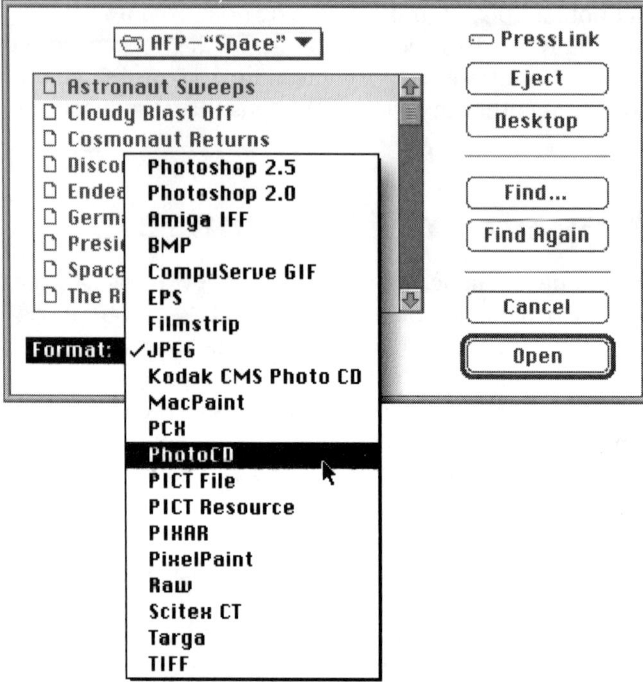

Figure 5-3: Choose the Open As command to access any document regardless of its four-character type code. To open the image, select the file format under which the image was saved.

The preceding explanation of saving an image applies to Photoshop 2.5. If you use Photoshop 2.0, the Save dialog box continues to appear if you save the foreground image in any format other than the native Photoshop format. It's a real pain in the neck.

Choose File ⇨ Save As to change the name, location, or format of the image stored on disk. By the way, if your only reason for choosing the Save As command is to change the file format, it's perfectly acceptable to overwrite (save over) the original document, assuming that you no longer need that copy of the image. Granted, your computer could crash during the save-as operation, in which case you would lose both the new document and the original. But crashing during the save-as operation is extremely unlikely and no more likely than crashing during any other save operation.

To speed up the save process, I usually save an image in Photoshop's native format until I'm finished working on it. (In Photoshop 2.0, doing this also stops the Save dialog box from reappearing every time you save the image.) Before I close the image, I choose File ⇨ Save As and save the image in the compressed TIFF or JPEG format. By using this method, I only compress each image once during a session.

Image File Formats

As you can see back in Figure 5-3, Photoshop 2.5 supports a total of 19 file formats from inside its Open and Save dialog boxes. It can support even more through the addition of plug-in modules, which attach commands to the File ⇨ Acquire and File ⇨ Export submenus.

File formats represent different ways to save a file to disk. Some formats provide unique image *compression schemes,* which save an image in a manner that consumes less space on disk. Other formats enable Photoshop to trade images with different applications on the Mac and on different platforms.

The native formats

Photoshop 2.5 supports two *native formats* (that is, formats that are optimized for Photoshop's particular capabilities and functions), one for Version 2.0 and one for Version 2.5. Photoshop 2.0 and 2.0.1 support the Version 2.0 format only.

Adobe specifically optimized both these native formats to retain every smidgen of data, including additional masking channels and a few other elements that may be lost when saving to other formats. It's also worth noting that Photoshop can open and save in its native format more quickly than in any other format.

If you're a long-time Photoshop user, you may have noticed that an image stored in the Photoshop 2.5 format consumes considerably less room on disk than the same image stored in the Photoshop 2.0 format. This is because the Photoshop 2.5 format offers a compression option missing from the earlier format. The compression does *not* result in any loss of data.

Cross-platform formats

Photoshop 2.5 provides seven formats for saving an image you want to transfer to a different computer. Photoshop 2.0 supports (provides compatibility with) all but one of these formats — BMP. If your clients or co-workers use computers other than Macs, you'll find these formats essential.

Amiga's IFF and HAM

Popular among video enthusiasts, the Commodore Amiga is a variety of personal computer that offers an operating system similar to the Mac's. I owned the first-model Amiga 1000, a machine that Commodore almost immediately abandoned. You'd think I would have learned my lesson after having previously owned a Commodore Plus/4, possibly the worst computer ever made.

Nowadays, the only reason to use an Amiga is because it supports NewTek's much-celebrated Video Toaster. If you know someone who uses an Amiga, maybe you can talk the poor soul into hawking it at a yard sale and using the money to make a down payment on a Mac. Until then, you can trade images using the *IFF* (*Interchange File Format*) format, which is the Amiga's all-around graphics format and serves much the same function as PICT on the Mac.

Photoshop 2.0 includes a plug-in module that lets you export an image to a compressed variation of IFF called *HAM* (*Hold and Modify*) by choosing File ⇨ Export ⇨ Amiga HAM. The Photoshop 2.5 manual refers to this module as well, but Adobe didn't include the module on the program disks. Whoops. (Adobe promises not to forget the module when it ships Photoshop 2.5.1.) Anyway, no big loss. HAM is generally useless for images that don't conform to one of two standard image sizes — 320 × 200 pixels or 320 × 400 pixels. Most Amiga applications treat nonstandard images as having rectangular as opposed to square pixels, thus stretching the image out of proportion.

Photoshop can open HAM images whether the module is available or not. Photoshop 2.5 supports HAM images with up to 256 colors and IFF images with up to 16 million colors.

Windows Paint's BMP

Supported exclusively by Photoshop 2.5, *BMP* (*Windows Bitmap*) is the native format for Microsoft Paint (included with Microsoft Windows) and is supported by a variety of Windows and OS/2 applications. Photoshop supports BMP images with up to 16 million colors. You also can use *RLE* (*Run-Length Encoding*), a lossless compression scheme specifically applicable to the BMP format.

The term *lossless* refers to compression schemes such as BMP's RLE and TIFF's LZW (*Lempel-Ziv-Welch*) that enable you to save space on disk without sacrificing any data in the image. The only reasons *not* to use lossless compression are that it slows down the open and save operations and it may prevent less-sophisticated applications from opening an image. *Lossy* compression routines, such as JPEG, sacrifice a user-defined amount of data to conserve even more disk space.

CompuServe's GIF

CompuServe designed *GIF* (*Graphics Interchange Format*) as a means of compressing 8-bit images so that users can transfer photographs via their modems to and from the company's commercial bulletin board service more quickly. Like most on-line imagery, the lion's share of the world's GIF images are pornographic. Still, many folks do use GIF for purposes their mothers would approve. Like TIFF, GIF uses LZW compression, but unlike TIFF, GIF can't handle more than 256 colors.

PC Paintbrush's PCX

PCX doesn't stand for anything. Rather, it's the extension that PC Paintbrush assigns to images saved in its native file format. By all accounts, PCX is one of the most popular image file formats in use today, largely due to the fact that PC Paintbrush is the oldest painting program for DOS. Photoshop supports PCX images with up to 16 million colors.

PIXAR workstations

PIXAR has created some of the most memorable computer-animated shorts and commercials in recent memory. (That "recent memory" bit is just a saying, of course. *All* computer animation has occurred in recent memory.) Examples include the desk lamps playing with a beach ball from *Luxo, Jr.;* the run-amok toddler from the Oscar-winning *Tin Toy;* and the commercial adventures of a Listerine bottle that boxes Gingivitis one day and swings Tarzan-like through a spearmint forest the next. These folks are *the* reason I entered computer graphics. They're so awesome. Wow weezers.

PIXAR develops a few 3-D graphics applications for the Mac, including MacRenderMan, ShowPlace, and Typestry. But the company works its 3-D magic using mondo-expensive PIXAR workstations. Photoshop enables you to open a still image created on a PIXAR machine or save an image to the PIXAR format so you can integrate it into a 3-D rendering. The PIXAR format supports grayscale and RGB images.

Scitex image-processors

High-end commercial printers use Scitex computers to generate color separations of images and other documents. Photoshop can open images digitized with Scitex scanners and save the edited images to the *Scitex CT (Continuous Tone)* format. Because you need special hardware to transfer images from the Mac to a Scitex drive, you'll probably want to consult with your local Scitex printer — the human, not the machine — before saving to the CT format. It's very possible that your printer will prefer that you submit images in the native Photoshop, TIFF, or JPEG format. The Scitex CT format supports grayscale and CMYK images.

TrueVision's TGA

TrueVision's Targa and NuVista video boards let you overlay Macintosh graphics and animation onto live video. The effect is called *chroma keying* because typically, a key color is set aside to let the live video show through. TrueVision designed the *TGA (Targa)* format to support 32-bit images that include 8-bit *alpha channels* capable of displaying the live video. Though support for TGA is scarce among Macintosh applications, it is widely implemented among professional-level color and video applications on the PC.

Interapplication formats

In the name of interapplication harmony, Photoshop supports a few software-specific formats that enable you to trade files with programs that run on the Mac. Photoshop can trade images directly with two painting pioneers, MacPaint and PixelPaint. In addition, you can use Photoshop 2.5 to edit frames from a QuickTime movie created with Adobe Premier.

Rendering an EPS illustration

What the heck, why not start things off with a controversial entry? Technically speaking, *EPS* (*Encapsulated PostScript*) is anything but an interapplication format. Instead, EPS was specifically designed for saving object-oriented graphics that you intend to print to a PostScript output device. Every drawing program and most desktop publishers enable you to save EPS documents.

However — and here's where things get thick — Photoshop doesn't support just any run-of-the-mill EPS format. Photoshop only supports Adobe Illustrator's version of the EPS format. This means you can't open artwork saved in Aldus FreeHand's EPS format. And when creating a graphic in a drawing program such as Canvas or CorelDRAW, you must save it in the Illustrator format rather than generic EPS. Therefore, Photoshop's EPS format amounts to little more than a means of trading artwork between Photoshop and Illustrator. (For an exception, see the next section, "QuarkXPress DCS.")

When you open an Illustrator graphic, Photoshop *renders* (or *rasterizes*) the artwork — that is, it converts it from a collection of objects to a bitmapped image. During the open operation, Photoshop presents the EPS Rasterizer dialog box (see Figure 5-4), which enables you to specify the size and resolution of the image, just as you do in the New dialog box. Because the graphic is object-oriented, you can render it as large or as small as you want without any loss of image quality.

Though it's deselected by default, you should select the Anti-aliased check box unless you're rendering a very large image — say, 300 ppi or higher. *Antialiasing* blurs pixels to soften the edges of the objects so they don't appear jagged. When rendering a very large image, the difference between image and printer resolution is less noticeable, so antialiasing is unwarranted.

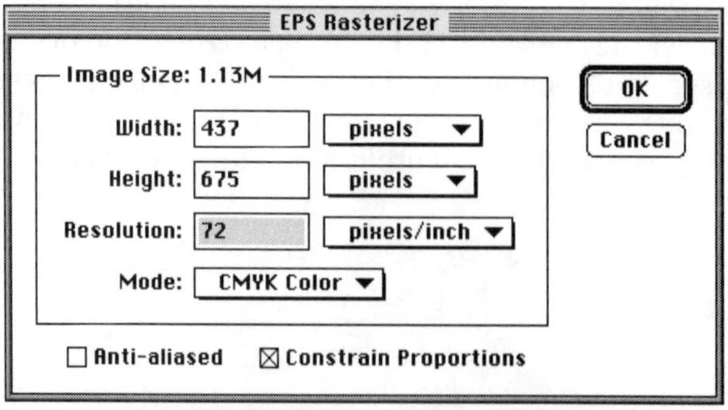

Figure 5-4: You can specify the size and resolution at which Photoshop renders an EPS illustration.

If you want to introduce an EPS graphic into the foreground image rather than rendering it into a new image window of its own, choose File ⇨ Place. Unlike other File menu commands, Place supports only the EPS format.

Rendering an EPS illustration is an extremely useful technique for resolving printing problems. If you work in Illustrator often, you no doubt have encountered *limitcheck errors,* which occur when an illustration is too complex for an imagesetter or other high-end output device to print. If you're frustrated with the printer and you're tired of wasting your evening trying to figure out what's wrong (sound familiar?), use Photoshop to render the illustration at 300 ppi and print it. Nine out of ten times, this technique works flawlessly.

Saving an EPS document

To use a Photoshop image inside Illustrator, you must save it in the EPS format. In my opinion, this is Illustrator's most prominent drawback. Photoshop can open 19 formats, acquire several more, and swap Sanskrit parchments among Buddhist monks. Meanwhile, Illustrator only supports EPS, which wouldn't be so bad if EPS weren't such a remarkably inefficient format for saving images. An EPS image may be three to four times larger than the same image saved to the TIFF format with LZW compression.

Griping aside, here's how the process works. When you save an image in the EPS format, Photoshop 2.5 displays the dialog box shown in Figure 5-5. The options in this dialog box are:

- **Preview:** Technically, an EPS document comprises two parts: a pure PostScript-language description of the graphic for the printer; and a bitmapped preview that enables you to see the graphic on-screen. If you want to use the image in Illustrator 3.2 or 5.0 on the Mac, select the 8-bit Macintosh radio button. If you want to import the image into Illustrator 4.0 or some other Windows application, select 8-bit IBM PC. The 1-bit options include black-and-white previews only, which are useful if you want to save a little room on disk. Select the None option to include no preview and save even more disk space.
- **Encoding:** If you're exporting an image for use with Illustrator, select the Binary encoding option (also known as *Huffman encoding*), which compresses an EPS document by substituting shorter codes for frequently used characters. The letter *a,* for example, receives the 3-bit code *010* rather than its standard 8-bit ASCII code, *01100001* (the binary equivalent of what we humans call *97*). Some programs don't recognize Huffman encoding, in which case you must select the ASCII option. (*ASCII* stands for *American Standard Code for Information Interchange,* which is fancy jargon for *text-only.* In other words, you can open and edit an ASCII EPS document in a word processor, provided you know how to read and write PostScript.) If you're exporting to an application other than Illustrator, however, you'll most likely want to use a file format other than EPS.

- **Include Halftone Screen:** I've been badmouthing EPS pretty steadily, but it does have one advantage over other image formats: it can retain printing attributes. If you specified a custom halftone screen using the Screen button inside the Page Setup dialog box, you can save this setting with the EPS document by selecting the Include Halftone Screen check box.
- **Include Transfer Function:** As described in Chapter 7, "Printing Images," you can change the brightness and contrast of a printed image by using the Transfer button inside the Page Setup dialog box. To save these settings with the EPS document, select the Include Transfer Function check box.

- **Transparent Whites:** When saving black-and-white EPS images in Photoshop 2.5.1, select this option to make all white pixels in the image transparent. Incidentally, the EPS format is the only format that offers this option. So if you're looking to create transparent images, black-and-white and EPS are the ways to go.

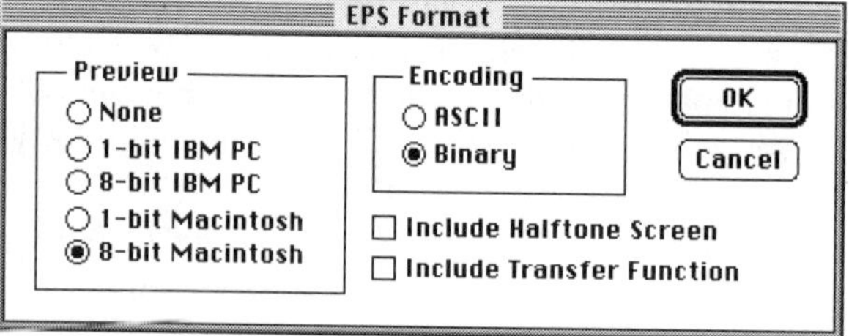

Figure 5-5: When saving an image in the EPS format, you can specify the type of preview to include and tack on some printing attributes.

Photoshop 2.5 provides a plug-in module that lets you compress images using the JPEG scheme when you save them in the EPS format. To do so, choose File ⇨ Export ⇨ Compress EPS JPEG. At the present time, very few programs other than Illustrator 5.0 support JPEG EPS. To open a compressed EPS image, choose File ⇨ Acquire ⇨ Decompress EPS. (More information on JPEG is presented later in this chapter.)

Photoshop 2.0 offers a slightly different dialog box for saving EPS images. Its dialog box features a Clipping Path and Flatness option. For information on both of these options, check out the "Swapping paths with Illustrator" section of Chapter 9.

QuarkXPress DCS

Quark developed a variation on the EPS format called *DCS (Desktop Color Separation)*. When you work in QuarkXPress, this format enables you to print color separations of imported artwork. If you save a CMYK image in the EPS format, Photoshop 2.5 displays the additional Desktop Color Separation options shown in Figure 5-6. When you save to the DCS format, Photoshop creates five files on disk: one master document plus one file each for the cyan, magenta, yellow, and black color channels. Select Off to save the image as a single standard EPS document. Select one of the Master File options to save the five DCS files.

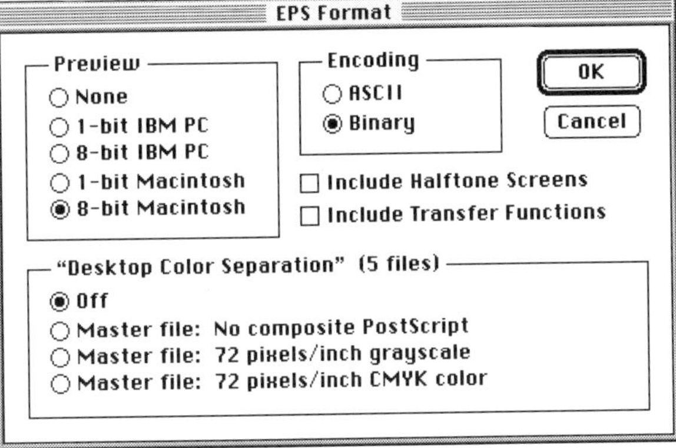

Figure 5-6: Photoshop 2.5 offers four DCS options when you save a CMYK image in the EPS format.

Photoshop also gives you the option of saving a 72 ppi PostScript-language version of the image inside the DCS master document. Independent from the bitmapped preview — which you specify as usual by selecting a Preview option — the 72 ppi *composite* image enables you to print a low-resolution version of a DCS image imported into QuarkXPress to a consumer-quality printer such as a LaserWriter. If your printer is black-and-white, select the 72 pixels/inch grayscale option; if your printer is color, select the final option. Note that the composite image significantly increases the size of the master document on disk.

You can convert an image to the CMYK mode by choosing Mode ⇨ CMYK Color. Do not choose this command casually. Converting back and forth between RGB and CMYK results in a loss of color information. You only want to use the CMYK Color command if you want to convert an image to CMYK color for good. For more information, read Chapter 14, "Defining Colors."

Premier Filmstrip

Adobe Premier is the foremost QuickTime movie editing application for the Mac. The program is a wonder when it comes to fades, frame merges, and special effects, but it offers no frame-by-frame editing capabilities. For example, you can't draw a mustache on a person in the movie, nor can you make brightly colored brush strokes swirl about in the background — at least, not inside Premier.

You can, however, export the movie to the Filmstrip format, which is a file-swapping option exclusive to Photoshop 2.5 and Premier 2.0. A Filmstrip document organizes frames in a long vertical strip, as shown in Figure 5-7. (The scene is from the early '60s, but I think you'll agree that the raw emotional power of these frames transcends the generations.)

A gray bar separates each frame. The number of each frame appears on the right; the *SMPTE* (*Society of Motion Picture and Television Engineers*) time code appears on the left. The structure of the three-number time code is *minutes:seconds:frames,* with 30 frames per second.

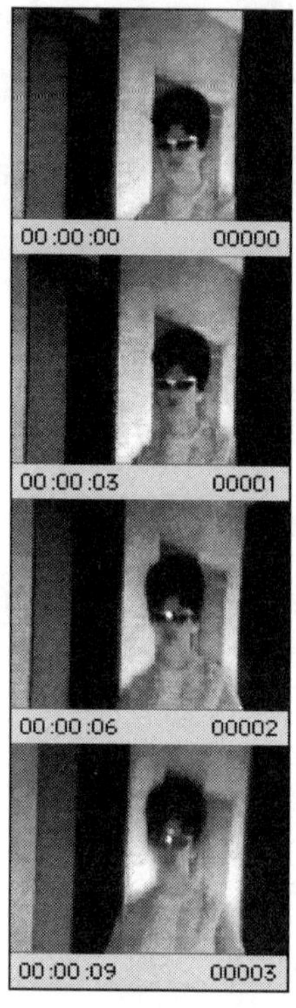

Figure 5-7: Four frames from a rollicking QuickTime movie as they appear in the Filmstrip format.

If you change the size of a Filmstrip document inside Photoshop 2.5 in any way, you cannot save the image back to the Filmstrip format. Feel free to paint and apply effects, but stay the heck away from the Image Size and Canvas Size commands.

After you open the Filmstrip document, you can edit individual frames to your heart's content. This process, sometimes called *rotoscoping,* is named after the traditional technique of combining live-action film with animated sequences. You also can emulate *scratch-and-doodle* techniques, in which an artist scratches and draws directly on frames of film. In addition, you can emulate *xerography,* in which an animator makes xerox copies of photographs, enhances the copies using markers or whatever else is convenient, and shoots the finished artwork, frame by frame, on film. In a nutshell, Photoshop extends Premier's functionality by adding animation to its standard supply of video-editing capabilities.

You can save an image in the Filmstrip format only if you opened the image as a Filmstrip document and did not change the size of the image.

MacPaint

Now in the hands of Claris, Apple's lethargic software subsidiary, MacPaint was the first painting program for the Mac. In fact, MacPaint and MacWrite preceded all other Macintosh applications and shipped with the first 128K Mac. Last updated in 1987, MacPaint 2.0 is severely lacking by today's standards.

The MacPaint format accommodates 1-bit (black-and-white) images on vertically-oriented, 7½ × 10½-inch pages. End of story. It's no wonder Photoshop can open MacPaint images but can't save to the MacPaint format. What would be the point? If you dig, you can find truckloads of old clip art in the MacPaint format, which is the only reason Photoshop bothers to support it at all.

PixelPaint

PixelPaint from Pixel Resources was the first color painting application for the Mac. In its day, it was a show-stopper, easily as remarkable as Photoshop is now. In fact, PixelPaint's demise started about the same time that Photoshop arrived on the scene. Some coincidence, huh?

Photoshop supports the old 8-bit PixelPaint format, the native format for the standard PixelPaints 1.0 and 2.0. PixelPaint Professional offers a 24-bit format that Photoshop does not support. I guess Adobe figures most of its users gave up on PixelPaint when Photoshop arrived on the scene. However, the newest upgrade, PixelPaint Professional 3.0, provides a number of capabilities that Photoshop 2.5 lacks, including greatly expanded selection capabilities and a scripting option for recording operations. To trade images with Pixel Paint Professional 3.0, your best option is to save images to the TIFF or PICT formats.

The mainstream formats

The formats discussed so far are mighty interesting, and they all fulfill their own niche purposes. But the following formats — JPEG, PICT, and TIFF — are the all-stars of Macintosh imagery. You'll use these formats the most because of their outstanding compression capabilities and almost universal support among Macintosh graphics applications.

JPEG

Photoshop 2.5 provides support for the *JPEG* format — named after the folks who designed it, the Joint Photographic Experts Group — via the Open and Save dialog boxes. To open or save JPEG images in Photoshop 2.0, you must use commands under the File ⇨ Acquire and File ⇨ Export submenus.

JPEG is the most efficient and essential compression format currently available and is likely to be the compression standard for years to come. It is a lossy compression scheme, which means that it sacrifices image quality to conserve space on disk. However, you can control how much data is lost during the save operation.

When you save an image in the JPEG format, Photoshop displays the dialog box in Figure 5-8, which offers nine compression settings. By dragging the up-pointing arrowhead control, you specify whether you want high compression, which reduces image quality but takes up less space on disk, or low compression, which retains a reasonable amount of image quality but consumes more disk space.

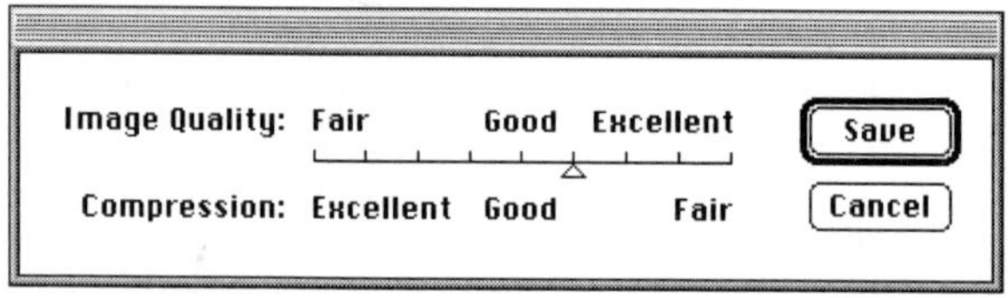

Figure 5-8: Photoshop provides nine JPEG compression settings, ranging from excellent compression (fair image quality) to fair compression (excellent image quality).

JPEG evaluates an image in 8 × 8-pixel blocks, using a technique called *Adaptive Discrete Cosine Transform* (or ADCT, as in *Yes, I'm an acronym ADCT*). It averages the 24-bit value of every pixel in the block (or 8-bit value of every pixel in the case of a grayscale image). It then stores the average color in the upper left pixel in the block and assigns the remaining 63 pixels smaller values relative to the average.

Next, JPEG divides the block by an 8 × 8 block of its own called the *quantization matrix,* which homogenizes the pixels' values by changing as many as possible to zero. It's this process that saves the majority of disk space and loses data. When Photoshop opens a JPEG image, it can't recover the original distinction between the zero pixels, so the pixels become the same or similar colors. Finally, JPEG applies lossless Huffman encoding to translate repeating values to a single symbol.

In most instances, I recommend that you use JPEG only at its highest quality setting, at least until you gain some experience with it. The smallest amount of JPEG compression saves more space on disk than any other compression format and still retains nearly every bit of detail from the original image. Figure 5-9 shows a grayscale image saved at each of the nine compression settings.

The samples are arranged in rows from highest image quality (upper left) to lowest quality (lower right). Below each sample is the size of the compressed document on disk. Saved in the only moderately compressed Photoshop 2.5 format, the image consumes 57K on disk. Without any compression, the file consumes 61K. From 61K to 6K — the result of the highest compression — is a remarkable savings, but it comes at a price.

I have taken the liberty of sharpening the focus of strips in each image so you can see more easily how JPEG averages neighboring pixels to achieve smaller file sizes. The first strip is normal focus, the second strip is sharpened once by choosing Filter ⇨ Sharpen ⇨ Sharpen More, and the third strip is sharpened twice. You can see that although the lower image quality settings lead to dramatic savings in file size, they also gum up the images excessively. The effect, incidentally, is more obvious on screen. And believe me, after you familiarize yourself with JPEG compression, you'll be able to spot other people's overly compressed JPEG images a mile away. It's not something you want to exaggerate in your images.

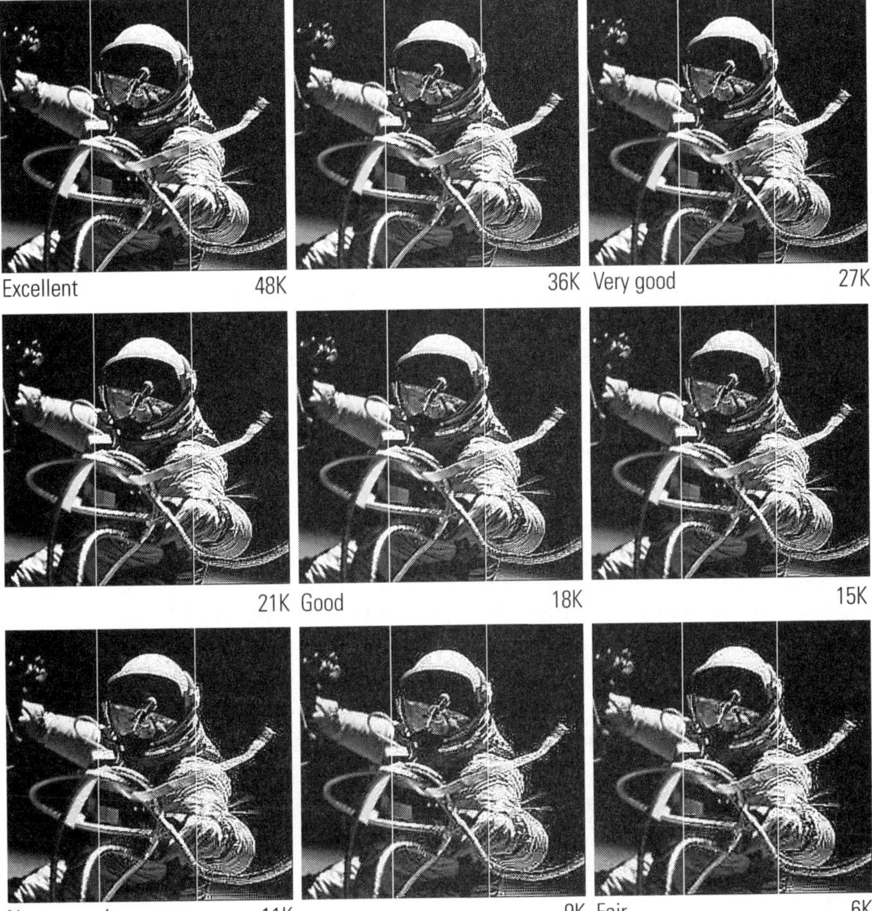

Figure 5-9: The nine JPEG settings from the preceding figure applied to a single image, with the highest image quality setting illustrated at the upper left and the lowest at the bottom right.

JPEG is a *cumulative compression scheme,* meaning that Photoshop recompresses an image every time you save it in the JPEG format. There's no disadvantage to repeatedly saving an image to disk during a single session, because JPEG always works from the on-screen version. But if you close an image, reopen it, and save it in the JPEG format, you inflict a small amount of damage. (For a JPEG alternative that is less cumulative, see the "Storm JPEG" section later in this chapter.) Therefore, use JPEG sparingly. In the best of all possible worlds, you should only save to the JPEG format after you finish *all* work on an image. Even in a pinch, you should apply all filtering effects before saving to JPEG, because these have a habit of exacerbating imperfections in image quality.

JPEG is best used when compressing *continuous-tone* images (images in which the distinction between immediately neighboring pixels is slight). Any image that includes gradual color transitions, as in a photograph, qualifies for JPEG compression. JPEG is not the best choice for saving screen shots, line drawings (especially those converted from Illustrator EPS graphics), and other high-contrast images. These are better served by a lossless compression scheme such as TIFF with LZW. The JPEG format is available when saving grayscale, RGB, and CMYK images.

Photoshop's built-in JPEG format is not the only way to access JPEG compression. Read the "PICT" and "Storm JPEG" sections in this chapter for more information.

PICT

PICT (*Macintosh Picture*) is the Macintosh system software's native graphics format. Based on the QuickDraw display language the system software uses to convey images on screen, PICT is one of the few file formats that handles object-oriented artwork and bitmapped images with equal aplomb. It supports images in any bit depth, size, or resolution. It even supports 32-bit images, so you can save a fourth masking channel when working in the RGB mode.

If you have installed QuickTime, you can subject PICT images to JPEG compression. When you save an image in the PICT format, Photoshop 2.5 offers several compression options in the dialog box shown in Figure 5-10. (Photoshop 2.0 provides only three compression options.) Although this dialog box provides fewer compression settings than the one shown in Figure 5-8, it represents the more viable solution because more Macintosh applications recognize QuickTime JPEG than Photoshop's built-in JPEG format. Heck, you can open JPEG PICT files inside a word processor, including everything from TeachText to Microsoft Word.

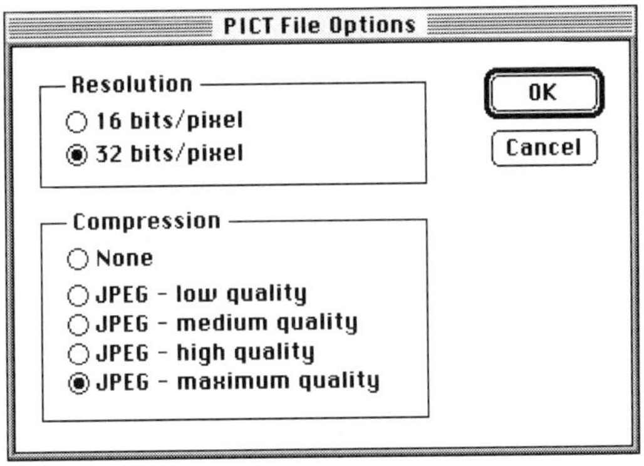

Figure 5-10: If QuickTime is installed, Photoshop provides JPEG compression options when you save an image in the PICT format.

TIFF

Developed by Aldus back in the early days of the Mac to standardize an ever-growing population of scanned images, *TIFF* (*Tag Image File Format*) is the most widely supported bitmapped format across both the Macintosh and PC platforms. Unlike PICT, it can't handle object-oriented artwork and doesn't support JPEG compression, but it is otherwise unrestricted. In fact, TIFF offers a few tricks of its own that are worth mentioning. When you save an image in the TIFF format, Photoshop displays the TIFF Options dialog box (see Figure 5-11), which offers these options:

- **Byte Order:** Leave it to Photoshop to name a straightforward option in the most confusing way possible. Byte Order? No, this option doesn't have anything to do with how you eat your food. Rather, because Macintosh TIFF and PC TIFF are two slightly different formats, this option permits you to specify whether you want to use the image on the Mac or on an IBM PC-compatible machine. I'm sure it has something to do with the arrangement of 8-bit chunks of data, but who cares? You want Mac or you want PC? It's that simple.
- **LZW Compression:** Like Huffman encoding (described earlier in the "Saving an EPS document" section), the LZW (Lempel-Ziv-Welch) compression scheme digs into the computer code that describes an image and substitutes frequently used codes with shorter equivalents. But instead of substituting characters, as Huffman does, LZW substitutes strings of data. Because LZW doesn't so much as touch a pixel in your image, it's entirely lossless. Most image editors and desktop publishing applications — including FreeHand, PageMaker, and QuarkXPress — import LZW-compressed TIFF images, but a few still have yet to catch on.
- **Save Alpha Channels:** If you added masking channels to an image, you can save those channels along with the TIFF document by selecting the Save Alpha Channels check box. Aside from PICT and Photoshop's native format, TIFF is the only format that lets you save masking channels. And with PICT, you can't save masking channels with CMYK images and you can save only one channel in RGB images.

Figure 5-11: Photoshop lets you save TIFF files in either the Mac or PC format and compress the image using LZW.

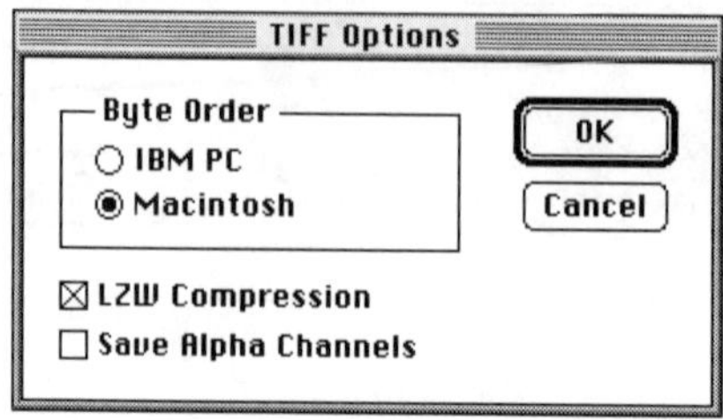

If names like Huffman and LZW ring a faint bell, it may be because these are the same compression schemes used by Aladdin's StuffIt, Salient's AutoDoubler, Bill Goodman's Compact Pro, and other compression utilities. For that reason, there's no sense in stuffing a TIFF image that was compressed using LZW. Neither do you want to stuff a JPEG image, because JPEG takes advantage of Huffman encoding. You may shave off a couple of K, but it's not enough space to make it worth your time and effort.

The oddball formats

Can you believe it? Sixteen formats down and I still haven't covered them all. The last three are the odd ones out. Few programs other than Photoshop support these formats, so you won't be using them to swap files with other applications. Also, these formats don't let you compress images, therefore you can't use them to conserve disk space. What can you do with these formats? Read the following sections and find out.

Photo CD YCC images

Photoshop 2.5 can open Eastman Kodak's Photo CD format directly. This capability is not essential, because a Photo CD contains compressed PICT versions of every image in each of the five scan sizes provided on Photo CDs — from 128 × 192 pixels (74K) to 2048 × 3072 pixels (18MB). However, these PICT files are RGB images. The Photo CD format uses the *YCC color model,* a variation on CIE (Commission Internationale de l'Eclairage) color space (discussed in Chapter 14, "Defining Colors"). YCC provides a broader range of color — theoretically, every color your eye can see.

By opening Photo CD files directly, you can translate the YCC images directly to Photoshop's Lab color mode, another variation on CIE color space that ensures no color loss. The Photo CD files are found inside the IMAGES folder in the PHOTO_CD folder, as shown in Figure 5-12. The PICT images are located inside the Photos folder.

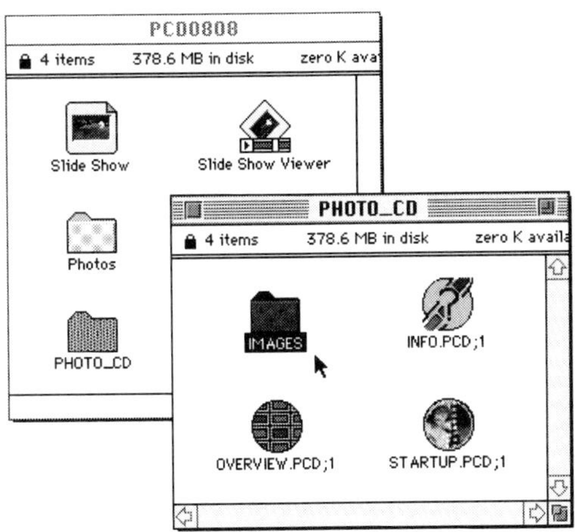

Figure 5-12: On a Photo CD disk, the YCC documents are in the IMAGES folder inside the PHOTO_CD folder.

When you open a Photo CD image, Photoshop displays the PhotoCD Options dialog box shown in Figure 5-13. You can open the image in one of three color modes. Select the Lab Color option to retain all YCC colors. Then select the image size you want to open. Unless you have 32MB or more of RAM, you may have problems opening image sizes larger than 1024 × 1536 pixels; a 1024 × 1536-pixel image consumes nearly 5MB in memory.

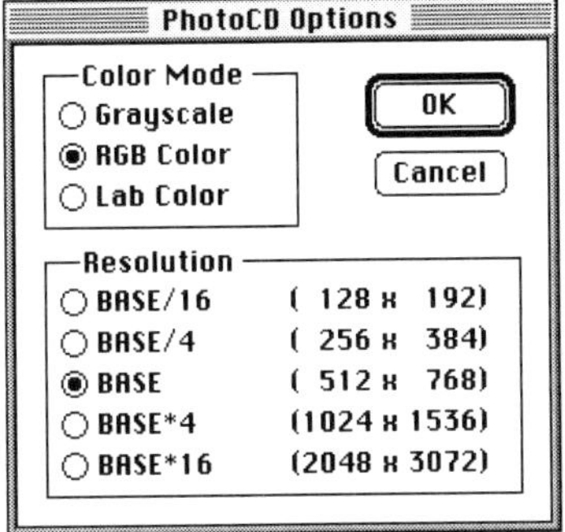

Figure 5-13: When opening a Photo CD image, you can specify the color mode and resolution of the image.

To access Photo CD images, you need a single-session or multi-session CD-ROM device. For more information on Kodak's Photo CD, read the "Using Images on CD-ROM" section of Chapter 6. For more information on the relationship between YCC, Lab, RGB, and every other color mode you ever thought you might want to learn about, read Chapter 14, "Defining Colors."

Photoshop 2.5 cannot save to the Photo CD format. So far, Kodak hasn't licensed other vendors to write images using its proprietary code.

Kodak CMS support

Photoshop 2.5.1 includes the new Kodak Color Management Software (CMS), which tweaks colors in Photo CD images based on the kind of film from which they were scanned. In order to use this software, the Kodak Precision CP system extension and the support files CP1 and CP2 must be inside the Extensions folder in the System folder. You should also find a KPCMS folder inside the System folder, chock full of additional support files.

When you open a Photo CD image while the Kodak Precision CP system extension is active, Photoshop bypasses the PhotoCD Options dialog box in favor of the one shown in Figure 5-14. Here you can specify the image size you want to open by selecting an option from the Resolution pop-up menu. The dialog box even shows you a preview of the image. But the options that make a difference are the Source and Destination buttons.

- **Source:** Click on this button to specify the kind of film from which the original photographs were scanned. You can select from two specific Kodak brands — Ektachrome and Kodachrome — or settle for the generic Color Negative Film option. Your selection determines the method by which Photoshop transforms the colors in the image.
- **Destination:** After clicking on this button, select an option from the Device pop-up menu to specify the color model you want to use. Select Adobe Photoshop RGB to open the image in the RGB mode; select Adobe Photoshop CIELAB to open the image in the Lab mode. A CMYK profile is available direct from Kodak.

Figure 5-14: Use these options to select a resolution and calibrate the colors in the Photo CD image.

Image: IMG0057.PCD;1
Resolution: 512 by 768
File Size: 1.13M
☒ Landscape (faster)
Source Kodak Photo CD Universal
Destination Adobe Photoshop RGB
Image Info Cancel OK

PICT resource (startup screen)

If you really want to open a *PICT resource,* such as the splash screen included with Photoshop or the contents of the Scrapbook, choose File ⇨ Acquire ⇨ PICT Resource, included with Photoshop 2.5, as described in the upcoming "Lifting PICT resources" section. The PICT Resource option provided by the Open As and Save dialog boxes is useful only for opening, editing, and saving *startup screens.*

What is a startup screen? Well, when you boot your computer, a message appears welcoming you to the great big wonderful Macintosh experience. This is the default startup screen included with the system software. However, you can change the startup screen by creating an image and saving it in the PICT Resource file format under the name *StartupScreen* in the root directory of your System Folder. The PICT Resource format automatically dithers your image to the 256-color system palette. A sample startup screen appears in Figure 5-15. I drew this image about three years ago and immediately assigned it as my startup screen. Since then, I've been too lazy to change it. Besides, it makes me feel so doggone patriotic.

For best results, create a startup screen that conforms to the exact dimensions of your screen. If you're unsure what those dimensions are, consult Table 5-1 near the beginning of this chapter.

Figure 5-15: An example of a custom startup screen.

Opening a raw document

A *raw document* is a plain binary file stripped of all extraneous information. It contains no compression scheme, it specifies no bit depth or image size, and it offers no color mode. Each byte of data indicates a brightness value on a single color channel, and that's it. Photoshop offers this function specifically so you can open images created in undocumented formats, such as those created on mainframe computers.

To open an image of unknown origin, choose File ➪ Open As and select Raw from the File Format pop-up menu. Then select the desired image and click on the Open button or press Return. The dialog box shown in Figure 5-16 appears and features these options:

- **Width, Height:** If you know the dimensions of the image in pixels, enter the values in these option boxes.
- **Swap:** Click on this button to swap the Width value with the Height value.
- **Channels:** Enter the number of color channels in this option box. If the document is an RGB image, enter 3; if it is a CMYK image, enter 4.
- **Header:** This value tells Photoshop how many bytes of data at the beginning of the file comprise header information that it can ignore.
- **Retain Header When Saving:** If the Header value is greater than zero, you can instruct Photoshop to retain this data when you save the image in a different format.
- **Guess:** If you know the Width and Height values but you don't know the number of bytes in the header — or vice versa — you can ask Photoshop for help. Fill in either the size or header information and then click on the Guess button to ask Photoshop to take a stab at the unknown value. Photoshop estimates all this information when the Raw Options dialog box first appears. Generally speaking, if it doesn't estimate correctly the first time around, you're on your own. But hey, the Guess button is worth a shot.

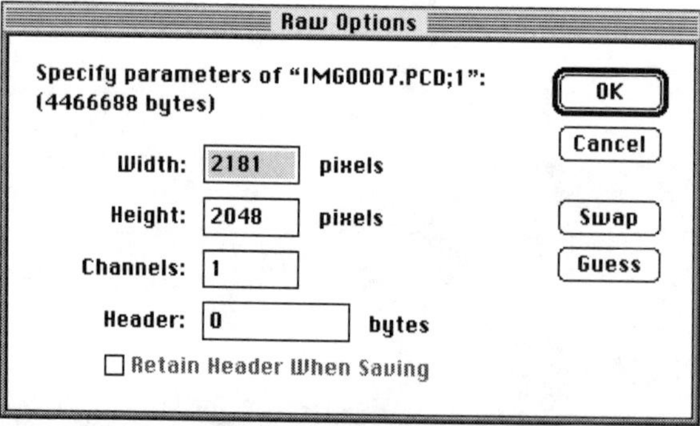

Figure 5-16: Photoshop requires you to specify the size of an image and the number of color channels when you open an image that does not conform to a standardized file format.

If a raw document is a CMYK image, it opens as an RGB image with an extra masking channel. To correctly display the image, choose Mode ➪ Multichannel to free the four channels from their incorrect relationship. Then recombine them by choosing Mode ➪ CMYK Color.

Saving a raw document

Photoshop also allows you to save to the raw document format. This capability is useful when you create files that you want to transfer to mainframe systems or output to devices that don't support other formats, such as the Kodak XL7700 or Hewlett PaintWriter XL.

Do not save 256-color indexed images to the raw format, or you will lose the color lookup table and therefore lose all color information. Be sure to first convert such images to RGB or one of the other full-color modes before saving.

When you save an image in the raw document format, Photoshop presents the dialog box shown in Figure 5-17. The dialog box options work as follows:

- **File Type:** Enter the four-character file type code (TIFF, PICT, and so on) in this option box. (You may want to check the documentation for the application you plan to use to open the raw document.) If you plan to use this file on a computer other than a Mac, you can enter any four characters you like; only Macs use this code.
- **File Creator:** Enter the four-character *creator code,* which tells the system software which application created the file. By default, the creator code is 8BIM, Photoshop's code. Ignore this option unless you have a specific reason for changing it — for example, to open the image in a particular Macintosh application. (You won't hurt anything by changing the code, but you will prevent Photoshop from opening the image when you double-click on the document icon at the Finder desktop.)
- **Header:** Enter the size of the header in bytes. If you enter any value but zero, you must fill in the header using a data editor such as Norton Disk Editor or Central Point Software's MacTools.
- **Save Image In:** Select the Interleaved Order option to arrange data in the file sequentially by pixels. In an RGB image, the first byte represents the red value for the first pixel, the second byte represents the green value for that pixel, the third the blue value, and so on. To group data by color channel, select Non-interleaved Order. When you select this option, the first byte represents the red value for the first pixel, the second value represents the red value for the second pixel, and so on. When Photoshop finishes describing the red channel, it describes the green channel and then the blue channel.

Figure 5-17: When saving a raw document, enter file type and creator codes and specify the order of data in the file.

How to import PICT elements

I don't think I ever want to see another format again — I thought my brain was going to dissolve during that last section. Talk about your raw topics! Well, I certainly hope I conveyed my enthusiasm to you. Really, it's the least I could do. (Yawn.) Anyway, on to bigger and better things, including — do you believe it — more formats! But these formats are more interesting. Honest.

The first topic of discussion is importing PICT images into Photoshop 2.5 via the File ⇨ Acquire submenu. You can do this using two different methods. These functions enable you to open Canvas and MacDraw Pro documents and extract PICT images from places where you never expected to find them.

Photoshop 2.0 users will probably want to skip ahead to the "Storm JPEG" section, which explains some amazing JPEG import and export functions. Although you have to purchase the required JPEG plug-in modules separately, I can attest from personal experience that they are well worth the price.

Rendering a PICT drawing

As I mentioned back in "The mainstream formats" section, Apple designed the PICT format to handle both images and object-oriented drawings. In fact, if you use Canvas, MacDraw Pro, or some other QuickDraw drawing program, you probably save a fair amount of your images to the PICT format. Photoshop 2.5 provides a plug-in module that lets you render an object-oriented PICT file and convert it to an antialiased image, just as you can render an EPS graphic.

Choose File ⇨ Acquire ⇨ Anti-aliased PICT, select the desired drawing, and click on the Open button or press Return. Photoshop displays the Anti-aliased PICT dialog box, shown in Figure 5-18, which allows you to specify the size of the image. The drawing is object-oriented, so you can render it as large or as small as you want without any loss of image quality. Select the Constrain Proportions check box to preserve the width-to-height ratio of the drawing. You also can change the colors in the drawing to gray values or open the drawing as an RGB image. Photoshop automatically antialiases objects to give them soft edges.

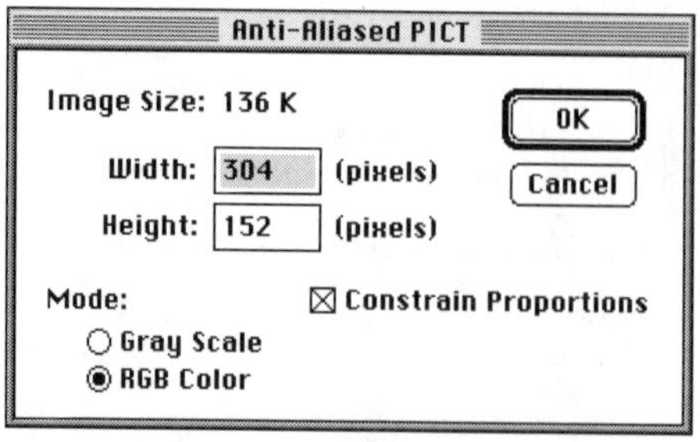

Figure 5-18: You can specify the size and colors of a PICT drawing rendered inside Photoshop.

Photoshop renders PICT drawings remarkably well, especially compared to other applications that import PICT — mostly notably PageMaker and QuarkXPress, both of which do a pretty lousy job. However, Photoshop does not support bitmapped patterns in a PICT drawing; any patterns render to solid color.

Lifting PICT resources

When you choose File ➪ Acquire ➪ PICT Resource, Photoshop lets you open an application or other resource file on disk and browse through any PICT images it may contain. Figure 5-19 shows the dialog box that appears after you select a file to open. You use the double arrow symbols to advance from one PICT image to the next. Click on the Preview button to display the image in the preview box.

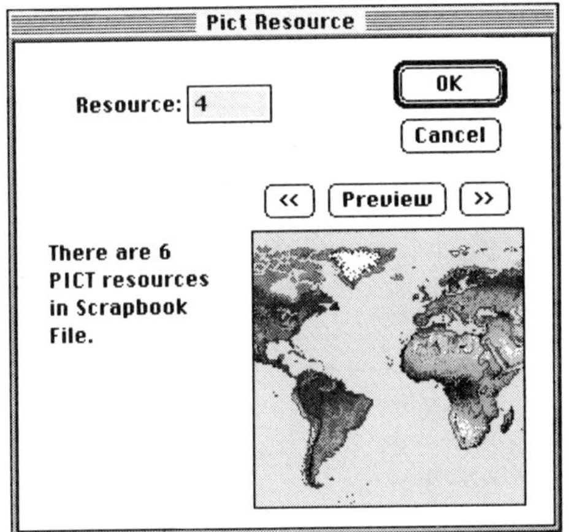

Figure 5-19: Choose File ➪ Acquire ➪ PICT Resource to browse through the PICT images inside an application or other file that contains a resource fork, such as the Scrapbook.

The manual shows how you can use this command to open the Photoshop application, which contains a number of PICT images, including those from the various splash screens shown back in Figure 4-1, Chapter 4. In fact, many applications include PICT images in their *resource forks,* a special section of code available to some files, usually applications. Most of these images are screen controls and other items you'll probably never want to access.

A better use for the File ➪ Acquire ➪ PICT Resource command is to open images directly from the Scrapbook. In fact, this function becomes phenomenally practical if you use a commercial or shareware screen-capture utility (such as Mainstay's Capture) that can store screens in the Scrapbook, as demonstrated in Figure 5-20. You can process your screen shots *en masse* at your leisure. In fact, I created every screen shot in this book this way.

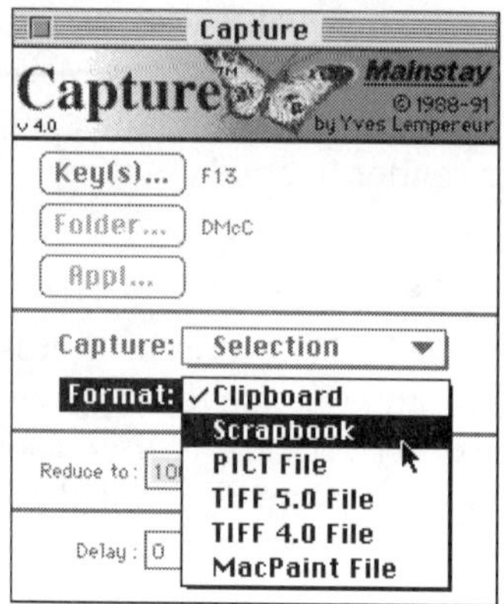

Figure 5-20: Use a commercial or shareware screen capture utility to save your screen shots to the Scrapbook and then use Photoshop to process them in a single sitting.

Storm JPEG

If you're serious about JPEG compression, you may find that neither QuickTime JPEG nor Photoshop's built-in JPEG sufficiently meets your needs. Although various companies, such as Apple and Adobe, support JPEG, only one company — Storm Technology — has made JPEG its corporate mission. Storm is one of the key members of Joint Photographics Experts Group that developed JPEG and is the leading developer of JPEG products.

Its first product of note is a software package called PicturePress. The second is a *digital-signal processor* (DSP) board called ThunderStorm, co-developed and sold by SuperMac. By itself, PicturePress boosts Photoshop's compression capabilities dramatically. Combined with ThunderStorm or an equivalent product, such as DayStar's Charger, PicturePress enables you to open and save in JPEG as quickly as you open and save in Photoshop's native format.

PicturePress

In addition to an independent utility that lets you open and compress JPEG images, PicturePress provides a plug-in module that adds commands to Photoshop's File ⇨ Acquire and File ⇨ Export submenus. Figure 5-21 shows the dialog box that appears when you choose File ⇨ Export ⇨ Storm JPEG Compress.

Storm JPEG Compress
Selected Area Quality: Slider
67
Fair Good High Excellent
☒ Channel #4 contains Selection
Unselected Area Quality: 80% of Selected
Compression Method: Hardware
☒ Include Thumbnail
☒ Include Caption Text Edit...
☐ Include Photoshop Paths
Last Decompressed Image: Cloudy Blast Off
Cancel Save

Figure 5-21: The PicturePress plug-in module, sold separately, provides a range of JPEG functions you won't find anywhere else.

The options in this dialog box provide access to several functions missing from Photoshop's built-in JPEG:

- **Wider range of quality settings:** The Storm JPEG Compress dialog box provides a slider bar that lets you compress an image at any of 100 different settings. Using the independent PicturePress utility, you can design custom compression settings.
- **Better compression:** Storm JPEG prevents degradation of images after repeated openings and recompressions. Figure 5-22 shows an image opened and recompressed multiple times using QuickTime JPEG, Photoshop's JPEG, and PicturePress JPEG. PicturePress provides a dramatic improvement over QuickTime and a slight improvement over Photoshop. Also, PicturePress can detect how the current image was previously compressed and offers the option of reapplying that compression setting to retain as much data as possible in the smallest amount of disk space.
- **Selective compression:** You can specify the exact portions of an image you want to compress and to what extent you want to compress them. To do so, you mask the area that you want to save at the highest quality and transfer it to a separate mask channel (a trick I explain in the "Selection Masks" section of Chapter 9). PicturePress saves the masked area at one quality setting and the unmasked area at a percentage of that setting. This feature enables you to preserve a foreground element of your image at the highest quality setting possible but conserve space on disk by saving the background at a lower quality setting.
- **Thumbnails and captions:** If you like, PicturePress can include a thumbnail of your image so that you can view it in a dialog box before you go to the trouble of opening the image. You also can include a caption of explanatory text that provides an image description, copyright information, or whatever you please.

Most JPEG modules are compatible with each other's documents. For example, you can open a Storm JPEG file using Photoshop's File ⇨ Open command whether or not you have the PicturePress plug-in module installed. Likewise, you can open a Photoshop JPEG image using the PicturePress module. QuickTime JPEG is the only exception. To open a PICT file compressed with JPEG, the QuickTime system extension must be installed and you must use Photoshop's File ⇨ Open command.

ThunderStorm

Like a 24-bit video board, a DSP board fits inside any computer with a NuBus slot (refer to the "External video boards" section of Chapter 3). Its purpose is to speed up specific Photoshop operations. For example, the ThunderStorm board ships with a handful of filters — including substitutes for Photoshop's Gaussian Blur and Unsharp Mask — that speed up common focus-adjustment functions by as much as 1,000 percent. If you work with very large images on a regular basis, the speed improvement may justify the $1,000 retail price tag.

Figure 5-22: Images compressed with three different varieties of JPEG multiple times. All JPEG images eventually degrade, but QuickTime JPEG is the worst offender.

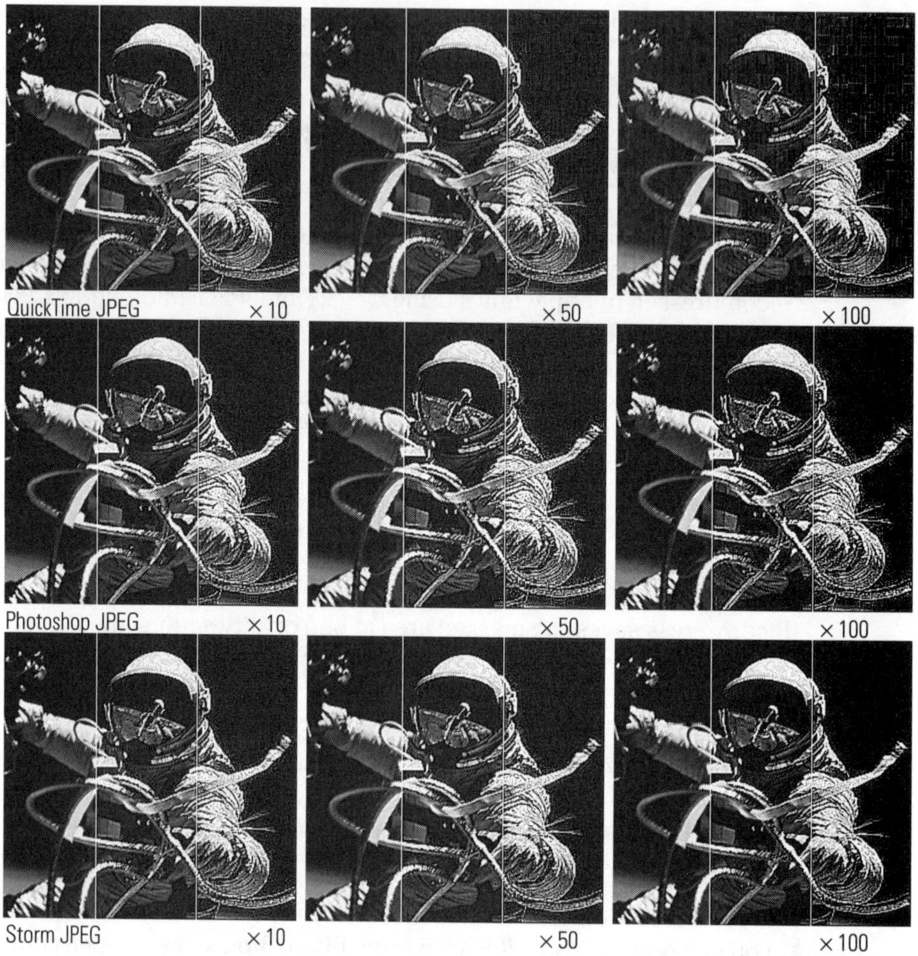

QuickTime JPEG ×10 ×50 ×100

Photoshop JPEG ×10 ×50 ×100

Storm JPEG ×10 ×50 ×100

Both ThunderStorm and DayStar's Charger speed up the opening and saving of Storm JPEG files. They even bundle PicturePress, so you don't have to purchase the software separately. However, in order to take advantage of a DSP board's speed enhancements, you must compress an image at one of the four preset quality settings — Excellent, High, Good, or Fair. PicturePress also includes a module called QuickPress that speeds the opening of PICT files subject to QuickTime JPEG compression.

The next generation of high-end Macintosh computers, beginning with the Centris 660AV and the Quadra 840AV, will sport digital-signal processors built into the motherboards. They'll also include miniature video cameras for shooting 360 × 288-pixel grayscale images.

Resampling and Cropping Methods

After you bring up an image — whether you created it from scratch or opened an existing image stored in one of the five billion formats discussed in the preceding pages — its size and resolution are established. However, neither size nor resolution is set in stone. Photoshop provides two methods for changing the number of pixels in an image: resampling and cropping.

Resizing versus resampling

Typically, when folks talk about *resizing* an image (as they're so prone to do these days), they mean enlarging or reducing it without changing the number of pixels in the image, as demonstrated back in Figure 5-1. By contrast, to *resample* an image is to scale it so that it contains a larger or smaller number of pixels. Resizing affects size and resolution inversely — size goes up when resolution goes down, and vice versa — while resampling affects either size or resolution alone. Figure 5-23 shows an image resized and resampled to 50 percent of its original dimensions. The resampled and original images have identical resolutions, but the resized image has twice the resolution of its companions.

Resizing an image

To resize an image, use one of the techniques discussed in the "Printed resolution" section near the beginning of this chapter. To briefly recap, you can either choose File ⇨ Page Setup and enter a percentage value into the Reduce or Enlarge option box, or you can choose Image ⇨ Image Size and enter a value into the Resolution option box (assuming the File Size check box is selected). Neither technique affects the appearance of the image on screen, only the way it prints.

Resampling an image

You also use Image ⇨ Image Size to resample an image. The difference is that you turn off the File Size check box, as shown in Figure 5-24. In fact, the File Size option is the key to this dialog box.

When selected, File Size ensures that the number of pixels in the image remains fixed. Any change to the Resolution inversely affects the Width and Height values if they are set to any measurement unit but pixels (see the following note).

Figure 5-23: An image (top) resized (bottom left) and resampled (bottom right) down to 50 percent.

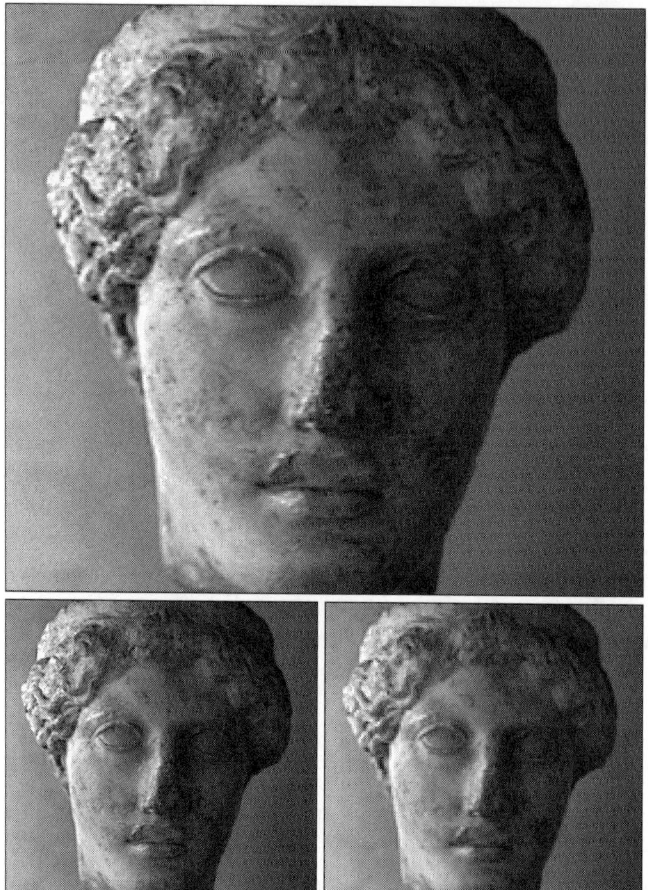

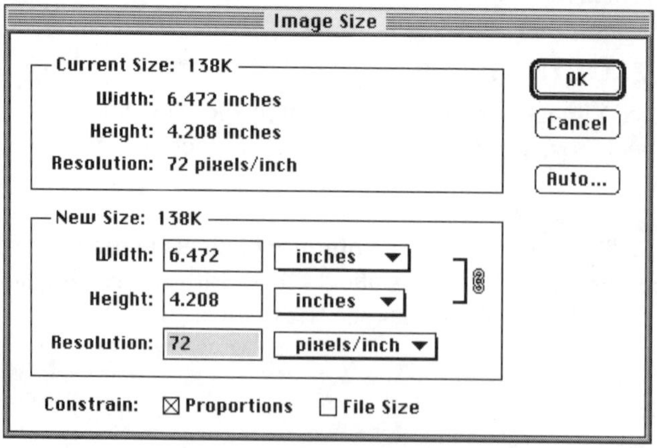

Figure 5-24: The setting of the File Size option determines whether you resize or resample an image.

Image Size

Current Size: 138K
Width: 6.472 inches
Height: 4.208 inches
Resolution: 72 pixels/inch

OK
Cancel
Auto...

New Size: 138K
Width: 6.472 inches
Height: 4.208 inches
Resolution: 72 pixels/inch

Constrain: ☒ Proportions ☐ File Size

When File Size is deselected, the Resolution value is independent of the Width and Height values. You then can increase the number of pixels in an image by increasing any of the three values or decrease the number of pixels by decreasing the values. Photoshop stretches or shrinks the image according to the new size specifications. To do so, it must interpolate the pixels in the image, as explained in the "General environmental preferences" section of Chapter 4 (see Figure 4-16).

If the unit of measurement is pixels, the Resolution option does not affect the Width or Height values regardless of whether File Size is on or off. In fact, the rules change completely. To resize an image, you change the Resolution value. To resample an image, you change the Width and Height values.

Cropping

You also can change the number of pixels in an image by *cropping* it, which means to clip away pixels around the edges of an image without changing the color of any remaining pixel. (The one exception occurs when you rotate a cropped image, in which case pixels in the image change color because Photoshop has to interpolate pixels to account for the rotation.)

Cropping enables you to focus in on an element in your image. For example, Figure 5-25 shows an image my sister photographed for me. It has good color balance, but the image is crooked and we're too far away from the central character, the apprehensive lion. (At least he looks apprehensive. I worry about the guy.) No problem. All I do is crop around the lion's head to delete all the extraneous image elements and focus right in on Mr. Scaredy Cat, as shown in Figure 5-26.

Figure 5-25: This image has too much extraneous information in it.

Figure 5-26: Cropping allows you to focus in on the essential image elements.

Changing the canvas size

One way to crop an image is to choose Image ⇨ Canvas Size, which displays the Canvas Size dialog box shown in Figure 5-27. The options in this dialog box enable you to scale the imaginary *canvas* on which the image rests separately from the image itself.

If you enlarge the canvas, Photoshop surrounds the image with a white background (assuming the background color is white). If you reduce the canvas, you crop the image. Click inside the Placement grid to specify the image placement on the new canvas. For example, if you want to add space to the bottom of an image, enlarge the canvas size and then click inside the upper middle square. If you want to crop away the upper left corner of an image, create a smaller canvas size and then click on the lower right square.

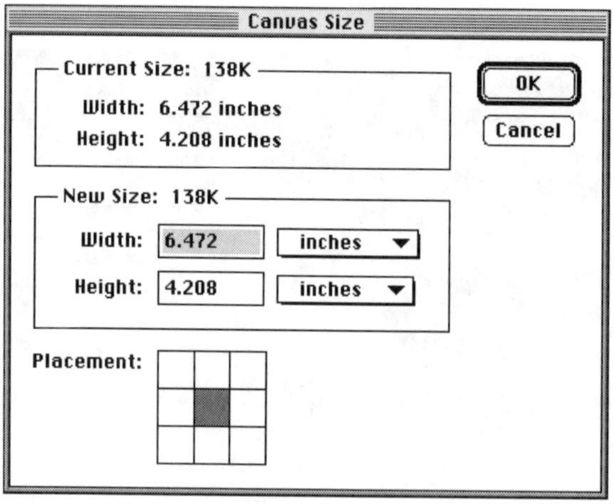

Figure 5-27: Choose Image ⇨ Canvas Size to crop an image or add empty space around the perimeter of an image.

Canvas Size
Current Size: 138K
Width: 6.472 inches
Height: 4.208 inches
OK
Cancel
New Size: 138K
Width: 6.472 inches
Height: 4.208 inches
Placement:

Using the crop tool

Generally speaking, the Canvas Size command is most useful for enlarging the canvas or shaving a few pixels off the edge of an image. If you want to crop away a large portion of an image, using the crop tool is a better choice.

To crop the image, drag with the crop tool to create a rectangular marquee that surrounds the portion of the image you want to retain. If you don't get it right the first time, you can change the horizontal and vertical dimensions of the marquee by dragging any one of the four *corner handles,* as shown in Figure 5-28. When the marquee surrounds the exact portion of the image you want to keep, click inside it with the scissors cursor. This action clips away all pixels except those that lie inside and along the border of the crop marquee.

Figure 5-28: Drag a corner handle to resize the crop marquee.

Rotating a crop marquee

Photoshop enables you to rotate a crop marquee by Option-dragging a corner handle prior to clicking inside the marquee with the scissors cursor. Straightening out an image by Option-dragging the corner handle of a crop marquee can be a little tricky, however. I wish I had a certified check for every time I thought I had the marquee rotated properly, only to find that the image was still crooked after I clicked inside it with the scissors cursor. If that happens to you, choose Edit ⇨ Undo and try again. Do *not* try using the crop tool a second time to rotate the already rotated image. If you do, Photoshop sets about interpolating between already interpolated pixels, resulting in more lost data. Every rotation gets farther away from the original image.

A better solution is to do it right the first time. Locate a line in your image that should be straight up and down. Option-drag the crop marquee so that it aligns *exactly* with that line, as shown in Figure 5-29. Don't worry that this isn't how you want to crop the image — you're just using the line as a reference. After you arrive at the correct angle for the marquee, release the Option key and drag the handles normally to specify the crop boundary. The angle of the marquee remains fixed throughout.

Figure 5-29: Option-drag exactly over a long line in your image to determine the proper angle of rotation.

Cropping a selection

You also can crop an image by dragging with the rectangular marquee tool around the portion of the image you want to keep and choosing Edit ⇨ Crop. One of the advantages of this technique is that it lets you crop the canvas to the boundaries of an image pasted from the Clipboard. As long as the boundaries of the pasted image are rectangular, as in the case of an image copied from a different application, you can choose Edit ⇨ Paste followed by Edit ⇨ Crop to both replace the former image and to crop the window to fit the new image.

Summary

- The resolution of an image is measured in pixels per inch; the resolution of a printer is measured in dots per inch.
- You can control the resolution at which an image prints by changing the Resolution value in the Image Size dialog box and/or the Reduce or Enlarge value in the Page Setup dialog box.
- The New dialog box automatically scales a prospective image window to the size of the image in the Clipboard (if any).
- If you can't get a PICT or EPS drawing to print or you simply want to be able to edit a drawing as a bitmapped image, you can render it at any size or resolution inside Photoshop 2.5.
- To import an image into Adobe Illustrator, you must save it in the EPS format.
- JPEG is a lossy image compression format, meaning that it sacrifices a minimal amount of data to conserve space on disk.
- With QuickTime installed, you can apply JPEG compression to a PICT image.
- The TIFF format is the most popular image format in use across both the Mac and PC platforms.
- Photoshop 2.5 enables you to open images directly while inside the Scrapbook by using File ⇨ Acquire ⇨ PICT Resource.
- PicturePress can selectively compress portions of an image so thats you can retain detail in the foreground and sacrifice detail in the background.
- A DSP board, such as SuperMac's ThunderStorm, increases the speed at which Photoshop opens and saves JPEG images.
- You can crop an image by choosing Image ⇨ Canvas Size or by using the crop tool.
- Option-drag a corner handle to rotate a crop marquee.
- The time-worn scribblings of Dionysius of Halicarnassus contain no information about Photoshop, except to say that the PICT format was very popular among the plebeians. I think there's something to that.

Acquiring the Raw Materials

CHAPTER 6

In This Chapter

- Quick introductions to the different varieties of scanners
- A look at plug-in modules, TWAIN, and Light Source's Ofoto
- How video capture boards and digital cameras work
- A detailed explanation of Kodak's Photo CD technology
- A primer on the different varieties of CD-ROM devices
- An analysis of PhotoDisc, ColorBytes, and other image collections
- How to access professional-quality stock photos from CD collections and on-line services such as PressLink

Turning Photographs into Computer Images

Before you can do anything with a digital photo, you must find one. I constantly hear friends say, "Where can I get a sky?" "I'm looking for a picture of a fire engine." "Quick, I need a shot of the Eiffel Tower!" Unfortunately, your computer can't generate images out of thin air. A computer is no better at conjuring up an image than any other device you may have had at your disposal 20 years ago — or, for the youngsters in the audience, *would* have had 20 years ago. Crude as it may be, someone still has to go out and take a picture with a camera.

But computers do provide you with a tremendous range of options when it comes to acquiring images. Some photographic agencies distribute images on CD-ROM, and others provide photos via on-line services. If you prefer to use your own photos, you can scan them, shoot them with digital cameras, capture them from high-resolution videotape, or have them transferred to Photo CDs. None of this means that you can find a specific image at the drop of a hat, but after you have an image in hand, you can transfer it to computer in a variety of ways. This chapter discusses several photographic resources and methods of feeding images into your computer.

Scanning

I'll start with scanning, because it's the oldest and currently the most reliable way to transfer an original photograph or piece of art to computer. But if you want my frank opinion, scanning is on its way out. Transferring an image to Photo CD (described later in this chapter) is less expensive, less labor-intensive, and almost always provides images of equal or better quality.

Before I proceed any farther, I'd better explain exactly what a *scanner* is and what it does. It's a device that captures a photograph and stores it on disk in PICT, TIFF, or another format of your choosing. Such an image is called a *digitized photograph* because scanning converts an image into a network of colored pixels. All photographs on disk have been digitized at one time or another.

Certainly, scanning offers some advantages. You can scan an image that is lying around the office in a matter of minutes as opposed to waiting several days for an image to be transferred to Photo CD. Scanning also provides a degree of hands-on control that you sacrifice when you place your film in the hands of a Photo CD technician. However, most folks — including professionals — have so many problems capturing a decent scan that the prospect of unloading this step for a small fee will make up for almost any inconvenience. If I were faced with the option of buying a $1,700 flatbed scanner or a $600 multi-session CD-ROM drive, I'd purchase the drive.

Color options

Scanners come in three color varieties, listed here in order of capability and expense:

- **Monochrome (black and white):** A 1-bit scanner is acceptable for scanning pages of text that you want to save as a word-processing document. You can do this using an *OCR* (*optical character recognition*) program such as Caere's OmniPage. But a monochrome scanner does *not* suffice for image editing.
- **Grayscale:** A grayscale scanner is more than adequate if you plan on printing only grayscale images or their equivalents (duotones, tritones, and quadtones). Grayscale scanners typically are less expensive than their full-color counter-

parts. Supposedly, you can create full-color scans with a flatbed grayscale device by scanning the image three times and placing colored transparencies between the photograph and the scanning instrument. You scan once using a red transparency, once using a green transparency, and once using a blue transparency. But because this requires moving the image between each scan, correctly aligning the separate color channels is a cumbersome and sometimes impossible task.

- **Full-color:** A 24-bit scanner is warranted only if you plan on producing full-color images, either for the screen or for output to a film processor or to CMYK separations. Most full-color scanners scan an image in three passes, once for each of the three color channels (red, green, and blue). Newer models can scan a photo in a single pass, which helps to keep color channels in precise alignment. As you might expect, these models are called *one-pass scanners.*

Scanner models

Beyond color, you can measure the sophistication of a scanner according to how it scans an image. The four basic scanner models, listed in order of capability and expense, are as follows:

- **Hand-held:** The most common type of *hand-held scanner* is about the size of a shoe and is shaped like a *T.* You hold the stem and drag the scanner bar across the page. If the page is wider than approximately four inches, you must scan it in two passes and splice the results together. The quality of the scan is largely dependent on how steadily you drag the scanner over the page. I have an unusually steady hand, but I'll be darned if I ever produced anything that didn't look like it came from a fun-house mirror. On the plus side, hand-held scanners are inexpensive. Currently, hand-helds are available only in monochrome and grayscale varieties. If you need an inexpensive solution and you have the time and patience to experiment, the grayscale model is acceptable for scanning snapshots and Polaroids.
- **Sheet-fed:** To use a *sheet-fed scanner,* you insert the page you want to scan into the top of the device, much as you load a page into a typewriter or fax machine. Color sheet-fed scanners, such as PlusTek's ScanPlus, are invariably one-pass devices. The scanner automatically feeds the image past the scanning sensor. The problem with this arrangement is that the page, and not the machine, moves. The page can tilt, slip, misfeed, jam, or wrinkle. You can do permanent damage to the page just by trying to scan it. Feeding problems are more likely for photographs with a glossy finish. When I worked at a service bureau, I had to tape photos to a page just to get them to go through the machine. It's no wonder sheet-fed models are a dying breed.

- **Flatbed:** Prices for full-color *flatbed scanners* start at about $1,200, but you get automation and reliability for your investment. To use a flatbed scanner, you set a page or photograph face down on the sheet of glass and close the cover. A scanning sensor moves back and forth under the surface of the page. Meanwhile, you can go out and have a cigarette, breath someone else's smoke, bug the person in the next cubicle, or whatever.

  The process is entirely automated, and the results range anywhere from good to splendid. Casual users and desktop publishers usually are satisfied with any image produced by a flatbed scanner. If you're a professional, you can use the scanner's software options to tweak colors and boost highlights and shadows.

- **Slide or transparency:** The preceding scanners are designed to digitize *paper positives* — that is, photographs or artwork printed on paper, such as a magazine picture or a standard photograph. If you want to scan a slide or other transparent photo, the cost goes up. Many flatbed scanners, such as the $4,000 Agfa Arcus, include optional transparency units. In the case of the Arcus, the additional unit costs about $1,000. Because transparent slides can't reflect light like paper positive, the transparency unit is required to light the slide from the back.

  A second option is to purchase a 35mm slide scanner. Prices range from $4,500 for a Barneyscan CIS 3515 to $10,000 for a LeafScan 35. A slide scanner can scan slides only and therefore is less versatile than a flatbed scanner with a transparency option. However, slide scanners tend to deliver the best results.

The colors of a scanned transparency almost invariably are more vivid and more true-to-life than the colors of a scanned paper positive. This fact is no real surprise, because the same holds true when you print and separate images in the traditional manner. Color Plate 6-1 compares a paper positive and a film transparency of the same image digitized with an Arcus 600 × 1200 dpi scanner. Except for slightly adjusting the focus with a single pass of the Unsharp Mask filter, both images appear exactly as scanned.

Resolutions

Typically, color flatbed scanners priced under $8,000 advertise resolutions between 300 and 1200 dpi. Most 600 dpi and higher resolution scanners are nonproportional, which means that they actually offer two different resolutions: the full resolution vertically, and half that resolution horizontally. The scanner interpolates between the horizontal pixels to create the full-resolution image. But by definition, interpolation is imperfect, which results in an image with about as much detail as one scanned with a resolution midway between the nonproportional rates. For example, a 600 × 300 dpi scanner delivers a 600 ppi image with as much clarity and detail as one scanned with a 450 × 450 dpi scanner. Unfortunately, the interpolated image consumes 75 percent more room on disk because of its higher resolution. Therefore, when possible, avoid interpolation by scanning the image at the lower of the two resolutions.

Scanning software

A scanner is only as good as the software behind it. How many times have you heard that old saw? I believe it's called segue number 14. But in this case, it's true. Umax, for example, makes a couple of high-quality, relatively inexpensive scanners, but the software is awful. You choose brightness values from a menu; you can increase the level of contrast but you can't decrease it; and you have no control over the adjustment of midrange colors (anything between black and white). Just to keep things interesting, the software even has a few perpetually dimmed options.

The point is, you should test a scanner's software before purchasing it. Most scanners include several kinds of software — desk accessories, stand-alone utilities, and so forth — but I'll explain only two. Either a plug-in scanning module or support for the TWAIN interface standard is sufficient to provide a direct link between your scanner and Photoshop.

Plug-in modules

The Macintosh image editing world revolves around Photoshop. Almost since Photoshop was introduced, I haven't seen a single scanner that doesn't provide a Photoshop plug-in module. Installing the module is as simple as dragging it into Photoshop's Plug-ins folder. The next time you launch the Photoshop application, a new command appears in the File ⇨ Acquire submenu that enables you to scan directly into Photoshop. The scanned image appears inside a new image window.

For example, Figure 6-1 shows the dialog box that appears when you choose File ⇨ Acquire ⇨ Agfa PhotoScan, the plug-in module for the Agfa Arcus. (Unless you own the Arcus, this command does not appear in your Acquire submenu.)

The dialog box provides access to the basic collection of options you need to acquire a quality scan. The most essential options fall into the following categories:

- **Color mode:** Color scanning software enables you to scan black-and-white, grayscale, or full-color images. The black-and-white setting is most useful for capturing line art that you want to convert into an object-oriented graphic by tracing the image inside a drawing program.
- **Resolution:** In the "Printed resolution" section of Chapter 5, I discuss the fact that both the Resolution and Reduce or Enlarge options affect the number of pixels per inch in a printed image. The same holds true for scanning. In the case of the Arcus, you control the number of pixels scanned by adjusting the Input value and change the printed resolution by using the Scale To value. If you set the resolution to 200 ppi and the scale to 200 percent, the scanner captures 200

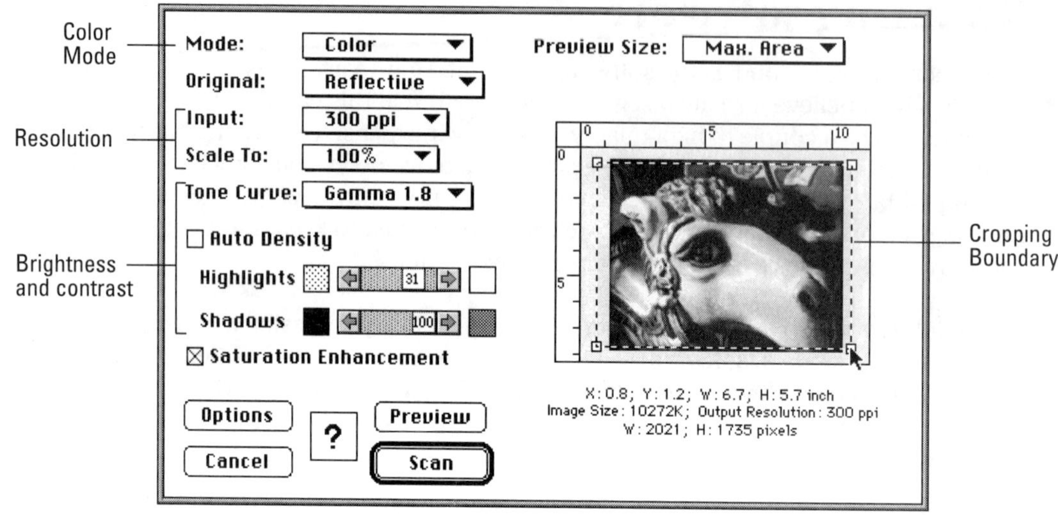

Figure 6-1: The plug-in module for the Arcus scanner enables you to change the color mode, select a resolution, adjust the brightness and contrast of colors in an image, and crop the portion of the image you want to scan.

pixels per every inch of a photograph. Next, the scanner reduces the resolution of the image inside Photoshop by half, to 100 ppi, so it prints twice as large as the original photo.

Scan a photo at the highest resolution possible. Then you can sample the image down inside Photoshop to gain clarity and eliminate *scanning artifacts* (dust, hairs, moiré patterns, and the like). Keep in mind, however, that Photoshop needs room to operate. If you scan a 16MB image and you plan to reduce it 50 percent, you need a minimum of 20MB of memory or disk space — that is, an extra 4MB for the 50 percent resolution image. (Recall that at 50 percent, an image consumes ¼ as much area and thus ¼ as much memory as the original, as demonstrated back in Figure 5-1.)

- **Brightness and contrast:** Chapter 16, "Mapping and Adjusting Colors," describes a number of ways you can adjust the brightness and contrast of an existing image inside Photoshop. The disadvantage to making adjustments inside Photoshop is that you sacrifice data. Photoshop takes two colors, maps them into one, and throws away the other. This method is your only choice if you want to adjust the colors in an existing image. During the scanning phase, however, you have the option of controlling how the scanner perceives brightness and contrast. Rather than throwing away colors, the scanner rearranges them. You can increase the range of colors in the highlights, lighten up on the shadows, and control colors in the midrange by editing the tonal curve.

Brightness, contrast, highlights, shadows, and tonal curves are all discussed at length in Chapter 16. Although Photoshop's specific color-mapping options no doubt differ from those provided by your scanning software, the fundamental concepts behind the options are the same.

- **Cropping boundary:** Flatbed scanners enable you to preview a document or photograph before scanning it. By dragging the handles of a cropping boundary, you can specify the portion of the preview that you want to scan.

As a general rule of thumb, always crop large — in other words, leave a generous margin around the portion of the image you want to use. If you end up scanning a few extraneous elements, you can always delete them using Photoshop's cropping capabilities.

For comparative purposes, Figure 6-2 shows the dialog box that appears when you choose File ⇨ Acquire ⇨ PlugInScan, the module for the medium-resolution Umax UC630. The color mode, resolution, and cropping boundary options are adequate, but the brightness and contrast options are less capable. You must choose highlight and shadow values from a pop-up menu and you have no control over colors in the midrange.

The disparity between the options and capabilities offered by different scanning software is the primary reason for the development of TWAIN, the subject of the next section.

TWAIN

If you select the TWAIN plug-in module at the Finder desktop and choose File ⇨ Get Info, you see the joke, `TWAIN, The spec With An Interesting Name.` That's not really what TWAIN stands for, but it might as well be. I'm pretty sure Aldus, Hewlett-Packard, and the rest of the folks who designed TWAIN drew the name from a hat.

TWAIN is an interface standard designed to facilitate the process of scanning images and text from inside any Macintosh or Windows application. The idea is that no matter which Mac program or which brand of scanner you use, you can access a familiar dialog box of scanning options every time you try to scan a document or photo. After all, the printing process is standardized among all Macintosh programs. You press Command-P, press the Return key, and you're off and running. TWAIN seeks to similarly standardize the scanning process.

It's a great idea. But although TWAIN is slowly but surely catching on with Windows software developers, Macintosh scanner vendors are jumping on the TWAIN bandwagon with about as much gusto as if a skunk were aboard. As I write this, TWAIN has been around for a full year, and to my knowledge, it's integrated into only one scanner,

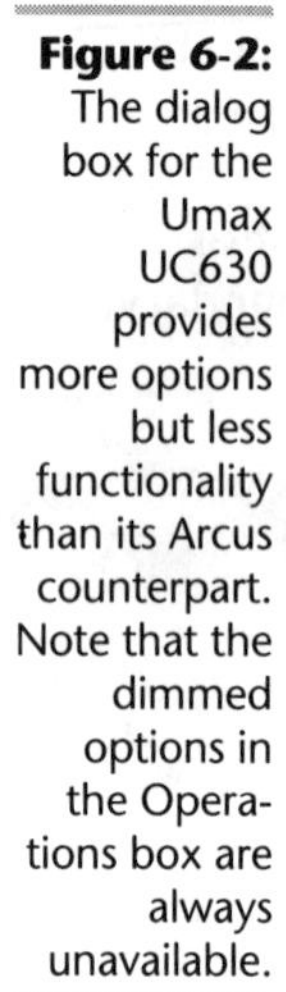

Figure 6-2: The dialog box for the Umax UC630 provides more options but less functionality than its Arcus counterpart. Note that the dimmed options in the Operations box are always unavailable.

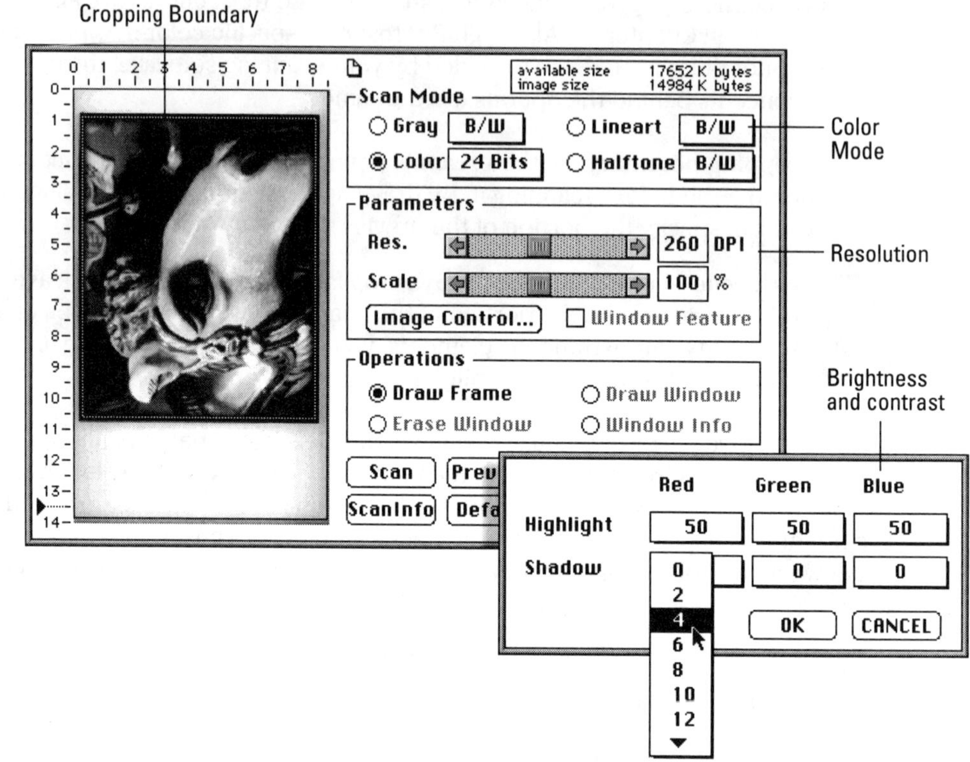

the $1,000 grayscale HP ScanJet IIp. Other scanner manufacturers claim TWAIN support, but they fail to provide a *source manager,* a key piece of software that acts as the translator between the scanner (the *source*) and the TWAIN-compatible application. Hopefully, more vendors will get with the program in the future. In the meantime, if you happen to come across a TWAIN-compatible device, you can use it to scan an image into Photoshop 2.5 only as outlined in the following steps.

STEPS: Scanning from a TWAIN-compatible Device

Step 1. Copy the TWAIN source manager provided with your scanner to the System Folder or other location specified by the scanner documentation. (***Note:*** Most scanner vendors provide Photoshop plug-in modules, but these modules do not qualify as TWAIN source managers. If the scanner does not include a source manager, Photoshop 2.5's TWAIN commands do not work.)

Step 2. Choose File ➪ Acquire ➪ TWAIN Select Source and then select the desired TWAIN device. You only need to perform this step the first time you use the scanner with Photoshop.

Step 3. Choose File ➪ Acquire ➪ TWAIN Acquire to access the standardized dialog box of options required to use your scanner. Then follow the instructions provided with your scanner.

I must level with you — I've never seen Photoshop interact with a TWAIN-compatible scanner in my short life. I feel so . . . so *naive.* If you ever use the two together, let me know how it works out. Send me some screen shots too, would you? And a box of Cuban cigars. Your fellow Photoshop users thank you.

Ofoto

If you outgrow the capabilities of your scanning software and TWAIN either isn't available or doesn't deliver what you want — and you have about $400 burning a hole in your pocket — then you're in the market for Light Source's Ofoto, which is shown in Figure 6-3. Arguably the best thing to happen to Macintosh image editing since Photoshop, Ofoto provides a wealth of options that automatically enhance scanned images. And unlike the previous grayscale version, Ofoto Version 2.0 supports 24-bit color.

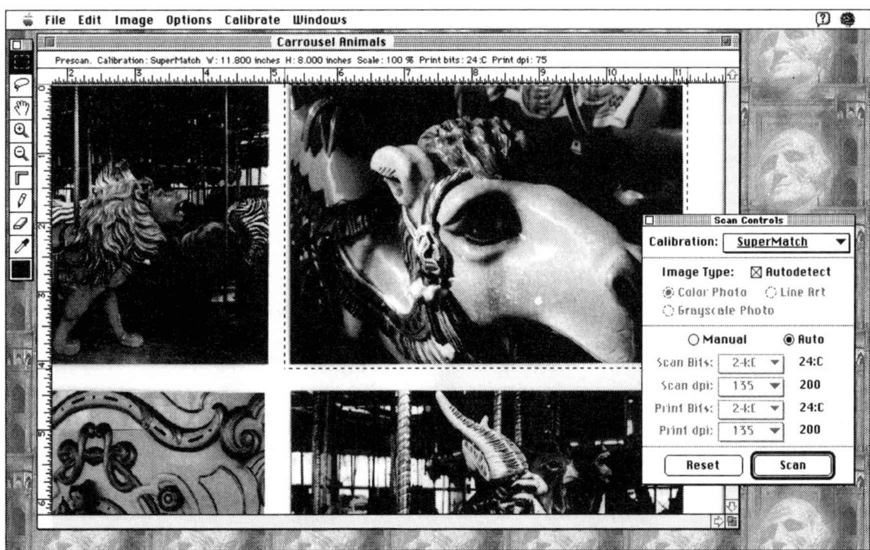

Figure 6-3: Unlike a Photoshop plug-in module, Ofoto provides a dedicated scanning interface with full-color previews and automated image-correction functions.

Here's a brief list of the capabilities provided by Ofoto:

- **Automatic adjustments:** Ofoto is capable of determining whether an image is line art (black and white), grayscale, or color. It doesn't always guess correctly, but at least it tries. If you so specify, Ofoto also can automatically straighten or crop an image and correct exposure and focus problems.
- **Adaptive printer calibration:** By scanning a test chart printed on a specific output device, Ofoto learns how to compensate for that device when correcting colors in future images. Ofoto is even sensitive enough to compensate for the paper stock you use.
- **ColorSync:** If you prefer to calibrate an image for your screen, Ofoto 2.0 bundles Apple's ColorSync system extension, which enables Ofoto and other applications to fine-tune a scanned image for a variety of monitors. You can then calibrate between screen and printer at a later time.
- **AeQ:** As if there aren't enough color models in the world, Ofoto throws in yet another one. *AeQ (Appearance Equivalence)* is Ofoto's answer to CIE, a color model which theoretically represents every color the human eye can see (read Chapter 14, "Defining Colors," for more information). Light Source claims that CIE, developed in the 1930s, is outdated when compared with modern research into human vision. AeQ supposedly addresses CIE's inadequacies.

Because I spent so much time trying to get a double major in math and art, I totally missed out on that Ph.D. in advanced color theory. As a result, I can't tell you whether AeQ is better than CIE — or for that matter, whether CIE is better than RGB. But I can tell you that Ofoto is superb at matching the colors in an original image. Color Plate 6-2 compares a page from *Macworld* magazine that was scanned using a Photoshop plug-in module with the same page scanned with Ofoto. For comparison purposes, Color Plate 6-3 shows the original image as I created it in Color It, the low-end image editor from Timeworks. (Yes, you can create cool stuff in programs other than Photoshop.)

Although it may appear that the colors in the plug-in scan more closely resemble those in the original image, the colors in the Ofoto scan are truer to the *Macworld* page. The Ofoto image also is sharper and more vivid. Moiré patterns are evident in both scans.

Shooting Photos to Disk

Scanning is only one option for transferring photographs to disk. You also can capture frames from videotape and take pictures with a digital camera. Both these options enable you to avoid the middleman: you can go directly from photograph to disk-based imagery without the delay or additional charge associated with film development.

However, these options also have disadvantages. Although video-input boards, such as SuperMac's VideoSpigot and Digital Vision's ComputerEyes/Pro, are inexpensive (less than $500), video frames don't begin to live up to the resolution standards set by scanned images. The situation is exactly opposite with digital cameras. You can shoot high-resolution images — nearly equivalent to the highest-resolution image on a Photo CD — but you pay an arm and a leg for the privilege. Costing upwards of $10,000, digital cameras are currently the stuff of big ad studios, news periodicals, and the occasional well-funded in-house design department.

Video capture

To transfer images from video to computer, you need two pieces of hardware: a *video-input device,* installed in your computer, and a *video source,* which can be a VCR, laser disc player, or video camera. Most video-input devices come in the form of NuBus boards (refer to the "External video boards" section of Chapter 3). But a few, including the VideoSpigot, are available as PDS boards to accommodate specific Macintosh models, such as the LC and IIsi. One video-input device, the MacVision Color Video Digitizer from Koala, isn't a board at all, but rather a box that attaches to your computer's SCSI port, just like an external hard drive or scanner.

Video-input devices

Many video-input devices — including TrueVision's NuVista+ and RasterOps MediaTime — can lift a single frame from a playing movie. For example, when the NuVista+ board is installed, you can choose File ➪ Acquire ➪ NuVista Capture inside Photoshop to load a frame into a new image window.

Other devices can capture only still images. Because the MacVision box connects to the SCSI port, it takes two full seconds to transfer an image to Photoshop. This limits your source options to a still-video camera, a VCR or laser disc player with a frame-accurate pause feature, or a live camera pointed at a stationary scene.

Deinterlacing

If a movie features a lot of movement or if your video camera provides a weak synchronization signal, the even and odd interlace fields may appear poorly matched, as shown in Figure 6-4. That statement might sound like a lot of gibberish, but stick with me for a moment, and I'll explain.

To display moving images, a television draws each frame one horizontal *scan line* at a time. The television signal is divided into two *fields* of scan lines — one for the even-numbered lines and one for the odd-numbered lines (counting down from the top). The TV draws the even field first and then starts over at the top of the frame and draws the odd field. Termed *interlaced video,* this rapid succession of even and odd fields produces the illusion of movement.

I captured the frame from Figure 6-4 using a standard 8mm video camera, which doesn't do such a hot job of synchronizing the even and odd fields. Despite the fact that I hardly moved the camera when shooting this tranquil Italian scene, the even and odd fields appear out of alignment.

Photoshop can patch up this problem by deleting either the even or odd field and interpolating between the scan lines of the remaining field. To access this feature, choose Filter ➪ Video ➪ De-Interlace. Photoshop then displays the De-Interlace dialog box shown in Figure 6-5.

You can't predict which field you should delete and which field you should retain. I generally experiment to see which option is best. I eliminate the odd field, see how that looks, and choose Edit ➪ Undo. Next I eliminate the even field, take a look at the results, and choose Edit ➪ Undo again. After I view both options, I apply the one I disliked least. Yes, you sacrifice data when you use this command. But because the only other choice is to upgrade your video source, you may have to settle for this compromise solution.

The video source

Different kinds of video sources provide different image resolutions. The American *NTSC* (*National Television Standards Committee*) protocol allows up to 525 scan lines per

Figure 6-4: The even and odd horizontal scan lines in this video frame are out of alignment, thanks to a weak synchronization signal.

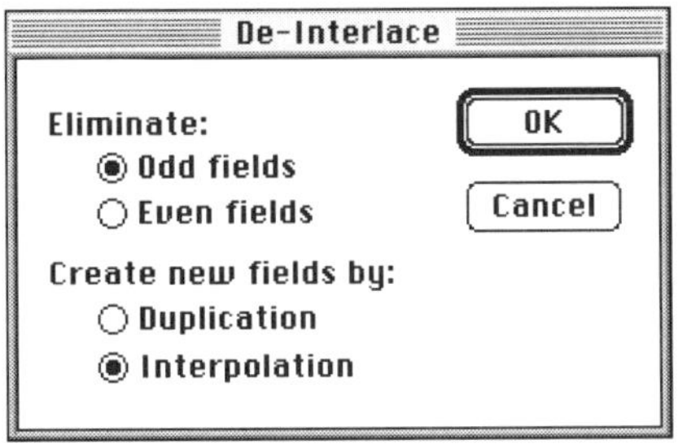

Figure 6-5: Photoshop can account for badly aligned scan lines by eliminating the even or odd field and interpolating between the remaining lines.

De-Interlace

Eliminate:
- (•) Odd fields
- ( ) Even fields

Create new fields by:
- ( ) Duplication
- (•) Interpolation

OK

Cancel

frame, top to bottom. But only professional decks achieve that resolution. Among consumer devices, laser discs fare the best, providing up to 450 scan lines. Super VHS and Hi8 video decks provide 400 scan lines, consumer video cameras provide about 300 scan lines, and standard VHS and 8mm tape players top out at a mere 240.

High-end devices, such as Super VHS and Hi8 players, also offer *S-Video* or *component video* output, which separates the *chrominance signal* (the part that contains the red, green, and blue color information) from the *luminance* signal, which specifies the highlights and shadows in an image. The result is a crisp image with a minimal amount of *color bleeding* — an effect in which red and blue elements appear to glow. Low-end decks provide a single *composite signal,* which mixes chrominance and luminance together to create fuzzy, glowy images.

Figure 6-6: The image from Figure 6-5 after eliminating the odd field. Photoshop interpolates between the odd scan lines and delivers an image that is more blocky but no longer looks like something out of a 3-D house of horrors.

Digital cameras

Digital cameras promise a degree of immediacy that no other device or technology currently matches. Scenarios for their application range from the convenient to the essential. As a designer, if you need an asphalt texture, you can walk outside, take a picture of the street, walk back inside, and download the image to your hard drive. How much easier can it get? If you're a news editor with a late-breaking story and an imminent deadline, you send a photographer out with a digital camera, he or she brings back a device full of images, you pilfer through the photos in a matter of minutes, grab the image you want, and store the rest on an archiving system — saving time and film-processing fees. Another triumph for the print media. Let CNN eat its heart out.

A digital camera — whether it's a complete camera or a product like the Leaf Digital Camera Back, an adapter that fits on a traditional 35mm camera — has two components: an *imaging system* that controls picture quality and a *storage system* that holds the images you shoot. The heart of most imaging systems is the *charge-coupled device* (*CCD*), a chip that converts light to electrical signals. The best CCDs provide resolutions up to 2048 × 2048 pixels, which is larger than a letter-sized page at 200 ppi. As with high-end video devices, some digital cameras separate the chrominance and luminance signals by providing two separate CCD chips. Some others include three chips, one each for the red, green, and blue color channels.

Storage systems for digital cameras vary widely. Low-resolution cameras offer RAM chips that can hold a handful of images at a time. High-resolution cameras require built-in hard drives that are bulky and prone to breakdowns. Transferring an image to a hard drive is a much slower process than saving it to memory, which prohibits rapid-fire shooting. Using a digital camera, therefore, requires that you compromise either resolution or speed and reliability. These are extremely expensive machines that demand patience and care.

Using Images on CD-ROM

If you can't operate a scanner, can't bear the low resolution of a video image, and can't afford a digital camera, all is not lost — thanks to the new world of image options emerging on CD-ROM. In most instances, these options are cheap and yield marvelous results. Assuming you own a compatible CD-ROM player, you can access a huge variety of images.

Kodak Photo CD

Photo CD is a new technology that enables you to transfer 35mm slides, negatives, and undeveloped film to CD-ROM. The process costs about $1 per photo, more if you mix your media by turning in slides, negatives, and undeveloped film all at once or if you request specific photos rather than processing a whole roll of film.

A single CD holds 100 images, which means that $100 buys you a supply of photos that would take you three or four days to scan. And, in most instances, Photo CD images look a heck of a lot better than their scanned counterparts, particularly if you scan from paper positives. Figure 6-7 shows grayscale versions of an image scanned from film to Photo CD and the same image scanned from a consumer-grade paper positive using an Arcus scanner and Ofoto. The wider range of brightness values in the Photo CD image give it greater depth and superior detail.

Color Plate 6-4 shows the same images in color. The Photo CD image leans a little heavily toward green, while the scanned image leans excessively toward orange. But the Photo CD image is without a doubt the superior photograph.

Figure 6-7: The $1 Photo CD image (top) provides greater depth and detail than the image I scanned (bottom) using a $4,000 scanner, a $400 application, and an hour of my time.

The fact is, unless you have access to a $10,000 slide scanner and are a red-hot expert at using the thing, Photo CD represents a better product at a better price. The only tradeoff is lag time. Most service bureaus and photographic developers do not provide Photo CD scanning services in-house. It takes a week or more to have a CD made, with most of that time spent in shipping. But if you can find a Photo CD lab — most major cities have at least one or two, and I'm sure they'll eventually catch on in less populated regions — you can have a CD made in a couple days, which is about the same amount of time it takes to get film developed.

Hardware requirements

To use a Photo CD, you need one of the following kinds of drives, listed here in order of preference:

- **Multi-session:** The best device is a *multi-session* CD-ROM drive, which can read data that was recorded to a disk at different times. This feature means you don't have to fill up the disk in a single session. Instead, you can keep adding images to a disk — 10 photos here, 20 more there, and so on — until the disk is full. Only certain drives manufactured after October 1992 have this capability.
- **Single-session:** A *single-session* drive lets you read a block of images that were recorded to disk in one sitting. If you try to open a multi-session disk on a single-session drive, you can only see the first block of images recorded.
- **Older models with CD-ROM Toolkit:** If you own an older model drive that is not single-session compatible and therefore cannot read Photo CDs, such as the original Apple CD SC, you can upgrade it using a separately-sold piece of software such as FWB's CD-ROM Toolkit. For $79, this program won't boost your drive to multi-session compatibility — only a hardware upgrade can accomplish that — but it will allow you to read Photo CD disks on most Macintosh drives.

Single-session drives support *ISO 9660,* a platform-independent CD-ROM standard that can be used on the IBM PC and other computers. Multi-session drives go a step farther by conforming to the *CD-ROM XA* (Extended Architecture) standard, which permits *data interleaving.* Whereas most drives expect to find a single directory of files around the innermost ring of the disk, XA drives look for multiple directories throughout the disk.

Whether they play music or CD-ROM disks, CD players read the underside of a disk. That's why the tops of most disks have writing on them and the bottoms are pristine. Because one Photo CD disk looks exactly like another, you can label the tops of disks by writing directly on them or adhering a label, as shown in Figure 6-8. Do *not* write on the underside of any CD.

Figure 6-8: You can label a Photo CD by writing on the top side of the disk.

Software requirements

To properly view the contents of a Photo CD, your Mac should be equipped with the following system extensions:

- **Foreign File Access:** This is the primary system extension for mounting and viewing the contents of non-Macintosh CDs. On its own, Foreign File Access is just a shell. It relies on other files — including Audio CD Access, High Sierra File Access, and the two following files — to recognize specific non-Macintosh formats.
- **ISO 9660 File Access:** This extension enables Foreign File Access to recognize single-session and multi-session CD-ROM disks.
- **Apple Photo Access:** You don't need this extension loaded to access Photo CD images. Because Photoshop 2.5 provides direct support for the Photo CD file format, you can open and edit images whether Photo Access is available or not. However, Photo Access does serve a purpose, especially when you work outside of Photoshop. Because Photo CD is a device-independent format, its file structure doesn't make a whole lot of sense at the Finder desktop. Photo Access hides some files, creates others, and generally makes the interface more straightforward, as demonstrated in Figure 6-9. Photo Access also makes QuickTime-compressed PICT versions of each image available so that you can open them in a wide assortment of Macintosh applications.

Figure 6-9: The contents of a Photo CD viewed normally (top) and when the Apple Photo Access system extension is loaded (bottom).

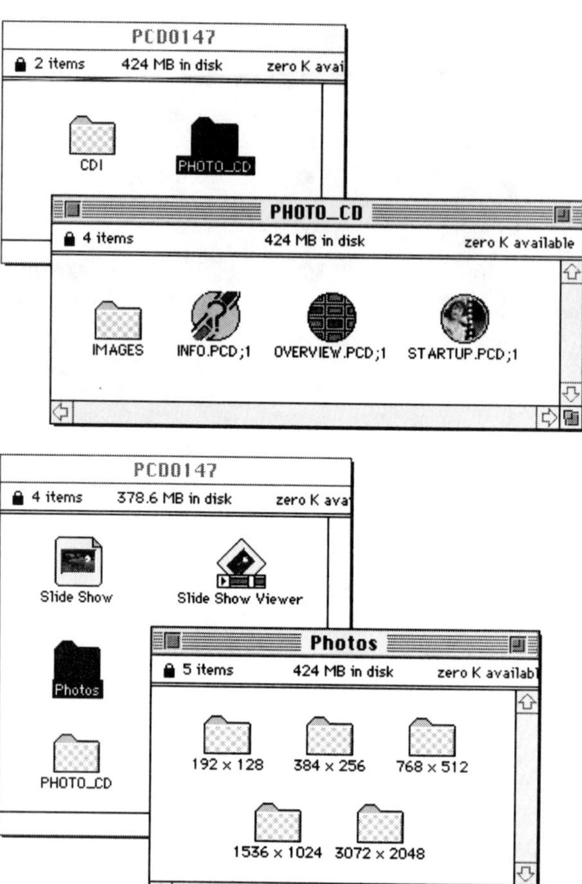

Apple developed and distributes all the CD extensions. One day, the extensions no doubt will be built into the system software. In the meantime, you might find them on the disk that accompanied your CD-ROM device, especially if you purchased the device in 1992 or later. If not, you can download the extensions from a bulletin board, purchase them in a commercial CD-ROM utility package such as FWB's CD-ROM Toolkit, or request them directly from Apple.

Commercial image collections

Commercial image collections on CD-ROM are becoming increasingly popular. One day, they'll probably be as common as fonts. In the meantime, here are a few of the image collections I discovered in the course of writing this book.

Collections offering unlimited reproduction rights

In a way, editing an image is like producing a rap song. In many cases, you take someone else's photography, mess it up, and put your name on it. Some photographic agencies don't mind what you do with their photos, while others are very picky and license an image only for a single use. Unless you want to be slapped with a lawsuit, you'll do well to learn the difference.

The first kind of photographic agency provides 200 or so high-resolution images per CD. For about $300, you can purchase not only the disk, but also a license to use the images on that disk as many times as you want in as many custom situations as you want. In other words, you have *unlimited reproduction rights.* Some agencies do restrict you from associating their images with pornography. And of course, it's no more legal to distribute digital images on disk to other users than it is to pirate any other kind of software. But otherwise, you're free and clear to publish the images as you like.

The best sources for images with unlimited reproduction rights are the Photoshop Deluxe Edition CD-ROM, PhotoDisc, and ColorBytes.

- **Photoshop Deluxe Edition:** The Photoshop CD contains images from PhotoDisc and ColorBytes as well as a handful of Photo CD scans from Eastman Kodak. You can publish all these images without paying any additional fees. The CD also includes some original artwork that you can view but not publish.
- **PhotoDisc:** As I write this, PhotoDisc provides six different sets of CD-ROM images under the titles *Business and Industry; People and Lifestyles; Backgrounds and Textures; Science, Technology, and Medicine; World Commerce and Travel; and Nature, Wildlife, and the Environment.* Each disc contains as many as 400 images in resolutions as high as 2000 × 3000 pixels — roughly the size of the largest Photo CD image. Retail prices vary from $300 to $400. Figure 6-10 and Color Plate 6-5 show examples from the *People and Lifestyles* disk. You'll find examples from other disks sprinkled throughout the book.
- **ColorBytes:** ColorBytes is new to the photo-licensing game, but its images are magnificent. The only ColorBytes disk available so far, the $400 Sampler One, includes 100 images with resolutions equal to those provided by PhotoDisc. But whereas PhotoDisc has the obvious advantages of quantity and variety, Sampler One images tend to be more dramatic and more carefully rendered. ColorBytes claims to edit every one of its images by hand to eliminate dust and other artifacts, and it shows. Figure 6-11 and Color Plate 6-6 show examples from Sample One.

Figure 6-10: Images from PhotoDisc's *People and Lifestyles* disk.

CD-ROM texture collections are as popular as image collections. For information about Wraptures and D'pix, see the "How to create patterns" section of Chapter 10.

Stock photo agencies

Stock photo agencies have been around for years, which is one of the reasons they work differently than you may expect. Rather than distributing 200 or so images that you can use as many times as you want, a stock photo agency sends you a CD with thousands of low-resolution images that you can view but not publish. After you find images you want to publish, you must license each photo individually for a single use.

Consider, for example, 3M's CD Stock collection. Priced at $650, CD Stock comprises four disks, each from a different stock photo company: The Stock Market, Tony Stone Worldwide, AllStock, and FPG International. Your $650 buys you access to a 20,000-

Figure 6-11: The vast majority of images on the ColorBytes disk are bold and exciting. To date, the company offers two 100-image disks — a small selection compared to PhotoDisc's 2,000-image collection.

photo catalog of images, but not the right to use any of them. You probably wouldn't want to publish any of the images on these disks anyway, because of their negligible resolutions (about 400 × 500 pixels).

The tie that binds the four disks is 3M's CD Stock utility, which lets you search the catalog included with each disk by browsing through thumbnails or entering keywords that interest you. As shown in Figure 6-12, each catalog page features one or more images. You can double-click on an image to view it in greater detail. By dragging on the scroll box, you can move to another section of the catalog. The topic and page number of the prospective section appear in the lower right corner of the window.

After you find an image you want to use, you telephone the specific stock photo agency and ask to license the image. For a hefty fee, the agency sends you a 70mm or 4 × 5-inch transparency of the image. You then must either scan the image yourself or have it traditionally separated and stripped into your document by hand.

Figure 6-12: A catalog page from one of the disks included in 3M's CD Stock collection.

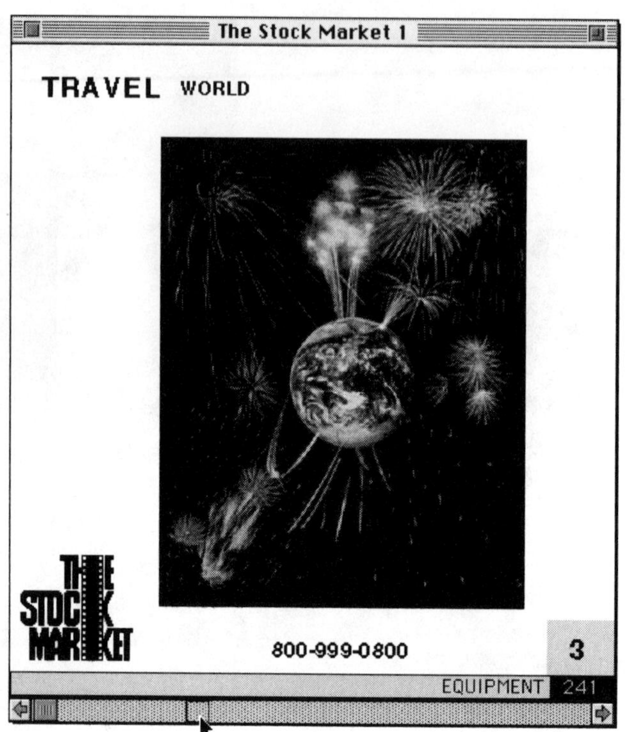

Soon, you may also have the option of transferring the image to a Photo CD. By the time you read this, Kodak may have introduced its Pro Photo CD Mastering system, which will handle professional film formats. But even so, you probably won't be able to take advantage of this technology. No stock photo agency will encourage you to digitize one of their images for your permanent image collection; more than likely, you will be prohibited from scanning stock-agency images to a Photo CD.

As far as the fee is concerned, stock agencies charge you according to several factors, including the size at which you reproduce an image; where the image appears (inside the publication or on the cover); whether the image is used for advertising or editorial purposes; and the size of the print run. For example, to reproduce an image from The Stock Market at half-page size inside a publication with a 50,000-copy print run, you pay somewhere in the neighborhood of $400.

Although stock photo agencies demand a professional price, they likewise deliver a professional product. Figure 6-13 and Color Plate 6-7 show a sampling of the low-resolution images from the CD Stock disks. Unfortunately, the image acquisition process is still a little rough around the edges. When the stock agencies get their acts together and when the companies are willing to provide disk-based versions of the licensed images, this scenario may grow into a viable solution for the electronic publishing professional.

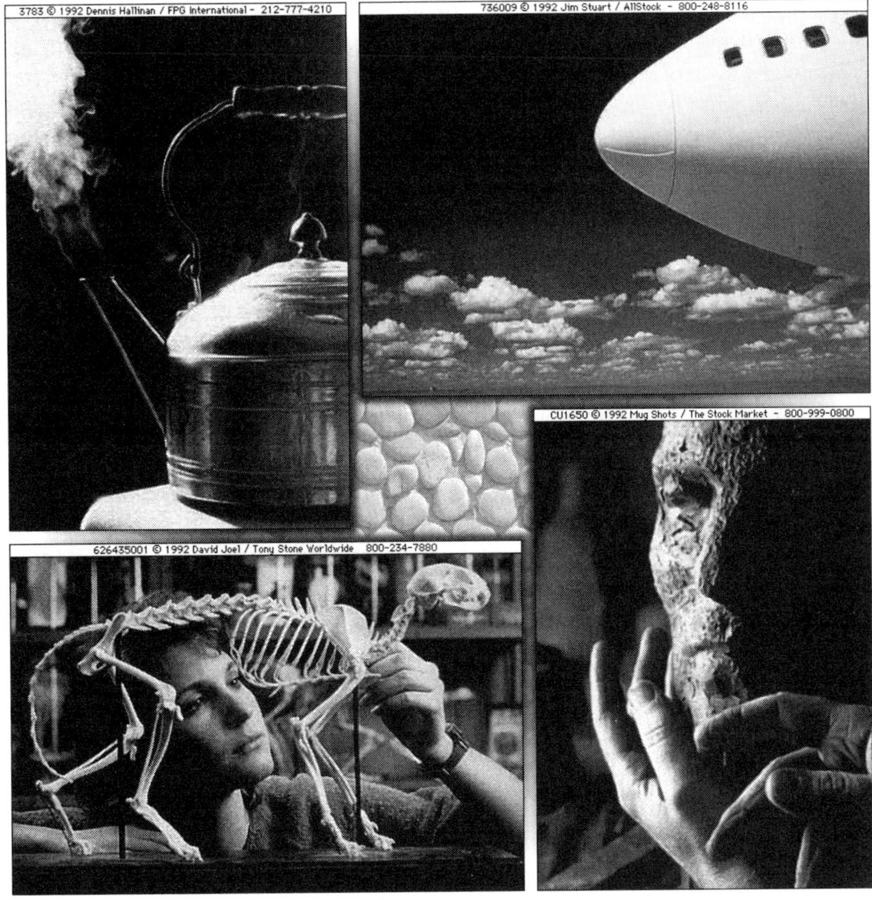

Figure 6-13: You pay $100 and up to license a CD Stock image, but the quality of the photography is in many cases a step up from the standard unlimited reproduction-rights fare.

Using On-Line Image Libraries

If you have a 9,600-baud or faster modem, you may want to consider downloading images from an on-line *bulletin-board service* (*BBS*). Popular BBSs, such as CompuServe and America Online, contain thousands of images scanned and uploaded by other users. (In case you aren't familiar with on-line lingo, to *upload* a file is to submit it to the BBS; to *download* a file is to copy it from the BBS.) However, consumer services are a crap shoot. At the risk of sounding repetitive, at least half of these images are pornographic and half of the others are of poor quality or questionable merit.

If you need a source of reliable and consistent on-line imagery, two professional services, Comstock and PressLink, are currently available to Macintosh users. Both companies charge startup fees (Comstock, $99; PressLink, $50) and per-image download fees. For this book, I tested out PressLink services.

Of all the image options available to professional users, PressLink is my favorite. A division of the Knight-Ridder news service, PressLink is an on-line bulletin board that contains news stories, information graphics (created in FreeHand for the most part), and historic and news photos. It functions primarily as a service for magazines and newspapers, but it plans to open its doors to designers sometime in 1994.

Several news services offer photos via PressLink, but the following are the best:

- **Reuters:** Along with Knight-Ridder, Reuters distributes a daily barrage of up-to-the-minute color news photos. Color Plate 6-8 shows examples from the Reuters library.
- **Bettmann:** The Bettmann Archive provides access to an amazing library of classic movie stills and historical grayscale images. Just about every memorable event from the civil war onward is represented in this unique collection. In Figure 6-14, you see two of Bettmann's icons from the 20th century.
- **Allsport:** As its name suggests, Allsport deals strictly in sports images, offering everything from action shots to sideline photos. As illustrated by Color Plate 6-9, much of the Allsport library goes beyond the usual ball-oriented team fare.
- **Agence France-Presse:** AFP is an international service that provides dramatic news photos. You might think of AFP as Reuters with a decidedly artistic slant. I was unable to secure the rights to publish AFP's photos, which is a shame because they represent some of PressLink's finest images.

In order to access images from a service such as Bettmann or Allsport, you must subscribe both to PressLink and to the specific service. (On its own, PressLink lets you download images from the U.S. Military service, in which case you can get all the Gulf War and humvee photos you want.) The fee structures for the services are as unique as they are complex. But to give you an idea, Reuters estimates that it charges a small weekly newspaper about $50 per month and $10 per photo. Large publications can expect to pay somewhere in the neighborhood of $100 per photo, which is quite a savings when compared with the prices charged by the stock agencies included in the 3M CD Stock collection.

To save time, the various PressLink services provide keyword search functions for locating thumbnail versions of their photos. After you download a handful of thumbnails, you can browse through them off-line using the PressLink Access utility, as demonstrated in Figure 6-15.

Each image includes a caption that explains the photo and lists the date it was taken. If a thumbnail appeals to you, you can add it to a TeachText report that lists the name of the file and its location on disk. Provided that you organize your thumbnails in folders named after the key words you used to find them, you can easily go back on-line and retrieve the full-resolution image.

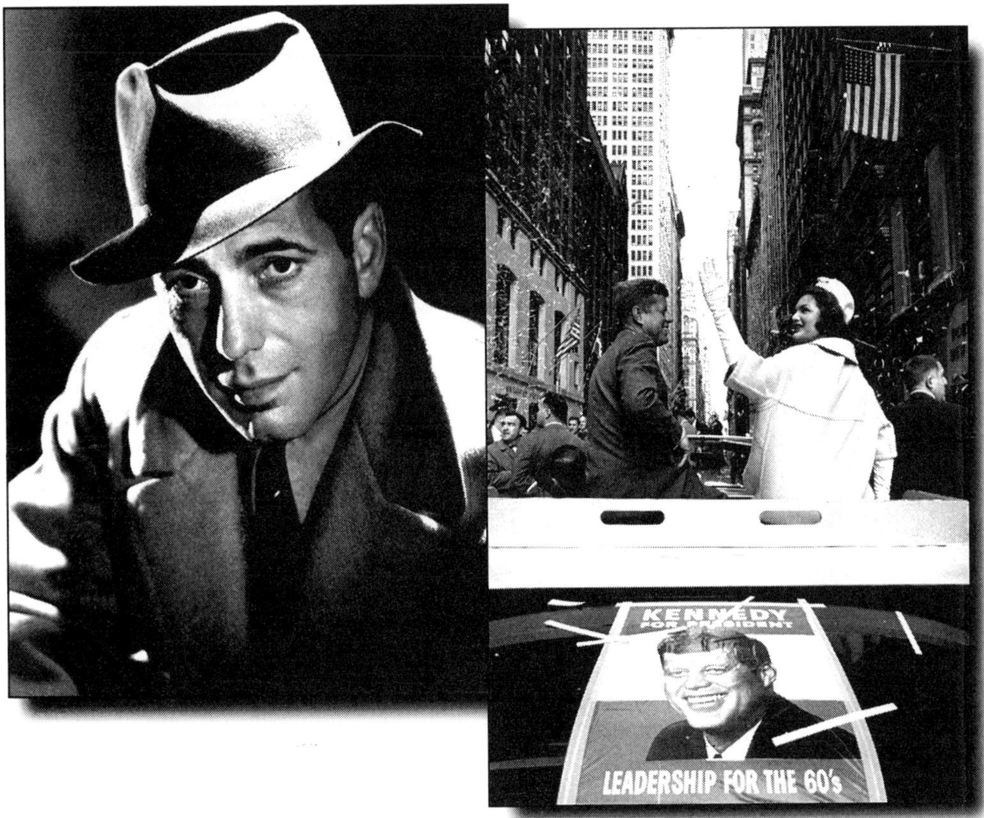

Figure 6-14: Bettmann serves up mesmerizing images of classic movie stills and historical photos.

One caveat: To shorten transmission time, all PressLink images are compressed using PicturePress or some other JPEG utility. Frequently, the compression is extensive enough that you can clearly see patterns in the image on-screen. As a result, the images are adequate for printing to newsprint, but may be unsuited to glossy magazine stock except at small sizes (¼ page and under).

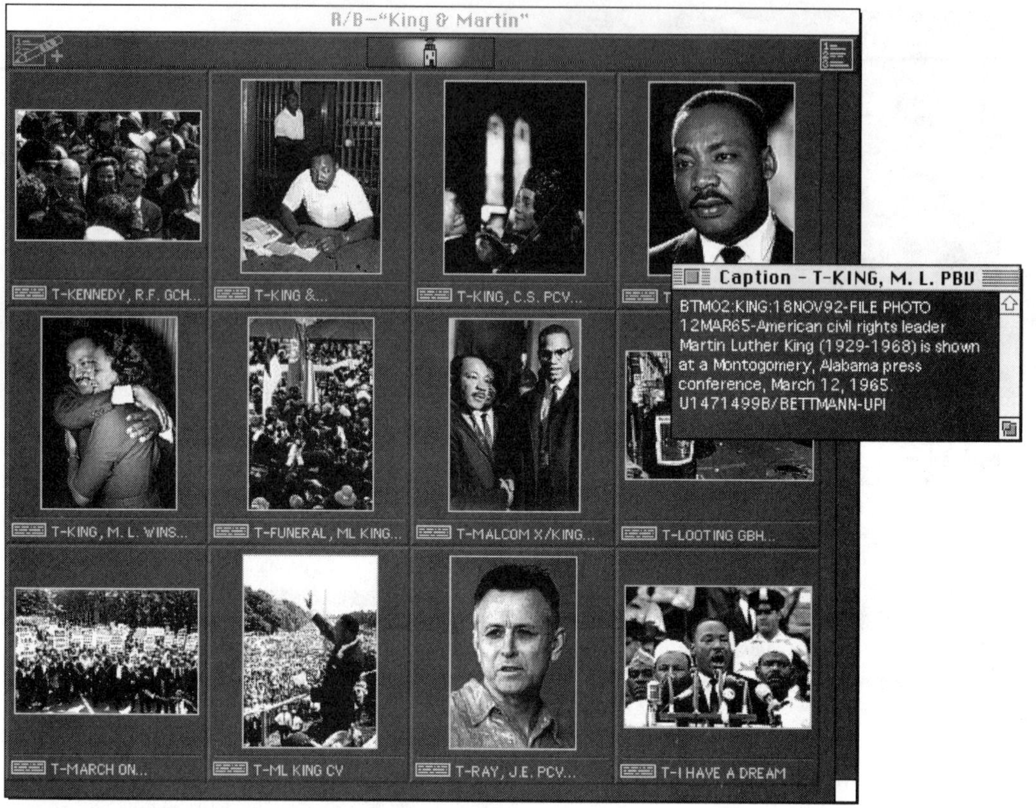

Figure 6-15: The thumbnail results of searching the Reuters and Bettmann services using the key words *King* and *Martin*.

Summary

- Grayscale scanners are adequate for casual users who plan to print primarily monochrome images or duotones, tritones, or quadtones.
- Monochrome, hand-held, and sheet-fed scanners are almost entirely unacceptable for scanning images for use in Photoshop.
- Nearly all scanners provide plug-in modules so that you can scan directly to a new image window inside Photoshop.
- TWAIN is a means for standardizing scanning from any device inside any Macintosh or Windows application. Currently, only one scanner supports TWAIN.
- Ofoto automatically calibrates a scan to match your printer model, automatically straightens and crops an image, and eliminates moiré patterns.
- If you capture a video image and every other row of pixels appears misaligned — like a badly-tuned television image — you can fix it by choosing Image ⇨ Video ⇨ De-interlace inside Photoshop.
- You can transfer 35mm slides, processed negatives, and undeveloped film to a Photo CD for about $1 per image.
- Any single-session CD-ROM drive lets you mount a Photo CD. Only multi-session drives can read all images on CDs that were written to more than once.
- FWB's CD-ROM Toolkit makes most older model CD-ROM drives Photo CD compatible.
- When you purchase a disk from a vendor that sells unlimited reproduction rights, such as PhotoDisc or ColorBytes, you can use the images as many times and in as many ways as you want. Stock photo agencies require you to license each photo independently.
- On-line photo services such as PressLink provide access to volumes of images for a per-image fee.

CHAPTER 7

Printing Images

In This Chapter

- A glossary of essential terms you need to know in order to communicate with a commercial printer
- How to print grayscale and color composites
- A complete guide to the Page Setup dialog box
- The theory behind halftone screens
- How to assign transfer functions to distribute brightness values
- A discussion of the color separation process
- How to apply color trapping
- How to convert a grayscale image into a duotone, tritone, or quadtone

Welcome to Printing

On one hand, printing can be a very straightforward topic. You choose the Print command, press the Return key, wait for something to come out of your printer, and admire yet another piece of forestry you've gone and destroyed. On the other hand, printing can be a ridiculously complicated subject, involving dot gain compensation, hardware calibration, under color removal, toxic processor chemicals, separation table generation, and so many infinitesimal color parameters that you're liable to spend half your life trying to figure out what's going on.

This chapter is about finding a middle ground. Although it is in no way intended to cover every possible facet of printing digitized images, it walks you through the process of preparing and printing the three major categories of output: composites, color separations, and duotones. By the end of the chapter, you'll be familiar with all of

Photoshop's printing options. You'll also be prepared to communicate with professionals at your service bureau or commercial printer, if need be, and to learn from their input and expertise.

Understanding Printing Terminology

I'm not a big believer in glossaries. Generally, they contain glib, jargony, out-of-context definitions that are about as helpful in gaining understanding of a concept as a seminar in which all the presenters speak in pig latin. But before I delve into the inner recesses of printing, I thought I should introduce, in a semilogical, sort of random order, a smattering of the printing terms you'll encounter. Oodgay ucklay:

- **Service bureau:** A service bureau is a shop filled with earnest young graphic artists (at least they were young and earnest when *I* worked there), printer operators, and about a billion dollars worth of hardware. A small service bureau is usually outfitted with a few laser printers, photocopiers, and self-service computers. Big service bureaus offer scanners, imagesetters, film recorders, and other varieties of professional-quality input and output equipment.
- **Commercial printer:** Generally speaking, a commercial printer takes up where the service bureau leaves off. Commercial printers reproduce black-and-white and color pages using offset presses, web presses, and a whole bunch of other age-old technology that I don't cover in this mini-glossary (or anywhere else in this book, for that matter). Suffice it to say, the process is less expensive than photocopying when you're dealing with large quantities — say, more than 100 copies — and it delivers professional-quality reproductions.
- **Output device:** This is just another way to say *printer.* Rather than writing *Print your image from the printer,* which sounds repetitive and a trifle obvious, I write *Print your image from the output device.* Output devices also include laser printers, imagesetters, film recorders, and a whole bunch of other machines I can't think of right at this moment.
- **Laser printer:** A laser printer works much like a photocopier. First, it applies an electric charge to a cylinder, called a *drum,* inside the printer. The charged areas, which correspond to the black portions of the image being printed, attract fine, petroleum-based dust particles called *toner.* The drum transfers the toner to the page and a heating mechanism fixes the toner in place. Most laser printers have resolutions of 300 dots (or *printer pixels*) per inch. A few offer higher resolutions, such as 600 and 1200 dots per inch (*dpi*).

- **Color printers:** Color printers fall into three categories: *ink-jet* and *thermal-wax* printers at the low end and *dye-sublimation* printers at the high end. Ink-jet printers deliver colored dots out of disposable ink cartridges. Thermal-wax printers apply wax-based pigments to a page in multiple passes. Both kinds of printers mix cyan, magenta, yellow, and, depending on the specific printer, black dots to produce full-color output. Generally speaking, these printers produce mediocre detail and acceptable, though not necessarily accurate, color. If you want photographic quality prints — the kind you'd be proud to hang on your wall — you must migrate up the price ladder to dye-sublimation printers. Dye-sub inks permeate the surface of the paper, literally dying it different colors. Furthermore, the cyan, magenta, yellow, and black pigments mix in varying opacities from one dot to the next, resulting in a continuous-tone image that appears nearly as smooth on the page as it does on-screen.
- **Imagesetter:** A typesetter that is equipped with a graphics page-description language such as PostScript is called an *imagesetter.* Unlike a laser printer, an imagesetter prints photosensitive paper or film by exposing the portions of the paper or film that correspond to the black areas of the image. The process is a lot like exposing film with a camera, but an imagesetter only knows two colors, black and white. The exposed paper or film collects in a light-proof canister. In a separate step, the printer operator develops the film in a *processor* that contains two chemical baths — developer and fixer — a water bath to wash away the chemicals, and a heat dryer to dry off the water. Developed paper looks like a typical glossy black-and-white page. Developed film is black where the image is white and transparent where the image is black. Imagesetters typically offer resolutions between 1200 and 2600 dpi. But the real beauty of imageset pages is that blacks are absolutely black (or transparent), as opposed to the deep, sometimes irregular gray you get with laser-printed pages.
- **Film recorder:** This device transfers images to full-color 35mm slides that are perfect for professional presentations. Slides also can be useful as a means for providing images to publications and commercial printers. Many publications can scan from slides, and commercial printers can use slides to create color separations. So if you're nervous that a color separation printed from Photoshop won't turn out well, ask your service bureau to output the image to a 35mm slide. Then have your commercial printer reproduce the image from the slide.
- **PostScript:** The PostScript page-description language was the first project developed by Adobe, the same folks who sell Photoshop, and is now a staple of hundreds brands of laser printers, imagesetters, and film recorders. A *page-description language* is a programming language for defining text and graphics on a page. PostScript specifies the locations of points, draws line segments between them, and fills in areas with solid blacks or *halftone cells* (dot patterns that simulate grays). PostScript Level 2, an updated version of the original PostScript,

speeds up output time and provides improved halftoning options, better color separations, automated antialiasing of jagged images, and direct support for Lab images (discussed in the "CIE's Lab" section of Chapter 14).

- **QuickDraw:** QuickDraw is a competing page-description language developed by Apple. It is the language that displays images on any Macintosh screen. It is also built into a few laser printers, including the LaserWriter SC. QuickDraw GX, a new version that may be available by the time you read this, will automate kerning and other typographic functions, provide better printer spooling, offer new graphics capabilities previously exclusive to PostScript, and integrate Apple's ColorSync color-matching technology to ensure smooth transitions from scanner to screen to printer.
- **Spooling:** Printer *spooling* allows you to work on an image while another image prints. Rather than communicating directly with the output device, Photoshop describes the image to the system software. Under System 7, this function is performed by a program called *PrintMonitor.* When Photoshop finishes describing the image — a relatively quick process — you are free to resume working while the system software prints the image in the background.
- **Calibration:** Traditionally, *calibrating* a system means to synchronize the machinery. However, in the context of Photoshop, it means to adjust or compensate for the color displays of the scanner, monitor, and printer so that what you scan is what you see on-screen, which in turn is what you get from the printer. Colors match from one device to the next. Empirically speaking, this is impossible; a yellow image in a photograph won't look exactly like the yellow on-screen or the yellow printed from a set of color separations. But calibrating is designed to make them look as much alike as possible, taking into account the fundamental differences in hardware technology. Expensive hardware calibration solutions seek to change the configuration of scanner, monitor, and printer. Less expensive software solutions, including those provided by Photoshop, manipulate the image to account for the differences between devices.
- **Brightness values/shades:** As described at length in Chapter 14, there is a fundamental difference between the way your screen and printer create gray values and colors. Your monitor shows colors by lightening up an otherwise black screen; the printed page shows colors by darkening an otherwise white piece of paper. Therefore, on-screen colors are measured in terms of *brightness values.* High values equate to light colors; low values equate to dark colors. On the printed page, colors are measured in percentage values called *shades,* or if you prefer, *tints.* High percentage values result in dark colors, and low percentage values result in light colors.
- **Composite:** A *composite* is a page that shows an image in its entirety. A black-and-white composite printed from a standard laser printer or imagesetter translates all colors in an image to gray values. A color composite printed from a

color printer or film recorder shows the colors as they actually appear. Composites are useful any time you want to proof an image or print a final grayscale image from an imagesetter, an overhead projection from a color printer, or a full-color image from a film recorder.

- **Proofing:** To *proof* an image is to see how it looks on paper in advance of the final printing. In professional circles, laser printers are considered proofing devices because they lack sufficient quality or resolution to output final images. Color printers are necessarily proofing devices because commercial printers can't reproduce from any color composite output except slides. (Well, they *can* reproduce from other kinds of color composites, but you don't get the same quality results.)
- **Color separations:** To output color reproductions, commercial printers require color separations (or slides, which they can convert to color separations for a fee). A color-separated image comprises four printouts, one each for the cyan, magenta, yellow, and black primary printing colors. The commercial printer transfers each printout to a *plate* that is used in the actual reproduction process.
- **Duotone:** A grayscale image in Photoshop can contain as many as 256 brightness values, from white on up to black. A printer can convey significantly fewer shades. A typical laser printer, for example, provides 26 shades at most. An imagesetter typically provides from 150 to 200 shades, depending on resolution and screen frequency. And that's assuming perfect printing conditions. You can count on at least 30 percent of those shades getting lost in the reproduction process. A *duotone* helps to retain the depth and clarity of detail in a grayscale image by printing with two inks. Suddenly, the number of shades available to you jumps from 150 to 22,000 (150^2). Photoshop also permits you to create *tritones* (three inks) and *quadtones* (four inks). Note, however, that using more inks translates to higher printing costs. Color Plate 7-1 shows a quadtone.

Printing Composites

Now that you've picked up a bit of printer's jargon, you're ready to learn how to put it all together. This section explores the labyrinth of options available for printing composite images. Later in this chapter, I cover color separations and duotones.

Like any Macintosh application, Photoshop can print composite images to just about any output device you hook up to your Mac. Assuming that your printer is turned on, properly attached, and in working order, printing a composite image from Photoshop is a five-step process, as outlined in the following steps.

STEPS: Printing a Composite Image

Step 1. Use the Chooser desk accessory to select the output device to which you want to print. Unless your computer is part of a network that includes multiple printers, you probably rely on a single output device, in which case you can skip this step.

Step 2. Choose File ⇨ Page Setup to specify the page size and the size and orientation of the image on the page. (You can also use Image ⇨ Image Size to control the size of the image by changing its resolution, as explained in the "Printed resolution" section of Chapter 5.)

Step 3. Click on the Screens button to change the size, angle, and shape of the halftone screen dots. This step is purely optional, useful mostly for creating special effects.

Step 4. Click on the Transfer button to map brightness values in an image to different shades when printed. This step is also optional, though frequently very useful.

Step 5. Choose File ⇨ Print (Command-P) to print the image according to your specifications.

The following sections describe each of these steps in detail.

Choosing a printer

To select a printer, choose the Chooser desk accessory from the list of desk accessories under the Apple menu. The Chooser dialog box appears, as shown in Figure 7-1. The dialog box is split into two halves, with the left half devoted to a scrolling list of printer driver icons and the right half to specific printer options.

Select the printer driver icon that matches your model of printer. *Printer drivers* help the Macintosh hardware, system software, and Photoshop translate the contents of an image to the printer hardware and the page-description language it uses. If you intend to use a PostScript-compatible printer, you'll generally want to select the LaserWriter driver (although some PostScript printers include drivers of their own). You even can prepare an image for output to a PostScript printer when no such printer is currently hooked up to your computer. For example, you can use this technique prior to submitting a document to be output on an imagesetter at a service bureau.

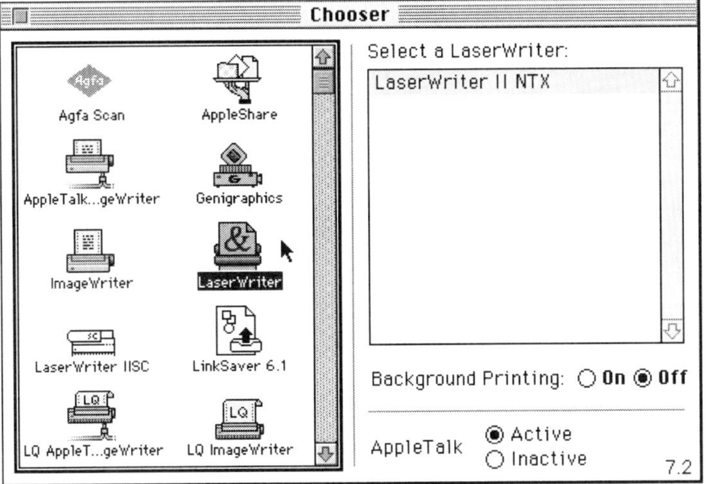

Figure 7-1: Use the Chooser desk accessory to select the desired output device.

If your computer is connected to one or more printers via AppleTalk or some other brand of network — as is required when printing to a PostScript device — select the name of the printer from the scrolling list on the right side of the dialog box. For example, in Figure 7-1, the printer name is *LaserWriter II NTX*.

If your printer does not require AppleTalk cabling, as is generally the case with ImageWriters, StyleWriters, and other low-end devices, the right-hand scrolling list contains two icons: one for the printer port, and the second for the modem port. Select the icon that corresponds to the serial port in the back of your Mac that connects to your printer.

Under System 7, many printer drivers provide a Background Printing option that lets you print an image in the background while you continue to work in Photoshop or some other application. If you read the preceding "Understanding Printing Terminology" section, you'll recognize this option from the *spooling* definition.

Spooling can interrupt foreground tasks and increase the likelihood of printing errors. I have found that Photoshop images are particularly prone to spooling problems. For example, a half inch across the middle of the image may print out of alignment with the rest of the image. For perfect image printing, turn off the Background Printing option.

When you finish selecting options in the Chooser dialog box, click on the close box in the upper left corner of the title bar to return to the Photoshop desktop.

Setting up the page

The next step is to define the relationship between the current image and the page on which it prints. Assuming that you're using a PostScript output device, choosing File ➪ Page Setup displays the LaserWriter Page Setup dialog box shown in Figure 7-2.

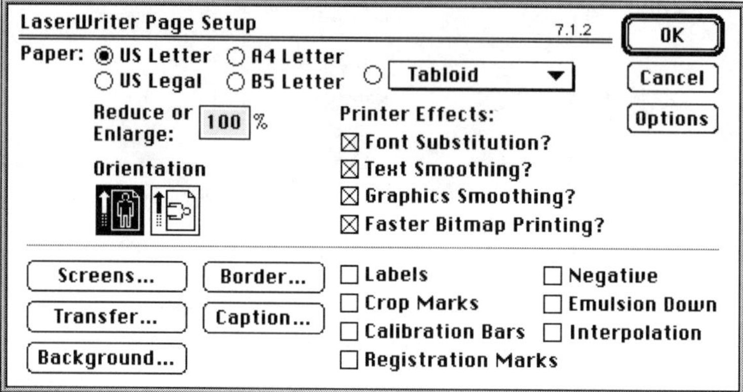

Figure 7-2: Use this dialog box to specify the relationship between the printed image and the page on which it appears.

This dialog box provides the following options:

- **Paper:** Select the Paper radio button that corresponds to the size of the paper loaded into your printer's paper tray. The paper size you select determines the *imageable area* of a page — that is, the amount of the page that Photoshop can use to print the current image. For example, the US Letter option calls for a page that measures 8.5 × 11 inches, but only 7.7 × 10.2 inches is imageable.

To slightly enlarge the imageable area of a page without changing paper sizes, click on the Options button to display the LaserWriter Options dialog box and select the Larger Print Area check box, as shown in Figure 7-3. For example, when you print to a letter-sized page, this option increases the size of the imageable area from 7.7 × 10.6 inches to 8.0 × 10.8 inches. The dotted line in the page preview on the left side of the dialog box enlarges slightly to demonstrate the option's effect.

- **Reduce or Enlarge:** Enter a percentage value into this option box to enlarge or reduce the size of the image when printed. For more information on this option, read the "Printing versus screen display" section of Chapter 5.
- **Orientation:** You can specify whether an image prints upright on a page (called the *portrait setting*) or on its side (called the *landscape setting*) by selecting the corresponding Orientation icon. The landscape setting is useful when an image is

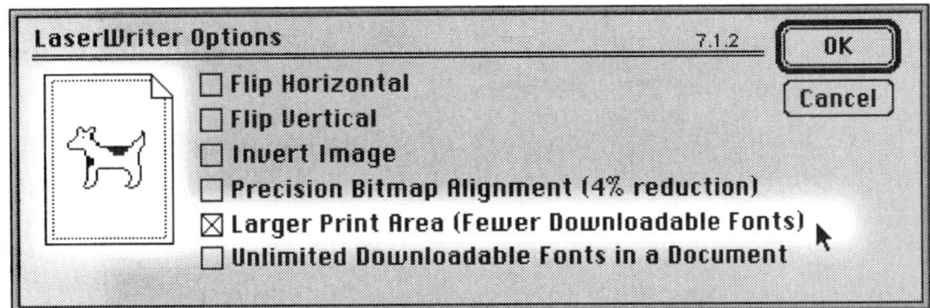

Figure 7-3: Select the Larger Print Area check box to enlarge the size of the imageable area of a page printed from a laser printer.

wider than it is tall. (In the Photoshop 2.5 manual, Adobe recommends that you rotate the image 90 degrees by choosing Image ⇨ Rotate ⇨ 90° CCW and print it at the portrait setting in order to save on printing time. I personally don't subscribe to this technique because rotating the image takes time, and you have to re-rotate it if you want to edit it again. But I suppose it's an option.)

After specifying the Reduce or Enlarge percentage and Orientation icon, you can check to see how the image fits on the page. To do so, press Return to exit the LaserWriter Page Setup dialog box and drag on the preview box in the lower left corner of the image window. The rectangle with the inset X that appears inside the pop-up window represents the image on the page. If the rectangle extends outside the page, you need to further reduce the image or change the page orientation.

- **Printer Effects:** All the Printer Effects check boxes are utterly and completely useless when you print from Photoshop. Select them, deselect them, wear a funny hat. It won't make any difference.

Nearly every Macintosh application offers the options described so far because they're a function of the Macintosh system software. However, it's a different story when you descend below the dotted line to the options at the bottom of the LaserWriter Page Setup dialog box. These options are specific to Photoshop. First I'll describe how to use the buttons on the left and then I'll explain the check boxes on the right.

- **Screens:** Click on this button to enter a dialog box that allows you to change the size, angle, and shape of the printed halftone cells, as described in the upcoming "Changing the halftone screen" section.
- **Transfer:** The dialog box that appears when you click on this button allows you to redistribute shades in the printed image, as explained in the upcoming "Specifying a transfer function" section.
- **Background:** To assign a color to the area around the printed image, click on this button and select a color from the Color Picker dialog box, which is described in the "Using the Color Picker" section of Chapter 14. This button and the one that follows (Border) are designed specifically for use when printing slides from a film recorder.

- **Border:** To print a border around the current image, click on this button and enter the thickness of the border into the Width option box. The border automatically appears in black.
- **Caption:** To print a caption beneath the image, click on this button and enter the text into the Caption dialog box. The text prints in 9-point Helvetica whether you like it or not. Except for annotating a printed image, this option is utterly useless.

Now for the check boxes on the bottom right side of the dialog box. Except for Labels and Interpolation, the check boxes are of use only to imagesetter operators and commercial printers. But just for the record, the options work as follows:

- **Labels:** When you select this check box, Photoshop prints the name of the image and the name of the printed color channel in 9-point Helvetica. If you process lots of images, you'll find this option extremely useful for associating printouts with documents on disk.
- **Crop Marks:** Select this option to print eight hairline *crop marks,* which indicate how to trim the image in case you anticipate engaging in a little traditional paste-up work. Two crop marks appear at each of the image's four corners.
- **Calibration Bars:** A calibration bar is a 10-step grayscale gradation that starts at 10 percent black and ends at 100 percent black. The function of the calibration bar is to ensure that all shades are distinct and on target. If not, the output device isn't properly calibrated, which is a fancy way of saying that the printer's colors are out of whack and need realignment by a trained professional armed with a hammer and hacksaw. When you print color separations, the Calibration Bars check box instructs Photoshop to print a gradient tint bar and progressive color bar, also useful to printing professionals.
- **Registration Marks:** Select this option to print eight crosshairs and two star targets near the four corners of the image. Registration marks are absolutely imperative when you print color separations, because they provide the only reliable means for ensuring exact registration of the cyan, magenta, yellow, and black printing plates. When printing a composite image, however, you can ignore this option.
- **Negative:** When you select this option, Photoshop prints all blacks as white and all whites as black. In-between colors switch accordingly. For example, 20 percent black becomes 80 percent black. Imagesetter operators use this option to print composites and color separations to film negative.
- **Emulsion Down:** The *emulsion* is the side of a piece of film on which an image is printed. When the Emulsion Down check box is turned off, film prints from an imagesetter emulsion side up; when the check box is turned on, Photoshop flips the image so that the emulsion side is down. Like the Negative option, this option is useful only when you print film from an imagesetter and should be set in accordance with the preferences of your commercial printer.
- **Interpolation:** If you own an output device equipped with PostScript Level 2, you can instruct Photoshop to antialias the printed appearance of a low-resolution

image by selecting this option. The output device samples the image up to 200 percent and then reduces it to its original size using bicubic interpolation (as described in the "General environmental preferences" section of Chapter 4), thereby creating a less jagged image. This option has no effect on older-model PostScript devices.

Changing the halftone screen

Before I go any farther, let me explain a bit more about how printing works. To keep costs down, commercial printers use as few inks as possible to create the appearance of a wide variety of colors. Suppose you want to print an image of a pink flamingo wearing a red bow tie. Your commercial printer could print the flamingos in one pass using pink ink, let that color dry, and then load the red ink and print all the bow ties. But why go to all that trouble? After all, pink is just a lighter shade of red. Why not imitate the pink by lightening the red ink?

Well, unfortunately, with the exception of dye-sublimation printers, output devices can't print lighter shades of colors. They recognize only solid ink and the absence of ink. So how do you print the lighter shade of red necessary to represent pink?

The answer is *halftoning*. The output device organizes printer pixels into spots called *halftone cells*. Because the cells are so small, your eyes cannot quite focus on them. Instead, the cells appear to blend with the white background of the page to create a lighter shade of an ink. Figure 7-4 shows a detail of an image enlarged to display the individual halftone cells.

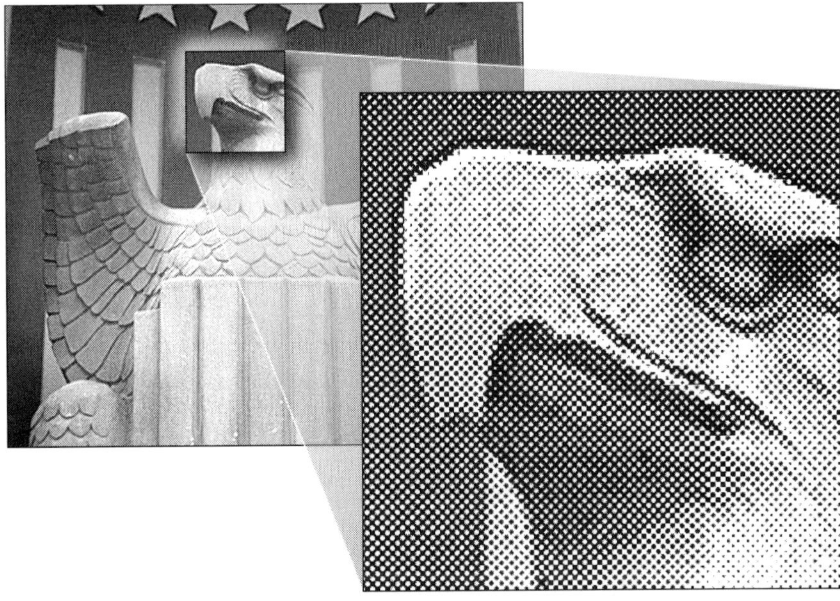

Figure 7-4: A detail from an image (left) enlarged so you can see the individual halftone cells (right).

The cells grow and shrink to emulate different shades of color. Large cells result in dark shades; small cells result in light shades. Cell size is measured in printer pixels. The maximum size of any cell is a function of the number of cells in an inch, called the *screen frequency.*

For example, the default frequency of the Apple LaserWriter is 60 halftone cells per linear inch. Because the resolution of the LaserWriter is 300 printer pixels per linear inch, each halftone cell must measure 5 pixels wide by 5 pixels tall (300 ÷ 60 = 5), for a total of 25 pixels per cell (5^2). When all pixels in a cell are turned off, the cell appears white; when all pixels are turned on, you get solid ink. By turning on different numbers of pixels — from 0 up to 25 — the printer can create a total of 26 shades, as demonstrated in Figure 7-5.

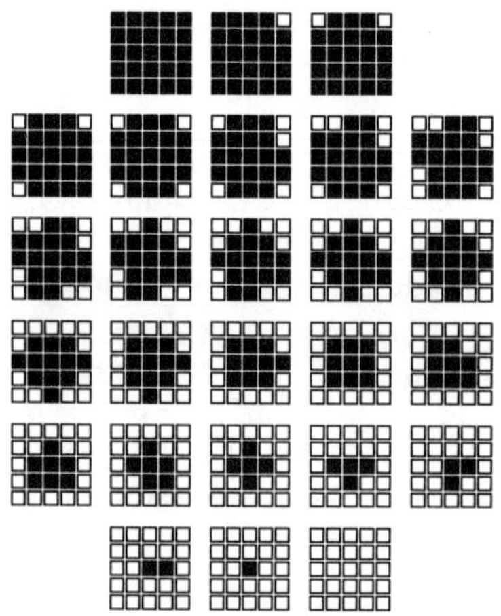

Figure 7-5: 5 × 5-pixel halftone cells with different numbers of pixels activated, ranging from 25 (top left) to 0 (bottom right). Each cell represents a unique shade from 100 to 0 percent black.

Photoshop lets you change the size, angle, and shape of the individual *halftone cells* used to represent an image on the printed page. To do so, click on the Screens button in the LaserWriter Page Setup dialog box. The Halftone Screens dialog box shown in Figure 7-6 appears. (In Photoshop 2.0, the format of the dialog box is different, but the functions are the same.)

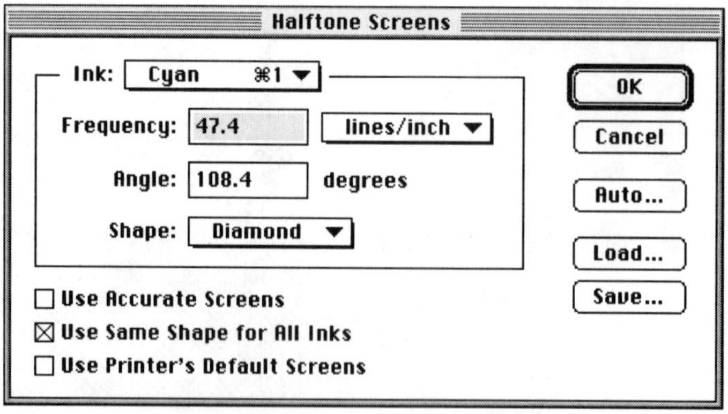

Figure 7-6: Use the Halftone Screens dialog box to edit the size, angle, and shape of the halftone cells for any one ink.

In the dialog box, you can manipulate the following options:

- **Ink:** If the current image is in color, you can select the specific ink that you want to adjust from the Ink pop-up menu. When you work with a grayscale image, no pop-up menu is available.
- **Frequency:** Enter a new value into this option box to change the number of halftone cells that print per linear inch. A higher value translates to a larger quantity of smaller cells; a smaller value creates fewer, larger cells. Frequency is traditionally measured in *lines per inch,* or *lpi* (as in lines of halftone cells), but you can change the measurement to lines per centimeter by selecting Lines/cm from the pop-up menu to the right of the option box.

Higher screen frequencies result in smoother-looking printouts. However, raising the Frequency value also decreases the number of shades an output device can print because it decreases the size of each halftone cell and likewise decreases the number of printer pixels per cell. Fewer printer pixels means fewer shades. You can calculate the precise number of printable shades using the following formula:

$$\text{Number of shades} = (\text{printer resolution} \div \text{frequency})^2 + 1$$

- **Angle:** To change the orientation of the lines of halftone cells, enter a new value into the Angle option box. In the name of accuracy, Photoshop accepts any value between negative and positive 180.0000 degrees.

When printing color composites to ink-jet and thermal-wax printers and when printing color separations, Photoshop calculates the optimum Frequency and Angle values required to print seamless colors. In such a case, you should change these values only if you know *exactly* what you're doing. Otherwise, your printout may exhibit moiré patterns, as defined in the "Moiré patterns" section of Chapter 5. When printing grayscale images, however, you can edit these values to your heart's content.

- **Shape:** By default, most PostScript printers rely on roundish halftone cells. You can change the appearance of all cells for an ink by selecting one of six alternate shapes from the Shape pop-up menu. (For a demonstration of four of these shapes, see Figure 14-12 in the "Black and white (bitmap)" section of Chapter 14.) If you know how to write PostScript code, you can select the Custom option to display a text-entry dialog box and code away.
- **Use Accurate Screens:** If your output device is equipped with PostScript Level 2, select this option to subscribe to the updated screen angles for full-color output. Otherwise, don't worry about this option.
- **Use Same Shape for All Inks:** Select this option if you want to apply a single shape option to the halftone cells for all inks used to represent the current image. The option is not available when you are printing a grayscale image.

- **Use Printer's Default Screens:** Select this check box to accept the default size, angle, and shape settings built into your printer's ROM. All other options in the Halftone Screens dialog box automatically become dimmed to show they are no longer in force.
- **Auto:** Click on this button to display the Auto Screens dialog box shown in Figure 7-7, which automates the halftone editing process. Enter the resolution of your output device in the Printer option box. Then enter the screen frequency you would like to use in the Screen option box. After you press the Return key to confirm your change, Photoshop automatically calculates the optimum screen frequencies for all inks. This technique is especially useful when you print full-color images; because Photoshop does the work for you, you can't make a mess of things.

Auto Screens

Printer: 2400 dots/inch OK

Screen: 133 lines/inch Cancel

Use Accurate Screens

Figure 7-7: To automate the halftone editing process, enter the resolution of the output device and the screen frequency you want to use into the Auto Screens dialog box.

- **Load/Save:** You can load and save settings to disk in case you want to reapply the options to other images. These buttons are especially useful if you find a magic combination of halftone settings that results in a really spectacular printout.

You can change the default size, angle, and shape settings that Photoshop applies to all future images by Option-clicking on the Save button. When you press Option, the Save button changes to read → *Default.* To restore the default screen settings at any time, Option-click on the Load button (← *Default*).

Specifying a transfer function

A *transfer function* enables you to change the way brightness values on-screen translate — or *map* — to printed shades. By default, brightness values print to their nearest shade percentages. A 30 percent gray on-screen pixel (which equates to a brightness value of roughly 180) prints as a 30 percent gray value.

Problems arise, however, when your output device prints lighter or darker than it should. For example, in the course of using my LaserWriter NTX over the last three years or so, I've discovered that all gray values print overly dark. Dark values fill in and become black; light values appear a dismal gray, muddying up any highlights. The problem increases if I try to reproduce the image on a photocopier.

To compensate for this over-darkening effect, I click on the Transfer button in the LaserWriter Page Setup dialog box and enter the values shown in Figure 7-8. Notice that I lighten 30 percent on-screen grays to 10 percent printer grays. I also lighten 90 percent screen grays to 80 percent printer grays. The result is a smooth, continuous curve that maps each gray value in an image to a lighter value on paper.

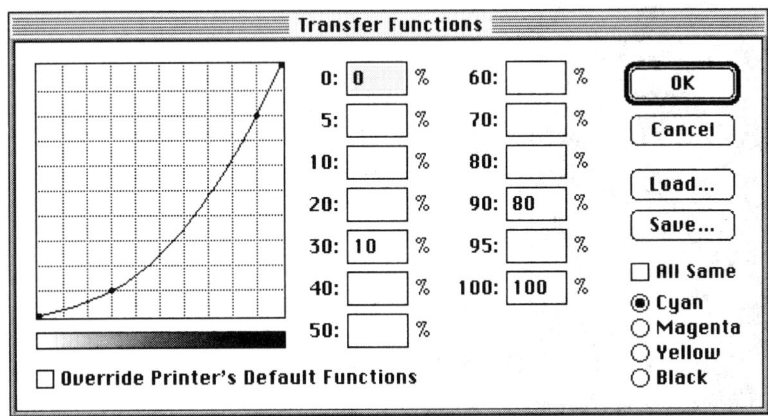

Figure 7-8: The transfer function curve lets you map on-screen brightness values to specific shades on paper.

The options in the Transfer Functions dialog box work as follows:

- **Transfer graph:** The *transfer graph* is where you map on-screen brightness values to their printed equivalents. The horizontal axis of the graph represents on-screen brightness values; the vertical axis represents printed shades. The *transfer curve* charts the relationship between on-screen and printed colors. The lower left corner is the origin of the graph — the point at which both on-screen brightness value and printed shade are white. Move to the right in the graph for darker on-screen values; move up for darker printed shades. Click in the graph to add points to the line. Drag up on a point to darken the output; drag down to lighten the output.

For a more comprehensive explanation of how to graph colors on a curve, read "The Curves command" section of Chapter 16.

- **Percentage option boxes:** The option boxes are labeled according to the on-screen brightness values. To lighten or darken the printed brightness values, enter higher or lower percentage values in the option boxes. Note that there is a direct correlation between changes made to the transfer graph and the option boxes. For example, if you enter a value in the 50 percent option box, a new point appears along the middle line of the graph.
- **Override Printer's Default Functions:** As an effect of printer calibration, some printers have custom transfer functions built into their ROM. If you have problems making your settings take effect, select this check box to instruct Photoshop to apply the transfer function you specify regardless of the output device's built-in transfer function.
- **Load/Save:** Use these buttons to load and save settings to disk. Option-click on the buttons to retrieve and save default settings.
- **Ink controls:** When you print a full-color image, five options appear in the lower right corner of the Transfer Functions dialog box. These options enable you to apply different transfer functions to different inks. Select the All Same check box to apply a single transfer function to all inks. To apply a different function to each ink, select one of the radio buttons and edit the points in the transfer graph as desired.

Printing pages

When you finish slogging your way through the mind-numbingly extensive Page Setup options, you can initiate the printing process by choosing File ⇨ Print (Command-P). The LaserWriter dialog box or its equivalent appears, as shown in Figure 7-9.

Most of the options of this dialog box are a function of the Macintosh system software, but a few at the bottom of the dialog box are exclusive to Photoshop. The options work as follows:

- **Copies:** Enter the number of copies you want to print in this option box. You can print up to 999 copies of a single image, although why you would want to do so is beyond me.

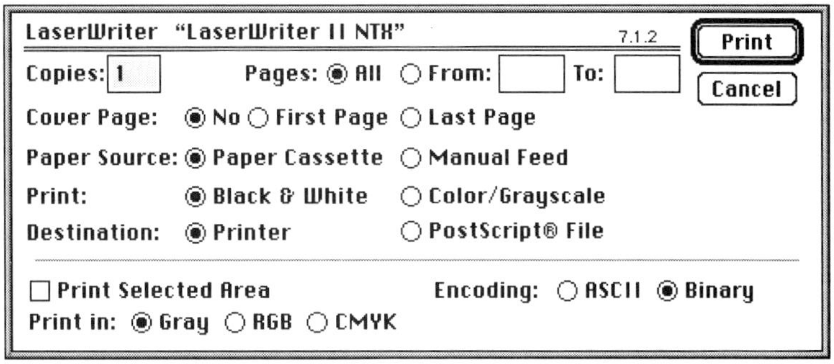

Figure 7-9: Use these options to specify how you want to print the current image to an output device.

LaserWriter "LaserWriter II NTX" 7.1.2 Print
Copies: 1 Pages: All From: To: Cancel
Cover Page: No First Page Last Page
Paper Source: Paper Cassette Manual Feed
Print: Black & White Color/Grayscale
Destination: Printer PostScript® File
Print Selected Area Encoding: ASCII Binary
Print in: Gray RGB CMYK

- **Pages:** There is no such thing as a multi-page document in Photoshop, so you can ignore the All, From, and To options.
- **Cover Page:** This option allows you to print an extra page that lists the user name, application, document name, date, time, and printer for the current image. What an obscene waste of paper! Leave this option alone, you would-be tree killer.
- **Paper Source:** If you want to feed special sheets of paper — such as letterheads — into your printer manually, one piece at a time, select the Manual Feed radio button. Your laser printer displays a manual feed light directing you to insert the special paper when it is ready to print. The Paper Source options are ignored when you print to a color printer, imagesetter, film recorder, or any other device that requires special paper or film.
- **Print:** Here's another option you can and should ignore. Photoshop is capable of printing both grayscale and color composites without the assistance of the system software. Furthermore, it accomplishes the task more quickly and more expertly than the system. Leave this option set to Black & White unless you want the system's assistance.
- **Destination:** If you use System 7, the dialog box includes two Destination radio buttons. Select the Printer option to print the image to an output device as usual. Select PostScript File to write a PostScript-language version of the image to disk. Because Photoshop offers its own EPS options via the Save dialog box, you'll probably want to ignore this option.
- **Print Selected Area:** Select this option to print the portion of an image that is selected with the rectangular marquee tool. You can use this option to divide an image into pieces when it's too large to fit on a single page.
- **Print In:** Select one of these radio buttons to specify the type of composite image Photoshop prints. Select the first radio button to print the image as a grayscale composite. Select the second radio button to let the printer translate the colors from the current color mode to CMYK. Select the third radio button to instruct

Photoshop to convert the image to CMYK colors during the print process. These options are not available when you print a grayscale image.

Relying on the output device to translate colors can result in printing errors, thanks to the low memory capabilities of most printers. If an image refuses to print, try selecting either the Gray or CMYK radio button. Use the first option when you print to black-and-white devices such as laser printers and imagesetters; use the last option when printing to color printers and film recorders.

- **Encoding:** If your network doesn't support binary encoding, select the ASCII option to transfer data in the text-only format. The printing process takes much longer to complete, but at least it's possible.

Press Return to start the printing process on its merry way. To cancel a print in progress, click on the Cancel button or press Command-period. If Photoshop ignores you, keep pressing away on those keys. I never have figured out if it does any good, but at least you feel like you're doing everything you can.

Creating Color Separations

If printing a composite image is moderately complicated, printing color separations is a terrific pain in the behind. Printer manufacturers and software developers are working to simplify this process, but for the present, Photoshop requires you to stagger through a maze of variables and obtuse options. I wish I could offer some conciliatory advice like "Hang in there and you'll make it," but every day that I work with Photoshop's color separation capabilities adds to my conviction that this is an unnecessarily complicated process, designed by people who are nearly as confused as we are.

On that cheery note, the upcoming steps explain how to muddle your way through the color-separation process. You'll recognize many of the steps from the process described for printing a grayscale or color composite.

If you're a prepress professional or computer artist looking for a means to enhance the printing process, you owe it to yourself to check out two substantial products, EFI's Cachet and Light Source's Ofoto. Cachet is capable of adjusting the colors in an image in keeping with a proven reference image that you know prints with superb color definition. Ofoto provides automatic calibration capabilities that match scanner, monitor, and printer at any stage in the image-editing process. Both programs simplify the color-separation process and offer a wealth of capabilities thus far missing from Photoshop.

STEPS: Printing CMYK Color Separations

Step 1. If your computer is part of a network that includes many printers, use the Chooser desk accessory to select the printer to which you want to print, as described previously in the "Choosing a printer" section.

Step 2. Calibrate your system to the specific requirements of your monitor and the selected printer using File ⇨ Preferences ⇨ Monitor Setup and File ⇨ Preferences ⇨ Printing Inks Setup. You only need to complete this step once for each time you switch hardware. If you always use the same monitor and printer combination, you need to repeat this step very rarely, say once every six months, to account for screen and printer degradation.

Step 3. Use File ⇨ Preferences ⇨ Separation Setup to control how Photoshop converts RGB and Lab colors to CMYK color space. Again, you need to perform this step only when you want to compensate for a difference in the output device or if you simply want to fine-tune Photoshop to create better separations.

Step 4. Choose Mode ⇨ CMYK Color to convert the image from its present color mode to CMYK. The CMYK mode is explained in the "CMYK" section of Chapter 14.

Step 5. Switching color modes can dramatically affect the colors in an image. To compensate for color and focus loss, you can edit the individual color channels as described in the "Editing Color Channels" section of Chapter 17.

Step 6. If your image features many high-contrast elements and you're concerned that your printer might not do the best job of registering the cyan, magenta, yellow, and black color plates, you can apply Image ⇨ Trap to prevent your final printout from looking like the color funnies.

Step 7. Choose File ⇨ Page Setup to specify the size of the pages and the size and orientation of the image on the pages, as described earlier in this chapter. Also select the Registration Marks option.

Step 8. Click on the Screens button to change the size, angle, and shape of the halftone screen dots for the individual color plates, as described earlier in the "Changing the halftone screen" section. This step and Step 9 are optional.

Step 9. Click on the Transfer button to map brightness values in each of the CMYK color channels to different shades on the printed plates, as described in the "Specifying a transfer function" section earlier in this chapter.

Step 10. Choose File ⇨ Print (Command-P) and select the Print Separations check box in the lower left corner of the dialog box. Photoshop then prints the color separations according to your specifications.

Steps 1 and 7 through 10 are repeats of concepts explained in earlier sections of this chapter. To fully understand Steps 4 and 5, read the larger color theory discussions contained in the chapters in Part V, "The Wonderful World of Color." That leaves Steps 2, 3, and 6, which I describe in detail in the following sections.

You also can create color separations by importing an image into a desktop publishing program like QuarkXPress. To do so, export the image in the DCS format, as described in the "QuarkXPress DCS" section of Chapter 5. Then print the separations directly from the desktop publishing program. Because DCS is a subset of the EPS format, it enables you to save halftone screen and transfer function settings.

Monitor calibration

Choose File ⇨ Preferences ⇨ Monitor to display the Monitor Setup dialog box shown in Figure 7-10. Along with the Gamma control panel, which offers the added capability of adjusting specific red, green, and blue color intensities, this dialog box represents the extent of Photoshop's monitor calibration capabilities. However, unlike Gamma, the Monitor Setup dialog box provides options that directly affect the conversion of scanned colors to their CMYK equivalents. These options advise Photoshop that certain on-screen color distortions are in effect and instruct the program to make accommodations when converting between the RGB and CMYK color modes.

The options in the Monitor Setup dialog box work as follows:

- **Monitor:** In the best of all possible worlds, you can select your exact model of monitor from this pop-up menu. Photoshop automatically changes the settings in the Monitor Parameters box — Gamma, White Point, and Phosphors — in accordance with the recommendations of the monitor's manufacturer. If you can't find your exact model, look for a model that is made by the same manufacturer and whose *only* difference from your model is screen size. If you can't find a suitable model, select the Other option.

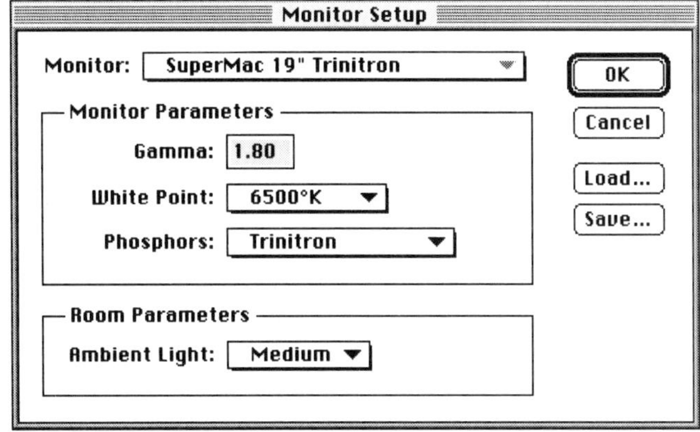

Figure 7-10: The options in the Monitor Setup dialog box tell Photoshop how to compensate for on-screen colors when preparing color separations.

Do *not* assume that all monitors from the same vendor are basically alike. Most vendors sell screens manufactured by different companies. For example, the SuperMac 19-inch Trinitron is manufactured by Sony, while the SuperMac 19-inch Color may come from Hitachi or Ikegami. More importantly, the two screens use different technology (Trinitron versus shadow-masked tridot). Do not select a monitor other than the one you use unless the only difference in the name is screen size.

- **Gamma:** This value represents the brightness of medium colors on-screen. Low values down to 0.75 darken the image to compensate for an overly light screen; high values up to 3.00 lighten the image to compensate for an overly dark screen. Generally speaking, 1.8 is the ideal value for Macintosh RGB screens. When you use an NTSC television monitor — as when editing video images using TrueVision's NuVista+ or RasterOps' ProVideo32 — set Gamma to 2.2.
- **White Point:** This value represents the temperature of the lightest color your screen can produce. Measured on the Kelvin temperature scale, it refers to the heat at which a so-called "black body" would turn to white. So theoretically, if you took the Maltese Falcon and heated it to 6,500 degrees Kelvin, it would turn white (if it didn't catch on fire first). The only way to achieve the correct value for this option is to consult the technical support department for your make of monitor or use a hardware testing device, such as Minolta's $10,000 Minolta CRT Color Analyzer CA-100.
- **Phosphors:** This pop-up menu lets you select the kind of screen used in your monitor. About half the monitors used with Macintosh computers — including all monitors sold by Apple — use Trinitron screens. (You can recognize Trinitron screens by the fact that they bow slightly outward horizontally but are flat vertically.) Select the NTSC option if you are using a television monitor. Otherwise, consult your vendor's technical support department.

- **Ambient Light:** Select the amount of light in your office or studio from this pop-up menu. In a dark room, Photoshop slightly darkens the image. In a light room, Photoshop lightens it so that you can see it clearly despite the ambient light.

When you finish setting the options, press Return to close the dialog box. Photoshop takes a few moments to adjust the display of the image on-screen.

Printer calibration

To prepare an image that is to be reproduced on a commercial offset or web press, choose File ⇨ Preferences ⇨ Printing Inks Setup to display the Printing Inks Setup dialog box shown in Figure 7-11.

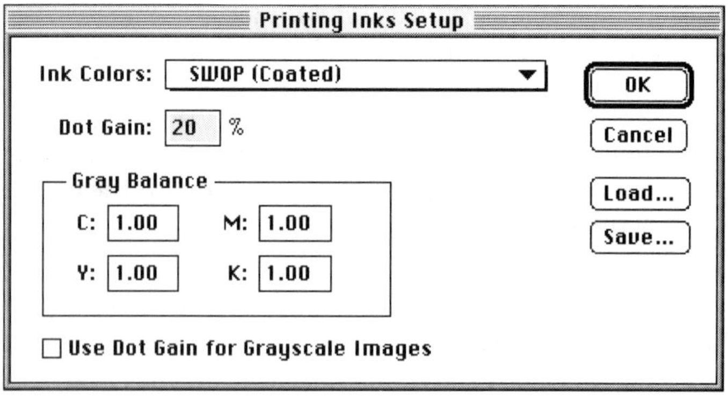

Figure 7-11: Use the options in the Printing Inks Setup dialog box to prepare an image for printing on a commercial offset or web press.

Like the Monitor Setup options, these settings are very technical and can be properly set only with the assistance of your commercial printer. But just so you have an inkling about inks, here's how the options work:

- **Ink Colors:** Select the specific variety of inks and paper stock that will be used to reproduce the current image. (Consult your commercial printer for this information.) Photoshop automatically changes the settings of the Dot Gain and Gray Balance options to the most suitable values.
- **Dot Gain:** Enter any value from – 10 to 40 percent to specify the amount by which you can expect halftone cells to shrink or expand during the printing process, a variable known as *dot gain.* When printing to newsprint, for example, you can expect halftone cells to bleed into the page and expand by about 30 percent. When you convert to the CMYK color mode, Photoshop automatically adjusts the brightness of colors to compensate for the dot gain.

- **Gray Balance:** Assuming that the inks are up to snuff, equal amounts of cyan, magenta, yellow, and black ink should produce gray. But inks can fade and become impure over time. To compensate for this, you can vary the amount of ink that mixes to produce medium gray by entering values from 0.50 to 2.00 in the Gray Balance option boxes. Think of it as a recipe — 0.75 parts cyan mixed with 1.50 parts magenta and so on. Again, consult with your commercial printer before changing these values.
- **Use Dot Gain for Grayscale Images:** When this option is turned off, the Dot Gain value only affects the creation and editing of CMYK images. If you select this check box, however, you also can apply the value to grayscale images. Then, any time you select a gray value, Photoshop automatically treats it as if it were lighter or darker depending on whether the Dot Gain value is negative or positive respectively.

In Photoshop 2.5, the Use Dot Gain for Grayscale Images check box is turned on by default, which I find highly confusing. Rather than getting 50 percent gray when you select 50 percent gray, for example, you might get 58 percent gray. This can cause problems when you want to create displacement maps, create precise gradations, or simply achieve exact brightness values. I strongly recommend that you turn this check box off unless you have some specific reason for turning it on.

How to prepare CMYK conversions

Now that you've told Photoshop how to compensate for the foibles of your screen and commercial printer, you need to explain what kind of separation process you intend to use. To do this, choose File ⇨ Preferences ⇨ Separation Setup to display the Separation Setup dialog box, shown in Figure 7-12. Unlike the options in the Printing Inks Setup dialog box, which describe the specific press belonging to your commercial printer, these options describe a general printing process. Even so, you'll probably find it helpful to consult with your commercial printer before changing the settings.

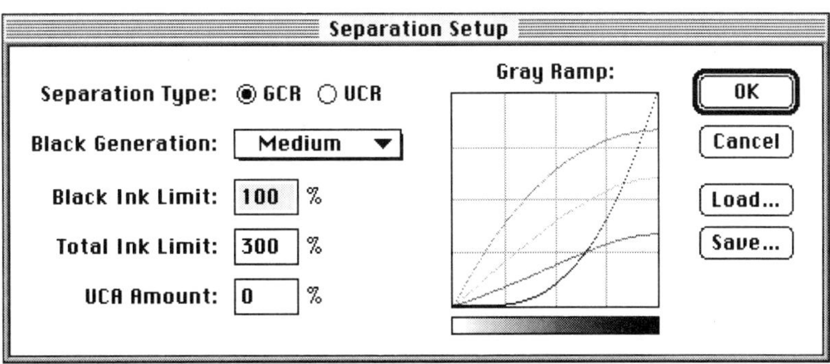

Figure 7-12: Describe the printing process using the options inside the Separation Setup dialog box.

The options in the Separation Setup dialog box work as follows:

- **Separation Type:** When the densities of cyan, magenta, and yellow inks reach a certain level, they mix to form a muddy brown. The GCR (*gray component replacement*) option avoids this unpleasant effect by overprinting these colors with black to the extent specified with the Black Generation option. If you select the UCR (*under color removal*) option, Photoshop removes cyan, magenta, and yellow inks where they overlap black ink. Generally speaking, GCR is the setting of choice except when you're printing on newsprint.
- **Black Generation:** Available only when the GCR option is active, the Black Generation pop-up menu lets you specify how dark the cyan, magenta, and yellow concentrations have to be before Photoshop adds black ink. Select Light to use black ink sparingly and Heavy to apply it liberally. The None option prints no black ink whatsoever, while the Maximum option prints black ink over everything. You may want to use the UCA Amount option to restore cyan, magenta, and yellow ink if you select the Heavy or Maximum option.
- **Black Ink Limit:** Enter the maximum amount of black ink that can be applied to the page. By default, this value is 100 percent, which is solid ink coverage. If you raise the UCA Amount value, you'll probably want to lower this value by a similar percentage to prevent the image from over-darkening.
- **Total Ink Limit:** This value represents the maximum amount of all four inks permitted on the page. For example, assuming that you use the default Black Ink Limit and Total Ink Limit values shown in Figure 7-12, the darkest printable color contains 100 percent black ink. Therefore, the sum total of cyan, magenta, and yellow inks is 200 percent. (You subtract the Black Ink Limit value from the Total Ink Limit value to get the sum total of the three other inks.)
- **UCA Amount:** The opposite of UCR, UCA stands for *under color addition,* which lets you add cyan, magenta, and yellow inks to areas where the concentration of black ink is highest. For example, a value of 20 percent raises the amount of cyan, magenta, and yellow inks applied with black concentrations between 80 and 100 percent. This option is dimmed when the UCR radio button is active.

The Gray Ramp graph demonstrates the effects of your changes to any option in the Separation Setup dialog box. Four lines, one in each color, represent the four inks. Though you can't edit the lines in this graph by clicking and dragging on them, as you can in the Transfer Functions dialog box, you can observe the lines to gauge the results of your settings.

Color trapping

If color separations misalign slightly during the reproduction process (a problem called *misregistration*), the final image can exhibit slight gaps between colors. Suppose an image features a 100 percent cyan chicken against a 100 percent magenta background. (Pretty attractive image idea, huh? Go ahead, you can use it if you like.) If the cyan and magenta plates don't line up exactly, you're left with a chicken with a white halo around it. Yuck.

A *trap* is a little extra bit of color that fills in the gap. For example, if you choose Image ⇨ Trap and enter 4 into the Width option box, Photoshop outlines the chicken with an extra 4 pixels of cyan and the background with an extra 4 pixels of magenta. Now the registration can be off a full 8 pixels without any halo occurring.

As you may already have figured out, there is a problem with this solution. Without trapping, you had a white halo, but *with* trapping, the cyan and magenta pixels overlap to create an obvious purple border around the chicken that's almost as distracting as the halo.

Well, because continuous-tone images don't feature such obvious amounts of contrast as those described in the chicken scenario, neither trap nor lack of it have such a marked affect on the final image. Furthermore, although Photoshop expands the darkest colors in each of the cyan, magenta, yellow, and black color channels to the full extent requested in the Trap dialog box, it expands midtones and light values to lesser extents, thereby distributing the trapping so it is less obvious to the viewer.

Still, trapping is anything but an ideal solution. It thickens up the borders and edges in an image, it smudges detail, and it generally dulls the focus. All that, and it doesn't remedy the number-one problem created by misregistration — moiré patterns. If the halftone screens don't line up properly, they create obvious patterns in an image that are twice as distracting as any halos that may occur.

I know a few folks who have made careers out of pitching the idea of trapping, but it's a get-by solution at best, especially in the context of image editing. The only sure-fire solution is to find a commercial printer who guarantees accurate registration. After all, you're the paying customer — you deserve professional-quality results.

Printing Duotones

It's been a few pages since the "Printing terminology" section, so here's a quick recap: A *duotone* is a grayscale image printed with two inks. This technique expands the depth of the image by allowing additional shades for highlights, shadows, and midtones. If you've seen one of those glossy Calvin Klein magazine ads, you've seen a duotone. Words like *rich, luxurious,* and *palpable* come to mind.

Photoshop also allows you to add a third ink to create a *tritone* and a fourth ink to create a *quadtone.* Color Plate 7-1 shows an example of an image printed as a quadtone. Figure 7-13 shows a detail from the image printed in its original grayscale form. See the difference?

Figure 7-13: This salute to all-around athlete Jim Thorpe looks pretty good, but if you want to see great, check out the quadtone in Color Plate 7-1.

Creating a duotone

To convert a grayscale image to a duotone, tritone, or quadtone, choose Mode ⇨ Duotone. Photoshop displays the Duotone Options dialog box shown in Figure 7-14. By default, Duotone is the active Type option, and the Ink 3 and Ink 4 options are dimmed. To access the Ink 3 option, select Tritone from the Type pop-up menu; to access both Ink 3 and Ink 4, select Quadtone from the pop-up menu.

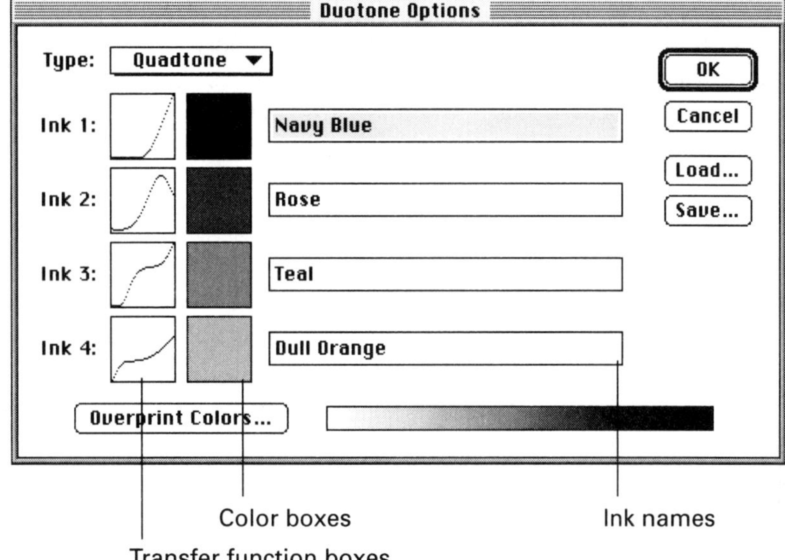

Figure 7-14: The Duotone Options dialog box allows you to apply multiple inks to a grayscale image.

You specify the color of each ink you want to use by clicking on the color box associated with the desired ink option. Select a color from the Custom Colors dialog box as described in the "Predefined colors" section of Chapter 14. (In some cases, Photoshop displays the Color Picker dialog box, described in the "Using the Color Picker" section of that same chapter.)

When creating duotones, tritones, and quadtones, prioritize your inks in order from darkest at the top to lightest at the bottom when you specify them in the Duotone Options dialog box. Because Photoshop prints inks in the order they appear in the dialog box, the inks will print from darkest to lightest. This ensures rich highlights and shadows and a uniform color range.

After selecting a color, you can use either of two methods to specify how the differently colored inks blend. The first and more dependable way is to click on the transfer function box associated with the desired ink option. Photoshop then displays the Transfer Functions dialog box, described back in the "Specifying a transfer function" section of this chapter. This enables you to emphasize specific inks in different portions of the image according to brightness values.

For example, Figure 7-14 shows the inks and transfer functions assigned to the quadtone in Color Plate 7-1. The Navy Blue color is associated only with the darkest brightness values in the image; Rose peaks at about 80 percent gray and then descends; Teal covers the midtones in the image; and Dull Orange is strongest in the light values. The four colors mix to form an image whose brightness values progress from light orange to olive green to brick red to black.

The second method for controlling the blending of colors is to click on the Overprint Colors button. An Overprint Colors dialog box appears, showing how each pair of colors will mix when printed. Other color swatches show how three and four colors mix, if applicable. To change the color swatch, click on it to display the Color Picker dialog box.

The problem with this second method is that it complicates the editing process. Photoshop doesn't actually change the ink colors or transfer functions in keeping with your new specifications; it just applies the new overprint colors without any logical basis. Secondly, you lose all changes made with the Overprint Colors dialog box when you adjust any of the ink colors or any of the transfer functions.

To go back and change the colors or transfer functions, choose Mode ⇨ Duotone again. Instead of reconverting the image, the command now enables you to edit the existing duotone, tritone, or quadtone.

Reproducing a duotone

If you want a commercial printer to reproduce a duotone, tritone, or quadtone, you must print the image to color separations, just like a CMYK image. However, because you already specified which inks to use and how much of each ink to apply, you don't have to mess around with all those commands in the File ⇨ Preferences submenu. Just take the following familiar steps:

STEPS: Printing a Duotone, Tritone, or Quadtone

Step 1. Select a printer with the Chooser desk accessory, as described previously in the "Choosing a printer" section.

Step 2. Choose File ⇨ Page Setup to specify the size of the pages and the size and orientation of the image on the pages, as described earlier in this chapter, in the "Setting up the page" section. Be sure to select the Registration Marks option.

Step 3. If you're feeling inventive, click on the Screens button to change the size, angle, and shape of the halftone screen dots for the individual color plates, as described previously in the "Changing the halftone screen" section.

Step 4. Choose File ⇨ Print (Command-P). Select the Print Separations check box in the lower left corner of the dialog box to print each ink to a separate sheet of paper or film.

Summary

- The Chooser desk accessory enables you to select a printer connected directly to your Mac or shared over a network.
- Use the Page Setup command to specify the size of the page and the orientation and size of the image on the page.
- Drag on the preview box in the lower left corner of the image window to preview how the image fits on the page before printing it.
- Output devices represent shades of color by printing thousands of tiny color spots called halftone cells.
- The number of distinct shades a printer can produce is dependent on the screen frequency. Higher frequencies result in smaller halftone cells and therefore fewer shades.
- A transfer function allows you to compensate for overly dark or overly light printouts by mapping brightness values in an image to lighter or darker printed shades.
- In order to properly calibrate your monitor, consult the technical support department for your make of monitor.
- Consult with your commercial printer before changing the settings in the Printing Inks Setup dialog box.
- Before printing color separations, you must convert an image to the CMYK mode by choosing Mode ⇨ CMYK.
- Be sure to turn on the Registration Marks check box in the LaserWriter Page Setup dialog box when printing color separations and duotones.
- Color trapping is a get-by solution that helps to eliminate gaps between colors by swelling up shades of ink, with emphasis on dark values.
- Duotones, tritones, and quadtones expand the number of shades available to a grayscale image. You also can add a modicum of color to otherwise drab grayscale images.

Retouching Images

PART III

Chapter 8:
Painting and Editing

Chapter 9:
Selections and Masks

Chapter 10:
Duplication and Reversion Techniques

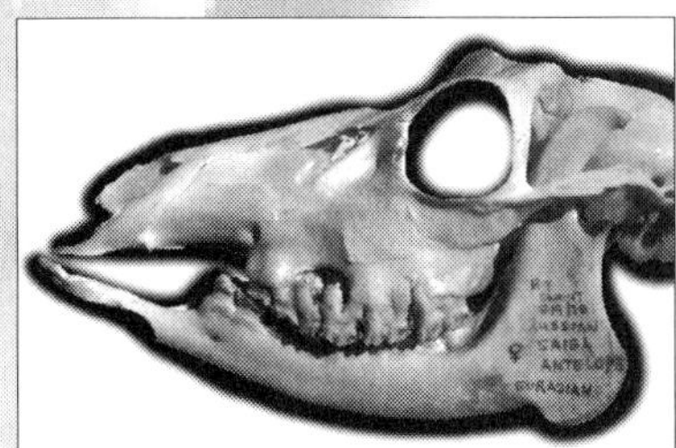

You can edit an image in Photoshop in three basic ways. You can retouch it to highlight or cover up details; you can apply special effects to change the image in measurable degrees; and you can adjust brightness values and colors to improve its overall appearance. Retouching is the subject of the three chapters in this section; special effects and color adjustments are covered in Parts IV and V respectively.

Retouching is perhaps the most controversial of image editing functions because an adept artist can dramatically alter the contents of a photo without the viewer being the least bit aware. The idea is particularly worrisome to news and action photographers, because any alteration to such a photo represents a departure from reality. After all, what's the point of risking personal injury to shoot a photo of an underwater shark encounter if some fool in the graphics department is going to enhance the photo by adding a few Great Whites?

In the following chapters, I explain how to edit photos as realistically as possible. However, I recommend that you temper the application of your skills with a smidgen of responsibility. Some retouching is perfectly acceptable. A photographer friend of mine, for example, runs an image editing service on the side so that he can edit his own photos according to a client's needs. Seems OK. Certainly, retouching is so rampant and blatant in advertising that most consumers have grown savvy enough not to mistake advertising for reality. Not ideal, but again, OK. Where the merit of retouching is most tenuous is in the depiction of real events. In this case, it's not enough to edit the photo with the approval of the photographer; you also need to bring the edit to the attention of the viewer. There has been talk of adopting a symbol to indicate manipulated news photos, such as an *M* in a circle. Even better is an addition to the credit line: *Photo by X. Photo manipulation by Y.*

Ultimately, the whens and whys of image editing are up to you. As I said before, my job, as I see it, is to show you how to retouch images without lecturing to you any more than I already have. So without further ado, the following chapters show you how to edit an image so that its own mother wouldn't recognize it.

Painting and Editing

CHAPTER 8

In This Chapter

- Explanations of Photoshop's paint and edit tools
- How to use the Shift key to create straight and perpendicular lines
- How to use and customize the smudge tool
- A thorough explanation of the Brushes palette
- How to create round and elliptical brush shapes and save any selection as a custom brush
- How to paint lines that gradually fade away or taper to a point
- An introduction to pressure-sensitive drawing tablets
- Brief descriptions of the 13 brush modes

Paint and Edit Tool Basics

Here it is Chapter 8, and I'm just now getting around to explaining how to use Photoshop's tools. You must feel like you're attending some kind of martial arts ritual where you have to learn to run away, cry, beg, and attempt bribery before you get to start karate-chopping bricks and kicking your instructor. "The wise person journeys through the fundamentals of image editing before painting a single brush stroke, Grasshoppa." *Wang, wang, wang.* (That's a musical embellishment, in case you didn't recognize it.) Now that you've earned your first belt or tassel or scouting patch or whatever it is you're supposed to receive for slogging this far through the book, you're as prepared as you'll ever be to dive into the world of painting and retouching images.

You may be thinking that using these tools requires artistic talent. In truth, each tool provides options for just about any level of proficiency or experience. Photoshop offers get-by measures for novices who just want to make a quick edit and put the tool down before they make a mess of things. If you have a few hours of experience with other painting programs, such as SuperPaint or PixelPaint, you'll find that Photoshop's tools provide as least as much functionality and, in many cases, more. And if you're a professional artist, well, come on now, you'll have no problem learning how to make Photoshop sing. Suffice it to say that no matter who you are, you'll find electronic painting and editing tools to be more flexible, less messy, and more forgiving than their traditional counterparts.

If you screw something up in the course of painting your image, stop and choose Edit ➪ Undo. If that doesn't work, try one of the reversion techniques described in the "Selectively Undoing Changes" section of Chapter 10. As long as a previous version of the image is saved on disk, you have a way out.

Meet your tools

Photoshop 2.5 provides three paint tools: the pencil, paintbrush, and airbrush. You also get five edit tools: smudge, blur, sharpen, burn, and dodge. Figure 8-1 shows all these tools. The burn and dodge tools are missing from Photoshop 2.0.

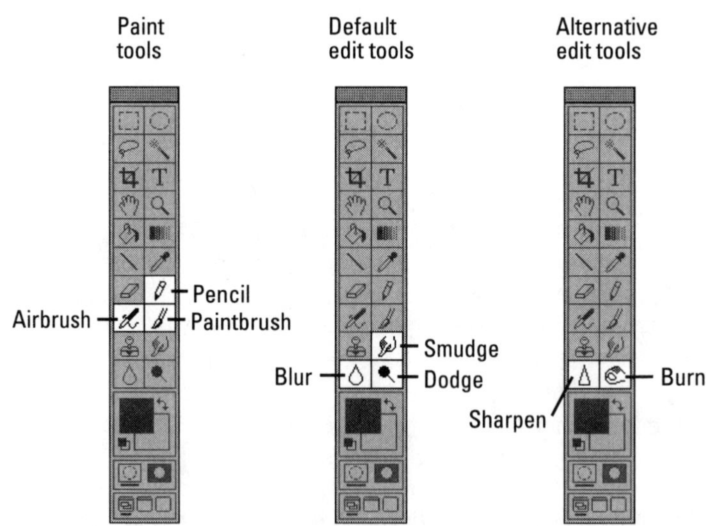

Figure 8-1: The three paint tools, the three edit tools that appear in the toolbox by default, and the two alternative edit tools.

In case you're wondering about all the other tools, Figure 8-2 segregates tools by category and lists the chapter in which you can find more information.

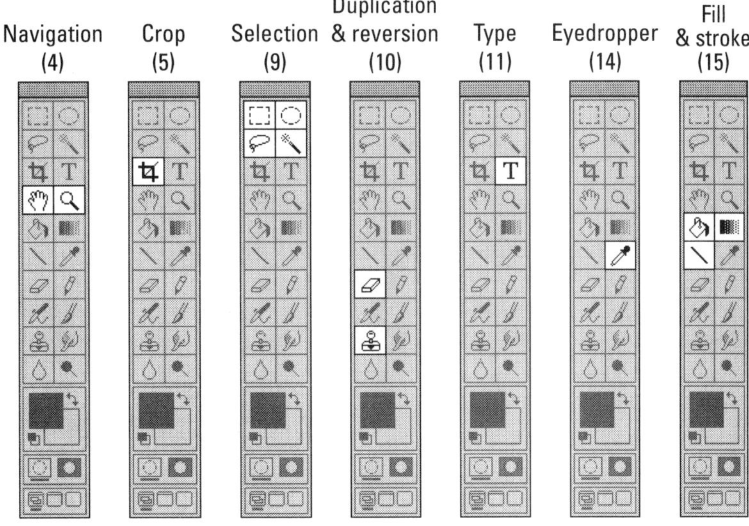

Figure 8-2: The rest of Photoshop's tools fall into the categories listed above each toolbox. The chapter in which I discuss each category of tools appears in parentheses.

The paint tools

The paint tools apply paint in the foreground color. In this and other respects, they work like their counterparts in other painting programs, you'll find the following few exceptions:

- **Pencil:** The pencil has been a Macintosh standard since the first version of MacPaint. Unlike pencil tools found in most other painting programs — which paint lines one pixel thick — Photoshop's pencil paints a hard-edged line of any thickness. Figure 8-3 compares the default single-pixel pencil line with a fatter pencil line, a paintbrush line, and an airbrush line.
- **Paintbrush:** The paintbrush works just like the pencil tool, except that it paints an antialiased line that blends in with its background.
- **Airbrush:** I'm tempted to describe Photoshop 2.5's airbrush tool as a softer version of the paintbrush, because it uses a softer brush shape by default. Photoshop's default settings also call for a lighter pressure so that the airbrush paints a semitranslucent line. But if you set the airbrush to the same brush shape and pressure as the paintbrush, you will notice only one distinction. The paintbrush stops applying paint when you stop dragging, but the airbrush continues to apply paint as long as you press the mouse button or stylus. Figure 8-3 shows the dark glob of paint that results from pressing the mouse button while holding the mouse motionless at the end of the drag.

In Photoshop 2.0, the difference between the paintbrush and airbrush tools is, well, different than it is in Version 2.5. If you double-click on the paintbrush or airbrush tool icon, you find a Repeat Rate value, which controls the rate at which the tool applies paint when motionless. This means that either the paintbrush or airbrush tool can be made to pump out color when you press the mouse button and hold the tool in place. The pressure of the two tools is the same by default. Therefore, the only difference is softness. The paintbrush cursor is antialiased, but the airbrush cursor looks like a fuzz ball with static cling.

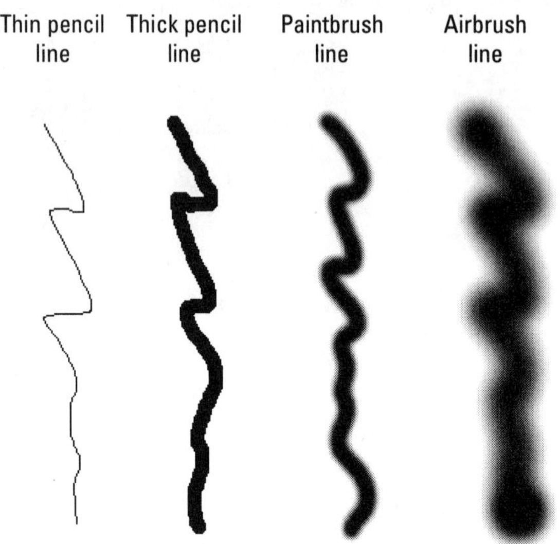

Figure 8-3: The pencil tool paints hard-edged lines, while the paintbrush and airbrush paint soft lines. Notice that I held the airbrush in place for a few moments at the end of the airbrush line.

The edit tools

The edit tools don't apply color; rather, they influence existing colors in an image. Figure 8-4 shows each of the five edit tools applied to a randomized background. The tools work as follows:

- **Smudge:** The smudge tool smears colors in an image. The effect is much like dragging your finger across wet paint.
- **Blur:** This tool blurs an image by lessening the amount of color contrast between neighboring pixels.
- **Sharpen:** This tool selectively sharpens by increasing the contrast between neighboring pixels. Generally speaking, I find both the blur and sharpen tools to be less useful than their command counterparts in the Filters menu. They provide less control and usually require scrubbing at an image. Maybe I've been using a computer too long, but my wrist starts to ache when I use these tools. If, unlike me, you like the basic principle behind the tools but you want to avoid Carpel Tunnel Syndrome, you can achieve consistent, predictable results without scrubbing by using the tools in combination with the Shift key, as described in the next section.

- **Dodge:** Available exclusively in Photoshop 2.5, the dodge tool lets you lighten a portion of an image by dragging across it. The dodge and burn tools are named after traditional film exposure techniques.
- **Burn:** The burn tool enables you to darken a portion of an image by dragging over it. The effect is similar to burning a film negative.

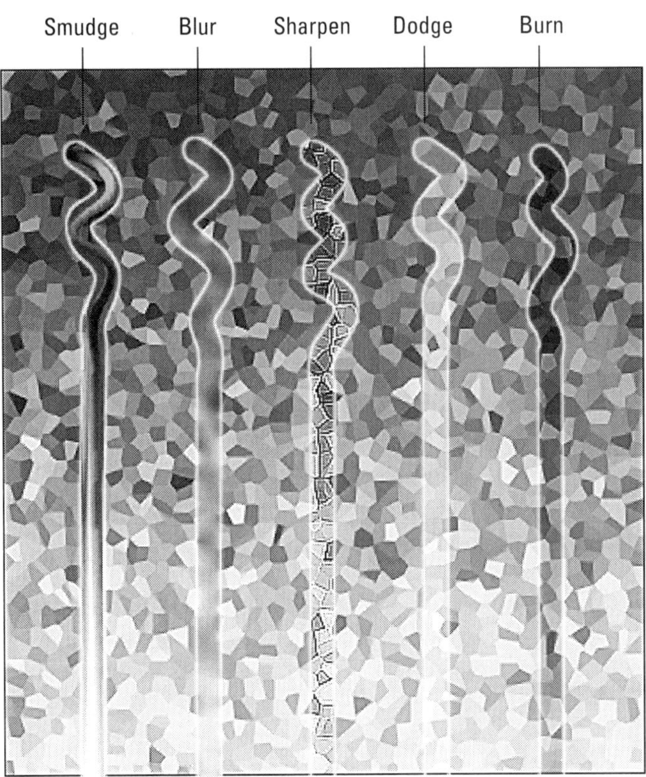

Figure 8-4: The effects of dragging with each of Photoshop 2.5's edit tools. The boundaries of each line are outlined so that you can clearly see the distinctions between line and background.

To temporarily access the sharpen tool when the blur tool is selected, press Option while using the tool. The sharpen tool remains available only as long as you press the Option key. You also can press Option to access the blur tool when the sharpen tool is selected, to access the burn tool when the dodge tool is selected, and to access the dodge tool when the burn tool is selected.

In Photoshop 2.5, you can replace the blur tool with the sharpen tool in the toolbox by Option-clicking on the tool's icon. To *toggle* (switch) back to the blur tool, Option-click on the sharpen icon. Likewise, you can Option-click on the dodge tool icon to toggle between the dodge and burn tools.

Basic techniques

I know several people who claim that they can't paint and yet they create beautiful work in Photoshop. The reason is that they have unique and powerful artistic sensibilities and they know lots of tricks that enable them to make judicious use of the paint and edit tools, even though they don't have sufficient hand-eye coordination to write their names on-screen. I can't help you in the sensibilities department, but I can show you a few tricks that will boost your ability and inclination to use the paint and edit tools.

Drawing a straight line

You're probably already aware that you can draw a straight line with the line tool. If not, try it out. The line tool is that diagonal line icon highlighted on the far right side of Figure 8-2. After selecting the tool, drag with it inside the image window to create a line. Pretty hot stuff, huh? Well, no, it's actually pretty boring. In fact, the only reason I ever use this tool is to draw arrows like those shown in the upcoming Figure 8-6. If you don't want to draw an arrow, you're better off using Photoshop's other means for drawing straight lines: the Shift key.

To access options that enable you to add an arrowhead to a line drawn with the line tool, double-click on the line tool icon in the toolbox. These options are explained in the "Applying Strokes and Arrowheads" section of Chapter 15.

To draw a straight line with any of the paint or edit tools, click on one point in the image and then press Shift and click on another point. Using the current tool, Photoshop draws a straight line between the two points.

To create free-form polygons, continue to Shift-click with the tool. Figure 8-5 shows an image drawn by Shift-clicking with the airbrush tool. I think it's supposed to be a cross between George Washington and Popeye. Don't ask me — I only drew the thing.

Figure 8-5: An image created by clicking and Shift-clicking with the airbrush tool. I traced this image over a lightened scan of Mount Rushmore.

The Shift key makes the blur and sharpen tools halfway useful. Suppose that you want to edit the perimeter of the car shown in Figure 8-6. The arrows in the figure illustrate the path your Shift-clicks should follow. Figure 8-7 shows the effect of Shift-clicking with the blur tool; Figure 8-8 demonstrates the effect of Shift-clicking with the sharpen tool.

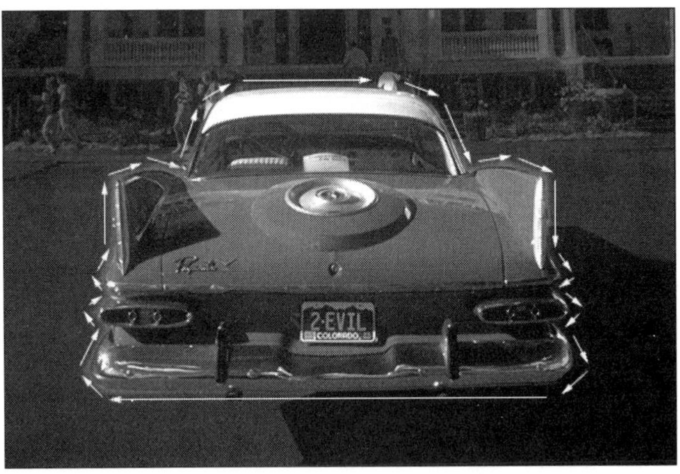

Figure 8-6: It takes one click and 24 Shift-clicks to soften or accentuate the edges around this car using the blur or sharpen tool.

Figure 8-7: The results of blurring the car's perimeter with the pressure set to 50 percent (top) and 100 percent (bottom). In Photoshop 2.5, you set the pressure by using the Brushes palette. In Version 2.0, you double-click on the tool icon.

Drawing a perpendicular line

To draw a perpendicular line — that is, one that is either vertical or horizontal — with any of the paint or edit tools, press and hold the mouse button, press the Shift key, and begin dragging in a vertical or horizontal direction. Don't release the Shift key until you finish dragging or until you want to change the direction of the line, as demonstrated in Figure 8-9. Notice that pressing the Shift key in mid-drag snaps the line back into perpendicular alignment.

Figure 8-8: The results of sharpening the car with the pressure set to 50 percent (top) and 100 percent (bottom).

One way to exploit the Shift key's penchant to snap to the perpendicular is to draw "ribbed" structures. Being left-handed, I dragged from right to left with the paintbrush to create both of the central outlines around the skeleton that appears at the top of Figure 8-10. I painted each rib by pressing and releasing the Shift key as I dragged with the paintbrush tool. Pressing Shift snapped the line to the horizontal axis, whose location was established by the beginning of the drag.

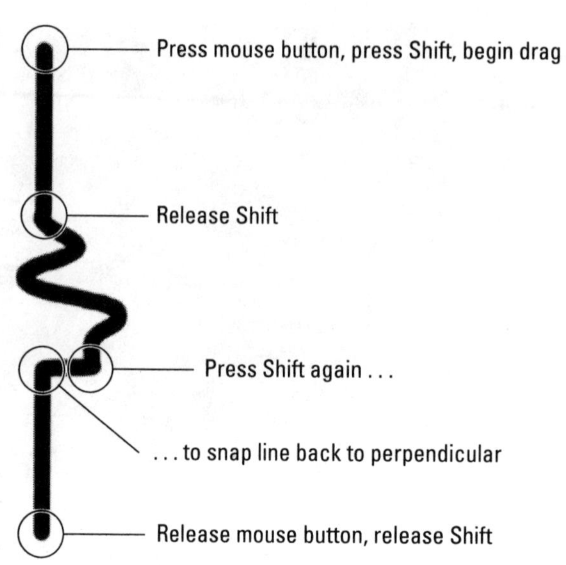

Figure 8-9: Pressing the Shift key after you start to drag with a paint or edit tool results in a perpendicular line for as long as the key is pressed.

In the figure, I represented the axis for each line in gray. After establishing the basic skeletal form, I added some free-form details with the paintbrush and pencil tools, as shown in the middle image in Figure 8-10. I then applied the Emboss filter to create the finished fossil image. Nobody's going to confuse my painting with a bona fide fossil — "Hey Marge, look what I done tripped over in the back forty!" — but it's not half bad for a cartoon.

It's no accident that Figure 8-10 features a swordfish instead of your everyday round-nosed carp. In order to snap to the horizontal axis, I had to establish the direction of my drag as being more horizontal than vertical. If I had instead dragged in a fish-faced convex arc, Photoshop would have interpreted my drag as vertical and snapped to the vertical axis.

Painting with the smudge tool

Lots of first-time Photoshop artists misuse the smudge tool to soften color transitions. In fact, softening is the purpose of the blur tool. The smudge tool *smears* colors by shoving them into each other. The process bears more resemblance to the finger painting you did in grade school than to any traditional photographic editing technique.

In Photoshop 2.5, the performance of the smudge tool depends on the settings of the Pressure and Finger Painting options. The Pressure slider bar, displayed in Figure 8-11,

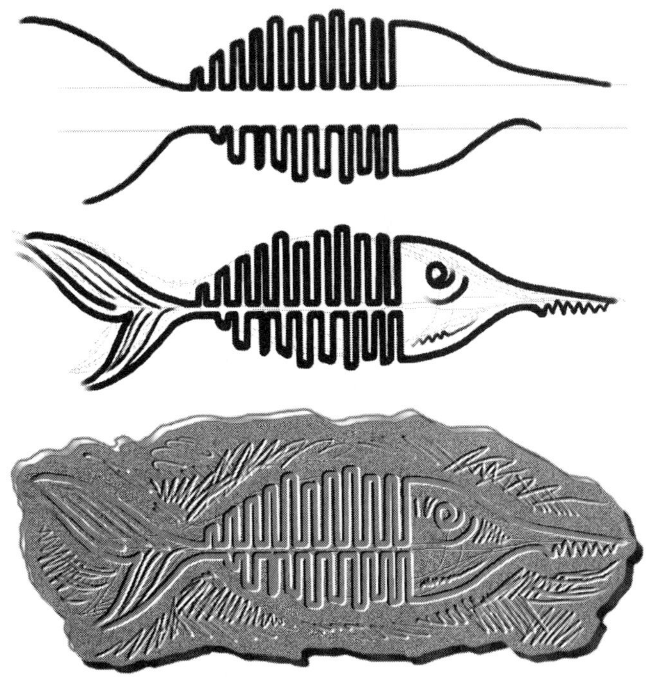

Figure 8-10: To create the basic structure for our bony pal, I periodically pressed and released the Shift key while dragging with the paintbrush tool (top). Then I embellished the fish using the paintbrush and pencil tools (middle). Finally, I selected a general area around the image and chose Filter ⇨ Stylize ⇨ Emboss to transform fish into fossil (bottom).

resides in the Brushes palette. You access the Finger Painting check box by double-clicking on the smudge tool icon. These two options work as follows:

- **Pressure:** Measured as a percentage of the brush shape, this option determines the distance that the smudge tool drags a color. Higher percentages and larger brush shapes drag colors farthest. A Pressure setting of 100 percent equates to infinity, meaning that the smudge tool drags a color from the beginning of your drag until the end of your drag, regardless of how far you drag. Cosmic, Daddy-O.
- **Finger Painting:** The folks at Adobe used to call this effect *dipping,* which I think more accurately expressed how the effect works. When you select this option, the smudge tool begins by applying a smidgen of foreground color, which it eventually blends in with the colors in the image. It's as if you dipped your finger in a color and then dragged it through an oil painting. Use the Pressure setting to specify the amount of foreground color applied. If you turn on Finger Painting and set the Pressure to 100 percent, the smudge tool behaves exactly like the paintbrush tool.

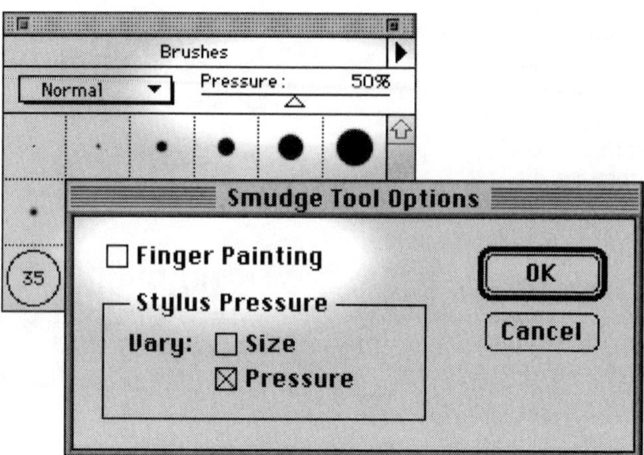

Figure 8-11: Combined with brush shape, the Pressure and Finger Painting options are the most important considerations when using the smudge tool.

For some examples of the smudge tool in action, take a look at Figure 8-12. The figure shows the effects of using the smudge tool set to four different Pressure percentages and with the Finger Painting option both off and on. In each instance, the brush shape is 13 pixels in diameter and the foreground color is set to black.

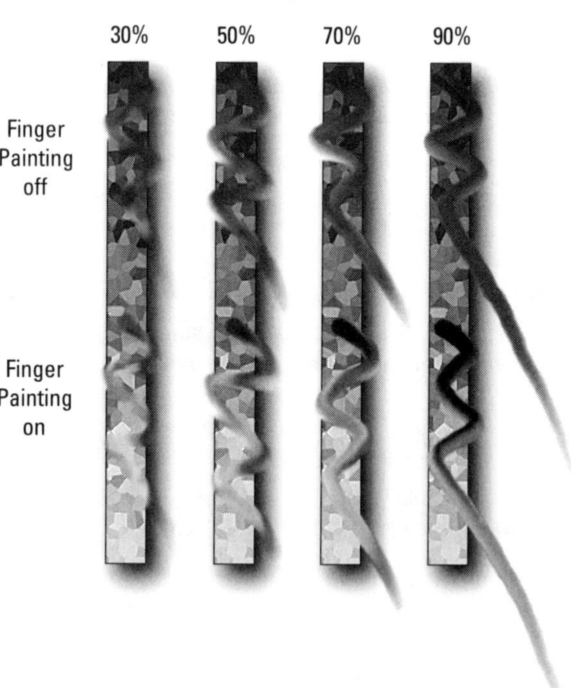

Figure 8-12: Eight drags with the smudge tool subject to different Pressure and Finger Painting settings.

To access the Pressure option in Photoshop 2.0, double-click on the smudge tool icon. Rather than dragging a slider bar to change the Pressure setting, you enter a value into an option box.

Although Version 2.0 lacks a Finger Painting check box, you can achieve the same effect by Option-dragging with the smudge tool. In Version 2.5, you reverse the Finger Painting setting by Option-dragging.

Brush Shape and Opacity

So far, I mentioned the words *brush shape* seven times and I have yet to explain what the Sam Hill I'm talking about. Luckily, it's very simple. The *brush shape* is the size and shape of the tip of your cursor when you use a paint or edit tool. A big, round brush shape paints or edits in broad strokes. A small, elliptical brush shape is useful for performing hairline adjustments.

When you use a paint or edit tool in most other painting programs, the outline of your cursor reflects the selected brush shape. Photoshop, on the other hand, displays a little cursor icon that may interrupt your view of an image. If the icon starts to get in your way, bid it a fond farewell by pressing the Caps Lock key. With Caps Lock down, Photoshop shows you a crosshair cursor that helps you focus in on the center of your brush. It's not as helpful as seeing an outline of the brush shape, but it's better than a meaningless icon.

The Brushes palette

In Photoshop 2.0, you change the brush shape for any paint or edit tool by double-clicking on the tool's icon in the toolbox. In Version 2.5, you access brush shapes by choosing Window ⇨ Show Brushes to display the Brushes palette. Figure 8-13 compares the brush shape options in the Brushes palette with those that appear when you double-click on a tool icon in Version 2.0.

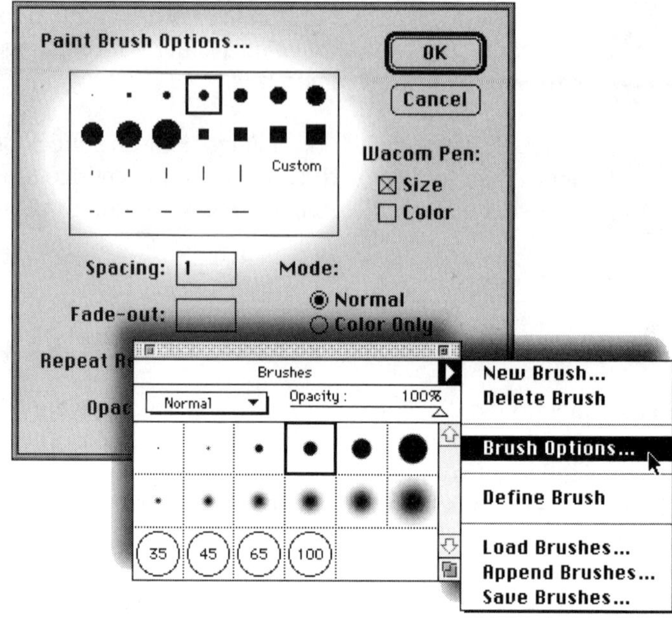

Figure 8-13: The brush shape options from Photoshop 2.0 (top) compared to the leaner and more functional Brushes palette found in Photoshop 2.5 (bottom).

Editing a brush shape

Photoshop 2.0 provides almost nothing in the way of brush editing functions. You can introduce a custom brush shape but you can't edit the existing shapes, one of Version 2.5's most powerful features. Also, whereas you can add several custom brushes to 2.5's Brushes palette, you can add only one at a time in Version 2.0. Thus, with the exception of the Spacing option, this section is meaningless to Version 2.0 users.

To edit a brush shape in the Brushes palette, select the brush you want to change and choose Brush Options from the palette menu (as in Figure 8-13). To create a new brush shape, choose New Brush. Either way, the dialog box shown in Figure 8-14 appears.

If you hate menus, you can more conveniently edit a brush shape by simply double-clicking on it. To create a new brush shape, click once on an empty brush slot, as shown in Figure 8-15.

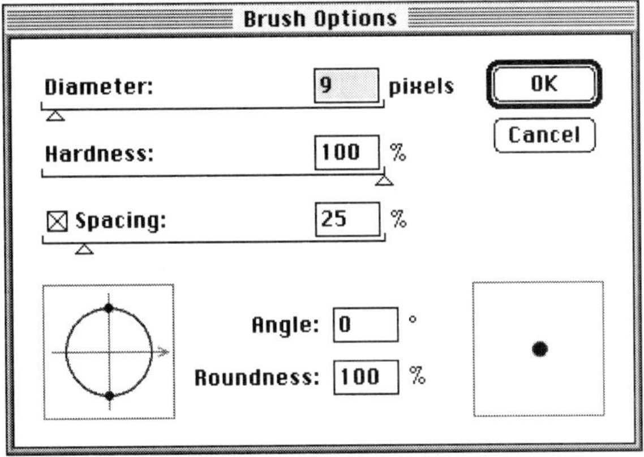

Figure 8-14: The Brush Options dialog box lets you change the size, shape, and hardness of the brush shape. If you choose the New Brush command, the title bar is different but the options are the same.

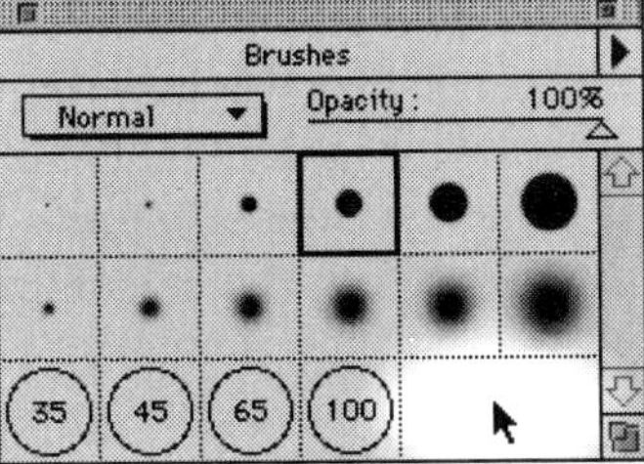

Figure 8-15: Clicking on an empty brush slot brings up the New Brush dialog box so you can create a new brush shape.

Whether you're editing an existing brush or creating a new one, you have the following options at your disposal:

- **Diameter:** This option determines the width of the brush shape. If the brush shape is elliptical instead of circular, the Diameter value determines the longest dimension. You can enter any value from 1 to 999 pixels. Brush shapes with diameters of 30 pixels or higher are too large to display accurately in the Brushes palette and instead appear as circles with inset Diameter values.
- **Hardness:** Except when you use the pencil tool, brush shapes are always antialiased. However, you can further soften the edges of a brush by dragging the Hardness slider bar away from 100 percent. The softest setting, 0 percent, gradually tapers the brush from a single solid color pixel at its center to a ring of transparent pixels around the brush's perimeter. Figure 8-16 demonstrates how low Hardness percentages expand the size of the brush beyond the Diameter value. Even a 100 percent hard brush shape expands slightly because it is antialiased. The Hardness setting is ignored when you use the pencil tool.
- **Spacing:** Of all the options in the Brush Options dialog box, Spacing is the only one available in Photoshop 2.0 (refer back to Figure 8-13). The Spacing option controls how frequently a tool affects an image as you drag, measured as a percentage of the brush shape. Suppose that the Diameter of a brush shape is 12

pixels and the Spacing is set to 25 percent (the setting for all default brush shapes). For every 3 pixels (25 percent of 12 pixels) you drag with the paintbrush tool, Photoshop lays down a 12-pixel wide spot of color. A Spacing of 1 percent provides the most coverage, but may also slow down the performance of the tool. If you deselect the Spacing check box, the effect of the tool is wholly dependent on the speed at which you drag, which can be useful for creating nonuniform or splotchy lines. (To get this effect in Photoshop 2.0, enter a Spacing value of 0.) Figure 8-17 shows examples.

- **Angle:** This option enables you to pivot a brush shape on its axes. However, it won't make a difference in the appearance of the brush shape unless the brush is elliptical.
- **Roundness:** Enter a value of less than 100 percent into the Roundness option to create an elliptical brush shape. The value measures the width of the brush as a percentage of its height, so a Roundness value of 5 percent results in a long, skinny brush shape.

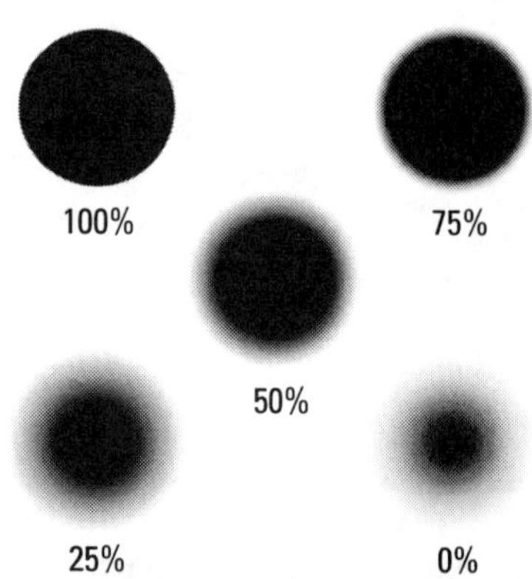

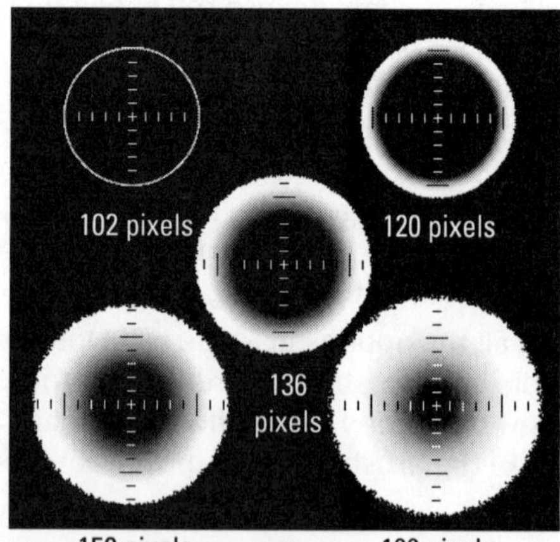

Figure 8-16: A 100-pixel diameter brush shown as it appears when set to a variety of Hardness per-centages top. On the bottom, I changed the background pixels from white to black so that you can see the actual diameter of each brush shape. The tick marks indicate 10-pixel incre-ments. As you can see, the lower the Hardness value, the more the brush perimeter expands beyond the 100-pixel diameter.

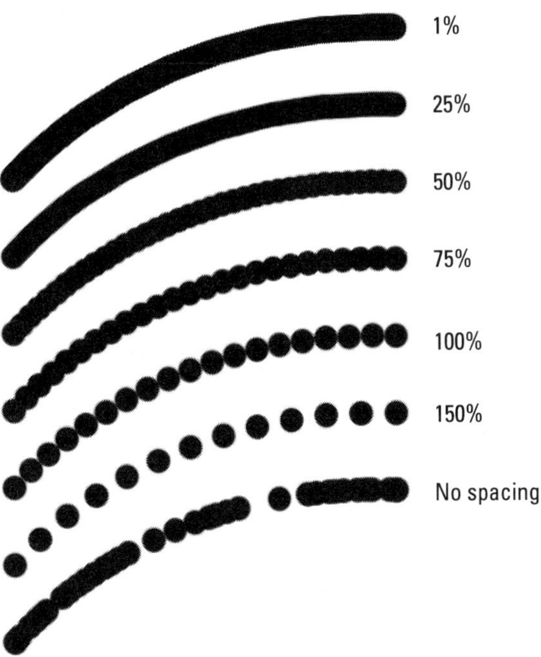

Figure 8-17: Examples of lines drawn with different Spacing values in the Brush Options dialog box. Gaps or ridges generally begin to appear when the Spacing value exceeds 30 percent. The final line was created by turning off the Spacing option.

You can adjust the angle of the brush dynamically by dragging the gray arrow inside the box to the left of the Angle and Roundness options. Drag the handles on either side of the black circle to make the brush shape elliptical, as demonstrated in Figure 8-18.

Brush Options
Diameter: 40 pixels
OK
Cancel
Hardness: 100 %
Spacing: 25 %
Angle: 46 °
Roundness: 44 %

Figure 8-18: Drag the gray arrow or the black handles to change the angle or roundness of a brush, respectively. The Angle and Roundness values update automatically, as does the preview of the brush in the lower right corner of the dialog box.

I heartily recommend that you take a few moments one of these days to experiment at length with the Brush Options dialog box. By combining paint and edit tools with one or more specialized brush shapes, you can achieve artistic effects unlike anything permitted via traditional techniques. Except for a few sketch lines drawn with the pencil tool, I painted the image in Figure 8-19 using *only* the flat, 45-pixel brush shape shown in the dialog box. Not one filtering effect was applied. Think of what you can accomplish if you don't limit yourself as ridiculously as I did.

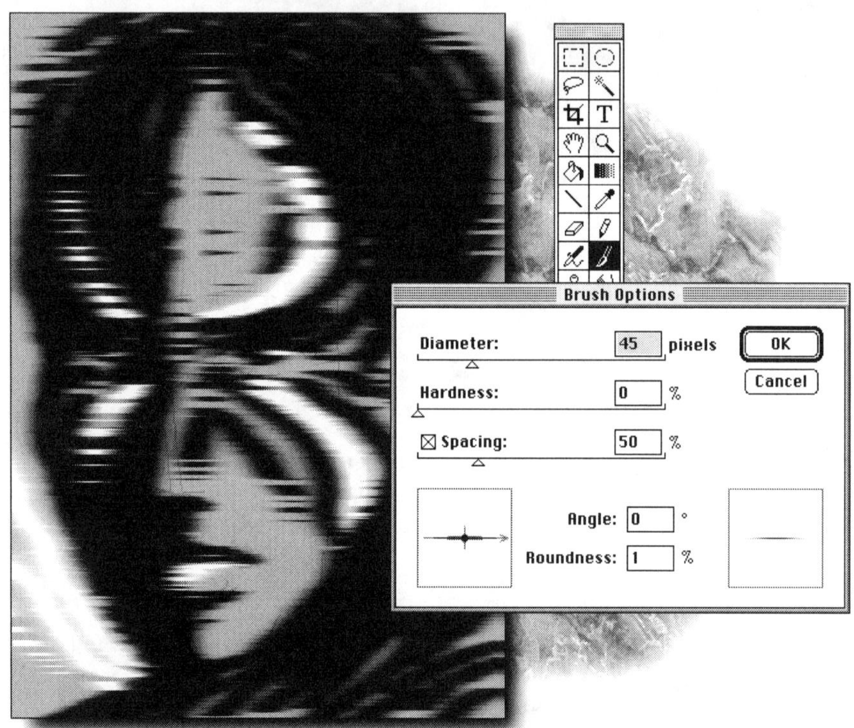

Figure 8-19: Just to show off, I painted the image on the left with the paintbrush tool, using the brush shape shown in the dialog box. Except for the sketch lines, no other tool so much as touched the canvas. If you come up with something better, feel free to mail it to me with the inscription "Neener, neener."

Creating and using custom brushes

Photoshop 2.0 and 2.5 both enable you to define a custom brush shape. All you do is select a portion of your image that you want to change to a brush and choose the Define Brush command, either from the Edit menu in the case of Version 2.0 or from the palette menu in Version 2.5.

In addition to giving you the flexibility to create a brush out of some element in your imagination, Photoshop 2.0 provides a file called Custom Brushes, which contains all kinds of little symbols and doodads you can assign as custom brush shapes. Photoshop 2.5 offers an Assorted Brushes file that contains nearly identical symbols.

Because Version 2.5 permits multiple custom brushes at a time, you can load the contents of the Assorted Brushes file into the Brushes palette by choosing the Load Brushes command from the palette menu (or Append Brushes if you don't want to lose the brush shapes that currently occupy the palette). You'll find Assorted Brushes inside the Brushes and Patterns folder, which resides in the same folder as the Photoshop application. Figure 8-20 shows an inspirational image I created using Photoshop's predefined custom brushes.

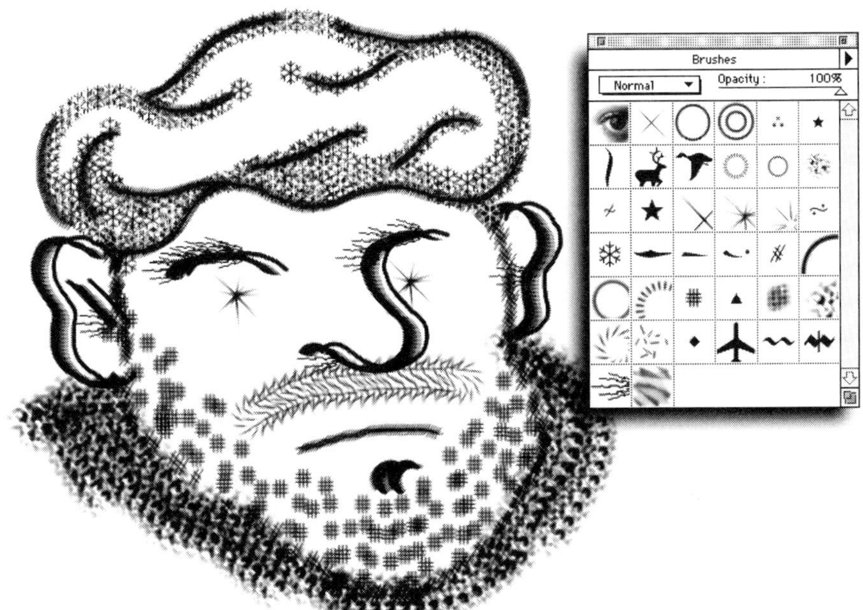

Figure 8-20: Yes, it's Boris, the sleeping custom-brush guy. If you suspect that this image is meant to suggest that custom brushes are more amusing than utilitarian, you're right. The brushes from the Assorted Brushes file appear on right.

In Photoshop 2.5, you can adjust the performance of a custom brush in the following ways:

- **Brush options:** Choose the Brush Options command from the palette menu or double-click on the custom brush in the Brushes palette to bring up the dialog box shown in Figure 8-21. Here you can adjust the spacing of the brush shape and specify whether Photoshop antialiases the edges or leaves them as is. If the brush is sufficiently large, the Anti-aliased check box appears dimmed. All custom brushes are hard-edged when you use the pencil tool.
- **Brush color:** The foreground color affects a custom brush just as it does a standard brush shape. To erase with the brush, select white as the foreground color. To paint in color, select a color. Only black paints the custom brushes exactly as they appear in the Brushes palette.

- **Opacity and brush mode:** The setting of the Opacity slider bar and the brush mode pop-up menu also affect the application of custom brushes. For more information on these options, keep reading this chapter.

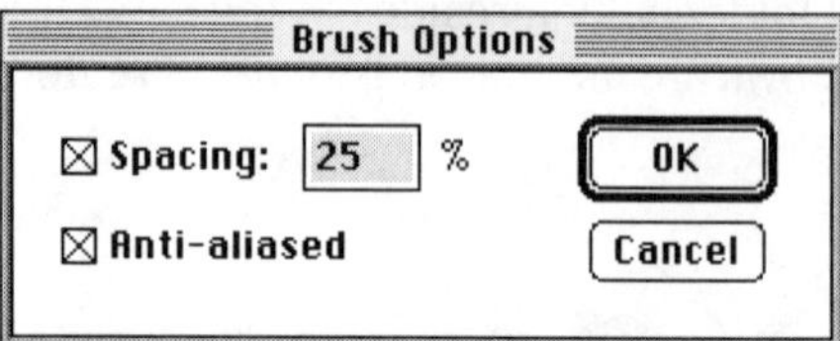

Figure 8-21: The dialog box that appears when you double-click on a custom brush.

You can achieve some unusual and sometimes interesting effects by activating the smudge tool's Finger Painting option and painting in the image window with a custom brush. At high Pressure settings, say 80 to 90 percent, the effect is rather like applying oil paint with a hairy paintbrush, as illustrated in Figure 8-22.

Figure 8-22: I created this organic, expressive image by combining the smudge tool's dipping capability with four custom brushes. I don't know what those finger-like growths are, but they'd probably feel right at home in an aquarium.

To restore the factory-default brush shapes, choose Load Brushes from the Brushes palette menu. Then open the Default Brushes file inside the Brushes and Patterns folder, which resides in the same folder as the Photoshop application.

Opacity, pressure, and exposure

The brush shapes in the Brushes palette affect only one tool other than the paint and edit tools — the rubber stamp, discussed in Chapter 10, "Duplication and Reversion Techniques." But the slider bar in the upper right corner of the Brushes palette additionally affects the type, paint bucket, gradient, and line tools. Photoshop assigns one of three labels to this slider bar, illustrated in Figure 8-23:

- **Opacity:** The Opacity slider bar determines the translucency of colors applied with the type, paint bucket, gradient, line, pencil, paintbrush, or rubber stamp tool. At 100 percent, the applied colors appear opaque, completely covering the image behind them. At lower settings, the applied colors mix with the existing colors in the image.
- **Pressure:** The Pressure slider bar affects different tools in different ways. When you use the airbrush tool, the slider bar controls the opacity of each spot of color the tool delivers. (In this case, the slider bar really ought to be labeled Opacity, because your settings produce the same results as the Opacity settings for the pencil or paintbrush tools. The effect appears unique because the airbrush spews out more color than the pencil or paintbrush.)

  When you use the smudge tool, the slider bar controls the distance that the tool drags colors in the image. And in the case of the blur or sharpen tool, the slider bar determines the degree to which the tool changes the focus of the image, 1 percent being the minimum and 100 percent being the maximum.
- **Exposure:** If you select the dodge or burn tool, the slider bar title changes to *Exposure.* A setting of 100 percent applies the maximum amount of lightening or darkening to an image, which is still far short of either absolute white or black.

The factory default setting for all Exposure and Pressure slider bars is 50 percent; the default setting for all Opacity sliders is 100 percent.

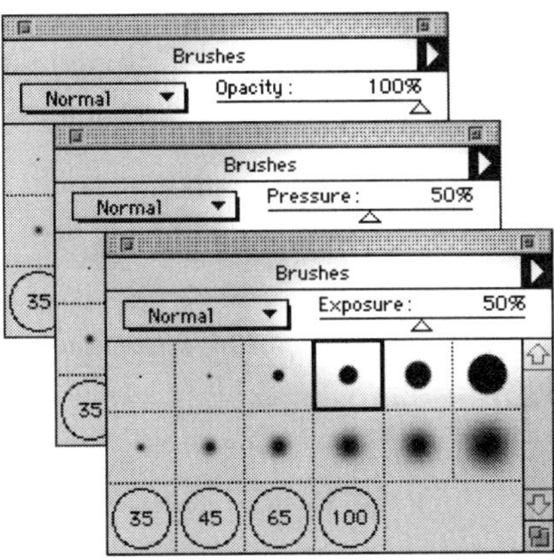

Figure 8-23: The slider bar in the upper right corner of the Brushes palette assumes one of these functions, depending on the selected tool. The slider disappears altogether when you select one of the navigation tools, one of the selection tools, the crop tool, or the eyedropper.

To access the Opacity or Pressure option in Photoshop 2.0, double-click on the toolbox icon of the tool you want to change. Version 2.0 lacks the dodge and burn tools, so it offers no Exposure option. Both Opacity and Pressure are presented as option boxes rather than slider bars.

You can change the Opacity, Pressure, or Exposure setting in 10 percent increments by pressing a number key on the keyboard or keypad. Press 1 to change the setting to 10 percent, press 2 for 20 percent, and so on, all the way up to 0 for 100 percent. This tip works in both Versions 2.0 and 2.5 whether or not the Brushes palette is visible. Believe me, this one of the best and most easily overlooked Photoshop tips ever. Get in the habit of using the number keys and you'll thank yourself later.

Tapered Lines

Photoshop provides two ways to create tapering lines that are reminiscent of brush strokes created using traditional techniques. You can specify the length over which a line fades by entering a value into the Fade-out option box, as described in the next section. Or, if you own a pressure-sensitive drawing tablet, you can draw brush strokes that fade in and out automatically according to the amount of pressure you apply to the stylus. Both techniques enable you to introduce an element of spontaneity into what otherwise seems at times like an absolute world of computer graphics.

Fade-out

In both Photoshop 2.0 and 2.5, all three paint tools offer Fade-out options that enable you to create lines that gradually fade away as you drag. To access the Fade-out option for a specific tool, double-click on the tool's icon in the toolbox. Figure 8-24 shows the Fade-out options that appear when you double-click on the paintbrush tool in Versions 2.5 and 2.0.

Enter a value into the option box to specify the distance over which the color fading should occur. The fading begins at the start of your drag and is measured in brush shapes.

For example, assume that the foreground color is black. If you enter 36 into the Fade-out option box — as in Figure 8-24 — Photoshop paints 36 brush shapes, the first in black and the remaining 35 in increasingly lighter shades of gray.

In Photoshop 2.5, you can paint gradient lines by selecting the To Background radio button. Photoshop fades the line from the foreground color to the background color, much the same way the gradient tool fades the interior of a selection. For more information on the gradient tool, see the "Applying Gradient Fills" section of Chapter 15.

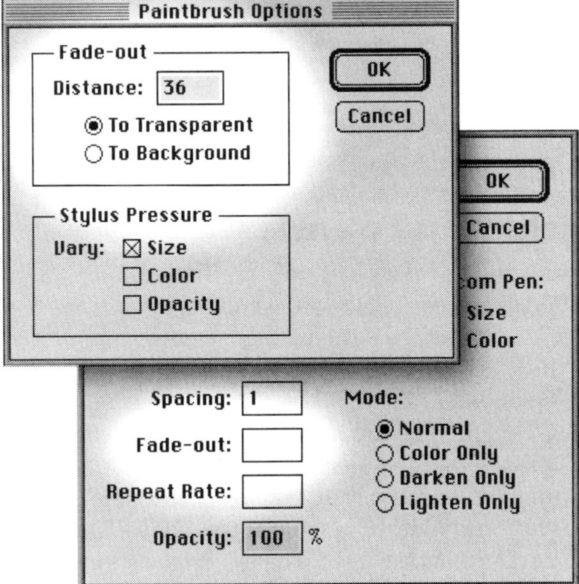

Figure 8-24: The Fade-out options in Photoshop 2.5 (top) and Photoshop 2.0 (bottom).

Fading and spacing

The physical length of a fading line is dependent both on the Fade-out value and on the value entered into the Spacing option box, discussed back in the "Editing a brush shape" section earlier in this chapter.

To recap, the Spacing value determines the frequency with which Photoshop lays down brush shapes, and the Fade-out value determines the number of brush shapes laid down. Therefore, as demonstrated in Figure 8-25, a high Fade-out value combined with a high Spacing value creates the longest line.

Figure 8-25: Five fading lines drawn with the paintbrush tool. In each case, the Fade-out option is set to 36 brush shapes. I changed the Spacing value incrementally from 1 to 50 percent, as labeled.

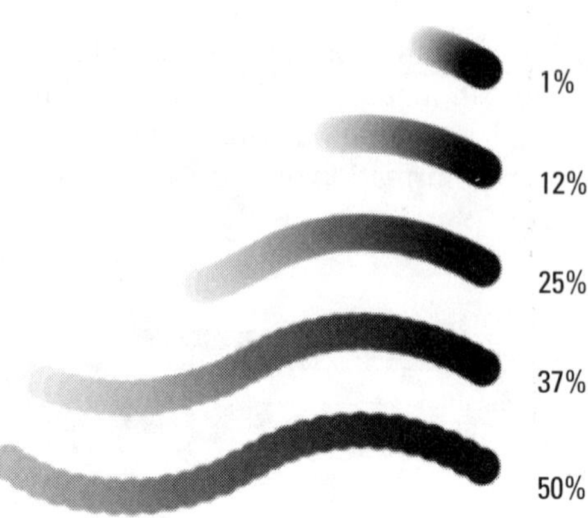

Creating sparkles and comets

Fading lines may strike you as pretty ho-hum, but they enable you to create some no-brainer, cool-mandoo effects, especially when combined with the Shift key techniques discussed earlier, in the "Drawing a straight line" section.

Figures 8-26 and 8-27 demonstrate two of the most obvious uses for fading straight lines: creating sparkles and comets. The top image in Figure 8-26 features two sets of sparkles, each made up of 16 straight lines emanating from the sparkle's center. To create the smaller sparkle on the right, I set the Fade-out value to 60 and drew each of the four perpendicular lines with the paintbrush tool. I changed the Fade-out value to 36 before drawing the four 45-degree diagonal lines. The eight very short lines that occur between the perpendicular and diagonal lines were drawn with a Fade-out value of 20. I likewise created the larger sparkle on the left by periodically adjusting the Fade-out value, this time from 90 to 60 to 42.

For comparison's sake, I used different techniques to add a few more sparkles to the bottom image in Figure 8-26. To achieve the reflection in the upper left corner of the image, I chose Filter ⇨ Stylize ⇨ Lens Flare and selected 50-300mm Zoom from the Lens Type options. I created the two tiny sparkles on the right edge of the bumper using a custom brush shape. I merely selected the custom brush, set the foreground color to white, and clicked once with the paintbrush tool in each location. So many sparkles make for an tremendously shiny image.

In Figure 8-27, I copied the car and pasted it on top of a NASA photograph of Jupiter. I then went nuts clicking and Shift-clicking with the paintbrush tool to create the comets — well, if you must know, they're actually cosmic rays — that you see shooting through and around the car.

After masking portions of the image (a process described at length in the following chapter), I drew rays behind the car and even one ray that shoots up through the car and out the spare tire. The three bright lights in the image — above the left fin, above the roof, and next to the right turn signal — are more products of the Lens Flare filter.

I drew all the fading lines in Figures 8-26 and 8-27 with the paintbrush tool, using a variety of default brush shapes. Because I didn't edit any brush shape, the Spacing value for all lines was a constant 25 percent.

Figure 8-26: I drew the sparkles in the top image using the paintbrush tool. The second image features a reflection applied with the Lens Flare filter (upper left corner) and two dabs of a custom brush shape (right edge of the bumper).

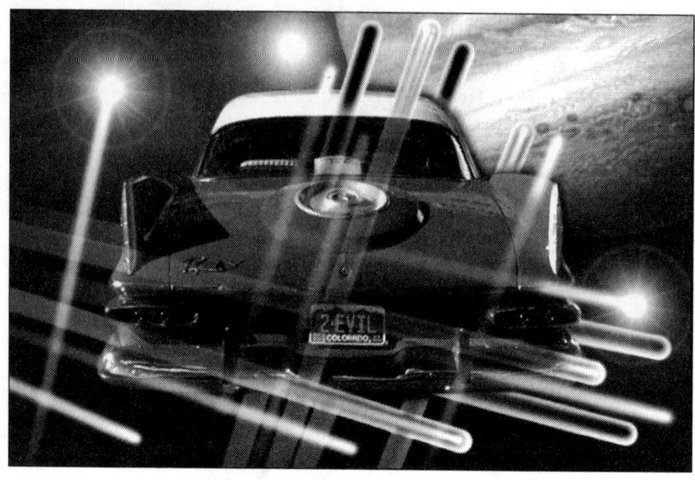

Figure 8-27: Remember when gas was cheap and you all piled in the car to go for a drive in space? Unfortunately, you always had to worry about those cosmic rays. Luckily, they're a cinch to draw: Set the Fade-out option to 110 and then click and Shift-click on opposite sides of the image with the paintbrush tool.

Lines created with pressure-sensitive tablets

The pressure-sensitive tablet has to be the single most useful piece of optional hardware available to computer artists. Not only can you draw with a pen-like *stylus* instead of a clunky mouse, you also can dynamically adjust the thickness of lines and the opacity of colors by changing the amount of pressure you apply to the stylus. As I write this, three vendors — Wacom, CalComp, and Kurta — manufacture pressure-sensitive tablets.

Of these, my favorite is Wacom's $450 ArtZ, a 6 × 8-inch tablet that plugs into your Mac's ADB port, which is the same port that accommodates the keyboard and mouse. The tablet offers 120 levels of pressure and a transparent overlay to hold pages you want to trace. It also has a cordless stylus that weighs less than an ounce and features both a pressure-sensitive nib and a side switch for double-clicking and choosing macros.

If you're an artist and you've never experimented with this or any other pressure-sensitive tablet, I recommend that you do so at your earliest convenience. You'll be amazed at how much it increases your range of artistic options. Minutes after I installed my first tablet, I was able draw the cartoon shown in Figure 8-28 (and in Color Plate 8-1) from scratch on a 13-inch monitor in about 30 minutes. Whether you like the image or not — I'll admit there is a certain troglodyte quality to the cut of his forehead, and that jaw could bust a coconut — it shows off the tablet's ability to paint tapering lines and accommodate artistic expression.

Figure 8-28: Though I painted this caricature years ago, it embodies the range of artistic freedom provided by a Wacom tablet.

How to undo pressure-sensitive lines

Pressure-sensitive lines can be hard to undo. Because a Wacom or other stylus is so sensitive to gradual pressure, you can unwittingly let up and repress the stylus during what you think is a single drag. If, after doing so, you decide don't like the line and choose Edit ⇨ Undo, Photoshop deletes only the last portion of the line because it detected a release midway through. As a result, you're stuck with half a line that you don't want or, worse, that visually mars your image.

Problems are even more likely to occur if you use a stylus with a side switch, such as the one included with Wacom's ArtZ or CalComp's DrawingPad. It's very easy to accidentally press your thumb or forefinger against the switch as you drag. If you have the switch set to some separate operation, such as double-clicking, you interrupt your line. This interruption not only creates an obvious break but also makes the error impossible to undo.

To prepare for this eventuality — and believe me, it *will* happen — make sure to save your image at key points when you're content with its appearance. Then if you find yourself stuck with half a line, you can remove the line by Option-dragging with the eraser tool, as discussed in the "Selectively Undoing Changes" section of Chapter 10.

Pressure-sensitive options

Photoshop Versions 2.5 and 2.0 handle pressure sensitivity in slightly different ways. For starters, Version 2.5 provides more options for interpreting pressure, as verified by Figure 8-29. These options work as follows (Figure 8-30 demonstrates the effects of each option):

- **Size:** If you select the Size check box, Photoshop varies the thickness of the line. The more pressure you apply, the thicker the line. The Size check box is selected by default. For a detailed discussion of this option, read the next section.
- **Color:** Select this option to create custom gradient lines. Full pressure paints in the foreground color; very slight pressure paints in the background color; medium pressure paints a mix of the two.
- **Opacity:** Exclusive to Version 2.5, this option paints an opaque coat of foreground color at full pressure that dwindles to transparency at very slight pressure.

Because Photoshop 2.5 presents its pressure options as check boxes, you can select more than one option at a time. For example, you can select both Size and Color to instruct Photoshop to change both the thickness and color of a line as you bear down or lift up on the stylus.

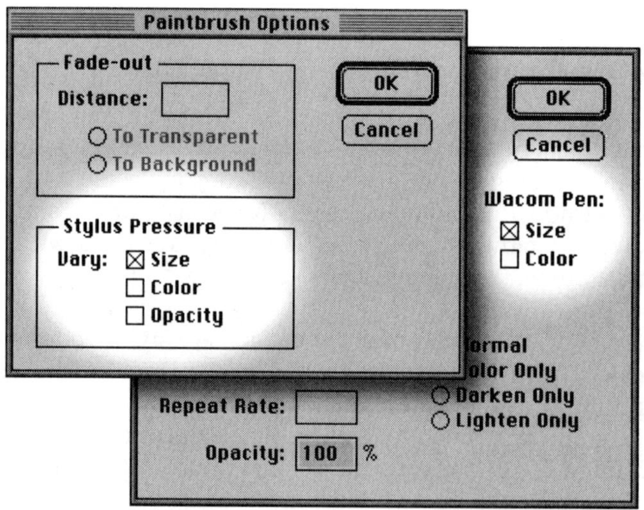

Figure 8-29: Photoshop 2.5 (left) provides an Opacity check box that's missing from Version 2.0 (right). (The Opacity option box in the Version 2.0 dialog box is unrelated to stylus pressure; it affects the opacity of color applied with brushes. For more information on this option, see "Opacity, pressure, and exposure," earlier in this chapter.)

The size disparity

Versions 2.5 and 2.0 differ in the way they apply pressure sensitivity to the size of the brush shape. In my opinion, Photoshop 2.5 dropped the ball in this area. In fact, the problem is so striking that you may want to use Photoshop 2.0 or some other more capable painting application, such as Fractal Design Painter, to do your pressure-sensitive work.

Figure 8-30 shows five lines subject to each of Photoshop's pressure-sensitive options. I applied varying amounts of pressure while drawing each line. The three lines on the left show the effects of the Size option. I drew the first line in Photoshop 2.5 using a hard brush shape — one of those in the first row of the Brushes palette. Despite the fact that only the Size check box was selected, the line varies more remarkably in opacity than in thickness. Compare this to the second line, created in Photoshop 2.0.1, which varies the thickness of the line just as you would expect. To get anything remotely resembling this effect in Version 2.5, you have to select a soft brush shape (second row of the Brushes palette), as witnessed by the third line. But even then, the effect is unsatisfactory. Whereas the 2.0.1 line is crisp and sharply focused, the 2.5 line is blurred, in keeping with the soft brush shape.

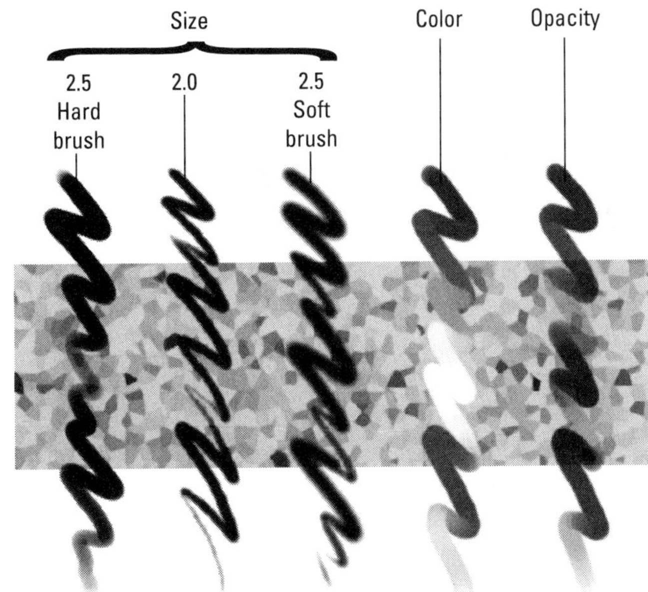

Figure 8-30: The effects of the Size, Color, and Opacity pressure-sensitivity options on lines drawn with a pressure-sensitive tablet. If you prefer the way Photoshop 2.0 handles pressure sensitivity, select a soft brush shape when drawing pressure-sensitive lines in Photoshop 2.5.

Brush Modes

The pop-up menu in the Brushes palette provides access to Photoshop 2.5's *brush modes,* which control how paint and edit tools affect existing colors in the image. Figure 8-31 shows which brush modes are available when you select various tools.

Brush modes have no influence over the performance of the navigation tools, the crop tool, the eyedropper, and the eraser. They are available when a selection tool is active only if an image is selected and floating in the image window, as explained in the "Overlaying Floating Selections" section of Chapter 15.

With the exception of the specialized brush modes provided for the dodge and burn tools, brush modes and the overlay modes described in Chapter 15 are varieties of the same animal. Read this section to get a brief glimpse of brush modes; read Chapter 15 for a more detailed account that should appeal to brush-mode aficionados.

Photoshop 2.0 provides only three brush modes: Color, Darken, and Lighten. To change the brush mode for a specific paint or edit tool, double-click on the tool's icon in the toolbox. The exception is the type tool, which provides no brush mode of its own. (You can apply an overlay mode to floating type by choosing Edit ⇨ Paste Controls.)

The 13 brush modes provided by Photoshop 2.5 work as follows:

- **Normal:** Choose this mode to paint or edit an image normally. A paint tool coats the image with the foreground color and an edit tool manipulates the existing colors in an image according to the setting of the Opacity or Pressure slider bar.
- **Darken:** If you choose this mode, Photoshop applies a new color to a pixel only if that color is darker than the present color of the pixel. Otherwise, the pixel is left unchanged.
- **Lighten:** The opposite of the previous mode, Lighten ensures that Photoshop applies a new color to a pixel only if the color is lighter than the present color of the pixel. Otherwise, the pixel is left unchanged.
- **Hue:** Understanding the next few modes requires a certain amount of color theory that I have yet to discuss. Quickly, the *HSL color model* calls for three color channels: one for *hue,* the value that explains the colors in an image; one for *saturation,* which represents the intensity of the colors; and one for *luminosity,* which explains the lightness and darkness of colors. If you choose Hue, Photoshop changes the colors themselves without changing any saturation or luminosity values. This option has no effect when you work on a grayscale image.

Figure 8-31: The number of options in the brush modes pop-up menu varies depending on whether you select a paint tool (top), an edit tool (middle), or the dodge or burn tool (bottom).

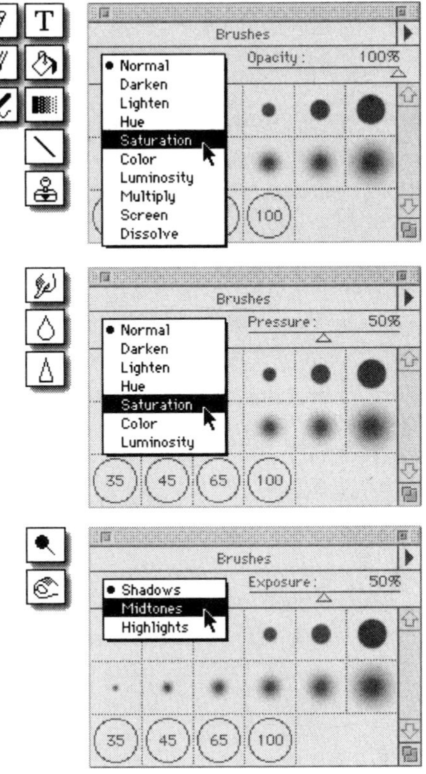

- **Saturation:** If you choose this mode, Photoshop changes the intensity of the colors in an image without changing the colors themselves or the lightness and darkness of individual pixels. This option has no effect on a grayscale image.
- **Color:** This mode might be more appropriately titled *Hue and Saturation.* It enables you to change the colors in an image and the intensity of those colors without changing the lightness and darkness of individual pixels. This option has no effect on a grayscale image.
- **Luminosity:** The opposite of the Color mode, Luminosity changes the lightness and darkness of pixels but leaves the hue and saturation values unaffected. When you work on a grayscale image, this mode operates identically to the Normal mode.
- **Multiply:** This mode and the two that follow are not applicable to the edit tools. The Multiply mode combines the foreground color with an existing color in an image to create a third color that is darker than the other two. Red times white is red, red times yellow is orange, red times green is brown, red times blue is violet,

and so on. The effect is almost exactly like drawing with felt-tipped markers, except that the colors don't bleed.

- **Screen:** The inverse of the Multiply mode, Screen combines foreground color with an existing color in an image to create a third color that is lighter that the other two. Red times white is white, red times yellow is off-white, red times green is yellow, red times blue is pink, and so on. The effect is unlike any traditional painting technique — not even chalk lightens an image in this way — but it can yield some pretty interesting results.
- **Dissolve:** This mode scatters colors applied with a paint tool randomly throughout the course of your drag. The Dissolve mode produces the most pronounced effects when used with soft brushes and the airbrush tool.
- **Shadows:** Along with the Midtones and Highlights modes (described next), Shadows is unique to the dodge and burn tools. When you select this mode, the dodge and burn tools affect dark pixels in an image more dramatically than they affect light pixels and shades in between.
- **Midtones:** Select this mode to apply the dodge or burn tools equally to all but the very lightest or darkest pixels in an image.
- **Highlights:** When you select this option, the dodge and burn tools affect light pixels in an image more dramatically than they affect dark pixels and shades in between.

Selecting Shadows when using the dodge tool or selecting Highlights when using the burn tool has an equalizing effect on an image. Figure 8-32 shows how using either of these functions and setting the Exposure slider bar to 100 percent lightens or darkens pixels in an image to very nearly identical brightness values.

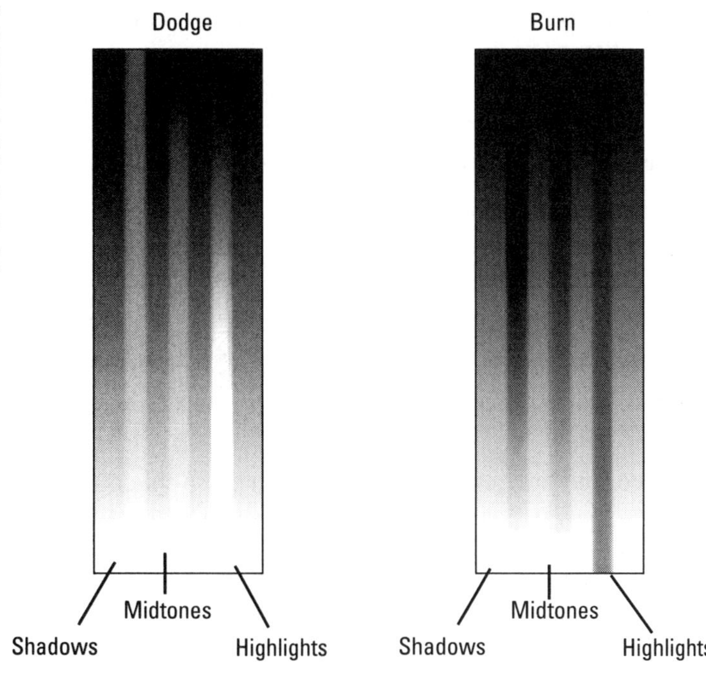

Figure 8-32: The dodge and burn tool applied at 100 percent Exposure settings subject to each of the three applicable brush modes.

Summary

- In Photoshop 2.5, you Option-click on the blur tool icon in the toolbox to replace it with the sharpen tool. Option-clicking a second time toggles back to the blur tool. You likewise can toggle between the burn tool and the dodge tool by Option-clicking on their icons.
- Click at one point and Shift-click at another with any paint or edit tool to draw a straight line between the two points. This technique is especially useful for controlling the behavior of an edit tool.
- Press Shift while dragging with any paint or edit tool to draw a perpendicular line.
- Option-drag with the smudge tool to dab on a bit of foreground color at the beginning of the drag.
- Double-click on a brush shape in the Brushes palette to edit the size, hardness, roundness, and angle of the brush. Click on an empty brush slot to create a new brush shape.
- You can convert any selection into a custom brush shape.
- Press a number key to change the setting of the Opacity, Pressure, or Exposure slider bar in 10 percent increments.
- You can use the Fade-out option in combination with Shift-click techniques to create sparkles and comets.
- A pressure-sensitive tablet enables you to draw variable-weight lines that swell and taper based on how hard you bear down on the stylus.

Selections and Masks

CHAPTER 9

In This Chapter

- How the magic wand's Tolerance setting works
- Ways to save a selection outline for later use
- How to move and clone selections and selection outlines
- The difference between antialiasing and feathering
- A comprehensive discussion of Photoshop's path tools
- The hows and whys of painting along an open path
- How to export paths for use in Adobe Illustrator
- How to use the quick mask mode and independent mask channels

Selection Fundamentals

Selections provide protection and automation. If it weren't for Photoshop's selection capabilities, you and I would be flinging paint on the canvas for all we were worth, like so many Jackson Pollock and Vasily Kandinsky wannabes, without any means to constrain, discriminate, or otherwise regulate the effects of our actions. Without selections, there'd be no filters, no color correction, no special effects. In fact, we'd all be dangerously close to real life, that dreaded environment we've spent so much time and money to avoid.

That's why this is the most important chapter in this book.

Pretty cool, huh? You put a provocative sentence like that on a line by itself and everyone reads it. Granted, it's a little overstated, but can you blame me? I mean, I can't have a sentence like, "If you want my opinion, I think this is possibly the most important chapter in the book," — at least, not on a line by itself. The other paragraphs would laugh at it.

At any rate, it's vital that you pay close attention to the selection concepts discussed in this chapter, because they're key to using Photoshop successfully. It's equally essential to understand how to apply masks in Photoshop, and this chapter covers that subject as well.

How selections work

Before you can edit a portion of an image, you must first *select* it — which is computerese for marking the boundaries of the area you want to edit. To *select* part of an image in a painting program, you must surround it with a *selection outline* or *marquee,* which tells Photoshop where to apply your editing instructions. The selection outline appears as a moving pattern of dash marks, lovingly termed *marching ants* by doughheads who've been using the Mac too long. (See Figure 9-1 for the inside story.)

Whether you use Version 2.0 or 2.5, Photoshop provides five tools for drawing selection outlines:

- **Rectangular marquee:** The rectangular marquee tool has been a staple of painting programs since the earliest MacPaint. It lets you select rectangular or square portions of an image.
- **Elliptical marquee:** This tool works just like the rectangular marquee except that it selects elliptical or circular portions of an image.
- **Lasso:** Another hand-me-down from MacPaint 1.0, the lasso tool lets you select a free-form portion of an image. You simply drag with the lasso tool around the area you want to edit. However, unlike the lasso tools in most Macintosh painting programs, which shrink selection outlines to disqualify pixels in the background color, Photoshop's lasso tool selects the exact portion of the image you enclose in your drag.
- **Magic wand:** Originally introduced by Photoshop, this tool enables you to select a contiguous region of similarly colored pixels by clicking inside it. For example, you might click inside the boundaries of a face to isolate it from the hair and background elements. Novices tend to gravitate toward the magic wand because it seems like such a miracle tool, but in fact, it's the least predictable and ultimately least useful of the bunch.
- **Pen:** Available from the toolbox in Photoshop 2.0 and from the Paths palette in Photoshop 2.5, the pen tool is both the most difficult to master and the most accurate and versatile of the selection tools. You use the pen tool to create a *path,* a special breed of selection outline. You click and drag to create individual points in the path. You can edit the path after the fact by moving, adding, and deleting points. You can even transfer a path via the Clipboard to or from Adobe Illustrator 5.0. For a discussion of the pen tool, read the "How to Draw and Edit Paths" section later in this chapter.

Technically, the type tool also is a selection tool, because Photoshop converts each character of type into its own floating selection boundary. However, the type tool automatically fills these boundaries with the foreground color and is otherwise sufficiently different from other selection tools to warrant its own chapter later in the book (see Chapter 11, "Text Effects").

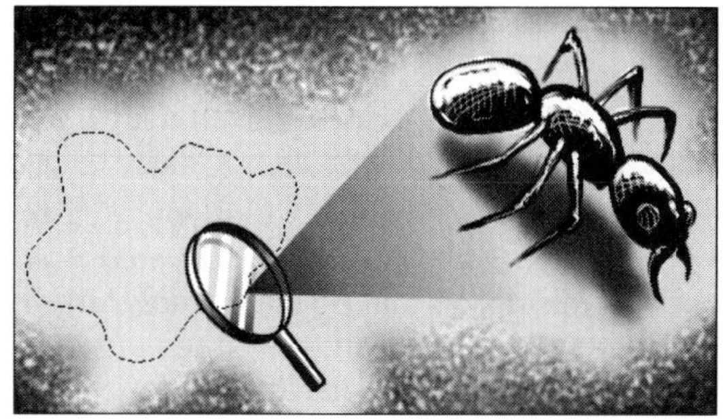

Figure 9-1: A magnified view of a dash mark in a selection outline reveals a startling discovery. No wonder the selection boundaries are nicknamed *marching ants.*

Selection tools in depth

If that's all there was to using the selection tools in Photoshop, the application would be on par with the average paint program for the Mac. Part of what makes Photoshop exceptional, however, is that it provides literally hundreds of little tricks to increase the functionality of each and every selection tool.

Furthermore, all of Photoshop's selection tools work together in perfect harmony. You can exploit the specialized capabilities of all five tools to create a single selection boundary. After you come to understand which tool best serves which purpose, you'll be able to isolate any element in an image, no matter how complex or how delicate its outline.

Geometric selection outlines

The rectangular and elliptical marquee tools are more versatile than they may appear at first glance. You can adjust the performance of each tool as follows:

- **Constraining to square or circle:** Press and hold Shift *after* beginning your drag to draw a perfect square with the rectangular marquee tool or a perfect circle with the elliptical marquee tool. (Pressing Shift *before* dragging adds to a selection, as explained in the "Ways to change existing selection outlines" section later in this chapter.)
- **Drawing out from the center:** Option-drag to draw the marquee from the center outward instead of from corner to corner. This technique is especially useful

when you draw an elliptical marquee. Frequently, it is easier to locate the center of the area you want to select than one of its corners — particularly because ellipses don't have corners.

- **Selecting a single-pixel line:** You can constrain the rectangular marquee tool so it selects a single row or column of pixels. To do so, double-click on the tool's icon in the toolbox to display the Rectangular Marquee Options dialog box and select the Single Row or Single Column radio button. I use this option to fix screw-ups such as missing a line of pixels when dragging a larger selection, to delete random pixels around the perimeter of an image, or to create perpendicular lines within a fixed space.
- **Constraining the aspect ratio:** If you know that you want to create an image that conforms to a certain height/width ratio — called an *aspect ratio* — you can constrain either marquee tool so that no matter how large or small a marquee you create, the ratio between height and width remains fixed. To accomplish this task, double-click on the appropriate marquee tool icon in the toolbox and select the Constrained Aspect Ratio check box. Then enter the desired ratio values into the Width and Height option boxes. For example, if you want to crop an image to the ratio of a 4 × 5-inch photograph, you double-click on the rectangular marquee tool icon, enter 4 and 5 respectively into the Width and Height option boxes, and press Return to confirm your changes. Then select the area of the image that you want to retain and choose Edit ⇨ Crop.
- **Sizing the marquee numerically:** If you're editing a screen shot or some other form of regular or schematic image, you may find it helpful to specify the size of a marquee numerically. To do so, double-click on the appropriate marquee tool icon in the toolbox and select the Fixed Size radio button. Suppose that you want to edit a screen shot of the Rectangular Marquee Options dialog box, like the one shown in Figure 9-2. You want to select and change the gray levels of the first four option boxes, all of which are the same size. You select one of them and note its size — 60 × 22 pixels — which is displayed in the last item of the Info palette (also shown in the figure). You enter 60 and 22 respectively into the Width and Height option boxes. You then Shift-click in the upper left corner of each remaining option box to add it to the selection and perform the desired color manipulations.

The Info palette can be extremely useful for making precise selections and image adjustments. For more information on this feature, read the "Making precision movements" section later in this chapter.

- **Drawing feathered selections:** In Photoshop 2.5, the Rectangular and Elliptical Marquee Options dialog boxes each provide a Feather option. To *feather* a selection is to soften its edges beyond the automatic antialiasing afforded by either marquee tool. For more information on feathering, refer to the "How to soften selection outlines" section later in this chapter.

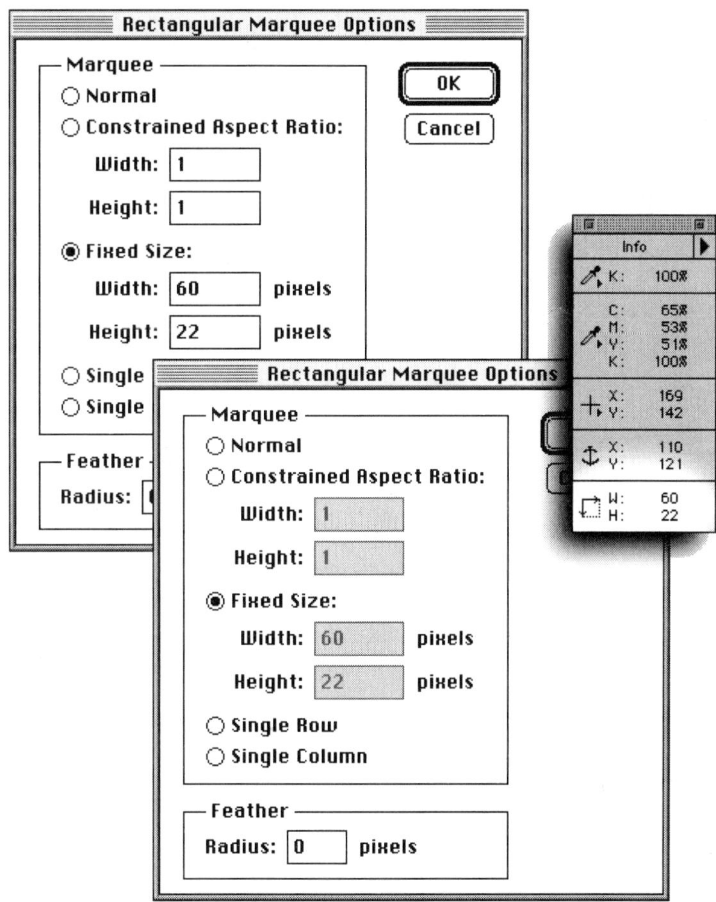

Figure 9-2: The Fixed Size option lets you select multiple equally-sized images — such as the option boxes in the forward dialog box — by entering their dimensions into the Width and Height option boxes. In this case, the option boxes measure 60 × 22 pixels, as indicated in the bottom section of the Info palette.

Frequently, Photoshop's lack of geometric shape tools throws novices for a loop. In fact, such tools do exist — you just don't recognize them. To draw a rectangle or ellipse in Photoshop, draw the shape as desired using the rectangular or elliptical marquee tool. Then choose Edit ⇨ Fill or Edit ⇨ Stroke respectively to color the interior or outline of the selection. It's that easy.

Free-form outlines

In comparison to the rectangular and elliptical marquee tools, the lasso provides a rather limited range of options. Generally speaking, you just drag in a free-form path around the image you want to select. The few special considerations are as follows:

- **Feathering and antialiasing:** To adjust the performance of the lasso tool, double-click on its icon in the toolbox to display the Lasso Options dialog box shown in

Figure 9-3. Just as you can feather rectangular and elliptical marquees, you can feather selections drawn with the lasso tool. However, although Photoshop automatically antialiases geometric marquees, it assigns lasso selections hard edges unless you select the Anti-aliased check box.

You should be aware that although you can adjust the feathering of any selection after you draw it by choosing Select ➪ Feather, you must specify antialiasing before you draw a selection. Unless you have a specific reason for doing otherwise, leave the Anti-aliased check box selected, as it is by default.

Although you can feather a selection outline in Photoshop 2.0, the program provides no means for antialiasing an outline drawn with the lasso tool.

- **Drawing polygons:** If you press and hold the Option key, the lasso tool works like a standard polygon tool. (*Polygon,* incidentally, just means a shape with multiple straight sides.) With the Option key down, you click to specify corners in a free-form polygon, as shown in Figure 9-4. If you want to add curves to the selection outline, just drag with the tool while still pressing the Option key. Photoshop closes the selection outline the moment you release both the Option key and the mouse button.

You can extend a polygon selection outline to the absolute top, right, or bottom edges of an image. To do so, Option-click with the lasso tool on the scroll bar or title bar of the image window, as illustrated by the gray lines and squares in Figure 9-4. (This technique does not work on the left side of an image, because the left side lacks a scroll bar or title bar.)

Figure 9-3: Double-click on the lasso tool icon to access the feathering and antialiasing options.

Lasso Options
Feather Radius: 0 pixels
OK
☒ Anti-aliased
Cancel

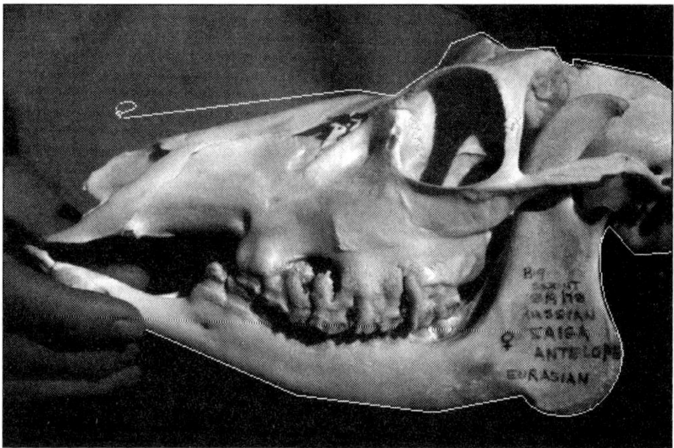

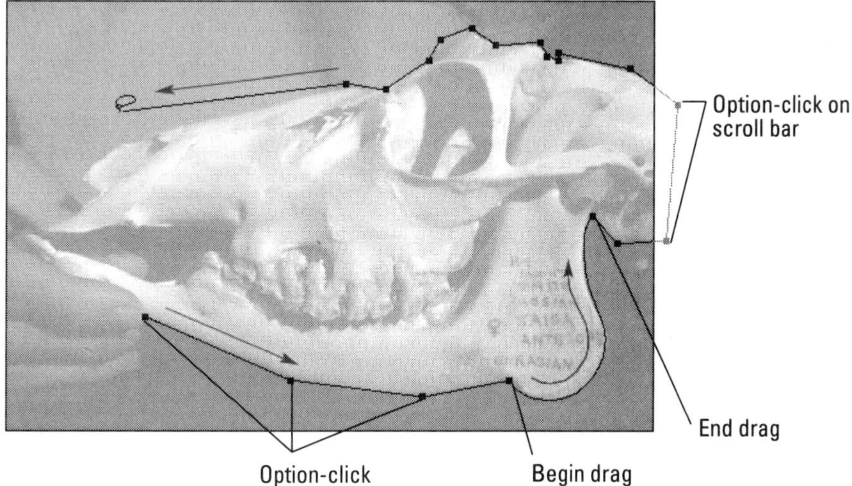

Figure 9-4: Option-click with the lasso tool to create corners in a selection outline, shown as black squares in the bottom image. Drag to create free-form curves. Surprisingly, you can Option-click on the scroll bar to add corners outside the boundaries of the image window.

Magic wand tolerance

As shown in Figure 9-5, Photoshop provides two options for adjusting the performance of the magic wand tool, both of which you access by double-clicking on the magic wand icon in the toolbox. The Anti-aliased option softens the selection, just as it does for the lasso tool described in the preceding section. The Tolerance value determines the range of colors the tool selects when you click with it in the image window.

You may have heard the standard explanation for adjusting the Tolerance value: you can enter any number from 0 to 255 in the Tolerance option box. Enter a low number to select a small range of colors; increase the value to select a wider range of colors.

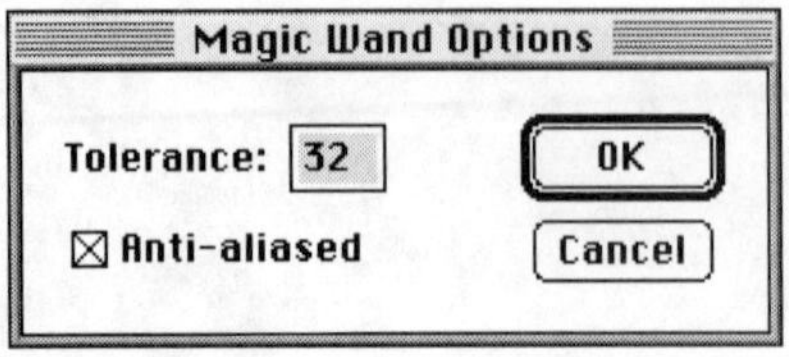

Figure 9-5: Double-click on the magic wand icon to specify the range of colors you want to select next time you use the tool.

Magic Wand Options	
Tolerance: 32	OK
☒ Anti-aliased	Cancel

There's nothing wrong with that explanation, mind you, except that it doesn't provide one iota of information you couldn't glean on your own. The fact is, if you really want to understand this option, you must dig a little deeper. So here goes. When you click on a pixel with the magic wand tool, Photoshop first reads the brightness value assigned to that pixel by each of the color channels. If you're working with a grayscale image, Photoshop reads a single brightness value from the one channel only; if you're working with an RGB image, it reads three brightness values, one each from the red, green, and blue channels; and so on. Because each color channel permits 8 bits of data, brightness values range from 0 to 255.

Next, Photoshop applies the Tolerance value, or simply *tolerance,* to the pixel. The tolerance describes a range that extends in both directions — lighter and darker — from each brightness value.

Suppose that you're editing a standard RGB image. The tolerance is set to 32 (as it is by default), and you click with the magic wand on a turquoise pixel whose brightness values are 40 red, 210 green, and 170 blue. Photoshop adds and subtracts 32 from each brightness value to calculate the magic wand range, which in this case is 8 to 72 red, 178 to 242 green, and 138 to 202 blue. Photoshop selects any pixel that both falls inside this range *and* can be traced back to the original pixel via an uninterrupted line of other pixels that also fall within the range.

From this information, we can draw the following basic conclusions about the magic wand tool:

- **Creating a contiguous selection:** The magic wand selects a contiguous region of pixels emanating from the pixel on which you click. If you're trying to select land masses on a globe, for example, clicking on St. Louis selects everything from Juno to Mexico City, but it doesn't select London because the cities are separated by a strip of water that doesn't fall within the tolerance range.
- **Clicking midtones maintains a higher range:** Because the tolerance range extends in two directions, you cut off the range when you click on a light or dark pixel. If the tolerance is 40 and you click on a grayscale pixel with a brightness value of 20, Photoshop calculates a range from 0 to 60. If you instead click on a

pixel with a brightness value of 40, you increase your range to 0 to 80. Therefore, clicking on a medium-brightness pixel permits the most generous range.

- **Selecting brightness ranges:** Many people have the impression that the magic wand selects color ranges. In fact, it selects brightness ranges within color channels. So if you want to select a flesh-colored region — regardless of shade — set against an orange or red background that is roughly equivalent in terms of brightness values, you probably should use a different tool.
- **Selecting from a single channel:** If the magic wand repeatedly fails to select a region of color that appears to be unique from its background, try isolating that region on a single color channel. You probably will have the most luck isolating a color on the channel that least resembles it. For example, to select a yellow flower petal set against an azure sky filled with similar brightness values, go to the blue channel (by clicking on the Blue option in the Channels palette). Because yellow contains no blue and azure contains lots of blue, the magic wand can distinguish the two relatively easily. Experiment with this technique and it will prove more and more useful over time.

In Photoshop 2.5, the magic wand tool reads brightness values from the single pixel on which you click. By contrast, Photoshop 2.0's wand reads values from all pixels that fall under the cursor, dramatically increasing your range. If you have problems isolating a color range in Version 2.0, try zooming in to the 800 percent view size so that a single pixel is as large as the magic wand cursor.

Ways to change existing selection outlines

If you don't draw a selection outline correctly the first time, you have two options. You either can draw it again from scratch, which is a real bore, or change your botched selection outline, which may indeed prove the more gratifying solution. You can deselect a selection, add to a selection, subtract from a selection, and even select the stuff that's not selected and deselect the selected stuff. (If that sounds like a load of nonsense, keep reading.)

Making automated adjustments

Some methods of adjusting a selection outline are automatic: you just choose a command and you're done. The following list explains how a few commands — all members of the Select menu — work:

- **Hide Edges (Command-H):** Get those marching ants out of my face! We're all grown ups, right? Do we really need these constant streams of marching ants to tell us what we've selected? We were there, we remember. My point is that although visible selection outlines can be helpful sometimes, they just as readily can impede your view of an image. When they annoy, press Command-H.

- **Deselect (Command-D):** You can deselect the selected portion of an image in three ways. You can select a different portion of the image; click anywhere in the image window with the rectangular marquee tool, the elliptical marquee tool, or the lasso tool; or choose Edit ⇨ Deselect. Remember, however, that when no part of an image is selected, the entire image is susceptible to your changes. If you apply a filter, choose a color-correction command, or use a paint tool, you affect every pixel of the foreground image.
- **Inverse:** Choose Edit ⇨ Inverse to reverse the selection. Photoshop deselects the portion of the image that was previously selected and selects the portion of the image that was not selected. This way, you can start out a selection by outlining the portion of the image that you want to protect rather than the portion you want to affect.

Manually adding and subtracting

Ready for some riddles? When editing a portrait, how do you select both eyes without affecting any other portion of the face? Answer: By drawing one selection and then tacking on a second. How do you select a doughnut and leave the hole behind? Answer: Encircle the doughnut with the elliptical marquee tool and then use that same tool to subtract the center.

Photoshop enables you to whittle away at a selection, add pieces back on, whittle away some more, ad infinitum, until you get it exactly right. Short of sheer laziness or frustration, there's no reason you can't eventually create the selection outline of your dreams.

- **Adding to a selection outline:** To increase the area enclosed in an existing selection outline, Shift-drag with the rectangular marquee, elliptical marquee, or lasso tool. You also can Shift-click with the magic wand tool or Shift-click with one of the marquee tools when the Fixed Size option is active (as described back in the "Geometric selection outlines" section earlier in this chapter). In Photoshop 2.0, you also can add to a selection by pressing Shift while using the pen tool. (For more pen tool information, read "How to Draw and Edit Paths," later in this chapter.)
- **Subtracting from a selection outline:** To take a bite out of an existing selection outline, press the Command key while using one of the selection tools.

You can make Photoshop's lasso tool behave like lassos in other Macintosh painting programs by applying a simple subtraction technique. First drag with the lasso around the portion of the image that you want to select. Then double-click on the magic wand tool icon in the toolbox, change the Tolerance value to zero, and deselect the Anti-aliased check box. Press Return to tell Photoshop to accept your changes and then Command-click with the magic wand tool on a portion of the selection that appears in the background color. Photoshop deselects this portion, as other programs do automatically.

- **Intersecting one selection outline with another:** Another way to subtract from an existing selection outline is to Command-Shift-drag around the selection with the rectangular marquee, elliptical marquee, or lasso tool. Command-Shift-dragging instructs Photoshop to retain only that portion of an existing selection that also falls inside the new selection outline. I frequently use this technique to confine a selection within a rectangular or elliptical border. Note that you cannot intersect a selection with the magic wand tool, though you can Command-Shift drag with the pen tool in Photoshop 2.0.

Adding to a selection by command

Photoshop provides two commands, Grow and Similar, that automatically increase the number of selected pixels in an image. Both commands resemble the magic wand tool in that they measure the range of eligible pixels by way of a Tolerance value. In fact, both tools rely on the Tolerance value found inside the Magic Wand Options dialog box. Therefore, if you want to adjust the impact of either command, you just double-click on the magic wand icon in the toolbox.

- **Grow (Command-G):** Choose Select ⇨ Grow to select all pixels that both neighbor an existing selection and resemble the colors included in the selection, in accordance with the Tolerance value. In other words, Select ⇨ Grow is the command equivalent of the magic wand tool. If you feel constrained by the fact you can click on only one pixel at a time with the wand tool, you may prefer to select a small group of representative pixels with a marquee tool and then choose Select ⇨ Grow to initiate the wand's magic.
- **Similar:** Another member of the Select menu, the Similar command works just like the Grow command except that the pixels don't have to be adjacent to one another. When you choose Select ⇨ Similar, Photoshop selects any pixel that falls within the tolerance range, regardless of its location in the foreground image.

One of the best applications for the Similar command is to isolate a complicated image set against a consistent background whose colors are significantly lighter or darker than the image. Consider Figure 9-6, which features a dark and ridiculously complex foreground image set against a continuous background of medium to light brightness values. Though the image features sufficient contrast to make it a candidate for the magic wand tool, I would never in a million years recommend that you use that tool because so many of the colors in the foreground image are discontiguous. The following steps explain how to separate this image using the Similar command in combination with a few other techniques I've described thus far.

STEPS: Isolating a Complex Image Set Against a Plain Background

Step 1. Use the rectangular marquee tool to select some representative portions of the background. In Figure 9-6, I selected the lightest and darkest portions of the background along with some representative shades in-between. Remember, you make multiple selections by Shift-dragging with the tool.

Step 2. Double-click on the magic wand tool icon to display the Tolerance option box. For my image, I entered a tolerance of 16, a relatively low value, in keeping with the consistency of the background. If your background is less homogenous, you may want to enter a higher value. Make sure the Anti-aliased check box is turned on. Then press Return to exit the dialog box.

Step 3. Choose Select ⇨ Similar. Photoshop should select the entire background. If it fails to select all of the background, choose Edit ⇨ Undo (Command-Z) and use the rectangular marquee tool to select more portions of the background. You may also want to increase the Tolerance value in the Magic Wand Options dialog box. If Photoshop's selection bleeds into the foreground image, try reducing the Tolerance value.

Step 4. Choose Select ⇨ Inverse. Photoshop selects the foreground image and deselects the background.

Step 5. If the detail you want to select represents only a fraction of the entire image, Command-Shift-drag around the portion of the image that you want to retain using the lasso tool. In Figure 9-7, I Command-Shift-Option-dragged to draw a polygon with the lasso.

If the technique in Step 5 sounds tempting but you have problems keeping three fingers planted on the keyboard as you draw, here's a little hint. You only have to press Command-Shift at the beginning of the drag or until after you complete the first click. After the selection process is established, you can release the Command and Shift keys. The Option key, however, must remain pressed if you want to draw a polygon.

Step 6. Congratulations, you've isolated your complex image. Now you can filter it, colorize it, or perform whatever operation inspired you to select this image in the first place. For myself, I wanted to superimpose the image onto a different background. To do so, I copied the image to the Clipboard (Edit ⇨ Copy), opened the desired background image, and then pasted the first image into place (Edit ⇨ Paste). The result, shown in Figure 9-8, still needs some touching up with the paint and edit tools, but it's not half bad for an automated selection process.

Figure 9-6: Before choosing Select ⇨ Similar, select a few sample portions of the background so that Photoshop has something on which to base its selection range.

Figure 9-7: Command-Shift-Option drag with the lasso tool to intersect the area that you want to select with a free-form polygon.

Figure 9-8: The completed selection superimposed onto a new background.

Saving selections

One of the most frightening experiences I ever endured was watching a selection go down in flames. After nearly 15 minutes of adding and subtracting, Shift-clicking here and Command-dragging there, I clicked with the lasso tool, the universal signal for the Big D (deselect, that is). Luckily, Photoshop can undo changes to selection outlines. Choose Edit ⇨ Undo and you should be back in business.

Of course, if you so much as click after deselecting an image, the Undo command does not retrieve your selection. For this reason, you should back up your selection if you've spent any amount of time on it. The following sets of steps describe a couple of ways to back up a selection.

STEPS: Protecting Your Selection in Photoshop 2.5

Step 1. Click on the quick mask mode icon in the toolbox (the right-hand icon directly under the color controls) to temporarily convert the selection outline to a grayscale image. Assuming that the default settings for the quick mask mode are in effect, deselected areas appear covered with a translucent coat of red paint; selected areas appear as normal.

Step 2. Choose Select ⇨ All (Command-A) to select everything.

Step 3. Choose Edit ⇨ Copy (Command-C) to transfer the image to the Clipboard.

Step 4. Provided you don't copy anything else, your selection is now backed up. However, stopping here isn't all that trustworthy; you can too easily forget and replace the contents of the Clipboard. To make sure you're 100 percent protected, choose the Scrapbook command from the Apple menu to display the Scrapbook desk accessory. Then choose Edit ⇨ Paste (Command-V) to transfer the image to the Scrapbook. Now you're protected.

Step 5. Close the Scrapbook by clicking on its close box. Then click on the marching ants icon (left icon directly under the color controls) to return to your selection outline in progress.

Step 6. If you later need to retrieve your selection, open the Scrapbook, choose Edit ⇨ Copy, close the Scrapbook, return to the quick mask mode, choose Edit ⇨ Paste, and then return to the marching ants mode to see your selection alive and well again.

If you're still using Photoshop 2.0 or you're looking for a way to store a selection permanently with your image, try the following steps instead. They're actually easier to perform — you don't have to go through all that rigmarole with the Scrapbook. But for some reason, the idea of using a *mask channel* — which is simply a portion of the image file in which you can save masks for later use — intimidates some users. At least try the steps out before you pass judgment.

STEPS: Transferring a Selection to a Mask Channel

Step 1. Choose Select ⇨ Save Selection, which converts the selection to a grayscale image and stores it in a separate mask channel, as demonstrated in Figure 9-9. If the current image already contains a mask channel, choosing Save Selection produces a submenu, enabling you to replace the contents of an existing channel or create yet another mask channel.

Step 2. To view the converted selection in Photoshop 2.0, choose the appropriate mask channel from the Mode ⇨ Channel submenu. In Photoshop 2.5, click on the channel name in the Channels palette. Provided this mask channel is the only one in the document, the channel is called #2 if you're editing a grayscale image or #4 if you're editing an RGB image. (In fact, you can press Command-2 or Command-4 to switch to the mask channel.)

Step 3. Return to the standard image-editing mode by choosing the first command from the Mode ⇨ Channel submenu or the first channel name from the Channels palette. Better yet, press Command-1 if you're editing a grayscale image or Command-0 if the image is RGB.

Step 4. Save the image to disk to store the selection permanently. In Photoshop 2.0, only the PICT and native formats accommodate mask channels. In Photoshop 2.5, the TIFF format also suffices. Only the TIFF and native formats can handle more than one mask channel.

Step 5. To later retrieve your selection, choose Select ⇨ Load Selection, which converts the grayscale image in the mask channel to a selection outline. The contents of the mask channel, incidentally, remain intact. If the current image contains more than one mask channel, choosing Load Selection produces a submenu, enabling you to select which of the mask channels you want to convert.

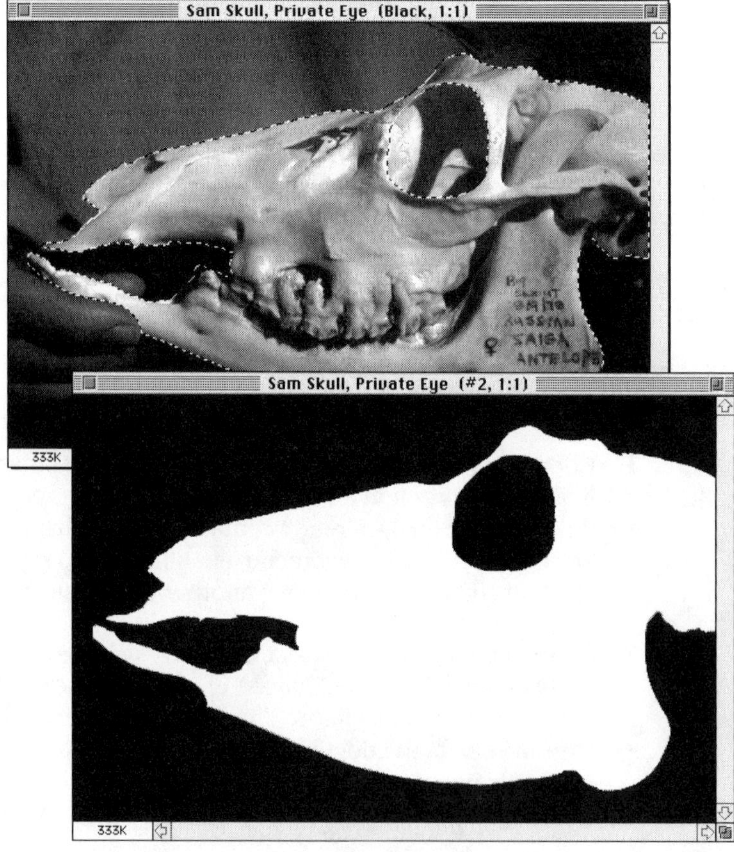

Figure 9-9: Two selection outlines (top) as they appear when stored in a mask channel (bottom). The selected areas appear white, the deselected areas appear black.

How to move and duplicate selections

After you select a portion of an image, you can move either the selection or selection outline to a new location. To do so, just drag the selection while any one of the selection tools is active, regardless of which tool you used to select the image in the first place. For example, after selecting part of an image with the rectangular marquee tool, you can drag it to a new location using the elliptical marquee, lasso, or magic wand tool. You also can move a selection with the pen tool in Photoshop 2.0 or the arrow tool found in Version 2.5's Paths palette.

Normally, both Photoshop 2.0 and 2.5 display the outline of the selected area during a move, as shown in the top image in Figure 9-10. Version 2.5 goes a step farther by also enabling you to preview the selected area in all its splendor as you move it (see the bottom image in Figure 9-10). As you might expect, this significantly slows down the screen refresh speed. It also prevents you from viewing the portion of the image behind the selection. But there are times when this capability comes in extremely handy.

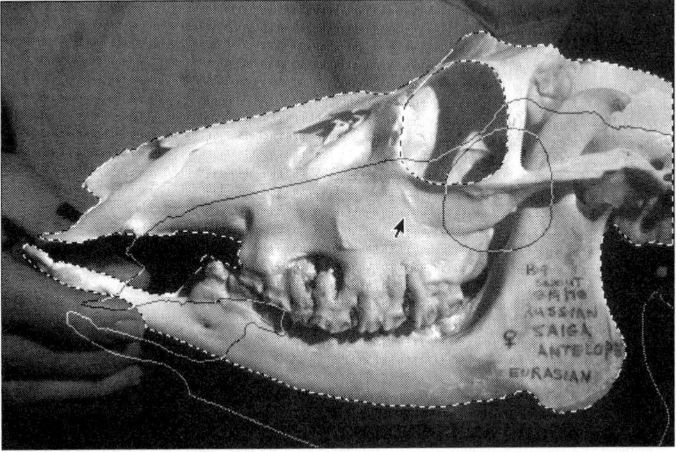

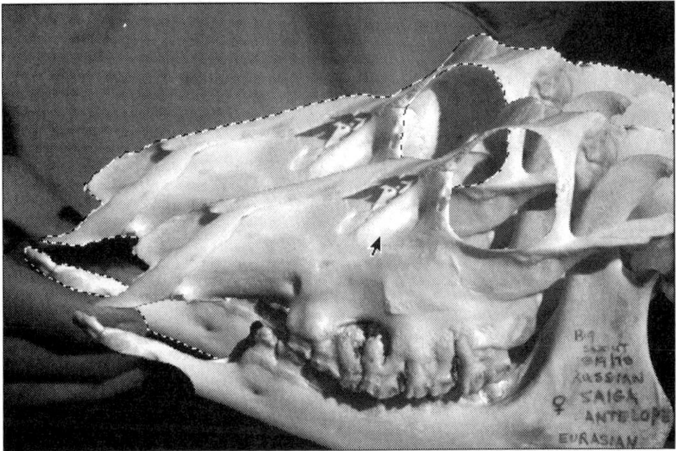

Figure 9-10: In Photoshop 2.5, you can drag a selection right off the bat to see only its outline (top) or you can press and hold the mouse button for a moment before beginning your drag to preview the selection (bottom).

To preview a selection as you move it, click and hold on the selection for a few moments before moving the mouse. The watch cursor appears. The moment the cursor changes back to a right-pointing arrow, you can start dragging.

Making precision movements

Photoshop provides three methods for moving selections in prescribed increments. First, you can nudge a selection in one-pixel increments by pressing an arrow key on the keyboard. This technique is useful for making precise adjustments to the position of an image. Second, you can press Shift during a drag to constrain a move to some 45-degree direction — that is, horizontally, vertically, or diagonally. And third, you can use the Info palette to track your movements and help you locate a precise position in the image.

To display the Info palette, choose Window ⇨ Show Info. Figure 9-11 shows the Info palette as it appears in Photoshop 2.5 and 2.0. The items at the bottom of the palette monitor movement, as follows:

- **X, Y:** These values show the coordinate position of your cursor. The distance is measured from the upper left corner of the image in the current unit of measure. The unit of measure in Figure 9-11 is pixels.
- **ΔX, ΔY:** These values indicate the distance of your move as measured horizontally and vertically.
- **A, D:** The A and D values reflect the angle and direct distance of your drag.
- **W, H:** Not displayed in Photoshop 2.0, these values reflect the width and height of your selection.

Figure 9-11: Though the Info palette for Photoshop 2.5 (left) appears to be different from that for Version 2.0 (right), both palettes provide virtually the same feedback when you move a selection.

Cloning a selection

When you move a selection, you leave a hole in your image in the background color, as shown in the top half of Figure 9-12. If you prefer instead to leave the original in place during a move, you have to *clone* the selection — that is, create a copy of the selection without upsetting the contents of the Clipboard. Photoshop provides three different means for cloning a selection:

- **Option-dragging:** Press the Option key and drag a selection to clone it. The bottom half of Figure 9-12 shows a selection that I Option-dragged three times. (Between clonings, I changed the gray level of each selection to make each one more uniquely identifiable.)
- **Option-arrowing:** Press Option in combination with one of the arrow keys to both clone the selection and nudge it one pixel away from the original. If you want to move the image multiple pixels, Option-arrow the first time only. Then just nudge the clone using the arrow key alone. Otherwise, you create a bunch of clones that you can't undo.
- **Floating:** In Photoshop 2.5, choose Select ⇨ Float (Command-J) to clone the selection in place. You then can move the clone to a new location as desired. (For more information about floating, read the upcoming "Floating a selection" section.)

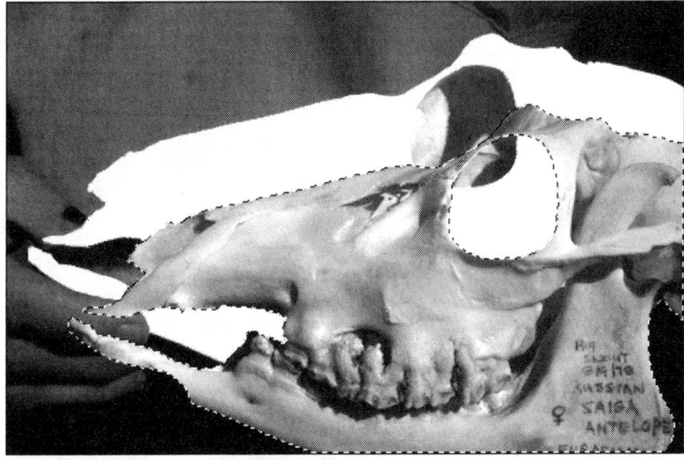

Figure 9-12: When you move a selection, you leave a gaping hole in the selection's wake (top). When you clone an image, you leave a copy of the selection behind. (The selection in the bottom image was cloned several times.)

Moving a selection outline

If a selection outline surrounds the wrong portion of an image, you can move it independently of the image by Command-Option-dragging. This technique serves as yet another means for manipulating inaccurate selection outlines. It also enables you to mimic one portion of an image in another portion of the image.

In the top image in Figure 9-13, I Command-Option-dragged the skull outline down and to the right so that it still overlapped the skull. Note that the image itself remains unaltered. I then lightened the new selection, applied a couple of strokes to set it off from its background, and gave it stripes. For all I know, this is exactly what a female Russian Saiga Antelope looks like.

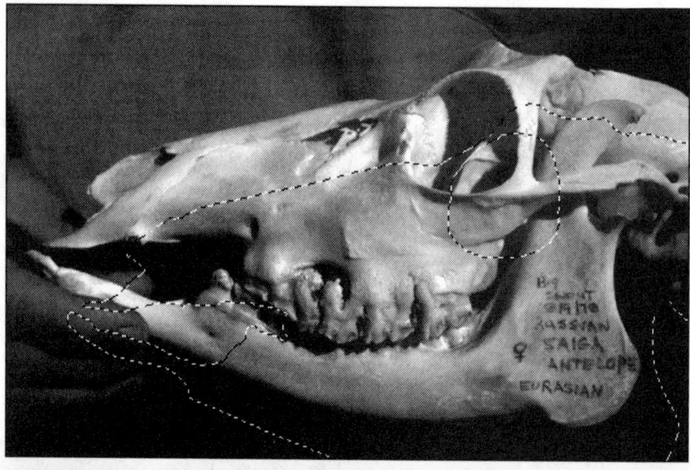

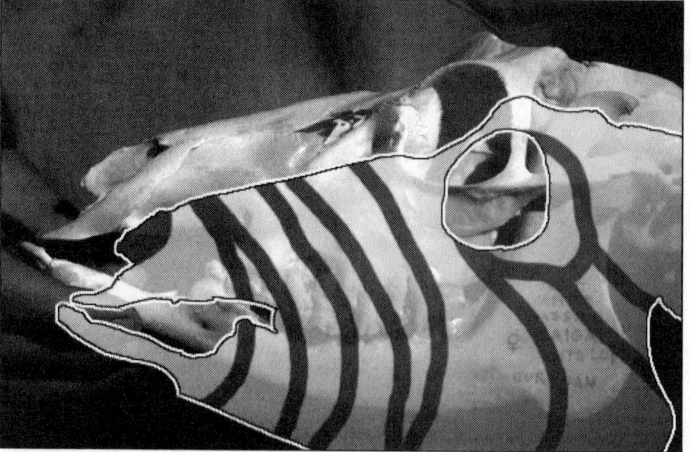

Figure 9-13: Command-Option-drag to move a selection outline independently of its image (top). The area to which you drag the selection outline becomes the new selection (bottom).

Floating a selection

A *floating selection* is a selection that hovers above the surface of the image. The beauty of a floating selection is that you can manipulate it by painting inside it, applying filters, coloring the image, and so on, all without affecting the underlying image itself. Then you can mix the floating selection with the underlying image by adjusting the Opacity slider bar in the Brushes palette, selecting an overlay mode from the brush mode pop-up menu (both functions of Photoshop 2.5), or choosing Edit ⇨ Composite Controls (Edit ⇨ Paste Controls in Photoshop 2.0).

You can float a selection in any of the following ways:

- **Paste:** When you paste an image from the Clipboard into the image window, the pasted image floats inside a selection outline, waiting for your next instructions.
- **Move:** When you move a selection by dragging it or pressing an arrow key, Photoshop floats the selection at its new location.
- **Clone:** Whether you clone a selection by Option-dragging it or pressing Option in combination with an arrow key, Photoshop floats the cloned selection.
- **Select ⇨ Float:** In Photoshop 2.5, you can clone a selection in place, which has the added effect of floating it, by choosing Select ⇨ Float (Command-J).

Conversely, any of the following techniques *defloat* a selection — that is, drop it in place — again making the image itself susceptible to changes:

- **Deselect:** Because a floating selection must remain selected to remain floating, choosing Select ⇨ None (Command-D) defloats a selection. Likewise, any operation that has the added effect of deselecting an image, such as selecting a different portion of the image, changing the canvas size, or choosing File ⇨ Revert, defloats the selection.
- **Add to the selection:** If you add to a selection outline by pressing Shift while using any of the selection tools (or adding a path to a selection outline from the Make Selection dialog box in Photoshop 2.5), Photoshop defloats the image. However, you can subtract from a selection outline and intersect it without defloating it.
- **Stroke the selection:** Photoshop automatically defloats a selection when you apply Edit ⇨ Stroke.
- **Editing a mask:** Photoshop retains selection outlines when you switch to a different color or mask channel. However, if you edit the selection in a different channel, you immediately defloat it. Furthermore, Photoshop 2.5 automatically defloats a selection when you switch to the quick mask mode, whether you edit the mask or not.
- **Select ⇨ Defloat:** In Photoshop 2.5, you can drop a selection by choosing Select ⇨ Defloat (Command-J).

Removing halos

One last note to lead you into the next discussion, which explains selection softening: When you move or clone an antialiased selection, you sometimes take with you a few pixels from the selection's previous background. These pixels can create a haloing effect if they clash with the selection's new background, as demonstrated in the top image in Figure 9-14.

You can instruct Photoshop to replace the fringe pixels with colors from neighboring pixels by choosing Select ⇨ Defringe. Enter the thickness of the perceived halo in the Width option box to tell Photoshop which pixels you want to replace. To create the image shown in the bottom half of Figure 9-14, I entered a Width value of 2. If you have to use a higher value than 2, you're probably better off redrawing your selection.

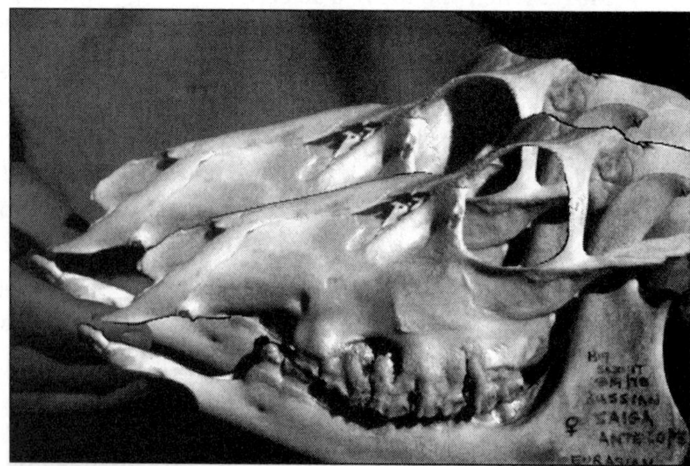

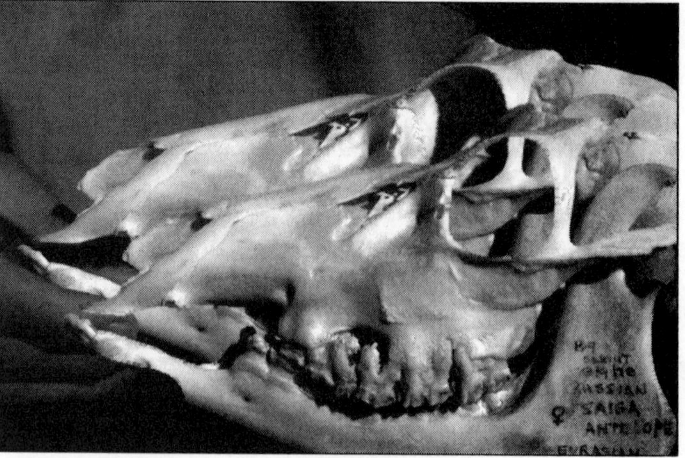

Figure 9-14: To remove the halo around the cloned skull (top), I used the Defringe command to replace the pixels around the perimeter of the selection with colors borrowed from neighboring pixels (bottom).

The Defringe command is applicable strictly to floating selections. Also, you'll generally only want to apply Select ⇨ Defringe to antialiased selections. The command performs some pretty hideous effects on feathered selections.

How to soften selection outlines

You can soften a selection in two ways. The first method is *antialiasing,* which I introduced in Chapter 5. Antialiasing is an intelligent and automatic softening algorithm that mimics the appearance of edges you'd expect to see in a sharply focused photograph. Where does the term *antialias* come from? Well, to *alias* an electronic signal is to dump essential data, thus degrading the quality of a sound or image. Antialiasing boosts the signal and condenses it in a way that preserves the overall quality.

When you draw an antialiased selection outline in Photoshop, the program calculates the hard-edged selection at twice its actual size. It then shrinks the selection in half using bicubic interpolation, as described in the "General environmental preferences" section of Chapter 4. The result is a crisp image with no visible jagged edges.

The second softening method, *feathering,* is less scientific. Feathering gradually dissipates the opacity of the pixels around the edge of a selection. You can specify the number of pixels affected — either before or after drawing a selection — by entering a value into the Feather Radius option box. To feather a selection before you draw it, double-click on the rectangular marquee, elliptical marquee, or lasso tool icon. (Only the lasso tool provides this option in Photoshop 2.0.) To feather a selection after drawing it, choose Select ⇨ Feather.

Although you can soften a selection after you draw it, you can't soften the selection after you paste it or drag it over another portion of the image. If you apply the Feather command to a floating selection, you see no immediate effect. This is because Photoshop adhered the selection to the image and feathered the outline of this new selection, very likely not what you intended. I recommend that you try feathering a floating selection for yourself to see the kind of interesting little messes you can create.

The Feather Radius value determines the distance over which Photoshop fades a selection, measured in pixels in both directions from the original selection outline. Therefore, if you enter a radius of 4 pixels, Photoshop fades the selection over an 8-pixel stretch. Figure 9-15 shows three selections lifted from the image at the bottom of the figure. The first selection is antialiased only. I feathered the second and third selections, assigning Feather Radius values of 4 and 12, respectively. As you can see, a small feather radius makes a selection appear fuzzy; a larger radius makes it fade into view.

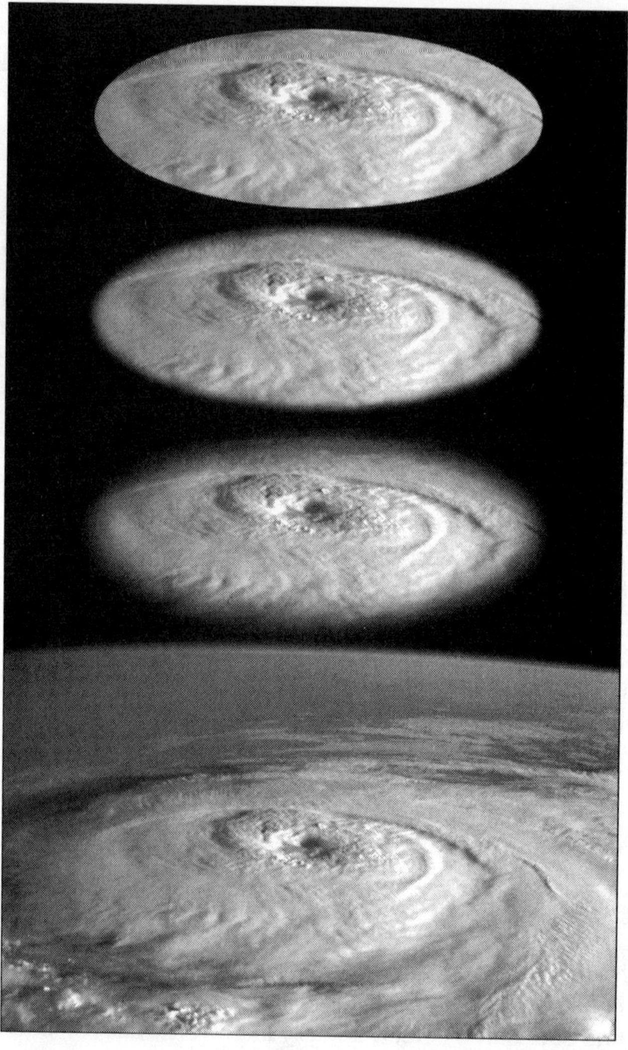

Figure 9-15: Three clones selected with the elliptical marquee tool. The top image is antialiased and not feathered; the next is feathered with a radius of 4 pixels; and the third is feathered with a radius of 12 pixels.

You can use feathering to remove an element from an image while leaving the background intact, a process I describe in the following steps. The image described in the steps, shown in Figure 9-16, is a NASA photo of a satellite with the earth in the background. I wanted to use this background with another image, but to do so I first had to get rid of that satellite. By Command-Option-dragging, feathering, and cloning, I covered the satellite with a patch so seamless you'd swear the satellite was never there.

Figure 9-16: The mission was to remove the satellite by covering it up with selections cloned from the background; the procedure is discussed in the section "STEPS: Removing an Element from an Image."

STEPS: Removing an Element from an Image

Step 1. Draw a selection around the element using the lasso tool. The selection doesn't have to be an exact fit; in fact, you want it to be rather loose, allowing a buffer zone of at least six pixels between the edges of the image and the selection outline.

Step 2. Now that you've specified the element you want to remove, you have to find some portion of the image that will cover the element in a manner that matches the surrounding background. In Figure 9-17, the best match seemed to be an area just below and to the right of the satellite. To select this area, move the selection outline independently of the image by Command-Option-dragging. Be sure to allow some space between the selection outline and the element you're trying to cover.

Step 3. Choose Select ⇨ Feather. Enter a small value (8 or less) in the Feather Radius option box — just enough to make the edges fuzzy. I, for example, entered 3. Then press Return to initiate the operation.

Step 4. Option-drag the feathered selection to clone and position the patch over the element you want to cover, as shown in Figure 9-18. To correctly align the patch, choose Select ⇨ Hide Edges (Command-H) to hide the marching ants and then nudge the patch into position with the arrow keys.

Step 5. My patch was only partially successful. The upper left corner of the selection matches clouds in the background, but the lower right corner is dark and cloudless, an obvious rift in the visual continuity of the image. The solution: try again. With the lasso tool still active, I drew a lose outline around the dark portion of the image and Command-Option-dragged it up and to the left as shown in Figure 9-19.

Step 6. It's all déjà vu from here on out. I chose Select ⇨ Feather, entered 6 into the Feather radius option box — thus allowing the clouds a sufficient range to taper off — and pressed Return. I then Option-dragged the feathered patch over the dark, cloudless rift; nudged, nudged, nudged; and voilà! No more satellite. Figure 9-20 shows $200 million worth of hardware vaporized in less than five minutes.

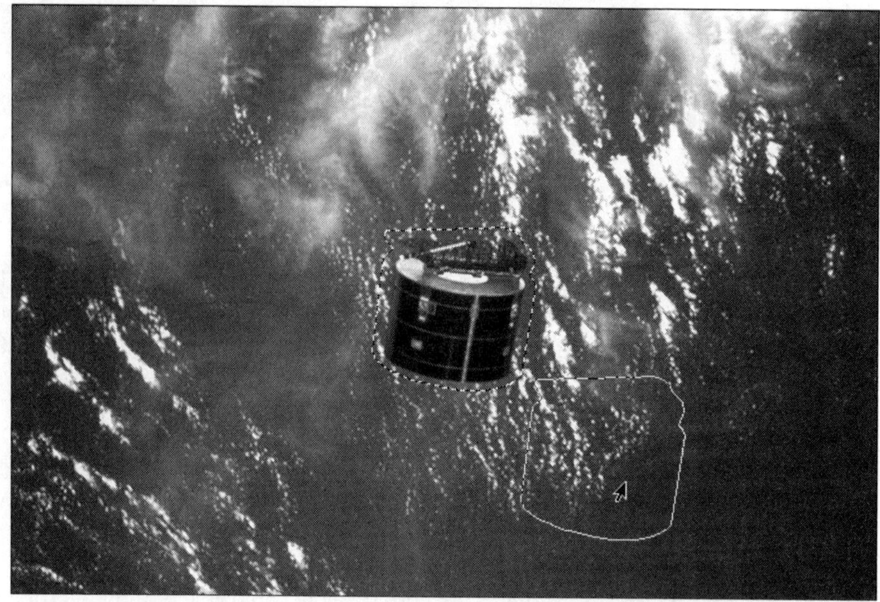

Figure 9-17: After drawing a loose outline around the satellite with the lasso tool, I Command-Option-dragged the outline to select a portion of the background.

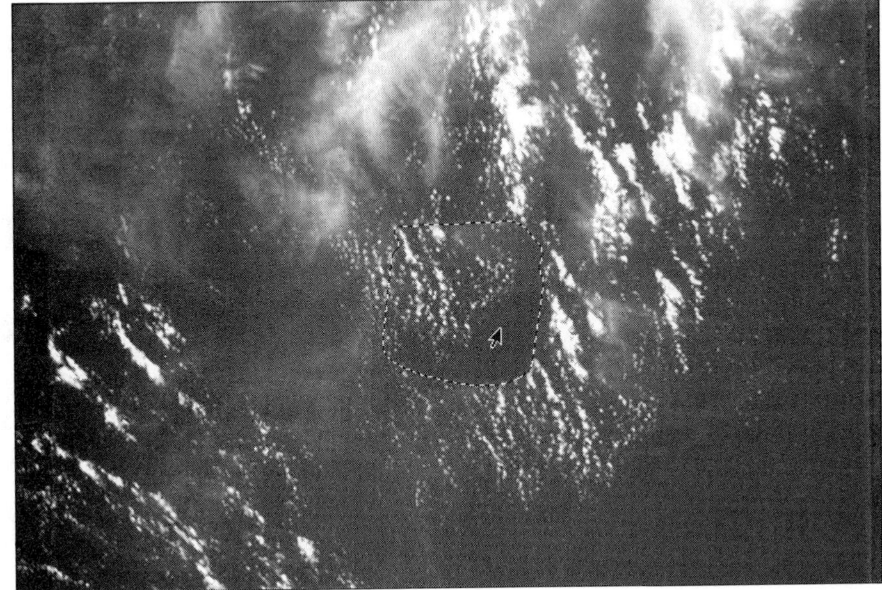

Figure 9-18: Next, I Option-dragged the feathered selection over the satellite. The patch was imperfect and required further adjustments.

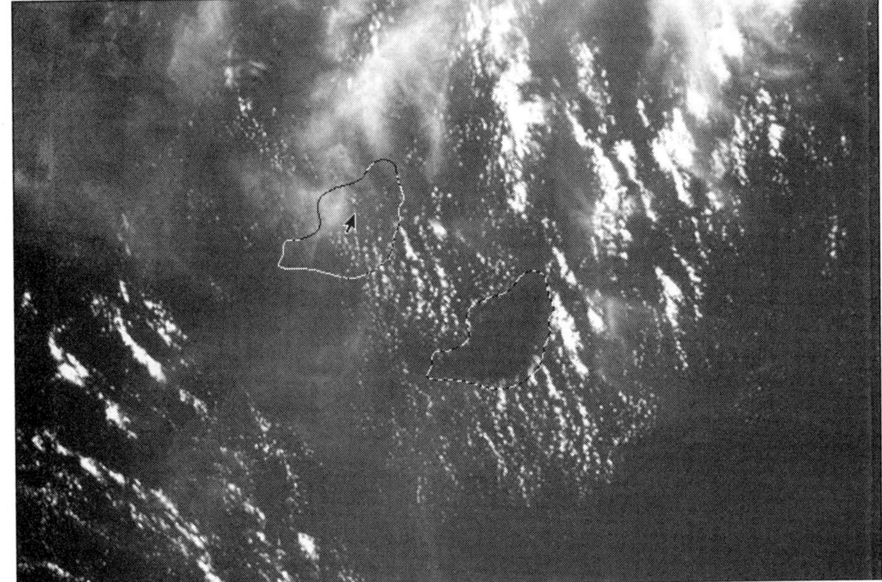

Figure 9-19: I drew a new outline around the dark, cloudless portion of the patch and Command-Option-dragged the outline to a different spot in the background.

Figure 9-20: I selected a new bit of cloudy sky and placed it over the formerly cloudless portion of the patch. Satellite? What satellite?

How to Draw and Edit Paths

The path tools represent Photoshop's most precise and arguably its most flexible selection function, far outpacing anything I've explained so far. (The only capability that even compares in the flexibility department is the quick mask mode, which I examine later in this chapter.) However, although a godsend to the experienced user, the path tools represent something of a chore to novices and intermediates. The fact is, it takes most users quite a while to get up and running with the path tools because you have to draw a selection outline one point at a time.

Luckily, this is one labor-intensive task that's worth every minute of effort. After you become familiar with these tools, I guarantee that you won't edit an image without turning to them at least once.

A first look at paths

Insofar as path creation functions are concerned, Photoshop 2.0 provides a pen tool, a couple of commands under the Select menu, and that's about it. By contrast, Version 2.5 provides five tools and an extensive palette of editing options, as shown in Figure 9-21. Because of its dramatically enhanced capabilities, my explanations focus on Version 2.5's Paths palette. Nevertheless, I'll also try to keep Version 2.0 users apprised of what they can and cannot accomplish.

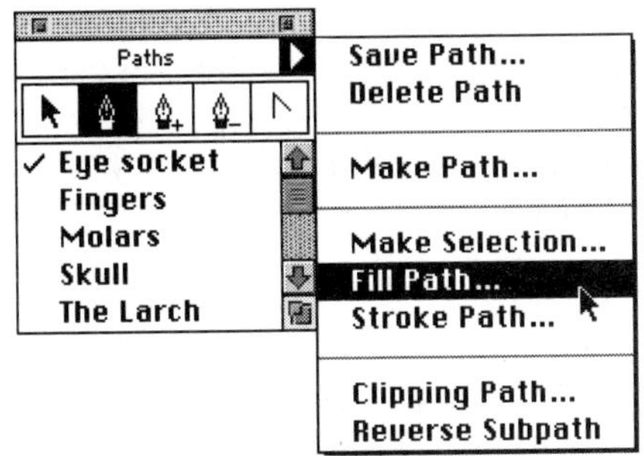

Figure 9-21: The Paths palette provides access to every one of Photoshop 2.5's path drawing and editing functions.

How paths work

Paths differ from normal selections in that they exist on the equivalent of a distinct object-oriented layer that sits in front of the bitmapped image. This setup enables you to edit a path with point-by-point precision after you draw it to make sure that it meets the exact requirements of your artwork. It also prevents you from accidentally messing up the image, as you can when you edit ordinary selection outlines. After creating the path, you convert it into a standard selection outline before using it to edit the contents of the image, as explained in the section "Converting and saving paths," later in this chapter.

The following steps explain the basic process of drawing a selection with the path tools.

STEPS: Drawing a Selection with the Path Tools

Step 1. Use the pen tool to draw the outline of your prospective selection.

Step 2. If the outline of the path requires some adjustment, reshape it using the other path tools in Photoshop 2.5 or using keyboard and mouse techniques in Photoshop 2.0.

Step 3. When you get the path exactly the way you want it, save the path in Photoshop 2.5 by choosing the Save Path command from the Paths palette menu. Skip this step if you're using Version 2.0.

Step 4. Convert the path to a selection by clicking inside it in Version 2.0 or by choosing the Make Selection command in Version 2.5. In Version 2.5.1, you can simply press the Enter key.

Be sure to save your path in Photoshop 2.5 before converting it to a selection. If you do not, Photoshop continues to display the path in front of your selection, which may prove a nuisance. The only way to hide an unsaved path is to delete it entirely — typically by pressing the Delete key twice — a rather drastic step. If you just take a moment to save the path, you can hide it and even bring it back later on.

That's all there is to it. After you convert the path to a selection, it works just like any of the selection outlines described earlier. You can feather a selection, move it, copy it, clone it, or apply one of the special effects described in future chapters.

Using the Paths palette tools

Before I get into my long-winded description of how you draw and edit paths, here is a quick introduction to the tools available from the Paths palette:

- **Arrow:** This tool lets you drag points and handles to reshape a path. To access the arrow tool cursor in Photoshop 2.0, press the Command key while using the pen tool.
- **Pen:** Use the pen tool to draw paths in Photoshop one point at a time. I explain this tool in detail in the following section.
- **Insert point:** Click on an existing path to add a point to it. To access this function in Photoshop 2.0, Command-Option-click on the path with the pen tool.
- **Remove point:** Click on an existing point in a path to delete the point without creating a break in the path's outline. To access this function in Photoshop 2.0, Command-Option-click on a point with the pen tool.
- **Convert point:** Click or drag on a point to convert it to a corner or smooth point. You also can drag on a handle to convert the point. This function is unavailable in Photoshop 2.0.

The terms *path, point, smooth point,* and others associated with drawing paths are explained in the upcoming section "Defining points and segments."

Drawing with the pen tool

When drawing with the pen tool, you build a path by creating individual points. Photoshop automatically connects the points with *segments* — which are simply straight or curved lines.

All paths in Photoshop are *Bézier* (pronounced *bay-zee-ay*) *paths,* meaning that they rely on the same mathematical curve definitions that make up the core of the PostScript printer language. The Bézier curve model allows for zero, one, or two levers to be associated with each point in a path. These levers are called *Bézier control handles,* or simply *handles.* You can move each handle in relation to a point, enabling you to bend and tug at a curved segment like a piece of soft wire.

The following list summarizes how you can use the pen tool to build paths in Photoshop. (Only the first two items are applicable to Photoshop 2.0.) I describe each of these methods in more detail in the upcoming sections.

- **Adding segments:** To build a path, create one point after another until the path is the desired length and shape. Photoshop automatically draws a segment between each new point and its predecessor.
- **Closing the path:** If you plan on eventually converting the path to a selection outline, you need to complete the outline by clicking again on the first point in the path. Every point will then have one segment coming into it and another segment exiting it. Such a path is called a *closed path* because it forms one continuous outline.
- **Leaving the path open:** If you plan on applying the Stroke Path command in Photoshop 2.5 (explained later), you may not want to close a path. To leave it open, so that it has a specific beginning and ending, deactivate the path by saving it. After you complete the save operation, you can click in the image window to begin a new path.
- **Extending an open path:** To reactivate an open path, click or drag on one of its endpoints. Photoshop draws a segment between the endpoint and the next point you create.
- **Joining two open paths:** To join one open path with another open path, click or drag on an endpoint in the first path and then click or drag on an endpoint in the second.

Defining points and segments

Points in a Bézier path act as little road signs. Each point steers the path by specifying how a segment enters it and how another segment exits it. You specify the identity of each little road sign by clicking, dragging, or Option-dragging with the pen tool. The following items explain the specific kinds of points and segments you can create in Photoshop. See Figure 9-22 for examples.

- **Corner point:** Click with the pen tool to create a *corner point,* which represents the corner between two straight segments in a path.
- **Straight segment:** Click at two different locations to create a straight segment between two corner points. Shift-click to draw a 45-degree-angle segment between the new corner point and its predecessor.
- **Smooth point:** Drag to create a *smooth point* with two symmetrical Bézier control handles. A smooth point ensures that one segment meets with another in a continuous arc.
- **Curved segment:** Drag at two different locations to create a curved segment between two smooth points.
- **Curved segment followed by straight:** After drawing a curved segment, Option-click on the smooth point you just created to delete the forward Bézier control handle. This step converts the smooth point to a corner point with one handle. Then click at a different location to append a straight segment to the end of the curved segment.
- **Straight segment followed by curved:** After drawing a straight segment, drag from the corner point you just created to add a Bézier control handle. Then drag again at a different location to append a curved segment to the end of the straight segment.
- **Cusp point:** After drawing a curved segment, Option-drag from the smooth point you just created to redirect the forward Bézier control handle, converting the smooth point to a corner point with two independent handles, sometimes known as a *cusp point.* Then drag again at a new location to append a curved segment that proceeds in a different direction than the previous curved segment.

Figure 9-22: The different kinds of points and segments you can draw with the pen tool.

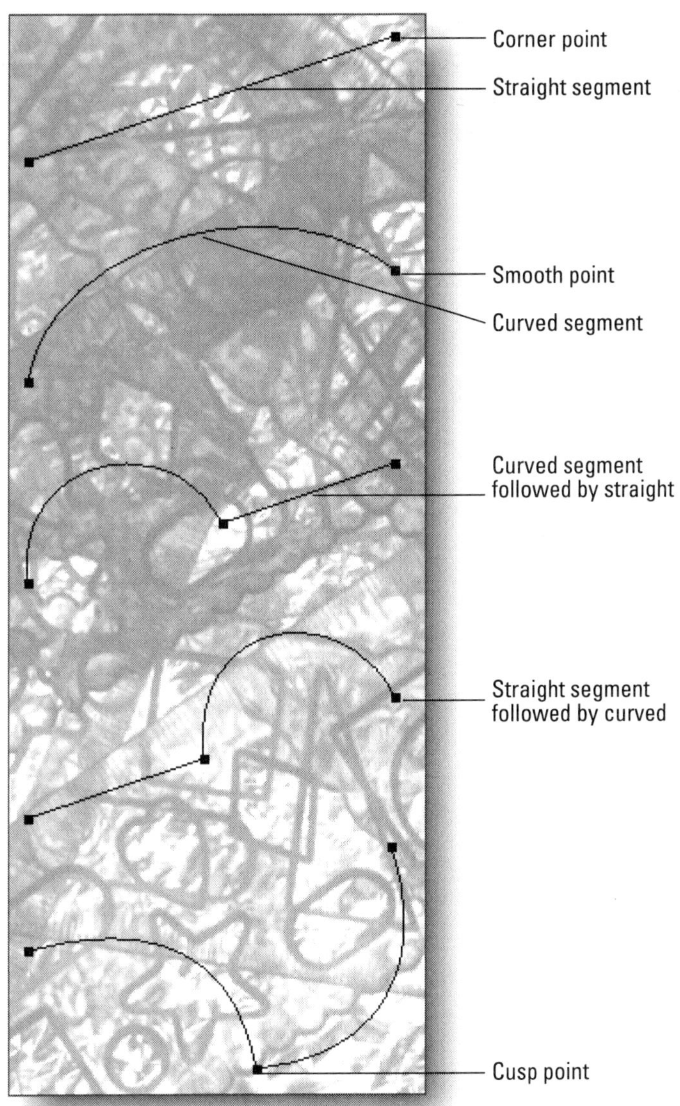

Test-driving the pen tool

It's one thing to read and even understand a list of ways to use Photoshop's most complicated tool, but it's another to actually put it to use. The best way to learn about the pen tool is to try it out for yourself. The following steps walk you through a simple pen-tool scenario. After that, I explain some of the pen tool's more complicated functions. May the Bézier be with you.

STEPS: Drawing a Straight-sided Polygon

Step 1. Select the pen tool and click at some location in the image window to create a corner point, which will represent a sharp corner in your path. The corner point appears as a tiny gray square to show that it is selected. It is also *open-ended,* meaning that it doesn't have both a segment coming into it and a segment going out from it. In fact, this new corner point — I'll call it point A — is associated with no segment whatsoever. It is a lone point, open-ended in two directions.

Step 2. Click at a new location in the image to create a new corner point — point B. Photoshop automatically draws a straight segment from point A to point B, as illustrated in Figure 9-23. Notice that point A now appears hollow rather than solid. This shows that point A is a member of a selected path but is itself deselected. Point B is selected and open-ended. Photoshop automatically selects a point immediately after you create it and deselects all other points.

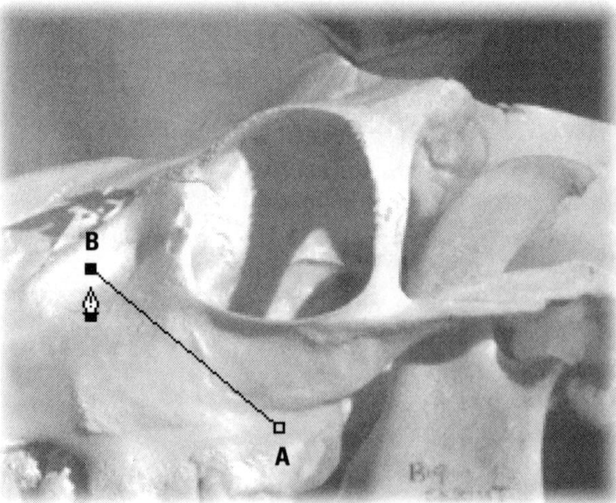

Figure 9-23: Draw a straight segment by clicking at each of two separate locations with the pen tool.

Step 3. Click a third time with the pen tool to create point C, yet another corner point. Because point B now has a segment coming into it and one emanating from it, it is no longer open-ended, as verified by Figure 9-24. Such a point is called an *interior point.* A point may be associated with no more than two segments.

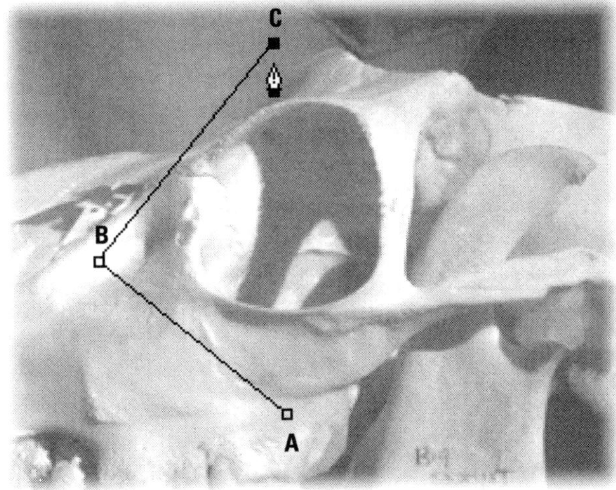

Figure 9-24: Point B is now an interior point, incapable of receiving additional segments.

Step 4. You can keep adding points to a path one at a time for a long as you like. When finished, you can *close* the path by again clicking on point A, as demonstrated in Figure 9-25. Because point A is open-ended, it willingly accepts the segment drawn between it and the previous point in the path. You see the closed path in Figure 9-26.

Step 5. All points in a closed path are interior points. Therefore, the path you just drew is no longer active, meaning that Photoshop will draw no segment between the next point you create and any point in the closed path. To verify this, click again with the pen tool. You create a new independent point, which is selected and open-ended in two directions — shown as point E in Figure 9-26. Meanwhile, the closed path becomes deselected. The path-creation process is begun anew.

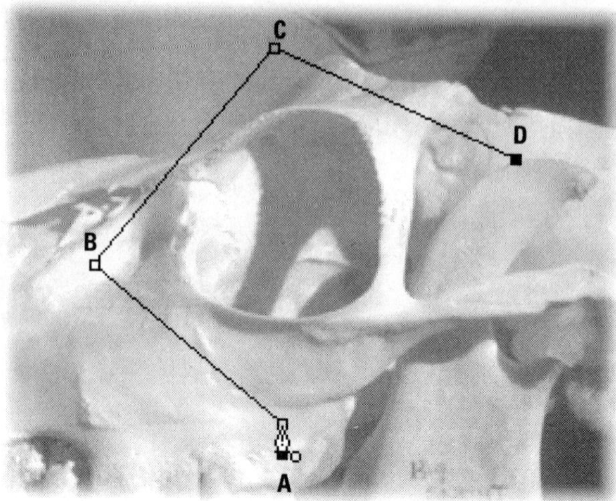

Figure 9-25: Clicking on the first point in a path closes the path and deactivates it. The next point you create begins a new path.

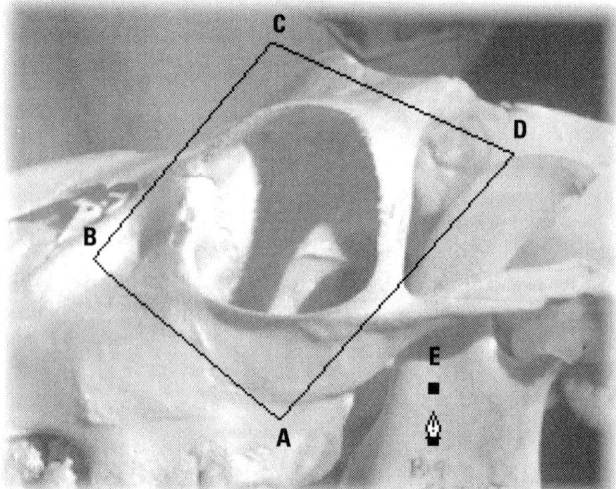

Figure 9-26: Creating a point E that is independent of the previous path deselects that path and begins a new one.

Drawing curved segments

All right, I admit it, you could have drawn that last outline by Option-clicking with the lasso tool. But the steps you just followed provide an important basis of knowledge you need to create more complicated paths. Now that you know your way around a Bézier polygon, you're ready to handle the good stuff.

The real advantage of the pen tool is that it enables you to draw very precise curves. When you drag to create a smooth point, for example, you specify the location of two Bézier control handles, each of which appear as a tiny circle perched at the end of a hairline that connects the handle to its point (see Figure 9-27). These handles act as levers, bending segments relative to the smooth point itself.

The point at which you begin dragging with the pen tool determines the location of the smooth point; the point at which you release becomes a Bézier control handle that affects the *next* segment you create. A second handle appears symmetrically about the smooth point to the first. This handle determines the curvature of the most recent segment, as demonstrated in Figure 9-27.

You might think of a smooth point as the center of a small seesaw, with the Bézier control handles acting as opposite ends. If you push down on one handle, the opposite handle goes up, and vice versa.

Smooth points act no differently than corner points when it comes to building paths. You can easily combine smooth and corner points in the same path by alternatively clicking and dragging. However, if the first point in a path is a smooth point, you should drag rather than click on the point when closing the path. Otherwise, you run the risk of altering the identity of the point, as discussed in the next section.

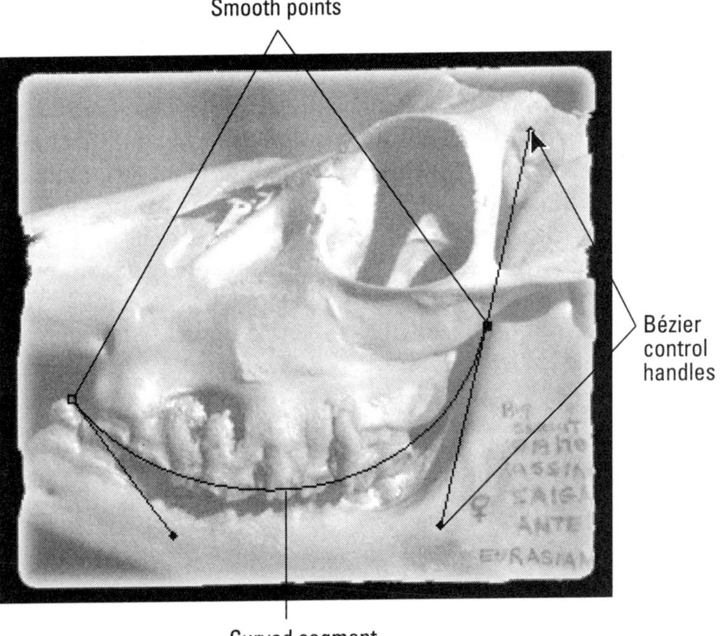

Figure 9-27: Drag with the pen tool to create a smooth point flanked by two Bézier control handles.

Creating cusps

A smooth point must *always* have two Bézier control handles, each positioned in an imaginary straight line with the point itself. A corner point, however, is much more versatile. It can have zero, one, or two handles. To create a corner point that has one or two Bézier control handles, you must manipulate an existing corner or smooth point while in the process of creating a path. The following steps provide three examples of how this technique can work.

STEPS: Deleting Handles from Smooth Points

Step 1. Begin by drawing the path shown in Figure 9-28. You do so by dragging three times with the pen tool. First, drag downward from the right point (A). Then drag leftward from the bottom point (B) and finally drag upward from the left point (C), which is selected in the figure. The result is an active path composed of three smooth points.

Step 2. Photoshop allows you to alter the most recent point while in the process of creating a path. Suppose that you want to change the semicircle into a bowl-shaped path like the one shown in Figure 9-29. Because smooth points can be associated only with curved segments, you must convert the top two smooth points to corner points. To convert the most recent point — the one on the left — press the Option key and click with the pen tool on the selected smooth point. In doing so, you amputate the forward handle, which does not yet control a segment.

Step 3. You now have an open path composed of two smooth points and a corner point. You still need to close the path and to amputate a handle belonging to the first smooth point (A). Both maneuvers are accomplished in a single operation, that of Option-clicking on the first smooth point. It's that simple. With one mouse operation, you close the path and amputate the Bézier control handle that would otherwise have controlled the most recent segment. Hence, the new segment is straight, bordered on both sides by corner points with one handle each, as shown in Figure 9-29.

Photoshop only shows handles that affect the active segment. Others are hidden, but still in effect. That's why you may not see some of the handles you expect to see in the figures that accompany this chapter.

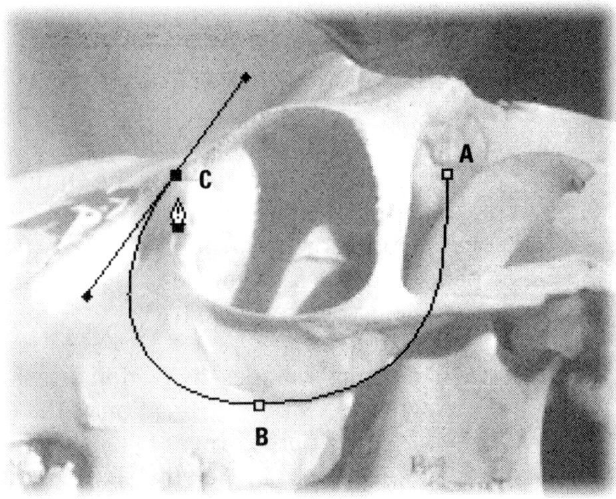

Figure 9-28: An active semicircular path with a selected, open-ended smooth point.

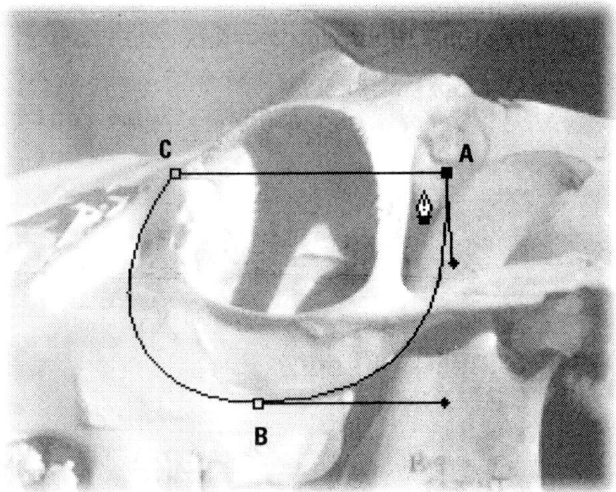

Figure 9-29: By Option-clicking with the pen tool on the two top points, you change the existing smooth points to corner points with one Bézier control handle apiece.

STEPS: Converting a Smooth Point to a Cusp

Step 1. Begin again by drawing the path shown in Figure 9-28, as described in the first step of the previous section.

Step 2. In this step and the next one, you close the path with a concave top, resulting in a crescent shape. All segments in a crescent are curved, but the upper and lower segments meet to form two cusps. This means that you must change the two top smooth points to corner points with two Bézier control handles apiece — one controlling the upper segment and one controlling a lower segment.

To subtract a handle from a smooth point and add a new handle to the resulting corner point in one operation, press the Option key and drag from the selected, open-ended smooth point on the left side of the path (C). The moment you begin to Option-drag, the point's identity changes to a corner point and a new handle emerges, as shown in Figure 9-30. This handle controls the next segment you create.

Step 3. You close the path in a similar manner, by Option-dragging from the first smooth point of the path (A). Notice the location of the cursor as you drag, as demonstrated in the upper right corner of Figure 9-31. You drag in one direction, but the handle emerges in the opposite direction. This effect occurs because when dragging with the pen tool, you always drag in the direction of the forward segment — that is, the one that *exits* the current point. Photoshop positions the handle controlling the newly created segment — the segment that *enters* the current point — symmetrically to your drag, even if it is the only handle being manipulated.

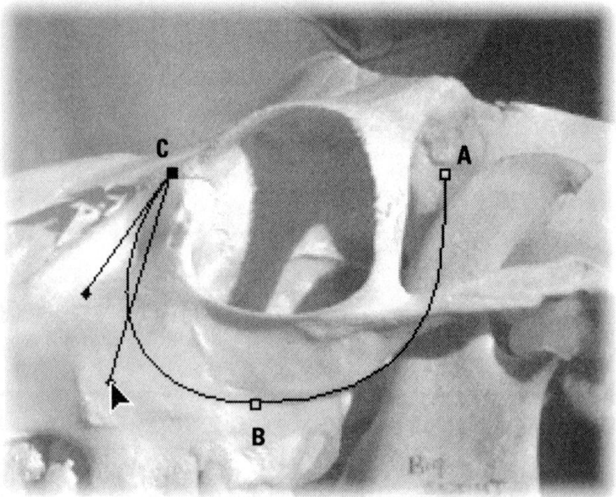

Figure 9-30: Press the Option key and drag from the selected smooth point to convert the point to a cusp.

Figure 9-31: Close the path by Option-dragging on the first point in the path.

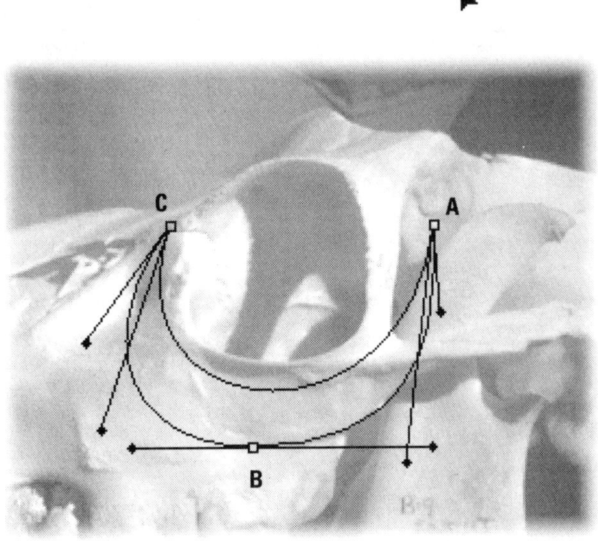

STEPS: Adding a Handle to a Corner Point

Step 1. This exercise demonstrates how you add a handle to an existing open-ended corner point that is so far associated only with straight segments. Begin by creating the straight-sided path shown in Figure 9-32. Well, create something like it, anyway. Actually, it doesn't matter how many points are in the path, as long as they're all corner points.

Step 2. By dragging from the selected, open-ended corner point, you extract a single Bézier control handle, as shown in Figure 9-33. Note that you don't convert the corner point to a smooth point by dragging from it. Although a smooth point can be changed to a corner point, a corner point can-not be changed to a smooth point using the pen tool. No doubt a more clever writer could come up with some kind of insightful XY chromosome analogy at this point, but I'll be darned if I can think of one.

Step 3. To close the path, drag on the first corner point in the path, as demonstrated in Figure 9-34. Once again, you drag in the opposite direction of the emerging Bézier control handle.

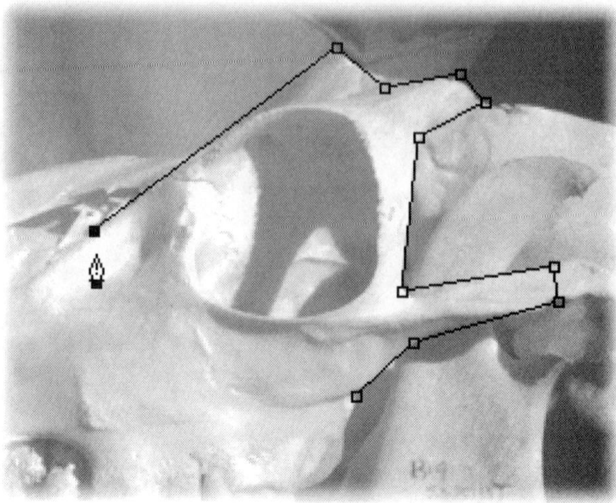

Figure 9-32: An active path composed entirely of straight segments with a selected, open-ended corner point.

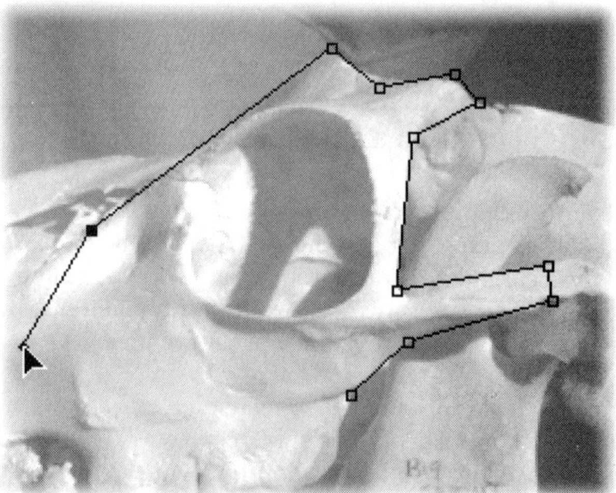

Figure 9-33: Drag from the selected corner point to add a Bézier control handle.

Reshaping existing paths

As you become more familiar with the pen tool, you'll draw paths correctly the first time around more and more frequently. But you'll never get it right 100 percent of the time or even 50 percent of the time. From your first timid steps until you develop into a seasoned pro, you'll rely heavily on Photoshop's ability to *reshape* paths by moving points and handles, adding and deleting points, and converting points to change the curvature of segments. So don't worry if you don't draw a path correctly the first time. The paths tools provide all the second chances you'll ever need.

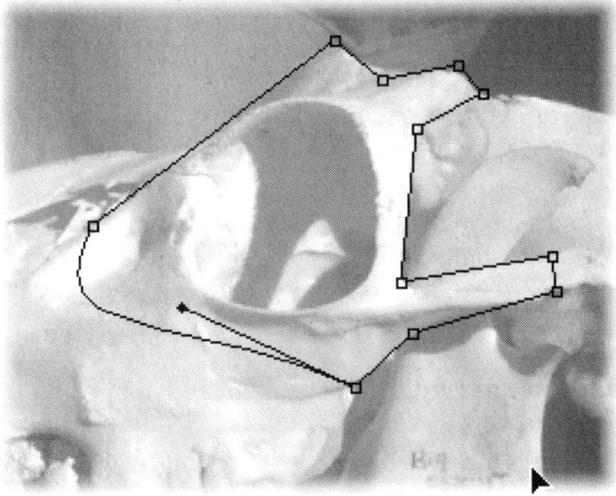

Figure 9-34: Close the path by dragging on the first corner point in the path.

Using the arrow tool

The arrow tool represents the foremost path reshaping function in Photoshop. After selecting this tool, you can perform any of the following functions:

- **Selecting points:** Click on a point to select it independently of other points in a path. Shift-click to add a point to a selection, even if the point belongs to a different path than other selected points. In Photoshop 2.5, you can Option-click on a path to select all of its points in one fell swoop. You can even marquee points by dragging in a rectangle around them. You *cannot,* however, apply commands from the Select menu, such as All or None, to the selection of paths.
- **Drag selected points:** To move one or more points in a path, select the points you want to move and drag one of the selected points. All selected points move the same distance and direction. When you move a point while a neighboring point remains stationary, the segment between the two points shrinks, stretches, and bends to accommodate the change in distance. Segments located between two selected or deselected points remain unchanged during a move.

You can move selected points in one-pixel increments by pressing arrow keys. If both a portion of the image and points in a path are selected, the arrow keys move the point only. Because paths reside on a higher layer, they take precedent in all functions that might concern them.

- **Drag a segment directly:** You also can reshape a path by dragging its segments. When you drag a straight segment, the two corner points on either side of the segment move as well. As illustrated in Figure 9-35, the neighboring segments stretch, shrink, or bend to accommodate the drag. When you drag a curved segment, however, you stretch, shrink, or bend that segment only, as demonstrated in Figure 9-36.

When you drag a curved segment, drag from the middle of the segment, approximately equidistant from both its points. This method provides the best leverage and ensures that the segment doesn't go flying off in some weird direction you hadn't anticipated.

- **Drag a Bézier control handle:** Select a point and drag either of its Bézier control handles to change the curvature of the corresponding segment without moving any of the points in the path. If the point is a smooth point, moving one handle moves both handles in the path. If you want to be able to move a smooth handle independently of its partner, you must use the convert point tool, as discussed in the "Converting points" section later in this chapter.
- **Clone a path:** To make a duplicate of a selected path, Option-drag it to a new location in the image window. Photoshop automatically stores the new path under the same name as the original.

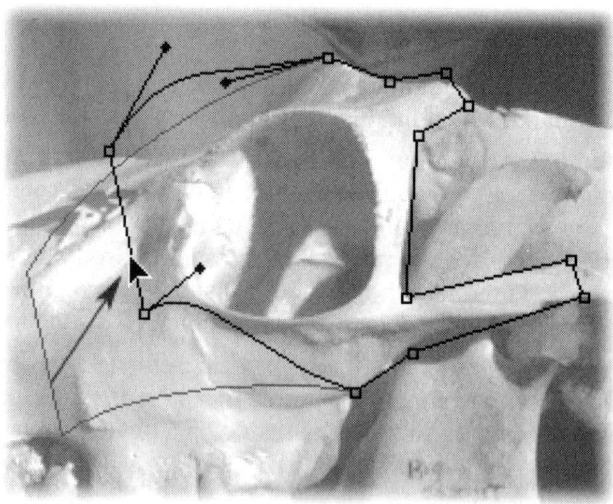

Figure 9-35: Drag a straight segment to move the segment and change the length, direction, and curvature of the neighboring segments.

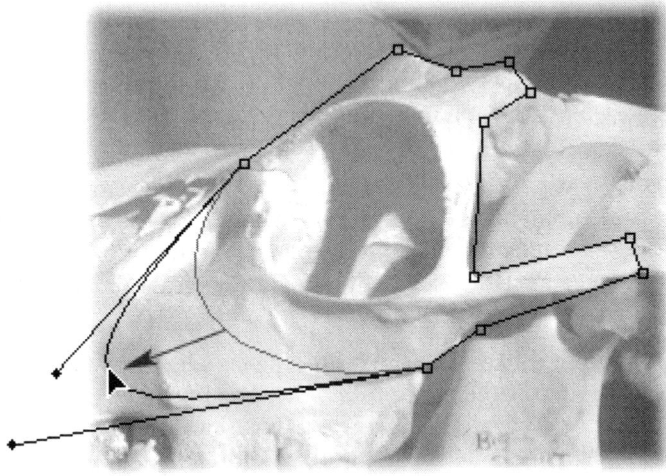

Figure 9-36: Drag a curved segment to change the curvature of that segment only and leave the neighboring segments unchanged.

Although Photoshop 2.0 doesn't provide an arrow tool per se, it does provide all the functionality of an arrow tool. To access the arrow tool cursor and perform any of the operations described in this section, press and hold the Command key while using the pen tool. You also can press the Command key to temporarily access the arrow tool in Photoshop 2.5.

Adding and deleting points

The quantity of points and segments in a path is forever subject to change. Whether a path is closed or open, you can reshape it by adding and deleting points, which in turn forces the addition or deletion of a segment. (For the most part, these techniques are inapplicable to Photoshop 2.0. See the upcoming Photoshop 2.0 note for exceptions.)

- **Appending a point to the end of an open path:** If an existing path is open, you can activate one of its endpoints by either clicking or dragging on it with the pen tool, depending on the identity of the endpoint and whether you want the next segment to be straight or curved. Photoshop is then prepared to draw a segment between the endpoint and the next point you create.
- **Closing an open path:** You also can use the technique I just described to close an open path. Just select one endpoint, click or drag on it with the pen tool to activate it, and then click or drag on the opposite endpoint. Photoshop draws a segment between the two endpoints, closing the path and eliminating both endpoints by converting them to interior points.
- **Joining two open paths:** You can join two open paths to create one longer open path. To do so, activate an endpoint of the first path and then click or drag with the pen tool on an endpoint of the second path.

- **Inserting a point in a segment:** Select the insert point tool and click anywhere along an open or closed path to insert a point and divide the segment on which you click into two segments. Photoshop automatically inserts a corner or smooth point, depending on its reading of the path. If the point does not exactly meet your needs, use the convert point tool to change it.

In Photoshop 2.0, you can access the insert point and remove point cursor by pressing the Command and Option keys when using the pen tool. In Photoshop 2.5, you press Command and Option when using the arrow tool. Command-Option-click on an existing segment to insert a point; Command-Option-click on a point to remove it.

- **Deleting a point and breaking the path:** The simplest way to delete a point is to select it with the arrow tool and press either the Delete or Clear key. You also can choose Edit ⇨ Clear, though why you would want to expend so much effort is beyond me. When you delete an interior point, you delete both segments associated with that point, resulting in a break in the path. If you delete an endpoint from an open path, you delete the single segment associated with the point.
- **Removing a point without breaking the path:** Select the remove point tool and click on a point in an open or closed path to delete the point and draw a new segment between the two points that neighbor it. The remove point tool ensures that no break occurs in a path.
- **Deleting a segment:** You can delete a single interior segment from a path without affecting any point. To do so, first click outside the path with the arrow tool to deselect the path. Then click on the segment you want to delete and press the Delete or Clear key. When you delete an interior segment, you create a break in your path.
- **Deleting a whole path:** To delete an entire path, select any portion of it and press the Delete or Clear key twice. The first time you press Delete, Photoshop deletes the selected point or segment and automatically selects all other points in the path. The second time you press Delete, Photoshop gets rid of everything it missed the first time around.

Converting points

Photoshop 2.5 allows you to change the identity of an interior point. You can convert a corner point to a smooth point and vice versa. You perform all point conversions using the convert point tool as follows:

- **Smooth to corner:** Click on an existing smooth point to convert it to a corner point with no Bézier control handle.
- **Smooth to cusp:** Drag one of the handles of a smooth point to move it independently of the other handle, thus converting the smooth point to a cusp.

- **Corner to smooth:** Drag from a corner point to convert it to a smooth point with two symmetrical Bézier control handles.
- **Cusp to smooth:** Drag one of the handles of a cusp point to lock both handles back into alignment, thus converting the cusp to a smooth point.

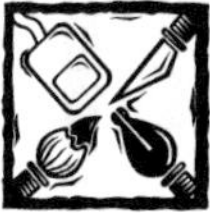

Press the Control key to temporarily access the convert point tool when the arrow tool is selected. Press both Command and Control to access the convert point tool when the pen tool is active.

Transforming a path

If you're used to using Illustrator — the program after which Photoshop's path tool is modeled — or some other drawing program such as FreeHand and Canvas, you may occasionally be frustrated by the fact that Photoshop provides no means for scaling, rotating, or flipping selected paths independently of an image. However, I have discovered a few workarounds you may find acceptable. These techniques work in Photoshop 2.5 only.

Flipping, scaling, and rotating by degree

You can transform an entire image in three ways in Photoshop. If you choose Select ⇨ None to ensure that no portion of the image is selected before applying one of these commands, you likewise transform any visible or saved paths. The three transformation options are as follows:

- **Scaling:** To scale both image and paths, choose Image ⇨ Image Size. (This option actually works whether or not some portion of the image is selected.)
- **Rotation:** To rotate both image and paths, deselect any portion of the image that is selected and then choose one of the commands from the Image ⇨ Rotate submenu. Image ⇨ Rotate ⇨ Free is unavailable.
- **Flipping:** To flip both image and paths, make sure that no portion of the image is selected and then choose one of the commands from the Image ⇨ Flip submenu.

The following steps show how to use the Image ⇨ Flip ⇨ Horizontal command to complete a roughly symmetrical path around the image shown in Figure 9-37. The beauty of this method is that you only have to draw half of the path by hand; you can reshape the other half to fit.

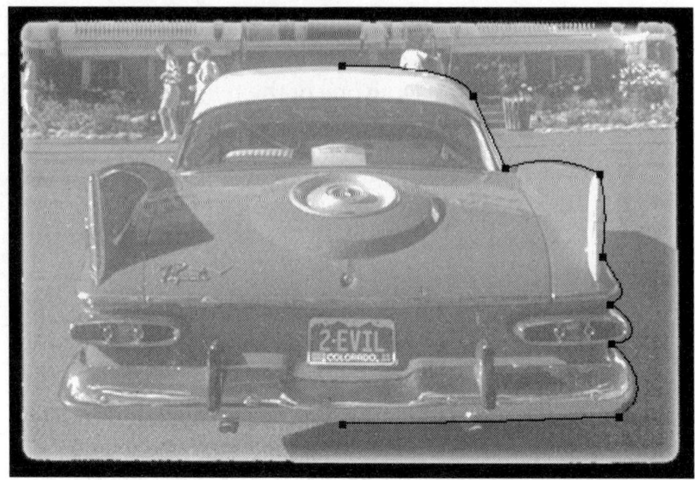

Figure 9-37: After tracing half of the path around a symmetrical image, you can automate the creation of the other half by using a standard transformation technique.

STEPS: Drawing a Symmetrical Path

Step 1. The car in Figure 9-37 is approximately symmetrical about the vertical axis. Therefore, you can begin by tracing around either the left or right half of the image. I began with the right half, which probably has something to do with my being left-handed.

Step 2. After you finish drawing the path, select the entire path by Option-clicking on it with the arrow tool. Then choose Edit ⇨ Copy (Command-C) to store a copy in the Clipboard.

Step 3. Choose Image ⇨ Calculate ⇨ Duplicate to create a duplicate version of the document in a new image window. When the dialog box appears, just press Return. (This dialog box is explained fully in Chapter 17, "Manipulating Channels.")

Step 4. The Duplicate command ignores paths, so it's a good thing you copied it in Step 2. (Talk about your blind luck!) Choose Edit ⇨ Paste (Command-V) and move the path into position using the arrow tool.

Step 5. Choose Image ⇨ Flip ⇨ Horizontal to flip both image and path about the vertical axis, as shown in Figure 9-38. (Make sure that the actual image is not selected; otherwise, only the image flips — the path stays the same.)

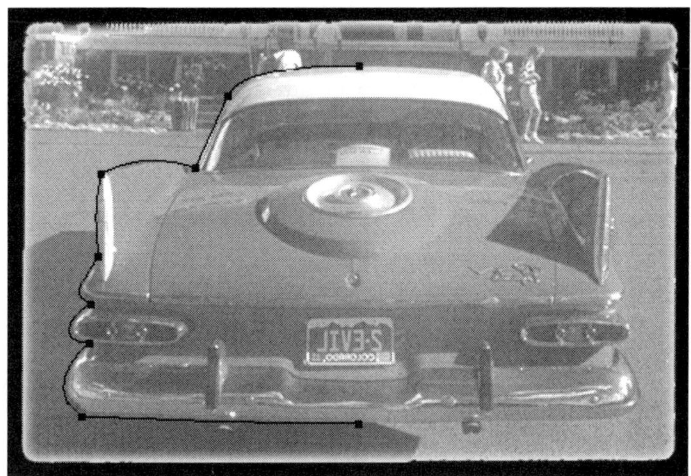

Figure 9-38: Duplicate the image and path and then choose Image ⇨ Flip ⇨ Horizontal to flip both about the vertical axis.

Step 6. Transfer the path to the Clipboard by choosing Edit ⇨ Cut (Command-X). Now that you have the flipped path, your use for the duplicate image is exhausted. Express your contempt and then close the image without saving it.

Step 7. Paste the flipped path into the original image. As shown in Figure 9-39, the path probably won't exactly conform to the outline of the image. You'll have to reshape it by relocating points with the arrow tool.

Step 8. After you finish reshaping the flipped path, join it with the original path. First, delete both of the flipped path's endpoints. I know this sounds drastic, but you have to get rid of the last segment on either end of the path so that you can redraw it while joining the flipped path to the original.

Step 9. To activate the original path, first select the pen tool. Then click or drag — depending on whether you want to draw a straight or curved segment — on one of the path's endpoints. Next, click or drag one of the new endpoints in the flipped path to join the two open paths into a single longer open path, as shown in Figure 9-40.

Step 10. You're now down to two endpoints. To connect these and close the path, click or drag on one endpoint with the pen tool and then click or drag on the other.

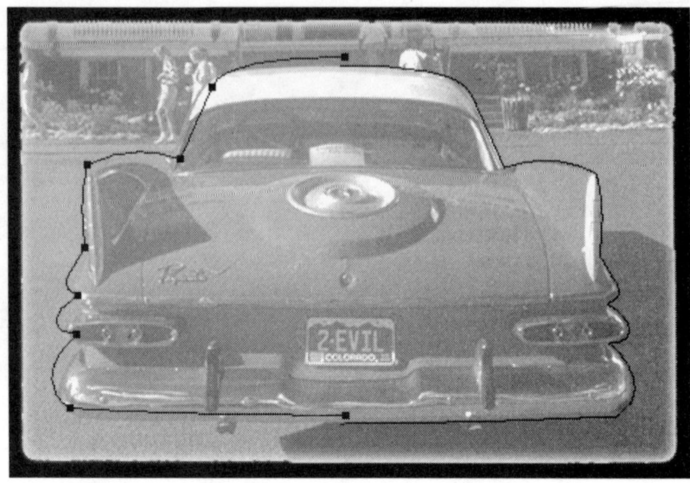

Figure 9-39: The flipped path usually requires reshaping before it conforms to the outline of the image.

Figure 9-40: Join the paths by dragging on the endpoint of one path and then dragging on the endpoint of the other. (Click on the endpoints if you want to connect them with a straight segment.)

Applying free rotation and other transformations

Several of Photoshop's transformation commands are applicable strictly to selected portions of an image. These commands include Free, found in the Image ➪ Rotate submenu, and all commands in the Image ➪ Effects submenu (Scale, Skew, Perspective, and Distort). If you absolutely must apply one of these commands to a path, read the following steps. Note that this technique may slightly degrade the path because it involves converting the path to a selection and then back again.

STEPS: Converting and Transforming a Path

Step 1. Select the path you want to transform. Save it by choosing the Save Path command from the Paths palette menu.

Step 2. Choose the Make Selection command from the palette menu. Enter 0 for the Feather Radius option and press Return.

Step 3. Copy the selection to the Clipboard.

Step 4. Choose File ⇨ New (Command-N) to create a new image window. Photoshop sets the options in the New dialog box to reflect the exact dimensions of the contents of the Clipboard. Add an inch or two to the height and width values to give yourself room to move. Press Return.

Step 5. Paste the selection into the new window.

Step 6. Apply the desired command from the Image ⇨ Rotate or Image ⇨ Effects submenu. Drag the corner handles of the transformation marquee until the selection outline meets with your approval. Keep in mind that you are concerned with the appearance of the selection outline, not the selection itself. Click inside the selection to confirm the transformation.

Step 7. Feel free to apply as many transformation commands as you want. Now's the time to get it out of your system.

Step 8. Choose the Make Path command from the Paths palette menu and press Return to convert the selection outline to a path.

Step 9. Cut the path to the Clipboard and close the image without saving it.

Step 10. Paste the transformed path into your original image.

You can use this technique to rotate or otherwise transform selections created with the rectangular marquee, elliptical marquee, and lasso tools as well. Just skip the first step and away you go.

Painting along a path

To be perfectly honest, I'm beginning to grow a little weary of the topic of paths. If you managed to read this far, I'll bet you feel the same way. But believe it or not, I have yet to cover a few essential path-editing capabilities provided by Photoshop 2.5. You Photoshop 2.0 users get off easy — you can skip to the "Selection Masks" section. Version 2.5 users still have a way to go.

Using the Stroke Path command

In Photoshop 2.5, you can paint a brush stroke along a path. OK, I admit, that may not sound like a big deal at first, but this feature enables you to combine the spontaneity of the paint and edit tools with the structure and precision of a path.

After drawing a path, choose the Stroke Path command from the Paths palette menu to display the Stroke Path dialog box shown in Figure 9-41. In this dialog box, you can choose the paint or edit tool with which you want to *stroke* the path — which means to paint a brush stroke along a path. Photoshop drags the chosen tool along the exact route of the path, retaining any tool or brush shape settings that were in force when you chose the tool.

If you prefer to bypass the Stroke Path dialog box, select a paint or edit tool before choosing the Stroke Path command. Instead of displaying the dialog box, Photoshop assumes that you want to use the selected tool and strokes away.

If the path is selected, the Stroke Path command becomes a Stroke Subpath command. Photoshop then only strokes the selected path, rather than all paths saved under the current name.

You may have noticed that the Paths palette menu provides a Fill Path command just above the Stroke Path command. Because this command is more in keeping with standard fill options available to any selection, I discuss it in Chapter 15, "Coloring Selections."

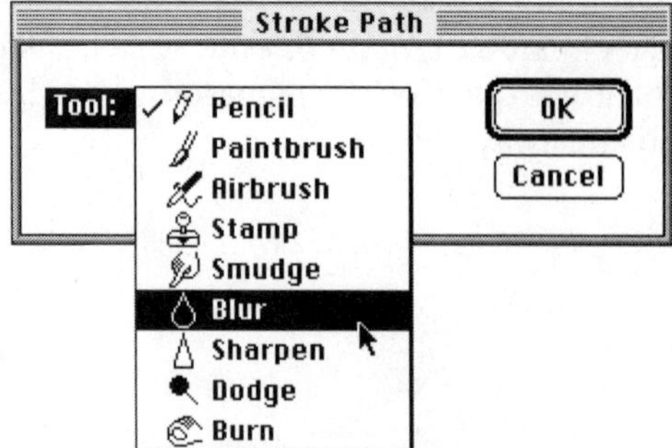

Figure 9-41: Photoshop displays this dialog box when you choose the Stroke Path command while a tool other than a paint or edit tool is selected.

Creating painted paths

The following steps walk you through a little project I created by stroking paths with the paintbrush and smudge tools. Figures 9-42 through 9-44 show the progression and eventual outcome of the image.

STEPS: Stroking Paths with the Paintbrush and Smudge Tools

Step 1. After opening a low-resolution version of a hurricane image from the PhotoDisc *Science, Technology, and Medicine* collection, I drew the zigzag path shown in Figure 9-42. As you can see, the path emits from the eye of the hurricane. I drew the path starting at the eye and working upward, which is very important because Photoshop strokes a path in the same direction in which you draw it.

If you ever decide you drew a path in the wrong direction or, for purposes of an effect, you want the freedom to be able to switch the direction back and forth, select the path with the arrow tool and choose the Reverse Subpath command from the Paths palette menu.

Step 2. I saved the path using the Save Path command from the Paths palette menu.

Step 3. I used the Brushes palette to specify three brush shapes, each with a Roundness value of 40. The largest brush had a diameter of 16, the next largest had a diameter of 10, and the smallest had a diameter of 4.

Step 4. I double-clicked on the paintbrush tool and set the Fade-out value to 400. Then I selected the To Background radio button so that Photoshop would draw gradient strokes between the foreground and background colors.

Figure 9-42: I drew this path starting at the eye of the hurricane and working my way upward.

Step 5. I stroked the path three times using the Stroke Path command with the paintbrush tool. The first time I stroked the path with the largest brush shape, the second time with the middle brush shape, and the final time with the smallest brush shape. I also changed the foreground and background colors between each stroke. In order of application, the foreground and background colors were: gray and white, black and white, and white and black. The result of all this stroking is shown in Figure 9-43.

Step 6. Next, I created two clones of the zigzag path by Option-dragging the path with the arrow tool. I pressed the Shift key while dragging to ensure that the paths aligned horizontally. I then clicked in an empty portion of the image window to deselect all paths so that they appeared as shown in Figure 9-43. This enabled me to stroke them all simultaneously in Step 8.

Step 7. I created a 60-pixel version of my brush shape and reduced its Hardness value to 0 percent. I then painted a single white spot at the bottom of each of the new paths. I painted a black spot at the bottom of the original path.

Step 8. I selected the smudge tool, moved the Pressure slider bar in the Brushes palette to 98 percent, and selected a brush shape with a radius of 16 pixels. At this setting, the tool has a tremendous range, but it eventually fades out.

Step 9. I chose the Stroke Path command to apply the smudge tool to all three paths at once. The finished image appears in Figure 9-44.

Figure 9-43: After stroking the path three times with the paintbrush tool, I cloned the path twice.

Figure 9-44: I stroked all three paths with the smudge tool set to 98 percent pressure in order to achieve this unusual extraterrestrial-departure effect. At least, I guess that's what it is. It could also be giant space slinkies probing the planet's surface. Hard to say.

If you're really feeling precise — I think they have a clinical term for that — you can specify the location of every single blob of paint laid down in an image. When the Spacing option in the Brush Options dialog box is deselected, Photoshop applies a single blob of paint for each point in a path. If that isn't sufficient control, then I'm a monkey's uncle. (What a terrible thing to say about one's nephew!)

Converting and saving paths

We're in the home stretch — just a few miles left until we see the last of Paths County. The sheriff's hot on our trail, but we'll make it.

In the meantime, Photoshop 2.5 provides two commands to switch between paths and selections, both of which are located in the Paths palette menu. The Make Selection command converts a path to a selection outline; the Make Path command converts a selection to a path.

Regardless of how you create a path, you can save it with the current image, which enables you not only to reuse the path later on down the line but also to hide and display it at will.

After you choose the Make Selection command in Photoshop 2.5 and establish the default settings, you can reapply the command by pressing the Enter key on the numeric keypad. In Version 2.5, the Enter key automatically repeats the last palette menu command without bringing up a dialog box. In Version 2.5.1, the Enter key converts the path to a selection regardless of the last command chosen.

Converting paths to selections

When you choose the Make Selection command, Photoshop displays the dialog box shown in Figure 9-45. You can specify whether or not to antialias or feather the selection and to what degree. You also can instruct Photoshop to combine the prospective selection outline with any existing selection in the image. The Operation options correspond to the keyboard functions discussed in the "Manually adding and subtracting" section earlier in this chapter.

You can combine paths with selections in Photoshop 2.0 as well, but you must make that decision when you begin drawing with the pen tool. Press Shift to add to the selection, Command to subtract, and Command-Shift to intersect, just as when using any other selection tool.

If you haven't saved a path by time you convert it, Photoshop leaves the path on-screen in front of the converted selection. If you try to copy, cut, delete, or nudge the selection, you perform the operation on the path instead. If, however, you save the path before converting it, Photoshop automatically hides the path and provides full access to the selection.

Make Selection

Rendering
Feather Radius: 0 pixels
☒ Anti-aliased

Operation
◉ New Selection
○ Add to Selection
○ Subtract from Selection
○ Intersect with Selection

OK
Cancel

Figure 9-45: When you choose the Make Selection command in Photoshop 2.5, you have the option of combining the path with an existing selection.

Converting selections to paths

When you choose the Make Paths command, Photoshop produces a single Tolerance option. Unlike the Tolerance options you've encountered so far, this one is accurate to 1/10 pixel and has nothing to do with colors or brightness values. Rather, it permits you to specify Photoshop's sensitivity to twists and turns in a selection outline. The value you enter determines how far the path can vary from the original selection. The lowest possible value, 0.5, ensures that Photoshop retains every nuance of the selection, but it can also result in overly complicated paths with an abundance of points. If you enter the highest value, 10, Photoshop rounds out the path and uses very few points. If you plan on editing the path, you probably won't want to venture any lower than 2.0, the default setting.

Saving paths with an image

I mentioned at the beginning of the paths discussion that saving a path is an integral step in the Photoshop 2.5 path-creation process. Although you can save paths to disk in Photoshop 2.0, Version 2.5 is structured to save multiple paths within a single image. You can store every path you draw and keep it on hand in case you decide later to select an area again. Because Photoshop defines paths as compact mathematical equations, they take up virtually no room when you save an image to disk.

You save one or more paths by choosing the Save Path command from the Paths palette menu. After you perform the save operation, the path name appears in the scrolling list in the lower portion of the palette. A path name can include any number of separate paths. In fact, if you save a path and then set about drawing another one, Photoshop automatically adds that path in with the saved path. To start a new path under a new name, you first have to hide the existing path. You can hide and display a saved path by merely clicking on its name.

To hide all paths, click in the empty portion of the scrolling list below the last saved path name. You can even hide unsaved paths in this way. However, once you hide an unsaved path, you can never retrieve it.

Swapping paths with Illustrator

Adobe promises that you'll be able to swap paths back and forth between Photoshop 2.5 and Illustrator 5.0, which is not yet shipping at the time I write this. All you'll have to do is copy a path to the Clipboard and paste it into the other program. This special cross-application compatibility feature will expand and simplify a variety of path editing functions. For example, instead of going through all that effort I described in the "Transforming a path" section earlier in this chapter, you will be able to simply copy a path, paste it into Illustrator, transform it as desired, copy it again, and paste it back into Photoshop.

The Photoshop manual mistakenly refers to Illustrator 4.0 as being the version that lets you swap paths with Photoshop. Illustrator 4.0 exists only on the Windows platform. On the Mac, Adobe skipped Version 4.0 and went straight to 5.0. Who can figure that crazy marketing department?

Of course, if you're working in Photoshop 2.5 for Windows, then the manual is correct. You can indeed swap paths between Photoshop and Illustrator 4.0 for Windows.

Exporting to Illustrator

As things stand now, you can export paths created in Photoshop for use in Illustrator. To export all paths in the current image, choose File ⇨ Export ⇨ Paths to Illustrator. Photoshop saves the paths as a fully editable Illustrator 3.0 document.

The potential use for this feature is a little different from the one I described a few paragraphs ago, however. Photoshop provides no capacity for importing Illustrator paths, so you can't use Illustrator to transform a path and reuse it in Photoshop. Rather, this scheme allows you to exactly trace images with paths in Photoshop and then combine those paths as objects with the exported EPS version of the image inside Illustrator. Although tracing an image in Illustrator 3.0 can prove a little tricky because of the program's previewing limitations, you can trace images in Photoshop as accurately as you like.

Masking an image

Illustrator and other object-oriented applications enable you to mask away unwanted portions of objects using *clipping paths.* Elements that fall inside the clipping path get printed; elements outside the clipping path do not. Photoshop lets you export an image in the EPS format with an object-oriented clipping path intact. When you import the image into Illustrator, it appears premasked with a perfectly smooth perimeter, as illustrated by the clipped image in Figure 9-46.

To assign a set of saved paths as clipping paths, choose the Clipping Path command from the Paths palette menu. Photoshop displays the Clipping Path dialog box shown in Figure 9-47, which enables you to select the saved paths and specify how the paths mask the image.

The options in the Clipping Path dialog box work as follows:

- **Path:** Choose the saved paths that you want to assign as clipping paths from the Path pop-up menu. You can only specify one set of saved paths per image.
- **Flatness:** This option permits you to simplify the clipping paths by printing otherwise fluid curves as polygons. The Flatness value represents the distance — between 0.2 and 100 — in printer pixels that the polygon may vary from the true mathematical curve. A higher value leads to a polygon with fewer sides. Unless you experience a *limitcheck* error when printing the image from Illustrator, don't even bother to enter a value for this option. Even then, try simplifying your illustration first. Only use the Flatness value as a last resort.

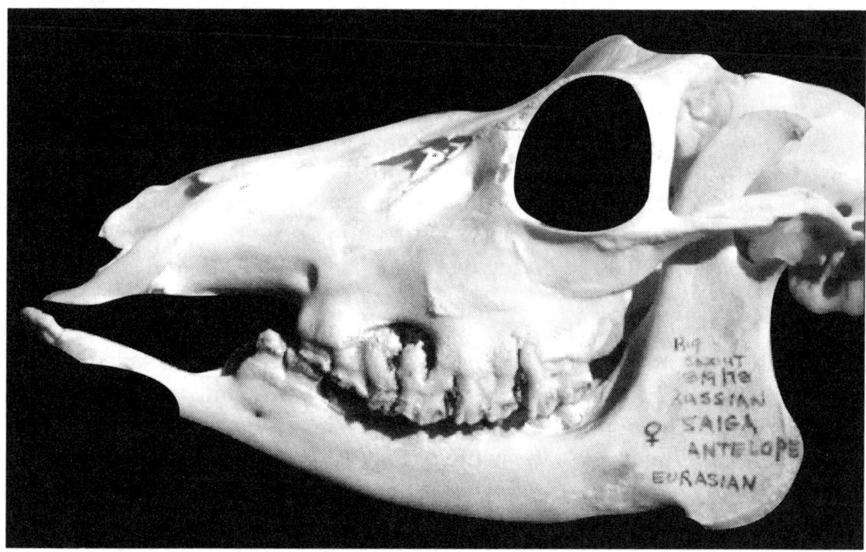

Figure 9-46: I drew one path around the perimeter of the skull and another around the eye socket. After defining the paths as clipping paths, I exported the image in the EPS format, imported it into Illustrator, and added a black background for contrast.

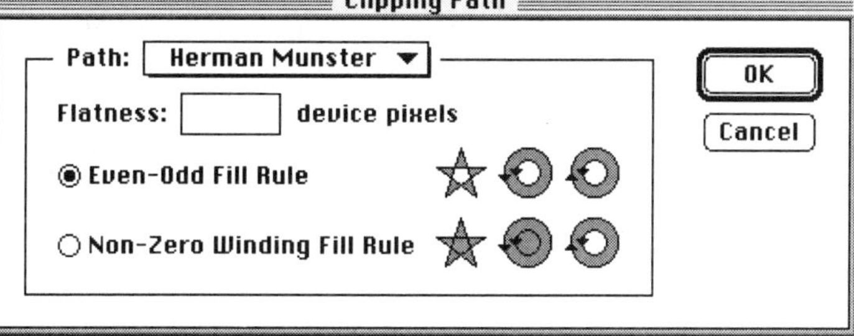

Figure 9-47: Choose the saved paths from the pop-up menu and specify how you want to mask the image.

- **Even-Odd Fill Rule:** The two radio buttons tell Photoshop how to determine which paths contain portions of the image and which paths serve as holes in the image. By default, any area in which two paths overlap is a hole; an area in which three paths overlap contains image; an area in which four paths overlap is another hole; and so on. Get it? The intersection of an even number of paths results in a hole; an odd number of paths displays the image. In Figure 9-46, the eye socket path intersects the skull path, so it creates a hole. If I were to draw another path inside the eye socket, you'd see some image.
- **Non-Zero Winding Fill Rule:** This option is less straightforward than its predecessor, but it cuts down pretty dramatically on print time and possible printing errors. In this scenario, a path only represents a hole if it was drawn in the opposite direction of the path that it intersects. In Figure 9-46, I drew the path

around skull in a clockwise fashion, but I drew the eye socket counterclockwise. Because the two paths proceed in opposite directions, one cuts a hole in the other.

To save on print time, select the Non-Zero Winding Fill Rule option whenever possible. If intersecting paths don't cut holes in the image in the way you anticipated when you import the image into Illustrator, return to Photoshop and apply the Reverse Subpath command from the Paths palette menu to the offending intersecting paths. If that still doesn't work, give up and select the Even-Odd Fill Rule option instead.

Figure 9-48 shows an enhanced version of the clipped skull from Figure 9-46. In addition to exporting the image with clipping paths in the EPS format, I saved the paths to disk by choosing File ⇨ Export ⇨ Paths to Illustrator. Inside Illustrator, I used the exported paths to create the outline around the clipped image. I also used them to create the shadow behind the image. The white of the eyeball is a reduced version of the eye socket, as are the iris and pupil. The background features a bunch of flipped and reduced versions of the paths. It may look like a lot of work, but the only drawing required was to create the two initial Photoshop paths.

Be prepared for your images to grow by leaps and bounds when imported into Illustrator. The EPS illustration shown in Figure 9-48 consumes a whopping 600K on disk. By contrast, the Photoshop image alone consumes only 100K when saved as an LZW-compressed TIFF file.

Figure 9-48: It's amazing what you can accomplish by combining scans edited in a painting program with smooth lines created in a drawing program.

Selection Masks

Phew, it's good to be through talking about paths. Now on to masks.

Rather than being a type of selection, *masks* give you a way to use selections to protect certain portions of an image and make other portions susceptible to changes. After you draw a selection outline, you can paint and edit within its confines. Using Photoshop's quick mask mode and mask channels, you can use paint and edit tools to manipulate the selection outline itself. Selection masks represent the coalescence of everything you've learned in this and the previous chapters.

Painting inside a selection outline

When you were in grade school, perhaps you had a teacher who nagged you to color within the lines. (I didn't. My teachers were more concerned about preventing me from writing on the walls and coloring on the other kids.) At any rate, if you don't trust yourself to paint inside an image because you're afraid you'll screw it up, selection masks are the answer. Regardless of which tool you use to select an image, you can paint only the selected area. The paint can't enter the deselected portion of the image. You can't help but paint inside the lines.

Figures 8-49 through 8-52 show the familiar skull image subject to some pretty free-and-easy use of the paint and edit tools. (You think I ought to lay off the heavy metal or what?) The following steps describe how I created these images using a selection mask.

STEPS: Painting and Editing Inside a Selection Mask

Step 1. Back in Figure 9-6, I created a selection that surrounded the skull and excluded the eye socket. I then used the quick mask mode to temporarily convert the selection to a grayscale image, as shown in the top portion of Figure 9-49. Speculating that I might use this selection again, I copied it and pasted it into the Scrapbook. To start this new project, I retrieved the grayscale image from the Scrapbook, clicked on the quick mask mode icon in the toolbox, and pasted the image.

Step 2. To restore the image to a selection, I clicked on the marching ants icon in the toolbox. Because I wanted to edit the area surrounding the skull, I chose Select ⇨ Inverse to reverse which areas were selected and which were not. I then pressed the Delete key to fill the selected area with the background color — in this case, white — as shown in the bottom half of Figure 9-49.

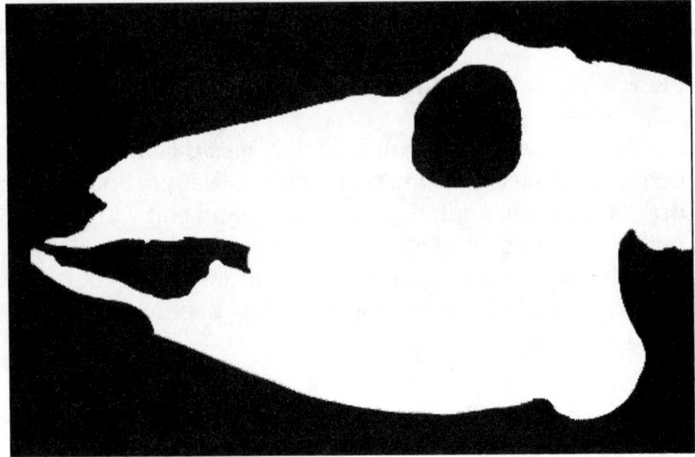

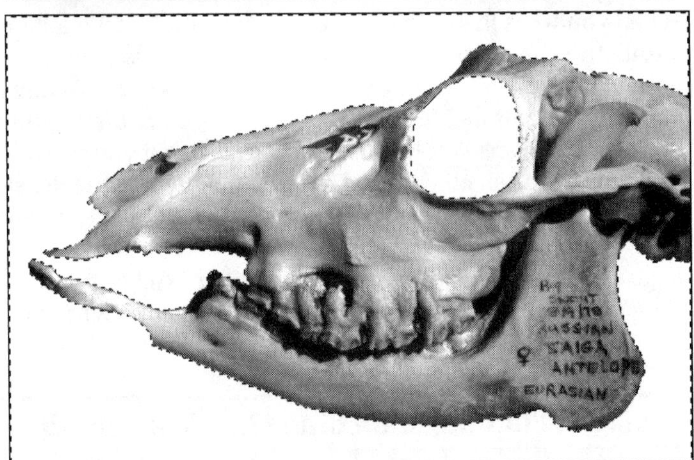

Figure 9-49: After retrieving the selection stored in the Scrapbook back in the first steps in this chapter (top), I reversed the selection and deleted the background (bottom).

Step 3. The next step was to paint inside the selection mask. But before I began, I chose Select ⇨ Hide Edges (Command-H). This step allowed me to paint without being distracted by those infernal marching ants. (In fact, this is one of the most essential uses for the Hide Edges command.)

Step 4. I selected the paintbrush tool and the 21-pixel soft brush shape in the Brushes palette. The foreground color was black. I dragged with the paintbrush around the perimeter of the skull to set it apart from its white background, as shown in Figure 9-50. No matter how sloppily I painted, the skull remained unscathed.

Step 5. I next selected the smudge tool and set the Pressure slider bar to 80 percent. I dragged from inside the skull outward 20 or so times to create a series of curlicues. I also dragged from outside the skull inward to create white gaps between the curlicues. As shown in Figure 9-51, the smudge tool can smear colors from inside the protected area, but it does not apply these colors until it reaches the selection mask. This is an important point to keep in mind, because it demonstrates that although the protected area is safe from all changes, the selected area may be influenced by colors from protected pixels.

Step 6. I double-clicked on the airbrush tool icon in the toolbox and set the Fade-out value to 20, leaving the To Transparent radio button selected. I then selected a 60-pixel soft brush shape and again dragged outward from various points along the perimeter of the skull. As demonstrated in Figure 9-52, combining airbrush and mask is as useful in Photoshop as it is in the real world.

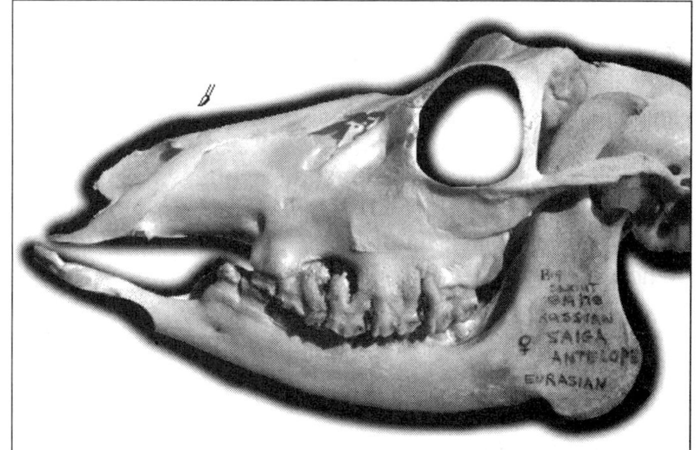

Figure 9-50: I painted inside the selection mask with a 21-pixel soft brush shape.

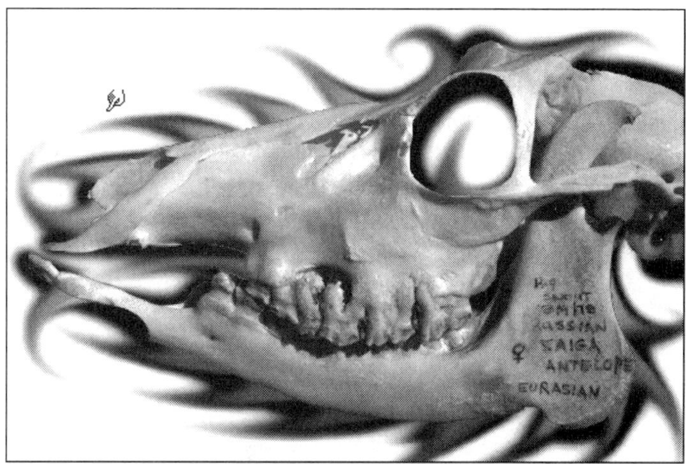

Figure 9-51: Dragging with the smudge tool smeared colors from pixels outside the selection mask without changing the appearance of those pixels.

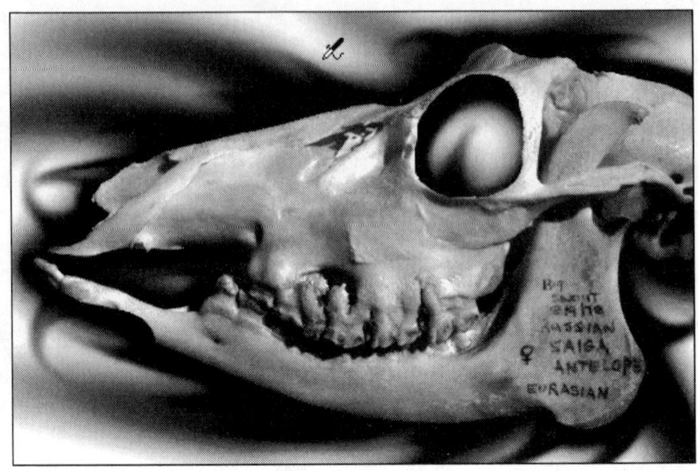

Figure 9-52: I dragged around the skull with the airbrush to further distinguish it from its background. Pretty cool effect, huh? Well, if it's not your cup of tea, maybe you can track down a teenager who will appreciate it.

Using the quick mask mode

If you're using Photoshop 2.5, select some portion of an image and click on the quick mask mode icon in the toolbox, which is the right-hand icon directly under the color controls. Go ahead, try it out. All the protected areas in your image appear covered in a translucent coat of red; the selected areas appear normally, with no red coating.

When I click on the quick mask icon, I get the image shown in Figure 9-53. I have now entered the *quick mask mode,* where you edit a selection as if it were a grayscale image. This relationship may not make much sense, because the selection you see on screen is red. But the translucent red coating is in reality an independent 8-bit image. You can edit it in the following ways:

- **Subtracting from a selection:** Paint with black to add red coating and thus deselect areas of the image, as demonstrated in the top half of Figure 9-54. Imagine, you can selectively protect portions of your image by merely painting over them.
- **Adding to a selection:** Paint with white to remove red coating and thus add to the selection outline. You can use the eraser tool to add hard-edged boundaries. Or you can swap the foreground and background colors so that you can paint in white with one of the painting tools.
- **Adding feathered selections:** If you paint with a shade of gray, you add feathered selections. You also can feather an outline by painting with black or white with a very soft brush shape, as shown in the bottom image in Figure 9-54.

- **Clone selection outlines:** You can clone a selection outline by selecting it with one of the five selection tools and Option-dragging it to a new location in the image, as shown in Figure 9-55. Although I use the lasso tool in the figure, the magic wand tool also works well for this purpose. To select an antialiased selection outline with the wand tool, set the tolerance to about 10 and be sure that the Anti-aliased check box is active. Then click inside the selection. It's that easy.
- **Transform selection outlines:** That's right, the quick mask mode provides yet another way to transform a selection outline independently of an image. Just select the outline with one of the five selection tools and transform it by choosing the desired command from the Select ⇨ Flip, Select ⇨ Rotate, or Select ⇨ Effects submenu.

These are just a few of the unique effects you can achieve by editing a selection in the quick mask mode. Others involve tools and capabilities I haven't yet discussed, so expect to hear more about this feature in future chapters.

Figure 9-53: Click on the quick mask mode icon (left) to instruct Photoshop to temporarily express the selection as a grayscale image.

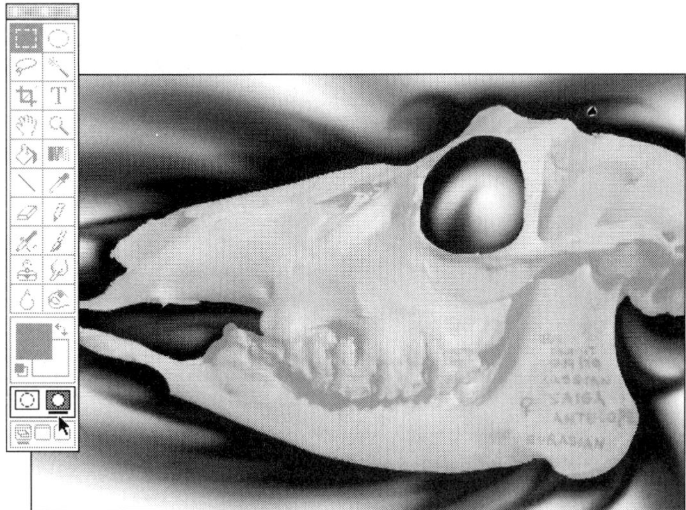

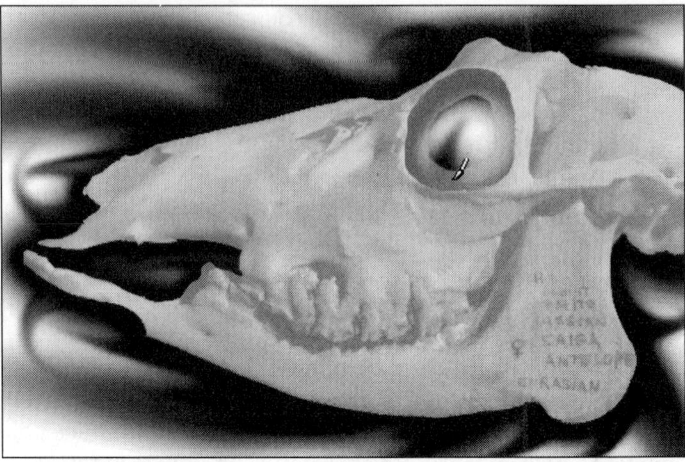

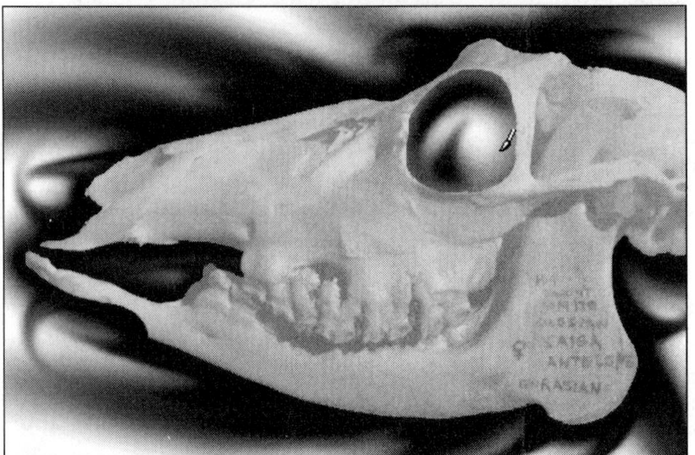

Figure 9-54: After subtracting some of the selected area inside the eye socket by painting in black with the paintbrush tool (top), I feathered the outline by painting with white using a soft 45-pixel brush shape (bottom).

When you finish editing your selection outlines, click on the marching ants mode icon (just to the left of the quick mask mode icon) to return to the standard image editing mode. Your selection outlines again appear flanked by marching ants and all tools and commands return to their normal image-editing functions. Figure 9-56 shows the results of switching to the marching ants mode and deleting the contents of the selection outlines created in the last examples of the previous two figures.

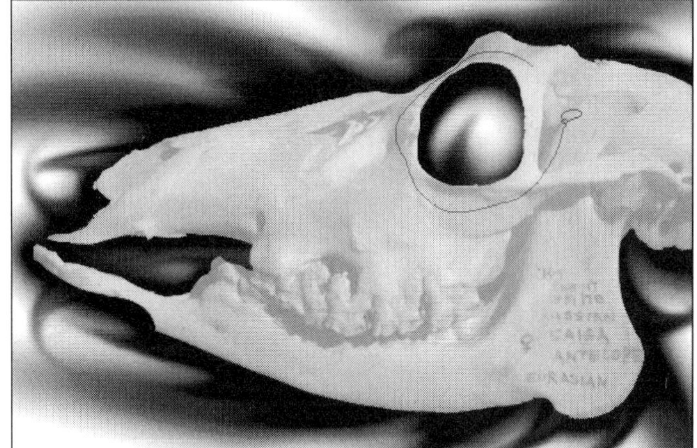

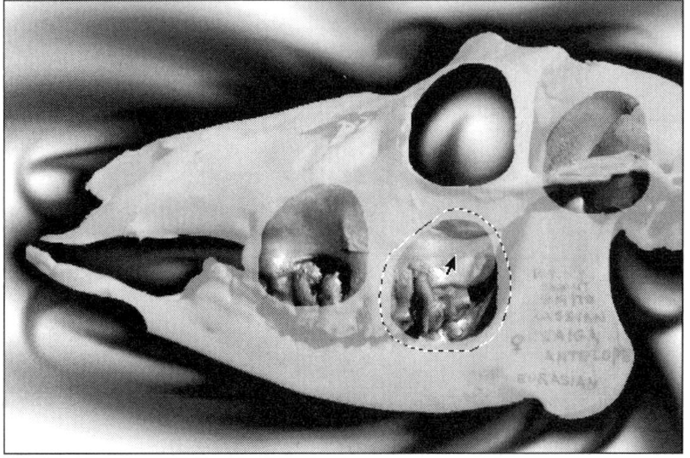

Figure 9-55: To clone the eye socket selection, I lassoed around it (top) and Option-dragged it (bottom).

As demonstrated in the top example of Figure 9-56, the quick mask mode offers a splendid environment for feathering one selection outline while leaving another hard-edged or antialiased. Granted, because most selection tools offer built-in feathering options, you can accomplish this task without resorting the quick mask mode. But only the quick mask mode lets you change feathering selectively after drawing selection outlines, and only the quick mask mode lets you see exactly what you're doing.

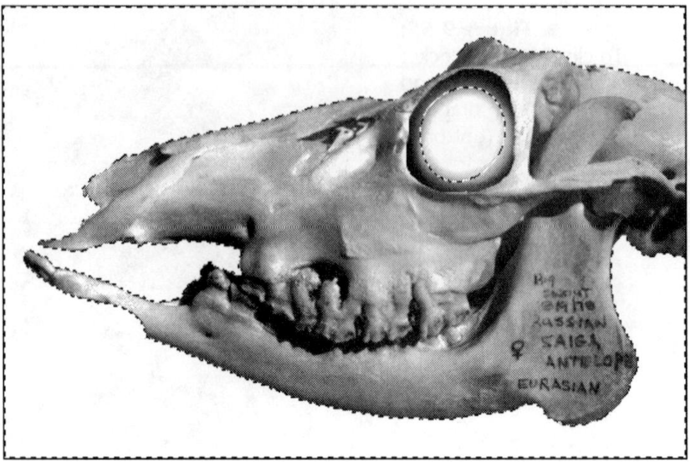

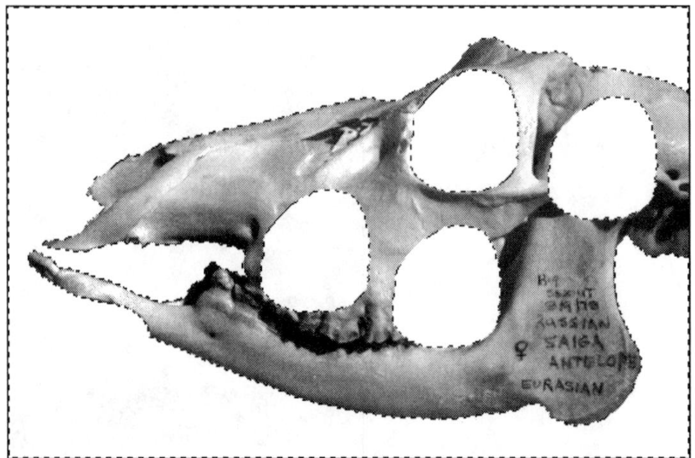

Figure 9-56: The results of deleting the regions selected in the final examples of Figures 9-54 (top) and 9-55 (bottom). Kind of makes me want to rent the video of *It's the Great Pumpkin, Charlie Brown.*

Changing the red coating

By default, the protected region of an image appears in translucent red in the quick mask mode, but you can change it to any color and any degree of opacity that you like. To do so, double-click on the quick mask icon in the toolbox to display the Mask Options dialog box shown in Figure 9-57.

- **Color Indicates:** Select the Selected Areas option to reverse the color coating — that is, to cover the selected areas in a translucent coat of red and view the protected areas normally. Select the Masked Areas option (the default setting) to cover the protected areas in color.

- **Color:** Click on the Color icon to display the Adobe Color Picker dialog box and select a different color coating. Color selection is the topic of Chapter 14, "Defining Colors."
- **Opacity:** Enter a value to change the opacity of the translucent color that coats the image.

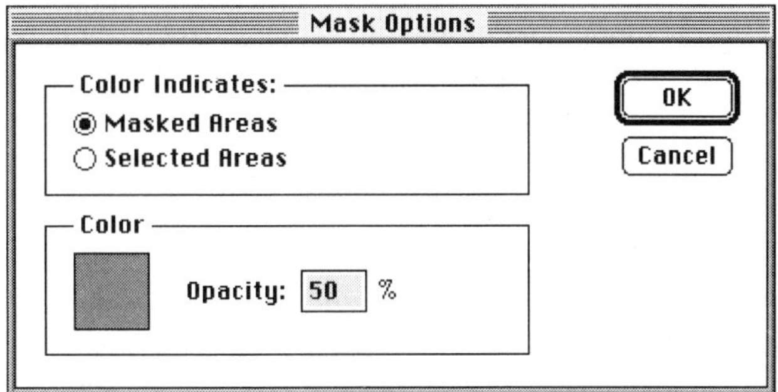

Figure 9-57: Double-click on the quick mask mode icon to access the Mask Options dialog box. You then can change the color and opacity of the protected or selected areas when viewed in the quick mask mode.

Change the color coating to achieve the most acceptable balance between being able to view and edit your selection and being able to view your image. For example, the red coating shows up badly on grayscale screen shots, so I changed the color coating to light blue and the Opacity value to 65 percent before shooting the screens featured in Figures 9-53 through 9-55.

Using a mask channel

A *mask channel* — which is simply a term for a portion of the file set aside to store the mask information — provides all the benefits of the quick mask mode, plus permanence. Provided that you save the image in an acceptable file format, you can permanently store the mask channel with your image on disk in the event that you might want to reuse it.

To copy one or more selection outlines to a mask channel, draw your selections and then choose Select ⇨ Save Selection. If a mask channel already exists, a submenu appears, enabling you to copy the selection over an existing mask channel or copy it to a new mask channel. After you copy the mask, you can view it in Photoshop 2.5 by choosing Window ⇨ Show Channels to display the Channels palette and clicking on the channel name, which will be a number such as *#2* or *#4*. In Photoshop 2.0, you view the new mask channel by choosing it from the Mode ⇨ Channel submenu. You can also switch channels in either program by pressing Command plus the number of the channel — for example, Command-2 or Command-4.

Unlike Version 2.5, Photoshop 2.0 does not allow you to view a mask channel and its image simultaneously. Although this limits your range of options, you can perform several invaluable selection outline adjustments by copying an image, pasting it into a mask channel, and editing it. For more information on this technique, skip to the upcoming "Deriving selections from images" section.

I mentioned this in the steps near the beginning of this chapter, but it bears repeating: Photoshop's native file format can accommodate as many mask channels as you like; the PICT format can accommodate one mask channel only; and, in Version 2.5, the TIFF format can save multiple mask channels. All other formats do not save mask channels.

Viewing mask and image

Photoshop 2.5 lets you view a mask channel and image together, just as you can view a mask and image together in the quick mask mode. This option enables you to see how your changes to the mask channel mesh with your image; in essence, you're tracing portions of the image you want to select.

To view the mask channel and image together, click in the first column of the Channels palette — called the *view column* — to toggle the display of the eyeball icon. An eyeball in front of a channel name indicates that you can see that channel. If you are currently viewing the image, click in front of the mask channel, as shown in the top half of Figure 5-58, to view the mask as a translucent color coating, just as in the quick mask mode. Alternatively, if you are currently viewing the mask channel, click in front of the image name in the view column.

Using mask channels is different from using the quick mask mode in that you can edit either the image or mask channel when viewing the two together. To decide which channel you want to edit, click in the *edit column* (see Figure 9-58) of the Channels palette to toggle the display of the pencil icon.

A pencil in front of a channel name indicates that any operations you perform will affect the contents of that channel. If you want to edit the selection only — as in the quick mask mode — click in front of the mask channel to display a pencil icon and click in front of the image name to hide its icon, as shown in the bottom half of Figure 9-58.

You can change the color and opacity of each mask independently of other mask channels and the quick mask mode. Click on the mask channel in the *channel name column* to select one channel exclusively and then choose the Channel Options command from the Channels menu. As shown in Figure 9-59, the ensuing dialog box enables you to change the name of the channel and provides access to the color coating options described a few pages ago.

Figure 9-58: Click in the view column to specify the channels you want to display (top); click in the edit column to specify the channel you want to edit (bottom).

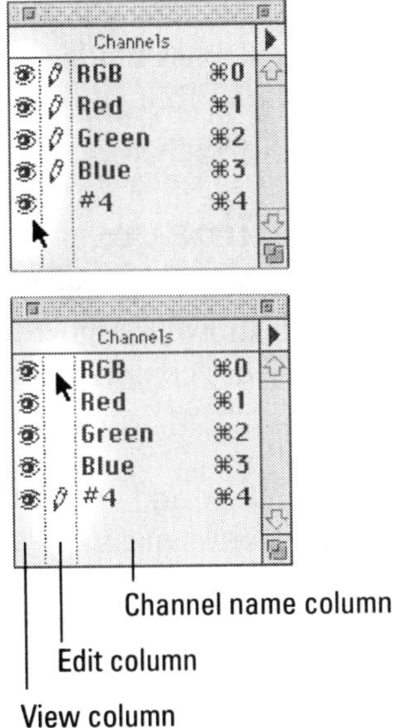

You can bypass the Channel Options command by double-clicking on the channel name in the scrolling list.

When you return to the image after editing the selection mask, Photoshop does not automatically copy the selection outlines from the mask channel as it does when you use the quick mask mode. Instead, you must manually copy the selection outlines by choosing Select ⇨ Load Selection. If the image contains more than one mask channel, a submenu appears asking you to specify the channel from which you want to copy the selection.

Figure 9-59: Click on the mask channel in the channel name column and choose the Channel Options command to access the Channel Options dialog box, shown here. You then can edit the name of the channel and change the color coating options.

Channel Options

Name: #4

OK

Cancel

Color Indicates:

Masked Areas

Selected Areas

Color

Opacity: 50 %

If you ever need to edit a selection outline inside the mask channel using paint and edit tools, click on the quick mask mode icon in the toolbox. This scheme may sound like a play within a play, but you can access the quick mask mode even when working in a mask channel.

Deriving selections from images

Here's your chance to see the mask channel in action. In the following steps, I start with the unadorned image of the Great Wall shown in Figure 9-60 and add the glow shown in Figure 9-63. Normally, this would be a fairly complex procedure. But when you employ a mask channel, it takes only minutes.

Rather than selecting a portion of the image and saving it to a channel, as described in the previous sections, I created the selection mask in the following steps by copying a portion of an image, pasting it into a mask channel, and editing it. This enabled me to create a selection without viewing image and mask together, making the steps equally applicable to Photoshop 2.0 and 2.5.

Figure 9-60: A 1940s photograph of the Great Wall from the Bettmann Archive.

I have yet to cover a couple of the techniques I use in the following steps, specifically those of filling a selection and applying the Threshold command. For more information, read Chapter 15, "Coloring Selections," and Chapter 16, "Mapping and Adjusting Colors."

STEPS: Using a Mask Channel to Enhance an Image

Step 1. I wanted to edit just the top third or so of the image, so I selected that portion and copied it to the Clipboard.

Step 2. The next step was to create a new mask channel. In Photoshop 2.5, I chose the New Channel command from the Channels palette menu. (If I had used Photoshop 2.0, I would have chosen Mode ⇨ New Channel to establish a new mask channel.) The application displayed the Channel Options dialog box, requesting that I name the channel. I pressed Return to accept the default name and color settings.

Step 3. I pasted the copied image into the mask channel, as shown in the top half of Figure 9-61. I then chose Image ⇨ Map ⇨ Threshold (Command-T), which changed all pixels in the mask channel to either white or black. This step enabled me to isolate gray values in the image and create a perfect selection outline. Inside the Threshold dialog box, you move a slider bar to specify a brightness value. All pixels lighter than that value turn to white, and all pixels darker than that value change to black. I used the value 233 to arrive at the image shown in the second example of Figure 9-61.

Step 4. The black-and-white image from Figure 9-61 was far from perfect, but it was as good as it was going to get using Photoshop's automated color mapping. From here on, I had to rely on my tracing abilities. I used the pencil tool to fill in the gaps in the wall and the eraser tool to erase the black pixels from the sky. Notice that I did not use the paintbrush or airbrush tools; at this stage, I wanted hard edges.

Step 5. I softened portions of the boundaries between the black and white pixels using the blur tool at the default 50 percent pressure and with a small brush shape.

Step 6. To create the glow, I Option-dragged with the elliptical marquee tool to draw the marquee from the center outward. Before releasing, I pressed and held Shift (as well as Option) to constrain the marquee to a circle. After I finished drawing the marquee, I Command-Option-dragged it to position it exactly where I wanted it, as shown in the top half of Figure 9-62.

Figure 9-61: After pasting a portion of the image into the mask channel (top), I changed all pixels to white or black using the Threshold command (bottom) and set about painting away the imperfections.

Step 7. I pressed Option-delete to fill the circular selection with black.

Step 8. I double-clicked on the paintbrush tool icon and set the Fade-out value to 40 pixels. I then drew several long rays about the perimeter of the circle.

Step 9. Using the smudge tool set to 50 percent pressure, I dragged outward from the circle to create the tapering edges shown in the bottom half of Figure 9-62.

Figure 9-62: I established the selection outline for the glow by Option-dragging with the elliptical marquee tool (top) and pressing Option-delete to fill the selection with black. I then used the paintbrush and smudge tools to paint in the rays (bottom).

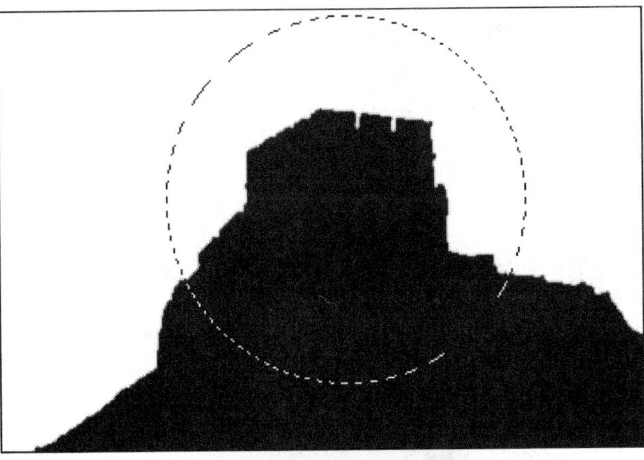

Step 10. To apply the finished selection to the image, I pressed Command-1 to return to the standard image mode. (This is a grayscale image. If it had been color, I would have pressed Command-0.) I then chose Select ⇨ Load Selection to copy the selection from the mask channel.

Step 11. Because I only edited the upper third of the image in the mask channel, the lower two thirds of the document appeared selected. To deselect this region, I Command-dragged around it with the rectangular marquee tool.

Step 12. Because Photoshop selects the portions of the mask channel that are white, only that portion of the sky outside the glow was selected. The rest of the image was masked. I pressed Option-delete to fill the selection with black. Figure 9-63 shows the result.

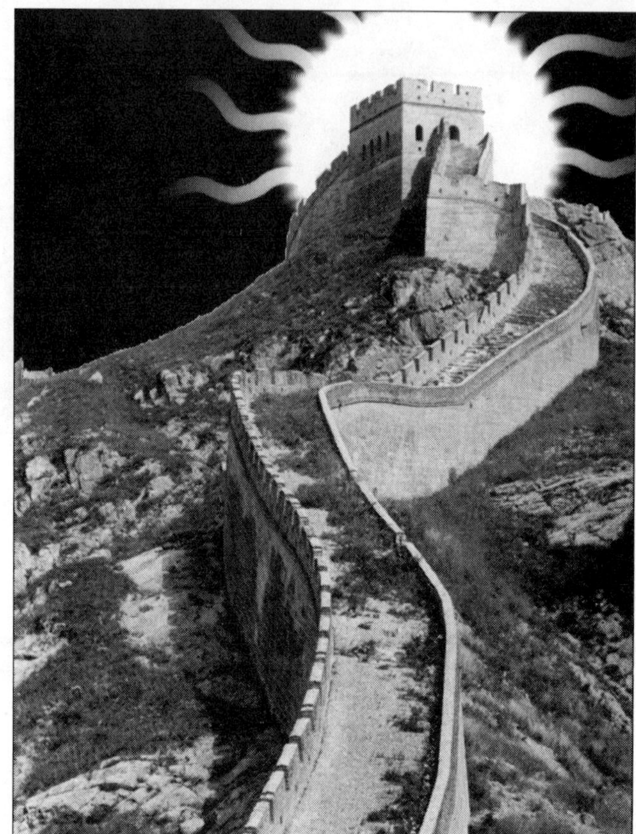

Figure 9-63: Returning to the standard image mode, I loaded the selection outlines from the mask layer and pressed Option-delete to fill the selected area with black.

Summary

- Option-drag with the rectangular or elliptical marquee tool to draw outward from the center of the shape. Press Shift after beginning your drag to constrain the shape to a square or circle.
- Option-click with the lasso tool to draw a selection outline with straight sides.
- It's a common misconception that the magic wand tool selects areas of similarly colored pixels. Rather, it distinguishes brightness values within color channels.
- Choose Select ⇨ Hide Edges to hide the marching ants and get an unobstructed view of your image.
- Shift-drag with a selection tool to add to a selection outline; Command-drag to subtract from a selection outline; Command-Shift-drag to intersect a selection.
- You can use the Similar and Inverse commands to automatically isolate a complex portion of an image.
- Option-drag a selection to clone it. Command-Option-drag to move a selection outline independently of the image.
- You can float a selection by pasting it, cloning it, or simply moving it. To drop a floating selection in Photoshop 2.5, press Command-J.
- You can use feathering to hide an element in an image while leaving its background intact.
- Photoshop's pen tool works identically to its counterpart in Adobe Illustrator, though Illustrator provides more options for editing a path.
- In Photoshop 2.5, be sure to save your path before converting it to a selection outline to prevent the path from obstructing your ability to edit the selection.
- The pen tool lets you combine precise straight and curved segments in a single path. Click to create a corner with the pen tool; drag to create a seamless arc in a curve.
- Use the arrow, insert point, remove point, and convert point tools in the Paths palette to edit a path after you draw it with the pen tool.
- You can transform a path by copying it to a new image, applying a transformation to the image, and copying the path back to the original image.

- Use the Stroke Path command to apply a paint or edit tool along the route of a path. This is especially useful for creating duplicate versions of a single brush stroke.
- Use the Clipping Path command to import a masked image with mathematically precise edges into Illustrator.
- Click on the quick mask mode icon to temporarily convert your selection to a grayscale image that you can manipulate by using the paint and edit tools.
- By creating an independent mask channel, you can save a selection for repeated use within an image.

Duplication and Reversion Techniques

10 CHAPTER

In This Chapter

- A complete description of the rubber stamp tool and its many settings
- How to clone portions of an image to touch up blemishes and eliminate elements from an image
- How to use the rubber stamp to paint with a repeating pattern
- A step-by-step guide to creating seamless patterns and textures
- Descriptions of the Undo and Revert commands
- Ways to use the magic eraser and rubber stamp tools to selectively revert portions of an image
- An explanation of the Take Snapshot command

Introducing the Amalgamated Rubber Stamp

This chapter is really about just one tool: the rubber stamp tool. Although the eraser figures into the reversion discussion in this chapter, and I even include a small reference to the pencil tool, the main ingredient — after you to boil it down at your local editorial content refinery — is the rubber stamp tool. This tool provides four loosely related but distinct capabilities, every one of which deserves to be split off into a tool of its own.

The name *rubber stamp* is pretty misleading, because this particular tool has nothing to do with rubber stamps. First of all, no tree sap is involved — let's get that sticky issue resolved right off the bat. Secondly, you don't use it to stamp an image. When I think of rubber stamps, I think of those things you see in stationery stores that plunk down laudatory exclamations and smiley faces and Pooh bears. Elementary school teachers and little girls use rubber stamps. I've never seen a professional image editor or artist walking around with a rubber stamp in my life.

So put rubber stamps entirely out of your mind for the moment. To discover exactly what the stamp tool does, you must double-click on its icon in the toolbox. Photoshop then displays the Rubber Stamp Options dialog box.

Figure 10-1 shows the Rubber Stamp Options dialog boxes presented by Photoshop 2.5 and 2.0. Each offers seven different settings for applying the rubber stamp tool. Although the settings differ slightly between the two programs, each setting falls into one of four basic categories:

- **Cloning:** Select one of the two Clone options to duplicate portions of an image by dragging over it. Option-click with the tool to specify a point of reference and then drag in a different area of the image to begin cloning.
- **Pattern application:** Select one of the two Pattern options to paint an image with a repeating pattern rather than the standard foreground color. Before using this option, you must establish a pattern by selecting a portion of the image and choosing Edit ⇨ Define Pattern.
- **Reversion:** Both the Revert option in Photoshop 2.0 and the From Saved option in Photoshop 2.5 enable you to revert portions of an image to the way they appeared when you last saved the image. Version 2.5 also offers a From Snapshot option that enables you to use the rubber stamp tool to revert portions of your image to the way they appeared when you last chose Edit ⇨ Take Snapshot.
- **Arbitrary, limited-use effects:** Photoshop 2.0's rubber stamp provides two special effects, Texture and Impressionist. The first paints in a stream of randomly colored pixels and the second merges the current image with its last saved version to create a smeared, gooey effect. The Texture option was such a hit that it was dropped from Photoshop 2.5 — and I haven't heard anyone complain. These are the least useful of the rubber stamp settings, and this is the last time I'll mention them.

If there is a tie that binds the rubber stamp's various capabilities, it is the fact that most enable you to paint with images. When you clone with the rubber stamp tool, for example, you paint with a displaced version of the image itself. When you paint a pattern, you paint with an image fragment. When you revert, you paint with the saved version of the image. Only the special effects settings violate this analogy.

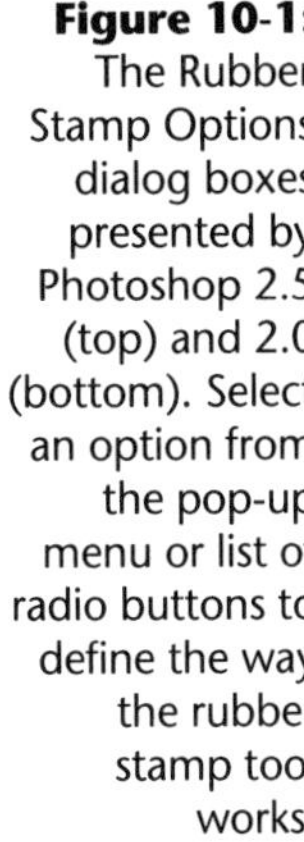

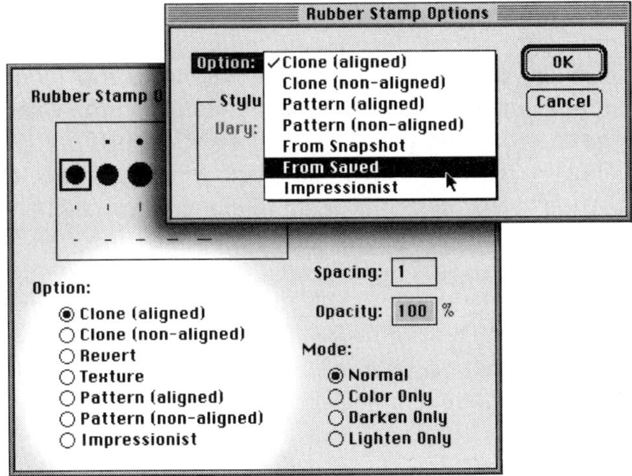

Figure 10-1: The Rubber Stamp Options dialog boxes presented by Photoshop 2.5 (top) and 2.0 (bottom). Select an option from the pop-up menu or list of radio buttons to define the way the rubber stamp tool works.

As you can see, a better name for the rubber stamp tool might be the clone/pattern/revert/stupid effects tool or maybe the junk-drawer tool. Then again, the mother of all mixed-up tools has a certain ring to it. Why don't you send me your favorite name, and we'll have a raffle or something — maybe give away some Tupperware.

In any case, the remainder of this chapter explores every one of the rubber stamp's capabilities.

Cloning Image Elements

So far, my take on the rubber stamp tool may sound a bit derogatory. But in truth, most of its capabilities can come in very handy.

Take cloning, for example. As any died-in-the-wool Photoshop user will tell you, the rubber stamp is an invaluable tool for touching up images, whether you want to remove dust fragments, hairs, and other blotches scanned with a photo or to eliminate portions of an image (as described in the "How to soften selection outlines" section of Chapter 9).

You also can use the rubber stamp to duplicate specific elements in an image, like flowers and umbrellas, as described in the Photoshop manual. But by all accounts, this is an inefficient use of the tool. If you want to duplicate an element, you'll have better luck if you select it and clone it by Option-dragging the selection. By taking that approach, you can specify the exact boundaries of the element, the softness of its edges, and the precise location of the clone. Cloning an element with the rubber stamp is more of an ordeal, because it's easy to accidently clone areas around the element and to begin a clone in the wrong location.

The cloning process

To clone part of an image, double-click on the rubber stamp tool icon and select either the Clone (Aligned) or Clone (Non-aligned) option. (The upcoming section explains the difference between the two.) After pressing Return or clicking OK to exit the Rubber Stamp Options dialog box, Option-click in the image window to specify a point of reference in the portion of the image you want to clone. Then click or drag with the tool in some other region of the image to paint a cloned spot or line.

In Figure 10-2, for example, I Option-clicked just above and to the right of the bird's head, as demonstrated by the appearance of the stamp pickup cursor. I then painted the line shown inside the white rectangle. The rubber stamp cursor shows the end of my drag; the cross-shaped clone reference cursor shows the corresponding point in the original image.

Photoshop lets you clone not only from within the image you're working on, but also from an entirely separate image window. This technique enables you to merge two different images together, as demonstrated in Figure 10-3. To achieve this effect, Option-click in one image, bring a second image to the foreground, and then drag with the rubber stamp tool to clone from the first image.

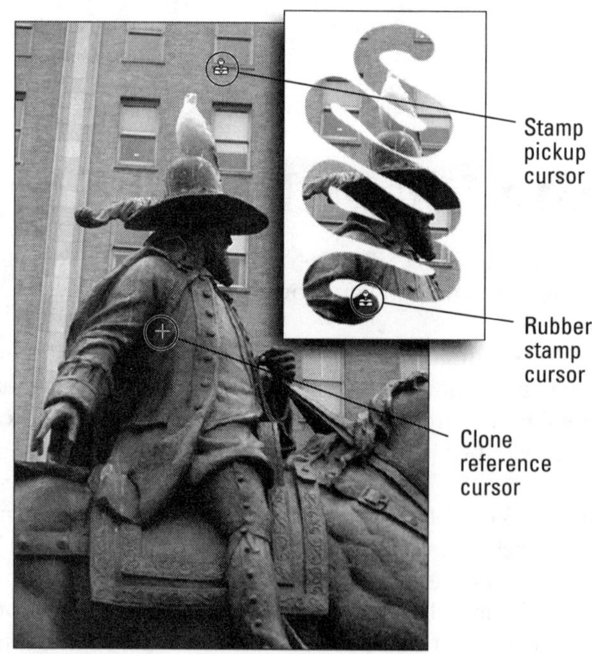

Figure 10-2: After Option-clicking at the point indicated by the stamp pickup cursor, I dragged with the rubber stamp tool to paint with the image. (The only reason I painted inside the white rectangle is to set off the line.)

Figure 10-3: I merged the area around horse and rider with a water image from another open window (see the upcoming Figure 10-6). The translucent effects were created by periodically adjusting the Opacity slider bar in the Brushes palette to settings ranging from 50 to 80 percent.

The Brushes palette affects the rubber stamp tool just as it does the paint and edit tools. Use the Opacity slider bar to paint with translucent versions of the cloned pixels. Select a brush shape to specify the thickness and softness of a cloned line. Finally, use the pop-up menu on the left side of the palette to access the ten brush modes discussed in the "Brush Modes" section of Chapter 8.

Aligned and nonaligned cloning

Now that I've explained how to use the tool, I'll return to the options in the Rubber Stamp Options dialog box:

- **Clone (Aligned):** To understand how this option works, think of the locations where you Option-click and begin dragging with the rubber stamp tool as opposite ends of an imaginary straight line (see the top half of Figure 10-4). The length and angle of that imaginary line remains fixed until you Option-click a second time. As you drag, Photoshop moves the line, cloning pixels from one end of the line and laying them down at the other. Regardless of how many times you start and stop dragging with the stamp tool, all lines match up as seamlessly as pieces in a puzzle.
- **Clone (Non-aligned):** If you want to repeatedly clone from a single portion of an image, select this option. The second example in Figure 10-4 shows how the length and angle of the imaginary line change every time you paint a new line with the rubber stamp tool.

Figure 10-4: Select the Clone (Aligned) option to instruct Photoshop to clone an image continuously, no matter how many lines you paint (top). If you select Clone (Non-aligned), Photoshop clones each new line from the point at which you Option-click.

Stamp differences

You should be aware of a difference between the way the rubber stamp clones an image in Photoshop 2.0 and 2.5. In Version 2.0, the rubber stamp clones the image as it exists before you start using the tool. Even when you drag over an area that contains a clone, the tool references the original appearance of the image to prevent recloning. This feature keeps you from creating more than one clone during a single drag, as witnessed in the first example of Figure 10-5.

In Photoshop 2.5, however, any changes you make to the image affect the tool as you use it, which can result in the repeating patterns like those shown in the second example of the figure. Although you can create some interesting effects, avoid cloning and recloning areas when retouching because it can result in obvious patterns that betray your adjustments.

Figure 10-5: Photoshop 2.0's rubber stamp tool clones the image as it exists before you start using the tool (top). In Version 2.5, the tool clones and reclones images during a single drag (bottom).

To avoid recloning areas in Photoshop 2.5, clone from a duplicate of the image. Begin by choosing Image ⇨ Calculate ⇨ Duplicate to create a copy of the current image. Option-click with the rubber stamp tool somewhere in the duplicate window. Then switch to the original image and drag freely with the tool to clone from the duplicate. Because your changes don't affect the duplicate image, there's no chance of recloning.

Touching up blemishes

One of the best uses for the rubber stamp tool is to touch up a scanned photo. Figure 10-6 shows a Photo CD image that desperately needs the stamp tool's attention. Normally, Kodak's Photo CD process delivers some of the best scans money can buy. But this particular medium-resolution image needs some work. It's a little late to go back to the service bureau and demand that they rescan the photo, so my only choice is to touch it up myself.

The best way to fix this image — or any image like it — is to use the rubber stamp over and over again, repeatedly Option-clicking at one location and then clicking at another. Begin by selecting a brush shape that's a little larger than the largest blotch. Of the default brushes, the hard-edged varieties with diameters of 5 and 9 pixels generally work best. (The soft-edged brush shapes have a tendency to incompletely cover the blemishes.)

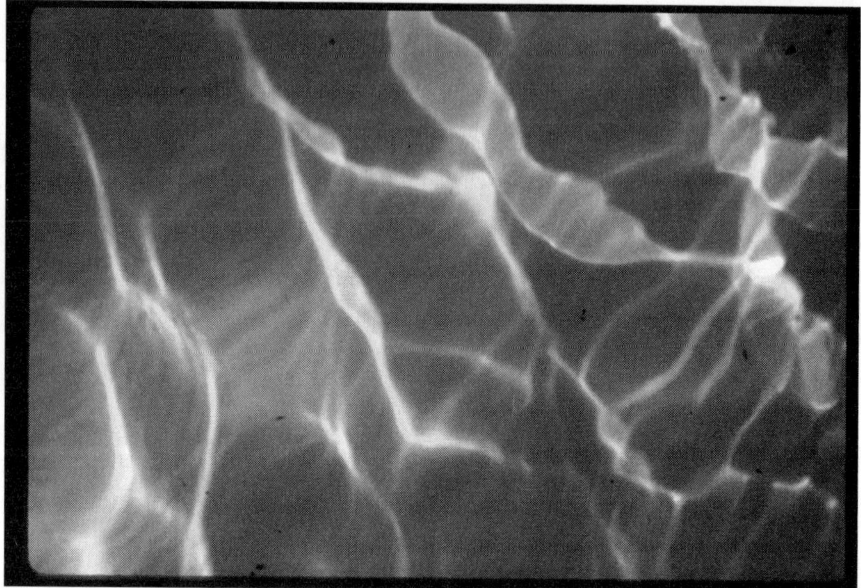

Figure 10-6: This appallingly bad Photo CD image is riddled with blotches and big hurky wads of dust that didn't exist on the original 35mm slide.

Option-click with the stamp tool at a location that is very close to the blemish and features similarly colored pixels. Then click — do not drag — directly on the blemish. The idea is to change as few pixels as possible.

If the retouched area doesn't look quite right, choose Edit ⇨ Undo (Command-Z), Option-click at a different location, and try again. If your touch-up appears seamless — *absolutely* seamless — move on to the next blemish, repeating the Option-click and click routine for every dust mark on the photo.

This process isn't necessarily time-consuming, but it does require patience. For example, although it took more than 40 Option-click and click combinations (not counting 10 or so undos) to arrive at the image shown in Figure 10-7, the process itself took less than 15 minutes. Boring but fast.

It's a little trickier to retouch hairs than dust and other blobs. That's because a hair, although very thin, can be surprisingly long. However, the retouching process is the same. Rather than dragging over the entire length of the hair, Option-click and click your way through it, bit by little bit. The one difference is brush shape. Because you'll be clicking so many times in succession and because the hair is so thin, you'll probably achieve the least conspicuous effects if you use a soft brush shape, such as the default 9-pixel model in the second row of the Brushes palette.

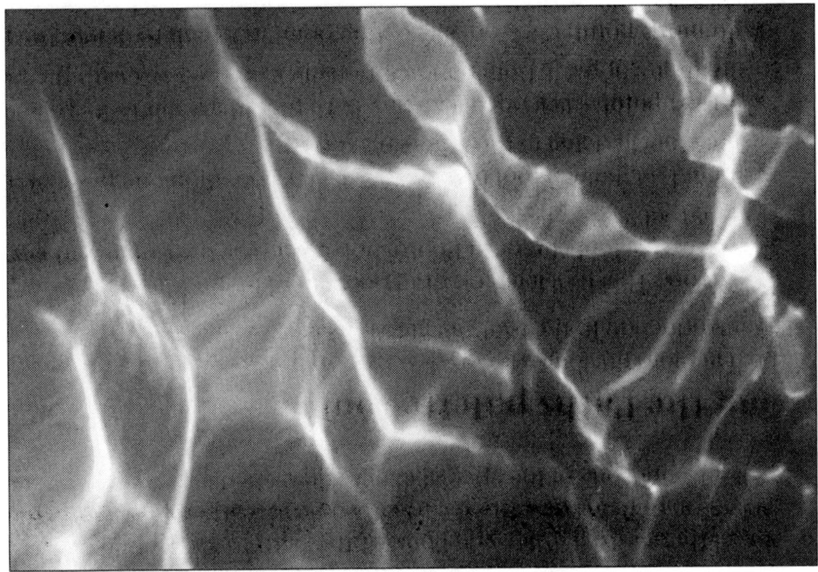

Figure 10-7: The result of Option-clicking and clicking more than 40 times on the photo shown in Figure 10-6. Notice that I also cropped the image and added a border. Now I can use the image as a background, as I did in Figure 10-3.

Personally, I find the rubber stamp cursor to be the most intrusive of all Photoshop's cursors. After all, when you're cloning an element, you need to see exactly what you're doing. You don't need to see a blocky icon that has nothing to do with the current operation. To get rid of this eyesore and view a simple crosshair cursor instead, press the Caps Lock key.

Eliminating distracting background elements

Another way to apply the stamp tool's cloning capabilities is to eliminate background action that competes with the central elements in an image. Figure 10-8, for example, shows a one-in-a-million news photo from the Reuters image library. Although the image is well-photographed and historic in its implications — in case you missed the last decade, that's Comrade V.I. Lenin (Vlad to his mom) — that rear workman doesn't contribute anything to the scene and in fact draws your attention away from the foreground drama. Simply put, the image would be better off without him.

The following steps explain how I eradicated the offending workman from the scene.

Keep in mind as you read the following steps that deleting an image element with the rubber stamp tool is something of an inexact science; it requires some trial and error. So regard the following steps as an example of how to approach the process of editing your image rather than a specific procedure that works for all images. You may need to adapt the process slightly depending upon your image.

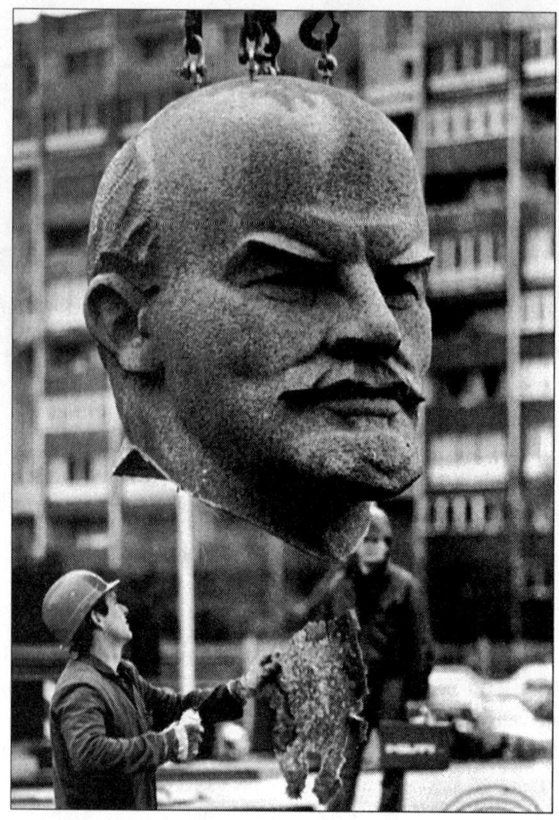

Figure 10-8: You have to love that old Soviet state-endorsed art. So bold, so angular, so politically intolerant. But you also have to lose that rear workman.

STEPS: Eliminating Distracting Elements from an Image

Step 1. I began by cloning the area around the neck of the statue with a soft brush shape. Abandoning the controlled clicks I recommended in the last section, I allowed myself to drag with the tool because I needed to cover relatively large portions of the image. The apartment building (or whatever that structure is) behind the floating head is magnificently out of focus, just the thing for hiding any incongruous transitions I might create with the rubber stamp. So I warmed up to the image by retouching this area first. Figure 10-9 shows my progress.

Notice that I covered the workman's body by cloning pixels from both his left and right sides. I also added a vertical bar where the workman's right arm used to be to maintain the rhythm of the building. Remember that variety is the key to using the rubber stamp tool: if you consistently clone from one portion of the image, you create an obvious repetition that the viewer can't help but notice.

Figure 10-9: Cloning over the background worker's upper torso was fairly easy because the background building is so regular and out of focus, providing a wealth of material from which to clone.

Step 2. The next step was to eliminate the workman's head. This was a little tricky because it involved rubbing up against the focused perimeter of Lenin's neck. I had to clone some of the more intricate areas using a hard-edged brush. I also ended up duplicating some of the neck edges to maintain continuity. In addition, I touched up the left side of the neck (your left, not Lenin's) and removed a few of the white spots from his face. You see my progress in Figure 10-10.

Step 3. Now for the hard part: eliminating the worker's legs and lower torso. See that fragment of metal that the foreground worker is holding? What a pain. Its edges were so irregular that there was no way I could restore it with the rubber stamp tool if I messed up while trying to eradicate the background worker's limbs. So I lassoed around the fragment to select it and chose Select ➪ Inverse to protect it. I also chose Select ➪ Feather and gave it a Radius value of 1 to slightly soften its edges. This prevented me from messing up the metal no matter what edits I made to the background worker's remaining body parts.

Figure 10-10: I eliminated the workman's head and touched up details around the perimeter of the neck.

Step 4. From here on out, it was just more cloning. Unfortunately, I barely had anything to clone from. See that little bit of black edging between the two "legs" of the metal fragment? That's it. That's all I had to draw the strip of edging to the right of the fragment that eventually appears in Figure 10-11. To pull off this feat, I double-clicked on the rubber stamp tool icon in the toolbox and chose the Clone (Non-aligned) option. Then I Option-clicked on the tiny bit of edging and click, click, clicked my way down to the street.

Step 5. Unfortunately, the strip I laid down in Step 4 appeared noticeably blobbular — it looked for all the world like I clicked a bunch of times. Darn. To fix this problem, I clicked and Shift-clicked with the smudge tool set to about 30 percent pressure. This step smeared the blobs into a continuous strip, but again, the effect was noticeable. It looked as if I had smeared the strip. So I went back and cloned some more, this time with the Opacity slider bar set to 50 percent.

Figure 10-11: After about 45 minutes worth of monkeying around with the rubber stamp tool, the rear workman is gone, leaving us with an unfettered view of the dubious one himself.

Step 6. To polish the image off, I chose Select ⇨ None (Command-D) and ran the sharpen tool along the edges of the metal fragment. This step helped to hide the fact that I retouched around it and further distinguished the fragment from the unfocused background. I also cropped away 20 or so pixels from the right side of the image to correct the balance of the image.

What I hope I demonstrated in this section is that cloning with the rubber stamp tool requires that you alternate between patching and whittling away. There are no rights and wrongs, no hard and fast rules. Anything you can find to clone is fair game. As long as you avoid mucking up the foreground image, you can't go wrong (so I guess there is *one* hard and fast rule). If you're careful and diligent, no one but you is going to notice your alterations.

Any time you edit the contents of a photograph, you tread on very sensitive ground. Though some have convincingly argued that electronically retouching an image is theoretically no different than cropping a photograph, a technique that has been available and in use since the first daguerreotype, photographers have certain rights under copyright law that cannot be ignored. A photographer may have a reason for including an element that you want to eliminate. So before you edit any photograph, be sure to get permission either from the original photographer or from the copyright holder.

Applying Repeating Patterns

Before you can use the rubber stamp tool to paint with a pattern, you must define a pattern by selecting a portion of the image with the rectangular marquee tool and choosing Edit ⇨ Define Pattern. For the Define Pattern command to work, you must use the rectangular marquee — no other selection tool will do. In addition, the selection cannot be feathered. Otherwise, the command is dimmed.

Figure 10-12 shows an example of how you can apply repeating patterns. I selected the single apartment window (surrounded by marching ants) and chose Edit ⇨ Define Pattern. I then applied the pattern with the rubber stamp tool at 80 percent opacity over the horse and rider statue.

Like the Clipboard, Photoshop can retain only one pattern at a time and remembers the pattern throughout a single session. Any time you choose Edit ⇨ Define Pattern, you delete the previous pattern as you create a new one. Photoshop also deletes the pattern when you quit the program. Therefore, each time you launch Photoshop, you must define the pattern from scratch.

Pattern options

To paint with a pattern, double-click on the rubber stamp tool icon and select either the Pattern (Aligned) or Pattern (Non-aligned) option. These options work as follows:

- **Pattern (Aligned):** Select this option to align all patterns you apply with the stamp tool, regardless of how many times you start and stop dragging. The two left examples in Figure 10-13 show the effects of selecting this option. The elements in the pattern remain exactly aligned throughout all the lines. I painted the top image with the Opacity slider bar set to 50 percent, which is why the lines darken when they meet.

Figure 10-12: After marqueeing a single window (top) and choosing Edit ⇨ Define Pattern, I painted a translucent coat of the pattern over the statue with the rubber stamp tool (bottom).

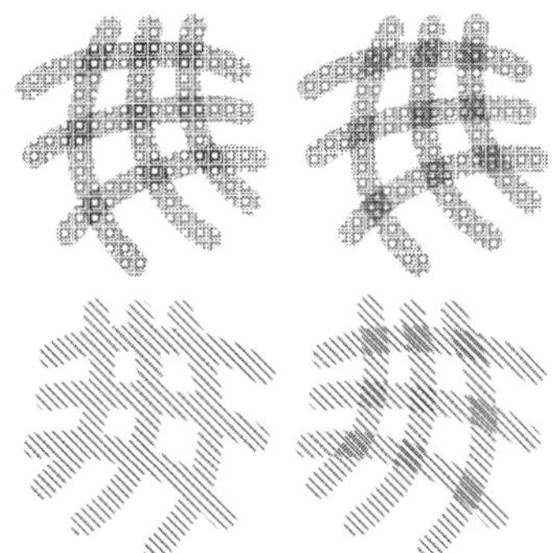

Figure 10-13: Select the Pattern (Aligned) option to align the patterns in all brush strokes painted with the stamp tool (left). If you select Pattern (Non-aligned), Photoshop aligns each pattern with the beginning of the line (right).

- **Pattern (Non-aligned):** To allow patterns in different lines to align randomly, select this option. The positioning of the pattern within each line is determined by the point at which you begin dragging. I dragged from right to left to paint the horizontal lines and from top to bottom to paint the vertical lines. The two right examples in Figure 10-13 show how nonaligned patterns overlap.

After you select Pattern (Aligned) or Pattern (Non-aligned), you're free to start dragging with the stamp tool. You don't need to Option-click or make any other special provisions, as you do when cloning.

How to create patterns

The biggest difficulty with painting patterns is not figuring out the rubber stamp tool, but creating the patterns in the first place. Ideally, your pattern should repeat continuously, without vertical and horizontal seams. Here are some ways to create repeating, continuous patterns:

- **Load a displacement map:** Both versions of Photoshop offer a Displacement Maps folder inside the Plug-ins folder. This folder contains several images, each of which represents a different repeating pattern, as illustrated in Figure 10-14. To use one of these patterns, open the image, choose Select ⇨ All (Command-A), and choose Edit ⇨ Define Pattern. (For more information on displacement maps, see Chapter 13.)

In addition to the displacement maps, Photoshop 2.0 ships with 22 Illustrator EPS patterns that you can open and render to any size you desire. You'll find these patterns in the PostScript Patterns folder on the ATM disk.

- **Using filters:** As luck would have it, you can create your own custom textures without painting a single line. In fact, you can create a nearly infinite variety of textures by applying several filters to a blank document. To create the texture shown in the bottom right box in Figure 10-15, for example, I began by selecting a 128 × 128-pixel area. I then chose Filter ⇨ Noise ⇨ Add Noise, entered a value of 32, and selected the Gaussian radio button. I pressed Command-F twice to apply the noise filter two more times. Finally, I chose Filter ⇨ Stylize ⇨ Emboss and entered 135 into the Angle option box, 1 into the Height option box, and 100 percent into the Amount option box. The result is a bumpy surface that looks like stucco. This is merely one example of the myriad possibilities filters afford. There's no end to what you can do, so experiment away. (For more information on using Add Noise, Emboss, and other filter commands, see Chapter 12, "Filtering Techniques.")

Color Plate 6-1: An image scanned from a paper positive (left) and a film transparency (right). For you film buffs, the paper positive is an 8 x 10-inch Cibachrome print and the film transparency is a 4 x 5-inch slide.

Color Plate 6-2: A page from *Macworld* magazine scanned using a Photoshop plug-in module (top) and Ofoto (bottom). The Ofoto scan is cripser and truer to the original printed page.

election tools, end bitmap graphics market all to itself.
t outperforms —DEKE McCLELLAND

Liberty Bowl I used Color It's paste controls to colorize the moon with a gradient and superimpose the face of the Stat-

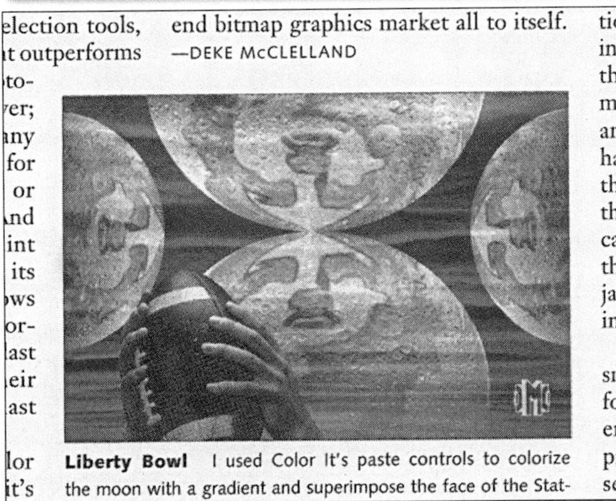

election tools, end bitmap graphics market all to itself.
t outperforms —DEKE McCLELLAND

Liberty Bowl I used Color It's paste controls to colorize the moon with a gradient and superimpose the face of the Stat-

Color Plate 6-3:
The original image as submitted to *Macworld* magazine.

Color Plate 6-4:
The detailing on the Camel's face and the shadows around the eyes are much clearer and more focused in the Photo CD image (top) than in the image I scanned (bottom).

Color Plate 6-5:
This hilarious little character comes from PhotoDisc's *People and Lifestyles* disk.

Color Plate 6-6:
Not all the images from the ColorBytes Sampler One disk are as eye-catching as this one, but they come very close.

Color Plate 6-7: Images from each of the four agencies represented on 3M's CD Stock catalog.

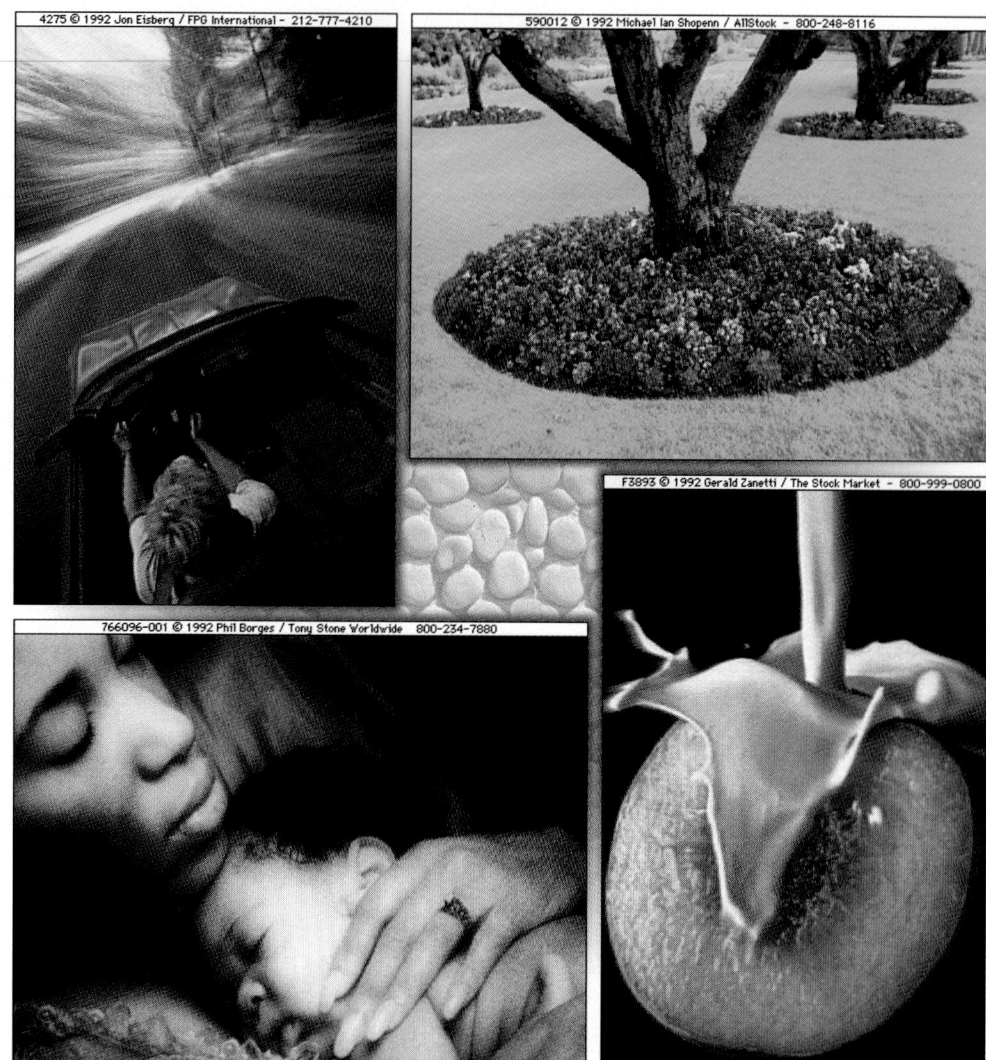

Color Plate 6-8:
Two Reuters news photos from the 1980's.

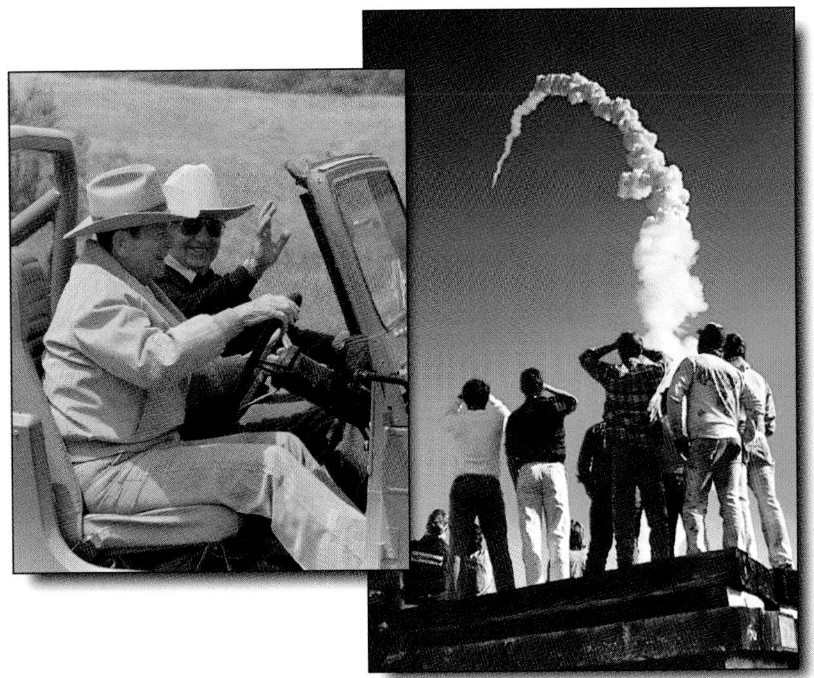

Color Plate 6-9:
Two dynamic images from the Allsport image library.

Color Plate 7-1: A grayscale image printed as a quadtone using the colors navy blue, rose, teal, and dull orange. All colors were defined and printed using CMYK pigments.

Color Plate 8-1: I painted this image for *Macworld* magazine in 1990 using a Wacom SD-510 pressure-sensitive tablet and Photoshop 1.0.7. A pressure-sensitive tablet transforms Photoshop into a fully functioning artist's studio.

Color Plate 10-1: Images from D' pix's Folio 1 collection (top) are designed to serve as single-shot background, no repetition required. By contrast, Wraptures images represent tiles in a repeating pattern. The bottom image shows how a single tile blends with its neighbors to create a seamless surface texture.

Color Plate 12-1: Clockwise from upper left, the effects of the Motion Blur, Sharpen Edges, Median, and High Pass corrective filters. Normally, the High Pass filter takes the saturation out of an image, leaving many areas gray, like an old, sun-bleached slide. To restore the colors, I pasted the original image in front of the filtered one and chose Color from the brush mode pop-up menu in the Brushes palette.

Color Plate 12-2: Clockwise from upper left, the effects of the destructive filters Crystallize, Lens Flare, Color Halftone, and Twirl. The Lens Flare filter is applicable to color images only. Perhaps surprisingly, you can apply the Color Halftone filter to grayscale and color images alike.

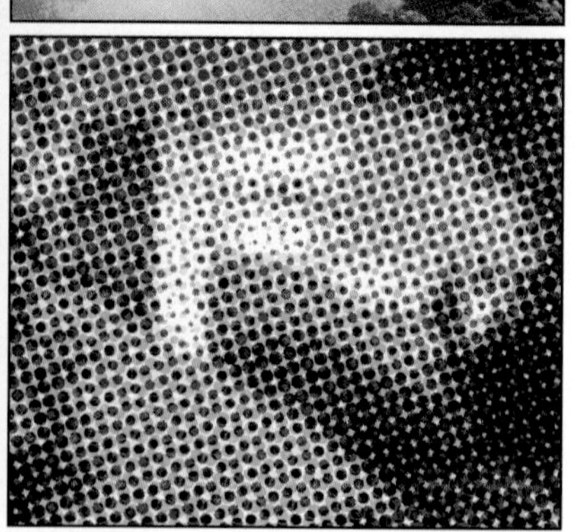

Color Plate 12-3: In this piece, titled Knowing Risk, Seattle artist Mark Collen combines a variety of distortion filtering effects to create a surrealistic landscape. The cat, the book, the mongoose, and the twigs are the only scanned images.

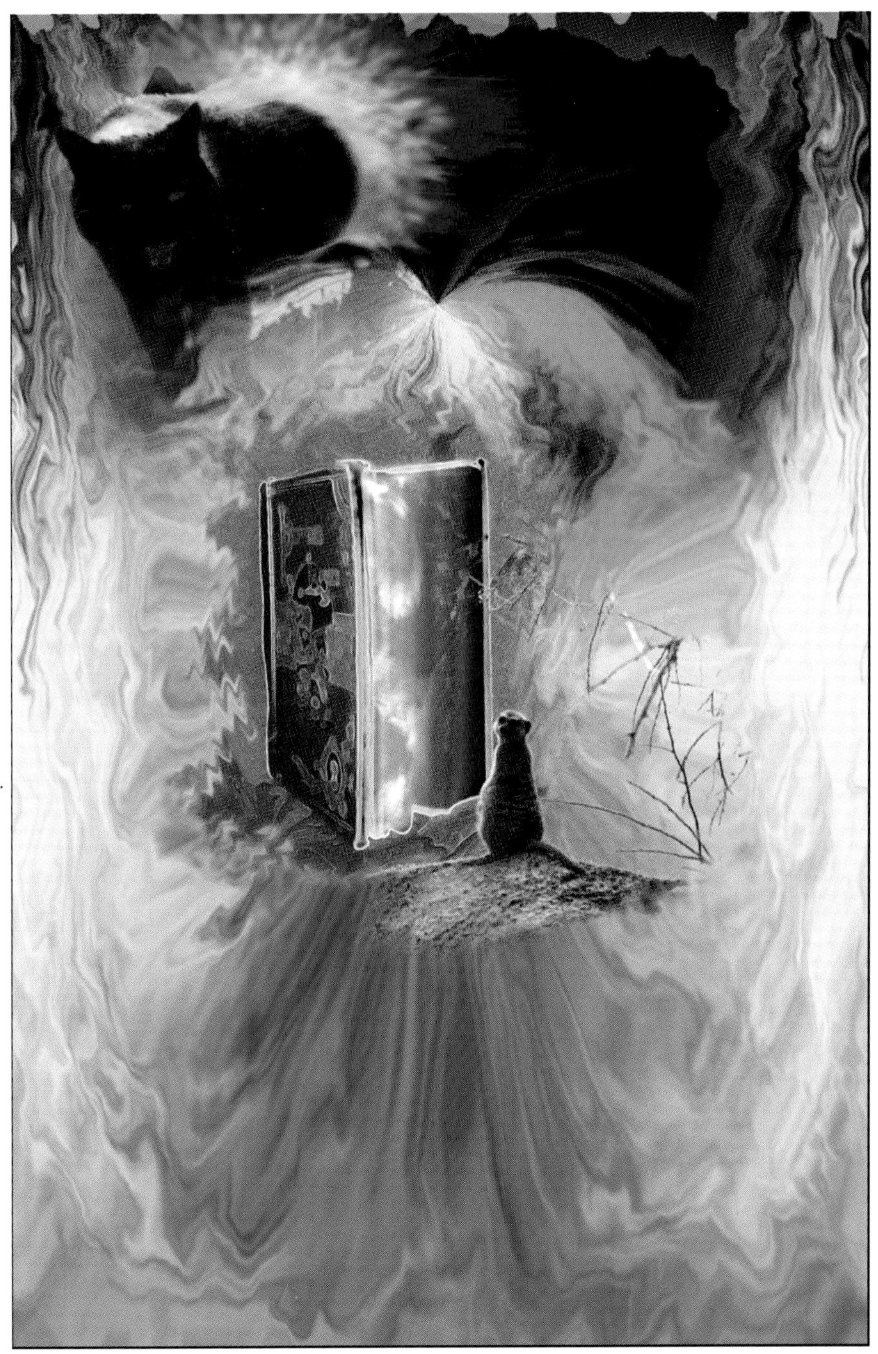

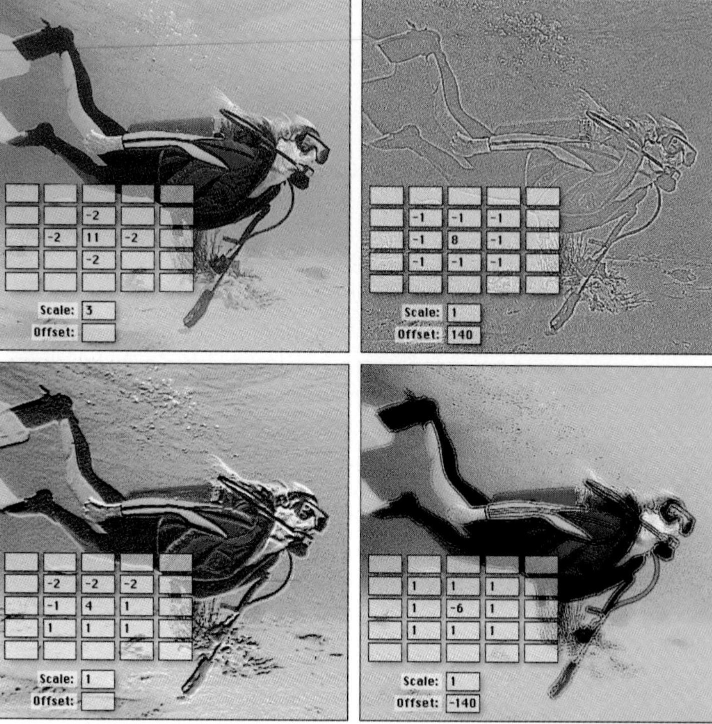

Color Plate 13-1: Color versions of four Custom filter effects, including (clockwise form upper left) mild sharpening, offset sharpening, edge-detection, and full-color embossing.

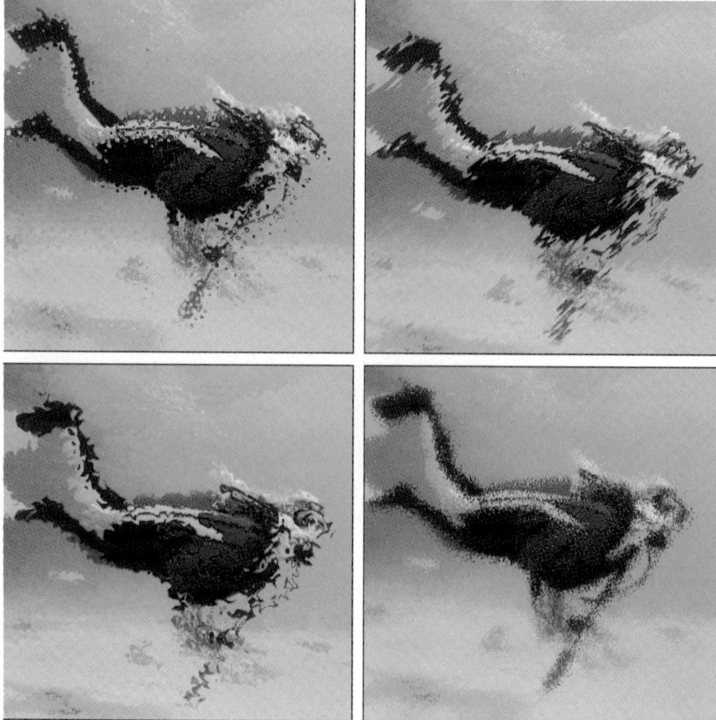

Color Plate 13-2: Examples of applying four patterns from the Displacement Maps folder with the Displace filter, including (clockwise from upper left) Crumbles, Streaks pattern, Mezzo effect, and Twirl pattern.

Color Plate 14-1: The colors inside the field and slider in the Color Picker dialog box change to reflect the selection of the H (Hue), S (Saturation), and B (Brightness) radio buttons.

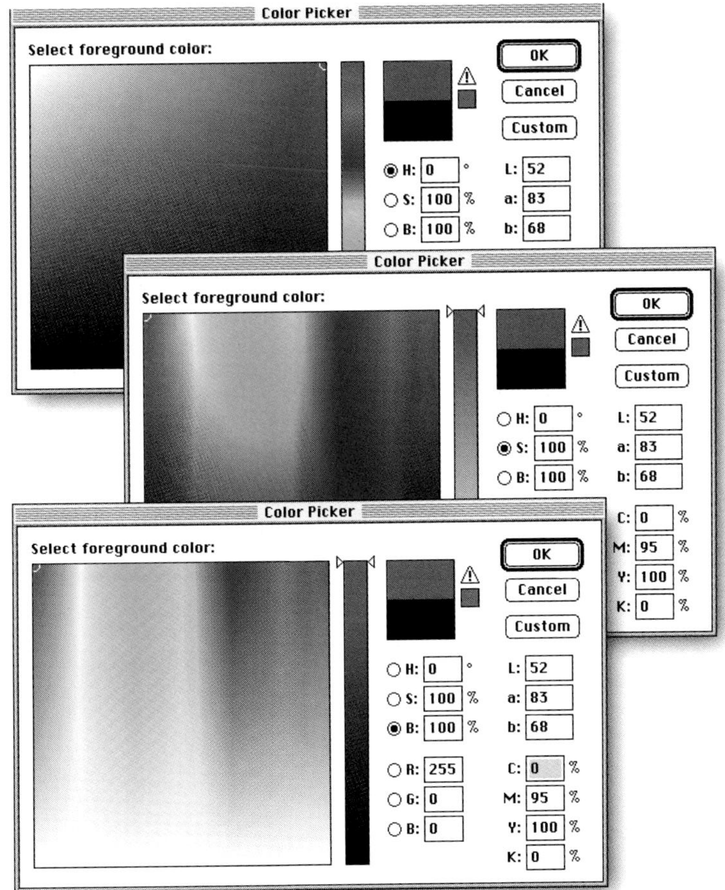

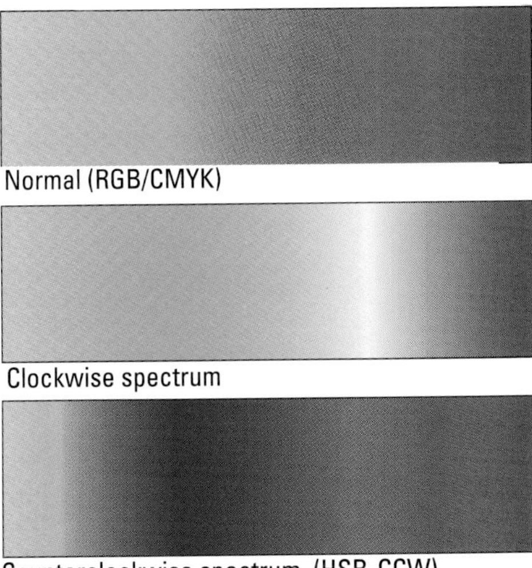

Color Plate 15-1: Three gradations between cyan and red created using each of the three Syle settings in the Gradient Tool Options dialog box.

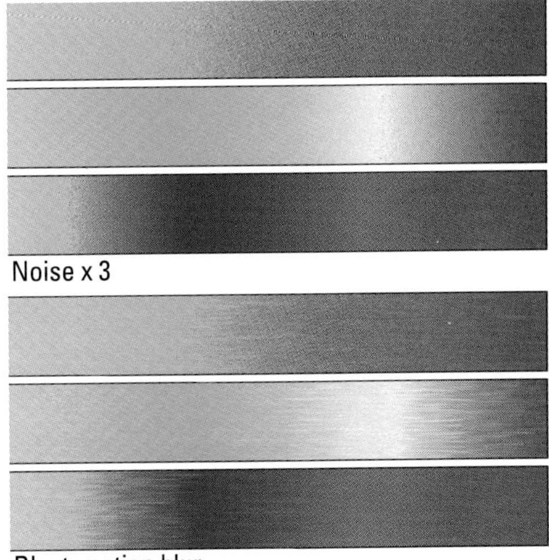

Color Plate 15-2: The results of filtering the three gradation styles from Color Plate 15-1 by applying the Add Noise filter three times in a row (top) and blasting the gradations with the Wind filter and applying the Motion Blur filter (bottom).

Color Plate 15-3: Examples of all but the last three overlay mode options in the Mode pop-up menu. Each overlay mode allows you to mix colors in a floating selection with colors in the underlying image in a unique way.

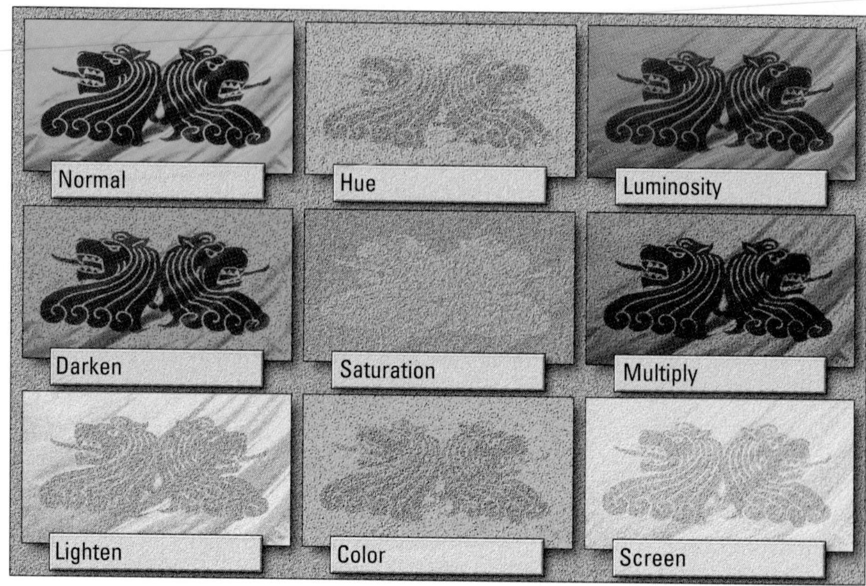

Color Plate 15-4: Ouch! Reckless combinations of bright colors like these ought to be forbidden outside of clown emporiums. Still, they're useful for demonstrating the effects of applying fuzziness ranges independently to the red (top row), green (middle), and blue (bottom) color channels by using the Floating slider triangles (left column) and Underlying slider triangles (right column).

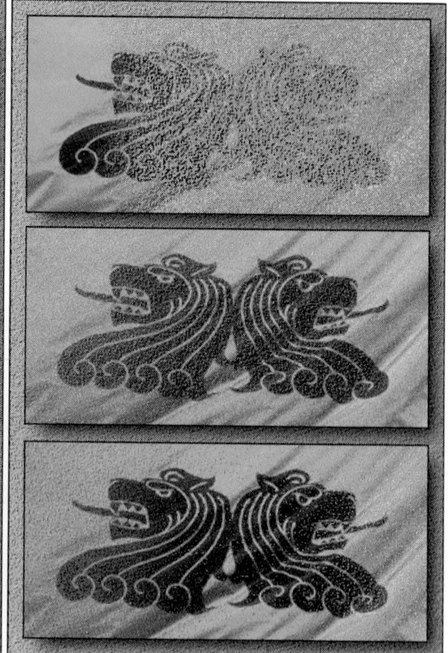

Color Plate 16-1: Sample results of the commands in the Image ⇨ Map submenu, including (clockwise from upper left) Invert, Equalize, Threshold, and Posterize. The Threshold example was applied to a floating selection set to 20 percent opacity and the Darken overlay mode.

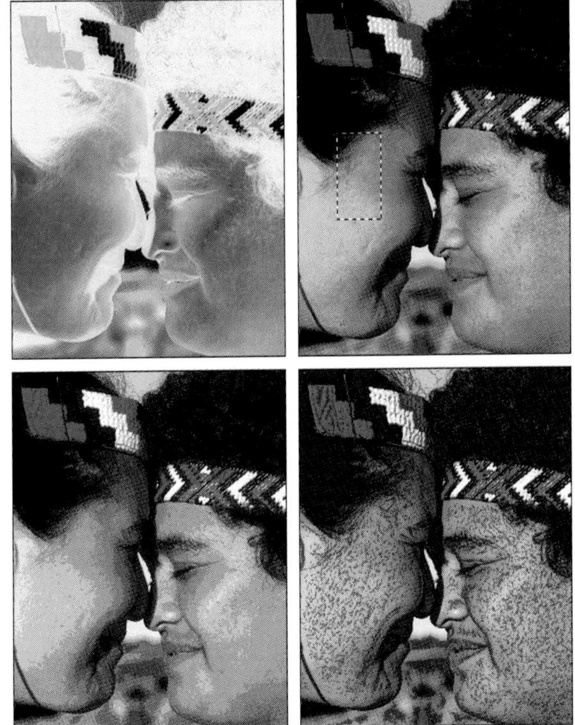

Color Plate 16-2: The results of choosing Image ⇨ Adjust ⇨ Hue/Saturation and applying various Hue values to an entire image (top row) and to only the red portions of the image (bottom row).

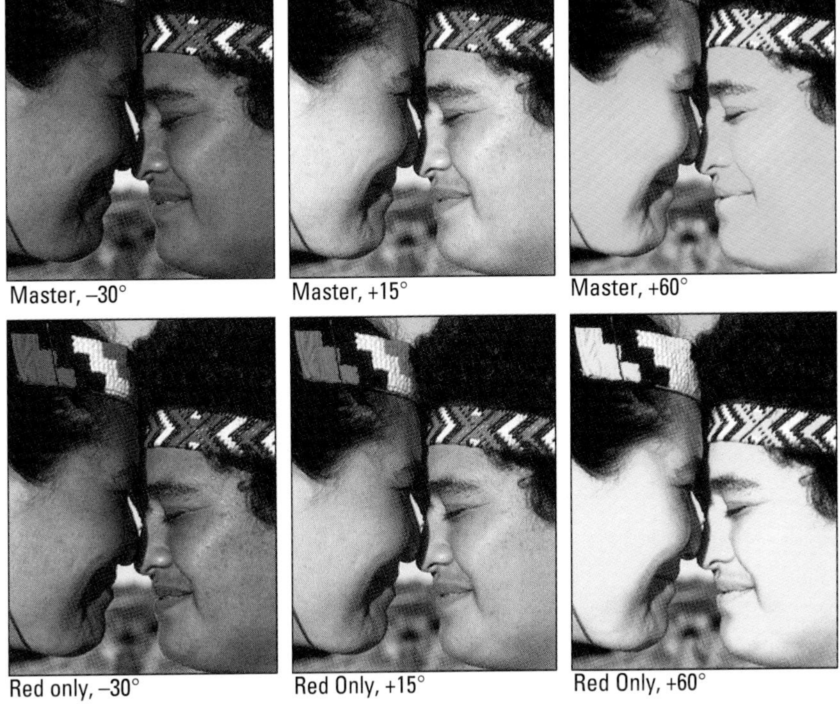

Color Plate 16-3: The results of applying various Saturation values to an entire image (top row) and to specified colors independently of others (bottom row).

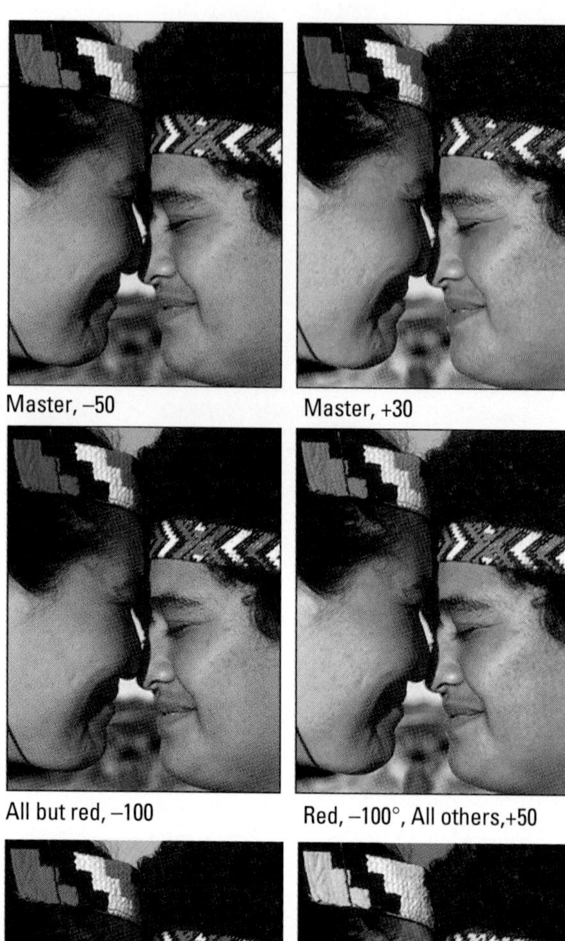

Master, –50

Master, +30

All but red, –100

Red, –100°, All others,+50

Color Plate 16-4: The results of applying various Hue values to an image when the Colorize option is inactive (top row) and active (bottom row).

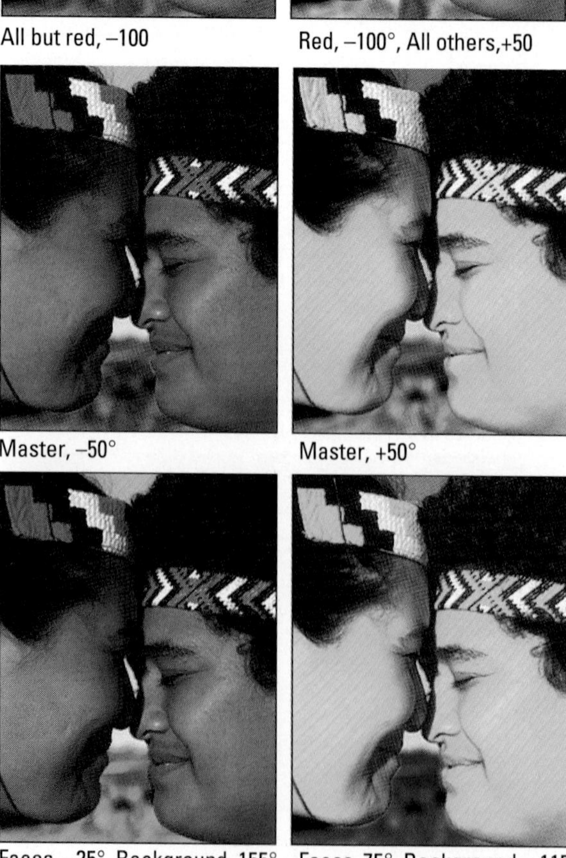

Master, –50°

Master, +50°

Faces, –25°, Background, 155°

Faces, 75°, Background, –115°

Color Plate 16-5: The results of using the Curves command to lighten the colors in the red channel (left), increase the level of contrast in the green channel (middle), and applying an arbitrary color map to the blue channel (right).

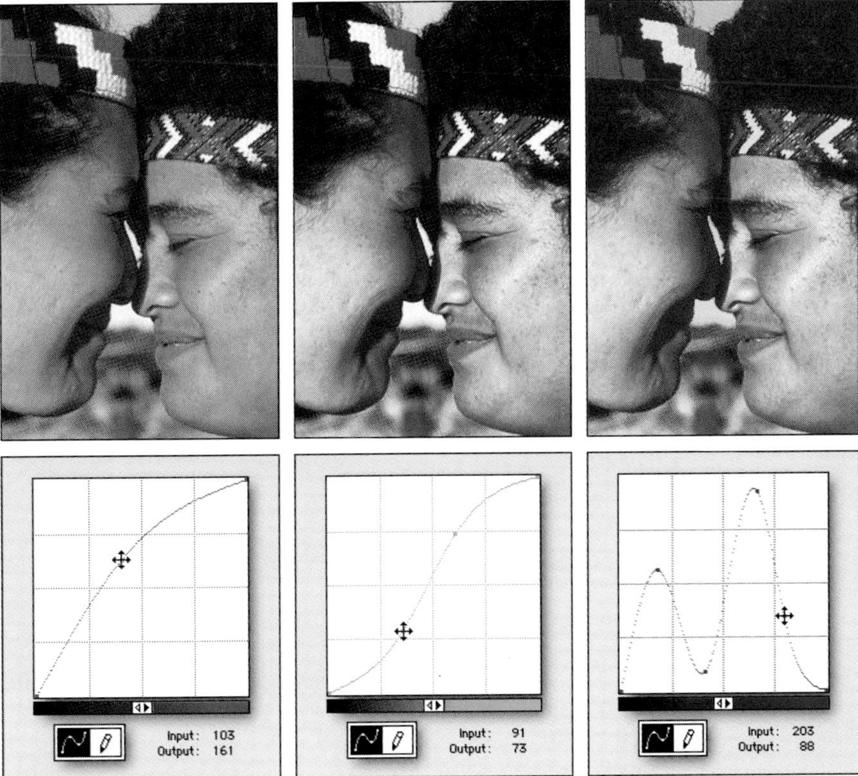

Color Plate 17-1: The U.S. Capitol building (a.k.a. National House of Filibuster) on a peaceful evening. Look at those tax dollars glow.

Figure 17-2: You can wreak some pretty interesting havoc on the colors in an image by copying the image from one channel and pasting it into another and by swapping images between color channels.

Replace red with blue

Replace blue with green

Replace green with red

Swap red and blue

Color Plate 17-3: The results of multiple applications of the Subtract (upper left) and Difference (upper right) commands, followed by the same images after swapping the red and blue color channels (bottom rows).

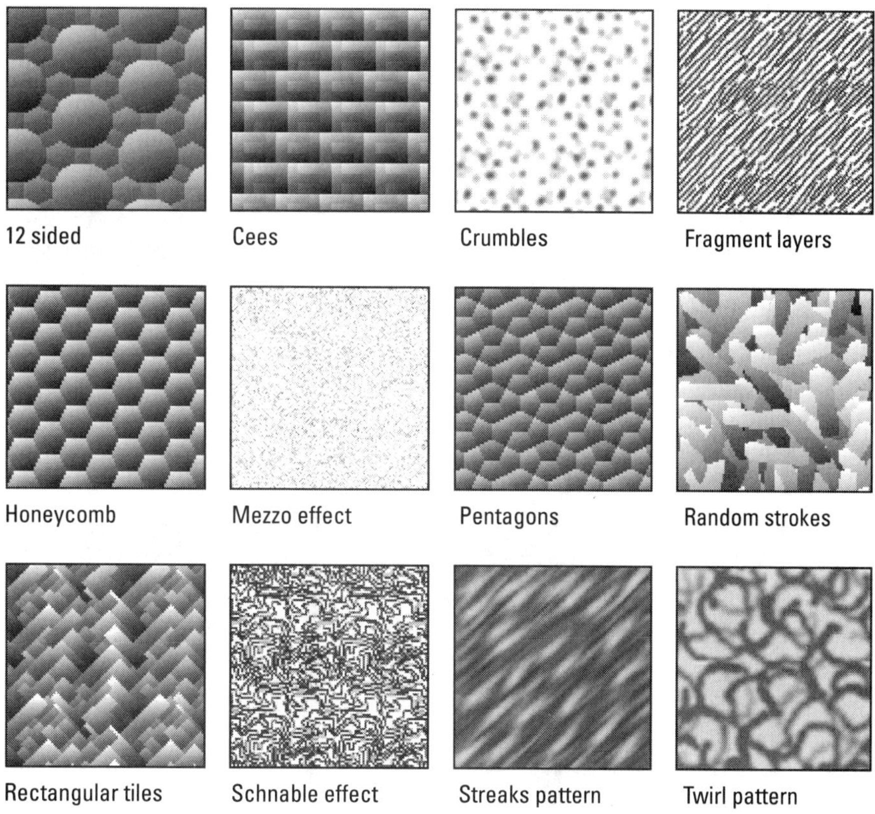

Figure 10-14: The 12 patterns contained in the Displacement Maps folder included with Photoshop 2.5. Only six of these patterns (12-sided, cees, honeycomb, pentagons, random strokes, and rectangular tiles) are included with Photoshop 2.0.

Figure 10-15: To create a stucco texture, apply Filter ⇨ Noise ⇨ Add Noise three times in a row (upper left, upper right, lower left). Then choose Filter ⇨ Stylize ⇨ Emboss and enter a Height value of 1 (lower right).

- **Marquee and clone:** You can use the rectangular marquee and rubber stamp tools to transform a scanned image into a custom pattern. Because this technique is more complicated as well as more rewarding than the others, I explain it in the upcoming section, "STEPS: Building a Repeating Pattern from a Scanned Image."
- **Texture collections:** If you don't have the time or energy to create your own custom patterns but you do have some extra cash lying around, all sorts of texture libraries are available on CD-ROM. My favorite is the Wraptures collection from Form and Function, because all patterns on these discs repeat seamlessly. The Folio collection from D'pix provides a wide range of images, but these do not repeat and are therefore more conducive to backgrounds than patterns. Figure 10-16 shows examples from both collections.

Figure 10-16: A repeating texture from Form and Function's Wraptures collection (top) and a non repeating background image from D'pix's Folio collection (bottom).

The following steps describe how to change a scanned image into a seamless, repeating pattern. To illustrate how this process works, Figures 10-17 through 10-20 show various stages in a project I completed. You need only two tools to carry out these steps: the rectangular marquee tool and the rubber stamp tool with the Clone (Aligned) option active.

STEPS: Building a Repeating Pattern from a Scanned Image

Step 1. Begin by marqueeing a portion of your scanned image and copying it to the Clipboard. For best results, specify the exact size of your marquee by double-clicking on the rectangular marquee icon in the toolbox, selecting the Fixed Size option, and entering specific values into the Width and

Height option boxes. This way, you can easily reselect a portion of the pattern in the steps that follow and use the fixed-size marquee to define the pattern when you are finished. To create the patterns shown in the example, I set the marquee to 128 × 128 pixels.

Step 2. Choose File ⇨ New (Command-N) and triple the values Photoshop offers as the default image dimensions. In my case, Photoshop offered 128 × 128 pixels because that was the size of the image I copied to the Clipboard. Therefore, I changed the image size to 384 × 384 pixels.

Step 3. Paste the marqueed image into the new image window. It appears smack dab in the center of the window, which is exactly where you want it. This image will serve as the central tile of your repeating pattern. Clone the selection by Option-dragging it eight times to create a 3 × 3-tile grid, as shown in Figure 10-17.

Figure 10-17: To build the repeating pattern shown in Figure 10-20, I started by creating a grid of nine image tiles. As you can see, the seams between the tiles in this grid are harsh and unacceptable.

Step 4. Drag the title bar of the new image window to position it so that you can see the portion of the image you copied in the original image window. If necessary, Command-drag the title bar of the original image window to reposition it as well. This way, you can clone from the original image without switching back and forth between windows.

Step 5. Double-click on the rubber stamp tool icon in the toolbox, select the Clone (Aligned) option, and press Return to exit the dialog box.

Step 6. To specify the image you want to clone, Option-click with the stamp tool in the original image window — no need to switch out of the new window — on an easily identifiable pixel that belongs to the portion of the image you copied. The *exact* pixel you click is very important. If you press the Caps Lock key, you get the crosshair cursor, which allows you to narrow in on a pixel. In my case, I clicked on the center of Lenin's right eye.

Step 7. Now click with the stamp tool on the matching pixel in the central tile of the new window. If you've clicked on the correct pixel, the tile should not change one iota. (If it does, choose Edit ⇨ Undo and repeat Steps 6 and 7.)

Step 8. Now that you've aligned the cloned image within the new window, use the stamp tool to fill in portions of the central tile. For example, in Figure 10-18, I extended the chin down into the lower row of tiles, I extended the central face to meet the Lenin on the left, and I extended the head upward into the jawline of the top-row Lenin.

Figure 10-18: I used the rubber stamp's cloning capability to extend the features in the central face toward the left and downward.

Step 9. After you establish one continuous transition between two tiles in any direction — up, down, left, or right — select a portion of the image with the rectangular marquee tool and clone the selection repeatedly to fill out a single row or column. In my case, I managed to create a smooth transition between the central and left-hand tiles. Therefore, I selected a region that includes half of the left tile and half of the central tile. Because I fixed the rectangular marquee to a 128 × 128-pixel square, I only had to click on an area to select it. (Drag to position the marquee exactly where you want it.) I then cloned that selection along the entire length of the middle row.

Step 10. If you started by creating a horizontal transition, now use the rubber stamp tool to create a vertical transition. (Likewise, if you started vertically, now go horizontally.) You may very well need to Option-click again on that special pixel in the original window. By Option-clicking, you allow yourself to build onto one of the perimeter tiles. In my case, I Option-clicked again in the original right eye. Next, I clicked on the matching pixel in the left tile and dragged around to build out the left Lenin's chin. To complete the vertical transition, I Option-clicked a third time and clicked on the matching pixel in the lower center tile, building a transition between the lower Lenin's head and the central Lenin's neck, as shown in Figure 10-19.

Figure 10-19: After completing a smooth transition between the central tile and the tiles below and to the left of it, I selected a portion of the image and choose Edit ⇨ Define Pattern.

Step 11. After you build up one set of both horizontal and vertical transitions, you can select a portion of the image and choose Edit ⇨ Define Pattern. Figure 10-19 shows where I positioned my 128 × 128-pixel selection boundary. It included both halves of the chin along with a smooth transition between head, jaw, and left side of the face (Lenin's left, that is). Don't worry that the image doesn't appear centered inside the selection outline. What counts is that the selection repeats seamlessly when placed beside itself.

Step 12. To confirm that the pattern is indeed seamless and every bit as lovely as you had hoped, double-click on the rubber stamp icon in the toolbox and select the Pattern (Aligned) option. After closing the Rubber Stamp Options dialog box, drag around inside the current image with the rubber stamp tool and a large brush shape. Figure 10-20 shows the seamless results of my dragging.

Figure 10-20: This Big Brother montage is the result of applying the Lenin pattern. I half expect him to say something about how the Great and Powerful Wizard of Oz has spoken, but I don't think that movie got out much in Russia.

Step 13. Be sure to save your completed image. You don't want to go to all this trouble for nothing.

Selectively Undoing Changes

Welcome to the second act of this chapter. It's a short act — more like a scene, really — so you'll have to forgo the intermission.

Now that I've explained the cloning and related patterning attributes of the rubber stamp tool, it's time to turn your attention — come on, turn, turn, just a little more, there you go — to a new topic. The rest of this chapter deals with *reversion,* which is a fancy word for returning your image to the way it looked before you went and made an unholy mess of it.

Using the traditional undo functions

Before I dive into the rubber stamp's reversion capabilities, allow me to introduce the more traditional reversion functions that are found in nearly all paint applications, including Photoshop:

- **Undo:** To restore an image to the way it looked before the last operation, choose Edit ⇨ Undo (Command-Z). You can undo the effect of a paint or edit tool, a change made to a selection outline, or a special-effect or color-correction command. You can't undo disk operations, such as opening or saving. However, Photoshop does let you undo an edit after printing an image. You can test out an effect, print it, and then undo it if you think it looks awful.
- **Revert:** Choose File ⇨ Revert to reload an image from disk. Most folks think of this as the last-resort function, the command you choose after everything else has failed. But really, it's quite useful as a stop-gap measure. Suppose that you're about to embark on a series of filtering operations that may or may not result in the desired effect. You're going to perform multiple operations, so you can't undo them if they don't work. Before choosing your first filter, choose File ⇨ Save. Now you're ready for anything. You can wreak a degree of havoc on your image no user in his or her right mind would dare. If everything doesn't go exactly as you planned or hoped, you can simply choose File ⇨ Revert and you're back in business.
- **The eraser tool:** Drag with the eraser tool to paint in white or some other background color. This procedure allows you to revert portions of your image back to bare canvas. The eraser is always hard-edged, like the pencil. You can't change the size of the eraser by selecting a different brush shape; it's always a 16 × 16-pixel square. The good news, however, is that the eraser is view-size independent. Therefore, you can magnify the image to erase small details or, more likely, reduce the view size to erase in gigantic sweeps. Double-click on the eraser icon in the toolbox to restore the entire image window to the background color, eliminating every vestige of line or image.
- **Erasing with the pencil:** If you double-click on the pencil icon in the toolbox and select the Auto Erase check box, the pencil draws in the background color any time you click or drag on a pixel colored in the foreground color. This feature can be very useful when you're drawing a line against a plain background. Set the foreground color to the color of the line; set the background color to the color of the background. Then use the pencil tool to draw and erase the line until you get it just right. Because you can change the size and shape of the pencil, many users prefer its erasing capabilities to those of the eraser tool.
- **Painting in the background color:** If you want to erase an image gradually using a soft-edged brush, click on the switch colors icon in the toolbox to swap the foreground and background colors. Then paint with the paintbrush or airbrush tool.

Reverting to the last saved image

The traditional reversion functions just described are all very well and good. But they don't hold a candle to Photoshop's *selective reversion* functions, which allow you to restore specific portions of an image to the way they looked when you last saved the image to disk.

The most convenient selective reversion function is the magic eraser tool. To access the magic eraser, press the Option key while using the standard eraser tool. A bunch of concentric squares appear inside the eraser cursor, as if Photoshop were trying to hypnotize you or something. Option-drag with the magic eraser to paint with the last saved image or, if you prefer to think of it in a different way, to scrape away paint laid down since the last time you saved the image to disk. The process is demonstrated in Figure 10-21.

Figure 10-21: After making a dreadful mistake (top), I Option-dragged with the eraser tool to restore the image to the way it looked when I last saved it (bottom).

Before Photoshop can begin to selectively revert an image, it must load the last saved version of the image into memory. This operation takes a little time — the same amount of time, in fact, that it took Photoshop to open the image in the first place. You probably won't want to hold the mouse button down for the entire time. Therefore, if this is the first time you've selectively reverted inside the current image, Option-click with the eraser tool and then wait for Photoshop to load the image. Your click won't effect the image in the slightest. After the load operation is completed, Option-drag with the eraser as described earlier.

Reverting with the rubber stamp tool

The rubber stamp tool offers a few advantages over the magic eraser. First, you can avail yourself of the Brushes palette when using the rubber stamp. This convenience means that you not only can change the brush shape, but also vary the translucency and brush modes. By reverting with a soft brush shape, you can soften the transition between reverted and acceptable portions of an image. By adjusting the Opacity slider bar, you can see through your changes to the way the image looks on disk. By choosing a different brush mode from the Brushes palette pop-up menu, you can mix changes and saved image to achieve interesting and sometimes surprising effects.

In addition, you don't have to press the Option key when reverting with the rubber stamp tool. Instead, you double-click on the rubber stamp icon in the toolbox and select the From Saved option in Photoshop 2.5 or the Revert option in Photoshop 2.0.

Reverting from a snapshot

Photoshop 2.5's rubber stamp tool offers yet another benefit, which is that it allows you to revert either from the last image saved to disk or the last image stored in memory as a *snapshot.*

To store the current version of an image in memory, choose Edit ➪ Take Snapshot. The operation takes no time to complete because the image is already in memory. By choosing the Take Snapshot command, you merely instruct Photoshop not to get rid of this image.

To selectively revert to the snapshot, double-click on the rubber stamp icon in the toolbox and select the From Snapshot option. Then drag in the image window. You don't have to wait for the image to load into memory as you do when reverting to a saved version, because it's already there. The function works instantaneously.

Photoshop can remember only one snapshot at a time. Therefore, when you choose the Take Snapshot command, you not only capture the current image, you abandon any snapshot previously stored in memory. You cannot undo the Take Snapshot command, so be careful how you use it.

Reverting selected areas

In Photoshop 2.5.1, you can revert selected areas of an image. After selecting the portion of the image you want to revert, choose Edit >> Fill to display the Fill dialog box. Select the Saved or Snapshot option from the Use pop-up menu, as shown in Figure 10-22; then press the Return key. The selected area reverts to the saved image or snapshot, according to your choice.

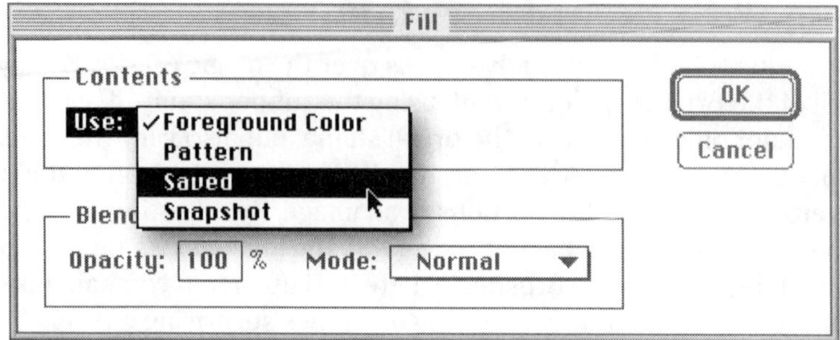

Figure 10-22: The Fill dialog box in Photoshop 2.5.1 lets you revert a selected area of your image.

Because you're actually filling the selected area with the saved image or snapshot, all the operations I mentioned in Chapter 9 are equally applicable to reversions. You can revert a feathered or antialiased selection; you can revert an area selected with the pen tool; you can even revert a floating selection and apply overlay modes (as described in Chapter 15). This capability has certainly been late in coming, but Photoshop's implementation is first rate.

Reversion limitations

Photoshop doesn't allow you to selectively revert from disk if you have in any way changed the number of pixels in the image since it was last saved. The process won't work if you have chosen Image ➪ Image Size or Image ➪ Canvas Size or if you have used the crop tool or Edit ➪ Crop command.

Photoshop also can't revert an image if you haven't yet saved it or if it can't read the document from disk (as when the image is saved in a format that requires conversion or can only be opened by means of a plug-in module).

You can, however, work around the image size problem by taking the following steps.

STEPS: Selectively Reverting a Resized Image

Step 1. Select the entire image and copy it to the Clipboard.

Step 2. Option-click on the preview box in the lower left corner of the window to view the size of the document in pixels. Write this information down or assign it to memory (the memory in your head, that is).

Step 3. Choose File ➪ Revert to load the last-saved version of the image into the image window.

Step 4. Choose Image ➪ Canvas Size to resize the image to the dimensions you noted when Option-clicking the preview box in Step 2.

Step 5. After completing the resize operation, save the image to disk.

Step 6. Paste the copied changes back into the image window and use the rubber stamp or magic eraser to selectively revert the image.

That's all there is to it. In fact, it's so simple that Photoshop should be able to revert from a resized image without your help. Hopefully, a future version will remedy this problem.

Summary

- The rubber stamp tool acts like four tools in one. It can clone images, paint in repeating patterns, revert portions of an image to their previous appearance, and apply goofy special effects.
- No matter how you use the tool, the rubber stamp reacts to the settings in the Brushes palette.
- To use the rubber stamp as a cloning tool, Option-click on the point in the image at which you want to begin cloning. Then drag to paint with the clone.
- The Clone (Aligned) and Pattern (Aligned) options ensure that images laid down with the rubber stamp tool match up with each other regardless of how many times you press and release the mouse button.
- If you are used to the way the rubber stamp clones in Photoshop 2.0, you will notice a significant difference in the tool in Version 2.5. In Photoshop 2.0, the tool always refers back to the image as it existed before you started cloning. In Photoshop 2.5, the tool refers back to the most recent version of the image. So any changes you make to the image with the tool affect how the tool clones from that point on.
- Press the Caps Lock key to replace the bulky rubber stamp cursor with a more serviceable crosshair.
- The rubber stamp is an ideal tool for touching up dust and hair scanned with an image and for eliminating distracting or non-essential elements.
- You can create repeating patterns by loading a displacement map, applying filters to an empty portion of an image (starting with Filter ⇨ Noise ⇨ Add Noise), marqueeing and cloning portions of a scan, or purchasing texture collections on CD-ROM.
- You can selectively revert portions of an image to the way they appeared when you last saved the image to disk by Option-dragging with the eraser tool or using the rubber stamp tool.

Special Effects

PART IV

Chapter 11:
Text Effects

Chapter 12:
Filtering Techniques

Chapter 13:
Constructing Homemade Effects

Special effects comprise a tremendous variety of automated functions that can change an image slightly or completely alter it beyond recognition. Photoshop's type tool, for example, provides one of the great means for applying special effects to an image. Each character is a predefined graphic that you can edit using any of the techniques described in previous and future chapters. If you're thinking that type effects probably aren't Photoshop's forte — after all, type created in a painting program is pretty jagged, right? — a quick browse through Chapter 11 should prove more than enough to change your mind.

All the special effect commands discussed in Chapter 12 and 13 reside under the Filters menu, but that doesn't mean they produce even vaguely similar effects. Chapter 12 starts off with a discussion of Photoshop's most subtle filters, those that affect the focus of an image. After you become familiar with commands like Unsharp Mask and Gaussian Blur, chances are you'll use one or the other at least once every time you edit an image in Photoshop.

In addition to showing you how to apply filters to images, Chapter 12 examines how filters work with selections. For example, you can dissipate the effect of a filter by applying it to a translucent floating selection. You also can use filters to edit selection outlines in the quick mask mode, which enables you to precisely select a complicated image with surprisingly little effort.

Chapter 13 shows you how to create your own special effects using the Custom and Displace filters, both of which provide access to all kinds of effects that you simply can't accomplish using any other Photoshop function. If you're like most Photoshop users, you've never so much as touched these filters. After reading Chapter 13, you'll wonder how you got by without them.

Text Effects

CHAPTER 11

In This Chapter

- Understanding the advantages and disadvantages of using bitmapped type
- Entering and editing type inside the Type Tool dialog box
- Specifying and measuring type size, leading, and spacing
- Kerning the space between two specific characters of type
- Selecting a portion of an image using character outlines
- Creating raised type and drop shadows
- Creating logos and other custom letterforms by using path tools to edit character outlines

Type Basics

What I'm about to say is going to shake you to the very core. I'm warning you — this is a biggie. You may want to sit down before you read any further. In fact, after you sit down, you might want to strap yourself in. Maybe go ahead and soundproof the room so no one's alarmed when you scream, "Oh, no, it can't be true!" and "Say it ain't so!"

(Ahem.) Type and graphics are the same thing.

There, there now. I understand. I reacted the same way when I heard the news. Dry your eyes while I explain. You see, your computer treats each character in a word as a little picture. The letter *O*, for example, is a big black oval with a smaller transparent oval set inside it. The only difference between a character of type and a standard graphic is that you don't have to draw type; every letter is already drawn for you. A font, therefore, is like a library of clip art you can access from the keyboard.

Qualities of bitmapped type

Now that you understand the realities of type, it should come as no surprise to learn that Photoshop treats type just like any other collection of pixels in an image. Type legibility is dependent upon the size and resolution of your image.

Figure 11-1, for example, shows four lines of type printed at equal sizes but at different resolutions. If these lines were printed at equal resolutions, each line would be twice as large as the line that precedes it. Hence, big type printed at a high resolution yields smooth, legible output, just as a big image printed at a high resolution yields smooth, detailed output. In fact, everything that you can say about an image is true of bitmapped type.

Figure 11-1: Four lines of type set in the TrueType font, Geneva, and printed at different resolutions.

Type = Graphics

Type = Graphics

Type = Graphics

Type = Graphics

You can create smooth, legible type in Photoshop only if you use TrueType fonts in combination with System 7 or if you use PostScript fonts with ATM (Adobe Type Manager) installed. To use a PostScript font, both the screen and printer version of the font must be installed on your machine. For a detailed introduction to the world of type on the Macintosh computer, see the "Using Fonts" section of Chapter 2.

The disadvantages of working with type in a painting program are obvious. First, the resolution of the type is fixed. Rather than matching the resolution of printed text to that of your printer — a function provided by drawing, word processing, and desktop publishing programs, just to name a few — Photoshop prints type at the same resolution it prints the rest of the image.

In addition, after you enter a line of type, you can't go back and add and delete characters from the keyboard as you can in an object-oriented program. If you misspell a word or just want to rephrase some text, you must erase the offending characters or words and start over again. In terms of entering type, Photoshop is more likely to remind you of a typewriter and a bottle of correction fluid than a typical computer program.

But although the disadvantages of creating type in a painting program may initially hamper your progress, the advantages are tremendous. You can do all of the following:

- **Create translucent type:** Photoshop enables you to change the translucency of type using the Opacity slider bar in the Brushes palette. (In Photoshop 2.0, you choose Edit ⇨ Paste Controls and enter a value into the Opacity option box.) By using this technique, you can merge type and images to create subtle overlay effects, as illustrated in the top example in Figure 11-2.
- **Use type as a selection:** As I mentioned in Chapter 9, text is just another variety of selection outline. You can mask portions of an image and even select elements and move, copy, or otherwise manipulate them using character outlines, as demonstrated in the middle example in Figure 11-2. I explore this option in detail in the upcoming "Character Masks" section.
- **Customize characters:** You also can customize a character of type by converting it to a path, editing the path using the tools in the Paths palette, and converting it back to a selection outline. Only high-end drawing programs such as Illustrator, Canvas, and FreeHand match this capability.
- **Edit type as part of the image:** You can erase type, paint over type, smear type, fill type with a gradation, draw highlights and shadows, and create a range of special text effects that fall well outside the capabilities of an object-oriented program. The last example in Figure 11-2 is just one of the bazillion possibilities.
- **Trade images freely:** If you've ever traded documents over a network or otherwise tried to share a file created in a word processor or desktop publishing program with associates and co-workers, you know what a nightmare fonts can be. If their machines aren't equipped with the fonts you used in your document — which seems to be the case more often than not — your document looks awful on their screens. "What's wrong with this file you gave me?" "Why did you use *this* font?" And "I liked what you wrote in your report, but it is sure ugly!" are only a few of the responses you can expect.

  When you work with images, however, your font worries are over, because type in an image is bitmapped. Other users don't need special screen or printer fonts to view your images exactly as you created them. Mind you, I don't recommend that you use Photoshop as a word processor, but it's great for creating headlines and short missives you want to fling about the office.

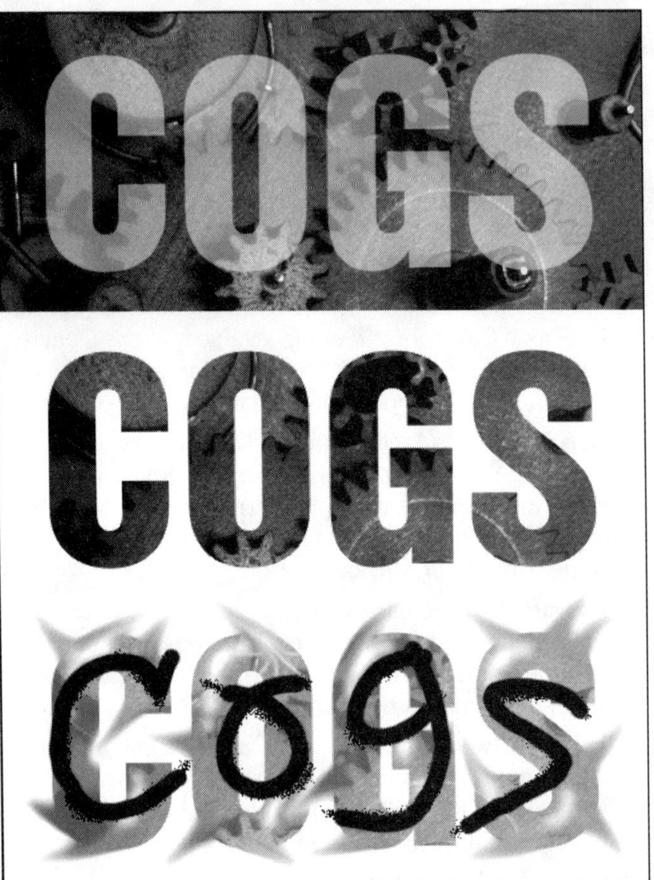

Figure 11-2: Examples of translucent type (top), type used as a selection (middle), and type enhanced with painting and editing tools (bottom). Taken as a whole, these effects are beyond the means of drawing and desktop publishing packages.

The type tool

In a drawing or desktop publishing program, the type tool typically serves two purposes. You can create text with the tool or you can edit the characters of existing text by highlighting them and either replacing characters or applying formatting commands. However, because Photoshop doesn't allow you to reword or reformat text after you add it to an image, its type tool serves one purpose only: to create type.

To carry out this function, click with the type tool in the image window. Instead of producing a blinking insertion marker in the window, as other graphics programs do, Photoshop displays the Type Tool dialog box shown in Figure 11-3. (In Photoshop 2.0, the title of the dialog box is simply *Type,* but the options are identical.)

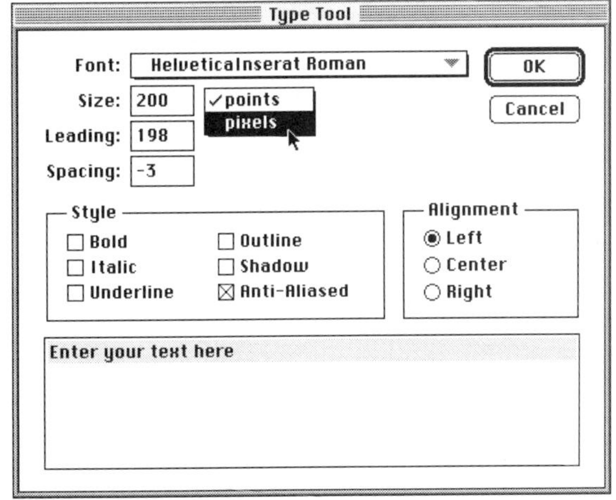

Figure 11-3: To create type in Photoshop, enter it into the Type Tool dialog box, which appears after you click in the image window with the type tool.

Entering and editing type

At the bottom of the Type Tool dialog box is the *text-entry box.* You enter and edit the text you want to add to the current image into this box.

You can edit text up to the moment you add it to the image. To make your edits, first select the characters you want to change by dragging over them with the cursor. Then enter new text from the keyboard. To select a whole word, double-click on it. You can also cut, copy, and paste text by choosing commands from the Edit menu or using keyboard equivalents.

If the text you are typing reaches the right edge of the text-entry box, the word in progress automatically drops down to the next line. However, when you click on the OK button or press Enter to exit the dialog box, all text appears on the same line unless you specifically entered carriage returns between lines (by pressing Return). Each carriage return indicates the end of one line and the beginning of the next, just as it does when you use a typewriter.

Get in the habit of pressing Enter rather than Return to exit the Type Tool dialog box, because pressing Return inserts a carriage return when the text-entry box is active. However, you can press Return to exit the dialog box when the Size, Leading, or Spacing option box is active.

If your text doesn't look the way you anticipated after you exit the Type Tool dialog box, choose Edit ⇨ Undo (Command-Z) or simply press Delete. Then start the process over again by clicking with the type tool. When the Type Tool dialog box appears, your previous text is displayed in the text-entry box.

Formatting type

Photoshop formats *all* text entered into the text-entry box identically according to the specifications in the Type Tool dialog box. You can't select a single character or word in the text-entry box and format it differently than its deselected neighbors.

The formatting options in the Type Tool dialog box work as follows:

- **Font:** Select the typeface and type style you want to use from the Font pop-up menu. Alternatively, you can just select the plain version of the font, such as Times Roman or Helvetica Regular, and apply styles using the Style options.
- **Size:** Type size is measured either in points (one point equals 1⁄72 inch) or pixels. You can select the desired measurement from the pop-up menu to the right of the Size option box, as shown in Figure 11-3. If the resolution of your image is 72 ppi, points and pixels are equal. However, if the resolution is higher, a single point may include many pixels. Select the points option when you want to scale text independently of image resolution; select pixels when you want to map text to an exact number of pixels in an image.

Type is measured from the top of its *ascenders* — letters like *b, d,* and *h* that rise above the level of most lowercase characters — to the bottom of its *descenders* — letters like *g, p,* and *q* that sink below the baseline. That's the way it's supposed to work, anyway. Characters from fonts in the Adobe Type Library, including those built into all PostScript laser printers and image setters, measure only 92 percent as tall as the specified type size.

The top two lines in Figure 11-4 contain 120-pixel type set in the Adobe versions of Times and Helvetica. All characters easily fit inside rectangular outlines that measure exactly 120 pixels tall. By contrast, the third and fourth lines of type are set in the TrueType fonts New York and Geneva. These characters are bursting their 120-point rectangular outlines at the seams.

- **Leading:** Also called line spacing, *leading* is the vertical distance between the baseline of one line of type and the baseline of the next line of type within a single paragraph, as illustrated in Figure 11-5. (You must separate lines of type manually by pressing the Return key in the text-entry box.) Leading is measured in the unit you selected from the Size pop-up menu. If you don't specify a leading value, Photoshop automatically inserts leading equal to 125 percent of the type size.

  Spacing: Each character in a font carries with it a predetermined amount of *side bearing* that separates it from its immediate neighbors. Although you can't change the amount of side bearing, you can insert and delete the overall amount of space between characters by entering a value into the Spacing option box. Enter a positive value to insert space; enter a negative value to delete space. The value is measured in the unit you selected from the Size pop-up menu.

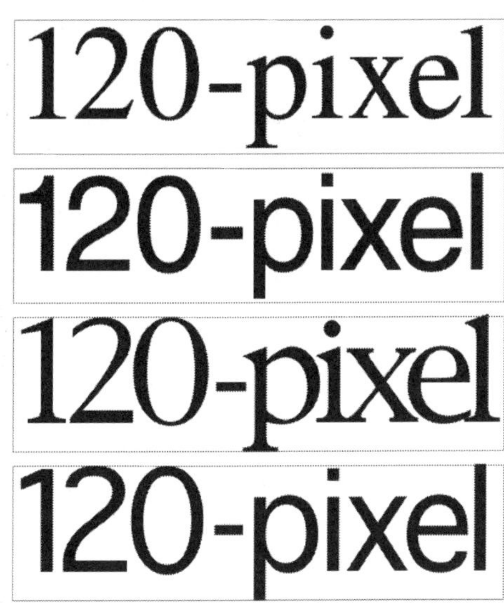

Figure 11-4: From top to bottom, I formatted these lines of type in the PostScript versions of Times and Helvetica from the Adobe Type Library and the TrueType versions of New York and Geneva that ship with System 7. The Adobe characters fit inside their 120-point rectangular outlines with room to spare, while the TrueType characters slightly overlap their outlines.

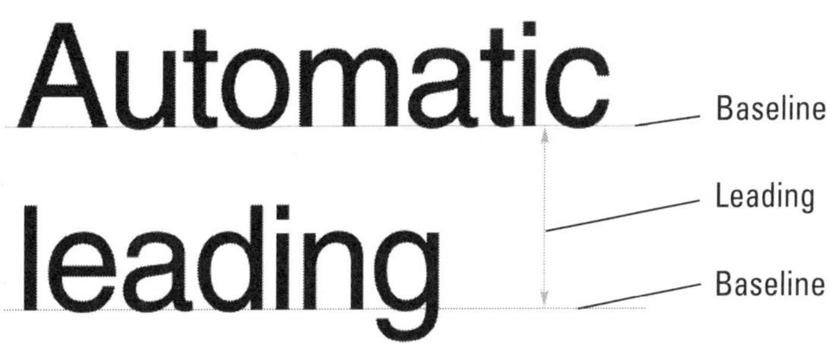

Figure 11-5: Leading is the distance between any two baselines in a single paragraph of text created with the typetool. By default, Photoshop inserts leading equal to 125 percent of the type size. Here, the type size is 120 pixels and the leading is 150 pixels.

- **Style:** Select one or more Style check boxes to specify the type styles you want to apply to your text. If you choose the plain version of a font, the Bold and Italic options call up the bold and italic PostScript or TrueType font definitions. If you apply the Bold option to a font that is already bold, such as Helvetica Bold or Helvetica Black (both shown in Figure 11-6), Photoshop makes the characters slightly heavier. If you apply the Italic option to a font that is already italicized, such as Helvetica Oblique (again, see Figure 11-6), Photoshop slants the characters even more.

Figure 11-6: Photoshop's Bold and Italic style options affect fonts that are already bold or italic. Bolding the regular style produces the same result as choosing the bold version of the font from the Font pop-up menu (second and third examples respectively), just as italicizing the regular style is the same as choosing the italic version of the font (seventh and eighth examples). However, you can achieve unique results by applying styles to already stylized fonts (fourth, sixth, and ninth examples).

Helvetica Regular
Helvetica Regular Bold
Helvetica Bold
Helvetica Bold Bold
Helvetica Black
Helvetica Black Bold
Helvetica Regular Italic
Helvetica Oblique
Helvetica Oblique Italic

The Outline option produces unspeakably ugly results, as demonstrated by the top two examples in Figure 11-7. You can create a better outline style using the Stroke command. First, create your text using the Type Tool dialog box as usual. (Don't you dare select the Outline option.) Press Enter to exit the dialog box. With the foreground color set to black, choose Image ⇨ Map ⇨ Invert (Command-I) to change the selected text to white. Finally, choose Edit ⇨ Stroke and enter the outline thickness of your choice. Figure 11-7 shows two stroked examples, one with a 1-pixel outline and the other with a 2-pixel outline.

The Shadow option produces equally unattractive results. To create attractive shadowed type, try out one of the techniques discussed in the "Character Masks" section of this chapter.

- **Anti-aliased:** This Style option is special enough to mention separately. When you select Anti-aliased, Photoshop softens characters by slightly blurring pixels around the perimeter, as shown in Figure 11-8. Unless you want to create very small type or intend to match the resolution of your output device — printing a 300 ppi image to a 300 dpi printer, for example — select this check box. Photoshop takes longer to produce antialiased type, but it's worth it. Unless otherwise indicated, I created all figures in this chapter with the Anti-aliased check box selected.
- **Alignment:** Select one of these radio buttons to specify the way lines of type in a single paragraph align to the point at which you originally clicked with the type tool. Examples appear in Figure 11-9.

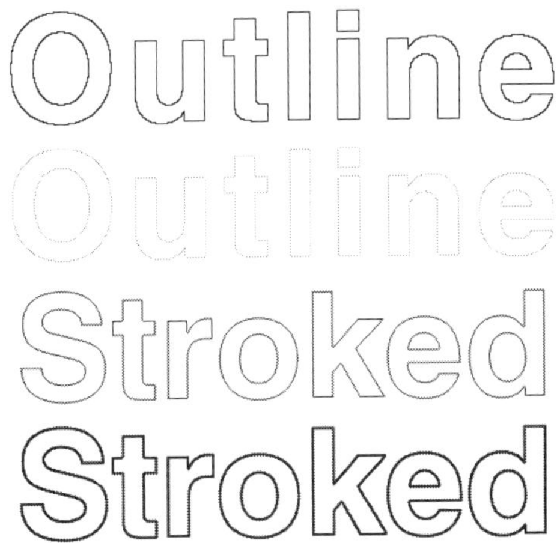

Figure 11-7: Photoshop's automated outline style, shown here when jagged (top) and antialiased (second line), is nothing short of hideous. You can get better results by stroking the characters with 1-pixel or 2-pixel outlines (third and bottom lines respectively).

Figure 11-8: The difference between 120-pixel type when the Anti-aliased option is selected (top line) versus deselected (bottom).

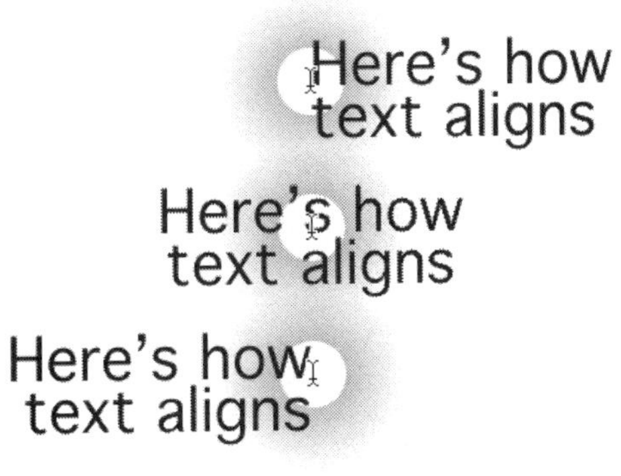

Figure 11-9: A single paragraph of type shown as it appears if you select Left Alignment (top), Center Alignment (middle), or Right Alignment (bottom). The I-beam cursor shows the point at which I clicked to display the Type Tool dialog box.

Manipulating type in the image window

After you confirm the contents of the Type Dialog box by clicking on the OK button or pressing Enter, the type appears selected in the image window. You can move it, clone it, copy it to the Clipboard, transform it by applying commands from the Image ⇨ Flip, Image ⇨ Rotate, or Image ⇨ Effects submenus, or perform any other operation that's applicable to a floating selection.

If you want to hide the marching ants that surround selected characters, choose Select ⇨ Hide Edges (Command-H). To make the selected text transparent, adjust the Opacity slider bar in the Brushes palette while the type tool or one of the four selection tools is active. You also can select a brush mode from the pop-up menu on the left side of the Brushes palette.

Pressing the Option key when the type tool is selected brings up the eyedropper cursor. Therefore, to clone selected text, you either have to switch to one of the selection tools (rectangular marquee, elliptical marquee, lasso, or magic wand) and Option-drag the text or press Option with an arrow key.

In addition, you can move characters of text independently of each other by Command-dragging with the type tool. When you press and hold the Command key, the standard I-beam cursor changes to a lasso cursor. Command-drag around the portions of the floating selection that you want to deselect and set in place. The rest of the text remains selected and floating.

This technique is ideal for *kerning* — that is, adjusting the amount of space between two neighboring characters. Suppose that you want to adjust the distance between the *P* and *a* in the last line of the novel-turned-top-40-song title shown in Figure 11-10. First, you position the paragraph in your image. You then Command-drag around the portion of the paragraph that you want to set down, as shown in the top example in the figure. To kern the text that remains floating, you Shift-drag it into place, as shown in the bottom half of the figure. Or, you can just as easily nudge the selected text with the left and right arrow keys.

Want an even better method of kerning? Create your text directly in the quick mask mode. This way, you can adjust the location of individual characters without deselecting any of them. Just switch to the quick mask mode, create your text, and then select individual characters and adjust their positioning as desired. When you finish, choose Image ⇨ Map ⇨ Invert (Command-I) to make the text white so that it will serve as the selection. Then switch back to the marching ants mode. Your text is both kerned and 100 percent selected.

A Tree Grows
in MacArthur
Park in the Rain

A Tree Grows
in MacArthur
Park in the Rain

Figure 11-10: After Command-dragging with the type tool around the text that I wanted to set down (top), I Shift-dragged the text that remained selected to close the gap between the *P* and *a* in *Park* (bottom).

You also can Command-drag around a portion of a floating selection with the rectangular marquee, elliptical marquee, or lasso tool. However, if you do so, you don't just deselect the portion of the selection around which you drag, you delete it. Try it out and you'll see what I mean. Click with the type tool, enter the word *Park,* and then press Enter. While the text remains floating, select the lasso tool and Command-drag around the *P.* The *P* disappears, leaving you stranded with an *ark.* After choosing Edit ⇨ Undo (Command-Z) to reinstate the *P,* select the type tool and Command-drag around the *P.* This time you deselect the *P* and make it part of your image, enabling you to nudge the *ark* into a better location.

You can Command-drag with the type tool to set down portions of any floating selection, not just text. You can also Command-Option-drag to draw a polygon around an area, as demonstrated in the first example of Figure 11-10, or Command-Shift-drag to intersect the portion of the floating selection that you want to remain selected and set down the portion outside your drag.

Character Masks

Recapping today's news: Type outlines are selections. Except for the fact that they arrive on the scene already filled with the foreground color, they act like any other selection outline. With that in mind, you can create an inexhaustible supply of special type effects.

The following sections demonstrate a few examples. Armed with these ideas, you should be able to invent enough additional type effects to keep you busy into the next millennia. Honestly, you won't believe the number of effects you can invent by screwing around with type outlines.

Filling type with an image

One of the most impressive and straightforward applications for text in Photoshop is to use the character outlines to mask a portion of an image. In fact, the only trick is getting rid of the foreground fill. You can accomplish this in a matter of a few straightforward steps.

STEPS: Selecting Part of an Image Using Character Outlines

Step 1. Begin by opening the image you want to mask. Then create your text by clicking with the type tool, entering the text you want to use as a mask, formatting it as desired, and pressing Enter to display the type in the image window. Large, bold characters work best. In Figure 11-11, I used the PostScript font Eras Ultra — an extremely bold type style — with a Size value of 260 and a Spacing value of negative 10.

Step 2. Choose Edit ➪ Cut (Command-X) to delete the text from the image and transfer it to the Clipboard.

Step 3. Choose Select ➪ All (Command-A) to marquee the entire image. Then choose Edit ➪ Paste Behind to paste the text in back of the image. The result is that you can see the character outlines without seeing the foreground fill, as demonstrated in Figure 11-12.

Step 4. Using the type tool, drag the character outlines into position. Because the selection is in back of the image, you move only the outlines without affecting the image itself. When you get the outlines where you want them, choose Select ➪ Defloat (Command-J) to set the selection down so it is no longer floating behind the image.

Photoshop 2.0 doesn't offer a Defloat command. To set down the selection in this program, select the rectangular marquee tool; then press Shift and draw a tiny marquee fully inside one of the character outlines. This procedure adds the marqueed portion of the image to the selection without changing the shape of the character outlines, which has the added effect of affixing the outlines to the image. (I know it sounds a little weird, but it works.)

Step 5. Selection and image are no longer separate entities. You now can clone the selected portion of the image and drag it to a new location, as demonstrated in Figure 11-13, or copy it to a new image.

Figure 11-11: When using type to mask an image, bold and blocky characters produce the best results because they enable you to see large chunks of unobstructed image.

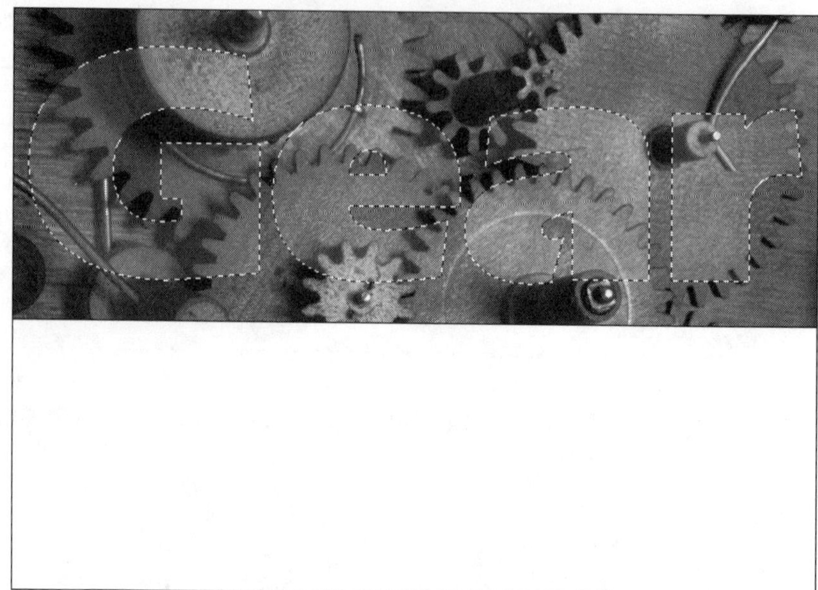

Figure 11-12: By pasting the text behind the image, you can use the selection outlines without worrying about the foreground fill of the characters.

Figure 11-13: The result of Option-dragging the selected image to an empty part of the image window by using one of the selection tools.

Painting raised type

Instead of moving the selected image or copying it to a different window, as suggested in Step 5 of the preceding section, you can paint around the character outlines to create a raised text effect, as illustrated in Figure 11-14.

To create this image, I carried out the first four steps described in the preceding section. I then prepared the characters by dragging inside them with the dodge tool. I used a 65-pixel soft brush shape and selected Shadows from the brush mode pop-up menu (on the left side of the Brushes palette) to concentrate the lightening effect on the very dark areas in the image.

As shown in the top image in Figure 11-15, this operation helps set the letters apart from the rest of the image. To give the letters depth, I set the foreground color to black and used the airbrush tool with a 35-pixel soft brush shape to apply shadows around the lower and right portions of each character, as shown in the middle row of Figure 11-15.

I next switched the foreground color to white and applied highlights around the upper and left portions of characters, which results in the image shown in the bottom row of Figure 11-15.

Figure 11-14: Raised type created by painting with the dodge and airbrush tools around the perimeter of the character outlines.

If you don't consider yourself an artist, you may find the prospect of painting around the edges of characters a little intimidating. But bear in mind that it's next to impossible to make a mistake. Because you're painting inside the selection, there's no danger of harming any portion of the image outside the character outlines. And if you mess up inside the selection, the problem is easily resolved.

If you look closely at the last image in Figure 11-15, for example, you can see that in applying white to the arch of the *a,* I accidentally got some on the right corner of the *e.* Hey, nobody's perfect. To fix the problem, all I need to do is select a smaller brush shape and paint over that area of the *e* with black.

So if you make a mistake, choose Edit ⇨ Undo or just keep painting. Give it a try. The process takes less than an hour and I bet you'll be pleasantly surprised with your results.

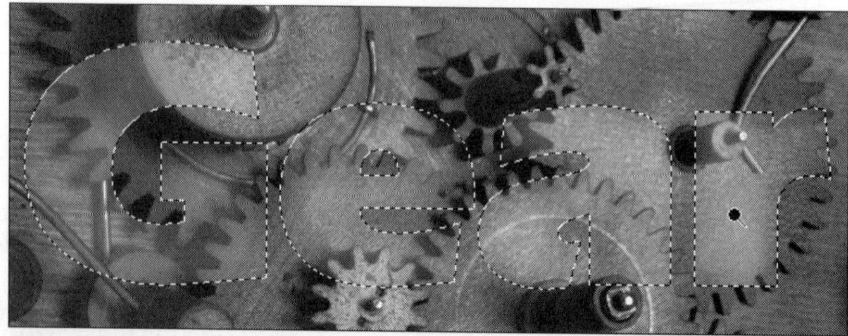

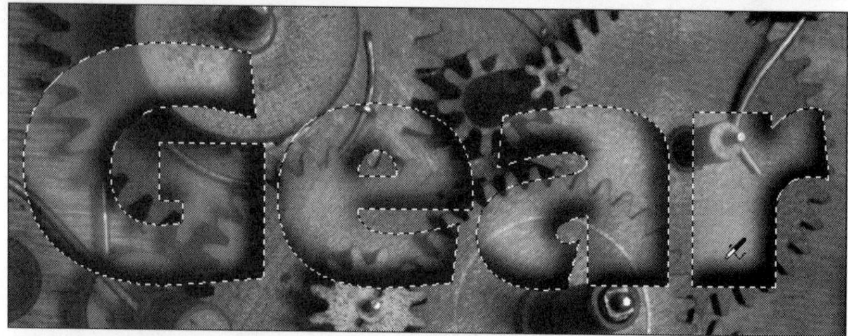

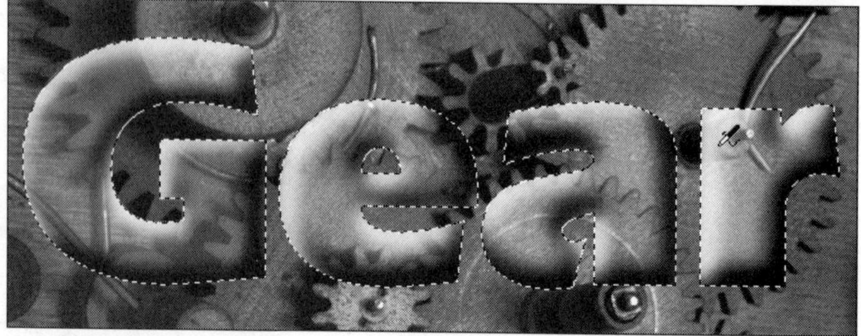

Figure 11-15: After using the dodge tool to lighten the darkest pixels inside the letters (top), I painted in the shadows by airbrushing in black around the right and bottom edges of the letters (middle). Finally, I painted in the highlights by airbrushing in white around the left and top edges of the letters (bottom).

Feathering effects

You can feather text outlines just as you can feather other kinds of selections. However, in doing so, you modify the shape of the selection and therefore set the characters down in the image area.

If you want to combine feathered text with an image, take care to paste the text behind the image as explained earlier, in Steps 2 and 3 in the section "STEPS: Selecting Part of an Image Using Character Outlines." (You don't have to perform Step 4, choosing Select ⇨ Defloat, because feathering automatically defloats the selection.) Otherwise, you leave behind deselected remnants of the foreground color that used to fill the characters.

The top example in Figure 11-16 shows the result of creating a line of type, feathering it with an 8-pixel radius, and deleting the feathered selection. You can plainly see that Photoshop leaves behind a harsh black outline after the deletion. If, on the other hand, you create the type, cut it to the Clipboard, select the image, paste the type in back of the image, and *then* feather it and delete it, you eliminate any chance that some of the type will be left behind, as demonstrated in the bottom example in Figure 11-16.

Figure 11-16: The results of feathering and deleting text positioned in front of an image (top) and in back of an image (bottom).

The following steps describe how to create a backlighting effect using Photoshop's feathering capability. Figure 11-17 shows the finished image. To simplify the process, the text appears in front of a plain black background. But you can just as easily apply this technique to an image as long as you take care to paste the text behind the image before choosing Select ⇨ Feather.

STEPS: Using Feathering to Backlight Text

Step 1. Create a new image window large enough to accommodate a single line of large text. I created an image 800 pixels wide by 300 pixels tall.

Step 2. Choose Select ⇨ All (Command-A) and press Option-Delete to fill the entire image with black. (I'm assuming here that black is the foreground color and white is the background color. If this is not the case, click on the default colors icon in the toolbox.)

Step 3. Create your text using the type tool and the Type Tool dialog box. The text in the figure is set in 240-pixel Helvetica Inserat, a member of the Adobe Type Library.

Step 4. Copy the text to the Clipboard (Command-C).

Step 5. Choose Select ⇨ Feather, enter a value somewhere between 6 and 8 into the Radius option box, and press Return.

Step 6. Press the Delete key to fill the feathered selection with white.

Step 7. Choose Edit ⇨ Paste (Command-V) to reintroduce the copied line of text to the image. Use the down arrow key to nudge the selection 3 to 5 pixels. The result is shown in the top half of Figure 11-17.

Step 8. For extra credit, set the foreground color to 50 percent black and then use the airbrush tool with the 100-pixel soft brush shape to paint a single line across the text. This step creates the effect of light seeping through a slightly open door, as shown in the bottom half of the figure.

Figure 11-17: You can create backlit text — also known as the movie-of-the-week effect — by deleting a feathered version of a line of type and then pasting the original, unfeathered type in front (top). A slash of the airbrush takes away some of the flatness of the image (bottom).

Creating drop shadows

I don't know of an artist who hasn't at some time or another made fun of drop shadows. By the same token, I know of no artist who hasn't employed a drop shadow or two at some weak moment. Let's face it — overused or not, the drop shadow is extremely functional. It helps to separate an element from its background by making it appear to hover above the surface. Quite frankly, there's no quicker or more reliable way to add depth to a flat image.

This section examines two methods for adding drop shadows: one that involves changing the translucency of type (demonstrated in Figure 11-18); and another that relies on feathering (Figure 11-19). The following sets of steps describe the techniques in detail.

STEPS: Creating Quick and Easy Hard-Edged Drop Shadows

Step 1. Create your text. In Figure 11-18, I used an unusual typeface called Remedy Single from Emigre Graphics. It's about the wildest font I've ever come across, so it lends itself well to this technique, which is by contrast quite simple.

Step 2. Select any selection tool and clone the selected type by Option-dragging it a few pixels down and to the right.

Step 3. Press 4 on the keyboard to lower the opacity of the cloned selection to 40 percent. The translucent clone serves as the drop shadow.

The benefit of this technique is that is takes about six seconds to complete. The downside is that it only works with text that is set in a solid color. You can't paint inside the text or fill it with an image because the drop shadow actually lies in front of the text.

The next steps describe a more functional, albeit slightly more complicated, drop shadow technique. The effect is illustrated in Figure 11-19.

Figure 11-18: I took two lines of type set in the font Remedy (yes, those lower characters are part of the font), cloned the paragraph, and changed the opacity of the clone to 40 percent.

STEPS: Creating a Feathered Drop Shadow

Step 1. For purposes of these steps, click on the default colors icon in the toolbox to change the foreground color to black and the background color to white.

Step 2. Create your type. Figure 11-19 features that old standby, 240-pixel Helvetica Inserat.

Step 3. Choose Image ➪ Map ➪ Invert (Command-I) to change the selected text to white. Then copy it to the Clipboard (Command-C).

Step 4. Choose Select ➪ Feather, enter 8 into the Radius option box, and press Return. The selection is now feathered.

Step 5. Press Option-Delete to fill the feathered text with black, as shown in the first example of Figure 11-19. This black text will serve as the drop shadow.

Step 6. Paste the white text in front of the drop shadow (Command-V) and nudge it slightly off center from the shadow, as demonstrated in the second row of Figure 11-19.

Step 7. From here on, what you do with the text is up to you. You can fill the selected type with a different color or gradation. I chose to paint inside my characters with the rubber stamp and airbrush tools. Previously, I had defined a pattern from a small selection in the familiar ColorBytes gears image (Figures 11-11 through 11-16). After double-clicking on the rubber stamp icon in the toolbox and selecting the Pattern (Aligned) option, I painted inside my text with a 65-pixel brush shape, taking care to leave some white spaces showing. I then dragged with the airbrush tool and a 35-pixel brush shape to create the bottom image shown in Figure 11-19.

Figure 11-19: Feather the text and fill it with black to create the drop shadow (top). Then paste the copied version of the text in front of the drop shadow (middle) and paint inside the characters as desired (bottom).

Converting characters to paths

Photoshop 2.5 allows you to create your own letterforms by editing selection outlines, using the tools in the Paths palette. After creating the text you want to edit, choose the Make Path command from the Paths palette menu, edit the selection outlines as desired, and choose the Make Selection command. This technique is perfectly suited to designing logos and other elements that call for custom characters. The following steps explain the technique in greater detail and describe how I created the type shown in Figure 11-22. (Figures 11-20 and 11-21 illustrate steps in the process.)

STEPS: Editing a Character Outline Using the Path Tools

Step 1. Begin by creating your text, as always. When inside the Type Tool dialog box, select a font that best matches the eventual letterforms you want to create. I selected Avant Garde Gothic because of its perfectly circular letterforms, which go well with the circular shapes in the ColorBytes gears image (see Figure 11-20).

Step 2. After creating your text, place it in back of your image so that you don't leave any deselected characters sitting around. Choose Edit ➪ Cut (Command-X) to send the text to the Clipboard. Then choose Select ➪ All (Command-A) followed by Edit ➪ Paste Behind.

Step 3. Applying one of Photoshop's transformation effects to alter the text is sometimes a good first step in creating custom letterforms. It enables you to prepare outlines for future edits by minimizing the number of point-by-point edits you have to perform later. In my case, I wanted to rotate my single character — a circular letter *e* — to a different angle. I chose Image ➪ Rotate ➪ Free and dragged the corner handles until the angle of the horizontal bar in the *e* matched the angle of the rod protruding from one of the gears, as demonstrated in Figure 11-20. Then I clicked inside the character with the gavel cursor to exit the transformation mode.

Figure 11-20: I rotated the angle of my character outline to match the angle of the rod coming out of the central gear.

Step 4. Choose the Make Path command from Paths palette menu and press Return to accept the default Tolerance setting. Photoshop converts the character outline to a Bézier path, as shown in the left example in Figure 11-21.

Step 5. Edit the Bézier path as desired using the tools in the Paths palette. I reduced the thickness of the circular perimeter of my *e* by dragging the inside edges of the paths outward with the arrow tool, as illustrated in the second example of Figure 11-21. I also simplified the structure of the paths by deleting some points with the remove point tool. Finally, I shortened the length of the *e*'s lip — that loose part that swings around to the right and makes the letter look like it's smiling.

Figure 11-21: After converting the letter to a path (left), I edited the outline by moving and deleting points (right).

Step 6. When you finish editing the character outlines, save them by choosing Save Path from the Paths palette menu. Then choose the Make Selection command and press Return to accept the default settings. The letters are again selection outlines.

Step 7. What you do from this point on is up to you. Want to know what I did? Sure you do. I copied the selection, created a new image window measuring about 500 × 500 pixels, and pasted the *e* into the window's center. I then clicked the switch colors icon in the toolbox to make white the foreground color and black the background color. I wanted to create a drop shadow for my character, so I pressed Option-delete to fill the selection with white and then chose Select ⇨ Feather and set the Radius value to 8. (Who can say why I'm so stuck on this value? I guess I'm in a rut.) To complete the drop shadow, I pressed the Delete key to fill the feathered selection with black. Next, I pasted the character again and nudged it a few pixels up and to the left to offset it in relation to shadow. Then, with the type tool still active, I selected the Dissolve option from the brush mode pop-up menu in the Brushes palette to rough up the edges of the floating character. The finished character appears in Figure 11-22.

Figure 11-22: I used the Dissolve option in the brush mode pop-up menu to randomize the pixels along the edges of the character.

Summary

- In Photoshop, the only way to fix typos and reword text after you create it is to choose Edit ➪ Undo and start over again.
- When entering text, you must press Return to specify the end of one line of type and the beginning of the next. Press Enter to confirm your text and exit the dialog box.
- To create outline type, choose Edit ➪ Stroke after creating your text; don't rely on Photoshop's automatic Outline style.
- To clone text, click on one of the selection tools in the toolbox and Option-drag the text to a new location in the image window.
- To deselect part of a floating selection without deleting it, Command-drag around that part of the selection with the type tool. This technique allows you to adjust the distance between characters — or *kern* them — by setting the characters down one at a time.
- To select part of an image by using character outlines, cut the outline to the Clipboard, select the image, paste the outlines behind the image by choosing Edit ➪ Paste Behind, and then set the outlines down by choosing Select ➪ Defloat.
- You can use the Feather command to create backlighting effects and drop shadows.
- If you want to edit a character outline, first convert it to a Bézier path. Then reshape the path using the tools from the Paths palette and convert the finished product back to a selection.

Filtering Techniques

CHAPTER 12

In This Chapter

- Comprehensive explanations of Photoshop's focus filters, including Unsharp Mask and Gaussian Blur
- How to establish a selection outline using the High Pass filter
- Creative uses for the Motion Blur, Wind, and Radial Blur filters
- A complete guide to the filters in the Noise submenu
- Everything you need to know about distortion filters
- A summary of third-party filter collections
- Information about DSP accelerations boards

Filter Basics

Photoshop offers two kinds of filters — those that enable you to open and save images in different file formats, as discussed back in Chapter 5, and those that provide access to special effects, which are the subject of this chapter.

At this point, a little bell should be ringing in your head, telling you to beware standardized special effects. Why? Because everyone has access to the same filters you do. If you rely on filters to edit your images for you, your audience will quickly recognize your work as poor or at least unremarkable art.

Think of it this way: You're watching MTV. You should be watching VH1 with the rest of the old folks, but when you were flipping through the channels you got stuck on Peter Gabriel's "Sledgehammer" video. Outrageous effects, right? He rides an imaginary roller coaster, bumper cars crash playfully into his face, fish leap over his head. You couldn't be more amused or impressed.

As the video fades, you're so busy basking in the glow that you neglect for a split second to whack the channel changer. Before you know it, you're midway through an advertisement for a monster truck rally. Like the video, the ad is riddled with special effects — spinning letters, a reverberating voice-over slowed down to an octave below the narrator's normal pitch, and lots of big machines.

In and of themselves, these special effects aren't bad. There was probably even a time when you thought spinning letters and reverberating voice-overs were hot stuff. But ever since you grew out of preadolescence, your taste has become, well, more refined. In truth, you're probably the same as you always were; you've simply grown tired of these particular effects. You've come to associate them with raunchy local car-oriented commercials. Certainly, these effects are devoid of substance, but more importantly, they're devoid of creativity.

This chapter, therefore, is about the creative application of special effects. Rather than trying to show an image subject to every single filter — a service already performed quite adequately by the manual included with your software — it explains exactly how the most important filters work and offers some concrete ways to use them.

You'll also learn how to apply several filters in tandem and how to use filters to edit images and selection outlines. My goal is not so much to teach you what filters are available — you can find that out by tugging on the Filters menu — but how and when to use filters.

A first look at filters

You access Photoshop's special-effects filters by choosing commands from the Filter menu. These commands fall into two camps: corrective and destructive.

Corrective filters comprise limited functions that you use to modify scanned images and prepare an image for printing or screen display. In most cases, the effects are subtle enough that a viewer won't even notice that you applied a corrective filter. As demonstrated in Figure 12-1 and Color Plate 12-1, these filters include those that change the focus of an image (Blur, Sharpen), enhance color transitions (High Pass), and randomize pixels (Add Noise).

Many corrective filters have direct opposites. Blur is the opposite of Sharpen, Despeckle is the opposite of Add Noise, and so on. This is not to say that one filter entirely removes the effect of the other; only reversion functions such as the Undo command provide that capability. Instead, two opposite filters produce contrasting effects.

Figure 12-1: Michelangelo's Moses from *Saint Peter in Chains* subject to four corrective filters, including (clockwise from upper left) Blur, Sharpen More, High Pass, and Add Noise. You have to love those old, uncopyrighted masterpieces, not to mention those explicit basilica names.

Destructive filters, found under the Filter ⇨ Distort and Filter ⇨ Stylize submenus, produce effects so dramatic that they can, if used improperly, completely overwhelm your artwork, making the filter more important than the image itself. A few examples of overwhelmed images appear in Figure 12-2 and Color Plate 12-2.

Destructive filters produce way-cool effects, and many people gravitate toward them when first experimenting with Photoshop. But the filters invariably destroy the original clarity and composition of the image. Yes, every Photoshop function is destructive to a certain extent, but destructive filters change your image so extensively that you can't easily disguise the changes later by applying other filters or editing techniques.

To get the best results from these filters, apply them to selected portions of an image rather than to the entire image. In addition, apply them partially, as described in the upcoming "Dissipating filtering effects" section. And make sure to save your image to disk before applying a destructive filter so you can revert to the saved image if your changes don't turn out the way you hoped.

Though I discuss both corrective and destructive filters throughout the course of this chapter, I spend most of my time — and yours, if you decide to read along with me — on corrective filters. They represent the functions you're most likely to use on a day-to-day basis.

Figure 12-2: The effects of applying four destructive filters (clockwise from upper left): Facet, Find Edges, Ripple, and Pointillize. These filters produce such dramatic effects that they are best used in moderation.

General filtering techniques

When you choose a command from the Filter menu, Photoshop applies the filter to the selected portion of the image. If no portion of the image is selected, Photoshop applies the filter to the entire image. Therefore, if you want to filter every nook and cranny of an image, choose Select ⇨ None (Command-D) and then choose the desired command.

Some filters are built into the Photoshop application. Others reside externally inside the Plug-ins folder. This feature allows you to add filters from third-party collections, such as Aldus Gallery Effects, Kai's Power Tools, and Xaos Tools. You can tell Photoshop 2.5 where to search for external filters by choosing File ⇨ Preferences ⇨ Plug-ins, specifying a new location on disk, and then quitting and relaunching Photoshop. Version 2.0 expects to find external filters inside the same folder as the preferences file.

To reapply the last filter used in the current Photoshop session, choose the first command from the Filter menu or simply press Command-F. If you want to reapply the filter subject to different settings, press Command-Option-F to redisplay that filter's dialog box. Both techniques work even if you undo the last application of a filter. However, if you cancel a filter while in progress, pressing Command-F or Command-Option-F applies the last uncanceled filter.

Previewing filters

Along with opening and saving images, importing and exporting the Clipboard, printing an image, and changing color modes, applying a filter is one of Photoshop's most time-consuming operations. Depending on the size of your selection or image, filters can take anywhere from a few seconds to several minutes to complete. You can switch to a different application while a filter is in progress, instructing Photoshop to work in the background without monopolizing your machine. You can cancel a filter-in-progress at any time by pressing Command-period (or clicking the Cancel button if one appears).

However, neither of these options helps you regain time wasted applying a filter that doesn't produce the desired effect. That's why it pays to preview filters before applying them. Although you can't preview most Photoshop operations, you can test out a filter by applying it to a small area of your image. This technique may sound like an obvious one, but you'd be surprised how many people — even experienced users like me — blithely apply filters to entire images without thinking.

To preview a filter effect, select a small, representative region of your image (about 40 × 40 pixels) and apply the prospective filter settings. If you're not happy with the results, choose Edit ⇨ Undo (Command-Z) and try again. If you like what you see, choose Edit ⇨ Undo and apply the filter to the full image area as desired. If you suddenly remember this tip in the middle of applying a long filter, press Command-period to cancel the operation.

Photoshop 2.5 offers a special, undocumented technique for previewing commands in the Filter ⇨ Distort submenu. Press and hold the Option key while choosing Displace, Pinch, Polar Coordinates, or any of the other Distort filter names from the About Plug-in submenu under the Apple menu. Keep the Option key pressed until the splash screen shown in Figure 12-3 appears. Select the Show Previews & Sliders check box and then click anywhere on the splash screen to hide the screen. After you do this, the Pinch, Polar Coordinates, Ripple, Spherize, Twirl, Wave, and Zigzag dialog boxes feature image previews, as illustrated in Figure 12-4.

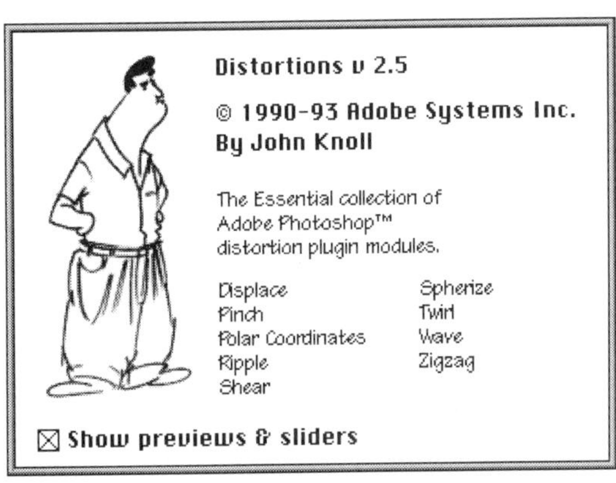

Figure 12-3: Press the Option key while choosing one of the Distort filter names from the Apple ⇨ About Plug-in submenu. Doing so displays the Show Previews & Sliders check box; selecting this check box lets you preview the effects of certain filters.

Figure 12-4: The Twirl dialog box shown as it appears before selecting the Show Previews & Sliders check box (top) and after (bottom).

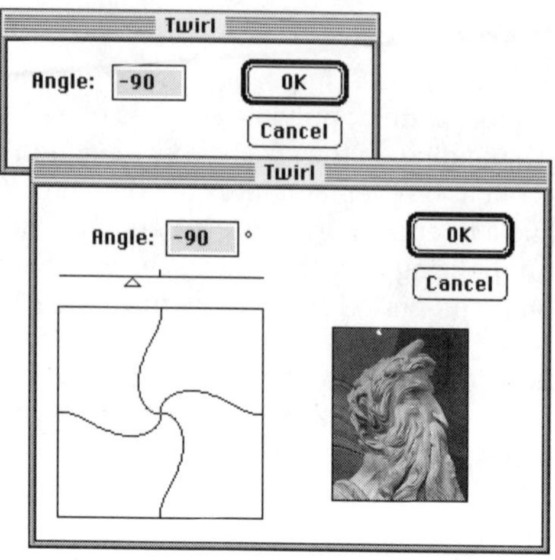

The original Photoshop 2.5 had a bug that prevented you from properly previewing the Polar Coordinates filter. Version 2.5.1 includes a new Distortion plug-in module that remedies this problem. If you subscribe to a bulletin board service such as America Online, you can download a patch for the old Distortion plug-in.

Though available from the Filter ⇨ Distort submenu, the dialog boxes for the Displace and Shear filters lack previews even after you select the Show Previews & Sliders check box.

Dissipating filtering effects

In many cases, you apply filters to a selection or image at *full intensity.* That is, you marquee an area using a selection tool, choose a filter command, enter whatever settings you deem appropriate if a dialog box appears, and sit back and watch the fireworks.

What's so "full intensity" about that? Sounds normal, right? Well, the fact is, you can dissipate the intensity of a filter either by floating the selection and then overlaying it onto the original image, in a translucent fashion, or by editing the selection in the quick mask mode.

For example, Figure 12-5 shows a series of applications of the Emboss filter (from the Filter ⇨ Stylize submenu). The original image appears in the upper left corner; the full-intensity effect of the filter appears in the lower right corner. To create the images in between, I floated the selection, applied the filter, and then changed the Opacity slider bar in the Brushes palette to the value that appears in the figure. (In Photoshop 2.0, choose Edit ⇨ Paste Controls and enter the value in the Opacity option box.)

An alternative method is to select the image, enter the quick mask mode, and fill the area that you want to select with a percentage of black equal to the opposite of the Opacity value. (Filling is the subject of the "Filling Portions of an Image" section of Chapter 15.) An 80 percent black results in the 20 percent filtering effect, a 60 percent black results in the 40 percent effect, and so on. This technique works because white in the quick mask mode equates to a full-intensity selection and 100 percent black equates to no selection. After filling the selection, you return to the marching ants mode and apply the filter.

Although the overlay method may sound less cumbersome, the quick mask method is more flexible. As you may remember from the "Selection Masks" section of Chapter 9, you can paint partial selections in the quick mask mode that are either exceedingly complex or impossible to duplicate in the marching ants mode. Figure 12-6 shows a row of selections as they appear in the quick mask mode followed by the result of applying the Emboss filter to each of these selections in the marching ants mode.

Mark Collen, an artist who contributed images to this book, tests out the dissipation of a filter by applying a gradient fill over the entire image in the quick mask mode, applying a filter, and specifying the portion of the operation that he likes the best. The following steps describe the process in detail.

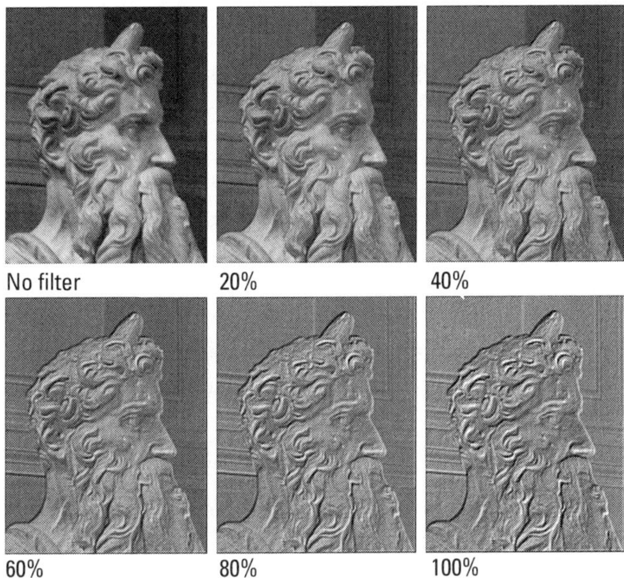

Figure 12-5: You can dissipate the effect of a filter by overlaying a translucent filtered image over the unfiltered original or by editing the selection in the quick mask mode.

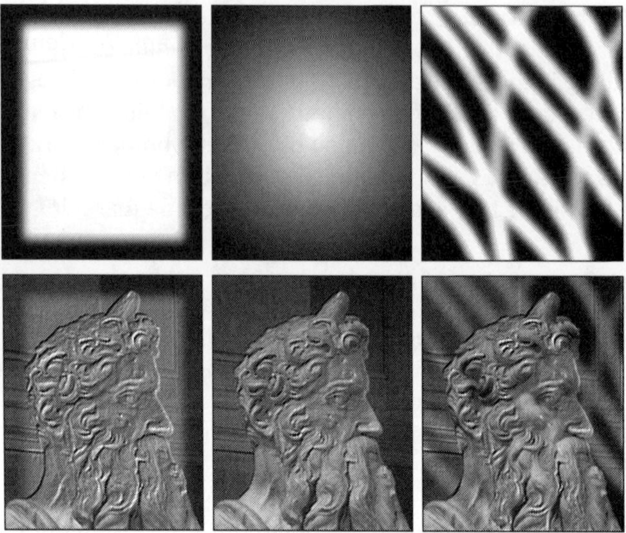

Figure 12-6: After creating a selection in the quick mask mode (top row), I applied the Emboss filter to each selection in the marching ants mode (bottom row).

STEPS: Previewing a Dissipated Filter

Step 1. Choose Select ⇨ None (Command-D) to deselect all portions of the current image. Then click on the default color icon in the toolbox to restore black and white as foreground and background colors. Save your image to disk by choosing File ⇨ Save (Command-S).

Step 2. Switch to the quick mask mode. Select the gradient tool and drag from the upper left corner of the image to the lower right corner to create an expansive gradation that covers the entire image, as demonstrated in the left example in Figure 12-7.

Step 3. Do not exit the quick mask mode. Instead, choose Window ⇨ Show Channels to display the Channels palette. Photoshop automatically adds a temporary channel titled *Mask* to the palette's scrolling list.

Step 4. Click on the first name in the list of channels in the palette. Then click in the view column in front of the Mask channel name to hide the eyeball icon. Now you can view and edit the image even though you're technically still inside the quick mask mode.

Step 5. Apply the filter as desired. The effect of the filter ranges from no intensity in the upper left corner to full intensity in the lower right corner.

Step 6. Select the eyedropper tool and position it on the point in your image where image and filter merge to produce the best effect, as demonstrated in the right example of Figure 12-7.

Step 7. With the eyedropper cursor in place, take your hand away from the mouse so that you don't accidentally jostle it. If you're editing a grayscale image, press Command-2 to view and edit the mask. If you're editing an RGB or Lab image, press Command-4. If you're in the CMYK mode, press Command-5.

Step 8. Click the mouse button without moving the mouse. You have now lifted the perfect brightness value and made it the foreground color.

Step 9. Choose File ⇨ Revert to restore the image to its appearance in Step 1. In addition to reverting the image, Photoshop returns to the marching ants mode.

Step 10. Return to the quick mask mode. Choose Select ⇨ All (Command-A) to select the entire image. Then press Option-Delete to fill the image with the foreground color.

Step 11. Switch to the marching ants mode and reapply your filter by pressing Command-F.

Figure 12-7: After creating a gradation across the entire image in the quick mask mode (left), display the image using options in the Channels palette, apply the filter, and use the eyedropper tool to isolate the ideal combination of image and dissipated filter (right).

Ways to Adjust Focus

If you've experimented at all with Photoshop, you've no doubt had your way with many of the commands in the Filter ⇨ Sharpen and Filter ⇨ Blur submenus. By increasing the contrast between neighboring pixels, sharpening filters enable you to compensate for image elements that were photographed or scanned slightly out of focus. Blur filters let you soften color transitions in images that include an excessive amount of artifacts, whether those artifacts were acquired during the scanning process or were simply the result of a poor original photograph.

Commands such as Sharpen Edges and Blur More are easy to use and immediate in their effect. However, you can achieve better results and widen your range of sharpening and blurring options if you learn how to use the Unsharp Mask, Gaussian Blur, and High Pass commands, which are all discussed at length in the following pages.

Sharpening an image using Unsharp Mask

The first thing you need to know about the Unsharp Mask filter is that it has a worthless name. The filter has nothing to do with "unsharpening" — whatever that is — nor has it anything to do with Photoshop's masking capabilities. It's named after a traditional film compositing technique (which is also oddly named) that highlights the edges in an image by combining a blurred film negative with the original film positive.

That's all very well and good, but the fact is most Photoshop artists have never touched a stat camera (an expensive piece of machinery, roughly twice the size of a washing machine, used by image editors of the late Jurassic, pre-Photoshop epoch). Even folks like me who used to operate them professionally never had the time to delve into the world of unsharp masking. In addition, the Unsharp Mask filter goes beyond traditional camera techniques, much to its credit.

To understand Unsharp Mask — or Photoshop's other sharpening filters, for that matter — you first need to understand some basic terminology. When you apply one of the sharpening filters, Photoshop increases the contrast between neighboring pixels. The effect is similar to what you see when you adjust a camera to bring a scene into sharper focus.

Two of Photoshop's sharpening filters, Sharpen and Sharpen More, affect whatever area of your image is selected. The Sharpen Edges filter, however, performs its sharpening operations only on the *edges* in the image — those areas that feature the highest amount of contrast.

Unsharp Mask gives you both sharpening options. It can sharpen only the edges in an image or it can sharpen any portion of an image according to your exact specifications, whether it finds an edge or not. It fulfills the exact same purposes as the Sharpen, Sharpen Edges, and Sharpen More commands, but it's much more versatile. Simply put, the Unsharp Mask tool is the only sharpening filter you'll ever need.

When you choose Filter ⇨ Sharpen ⇨ Unsharp Mask, Photoshop displays the Unsharp Mask dialog box, shown in Figure 12-8, which offers these options:

- **Amount:** Enter a value between 1 and 500 percent to specify the degree to which you want to sharpen the selected image. Higher values produce more pronounced effects.
- **Radius:** This option enables you to distribute the effect of the filter by applying it over a range of 0.1 to 100.0 pixels at a time. Low values produce crisp images. High values produce softer, higher contrast effects.
- **Threshold:** Enter a value between 0 and 255 to control how Photoshop recognizes edges in an image. The value indicates the numerical difference between the brightness values of two neighboring pixels that must occur if Photoshop is to sharpen those pixels. A low value sharpens lots of pixels; a high value excludes most pixels from the running.

The following sections explain the Amount, Radius, and Threshold options in greater detail and demonstrate the effects of each.

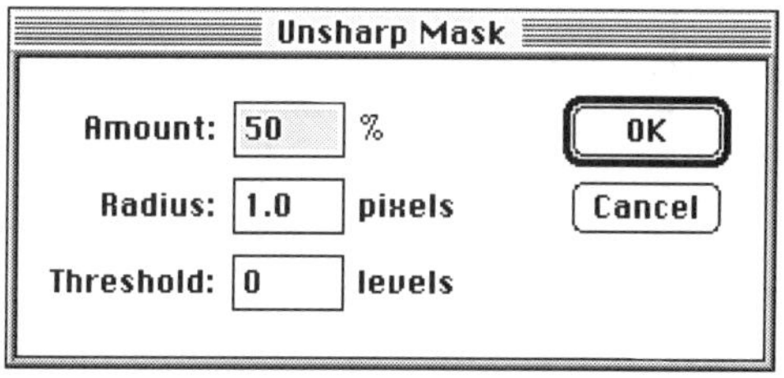

Figure 12-8: Despite any conclusions you may glean from its bizarre name, the Unsharp Mask filter sharpens images according to your specifications in this dialog box.

Specifying the amount of sharpening

If Amount were the only Unsharp Mask option, no one would have any problems understanding this filter. If you want to sharpen an image ever so slightly, enter a low percentage value. Values between 25 and 50 percent are ideal for producing subtle effects. If you want to sharpen an image beyond the point of good taste, enter a value somewhere in the 300 to 500 percent range. And if you're looking for moderate sharpening, try out some value between 50 and 300 percent. Figure 12-9 shows the results of applying different Amount values while leaving the Radius and Threshold values at their default settings.

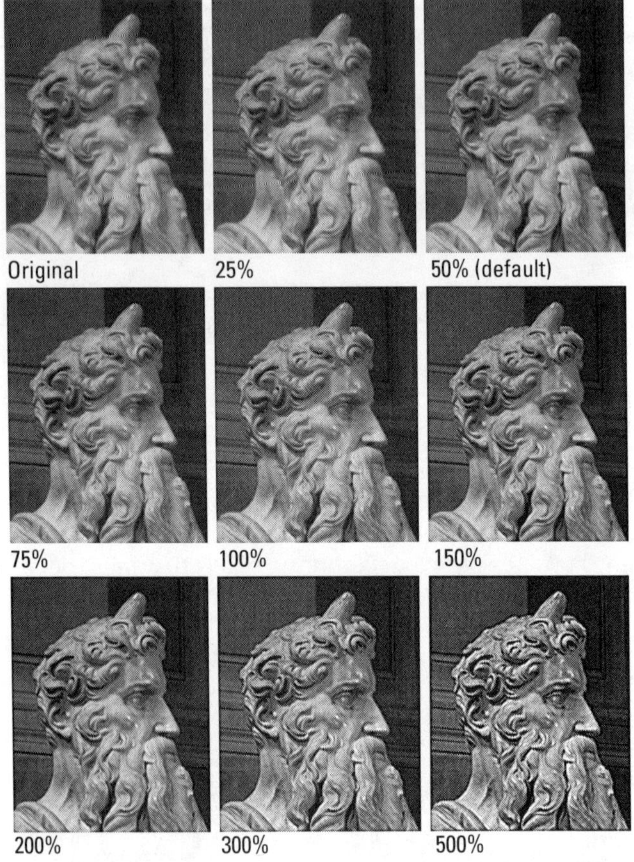

Figure 12-9: The results of sharpening an image with the Unsharp Mask filter using eight different Amount values. The Radius and Threshold values used for all images were 1.0 and 0 respectively (the default settings).

If you're not sure how much you want to sharpen an image, try out a small value, in the 25 to 50 percent range. Then reapply that setting repeatedly by pressing Command-F. As you can see in Figure 12-10, repeatedly applying the filter at a low setting produces a nearly identical result to applying the filter once at a higher setting. For example, you can achieve the effect shown in the middle image in the figure by applying the Unsharp Mask filter three times at 50 percent or once at 250 percent.

The benefit of using small values is that they allow you to experiment with sharpening incrementally. As the figure demonstrates, you can add sharpening bit by bit to increase the focus of an image. You can't, however, reduce sharpening incrementally if you apply too high a value; you must choose Edit ⇨ Undo and start again.

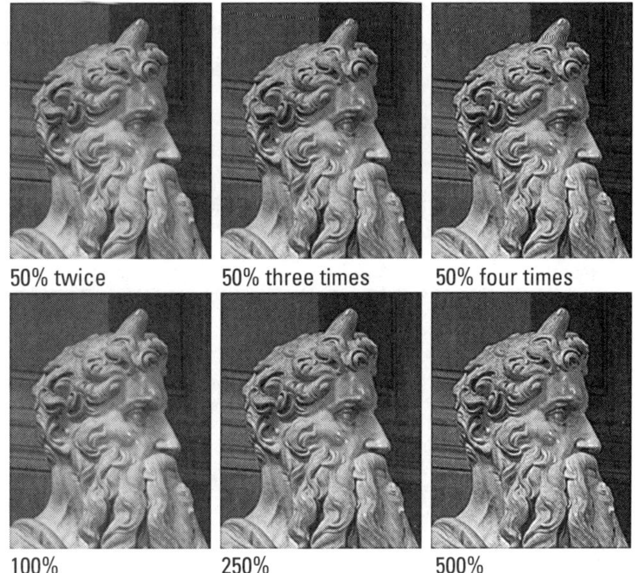

Figure 12-10: Repeatedly applying the Unsharp Mask filter at 50 percent (top row) is nearly equivalent on a pixel-by-pixel basis to applying the filter once at higher settings (bottom). The top row results were created using a constant Radius value of 1.0. In the second row, I lowered the Radius progressively from 1.0 (left) to 0.8 (middle) to 0.6 (right).

Distributing the effect

Understanding the Amount value is a piece of cake. It's a little more difficult to wrap the old noodle around the Radius value.

Here's the scoop: for each and every pixel Photoshop decides to sharpen, it distributes the effect according to the value you specify in the Radius option box. It's as if you selected the range of pixels identified by the Unsharp Mask filter's Threshold option, applied the Select ➪ Feather command to them, and then applied the Amount value.

In fact, the Radius value offered by the Unsharp Mask and Feather dialog boxes operate on the exact same principle. The result is that lower values concentrate the impact of the Unsharp Mask filter. Higher values distribute the impact and, in doing so, lighten the lightest pixels and darken the darkest pixels, almost as if the image had been photocopied too many times.

Figure 12-11 demonstrates the results of specific Radius values. In each case, the Amount and Threshold values remain constant at 100 percent and 0 respectively.

Most softening effects in Photoshop — including feathering, softened brush shapes, and the radius of the Unsharp Mask filter — work according to a bell-shaped *Gaussian distribution curve.* The curve slopes gradually in the beginning,

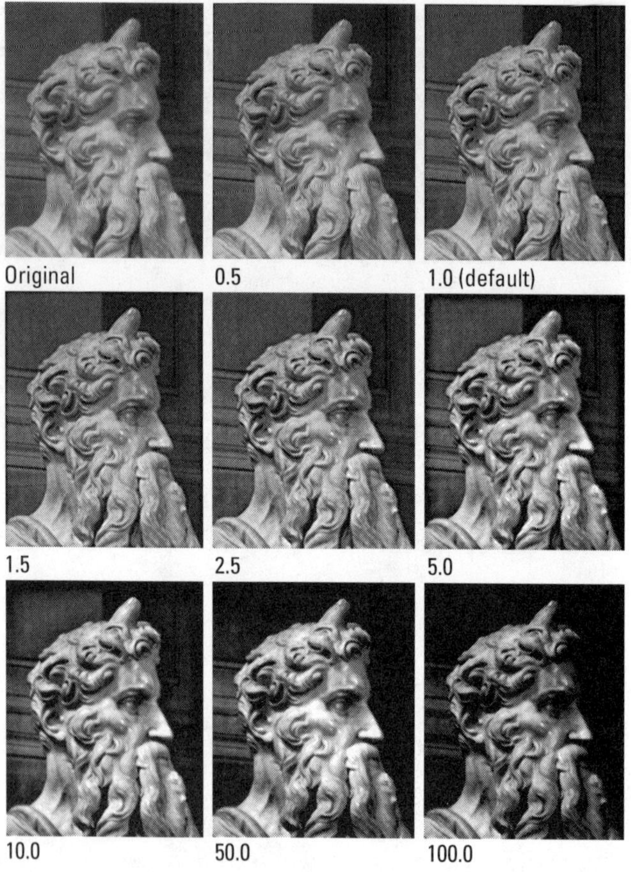

Figure 12-11: The results of applying eight different Radius values, ranging from precisely concentrated to overly generalized.

radically in the middle, and gradually at the end, thus softening the effect without altogether destroying its impact. The Unsharp Mask filter, however, conforms to the Gaussian curve only at Radius values of 2.0 and less. If you specify a radius greater than 2.0, the curve flattens out to accelerate the speed of the filter. The filter then destroys edges instead of working to retain edges as it does when the normal Gaussian curve is in effect. For this reason, I recommend that you use Radius values less than 2.0 to accomplish most of your sharpening effects.

Figure 12-12 shows the results of combining different Amount and Radius values. You can see that a large Amount value helps to offset the softening of a high Radius value. For example, when the Amount is set to 200 percent, as in the first row, the Radius value appears to mainly enhance contrast when raised from 0.5 to 2.0. However, when the Amount value is lowered to 50 percent, the higher Radius value does more to distribute the effect than boost contrast.

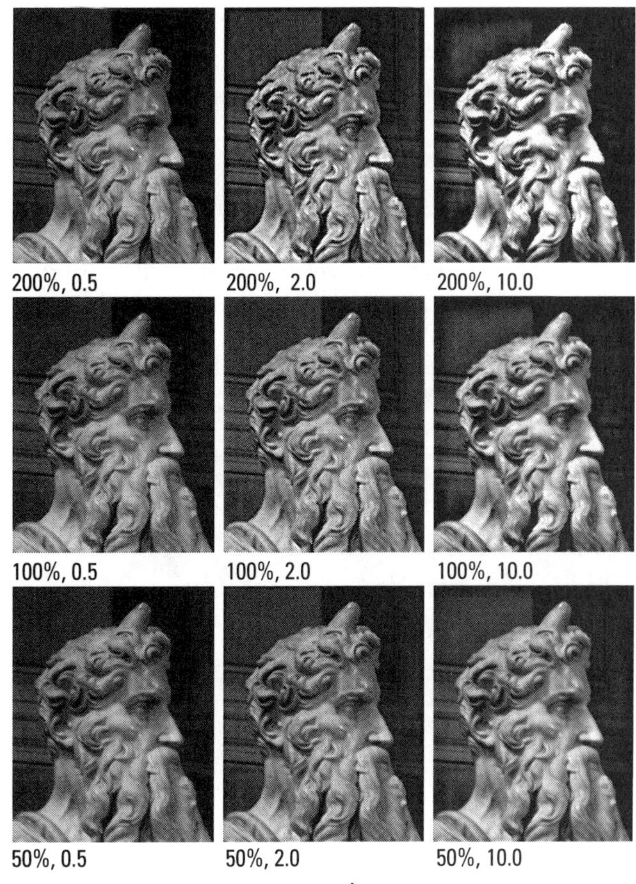

Figure 12-12: The effects of combining different Amount (first value) and Radius (second value) settings. Relatively high Amount and Radius values bring out the deep curls in the hair, as you can see in the top middle image. The Threshold value for each image was set to 0, the default setting.

By the way, in case you're wondering how Moses got that huge bump on his head — from this angle the growth looks rather like a finger — it wasn't because someone whacked him one. Ostensibly, the Hebrew word for the *shaft of light* and *horn* are one and the same. Naturally confused, Michelangelo opted for the latter interpretation. Great sculptor, that Michelangelo, but a poor translator of the world's languages.

Recognizing edges

By default, the Unsharp Mask filter sharpens every pixel in a selection. However, you can instruct the filter to sharpen only the edges in an image by raising the Threshold value from zero to some other number. The Threshold value represents the difference between two neighboring pixels — as measured in brightness levels — that must occur for Photoshop to recognize them as an edge.

Suppose that the brightness values of neighboring pixels A and B are 10 and 20. If you set the Threshold value to 5, Photoshop reads both pixels, notes that the difference between their brightness values is more than 5, and treats them as an edge. If you set the Threshold value to 20, however, Photoshop passes them by. A low Threshold value, therefore, causes the Unsharp Filter to affect a high number of pixels, and vice versa.

In the upper left image in Figure 12-13, the carved curls in the ravishing Moses hairdo stand out in stark contrast against the light gray of the poofier portions of the coiffure. I can sharpen the edges of the curls exclusively of other portions of the image by raising the Threshold value to 50 or even 30, as demonstrated in the second and third examples of the figure.

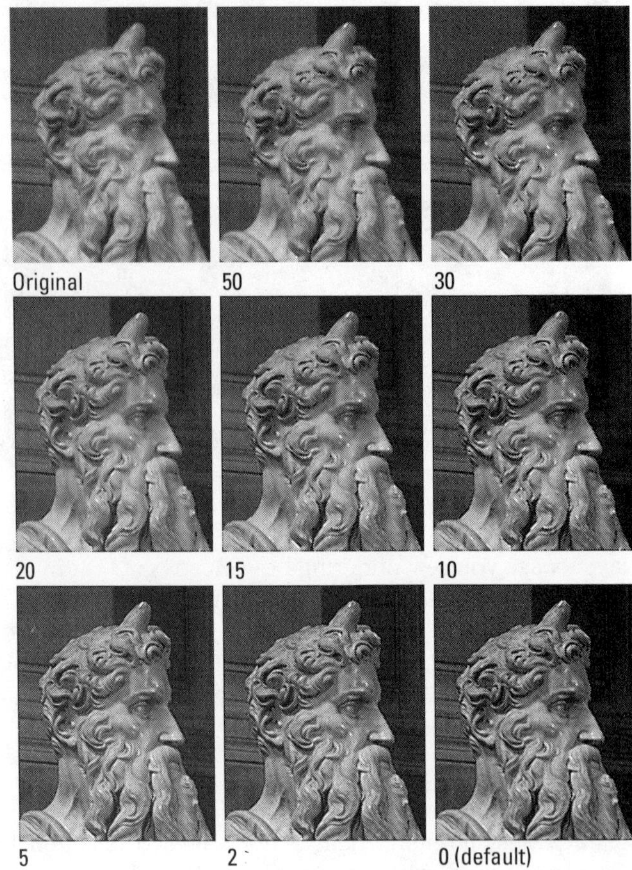

Figure 12-13: The results of applying eight different Threshold values. High Threshold values limit the effect of the Unsharp Mask filter to high-contrast regions; low values apply the filter more evenly. To best show off the differences between each image, I set the Amount and Radius values to 500 percent and 0.5 respectively.

Using the preset sharpening filters

So how do the Sharpen, Sharpen Edges, and Sharpen More commands compare with the Unsharp Mask filter? First of all, none of the preset commands can distribute a sharpening effect, a function provided by the Unsharp Mask filter's Radius option. Secondly, only the Sharpen Edges command can recognize high-contrast areas in an image. And third, all three commands are set in stone — you can't adjust their effects in any way. Figure 12-14 shows the effect of each preset command and the nearly equivalent effect created with the Unsharp Mask filter.

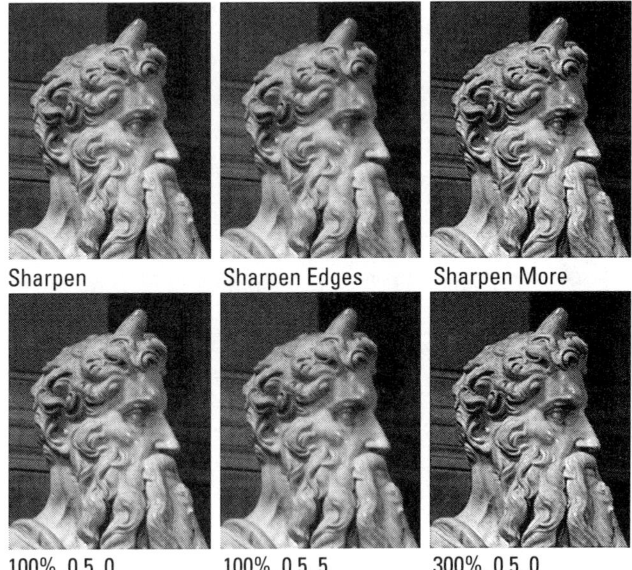

Figure 12-14: The effects of the three preset sharpening filters (top row) compared with their Unsharp Mask equivalents (bottom row). Unsharp Mask values are listed in the following order: Amount, Radius, Threshold.

Using the High Pass filter

The High Pass filter falls more or less in the same camp as the sharpening filters but is not located under the Filter ➪ Sharpen submenu. This frequently overlooked gem enables you to isolate high-contrast image areas from their low-contrast counterparts.

When you choose Filter ➪ Other ➪ High Pass, Photoshop offers a single option: the familiar Radius value, which can vary from 0.1 to 100.0. As demonstrated in Figure 12-15, high Radius values distinguish areas of high and low contrast only slightly. Low values change all high-contrast areas to dark gray and low-contrast areas to a slightly lighter gray. A value of 0.1, not shown in the figure, changes all pixels in an image to a single gray value and is, therefore, useless.

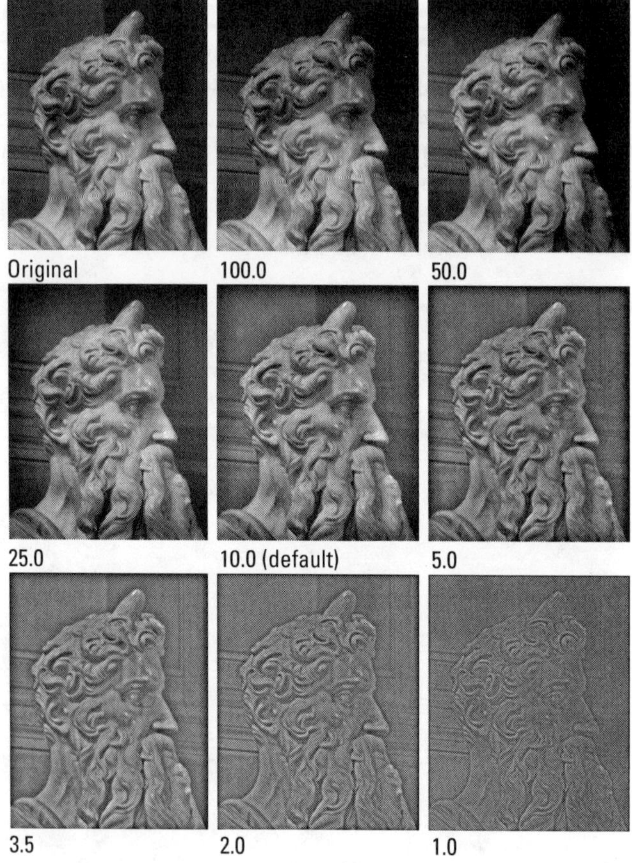

Figure 12-15: The results of separating high- and low-contrast areas in an image with the High Pass filter set at eight different Radius values.

The High Pass filter is especially useful as a precursor to choosing Image ➪ Map ➪ Threshold (Command-T), which converts all pixels in an image to black and white. As illustrated in Figure 12-16, the Threshold command produces entirely different effects on images before and after you alter them with the High Pass filter. Applying the High Pass filter with a Radius value of 1.0 and then issuing the Threshold command converts your image into a line drawing. The effect is similar to choosing Filter ➪ Stylize ➪ Find Edges, but the lines are crisper and, obviously, black and white. (An image filtered with the Find Edges command remains in color.)

Why change your image to a bunch of slightly different gray values and then apply Image ➪ Map ➪ Threshold? Why, to select portions of an image using a mask channel, of course. Because the High Pass filter sees an image in terms of contrast levels, which is one of the ways your eyes perceive images in real life, it can be a useful first step in selecting an image element that is clearly visually unique but has proved difficult to isolate.

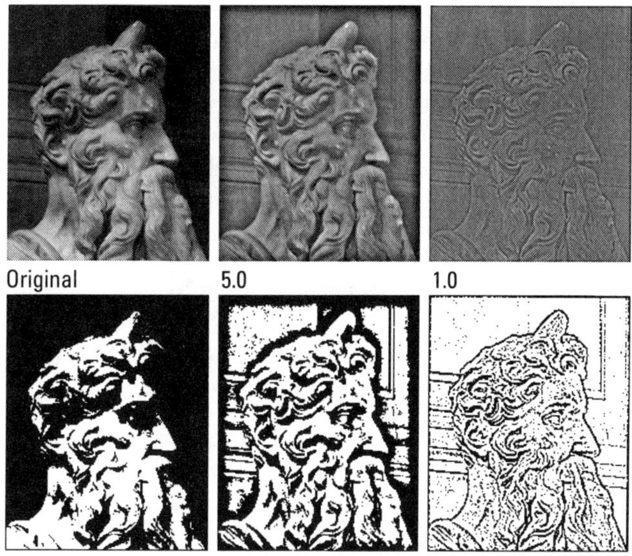

Figure 12-16: The original image and two counterparts edited with the High Pass command (top row) followed by the same images subject to the Threshold command set to 124 (bottom).

I introduced the idea of employing the Threshold command as a selection tool in the "Deriving selections from images" section of Chapter 9. The following steps explain how you can use the High Pass filter to help distinguish an image element from a busy background. The image shown in Figure 12-17 is used as an example.

STEPS: Selecting an Image Element Set Against a Busy Background

Step 1. Select the entire image and copy it to the Clipboard.

Step 2. Switch to the quick mask mode or an independent mask channel and paste the image.

Step 3. Choose Filter ⇨ Other ⇨ High Pass and enter the desired Radius value. To create the image shown in the bottom half of Figure 12-17, I entered a Radius value of 3.0, which isolates most of the high-contrast portions of the image while retaining some thick outlines of solid color that will prove useful during the editing process. Press Return to filter the image.

Step 4. Choose Image ⇨ Map ⇨ Threshold (Command-T). I found the best balance of black and white pixels by setting the slider bar in the Threshold dialog box to 124. The resulting image appears in the top half of Figure 12-18.

Step 5. You should now be able to eliminate the background elements fairly easily by dragging with the eraser tool. When working in the quick mask mode, you are likely to find it easier to edit the selection outline if you hide the image by clicking on its eyeball icon in the Channels palette. Next, use the pencil tool to close the gaps in the outline of the foreground elements, and click with the paint bucket tool to fill the elements with black, as demonstrated in the second example of Figure 12-18. You'll probably have to fill in some remaining gaps by painting with the pencil tool and a large brush shape.

Step 6. If you want to select the background, simply switch to the marching ants mode or switch to the image channel and choose Select ➪ Load Selection. If you prefer to select the foreground elements, choose Image ➪ Map ➪ Invert (Command-I) before switching out of the quick mask mode or independent mask channel.

Figure 12-17: A busy image before (top) and after (bottom) applying the High Pass filter with a Radius value of 3.0.

Figure 12-18: The result of applying the Threshold command set to 124 (top) and editing the black and white image with the eraser, pencil, and paint bucket tools (bottom).

Blurring an image

The commands under the Filter ⇨ Blur submenu produce the opposite effects of their counterparts under the Filter ⇨ Sharpen submenu, or, for that matter, the High Pass command. Rather than enhancing the amount of contrast between neighboring pixels, the Blur filters diminish contrast to create a softening effect.

Gaussian blur

The preeminent Blur filter is Gaussian Blur, which blends a specified number of pixels at a time incrementally, following the bell-shaped Gaussian distribution curve I touched on earlier.

When you choose Filter ⇨ Blur ⇨ Gaussian Blur, Photoshop produces a single Radius option box, in which you can enter any value from 0.1 to 100.0 (beginning to sound familiar?). As demonstrated in Figure 12-19, Radius values of 1.0 and smaller blur an image slightly; moderate values, between 1.0 and 5.0, turn an image into a rude approximation of life without my glasses on; and higher values blur the image beyond recognition.

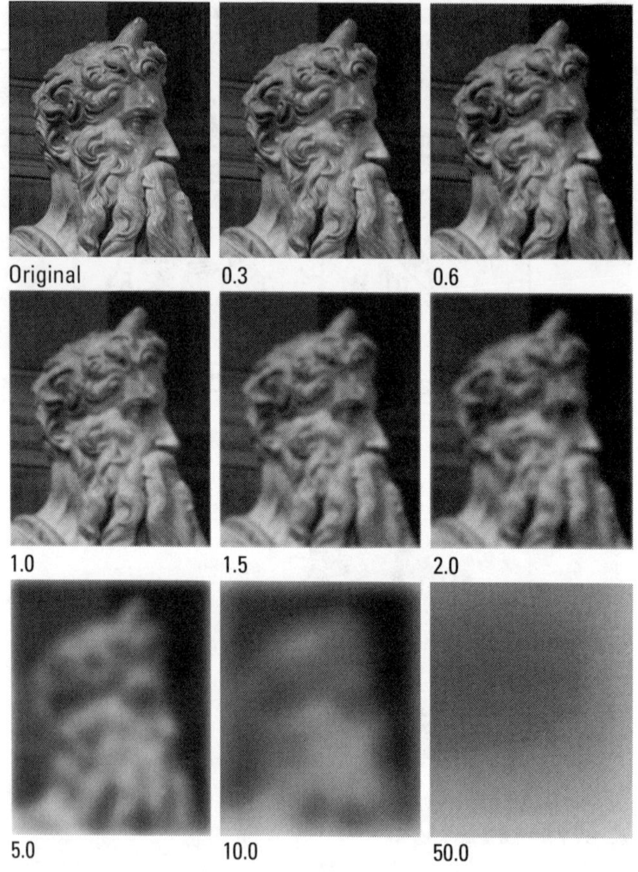

Figure 12-19: The results of blurring an image with the Gaussian Blur filter using eight different Radius values, ranging from slightly out of focus to Bad Day at the Ophthalmologist's Office.

Applying the Gaussian Blur filter to a selection in the quick mask mode is almost the exact equivalent of feathering the selection in the marching ants mode. The only difference is that the Radius option in the Gaussian Blur dialog box is accurate to 1/10 pixel, while its counterpart in the Feather dialog box accepts whole numbers only. To see this tip in action, read the "Softening a selection" section later in this chapter.

Moderate to high Radius values can be especially useful for creating that hugely amusing "Star Trek" Iridescent Female effect — you know, the one where some bewitching ambassador or scientist beams on board and Captain Kirk takes her hand in sincere welcome, all the while explaining how truly honored he is to have such a renowned guest in his transporter room, and so charming to boot, as he gives out with the grin. Then we see it — the close-up of the fetching actress shrouded in a kind of gleaming halo, which prevents us from discerning if her lips are chapped or if she's hiding an old acne scar, because some cockeyed cinematographer smeared Vaseline all over the camera lens. I mean, what *wouldn't* you give to be able to re-create this effect in Photoshop?

Unfortunately, I don't have any images of actresses adorned in futuristic go-go boots, so I'll use Moses, again. The following steps explain how to make Moses glow as demonstrated in Figure 12-20.

STEPS: The Wondrous Iridescent Effect

Step 1. Choose Select ⇨ All (Command-A) to select the entire image. If you only want to apply the effect to a portion of the image, be sure to feather the selection with a radius in the neighborhood of 5 to 8 pixels.

Step 2. Choose Select ⇨ Float (Command-J) to clone the image in place. (In Photoshop 2.0, press the Option key with the up arrow to clone it and nudge it slightly upward. Then press the down arrow to nudge it back into place.)

Step 3. Choose Filter ⇨ Blur ⇨ Gaussian Blur, enter 5.0 into the Radius option box, and press Return. This blurs the cloned image only; the original image remains unchanged.

Step 4. Press the 7 key to change the Opacity slider bar to 70 percent, making the blurred image slightly translucent. This setting enables you to see the hard edges of the original image beneath the cloned image, as demonstrated in the first example of Figure 12-20. (In Photoshop 2.0, choose Edit ⇨ Paste Controls, enter 70 into the Opacity option box, and press Return.)

Step 5. You can achieve additional effects by selecting options from the brush mode pop-up menu on the left side of the Brushes dialog box. For example, I created the image in the upper right corner of Figure 12-20 by selecting the Screen option, which combines colors in the original and floating images to create a lightening effect. I created the two bottom examples in the figure by choosing the Lighten and Darken options.

Figure 12-20: After floating the selection, blurring it, and changing the Opacity slider bar to 70 percent, I applied overlay modes to alter the image further. Clockwise from upper left, the overlay modes I used were Normal, Screen, Darken, and Lighten.

The preset blurring filters

Neither of the two preset commands in the Filter ➪ Blur submenu, Blur and Blur More, can distribute its blurring effect over a bell-shaped Gaussian curve. For that reason, these two commands are less functional than the Gaussian Blur filter. However, just so you know where they stand in the grand Photoshop focusing scheme, Figure 12-21 shows the effect of each preset command and the nearly equivalent effect created with the Gaussian Blur filter.

Figure 12-21: The effects of the two preset blurring filters (top row) compared with their Gaussian Blur equivalents (bottom row), which are labeled according to Radius values.

Directional blurring

On to bigger and better things. Photoshop provides two *directional blurring* filters, Motion Blur and Radial Blur. Instead of blurring pixels in feathered clusters like the Gaussian Blur filter, the Motion Blur filter blurs pixels in straight lines over a specified distance. The Radial Blur filter blurs pixels in varying degrees depending on their distance from the center of the blur. The following pages explain both of these filters in detail.

Motion blurring

The Motion Blur filter makes an image appear as if either the image or camera was moving when you shot the photo. When you choose Filter ⇨ Blur ⇨ Motion Blur, Photoshop displays the dialog box shown in Figure 12-22. You enter the angle of movement into the Angle option box. Alternatively, you can indicate the angle by dragging the straight line inside the circle on the right side of the dialog box, as shown in the figure.

You then enter the distance of the movement in the Distance option box. Photoshop permits any value between 1 and 999 pixels. The filter distributes the effect of the blur over the course of the Distance value, as illustrated by the examples in Figure 12-23.

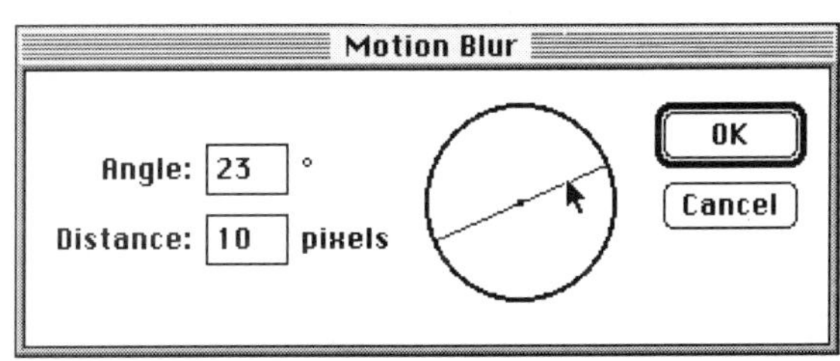

Figure 12-22: Drag the line inside the circle to change the angle of the blur.

Figure 12-23: A single black rectangle followed by five different applications of the Motion Blur filter. Only the Distance value varied, as labeled. A 0-degree Angle value was used in all five examples.

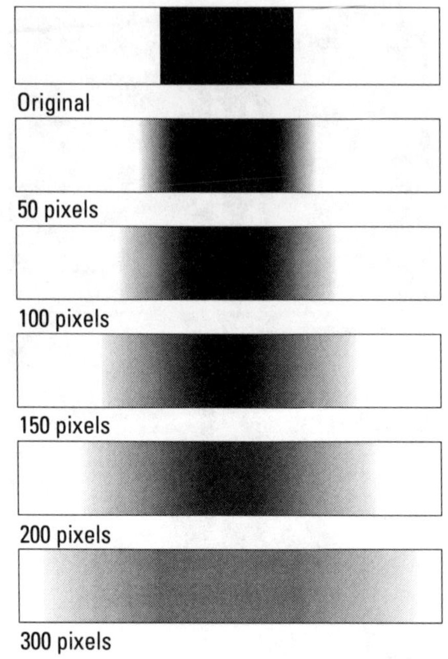

Mathematically speaking, Motion Blur is one of Photoshop's simpler filters. Rather than distributing the effect over a Gaussian curve, Photoshop creates as many copies of the selection as you specify in the Distance option, divides the opacity of each copy by the Distance value, and offsets each copy 1 pixel from its neighbors. The result is a linear distribution, peaking in the center and fading at either end.

Using the Wind filter

The problem with the Motion Blur filter is that it blurs pixels in two directions. If you want to distribute pixels in one absolute direction or the other, try out the Wind filter, which you can use either on its own or in tandem with Motion Blur.

When you choose Filter ⇨ Stylize ⇨ Wind, Photoshop displays the Wind dialog box shown in Figure 12-24. You can select from three methods and two directions to distribute the selected pixels. Figure 12-25 compares the effect of the Motion Blur filter to each of the three methods offered by the Wind filter. Notice that the Wind filter does not blur pixels. Rather, it evaluates a selection in 1-pixel-tall horizontal strips and offsets the strips randomly inside the image.

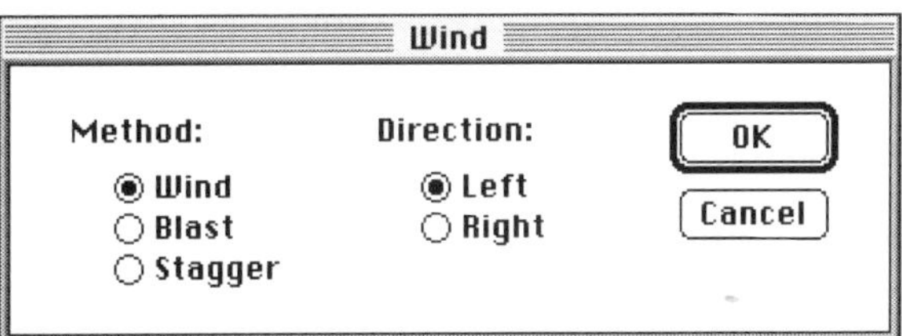

Figure 12-24: Use the Wind filter to randomly distribute a selection in 1-pixel horizontal strips in one of two directions.

Figure 12-25: The difference between the effects of the Motion Blur filter (top left) and the Wind filter. Clockwise from upper right, I applied the Wind filter using the Method options Wind, Blast, and Stagger.

To get the best results, try combining the Motion Blur and Wind filters with a translucent selection. For example, to create Figure 12-26, I floated the entire image and applied the Wind command twice, first selecting the Stagger option and then selecting Blast. Next, I applied the Motion Blur command with a 0-degree angle and a Distance value of 30. I then set the Opacity slider bar to 50 percent and selected Lighten from the brush mode pop-up menu. Unlike the example in Figure 12-25, the motion lines in the image in Figure 12-26 no longer completely obliterate the original image.

Figure 12-26: The result of combining the Wind and Motion Blur filters with a translucent selection.

Directional smudging

If you have problems creating an acceptable motion effect because the results of the filters are either too random or too generalized, you can create very precise motion lines using the smudge tool inside a translucent selection, as demonstrated in Figure 12-27. The following steps explain how to achieve this effect. The process has nothing to do with filters — I just thought I'd throw them in as an alternative to the Motion Blur and Wind commands. The steps assume you use Photoshop 2.5.

STEPS: Painting Motion Lines with the Smudge Tool

Step 1. Begin by using the rectangular marquee tool to select the area in which you want the motion lines to appear. Be sure to select all of the background area that will contain the motion lines as well as at least part of the foreground element that's responsible for the motion lines. Don't worry if you select too much of the image; you remedy that problem in the next step.

Step 2. Enter the quick mask mode. Use the paintbrush tool and a soft brush shape to trace along the edge of the foreground element, giving it a feathered selection outline. Then go ahead and fill in the rest of the foreground element so that only the background remains selected, as demonstrated in the top image in Figure 12-27.

Step 3. Return to the marching ants mode and clone the selection by choosing Select ⇨ Float (Command-J).

Step 4. Select the marquee tool or some other selection tool and press 7 to change the Opacity of the floating selection to 70 percent.

Step 5. Create a new, flat, vertical brush shape. You can specify any diameter with which you're comfortable. Enter 100 percent for the Hardness value, 1 percent for Spacing, and 0 percent for Roundness. Angle the brush perpendicularly to the prospective motion lines. When creating the image in Figure 12-27, I wanted to paint horizontal lines, so I made my brush vertical by entering an Angle value of 90 degrees.

Step 6. Select the smudge tool and set the Pressure slider bar to 95 percent.

Step 7. Apply the smudge tool repeatedly inside the floating selection. Be sure to drag in a consistent direction. In my case, I dragged from right to left, pressing the Shift key to constrain the drag so that it was perfectly horizontal. Drag as many times as you deem necessary. The result of my efforts appears in the bottom example in Figure 12-27.

Figure 12-27: I edited and softened the selection outline so that it followed the contours of the foreground image (top). Then I floated the selection, changed its Opacity setting to 70 percent, and dragged inside the selection in a consistent direction with the smudge tool (bottom).

Radial blurring

Choosing Filter ⇨ Blur ⇨ Radial Blur displays the Radial Blur dialog box shown in Figure 12-28. The dialog box offers two Blur Method options: Spin and Zoom.

If you select Spin, the image appears to be rotating about a central point. You specify that point by dragging in the grid inside the Blur Center box (as demonstrated in the figure).

If you select Zoom, the image appears to rush away from you, as if you were zooming the camera while shooting the photograph. Again, you specify the central point of the Zoom by dragging in the Blur Center box. Figures 12-29 and 12-30 feature examples of both settings.

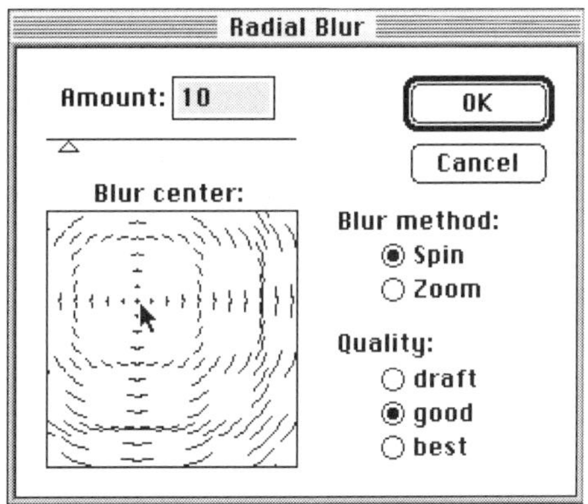

Figure 12-28: Drag inside the Blur Center grid to change the point about which the Radial Blur filter spins or zooms the image.

After selecting a Blur Method option, you can enter any value between 1 and 100 in the Amount option box to specify the maximum distance over which the filter blurs pixels. (You can enter a value of 0, but doing so merely causes the filter to waste time without producing an effect.) Pixels farthest away from the center point move the most; pixels close to the center point barely move at all. Keep in mind that large values take more time to apply than small values. The Radial Blur filter, incidentally, qualifies as one of Photoshop's most time-consuming operations.

Select a Quality option to specify your favorite time/quality compromise. The Good and Best Quality options ensure smooth results by respectively applying bilinear and bicubic interpolation (as explained in the "General environmental preferences" section of Chapter 4). However, they also prolong the amount of time the filter has to spend calculating pixels in your image.

The Draft option *diffuses* an image, which leaves a trail of loose and randomized pixels but takes less time to complete. I used the Draft setting to create the left images in Figures 12-29 and 12-30; I selected the Best option to create the images on the right.

Figure 12-29: Two versions of the Radial Blur filter set to Spin, using the Draft option (left) and Best option (right). In both cases, I specified Amount values of 5 pixels. Each effect is centered about Moses's eye.

Figure 12-30: Two versions of the Radial Blur filter set to Zoom, using the Draft (left) and Best (right) options. I entered 20 into the Amount option box because the Zoom option produces less-pronounced blurs than the Spin option. Again, the effects are centered about the eyes.

Combining sharpening and blurring

One of the best ways to combine commands from the Filter ⇨ Sharpen and Filter ⇨ Blur submenus is to differentiate foreground elements from their backgrounds. The foreground elements gets the sharpening, the background gets the blur.

For example, consider the image in Figure 12-31. On its own, it's not what I would call an inspirational image — just your standard everyday lady talking on the phone surrounded by your standard everyday urban landscape. Sure, the photo was shot in Japan, so it might stir up that world travel feeling in those of us who go in for that kind of thing. But I wouldn't call it exciting or provocative. In fact, it's a real snoozer.

The image does have one thing going for it, however. It features a distinct pair of foreground elements — the woman and the telephone — set against a clearly independent background, which includes everything else. This composition means that I can differentiate the two using sharpening and blurring effects.

To create the image in Figure 12-32, I selected the foreground elements and applied the Unsharp Mask filter. I used an Amount value of 75 percent, a Radius of 0.5, and a Threshold of 3. Then, just for laughs, I chose Select ⇨ Inverse and applied the Wind filter, selecting the Blast and Right radio buttons. Finally, I applied the Motion Blur filter, entering a Distance value of 20 pixels and a 0-degree angle.

Figure 12-31: This photo has potential that can be drawn to the surface using sharpening and blurring filters.

The Wind and Motion Blur filters produce the effect of moving the camera from right to left. By applying the Unsharp Mask filter, I kept the camera focused on the foreground elements throughout the move. This effect is extremely difficult to pull off in real life, but it's a simple matter in Photoshop.

Actually, I saw this technique applied once with great success to a photo of a baseball player preparing to bat in a big stadium. The crowds were swirling around him. But he looked cool, cocky, and, above all, completely stationary. Sadly, I didn't have any baseball photos lying around, so I picked the next best thing, a woman on the phone. I mean, hey, maybe her world's falling apart, you know. She feels the city spinning around her, closing in. Well, she looks a little calm for that, huh? OK, maybe she's trying to get her watch repaired and the store's about to close. Or maybe she's trying to order a pizza, but the clerk is being kind of surly, or at least unhelpful. Use your imagination.

Figure 12-33 shows a different take on the same scene. Again, I sharpened the foreground elements. But this time, instead of applying the Wind and Motion Blur filters to the background, I chose Filter ⇨ Blur ⇨ Radial Blur. I selected the Zoom option and raised the Amount value to 50. I also selected Draft from the Quality settings — not to save time, but to give the background a grainy appearance.

This image imitates the appearance of zooming the camera to a lower magnification while moving it forward, thus maintaining a constant focal distance between camera

Figure 12-32: The world swirls around this woman after liberal applications of the Wind and Motion Blur filters, yet she remains calm and collected, thanks to the use of Unsharp Mask.

and foreground elements. You may remember that Hitchcock used this effect to make the background appear as if it were moving independently of the acrophobic Jimmy Stewart in *Vertigo.* The effect looks a little different when applied to a still photo, but it nevertheless lends a dynamic quality to the image.

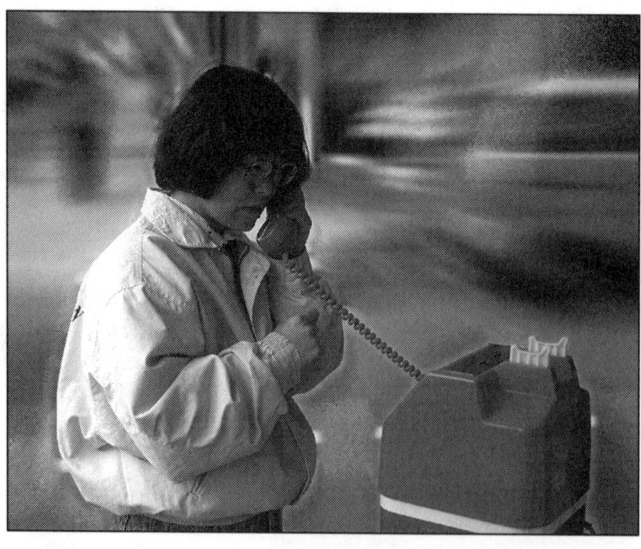

Figure 12-33: You can use the Radial Blur filter to zoom out from the background while retaining a constant focal distance between viewer and foreground elements.

Softening a selection

In Figures 12-32 and 12-33, the blurring filters had no effect on the foreground elements because those elements were not selected when the filters were applied. But rather than having the blurring start at the exact boundaries between the foreground and background elements, which would produce the highly unrealistic effect of drawing colors from the foreground elements into the background, the blurring becomes more pronounced a few pixels away from the foreground elements. This result occurs because the foreground is protected by a feathered buffer zone.

Now, if I had simply applied Select ⇨ Feather to my original selection boundary, displayed in progress back in Figure 12-18, the command would have feathered the selection in both directions — that is, inward and outward. In that case, the blurring would slightly affect the edges of the foreground elements, again producing an unrealistic effect. So instead, I edited the selection outline in the quick mask mode using two filters: Gaussian Blur, which I discussed earlier in this chapter; and Minimum, which you learn about in the next section.

Minimum and Maximum

The Minimum filter enhances the dark portions of an image, spreading them outward into other pixels. Its opposite, the Maximum filter, enhances the light portions of an image. In traditional stat photography, these techniques are known as *spread* and *choke* respectively.

When you are working in the quick mask mode or an independent mask channel, applying the Minimum filter has the effect of incrementally increasing the size of black areas, which deselects pixels evenly around the edges of a selection. The Radius value that you enter into the Minimum dialog box tells Photoshop how many edge pixels to deselect. Just the opposite, the Maximum filter incrementally increases the size of white areas, which adds pixels evenly around the edges of a selection.

How to feather outward from a selection

The following steps describe how to use the Minimum and Gaussian Blur filters to feather an existing selection outline outward only. These steps start where "STEPS: Selecting an Image Element Against a Busy Background," earlier in this chapter, left off. The steps assume you use Photoshop 2.5, but you can easily apply them to a mask channel in Version 2.0.

STEPS: Adding a Soft Edge in the Quick Mask Mode

Step 1. Start with a selection outline that exactly follows the boundaries of one or more foreground elements. Then switch to the quick mask mode. In Figure 12-34, the background is selected and the foreground is deselected.

Step 2. Choose Filter ⇨ Other ⇨ Minimum. Enter a Radius value of 4 to push back the boundaries of the selection outline 4 pixels and then press Return. (If you prefer to add 4 pixels to the selection outline, choose Filter ⇨ Other ⇨ Maximum.) The result appears in Figure 12-35.

Step 3. Choose Filter ⇨ Blur ⇨ Gaussian Blur and enter 3.9 to soften nearly all of the edge you added to your selection outline. The unaffected ⅒ pixel serves as a tiny insurance policy so that any effect you apply later doesn't harm the foreground elements. The Gaussian Blur filter feathers the selection outline, as shown in Figure 12-36.

Step 4. Switch back to the marching ants mode and apply your effect. In Figure 12-37, I deleted the selected area to demonstrate how the foreground elements remain entirely protected, with a feathered buffer zone to spare.

Figure 12-34: Begin in the quick mask mode with a selection that clearly distinguishes foreground and background elements.

Figure 12-35: Apply the Minimum filter to add a 4-pixel edge around the deselected area.

Figure 12-36: Use the Gaussian Blur filter to soften the 4pixel edge, thus feathering the selection outline.

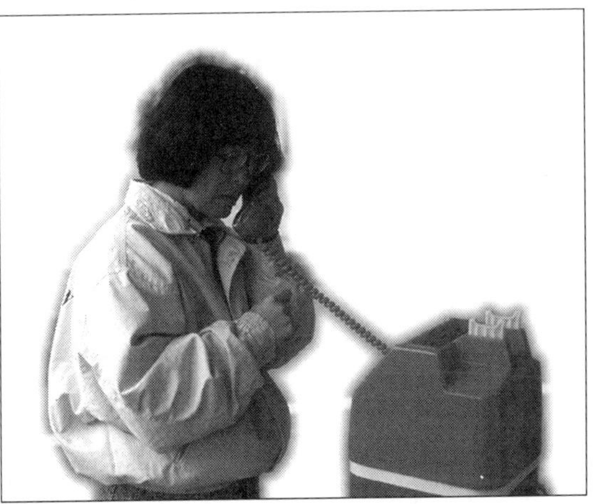

Figure 12-37: I deleted the selected background in the marching ants mode. The foreground elements remain intact and are surrounded by a soft halo of residual image data.

Noise Factors

Photoshop offers three loosely associated filters in its Filter ➪ Noise submenu. One filter adds random pixels — known as *noise* — to an image. The other two, Despeckle and Median, blur an image in ways that theoretically remove noise from poorly scanned images. In fact, they function nearly as well at removing essential detail as they do at removing extraneous noise. The only tried and true way to fix a badly scanned image is to chuck it and rescan. Garbage in, garbage out, as the lava lamp manufacturers used to say.

In the following sections, I show you how the Noise filters work, demonstrate a few of my favorite applications, and leave you to draw your own conclusions.

Adding noise

Noise adds grit and texture to an image. You can find examples of noise in grainy album covers, perfume commercials, Levi's 501 Blues ads . . . in short, anything that's trying to appeal to a hip, young, no-marbles-in-their-heads audience.

Noise makes an image look like I shot it in New York on the Lower East Side and was lucky to get the photo at all because someone was throwing sand in my face as I sped away in my chauffeur-driven jet-black Maserati Bora, hammering away at the shutter release. In reality, of course, a guy over at Sears shot the photo while I toodled around in my minivan trying to find a store that sold day-old bread. But, hey, if there's a moral to this book — which there most certainly is *not* — it's that impressions talk, reality walks.

You add noise by choosing Filter ➪ Noise ➪ Add Noise. Shown in Figure 12-38, the Add Noise dialog box features the following options:

- **Amount:** Enter any value between 1 and 999 to specify the amount that pixels in the image can stray from their current colors. The value itself represents a color range rather than a brightness range. For example, if you enter a value of 10, Photoshop can apply any color that is 10 shades more or less green, more or less blue, *and* more or less red than the current color. Any value over 255 allows Photoshop to select random colors from the entire 16-million color spectrum. The higher you go above 255, the more likely Photoshop is to pick colors at opposite ends of the spectrum — that is, white and black.
- **Uniform:** Select this option to apply colors absolutely randomly within the specified range. Photoshop is no more likely to apply one color within the range than another, thus resulting in an even color distribution.
- **Gaussian:** When you select this option, you instruct Photoshop to prioritize colors along the Gaussian distribution curve. The effect is that most colors added by the filter either closely resemble the original colors or push the boundaries of the specified range. In other words, this option results in more light and dark pixels, thus producing a more pronounced effect.

Figure 12-39 compares three applications of Gaussian noise to identical amounts of Uniform noise. Figure 12-40 features magnified views of the noise so you can compare the colors of individual pixels.

Figure 12-38: The Add Noise dialog box enables you to specify the amount and variety of noise you want to add to the selection.

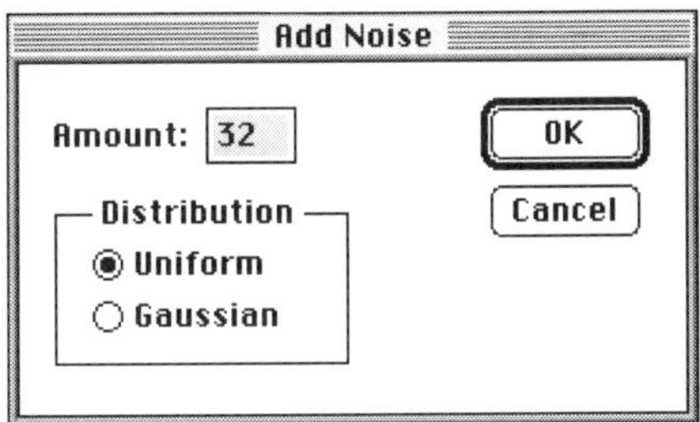

Figure 12-39: The Gaussian option produces more pronounced effects than the Uniform option at identical Amount values.

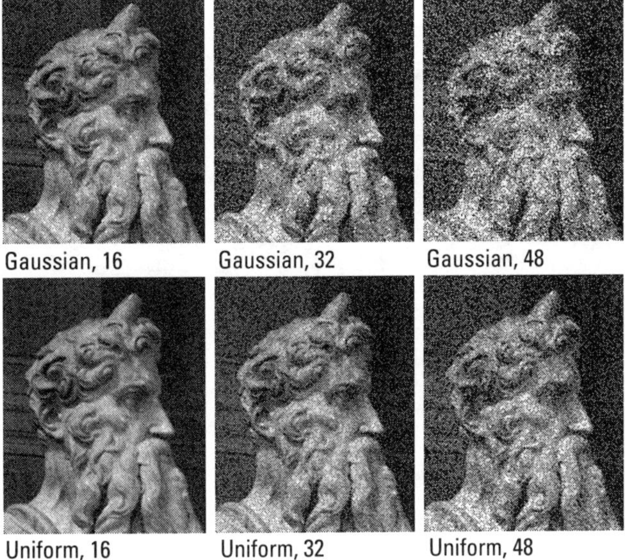

Figure 12-40: The upper left corners of the examples from Figure 12-39 enlarged to four times their original size.

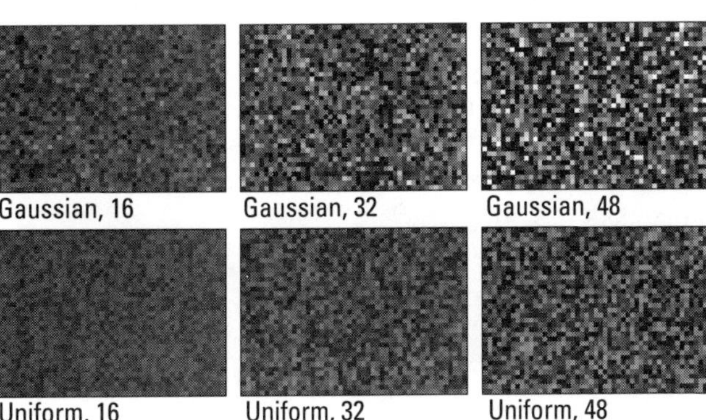

Noise variations

Normally, the Add Noise filter adds both lighter and darker pixels to an image. If you prefer, however, you can limit the effect of the filter to strictly lighter or darker pixels. To do so, float the selection before applying the filter and then select the Lighten or Darken overlay mode.

Figure 12-41 shows sample applications of lighter and darker noise. I began each example by selecting the entire image and choosing Select ⇨ Float (Command-J). I then chose Filter ⇨ Noise ⇨ Add Noise, entered an Amount value of 500, and selected Uniform. To create the left example in the figure, I changed the Opacity slider bar in the Brushes palette to 20 percent and selected Lighten from the brush mode pop-up menu. To create the right example, I changed the Opacity to 40 percent and selected Darken from the pop-up menu. In each case, I added a layer of strictly lighter or darker noise while at the same time retaining the clarity of the original image.

Figure 12-41: You can limit the Add Noise filter to strictly lighter (left) or darker (right) noise by applying the filter to a floating, translucent selection.

You can achieve a softened noise effect by applying one of the Blur filters to the floating selection before setting it down onto the original image. Figure 12-42, for example, shows images subject to the same amount of noise as those in Figure 12-41. But in this case, immediately following the application of the Add Noise filter, I chose Filter ⇨ Blur ⇨ Motion Blur, changed the angle to 30 degrees, and entered a Distance value of 3 pixels. I then changed the Opacity and brush mode settings as described in the preceding paragraph. In this way, I applied softened grains that are strictly lighter or darker than the original pixels in the image.

Figure 12-42: To create these rainy and scraped effects, I applied motion blurring to the noise in the floating selections from Figure 12-41.

Randomizing selections

As with any other filter, you can apply Add Noise to a selection in the quick mask mode. Suppose that I want to again edit the background of the woman-on-the-phone image, this time creating a static effect, as demonstrated in the top example in Figure 12-43. I enter the quick mask mode and draw the selection outline shown back in Figure 12-36. I only want to randomize the pixels within the selected background, so I use the magic wand tool to select the transparent areas of the mask that surround the woman and phone unit.

To soften the selection, I choose Select ⇨ Feather and enter a Radius value of 2. Next, I choose the Add Noise filter and enter a value of 500 to heavily randomize the selection. When I switch back to the marching ants mode, only random pixels in the background are selected. By pressing the Delete key, I achieve the effect shown in the top example of Figure 12-43.

The bottom example in Figure 12-43 features a blurred version of the static effect that looks vaguely like snow (more like a blizzard, really). After applying the Add Noise command in the quick mask mode — before switching to the marching ants mode and pressing Delete — I chose Filter ⇨ Blur ⇨ Gaussian Blur and entered a Radius value of 0.5. This softened the transition between random pixels in the selected region. I then switched back to the marching ants mode and pressed Delete to create the snow shown in the figure.

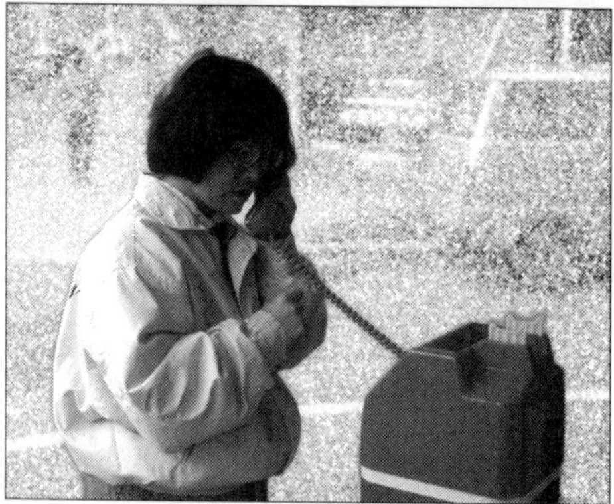

Figure 12-43: You can create a static effect (top) by randomizing pixels of a selection in the quick mask mode. To achieve a snow effect (bottom), apply the Gaussian Blur filter to the randomized selection.

Chunky noise

My biggest frustration with the Add Noise filter is that you can't specify the size of individual specks of noise. No matter how you cut it, noise only comes in 1-pixel squares. It may occur to you that you can enlarge the noise dots in a floating selection by applying the Minimum filter. But, in practice, doing so simply fills in the selection because there isn't sufficient space between the dark noise pixels to accommodate the larger dot sizes.

Luckily, Photoshop provides a Pointillize filter, which adds variable-sized dots and then colors those dots in keeping with the original colors in the image. Though Pointillize lacks the random quality of the Add Noise filter, you can use it to add texture to an image.

To create the left image in Figure 12-44, I selected the entire image and chose Select ⇨ Float. I then chose Filter ⇨ Stylize ⇨ Pointillize and entered 3 into the Cell Size option box. After pressing Return to apply the filter (for your information, it's a slow one), I changed the Opacity slider bar in the Brushes palette to 20 percent. The effect is rather like applying chunky bits of noise.

The problem with this technique is that it has the added effect of softening an image. To preserve image detail and create the right-hand image in Figure 12-44, I transferred the floating selection to the Clipboard — by choosing Edit ⇨ Cut (Command-X) — before setting it down. I then selected the original image and applied the Unsharp Mask filter. Because the Pointillized image contains its own color detail, I could sharpen with impunity by entering 500 percent for the Amount value, 0.5 for Radius, and 5 for Threshold. After pressing Return, I chose Filter ⇨ Other ⇨ High Pass and applied a Radius value of 20.0. I then chose Edit ⇨ Paste (Command-V) to restore the floating selection and pressed 4 to change the Opacity slider bar value to 40 percent. The resulting image is crisp, clear, and chunky. Yes, friends, it's Cream of Moses soup, so hearty you can eat it with a fork.

Figure 12-44: Two results of applying the Pointillize filter to a floating selection, one in front of a standard image (left) and the other in front of a highly-sharpened image (right).

Removing noise

Now for the noise removal filters. Strictly speaking, the Despeckle command belongs in the Filter ⇨ Blur submenu. It blurs a selection while at the same time preserving its edges — the idea being that unwanted noise is most noticeable in the continuous regions of an image. In practice, this filter is nearly the exact opposite of the Sharpen Edges filter.

The Despeckle command searches an image for edges using the equivalent of an Unsharp Mask Threshold value of 5. It then ignores the edges in the image and blurs everything else with the force of the Blur More filter, as shown in the upper left image in Figure 12-45.

The remaining command in the Filter ⇨ Noise submenu, Median, removes noise by averaging the colors in an image, one pixel at a time. When you choose Filter ⇨ Noise ⇨ Median, Photoshop produces a Radius option box, into which you can enter any value between 1 and 16. For every pixel in a selection, the filter averages the colors of the neighboring pixels that fall inside the specified radius — ignoring any pixels that are so different they might skew the average — and applies the average color to the central pixel. As verified by Figure 12-45, large values produce the most destructive effects.

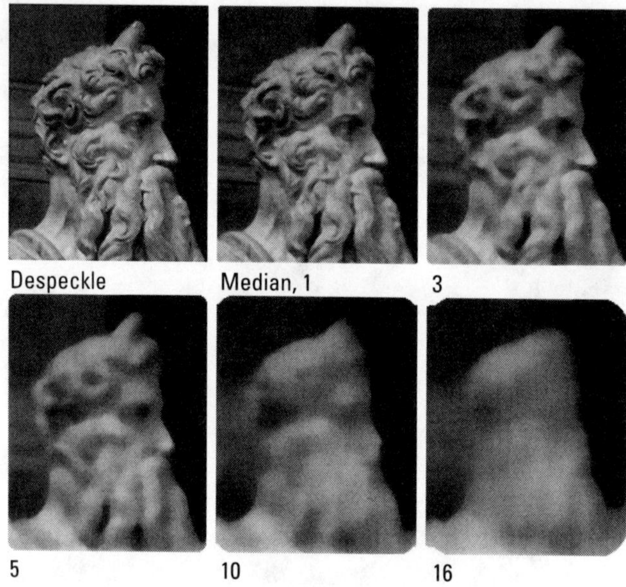

Figure 12-45: The effects of the Despeckle filter (upper left) and Median filter. The numbers indicate Median filter Radius values.

I mentioned at the beginning of the "Noise Factors" section that the Despeckle and Median filters are something of a wash for removing noise because they eliminate too much detail. However, you can apply the Median filter to a floating selection to mute an image and give it a plastic, molded quality, as demonstrated by the examples in Figure 12-46.

To create the left example, I cloned the image by selecting it and choosing Select ⇨ Float. I then chose Filter ⇨ Noise ⇨ Median and entered a Radius value of 3. After pressing Return, I pressed 6 to change the Opacity slider bar to 60 percent.

When used in this manner, the Median filter over-softens the image, even when constrained to a floating selection. To remedy this problem, I used the same tactics I used to fix the over-softening produced by the Pointillize filter in Figure 12-44. After applying Median, I cut the floating selection to the Clipboard, applied the Unsharp Mask filter to the original image at 500 percent, applied the High Pass filter with a 20-pixel radius, and pasted the floating selection back into place. To achieve the effect shown in the right-hand example of Figure 12-46, I pressed 8 to raise the opacity of the floating selection to 80 percent. The result is a gradually contoured image unlike anything you could accomplish using traditional techniques.

Figure 12-46: Two results of applying the Median filter to a floating selection, one in front of a standard image (left) and the other in front of a highly-sharpened image (right).

Destructive Filters

The first part of this chapter covered (in excruciating detail) all Filter menu commands under the Blur, Sharpen, and Noise submenus as well as the most important entries in the Other submenu. The "Deinterlacing" section of Chapter 6 covered Filter ⇨ Video ⇨ De-Interlace. That leaves the huge glut of commands in the Distort and Stylize submenus, which you learn about in the upcoming pages.

The Distort and Stylize commands are the destructive filters, as you may recall from the discussion near the beginning of this chapter. Don't get me wrong — they're a superb bunch of filters. But because they are arguably less utilitarian than the corrective filters covered so far, this book doesn't explain each and every one of them. Rather, I concentrate on the ones I think you'll use most often, breeze over a few others, and let you discover on your own the few that I ignore altogether.

The Wind and Pointillize filters, which reside under the Stylize submenus, are covered in greater depth in the discussion of the blur and noise filters earlier in this chapter. For complete information about Filter ⇨ Other ⇨ Custom and Filter ⇨ Distort ⇨ Displace, read the following chapter, "Constructing Homemade Effects."

The block filters

The Stylize submenu features a handful commands that rearrange your image into blocks of solid color:

- **Crystallize:** This filter organizes an image into irregularly shaped nuggets. You specify the size of the nuggets by entering a value from 3 to 999 pixels in the Cell Size option.
- **Facet:** Facet fuses areas of similarly colored pixels to create a sort of hand-painted effect.
- **Mosaic:** The Mosaic filter blends pixels together into larger squares. You specify the height and width of the squares by entering a value into the Cell Size option box.
- **Pointillize:** This filter is similar to Crystallize, except that it separates an image into disconnected nuggets set against the background color. As usual, you specify the size of the nuggets by changing the Cell Size value.

By applying one of these filters to a feathered selection, you can create what I call a Crystal Halo effect, named after the Crystallize filter, which tends to deliver the most successful results. (For a preview of these effects, sneak a peek at Figure 12-48.) The following steps explain how to create a Crystal Halo, using the images in Figures 12-47 and 12-48 as an example.

STEPS: Creating the Crystal Halo Effect

Step 1. Begin by selecting the foreground element around which you want to create the halo. Then choose Select ⇨ Inverse to deselect the foreground element and select the background.

Step 2. Enter the quick mask mode. Choose Filter ⇨ Other ⇨ Minimum to increase the size of the deselected area around the foreground element. The size of the Radius value depends on the size of the halo you want to create. For my part, I wanted a 15-pixel halo. Unfortunately, the Radius option box in the Minimum dialog box can't accommodate a value larger than 10. So I entered 10 the first time. When Photoshop finished applying the filter, I chose Filter ⇨ Other ⇨ Minimum again and entered 5.

Step 3. Choose Filter ⇨ Blur ⇨ Gaussian Blur and enter a Radius value 0.1 less than the amount by which you increased the size of the deselected area. In my case, I entered 14.9. The result appears in the left image in Figure 12-47.

Step 4. Choose Filter ➪ Stylize ➪ Crystallize and enter a moderate value into the Cell Size option box. I opted for the value 12, just slightly larger than the default value. After pressing Return, you get something along the lines of the selection outline shown in the right image in Figure 12-47. The filter refracts the softened edges, as if you were viewing them through textured glass.

Step 5. Switch back to the marching ants mode and use the selection as desired. I merely deleted the selection to produce the effect shown in the top left image in Figure 12-48. You may find this technique particularly useful for combining images. You can copy the selection and paste it against a different background or copy a background from a different image and choose Edit ➪ Paste Into to paste it inside the crystal halo's selection outline.

Figure 12-48 shows several variations on the Crystal Halo effect. To create the upper right image, I substituted Filter ➪ Stylize ➪ Facet for Filter ➪ Stylize ➪ Crystallize in Step 4. I also sharpened the result to increase the effect of the filter (which nevertheless remains subtle). To create the lower right image, I applied the Mosaic filter in place of Crystallize, using a Cell Size value of 8. Finally, to create the lower left image, I applied the Pointillize filter. Because Pointillize creates gaps in a selection, I had to paint inside Moses to fill in the gaps and isolate the halo effect to the background before returning to the marching ants mode.

Figure 12-47: Create a heavily feathered selection outline (left) and then apply the Crystallize filter to refract the feathered edges (right).

Figure 12-48: Which aura will Moses don today? The images illustrate the effects of applying each of four filters to a heavily feathered selection in the quick mask mode and pressing the Delete key. Clockwise from upper left, the filters used were Crystallize, Facet, Mosaic, and Pointillize.

The Emboss filter

Emboss adds dimension to an image by making it look like it was carved in relief. The filter works by searching for high-contrast edges (just like the Sharpen Edge and High Pass filters), highlighting the edges with black or white pixels, and coloring the low-contrast portions with medium gray.

When you choose Filter ⇨ Stylize ⇨ Emboss, Photoshop displays the Emboss dialog box shown in Figure 12-49. The dialog box offers three options:

- **Angle:** The value in this option box determines the angle at which Photoshop lights the image in relief. For example, if you enter a value of 90 degrees, you light the relief from the bottom straight upward. The white pixels therefore appear on the bottom sides of the edges, and the black pixels appear on the top sides. Figure 12-50 shows eight reliefs lit from different angles. I positioned the images so they appear lit from a single source.
- **Height:** The Emboss filter accomplishes its highlighting effect by displacing one copy of an image relative to another. You specify the distance between the copies using the Height option, which can vary from 1 to 10 pixels. Lower values produce crisp effects, as demonstrated in Figure 12-51. Values above 3 goop things up pretty good unless you also enter a high Amount value. Together, the Height and Amount values determine the depth of the image in relief.
- **Amount:** Enter a value between 1 and 500 percent to determine the amount of black and white assigned to pixels along the edges. Values of 50 percent and lower produce almost entirely gray images, as you can see in the top row of Figure 12-51. Higher values produce sharper edges, as if the relief were carved more deeply.

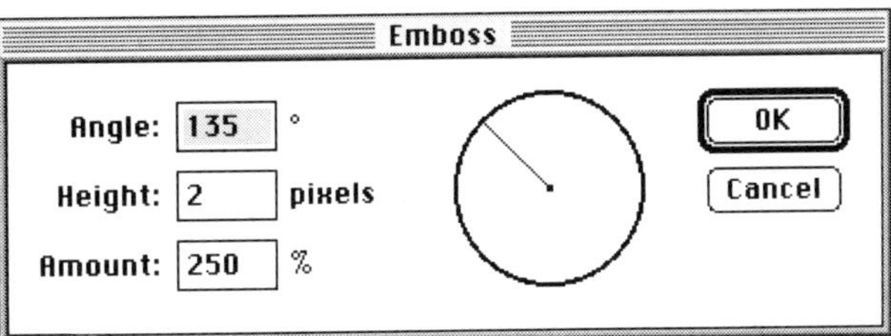

Figure 12-49: The Emboss dialog box allows you to control the depth of the filtered image and the angle from which it is lit.

As a stand-alone effect, Emboss is something of a dud. It's one of those filters that makes you gasp with delight the first time you see it but never quite lends itself to any practical application after you become acquainted with Photoshop. But if you think of Emboss as an extension of the High Pass filter, it takes on new meaning. You can use it to edit selection outlines in the quick mask mode, just as you might use the High Pass filter. You also can use it to draw out detail in an image.

Figure 12-52 shows Emboss applied to floating selections. To create the left example, I selected Darken from the brush mode pop-up menu in the Brushes palette in order to add shadows to the edges of the image, thus boosting the texture without unduly upsetting the original brightness values. I selected Lighten from the brush mode pop-up menu to create the right-hand example. In both cases, I applied the Emboss filter at an Angle of 135 degrees, a Height of 2 pixels, and an Amount of 250 percent. I also set the Opacity slider bar to 70 percent.

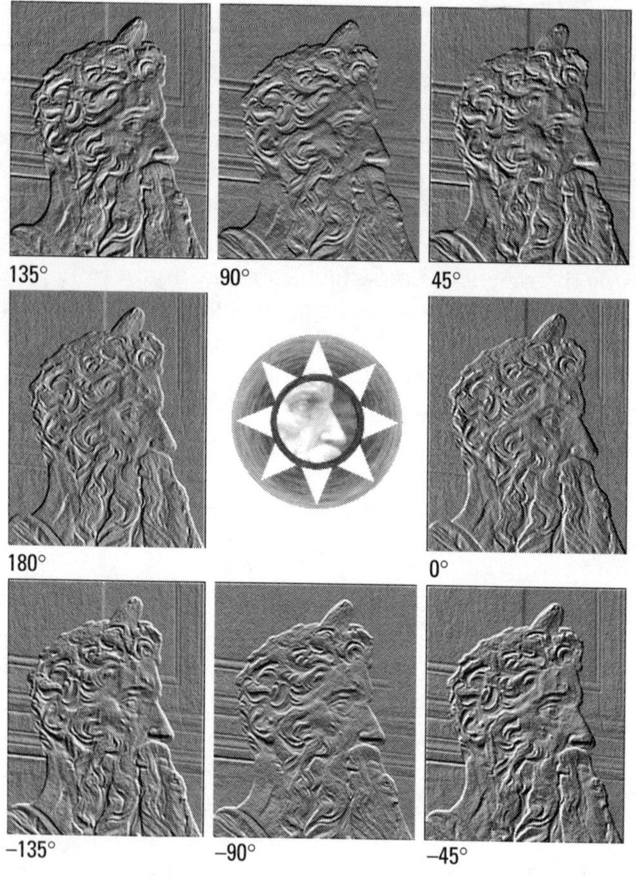

Figure 12-50: Reliefs lighted from eight different angles, in 45-degree increments. In all cases, the central sun image indicates the location of the light source. Height and Amount values of 1 pixel and 250 percent were used for all images.

To create a color relief effect, apply the Emboss filter to a floating selection and then select the Luminosity option from the brush mode pop-up menu. This sequence retains the colors from the original image while applying the lightness and darkness of the pixels from the floating selection. The effect looks something like an inked lithographic plate, with steel grays and vivid colors mixing together.

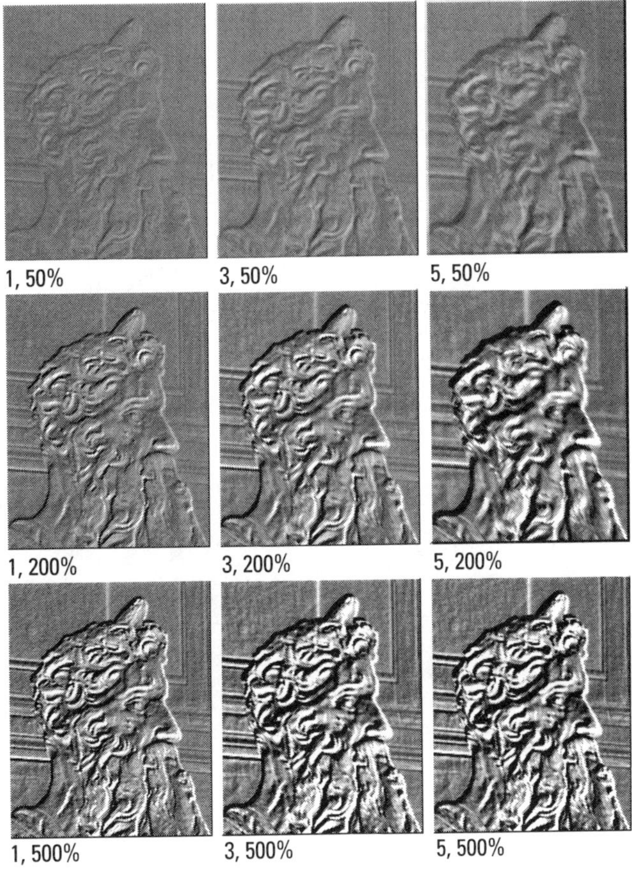

Figure 12-51: Examples of different Height settings (first value) and Amount settings (second value). The Angle value used for each image was 135 degrees.

Figure 12-52: I limited the effect of the Emboss filter to darkening the image (left) and then to lightening the image (right) by applying the filter to a floating, translucent selection.

Distortion filters

For the most part, commands in the Distort submenu are related by the fact that they move colors in an image to achieve unusual stretching, swirling, and vibrating effects. They're rather like the transformation commands from the Image ⇨ Effects submenu, in that they perform their magic by relocating and interpolating colors rather than by altering brightness and color values.

The distinction, of course, it that while the transformation commands let you scale and distort images by manipulating four control points, the Distort filters provide the equivalent of hundreds of control points, all of which you can use to affect different portions of an image. In some cases, you're projecting an image into a fun-house mirror; other times, it's a reflective pool. You can fan images, wiggle them, and change them in ways that have no correlation to real life, as illustrated in Figure 12-53.

Figure 12-53: Your image (left); your image on distortion filters (right).

Distortion filters are very powerful tools. Although they are easy to apply, they are extremely difficult to use well. Here are some rules to keep in mind:

- **Practice makes practical:** Distortion filters are like complex vocabulary words. You don't want to use them without practicing a little first. Experiment with a distortion filter several times before trying to use it in a real project. You may even want to write down the steps you take so you can remember how you created an effect.
- **Use caution during tight deadlines:** Distortion filters are enormous time-wasters. Unless you know exactly how you want to proceed, you may want to avoid using them when time is short. The last thing you need when you're working under the gun is to get trapped trying to pull off a weird effect.

- **Apply selectively:** The effects of distortion filters are too severe to inflict all at once. You can achieve marvelous, subtle effects by distorting feathered and floating selections. Although I wouldn't call the image in Figure 12-53 subtle, no effect was applied to the entire image. I applied the Spherize filter to a feathered elliptical marquee that included most of the image. I then reapplied Spherize to the eye. I selected the hair and beard and applied the Ripple filter twice. Finally, after establishing two heavily feathered vertical columns on either side of the image in the quick mask mode, I applied the Polar Coordinates filter, which reflected the front and back of the head. Turn the book upside down and you'll see a second face.
- **Combine creatively:** Don't expect a single distortion to achieve the desired effect. If one application isn't enough, apply the filter again. Try experimenting with combining different distortions.
- **Save your original:** Never distort an image until you save it. After you start down Distortion Boulevard, the only way to go back is File ⇨ Revert. If you have the disk space, you may even want to save your image under a different name after every distortion so you can back up a few steps if you run into a dead end.

Distortion filters interpolate between pixels to create their fantastic effects. Therefore, the quality of your filtered images is dependent on the setting of the Interpolation option in the General Preferences dialog box. If a filter is producing jagged effects, the Nearest Neighbor option may be selected. Try selecting the Bicubic or Bilinear option instead.

Reflecting an image in a spoon

Most folks take their first ventures into distortion filters by using Pinch and Spherize. Pinch maps an image onto the inside of a sphere or similarly curved surface; Spherize maps it onto the outside of a sphere. It's sort of like looking at your reflection on the inside or outside of a spoon.

You can apply Pinch to a scanned face to squish the features toward the center or you can apply Spherize to accentuate the girth of the nose. Figure 12-54 illustrates both effects. It's a laugh, and you pretty much feel as though you're onto something no one else ever thought of before. (At least that's how I felt — but I'm easily amazed.)

Figure 12-54: The stereotypical rookie applications for the Pinch (left) and Spherize (right) filters.

You can pinch or spherize an image using either the Pinch or Spherize command. As shown in Figure 12-55, a positive value in the Pinch dialog box produces the same effect as a negative value in the Spherize dialog box. In fact, the only difference between the two filters in terms of capabilities is that Spherize lets you wrap an image not only onto a sphere, but also onto the inside or outside of a horizontal or vertical cylinder. To try out these effects, select the Horizontal Only or Vertical Only radio button in the lower left corner of the Spherize dialog box.

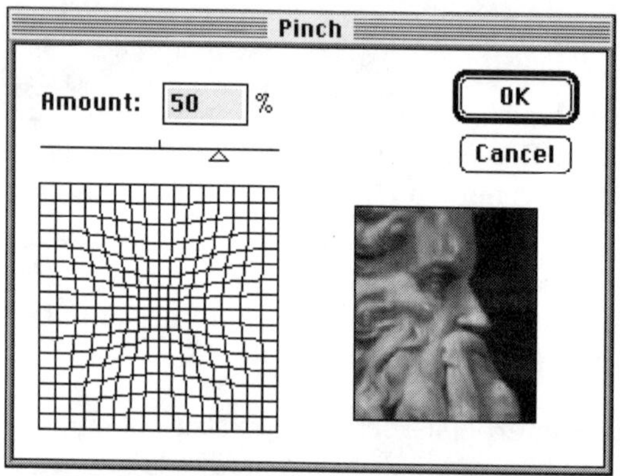

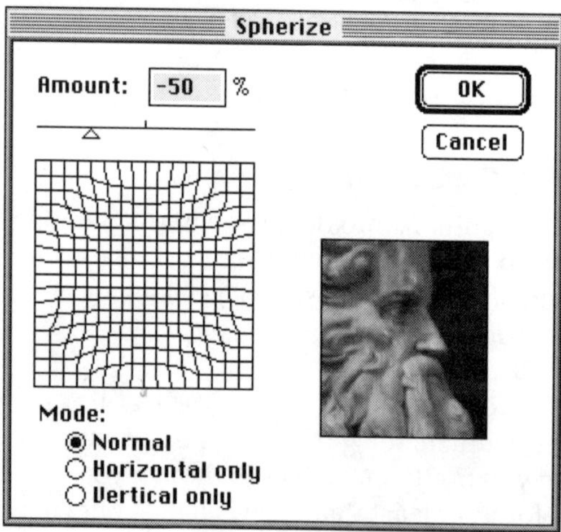

Figure 12-55: Both the Pinch and Spherize dialog boxes enable you to pinch or spherize an image.

Remember that the previews, grids, and slider bars shown in Figure 12-55 only show up if you're using Photoshop 2.5. Even then, they appear only if you Option-chose a distortion filter name from the Apple ⇨ About Plug-ins submenu and turned on the Show Previews & Sliders check box, as described in the "Previewing filters" section earlier in this chapter.

Both the Pinch and Spherize filters are applicable only to elliptical regions of an image. If a selection outline is not elliptical in shape, Photoshop applies the filter to the largest ellipse that fits inside the selection. As a result, the filter may leave behind a noticeable elliptical boundary between the affected an unaffected portions of the selection. To avoid this effect, select the region you want to edit with the elliptical marquee tool and then feather the selection before filtering it. This softens the effect of the filter and provides a more gradual transition.

One of the more remarkable properties of the Pinch filter is that it lets you turn any image into a conical gradation. Figure 12-56 illustrates how the process works.

First, blur the image to eliminate any harsh edges between color transitions. Then apply the Pinch filter at full strength (100 percent). Reapply the filter several more times. Each time you press Command-F, the center portion of the image recedes farther and farther into the distance, as shown in Figure 12-56. After 10 repetitions, the face in the example all but disappeared.

Next, apply the Radial Blur filter, set to Spin 10 pixels or so to mix the color boundaries a bit. The result is a type of gradation you can't create using Photoshop's gradient tool.

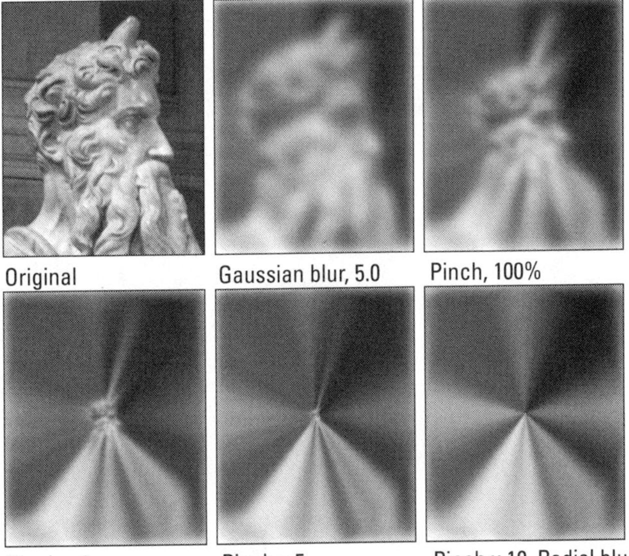

Figure 12-56: After applying the Gaussian Blur filter, I pinched the image 10 times and applied the Radial Blur filter to create a conical gradation.

Twirling spirals

The Twirl filter rotates the center of a selection while leaving the sides fixed in place. The result is a spiral of colors that looks for all the world as if you poured the image into a blender set to a very slow speed.

When you choose Filter ⇨ Distort ⇨ Twirl, Photoshop displays the Twirl dialog box, shown in Figure 12-57. Enter a positive value from 1 to 999 degrees to spiral the image in a clockwise direction. Enter a negative value to spiral the image in a counterclockwise direction. As you are probably already aware, 360 degrees make a full circle, so the maximum 999-degree value equates to spiral that circles around approximately three times, as shown in the bottom right example in Figure 12-58.

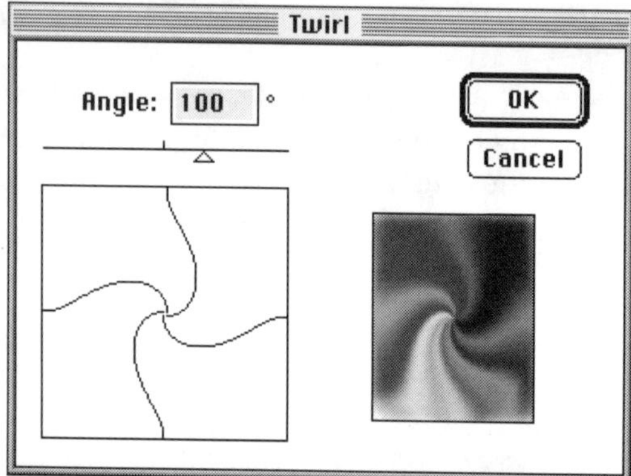

Figure 12-57: The Twirl dialog box lets you create spiraling images.

The Twirl filter produces smoother effects when you use lower Angle values. Therefore, you're better off applying a 100-degree spiral 10 times rather than applying a 999-degree spiral once, as verified by Figure 12-58.

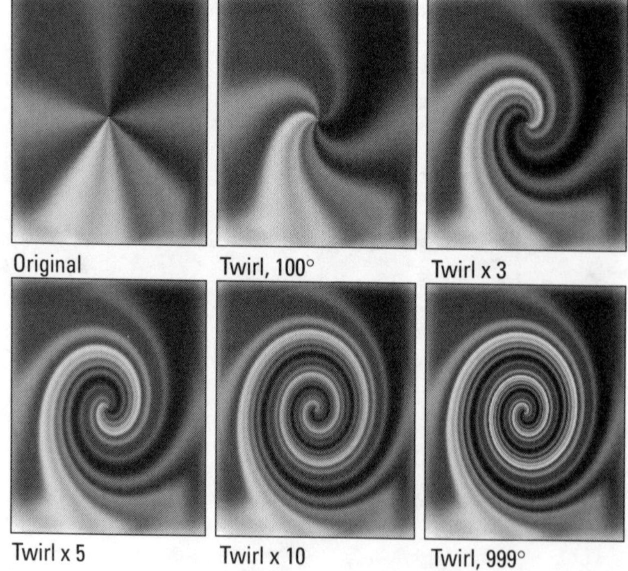

Figure 12-58: Effects of applying the Twirl filter. Repeatedly applying the Twirl filter at a moderate value (bottom middle) produces a smoother effect than applying the filter once at a high value (bottom right).

In addition to creating ice-cream swirls like those shown in Figure 12-58, you can use the Twirl filter to create organic images virtually from scratch, as witnessed by Figures 12-59 and 12-60.

To create the images shown in Figure 12-59, I used the Spherize filter to flex the conical gradation vertically by entering 100 percent in the Amount option box and selecting Vertical Only from the Mode radio buttons. After repeating this filter several times, I eventually achieved a stalactite-stalagmite effect, as shown in the center example of the figure. I then repeatedly applied the Twirl filter to curl the flexed gradations like two symmetrical hairs. The result merges the simplicity of pure math with the beauty of bitmapped imagery.

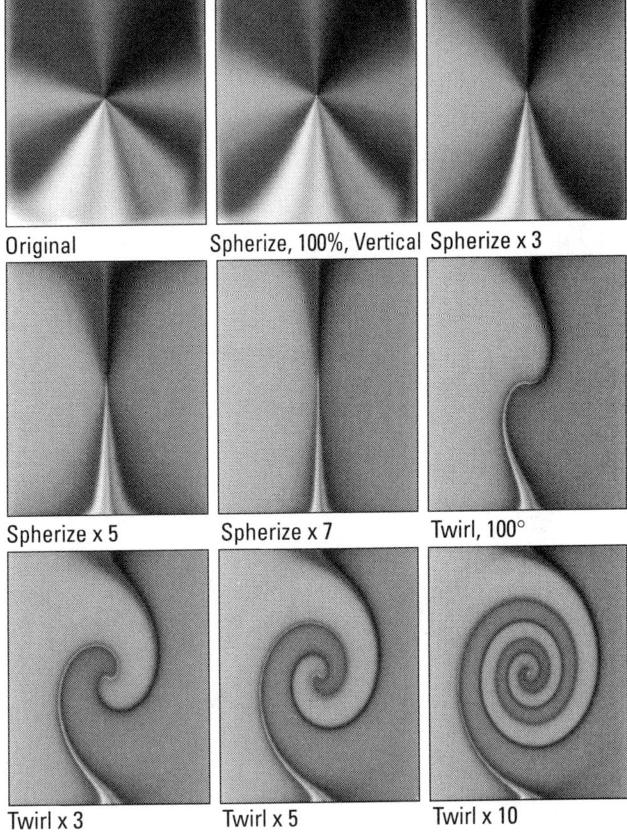

Figure 12-59: You can create surprisingly naturalistic effects using distortion filters exclusively.

Figure 12-60 illustrates a droplet technique designed by Mark Collen. I took the liberty of breaking down the technique into the following steps.

STEPS: Creating a Thick-liquid Droplet

Step 1. Click on the default colors icon to restore black as the foreground color and white as the background color. Select a square portion of an image by dragging with the rectangular marquee tool while pressing the Shift key.

Step 2. Drag inside the selection outline with the gradient tool. Drag a short distance near the center of the selection from upper left to lower right, creating the gradation shown in the top left box in Figure 12-60.

Step 3. Choose the Twirl filter and apply it at 360 degrees so that the spiral moves counterclockwise. To create the top right image in the figure, I applied the Twirl filter three times. Each repetition of the filter adds another ring of ripples.

Step 4. Choose Select ⇨ Float (Command-J) to clone the image. Then choose Image ⇨ Flip ⇨ Horizontal.

Step 5. Select the rectangular marquee tool. Press 5 to change the Opacity slider bar in the Brushes palette to 50 percent. The result is shown in the lower left image in Figure 12-60.

Step 6. Choose Image ⇨ Rotate ⇨ 90° CW to rotate the image a quarter turn, thus creating the last image in the figure. You can achieve other interesting effects by choosing Lighten, Darken, and others from the brush mode pop-up menu.

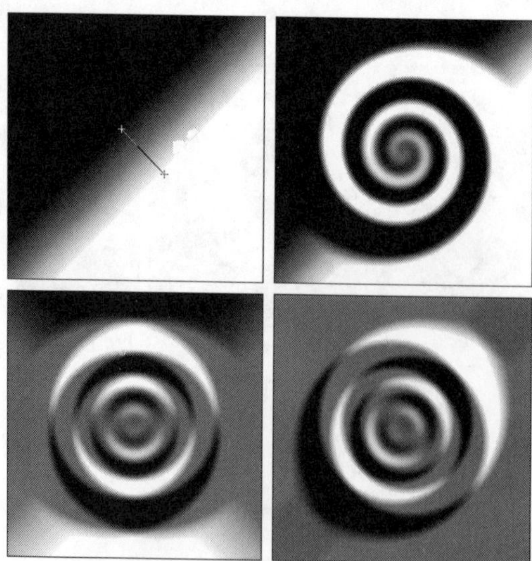

Figure 12-60: If you know your way around Photoshop, you may at first misinterpret the bottom two images as the result of the Zigzag filter, discussed in the next section. In fact, they were created entirely by using the gradient tool and Twirl filter and then applying a couple of transformations to a floating selection.

Creating concentric pond ripples

I don't know about you, but when I think of zigzags, I think of cartoon lighting bolts, wriggling snakes, scribbles — anything that alternately changes directions along an axis, like the letter *Z*. The Zigzag filter does arrange colors into zigzag patterns, but it does so in a radial fashion, meaning that the zigzags emanate from the center of the image like spokes in a wheel. The result is a series of concentric ripples. If you want parallel zigzags, check out the Ripple and Wave filters, described in the next section. (The Zigzag filter creates ripples and the Ripple filter creates zigzags. Go figure.)

When you choose Filter ⇨ Distort ⇨ Zigzag, Photoshop displays the Zigzag dialog box shown in Figure 12-61. The dialog box offers the following options:

- **Amount:** Enter an amount between negative and positive 100 in whole-number increments to specify the depth of the ripples. If you enter a negative value, the ripples descend below the surface. If you enter a positive value, the ripples protrude upward. Examples of three representative Amount values appear in Figure 12-62.
- **Ridges:** This option box controls the number of ripples in the selected area and accepts any value from 1 to 20. Figure 12-63 demonstrates the effect of three Ridges values.
- **Pond Ripples:** This option is really a cross between the two that follow. It moves pixels outward and rotates them around the center of the selection to create circular patterns. As demonstrated in the top rows of Figures 12-62 and 12-63, this option truly results in a pond ripple effect.
- **Out From Center:** When you select this option, Photoshop moves pixels outward in rhythmic bursts according to the value in the Ridges option box. Because the gradation image I created in Figure 12-56 was already arranged in a radial pattern, I brought in Moses to demonstrate the effect of the Out From Center option, as shown in the second rows of Figures 12-62 and 12-63.
- **Around Center:** Select this option to rotate pixels in alternating directions around the circle without moving them outward. This option is the only one that produces what I would term a zigzag effect. The last rows of Figures 12-62 and 12-63 show the effects of the Around Center option.

Figure 12-61: The Zigzag dialog box lets you add concentric ripples to an image, as if the image were reflected in a pond into which you dropped a pebble.

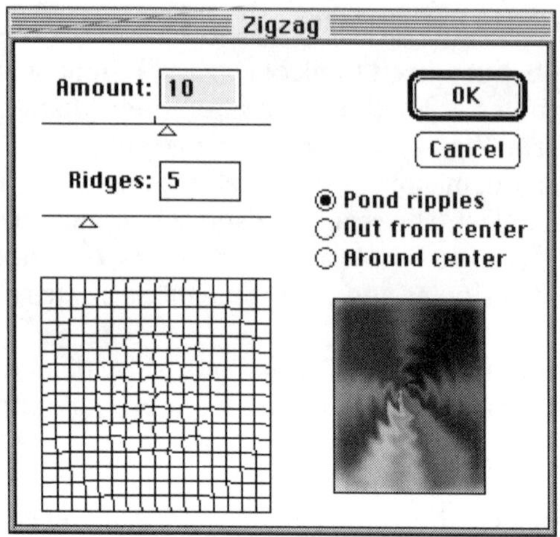

Figure 12-62: The effects of the Zigzag filter subject to three Amount values and the Pond Ripples, Out From Center, and Around Center settings. In all cases, the Ridges value was 5.

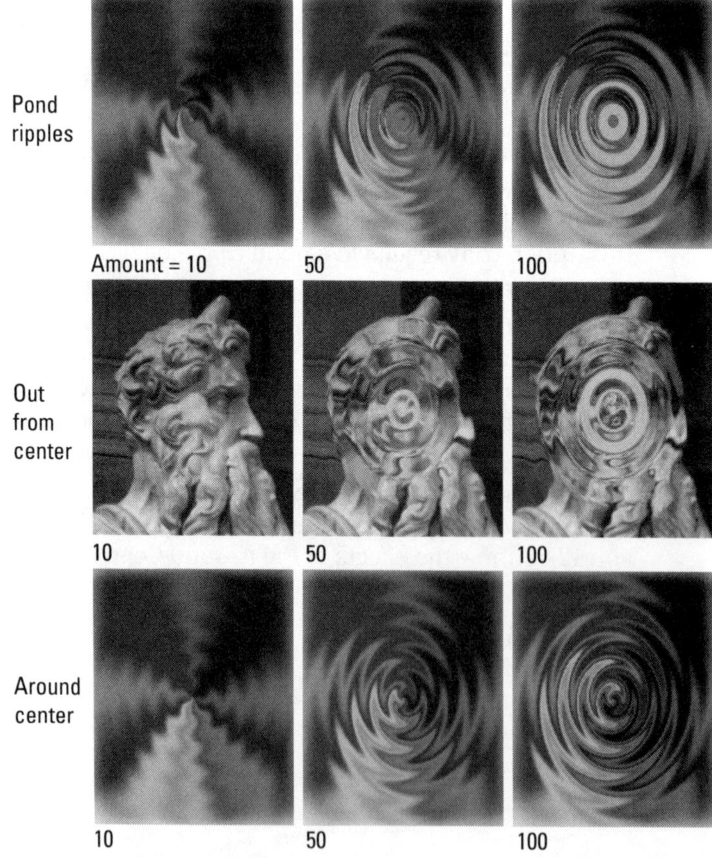

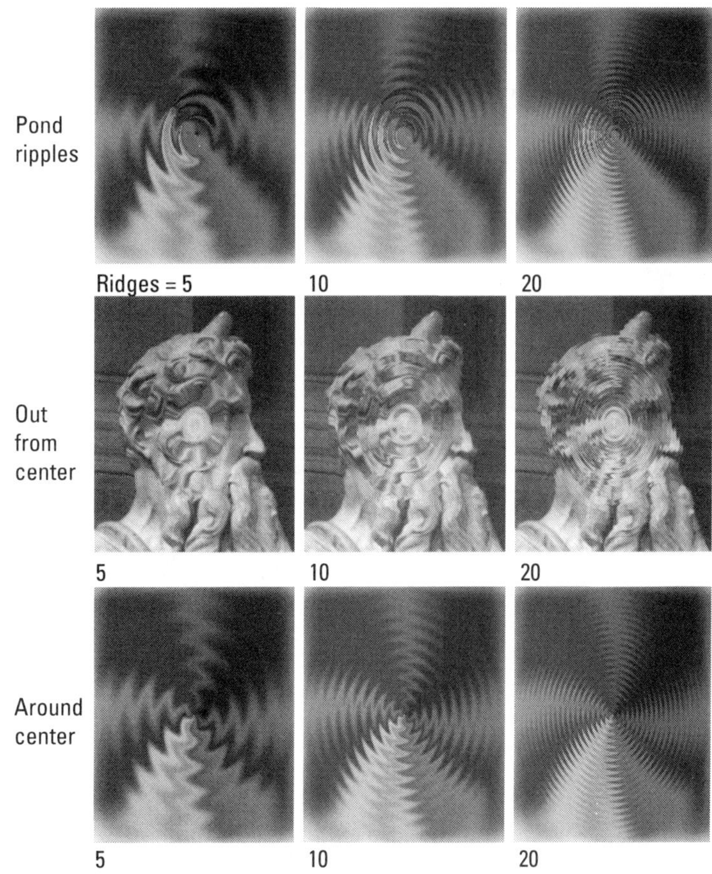

Figure 12-63: The effects of the Zigzag filter using three Ridges values and each of the three radio button settings. In all cases, the Amount value was 20.

Creating parallel ripples and waves

Photoshop provides two means to distort an image in parallel waves, as if the image were lying on the bottom of a shimmering or undulating pool. Of the two, the Ripple filter is less sophisticated, but it's also straightforward and easy to apply. The Wave filter affords you greater control, but its options are among the most complex Photoshop has to offer.

To use the Ripple filter, choose Filter ⇨ Distort ⇨ Ripple. Photoshop displays the Ripple dialog box shown in Figure 12-64. You have the following options:

- **Amount:** Enter an amount between negative and positive 999 in whole-number increments to specify the width of the ripples from side to side. Negative and positive values change the direction of the ripples, but visually speaking, they produce identical effects. The ripples are measured as a ratio of the Size value and the dimensions of the selection — all of which translates to, "Experiment and see what happens." You can count on getting ragged effects from any value over 300, as illustrated in Figure 12-65.

- **Size:** Select one of the three radio buttons to change the length of the ripples. The Small option results in the shortest ripples and therefore the most ripples. As shown in the upper right corner of Figure 12-65, you can create a textured glass effect by combining the Small option with a high Amount value. The Large option results in the longest and fewest ripples.

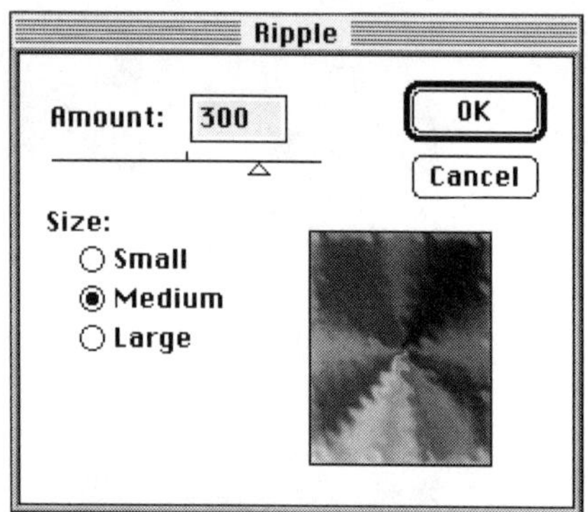

Figure 12-64: The Ripple filter makes an image appear as if it were refracted through flowing water.

You can create a blistered effect by overlaying a negative ripple onto a positive ripple. Try this: First, copy the selection. Then apply the Ripple filter with a positive Amount value — say, 300. Next, paste the copied selection and apply the Ripple filter at the exact opposite Amount value, in this case, –300. Press 5 to change the Opacity slider bar to 50 percent. The result is a series of diametrically opposed ripples that cross each other to create teardrop blisters.

Now that you're familiar with the Ripple filter, it's on to the Wave filter. I could write a book on this filter alone. It wouldn't be very big, nobody would buy it, and I'd hate every minute of it, but you never know what a free-lancer will do next. Keep an eye out at your local bookstore. In the meantime, I'm going to breeze though this filter like a little dog on the Oz-bound Kansas Express.

Here goes: Choose Filter ⇨ Distort ⇨ Wave (that's the easy part) to display the Wave dialog box shown in Figure 12-66. Photoshop presents you with the following options, which makes applying a distortion almost every bit as fun as operating an oscilloscope:

- **Number of Generators:** Right off the bat, the Wave dialog box boggles the brain. A friend of mine likened this option to the number of rocks you throw in the water to start it rippling. One generator means you throw in one rock to create one set of waves, as demonstrated in Figure 12-67. You can throw in two rocks to create two sets of waves (see Figure 12-68), three rocks to create three sets of

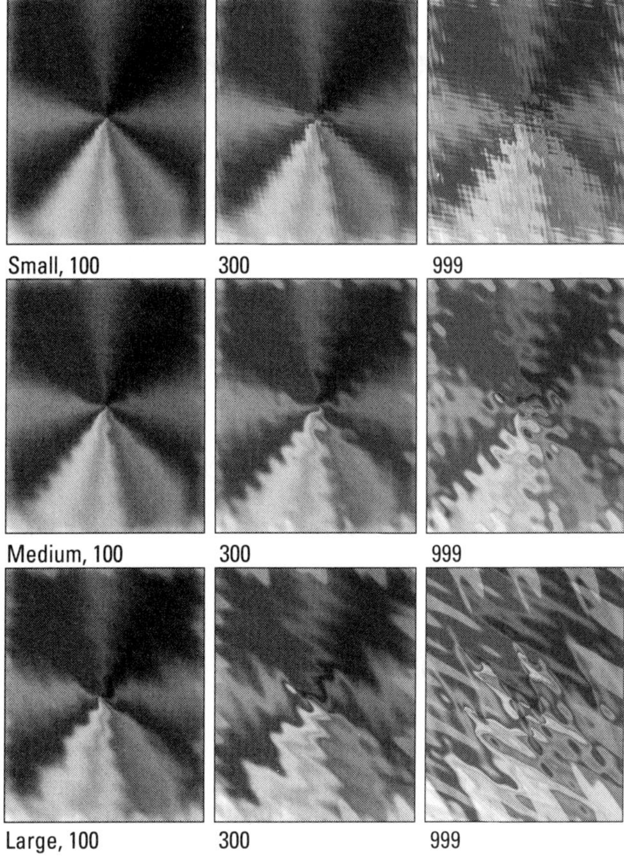

Figure 12-65: The effects of combining three different Ripple filter Amount values with three different Size settings.

waves, and all the way up to a quarry-full of 999 rocks to create, well, you get the idea. If you enter a high value, however, be prepared to wait a few years for the preview to update. If you can't wait, press Command-period, which turns off the preview until the next time you enter the dialog box.

- **Wavelength and Amplitude:** Beginning to feel like you're playing with a HAM radio? The Wave filter produces random results by varying the number and length of waves (Wavelength) as well as the width of the waves (Amplitude) between minimum and maximum values, which can range anywhere from 1 to 999. (The Wavelength and Amplitude options, therefore, correspond in theory to the Size and Amount options in the Ripple dialog box.) Figures 12-67 and 12-68 show examples of representative Wavelength and Amplitude values.

- **Scale:** You can scale the effects of the Wave filter anywhere between 1 and 100 percent horizontally and vertically. (The Photoshop 2.5 manual states that you can go all the way up to 9,999 percent and that negative values are possible. Neither statement is true.) All the effects featured in Figures 12-67 and 12-68 were created by setting both Scale options to 15 percent.
- **Undefined Areas:** The Wave filter distorts a selection to the extent that gaps may appear around the edges. You can either fill those gaps by repeating pixels along the edge of the selection, as in the figures, or by wrapping pixels from the left side of the selection onto the right side and pixels from the top edge of the selection onto the bottom.
- **Type:** You can select from three kinds of waves. The Sine option produces standard sine waves that rise and fall smoothly in bell-shaped curves, just like real waves. The Triangle option creates zigzags that rise and fall in straight lines, like the edge of a piece of fabric cut with pinking shears. The Square option has nothing to do with waves at all, but rather organizes an image into a series of rectangular groupings, reminiscent of Cubism. You might think of this option as an extension of the Mosaic filter. All three options are demonstrated in Figures 12-67 and 12-68.
- **Randomize:** The Wave filter is random by nature. If you don't like the effect you see in the preview box, click on the Randomize button to stir things up a bit. You can keep clicking on the button until you get an effect you like.

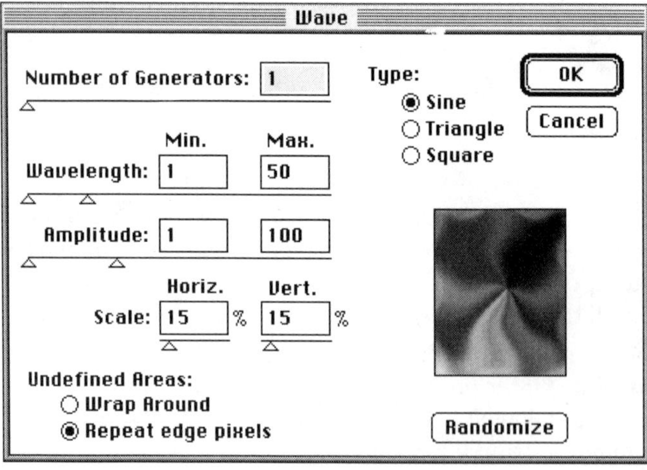

Figure 12-66: The Wave dialog box enables you to wreak scientific havoc on an image. Put on your pocket protector, take out your slide rule, and give it a whirl.

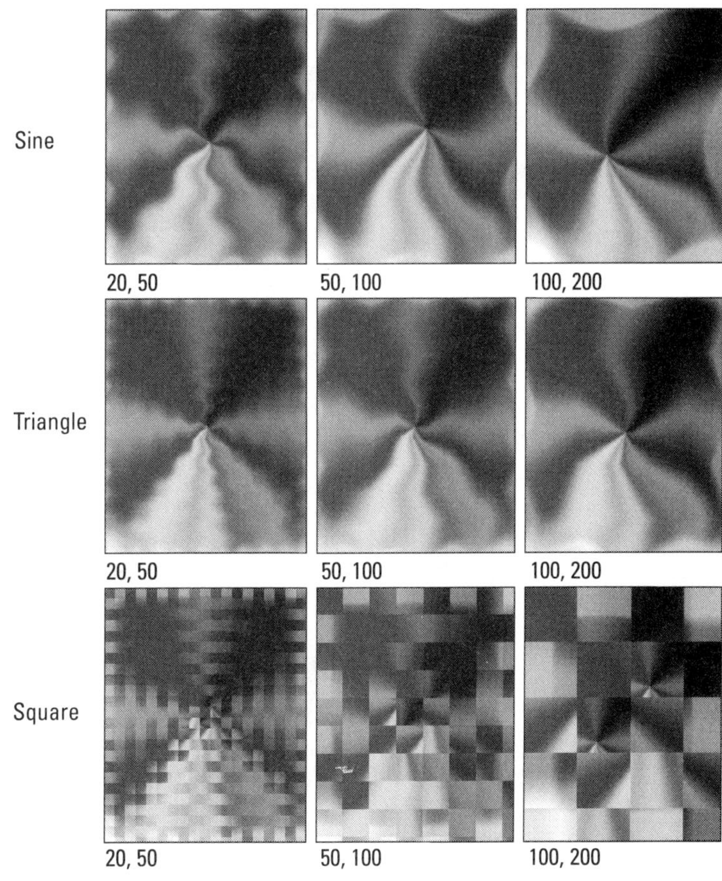

Figure 12-67: The effect of three sets of Maximum Wavelength (first value) and Amplitude (second value) settings when combined with each of the three Type settings. The Number of Generators value used was 1 in all cases.

If you have not activated Photoshop 2.5's distortion filter previewing capabilities (by Option-choosing a distortion filter name from the Apple ⇨ About Plug-ins submenu), a Randomize parameters check box appears in place of the button. When the check box is turned off, the Wave filter produces consistent results over the course of the selection. When the check box is turned on, the filter randomly changes the length and width of the waves within the ranges specified in the Wavelength and Amplitude options.

Figure 12-68: The only difference between these images and their counterparts in Figure 12-67 is that the Number of Generators value used for all images was 2.

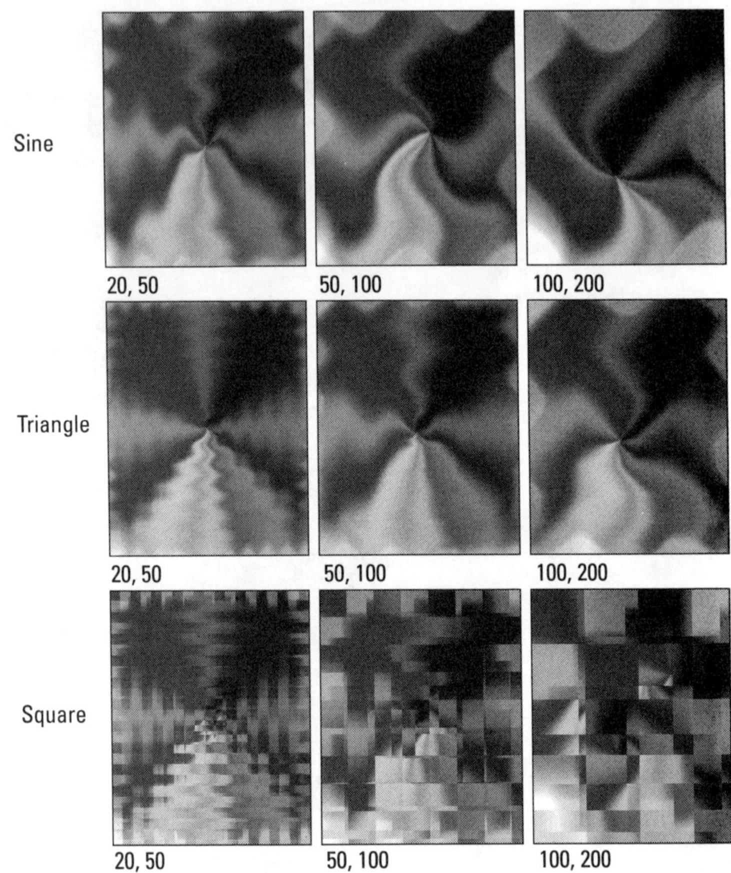

Changing to polar coordinates

The Polar Coordinates filter is another one of those gems that a lot of folks shy away from because it doesn't make much sense at first glance. When you choose Filter ⇨ Distort ⇨ Polar Coordinates, Photoshop presents two radio buttons, as shown in Figure 12-69. You can either map an image from rectangular to polar coordinates or from polar to rectangular coordinates.

All right, time for some global theory. The top image in Figure 12-70 shows a stretched detail of the world map included in the default System 7 Scrapbook file. Though a tad simplistic, this map falls under the heading of a *Mercator projection,* meaning that Greenland is all stretched out of proportion, looking as big as the United States and Mexico combined.

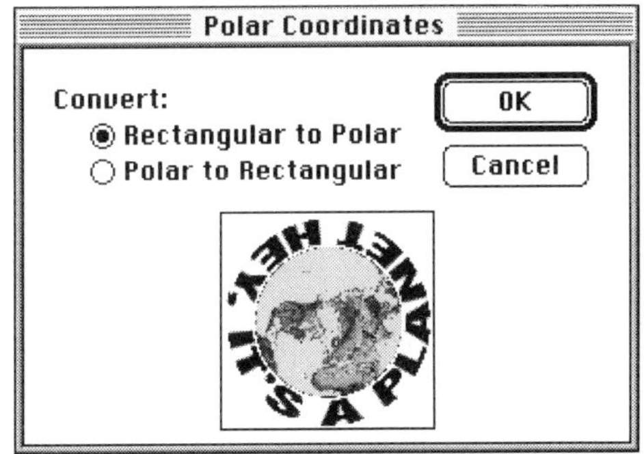

Figure 12-69: In effect, the Polar Coordinates dialog box lets you map an image onto a globe and view the globe from above.

The reason for this result has to do with the way different mapping systems handle longitude and latitude lines. On a spherical globe, lines of latitude converge at the poles. On a Mercator map, they run absolutely parallel. Because the Mercator map exaggerates the distance between longitude lines as you progress away from the equator, it likewise exaggerates the distance between lines of latitude. The result is a map that becomes infinitely enormous at each of the poles.

Figure 12-70: The world from the equator up expressed in rectangular (top) and polar (bottom) coordinates.

When you convert the map to polar coordinates (by selecting the Rectangular to Polar radio button in the Polar Coordinates dialog box), you look down on it from the extreme north or south pole. The entire length of the top edge of the Mercator map becomes a single dot in the exact center of the polar projection. The length of the bottom edge of the map wraps around the entire perimeter of the circle. The bottom example in Figure 12-70 shows the result. As you can see, the Rectangular to Polar option is just the thing for wrapping text around a circle.

If you select the Polar to Rectangular option, the Polar Coordinates filter produces the opposite effect. Imagine for a moment that the conical gradation shown in the upper left corner of Figure 12-71 is a fan spread out into a full circle. Now imagine closing the fan, breaking the hinge at the top, and spreading out the rectangular fabric of the fan. The center of the fan unfolds to form the top edge of the fabric, and what was once the perimeter of the circle is now the bottom edge of the fabric. Figure 12-71 shows two examples of what happens when you convert circular images from polar to rectangular coordinates.

Figure 12-71: Two familiar circular images (left) converted from polar to rectangular coordinates (right). The top example is simple enough that you can probably predict the results of the conversion in your head. The lower example looks cool, but you'd need a brain extension to predict the outcome.

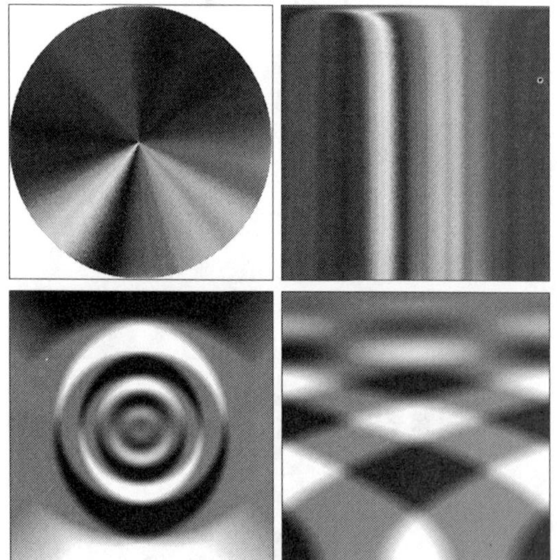

Distorting an image inside out

The following exercise describes how to achieve a sizzling Parting of the Red Sea effect. Though it incorporates several distortion filters, the star of the effect is the Polar Coordinates filter, which is used to turn the image inside out and then convert it back to polar coordinates after flipping it upside down. No scanned image or artistic talent is required. Rumor has it that Moses puts in a guest appearance in the final image.

This effect is the brainchild of Mark Collen, easily the most authoritative filtering expert I've had the pleasure of knowing. I already mentioned his name twice in this chapter, in connection with the "Previewing a Dissipated Filter" and "Creating a Thick-liquid Droplet" steps. To be perfectly honest, I probably should have mentioned him more than that, because many of the ideas conveyed in this chapter were based on long, expensive telephone conversations with the guy.

At any rate, Figures 12-72 through 12-77 show the progression of the image through the following steps, starting with a simplistic throwback to Dada (the art movement, not the family member) and continuing to the fabled sea rising in billowing streams. Color Plate 12-3 shows one of Mark's most vivid images, which was created in part using many of the techniques from the steps below. Obviously, a lot of other filtering and nonfiltering techniques were used to create that image, but gee whiz folks, you can't expect the guy to share everything he knows in one fell swoop. He has to make a living, after all.

STEPS: The Parting of the Red Sea Effect

Step 1. Draw some random shapes in whatever colors you like. My shapes appear against a black background in Figure 12-72, but you can use any shapes and any colors you like. To create each shape, I used the lasso tool to draw the outline of the shape and pressed Option-Delete to fill the lassoed selection with the foreground color. The effect works best if there's a lot of contrast between your colors.

Figure 12-72: Draw several meaningless shapes with the lasso tool and fill each with a different color.

Step 2. In Step 3, you apply the Wind Filter to add streaks to the shapes you just created, as shown in Figure 12-73. Because the Wind filter creates horizontal streaks only, and your goal is to add vertical streaks, you must temporarily reorient your image before applying the filter. To do so, choose Image ➪ Rotate ➪ 90° CCW, which rotates the entire image a quarter turn counterclockwise.

Step 3. Choose Filter ⇨ Stylize ⇨ Wind. Select Blast and Left and press Return. To randomize the image in both directions, choose the Wind filter again and select Blast and Right.

Step 4. Choose Image ⇨ Rotate ⇨ 90° CW to return the image to its original orientation.

Step 5. Choose Filter ⇨ Blur ⇨ Motion Blur. Enter 90 degrees into the Angle option and use 20 pixels for the Distance option. This blurs the image vertically to soften the blast lines, as demonstrated in Figure 12-73.

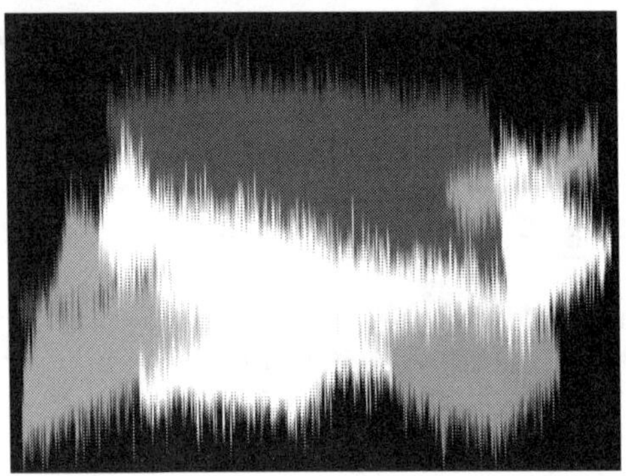

Figure 12-73: The result of rotating the image a quarter turn, blasting it in both directions with the Wind filter, rotating it back into place, and applying the Motion Blur filter vertically.

Step 6. Choose Filter ⇨ Distort ⇨ Wave and enter the values shown in Figure 12-74 into the Wave option box. Most of these values are approximate. You can experiment with other settings if you like. The only essential value is 0 percent in the Horiz. option box, which ensures that the filter waves the image in a vertical direction only.

Wave

Number of Generators: 3

Type: Sine / Triangle / Square

OK

Cancel

	Min.	Max.
Wavelength:	9	29
Amplitude:	1	18

	Horiz.	Vert.
Scale:	0 %	73 %

Undefined Areas:
Wrap Around
Repeat edge pixels

Randomize

Figure 12-74: Apply these settings from the Wave dialog box to wave the image in a vertical direction only.

Step 7. Choose Filter ➪ Distort ➪ Ripple. I entered 300 for the Amount value and selected the Medium radio button.

Step 8. To perform the next step, the Polar Coordinates filter needs lots of empty room in which to maneuver. If you filled up your canvas like I did, choose Image ➪ Canvas size and add 200 pixels both vertically and horizontally. The new canvas size, offering generous borders, appears in Figure 12-75.

Figure 12-75: After applying the Ripple filter, use the Canvas Size command to add a generous amount of empty space around the image.

Step 9. So far, you've probably been a little disappointed by your image. I mean, it's just this disgusting little hairy thing that looks like a bad rug or something. Well, now's your chance to turn it into something special. Choose Filter ➪ Distort ➪ Polar Coordinates and select the Polar to Rectangular radio button. Photoshop in effect turns the image inside out, sending all the hairy edges to the bottom of the screen. Finally, an image worth waiting for.

Step 10. Choose Image ➪ Flip ➪ Vertical to turn the image upside down. The hair now rises, as shown in Figure 12-76. This step prepares the image for the next polar conversion. Without it, you would just end up undoing the effect created in Step 9.

Step 11. Use the rectangular marquee tool to select the central portion of the image. Leave deselected about 50 pixels along the top and bottom of the image and 100 pixels along both sides. Then feather the selection with a 15-pixel radius.

Figure 12-76: Convert the image from polar to rectangular coordinates to turn it inside out. Then flip it vertically to prepare it for the next polar conversion.

Step 12. Press Command-Option-F to redisplay the Polar Coordinates dialog box. Select the Rectangular to Polar option and press Return. The pixels inside the selection now billow into a fountain.

Step 13. Add Moses to taste. The finished image appears in Figure 12-77.

Figure 12-77: Marquee the central portion of the image with a heavily feathered selection outline, convert the selection from rectangular to polar coordinates, and put Moses into the scene. My, doesn't he look natural in his new environment?

Third-Party Filtering Tools

Adobe has structured Photoshop so that third-party vendors can create specialized filters you can use inside the application. The program also allows vendors to produce hardware that speeds up various Photoshop functions. In fact, Photoshop is perhaps the only graphics program on the Mac that supports its own flourishing cottage industry of third-party solutions.

Filter collections

As I write this, four companies provide filters for use in Photoshop:

- **Aldus Gallery Effects:** A lot of folks love Gallery Effects. In my opinion, they're expensive and uninspired. Nevertheless, Aldus sells two Gallery Effects packages, Classic Art Volumes 1 and 2, which provide 17 and 16 filters respectively. Volume 2 assembles the better collection and it's slightly less expensive, but it remains a mixed bag, as demonstrated by Figure 12-78. The top two images illustrate the effects of the Patchwork and Underpainting filters. These filters provide access to interesting texturing techniques. But the Bas Relief filter (lower left) does more to block out detail than provide depth, like an overly softened Emboss filter. And the Stamp filter (lower right) just globs up an image and applies a Threshold effect. Neither Bas Relief nor Stamp provides sufficient controls, and the controls they do provide are unpredictable. In the final analysis, both Kai's Power Tools and Xaos Tools Paint Alchemy provide a wider range of more powerful options.
- **Andromeda Photography Series:** Sadly, I know next to nothing about these filters. The only examples I've seen are the two that are included with Photoshop 2.5. One creates specialized motion blurs; the other duplicates an image to create a network of reflections. Both filters are demos, meaning that you can preview effects but can't apply them. I made many attempts to reach the company to obtain a real-live version of their filters, but I was unsuccessful in getting a response.
- **Kai's Power Tools:** If I had to recommend only one third-party filter collection, it would be Kai's Power Tools from HSC Software. In addition to some enhancements to Photoshop's standard filter set, the package provides special color-manipulation effects (such as Cyclone, shown in Figure 12-79); distortion filters (Glass Lens, again shown in the figure); a texture explorer for creating seamless repeating patterns; unbelievable gradient fill and stroke tools; and a fractal designer. The interface takes some getting used to, but after you come to terms

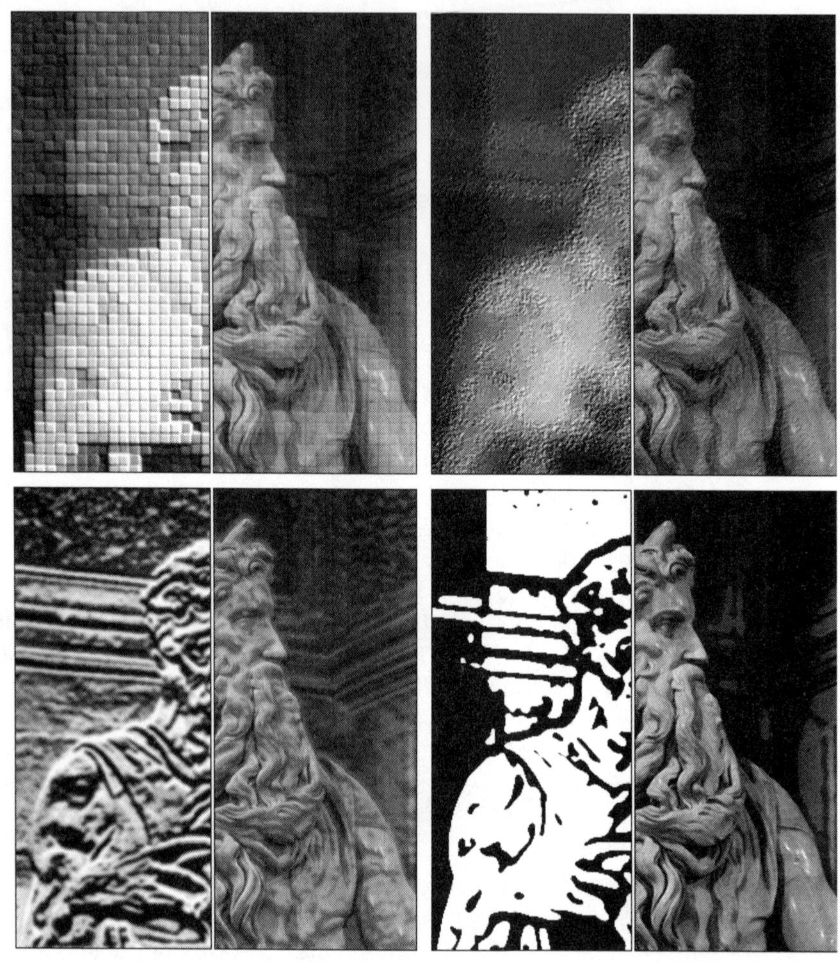

Figure 12-78: Four filters from Aldus Gallery Effects, Classic Art 2, including (clockwise from upper left) Patchwork, Underpainting, Stamp, and Bas Relief. The filters are demonstrated at full intensity on the left side of each image and applied to a translucent floating selection on the right side.

with it, you'll find the options logical and the application thoughtful. I can't begin to do justice to this package in a few words, so I think it's time I stopped trying. If you have $100 to spare, check it out for yourself.

- **Xaos Tools Paint Alchemy:** Paint Alchemy from Xaos (pronounced *chaos*) Tools is less a filtering tool than an effects studio. In a way, it introduces some of the free-form power of Fractal Design Painter to Photoshop. It filters a selection by applying hundreds of brush strokes of a specified shape, color, size, angle, and opacity. You also can apply custom brush strokes loaded from disk. If its extensive array of options proves too bewildering, you can choose from a palette of

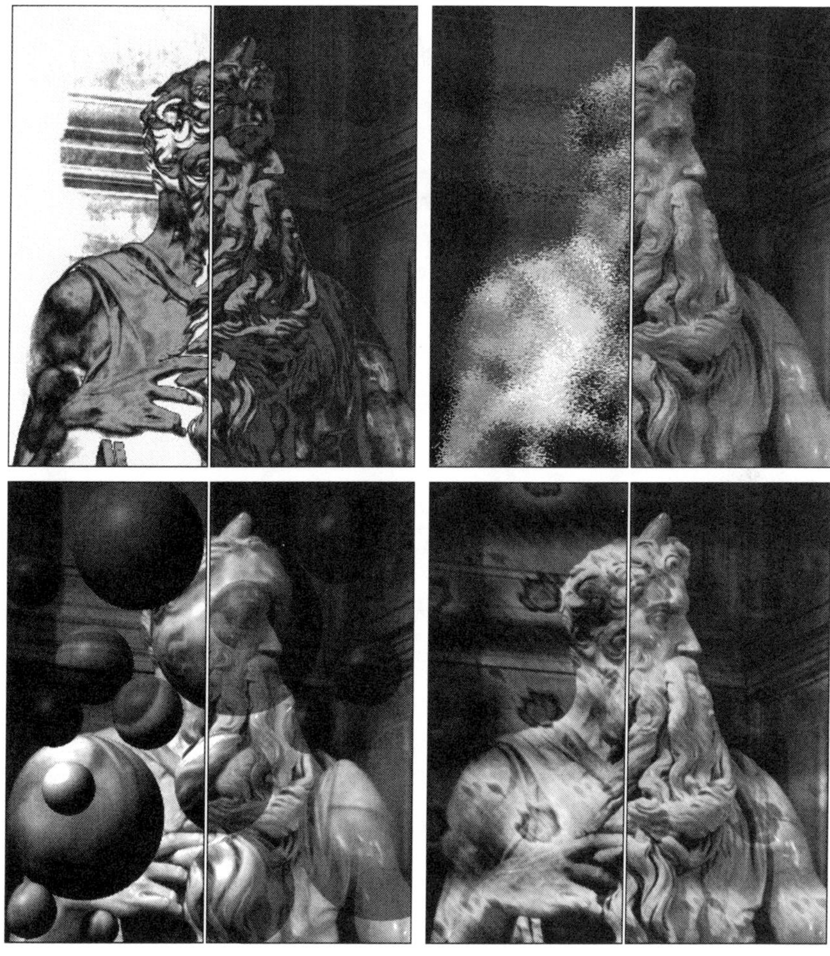

Figure 12-79: Four predefined effects from Kai's Power Tools, including (clockwise from upper left) Cyclone, Pixel Breeze, Texture Explorer, and Glass Lens. Again, I applied each effect at full intensity on the left side of the images and to a floating translucent selection on the right.

predefined effects, some of which are exhibited in Figure 12-80. Because I worked from a pre-release version of the program, I can't comment on its performance. But I can say that in addition to a cumbersome and sometimes confusing interface, the module requires you to work on color images, seemingly an arbitrary restriction. Even so, Paint Alchemy provides capabilities that are sufficiently unique from those offered by Photoshop to make it worth your attention.

Figure 12-80: Four predefined effects from Paint Alchemy, including (clockwise from upper left) Brush Strokes, Smoke, Crowd, and Weave Thatch. If you look closely, you may be able to see the little men that make up the Crowd effect (lower right). As in Figures 12-78 and 12-79, I applied each effect to the left half of the images at full intensity and to a floating translucent selection on the right.

DSP boards

If you have a thousand bucks lying around (and who isn't plagued by excess cash these days?), you can speed up some of Photoshop's filtering operations by investing in a *digital signal processor* (DSP) board. I introduced a couple of examples, SuperMac's ThunderStorm and DayStar's Charger, back in the "ThunderStorm" section of Chapter 5. Both boards are based on a DSP model from Storm Technology, the same folks who sell the PicturePress JPEG module. Other examples include Spectral Innovations' Lightning Effects and Newer Technology's Image Magic; future versions of these two products promise to be superior solutions based on their integration of a more capable processing chip.

How DSP acceleration works

A DSP board acts like a very fast, very dumb extension of the CPU. It can solve a narrow range of mathematical equations extremely quickly. DSP vendors license code for Photoshop's filters and other functions from Adobe, modify the code to fit their boards, and subsequently accelerate key Photoshop functions.

The difference between the two basic types of DSP processors — the Storm 16A found on the SuperMac and DayStar boards and the more capable AT&T 3210 offered by Spectral and Newer — is that the 16A chip can only solve equations that involve integers (numbers with no decimal points), while the 3210 can solve more complex equations involving floating-point values. This means that 3210 boards not only can enhance Photoshop's speed more dramatically, but also can enhance the speed of other programs, including Painter, Adobe Premier, and Kai's Power Tools. Some boards even feature multiple chips, in which case the software might break the equation in half and then put the solution together in about half the time it would take on a single-chip board.

I should state that so far, a good deal of this information is hypothetical. Much of the hardware is up and running, but the DSP software required to accelerate other programs and break up equations is still in a state of transition. As a result, there is presently no clear leader in the DSP market. One board speeds the Unsharp Mask filter better than others; another shaves an extra second off Gaussian Blur. But by the time you read this, new hardware and software solutions should be available, the most exciting of which will come from Newer Technology.

Newer will market a 3210 board available with either two or four chips that will be fully compatible with the DSP chip built into the motherboard of the new Macintosh Centris 660AV and Quadra 840AV. The board will be able to accelerate any software that is compatible with the AV's DSP. Because thousands of folks will own AV— conceivably, more people than own all the DSP boards put together — AV DSP will become the standard.

Newer also will sell rewritten versions of Photoshop code that will enable both the AV and Newer DSP chips to accelerate the program. This software will accelerate key filters as well as the open and save functions, Rotate and Image Size commands, painting tools, color conversions, and a host of other functions.

The SuperMac and DayStar Storm DSP boards are available exclusively as NuBus boards. Lightning Effects ships as a PDS board for the Macintosh Centris 650, Centris 660AV, and Quadra series. (PDS, as you will remembers, stands for *processor direct slot,* not to be confused with DSP. Same initials, different order.) Image Magic is available in both NuBus and PDS varieties; the PDS boards are compatible not only with the Centris 650, 660AV, and Quadra series, but also with the orphaned IIfx.

Who needs DSP?

My personal take on DSP boards is that they're unnecessary unless you do an awful lot of image processing, churning out several color images a day. All boards are expensive, listing between $700 and $1,000. And although vendors make claims of 1,000 percent speed enhancements, the amount of time you save will be significantly less.

In the first place, the 1,000 percent enhancement occurs only when you set a filter to its most radical setting — maximum values all around, for example, in the Unsharp Mask dialog box — and apply it to an entire 11 × 17-inch image in one fell swoop. Only a few of us work that way on a regular basis.

Secondly, DSP boards speed up specific functions only. Currently, you can expect to enhance the performance of the Unsharp Mask, Gaussian Blur, and a handful of other focus filters, as well as opening and saving JPEG files. As things stand now, no one DSP product speeds up the opening and saving of the TIFF format or other non-filter related functions.

Furthermore, DSP boards need an uninterrupted data stream going through them, meaning that you must be working entirely in RAM to achieve significant speed gains. If the board has to constantly swap data to and from disk space, you can kiss the speed gain goodbye.

My point is, if you're the head of a design firm and you need to boost Photoshop's performance, you should probably look into the various DSP options. If you're a free-lance Photoshop artist on a shoestring budget, don't even think about it. CPU, memory, and monitor size all are much more important considerations.

Changing the Location of a Filter Command

If you're unhappy with the way Photoshop organizes its plug-in filters, you can move commands to different hierarchical submenus within the Filter menu and even create submenus of your own. A special resource included inside every plug-in filter, called *PiMI,* specifies the name of the submenu under which the filter command appears. Using Apple's ResEdit utility, you change the name of the PiMI resource; if no such submenu exists, Photoshop creates a new submenu bearing the PiMI resource name. By way of an example, the following steps describe how to segregate the Radial Blur filter into a special submenu called General Wackiness.

STEPS: Editing the PiMI Resource with ResEdit

Step 1. Launch ResEdit (Version 2.1 or higher is recommended) and open the Radial Blur file located in the Photoshop Plug-ins folder.

Step 2. Double-click on the PiMI icon (between *DLOG* and *vers*). The PiMI window appears, displaying a single resource numbered *16,000.*

Step 3. Select resource number 16,000 and choose Resource ⇨ Get Resource Info (Command-I). The Info window appears.

Step 4. The Name option box near the top of the Info window contains the name of the submenu under which this filter appears, which is currently *Blur.* Enter the name *General Wackiness* into the Name option box, as shown in Figure 12-81.

Step 5. Quit ResEdit. When the message `Save Radial Blur before closing?` appears, press Return to save your changes.

Step 6. Launch Photoshop and create a new file. Now display the Filter menu. Choose the new General Wackiness command to display a submenu containing the single Radial Blur command. If you display the Blur submenu, the Radial Blur command is no longer there.

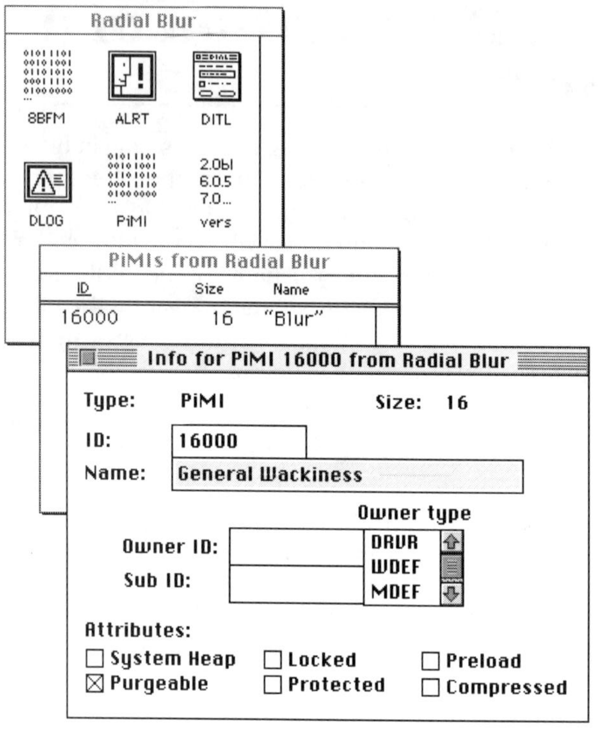

Figure 12-81: Enter a new name into the Name option of the Info for PiMI dialog box inside ResEdit to change the submenu under which a filter appears.

Summary

- Press Command-F to reapply the most recently used filter. Press Command-Option-F to display the dialog box for that filter.
- Option-choose one of the distortion filters from the Apple ⇨ About Plug-in submenu to preview the effects from inside the distortion filter dialog boxes in Photoshop 2.5.
- If you apply a filter to a floating selection, you can dissipate its effect by adjusting the translucency of the selection or changing the overlay mode.
- Use the Unsharp Mask filter to gain control over the sharpening process. The filter is exponentially more functional than the preset Sharpen, Sharpen Edges, and Sharpen More crowd.
- Use the High Pass filter in combination with Image ⇨ Map ⇨ Threshold to select the exact boundaries of a foreground element set against a busy background.
- The Gaussian Blur filter distributes the blurring effect along a bell-shaped curve, thus blending neighboring pixels while retaining the greatest amount of detail.
- Use the Wind filter in combination with Motion Blur to point the blur in one direction or the other. Use the smudge tools for even better control.
- The Minimum and Maximum filters are ideal for reducing and enlarging the area of a selection outline inside the quick mask mode or inside an independent mask channel.
- The Despeckle command blurs all but the edges in an image; Median averages the colors of neighboring pixels. Neither removes noise that well, but each can be useful for creating special effects.
- You can create unusual halo effects by applying the Crystallize or Mosaic filter to a heavily feathered selection.
- Get to know the distortion filters before trying to use them in a real project, especially if you're under a mean, grueling deadline.
- Apply the Pinch filter 10 times in succession at 100 percent to turn any image into a conical gradation.
- The Twirl filter results in spirals; the Zigzag filter results in concentric pond ripples; the Ripple filter results in smooth waves; and the Wave filter results in smooth waves, abrupt zigzags, and mosaic patterns.

- Use the Polar Coordinates filter to create text on a curve. The filter folds and unfolds images like they were patterns on a Japanese fan.
- Kai's Power Tools is the best filtering collection money can buy.
- A DSP board can accelerate specific Photoshop filters, but only if you have sufficient RAM to maintain the image entirely in memory.

Constructing Homemade Effects

13 CHAPTER

In This Chapter

- The mathematics behind the Custom filter
- Demonstrations of more than 70 custom sharpening, blurring, edge-detection, and embossing effects
- An in-depth analysis of the Displace filter
- A look at Photoshop's predefined displacement maps
- How to apply custom gradations and textures as displacement maps

Creating a Custom Effect

The last chapter was bigger than the Mexico City telephone directory. It took you so long to read it that Photoshop has since been updated twice and Apple is about to release a completely new line of computers with the code name *Elmer.* Nevertheless, the fact is that I skipped two very important filters, Custom and Displace, which enable you to create your own individualized special effects.

Both commands require some mathematical reasoning skills to fully understand, and even then, you'll probably have occasional difficulty predicting the outcomes. If math isn't your bag, if number theory clogs up your synapses to the extent that you feel like a worthless math wimp, then by all means don't put yourself through the torture. Skip all the mathematical background and read the "Applying Custom Values" and "Using Displacement Maps" sections to try out some specific no-brainer effects.

On the other hand, if you want to understand what's going on so that you eventually can create effects of your own, read on, you hearty soul.

The Custom filter

The Custom command enables you to design your own filter, which can be a variation on sharpening, blurring, embossing, or half a dozen other effects. You create your filter by entering numerical values into a matrix of options.

When you choose Filter ➪ Other ➪ Custom, Photoshop displays the dialog box shown in Figure 13-1. It sports a 5 × 5 matrix of option boxes followed by two additional options, Scale and Offset. The matrix options can accept values from negative to positive 999. The Scale value can range from 1 to 9,999, and the Offset value can range from negative to positive 9,999. The dialog box includes Load and Save buttons so that you can load settings from disk and save the current settings for future use.

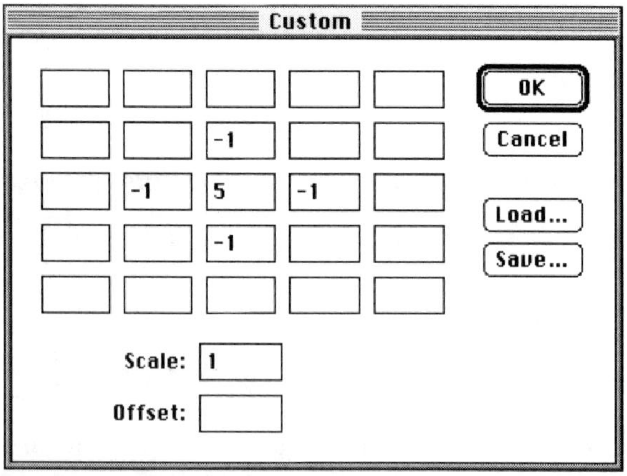

Figure 13-1: The Custom dialog box lets you design your own filter by multiplying the brightness values of pixels.

Here's how the filter works: When you press the Return key to apply the values in the Custom dialog box to a selection, the filter passes over every pixel in the selection one at a time. For each pixel being evaluated — which I'll call the PBE, for short — the filter multiplies the PBE's current brightness value by the number in the center option box (the one that contains a 5 in Figure 13-1). To help keep things straight, I'll call this value the CMV, for *central matrix value.*

The filter then multiplies the brightness values of the surrounding pixels by the surrounding values in the matrix. For example, Photoshop multiplies the value in the option box just above the CMV by the brightness value of the pixel just above the PBE. It ignores any empty matrix option boxes and the pixels they represent.

Finally, the filter totals the products of the multiplied pixels, divides the sum by the value in the Scale option, and adds the Offset value to calculate the new brightness of the PBE. It then moves on to the next pixel in the selection and performs the calculation all over again. Figure 13-2 shows a schematic drawing of the process.

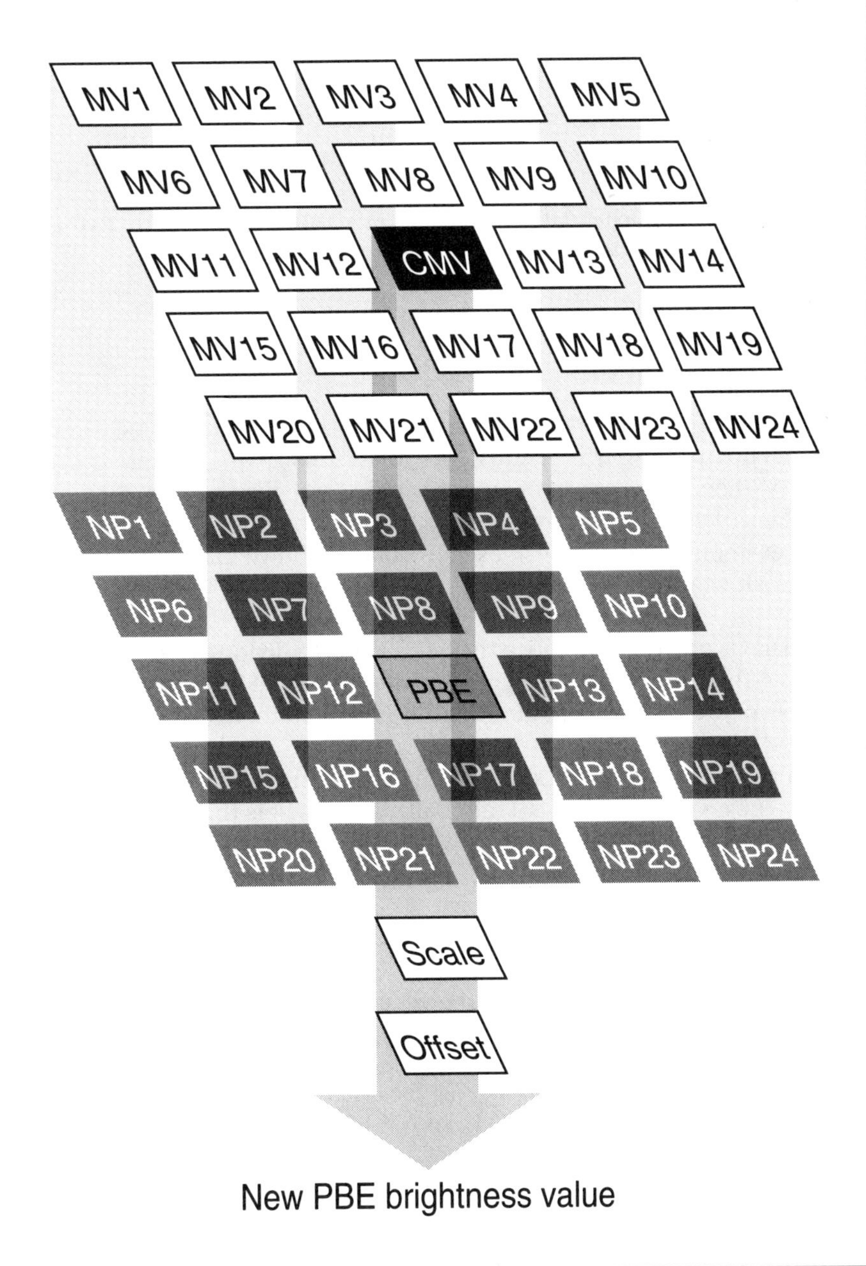

Figure 13-2: The Custom filter multiplies each matrix value by the brightness value of the corresponding pixel, adds the products together, divides the sum by the Scale value, adds the Offset value, and applies the result to the pixel being evaluated.

Perhaps seeing all of this spelled out in an equation will help you understand the process. Then again, perhaps not — but here it comes anyway. In the following equation, NP stands for *neighboring pixel* and MV stands for the corresponding matrix value in the Custom dialog box.

New brightness value = (((*PBE* × *CMV*) + (*NP1* × *MV1*) + (*NP2* × *MV2*) + . . .) ÷ *Scale*) + *Offset*

Luckily, Photoshop calculates the equation without any help from you. All you have to do is punch in the values and see what happens.

Custom filter advice

Now obviously, if you go around multiplying the brightness value of a pixel too much, you end up making it white. And a filter that turns an image white is pretty darn useless. The key, then, is to filter an image and at the same time maintain the original balance of brightness values. To achieve this, just be sure that the sum of all values in the matrix is 1. For example, the default values in the matrix shown back in Figure 13-1 are 5, –1, –1, –1, and –1, which add up to 1.

If the sum is greater than 1, use the Scale value to divide the sum down to 1. Figures 13-3 and 13-4 show the results of increasing the CMV from 5 to 6 and then 7. This step raises the sum of the values in the matrix from 1 to 2 and then 3.

In Figure 13-3, I entered the sum into the Scale option to divide the sum back down to 1 (any value divided by itself is 1, after all). The result is that Photoshop maintains the original color balance of the image while at the same time filtering it slightly differently. When I did not raise the Scale value, the image became progressively lighter, as illustrated in Figure 13-4.

If the sum is less than 1, increase the CMV until the sum reaches the magic number. For example, in Figure 13-5, I lowered the values to the left of the CMV and then above the CMV by 1 apiece to increase the sharpening effect. To ensure that the image did not darken, I also raised the CMV to compensate. When I did not raise the CMV, the image turned black, as shown in Figure 13-6.

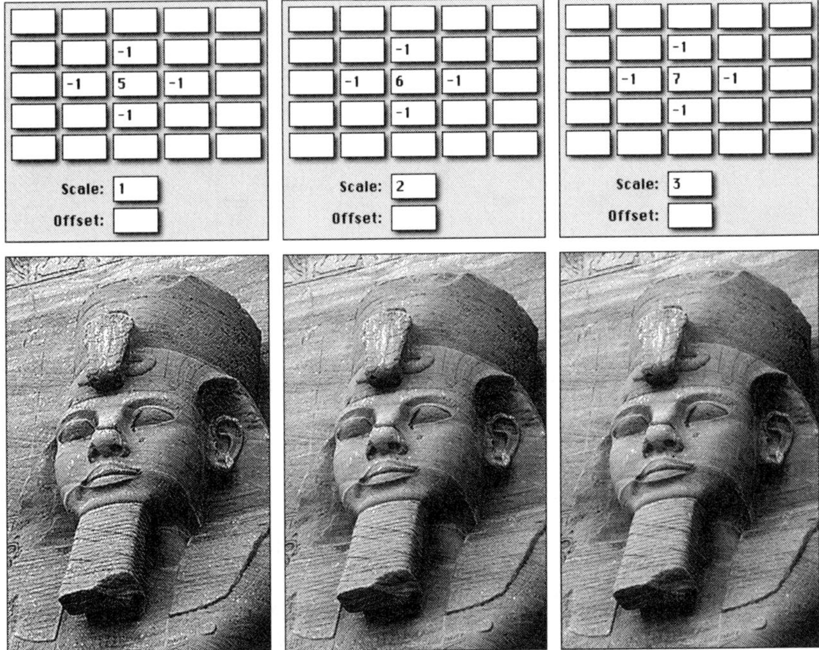

Figure 13-3: Raising the Scale value to reflect the sum of the values in the matrix maintains the color balance of the image.

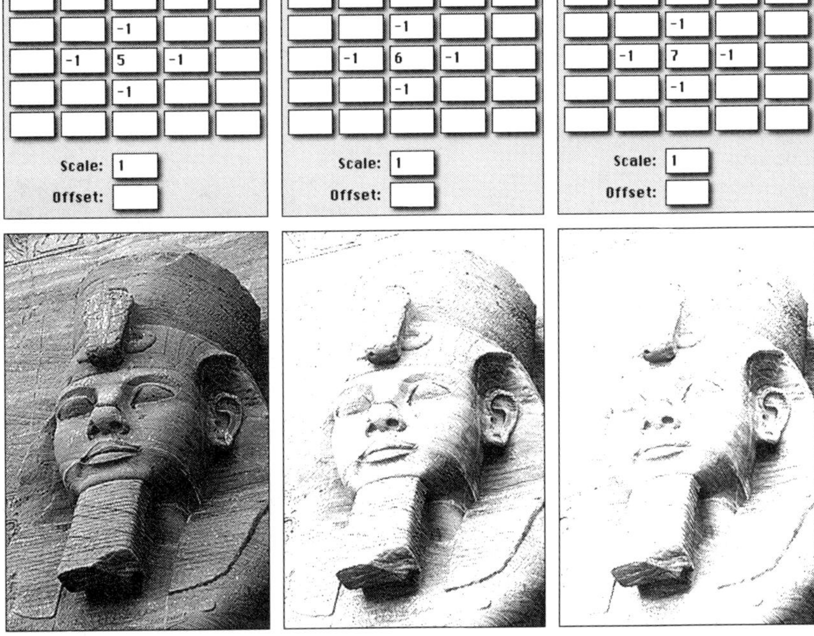

Figure 13-4: Raising the sum of the matrix values without counterbalancing it in the Scale option lightens the image.

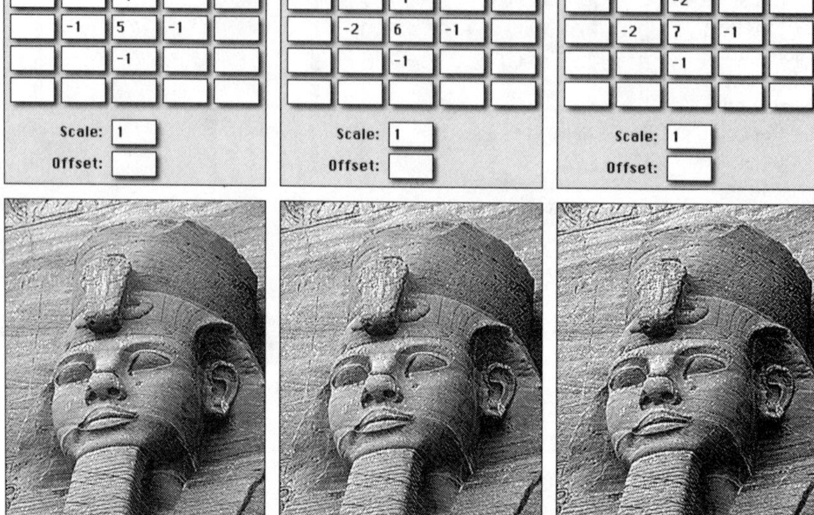

Figure 13-5: Raising the CMV to compensate for the lowered values in the matrix maintains the color balance of the image.

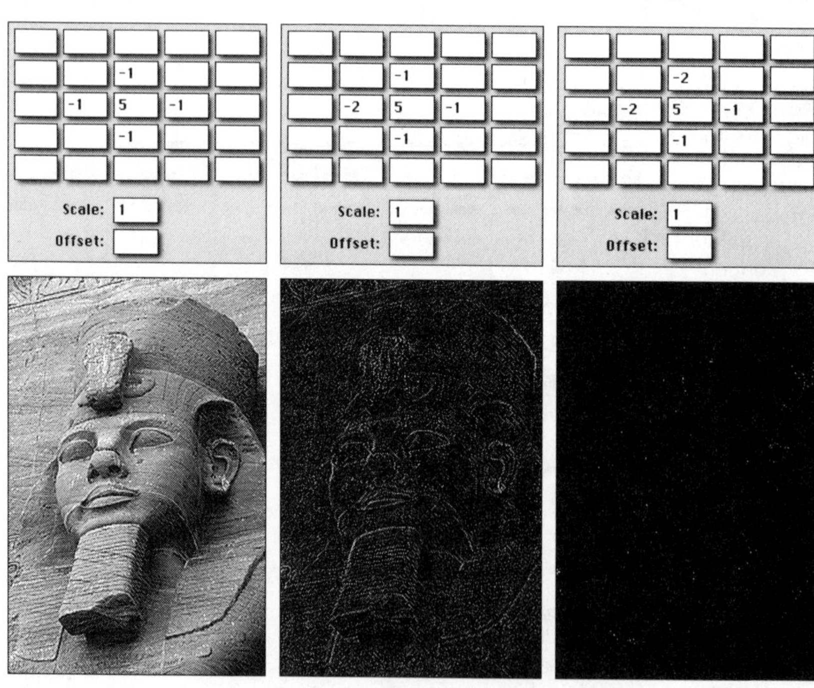

Figure 13-6: Lowering the sum of the matrix values without counterbalancing them with the CMV darkens the image.

Though a sum of 1 provides the safest and most predictable filtering effects, you can use different sums, such as 0 and 2, to try out more destructive filtering effects. If you do, be sure to raise or lower the Offset value to compensate. For some examples, see the "Non-one variations" section.

Applying Custom Values

The following sections show you ways to sharpen, blur, and otherwise filter an image using specific matrix, Scale, and Offset values. It is my sincere hope that by the end of the Custom filter discussions, you not only will know how to repeat my examples, but also how to apply what you've learned to design special effects of your own.

Symmetrical effects

Values that are symmetrical both horizontally and vertically about the central matrix value produce sharpen and blur effects:

- **Sharpening:** A positive CMV surrounded by symmetrical negative values sharpens an image, as demonstrated in the first example of Figure 13-7. Figures 13-3 through 13-6 also demonstrate varying degrees of sharpening effects.
- **Blurring:** A positive CMV surrounded by symmetrical positive numbers — balanced, of course, by a Scale value as explained in the preceding section — blurs an image, as demonstrated in the second example of Figure 13-7.
- **Blurring with edge-detection:** A negative CMV surrounded by symmetrical positive values blurs an image and adds an element of edge-detection, as illustrated in the last example of the figure. These effects are unlike anything provided by Photoshop's standard collection of filters.

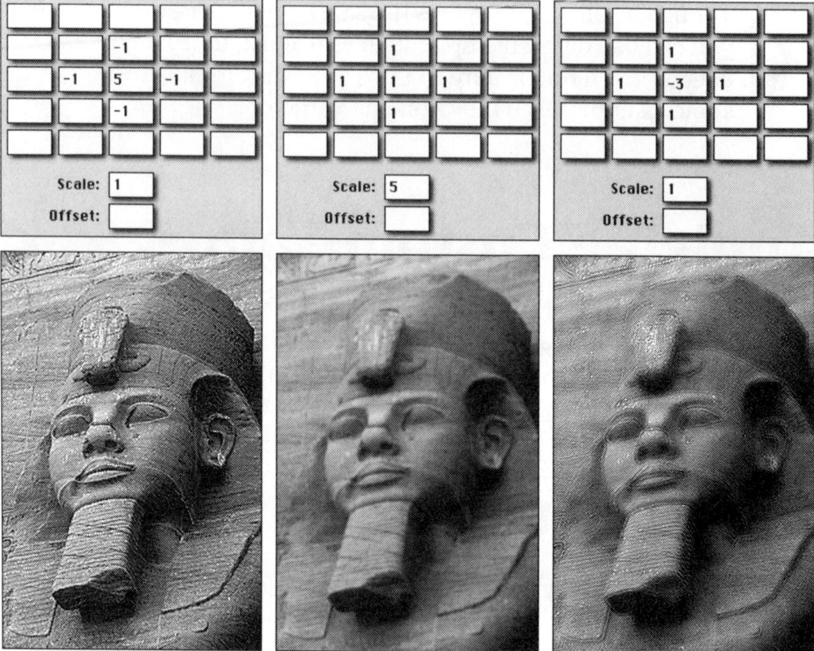

Figure 13-7: Symmetrical values can result in sharpening (left), blurring (middle), and edge-detection (right) effects.

Sharpening

The Custom command provides as many variations on the sharpening theme as the Unsharp Mask filter. In a sense, it provides even more, for whereas the Unsharp Mask filter requires you to sharpen an image inside a Gaussian radius, you get to specify exactly which pixels are taken into account when you use the Custom filter.

To create Unsharp Mask-like effects, enter a large number in the CMV and small values in the surrounding option boxes, as demonstrated in Figure 13-8. To go beyond Unsharp Mask, you can violate the radius of the filter by entering values around the perimeter of the matrix and ignoring options closer to the CMV, as demonstrated in Figure 13-9.

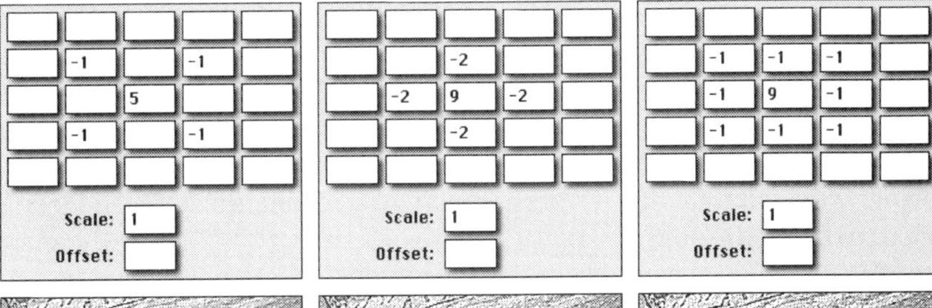

Figure 13-8: To create severe sharpening effects, enter a CMV just large enough to compensate for the negative values in the matrix.

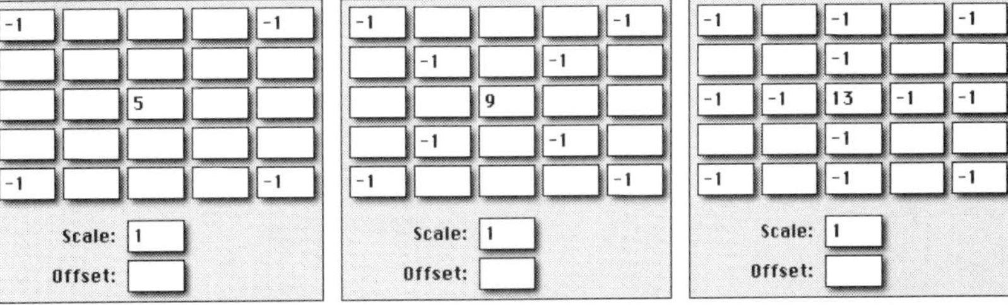

Figure 13-9: To heighten the sharpening effect even further, enter negative values around the perimeter of the matrix.

You can sharpen an image using the Custom dialog box in two basic ways. First, you can enter lots of negative values into the neighboring options in the matrix and then enter a CMV just large enough to yield a sum of 1. Radical sharpening effects result, as demonstrated throughout the examples in Figure 13-8 and 13-9.

Second, you can tone down the sharpening by raising the CMV and using the Scale value to divide the sum down to 1. Figures 13-10 and 13-11 show the results of raising the CMV to lessen the impact of the sharpening effects performed in Figures 13-8 and 13-9.

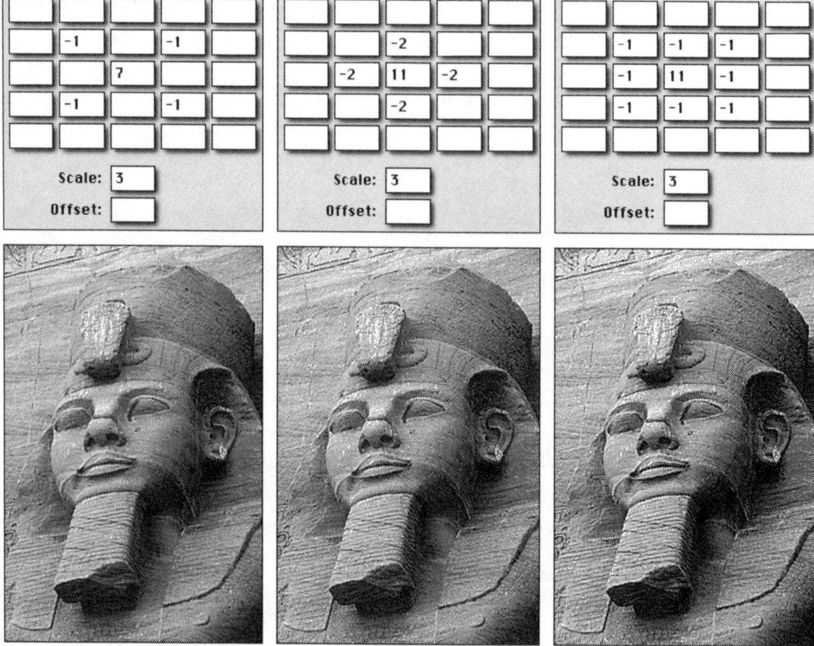

Figure 13-10: To sharpen more subtly, increase the central matrix value and then enter the sum into the Scale value.

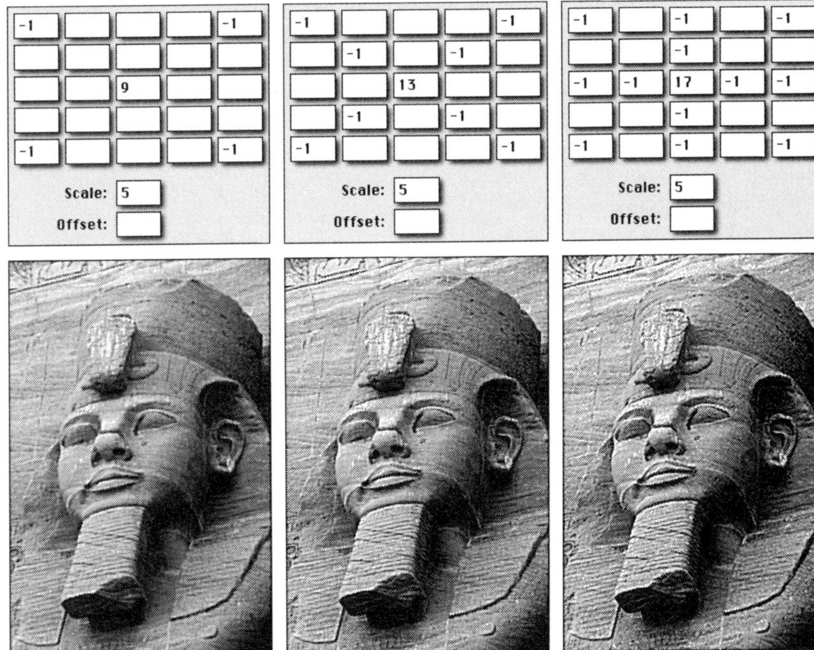

Figure 13-11: When you soften the effect of radical sharpening, you create a thicker, higher contrast effect, much as when raising the Radius value in the Unsharp Mask dialog box.

Blurring

The philosophy behind blurring is very much the same as that behind sharpening. To produce extreme blurring effects, enter lots of values or high values into the neighboring options in the matrix, enter 1 into the CMV, and then enter the sum into the Scale option. Examples appear in Figure 13-12. To downplay the blurring, raise the CMV and the Scale value by equal amounts. In Figure 13-13, I used the same neighboring values as in Figure 13-12, but I increased the CMV and the Scale value by 3 apiece.

Figure 13-12: To create severe blurring effects, enter 1 for the CMV and fill the neighboring options with 1s and 2s.

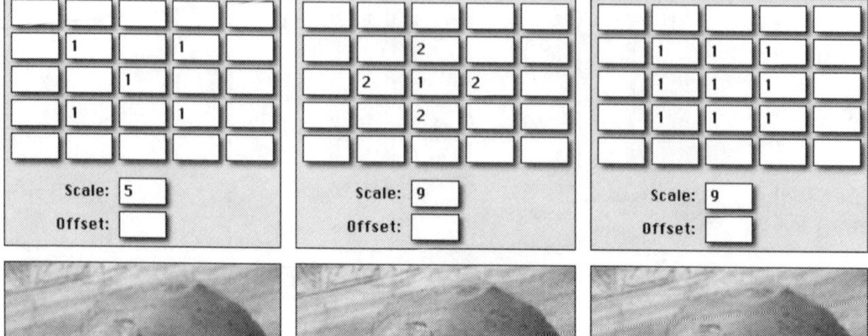

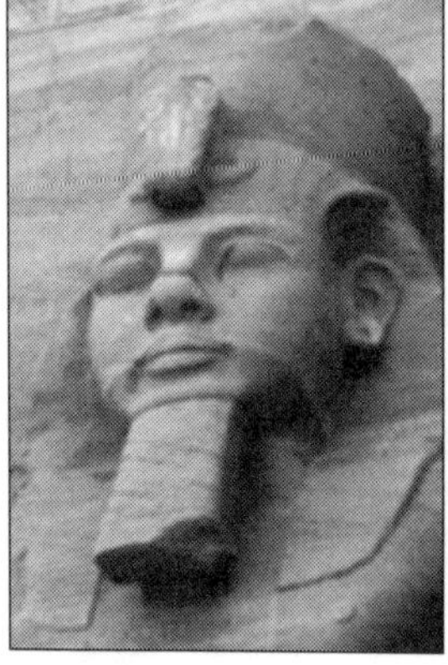

Figure 13-13: To blur more subtly, increase the central matrix value and the Scale value by equal amounts.

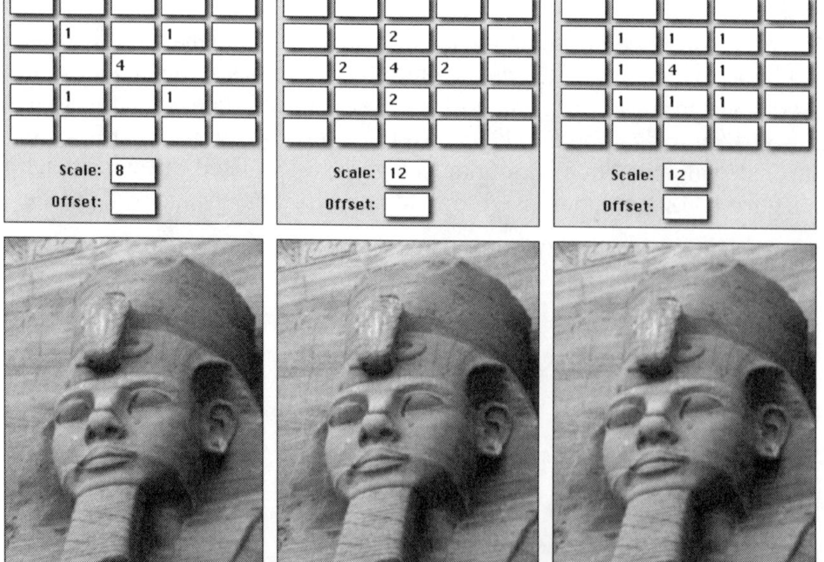

Edge-detection

Many of you are probably beginning to get the idea by now, but just in case you're the kind of person who believes that friends don't let friends do math, I breeze through it one more time in the venue of edge-detection. If you really want to see those edges, enter 1s and 2s into the neighboring options in the matrix and then enter a CMV just *small* enough — it's a negative value, after all — to make the sum 1. Examples appear in Figure 13-14 for your viewing pleasure.

To lighten the edges and bring out the blur, raise the CMV and enter the resulting sum into the Scale option box. The first example in Figure 13-15 pushes the boundaries between edge-detection and a straight blur.

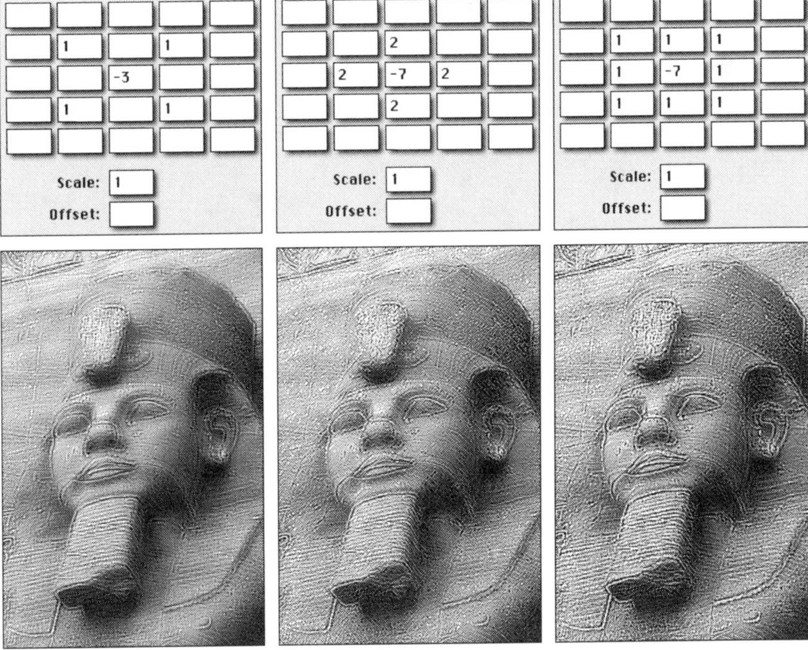

Figure 13-14: To create severe edge-detection effects, enter a negative CMV just small enough to compensate for the positive values in the matrix.

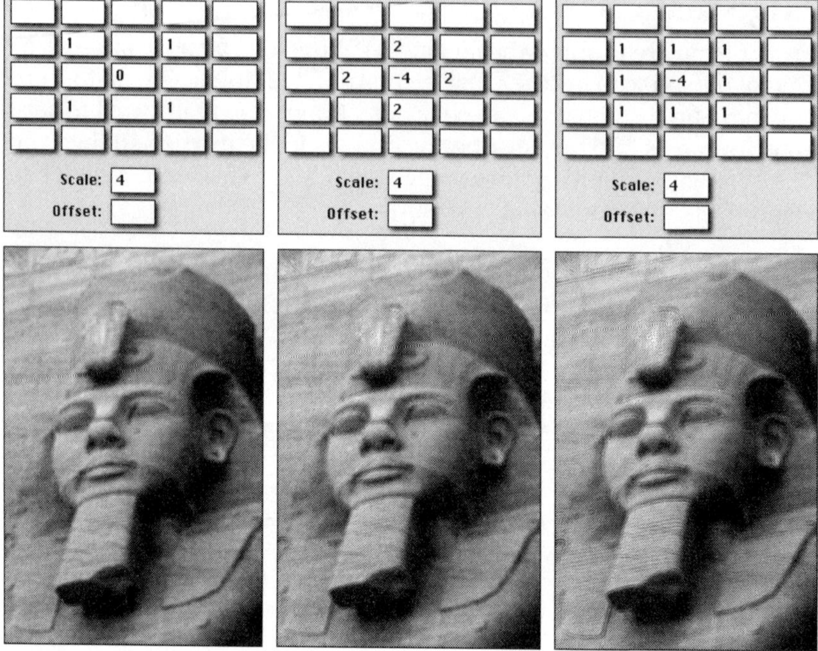

Figure 13-15: To blur the edges, increase the central matrix value and then enter the sum into the Scale value.

Non-1 variations

Every image shown in Figures 13-7 through 13-15 is the result of manipulating matrix values and using the Scale option to produce a sum total of 1. Earlier in this chapter, I showed you what can happen if you go below 1 (black images) or above 1 (white images). But I haven't shown you how you can use non-1 totals to produce interesting, if somewhat washed-out, effects.

The key is to raise the Offset value, thereby adding a specified brightness value to each pixel in the image. By doing this, you can offset the lightening or darkening caused by the matrix values to create an image that has half a chance of printing.

Lightening overly dark effects

The first image in Figure 13-16 uses nearly the exact same values used to create the extreme sharpening effect in the last image of Figure 13-8. The only difference is that the CMV is 1 lower (8, down from 9), which in turn lowers the sum total from 1 to 0.

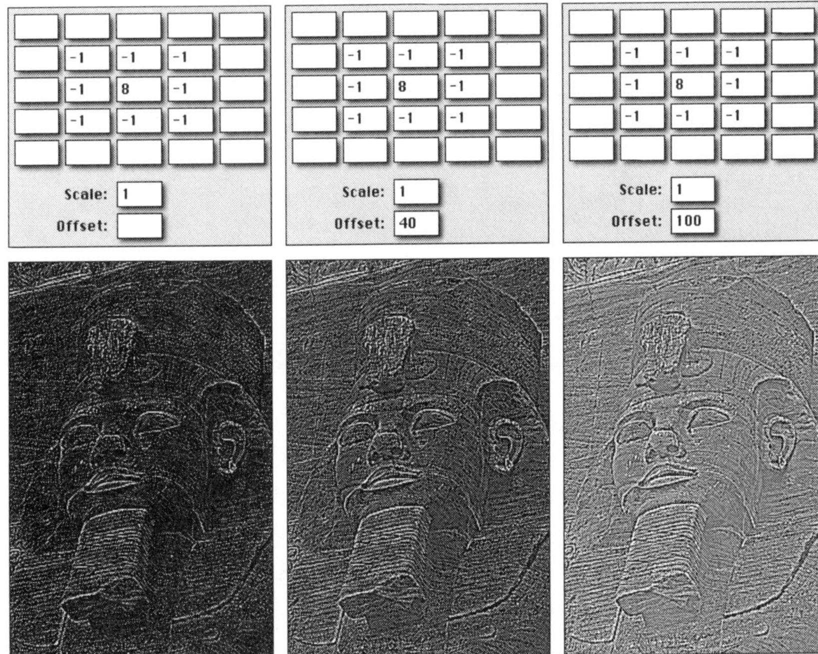

Figure 13-16: Three examples of sharpening effects with sum totals of 0. I lightened the images incrementally by entering positive values into the Offset option box.

The result is an extremely dark image with hints of brightness at points of high contrast. The image looks OK on-screen — actually, it looks pretty cool because of all those little star-like sprinkles in it — but it's likely to fill in during the printing process. If the first image in Figure 13-16 looks like anything but a vague blob of blackness, it's a credit to the printer of this book. Most printers who didn't have a giant publisher breathing down their necks would have kissed this image goodbye, and rightly so. It's too darn dark.

To prevent the image from filling in and to help head off any disputes between you and your printer, lighten the image using the Offset value. Photoshop adds the value to the brightness level of each selected pixel. A brightness value of 255 equals solid white, so you don't need to go too high. As shown in the last example of Figure 13-16, an Offset value of 100 is enough to raise most pixels in the image to a medium gray. Figure 13-17 shows the results of lightening an overly dark edge-detection effect using the Offset value.

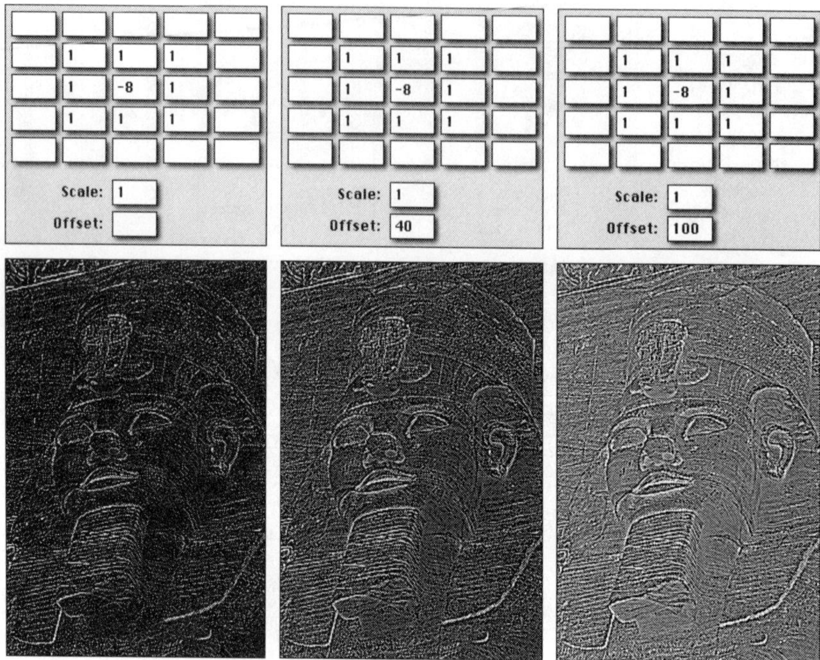

Figure 13-17: Three examples of edge-detection effects with sum totals of 0, lightened incrementally by using progressively higher Offset values.

Darkening overly light effects

You also can use the Offset value to darken filtering effects with sum totals greater than 1. The images in Figures 13-18 and 13-19 show sharpening and edge-detection effects whose matrix totals amount to 2. On their own, these filters produce effects that are too light. However, as demonstrated in the middle and right examples in the figures, you can darken the effects of the Custom filter to create high-contrast images by entering a negative value into the Offset option box.

Using extreme offsets

If a brightness value of 255 produces solid white and a brightness value of 0 is solid black, why in blue blazes does the Offset value permit any number between negative and positive 9,999, a number 40 times greater the solid white? The answer lies in the fact that the matrix options can force the Custom filter to calculate brightness values much darker than black and much lighter than white. Therefore, you can use a very high or very low Offset value to boost the brightness of an image in which all pixels are well below black or diminish the brightness when all pixels are way beyond white.

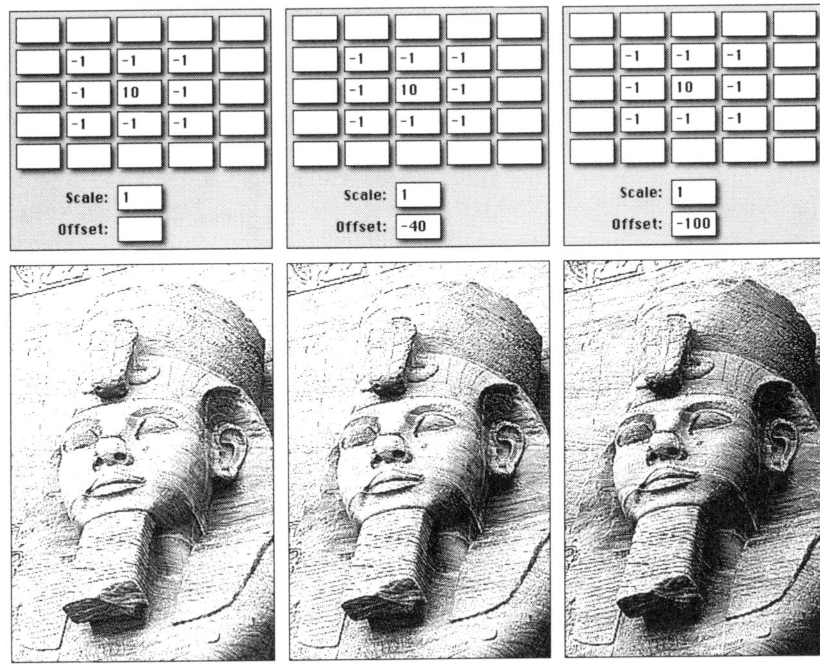

Figure 13-18: Three examples of sharpening effects with sum totals of 2. I darkened the images incrementally by entering negative values into the Offset option box.

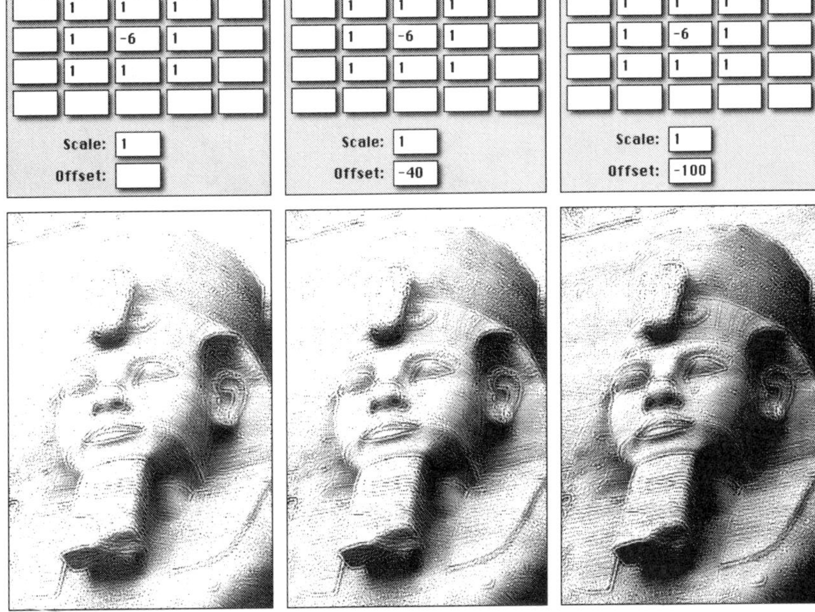

Figure 13-19: Three examples of edge-detection effects with sum totals of 2, darkened incrementally with progressively lower Offset values.

Figure 13-20 shows exaggerated versions of the sharpening, blurring, and edge-detection effects. The sum totals of the matrixes are – 42, 54, and 42 respectively. Without some help from the Offset value, each of these filters would turn every pixel in the image black (in the case of the sharpening effect) or white (blurring and edge-detection). But as demonstrated in the figure, using enormous Offset numbers brings out those few brightness values that remain. The images are so polarized that there's hardly any difference between the three effects, except that the first image is an inverted version of the other two. The difference is even less noticeable if you apply the effect to a translucent floating selection, as demonstrated in the second row of examples in Figure 13-20.

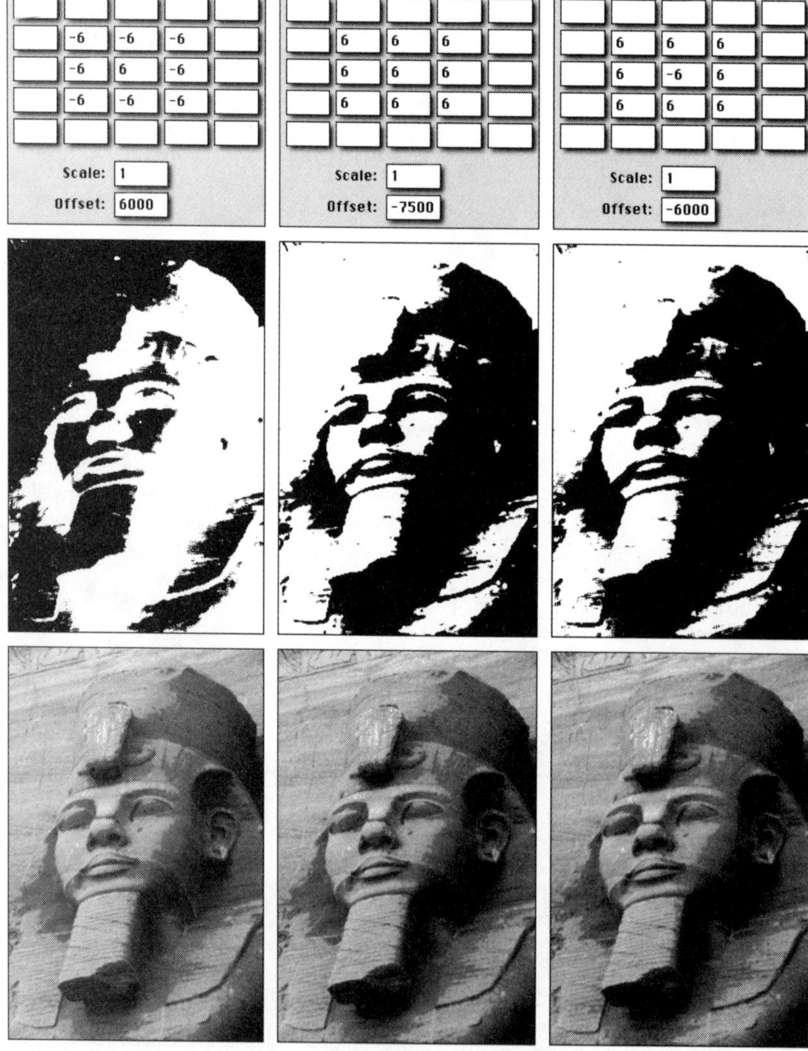

Figure 13-20: You can create high-contrast effects by exaggerating all values in the matrix and then compensating by entering a very high or very low Offset value (top row). When applied to translucent floating selections (bottom row), the sharpening, blurring, and edge-detection effects are barely discernible.

Other custom effects

By now, I hope you understand what an absolute trip the Custom filter can be, provided you immerse yourself in the old adventurous spirit. Quite honestly, I could keep showing you ways to use the Custom filter for another 20 or 30 pages. But then my publisher would come unglued because I'd never finish the book and you'd miss the pleasure of discovering variations on your own.

Nonetheless, you're probably wondering what happens if you just go absolutely berserk, in a computer-geek sort of way, and start entering matrix values in unusual or even arbitrary arrangements. The answer is that as long as you maintain a sum total of 1, you achieve some pretty interesting and even usable effects. Many of these effects will prove to be simple variations on sharpening, blurring, and edge-detection.

Directional blurs

Figure 13-21 shows examples of entering positive matrix values all in one row, all in a column, or in opposite quadrants. As you can see, as long as you maintain uniformly positive values, you get a blurring effect. However, by keeping the values lowest in the center and highest toward the edges and corners, you can create directional blurs. The first example resembles a slight horizontal motion blur, the second looks like a slight vertical motion blur, and the last example looks like it's vibrating horizontally and vertically.

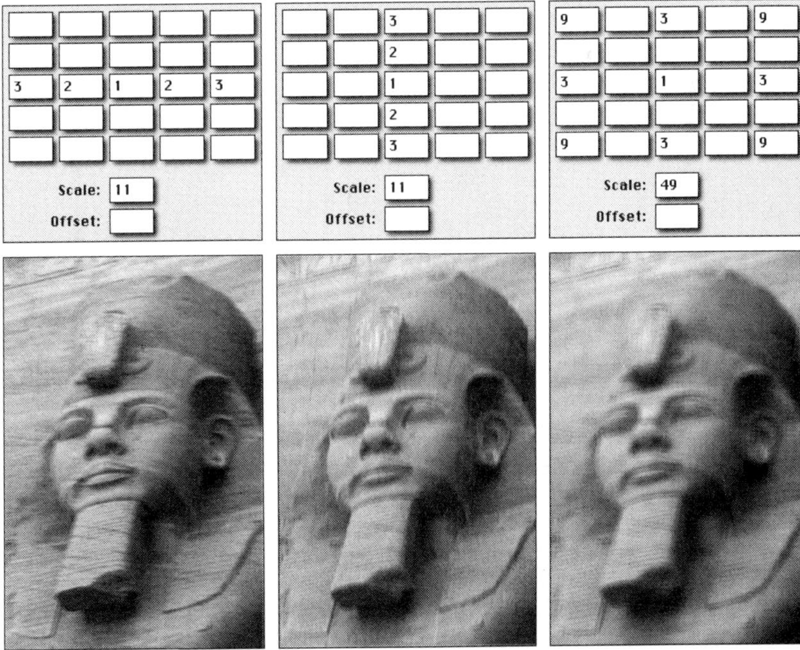

Figure 13-21: Enter positive matrix values in a horizontal formation (left) or vertical formation (middle) to create slight motion blurs. By positioning positive values in opposite corners of the matrix, you create a vibrating effect (right).

Directional sharpening

To selectively sharpen edges in an image based on the angles of the edges, you can organize negative and positive matrix values into rows or columns. For example, to sharpen only the horizontal edges in an image, fill the middle row of matrix options with positive values and the rows immediately above and below with negative values, as demonstrated in the left example in Figure 13-22. Similarly, you can sharpen the vertical edges only by entering positive values in the middle column and flanking the column on left and right with negative values, as shown in the middle example in the figure. In the last example, I arranged the positive values along a diagonal axis to sharpen only the diagonal edges.

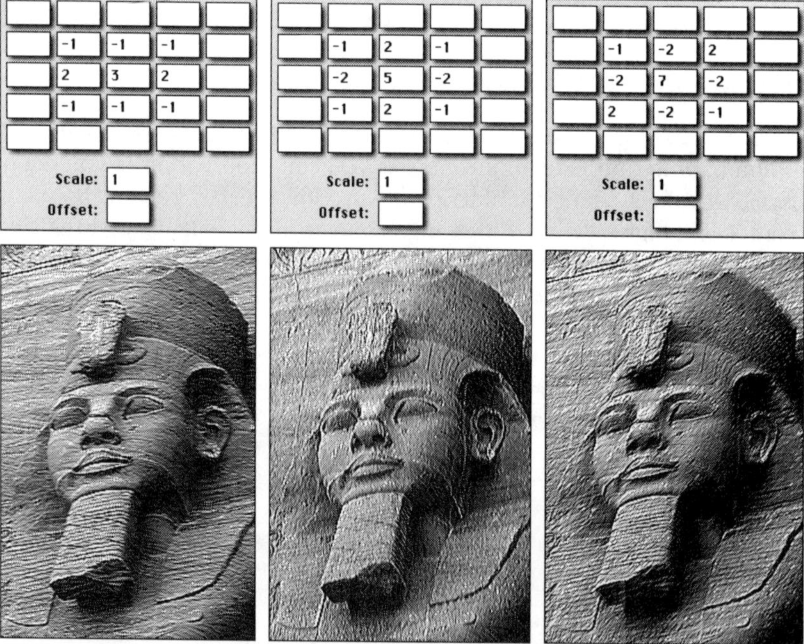

Figure 13-22: Arrange positive values in a row (left), column (middle), or along a diagonal axis (right) to sharpen horizontal, vertical, and diagonal edges exclusively.

You even can combine directional sharpening with directional blurring. Figure 13-23 shows the first example from Figure 13-22 blurred both horizontally and vertically. To blur the image horizontally, as in the middle example of Figure 13-23, I added positive values to the extreme ends of the middle row, thereby extending the range of the filter and creating a sort of horizontal jumbling effect. To blur the image vertically, as in the final example of the figure, I added positive values to the ends of the middle column.

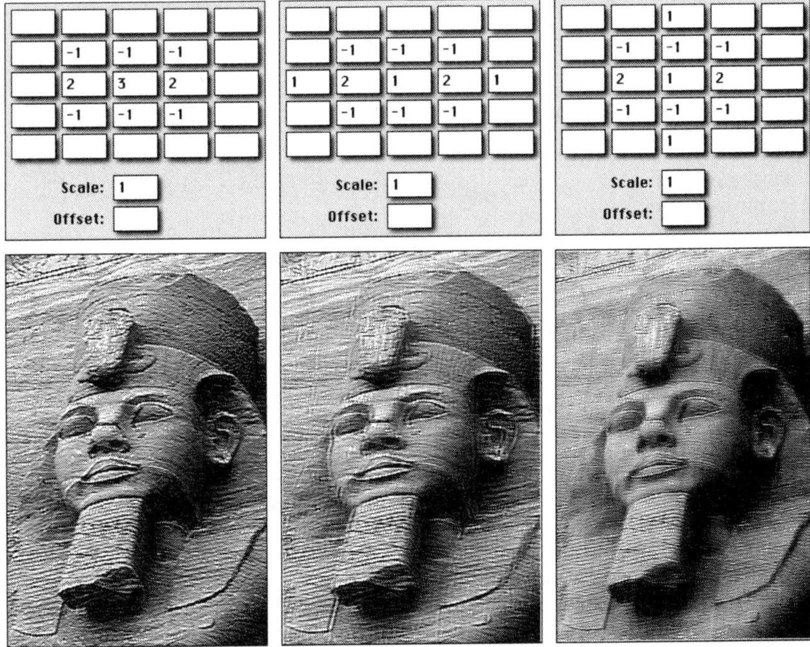

Figure 13-23: The image from Figure 13-22 (left) blurred horizontally (middle) and vertically (right).

Embossing

So far, we aren't going very nuts, are we? Despite their unusual formations, the matrix values in Figures 13-21 through 13-23 still manage to maintain symmetry. Well, now it's time to lose the symmetry, which typically results in an embossing effect.

Figure 13-24 shows three variations on embossing, all of which involve positive and negative matrix values positioned on opposite sides of the CMV. (The CMV happens to be positive merely to maintain a sum total of 1.)

This type of embossing has no hard and fast light source, but you might imagine that the light comes from the general direction of the positive values. Therefore, when I swapped the positive and negative values throughout the matrix (all except the CMV), I approximated an underlighting effect, as demonstrated by the images in Figure 13-25.

In truth, it's not so much a lighting difference as a difference in edge enhancement. White pixels collect on the side of an edge represented by positive values in the matrix; black pixels collect on the negative-value side. So when I swapped the locations of positive and negative values between Figures 13-24 and 13-25, I changed the distribution of white and black pixels in the filtered images.

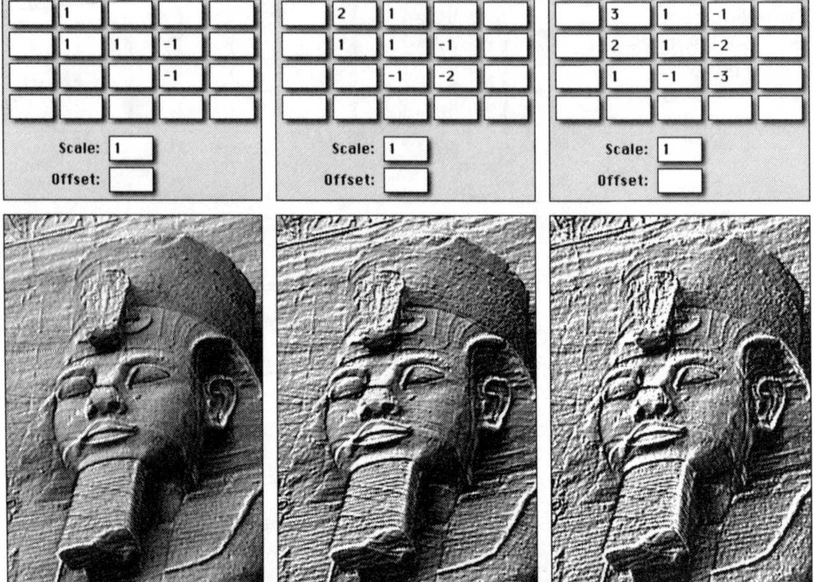

Figure 13-24: You can create embossing effects by distributing positive and negative values on opposite sides of the central matrix value.

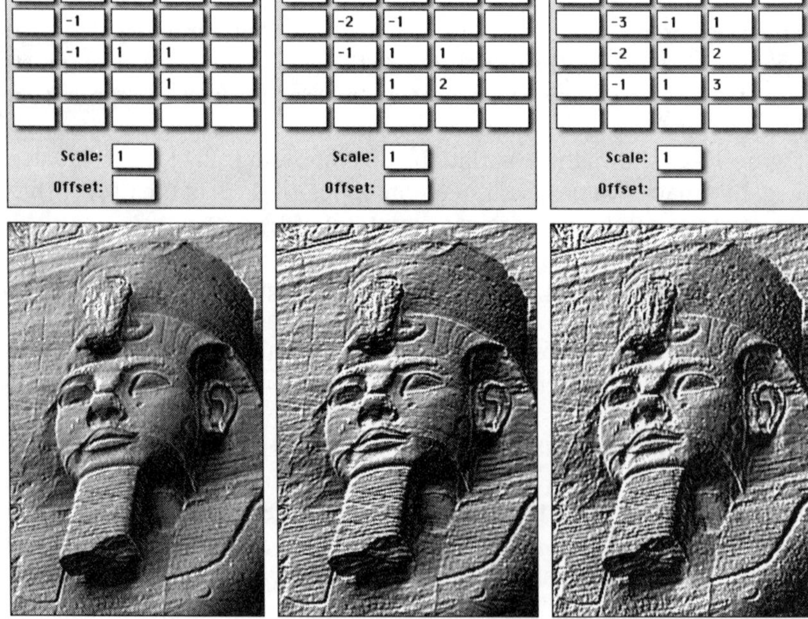

Figure 13-25: Change the location of positive and negative matrix values to change the general direction of the light source.

Embossing is the loosest of the Custom filter effects. As long as you position positive and negative values on opposite sides of the CMV, you can distribute the values in almost any way you see fit. Figure 13-26 demonstrates three entirely arbitrary arrangements of values in the Custom matrix. Figure 13-27 shows those same effects downplayed by raising the CMV and entering the sum of the matrix values into the Scale option box.

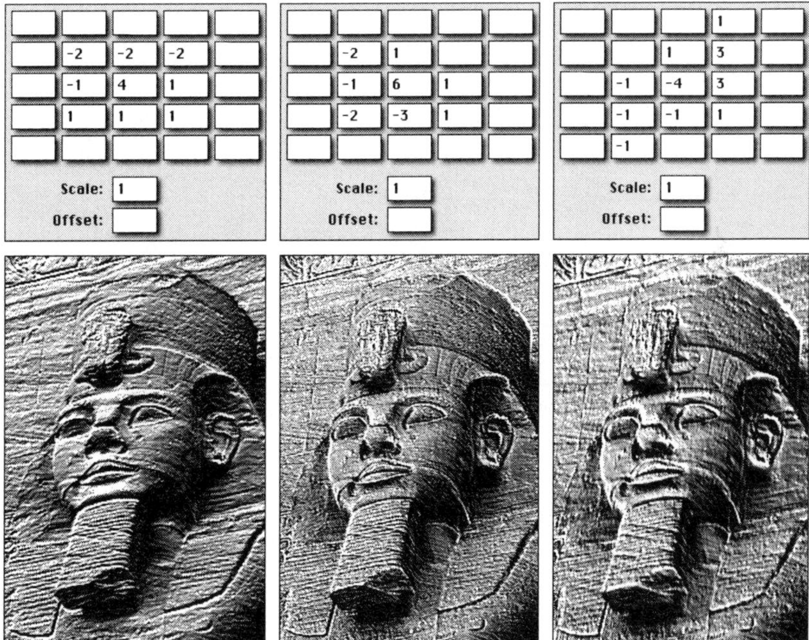

Figure 13-26: You can create whole libraries of embossing effects by experimenting with different combinations of positive and negative values.

Incidentally, the main advantage of using the Custom filter rather than Filter ⇨ Stylize ⇨ Emboss to produce embossing effects is that Custom preserves the colors in an image while Emboss sacrifices color and changes low-contrast portions of an image to gray. Color Plate 13-1 shows the matrix values from the first example of Figure 13-26 applied to a color image. It also shows examples of other Custom effects, including variations on sharpening and edge-detection.

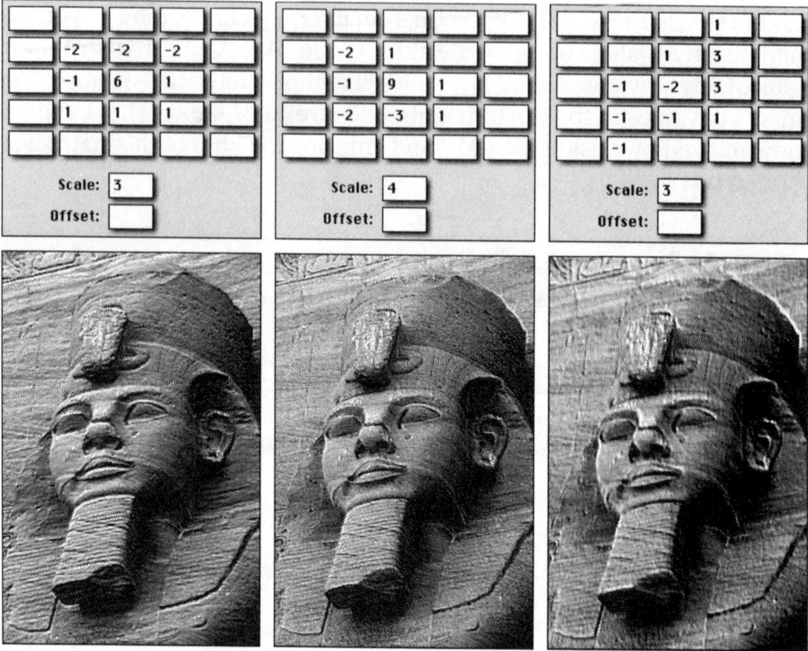

Figure 13-27: To emboss more subtly, increase the central matrix value and the Scale values by equal amounts.

Displacing Pixels in an Image

Photoshop's second custom-effects filter is Filter ⇨ Distort ⇨ Displace, which enables you to distort and add texture to an image by moving the colors of certain pixels in a selection. You specify the direction and distance that the Displace filter moves colors by creating a second image called a *displacement map,* or *dmap* (pronounced *dee-map*) for short. The brightness values in the displacement map tell Photoshop which pixels to affect and how far to move the colors of those pixels:

- **Black:** The black areas of the displacement map move the colors of corresponding pixels in the selection a maximum prescribed distance to the right and/or down. Lighter values between black and medium gray move colors a shorter distance in the same direction.
- **White:** The white areas move the colors of corresponding pixels a maximum distance to the left and/or up. Darker values between white and medium gray move colors a shorter distance in the same direction.
- **Medium gray:** A 50 percent brightness value, such as medium gray, ensures that the colors of corresponding pixels remain unmoved.

Suppose that I create a new image window the same size as the scan of the Egyptian temple carving that I've used about 60 times now in this chapter. This new image will serve as the displacement map. I divide the image into four quadrants. As shown in the middle example of Figure 13-28, I fill the upper left quadrant with black, the lower right quadrant with white, and the other two quadrants with medium gray. (The arrows indicate the direction in which the quadrants will move colors in the affected image. They do not actually appear in the dmap.)

When finished, I save the dmap to disk in the native Photoshop format so that the Displace filter can access it. I then return to the Egyptian carving image, choose Filter ⇨ Distort ⇨ Displace, edit the settings as desired, and open the dmap from disk. The result is the image shown in the last example of Figure 13-28. In keeping with the distribution of brightness values in the dmap, the colors of the pixels in the upper left quadrant of the carving image move rightward, the colors of the pixels in the lower right quadrant move to the left, and the colors in the upper right and lower left quadrant remain intact.

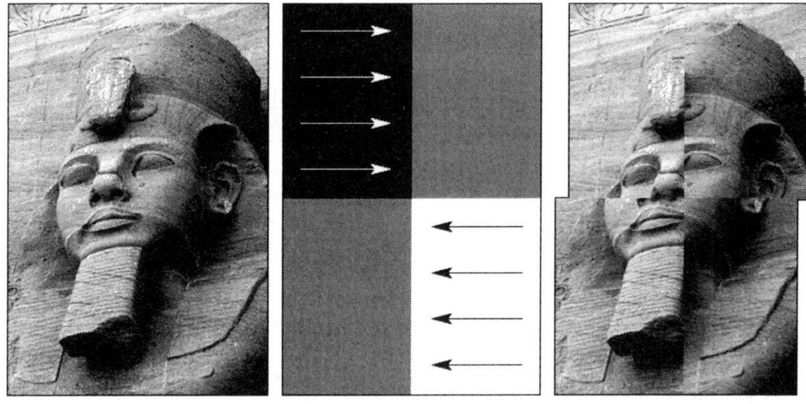

Figure 13-28: The Displace filter enables you to move colors in an image (left) according to the brightness values in a separate image, known as a displacement map (middle). The arrows indicate the direction in which the brightness values will move colors in the original image, as verified by the image on the right.

A dmap must be a color or grayscale image, and you must save the dmap in the native Photoshop 2.0 or 2.5 file format. The Displace command does not recognize PICT, TIFF, or any of the other non-native (albeit common) file formats. Who knows why? Those programmers move in mysterious ways.

At this point, you likely have two questions: How do you use the Displace filter and why in the name of all that is good would you possibly want to? The hows of the Displace filter are covered in the following section. To discover some whys — which should in turn help you dream up some whys of your own — read the "Using Displacement Maps" section later in this chapter.

Displacement theory

Like any custom filtering effect worth its weight in table salt — an asset that has taken something of a nose dive in the recent millennium — you need a certain degree of mathematical reasoning skills to predict the outcome of the Displace filter. Though I was a math major in college (well, actually, math and fine arts, and I must admit to paying the lion's share of attention to the latter), I frankly was befuddled by the results of my first few experiments with the Displace command. Don't be surprised if you are as well. With some time and a modicum of effort, however, you can learn to anticipate the approximate effects of this filter.

Direction of displacement

Earlier, I mentioned — and I quote — "The black areas of the displacement map move . . . colors . . . to the right and/or down . . . The white areas move . . . colors . . . to the left and/or up." Yikes, talk about your fragmented quotations. I think I'll sue! Anyway, the point is, you may have wondered to yourself what all this "and/or" guff was all about. "Is it right or is it down?" you may have puzzled, and rightly so.

The truth is that the direction of a displacement can go either way. It's up to you. If you like right, go with it. If you like down, don't let me stop you. If you like both together, by all means, have at it.

Beginning to understand? No? Well, it works like this: A dmap can contain one or more color channels. If the dmap is a grayscale image with one color channel only, the Displace filter moves colors that correspond to black areas in the dmap both to the right *and* down, depending on your specifications in the Displace dialog box. The filter moves colors that correspond to white areas in the dmap both to the left and up.

Figure 13-29 shows two examples of an image displaced using a single-channel dmap, which appears on the left side of the figure. (Again, the arrows illustrate the directions in which different brightness values move colors in the affected image. They are not part of the dmap file.) I displaced the middle image at 10 percent and the right image at 20 percent. Therefore, the colors in the right image travel twice the distance as those in the middle image, but all colors travel the same direction. (The upcoming section "The Displace dialog box" explains exactly how the percentage values work.)

However, if the dmap contains more than one channel — whether it's a color image or a grayscale image with an independent mask channel — the first channel indicates horizontal displacement and the second channel indicates vertical displacement. All other channels are ignored. Therefore, the Displace filter moves colors that correspond to black areas in the first channel of the dmap to the right and colors that correspond to white areas to the left. (Again, this depends on your specifications in the Displace dialog box.) The filter then moves colors that correspond to the black areas in the second channel downward and colors that correspond to white areas upward.

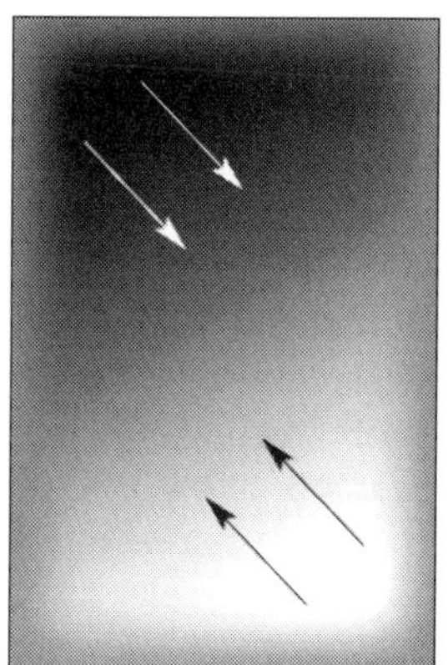

Figure 13-29: The results of applying a single-channel displacement map (left) to an image at 10 percent (middle) and 20 percent (right).

Figure 13-30 shows the effect of a two-channel dmap on our friend the pharaoh. The top row shows the appearance and effect of the first channel on the image at 10 percent and 20 percent. The bottom row shows the appearance and effect of the second channel.

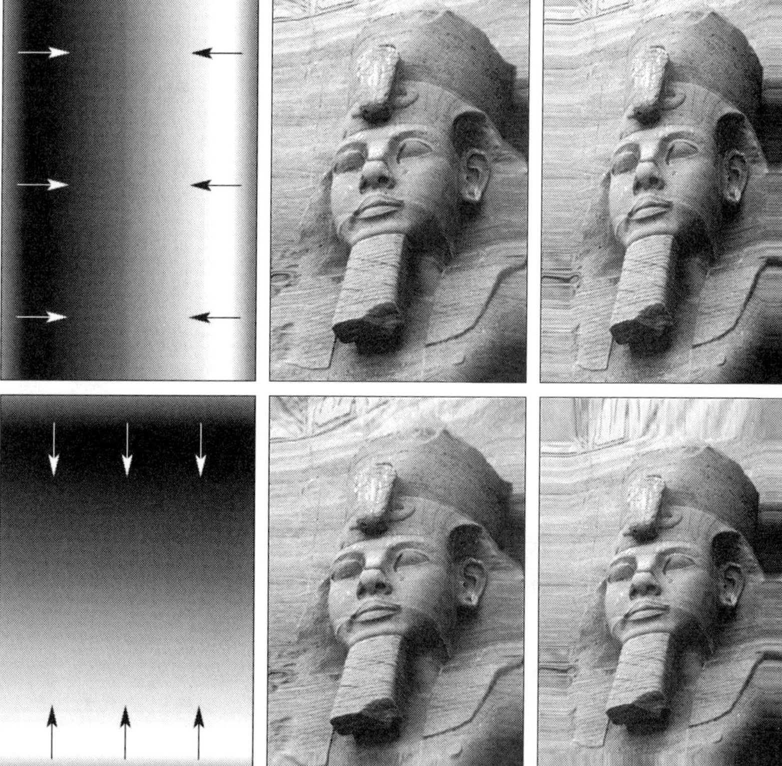

Figure 13-30: The horizontal (top row) and vertical (bottom row) results of applying a two-channel displacement map (left column) to an image at 10 percent (middle) and 20 percent (right).

Brightness value transitions

If you study Figure 13-30 for any length of time, you'll notice a marked stretching effect around the edges of the image, particularly around the two right-hand images. This is an effect you want to avoid.

The cause of the effect is twofold. First, the transition from gray to black and gray to white pixels around the perimeter of the dmap is relatively quick, especially compared with the gradual transitions in the central portion of the image. Second, transitions — reading from left to right, or top to bottom — produce a more noticeable effect when they progress from light to dark than from dark to light. The reason for this is that these transitions follow the direction of Photoshop's displacement algorithm. (I know, when I throw in a word like *algorithm,* everybody's eyes glaze over, but try to stick with me.)

For example, in the light-to-dark transition on the left side of the first-channel dmap in Figure 13-30, one gray value nudges selected colors slightly to the right, the next darker value nudges them an extra pixel, the next darker value another pixel, and so on, resulting in a machine-gun displacement effect that creates a continuous stream of the same colors over and over again. Hence, the big stretch.

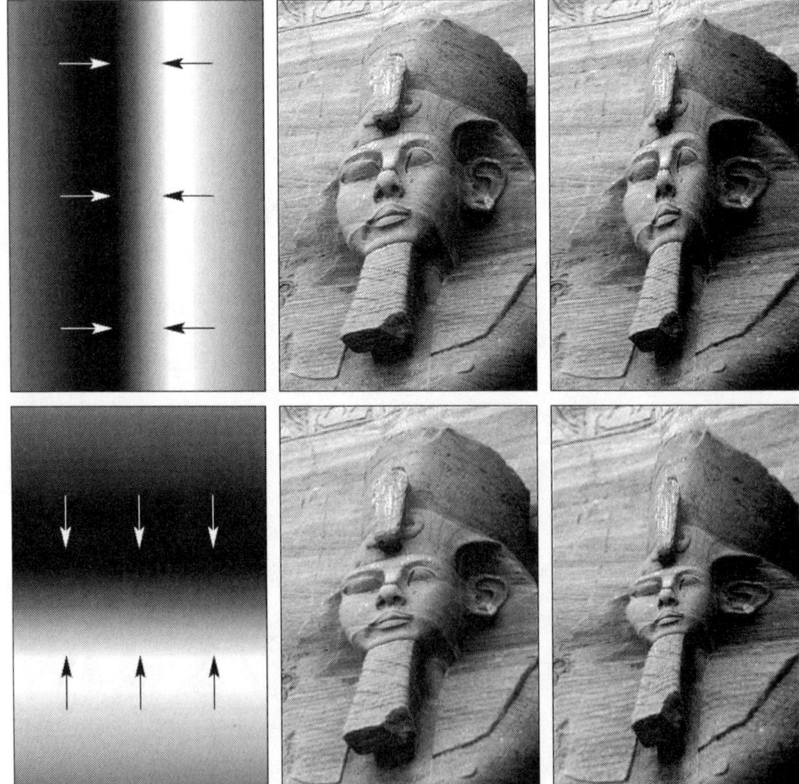

Figure 13-31: Changing the speeds of color transitions in the two-channel displacement map (left column) created smoother image distortions at both the 10 percent (middle) and 20 percent (right) settings.

Get it? Well, if not, the important part is this: to avoid stretching an image, make your dmap transitions slow when progressing from light to dark and quick when progressing from dark to light. For example, in the revised dmap channels shown in the left column of Figure 13-31, the gray values progress slowly from gray to black, abruptly from black to gray to white, and then slowly again from white to gray. Slow light to dark, fast dark to light. The results are smoother image distortions, as demonstrated in the middle and right columns of the figure.

To learn how to create and edit gradations, read the "Applying Gradient Fills" section of Chapter 15. However, as explained in the upcoming "Using Displacement Maps" section, most of the dmaps that you'll use will feature patterns rather than gradations. Pattern dmaps add texture to an image; gradient dmaps distort an image.

The Displace dialog box

When you choose Filter ➪ Distort ➪ Displace, Photoshop displays the Displace dialog box. ("Displays the Displace" is the modern equivalent of "Begin the Beguine," don't you know.) As shown in Figure 13-32, the Displace dialog box provides the following options:

- **Scale:** You can specify the degree to which the Displace filter moves colors in an image by entering percentage values into the Horizontal Scale and Vertical Scale option boxes. At 100 percent, black and white areas in the dmap each have the effect of moving colors 128 pixels. That's 1 pixel per each brightness value over or under medium gray. You can isolate the effect of a single-channel dmap vertically or horizontally — or ignore the first or second channel of a two-channel dmap — by entering 0 percent into the Horizontal or Vertical option box respectively.

  Figure 13-33 shows the effect of distorting an image exclusively horizontally (top row) and vertically (bottom row) at each of three percentage values: 5 percent, 15 percent, and 30 percent. In each case, I used the two-channel dmap from Figure 13-31.
- **Displacement Map:** If the dmap contains fewer pixels than the image, you can either scale it to match the size of the selected image by selecting the Stretch to Fit radio button or repeat the dmap over and over within the image by selecting Tile. Figure 13-34 shows a small two-channel dmap that contains radial gradations. In the first column, I stretched the dmap to fit the image. In the second column, I tiled the dmap. To create both examples in the top row, I set the Horizontal Scale and Vertical Scale values to 10 percent. To create the bottom-row examples, I raised the values to 50 percent.
- **Undefined Areas:** New to Photoshop 2.5, these radio buttons let you tell Photoshop how to color pixels around the outskirts of the selection that are otherwise undefined. By default, the Repeat Edge Pixels radio button is selected, which repeats the colors of pixels around the perimeter of the selection. This

selection can result in extreme stretching effects, as shown in the middle example of Figure 13-35. To instead repeat the image inside the undefined areas, as demonstrated in the final example of the figure, select the Wrap Around option.

The Repeat Edge Pixels setting was active in all displacement map figures prior to Figure 13-35. In these cases, I frequently avoided stretching effects by coloring the edges of the dmap with medium gray and gradually lightening or darkening the brightness values toward the center.

Figure 13-32: Use the options in the Displace dialog box to specify the degree to which the filter distorts the selection, how the filter matches the displacement map to the image, and how it colors the pixels around the perimeter of the selection.

Displace

Horizontal Scale: 10

Vertical Scale: 10

OK

Cancel

Displacement map:
- (•) Stretch to fit
- ( ) Tile

Undefined Areas:
- ( ) Wrap Around
- (•) Repeat edge pixels

Figure 13-33: The results of applying the Distort filter exclusively horizontally (top row) and exclusively vertically (bottom row) at 5 percent (left column), 15 percent (middle), and 30 percent (right).

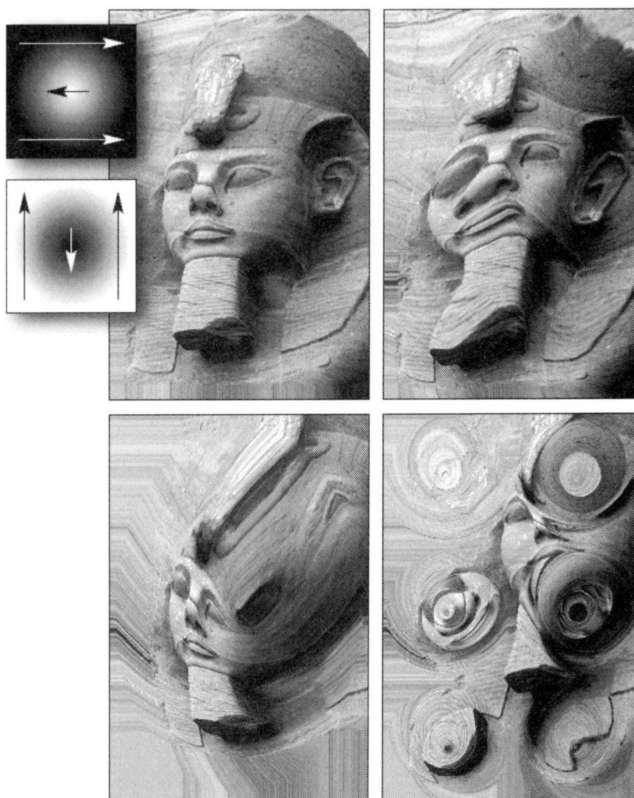

Figure 13-34: Using a small two-channel dmap (offset top left), I stretched the dmap to fit (left column) and tiled it (right column) at 10 percent (top row) and 50 percent (bottom row).

Figure 13-35: After creating a straightforward, single-channel displacement map (left), I applied the filter subject to two different Undefined Areas settings, Repeat Edge Pixels (middle) and Wrap Around (right).

After you finish specifying options in the Displace dialog box, click on the OK button or press Return to display the Open dialog box, which allows you to select the displacement map saved to disk. Only native Photoshop documents show up in the scrolling list.

Using Displacement Maps

So far, all of the displacement maps demonstrated involve gradations of one form of another. Gradient dmaps distort the image over the contours of a fluid surface, like a reflection in a fun-house mirror. In this respect, the effects of the Displace filter closely resemble those of the Pinch and Spherize filters described in the last chapter. But the more functional and straightforward application of the Displace filter is to add texture to an image.

Creating texture effects

Figure 13-36 shows the results of using the Displace filter to apply nine of the patterns from the Displacement Maps folder inside the Plug-ins folder. Color Plate 13-2 shows the effects of applying four of the patterns to color images. Introduced in the "How to create patterns" section of Chapter 10, this folder contains repeating patterns that Adobe Systems designed especially with the Displace filter in mind.

As shown in the figure and color plate, most of these patterns produce the effect of viewing the image through textured glass — an effect known in high-end graphics circles as *glass refraction.* Those few patterns that contain too much contrast to pass off as textured glass — including Fragment layers, Mezzo effect, and Schnable effect — can be employed to create images that appear as if they were printed on coarse paper or even textured metal.

To view each of the textures from the Displacement Maps folder on its own, see Figure 10-14 in the "How to create patterns" section of Chapter 10. Like Figure 13-36, Figure 10-14 is labeled so that you can easily match texture and effect.

Displacement Maps folder — as a dmap, be sure to select the Tile radio button inside the Displace dialog box. This option repeats the dmap rather than stretching it out of proportion.

I also explained in Chapter 10 that you can create your own textures from scratch using filtering effects. I specifically described how to create a stucco texture by applying the Add Noise filter three times in a row to an empty image and then using the Emboss filter to give it depth. (See the "Using filters" item in the "How to create patterns" section.) This texture appears in the first example of Figure 13-37. I applied the texture at 2 percent and 10 percent to create the windblown middle and right examples in the figure.

Figure 13-36: Examples of applying nine patterns from the Displacement Maps folder with the Displace filter at 10 percent horizontally and vertically.

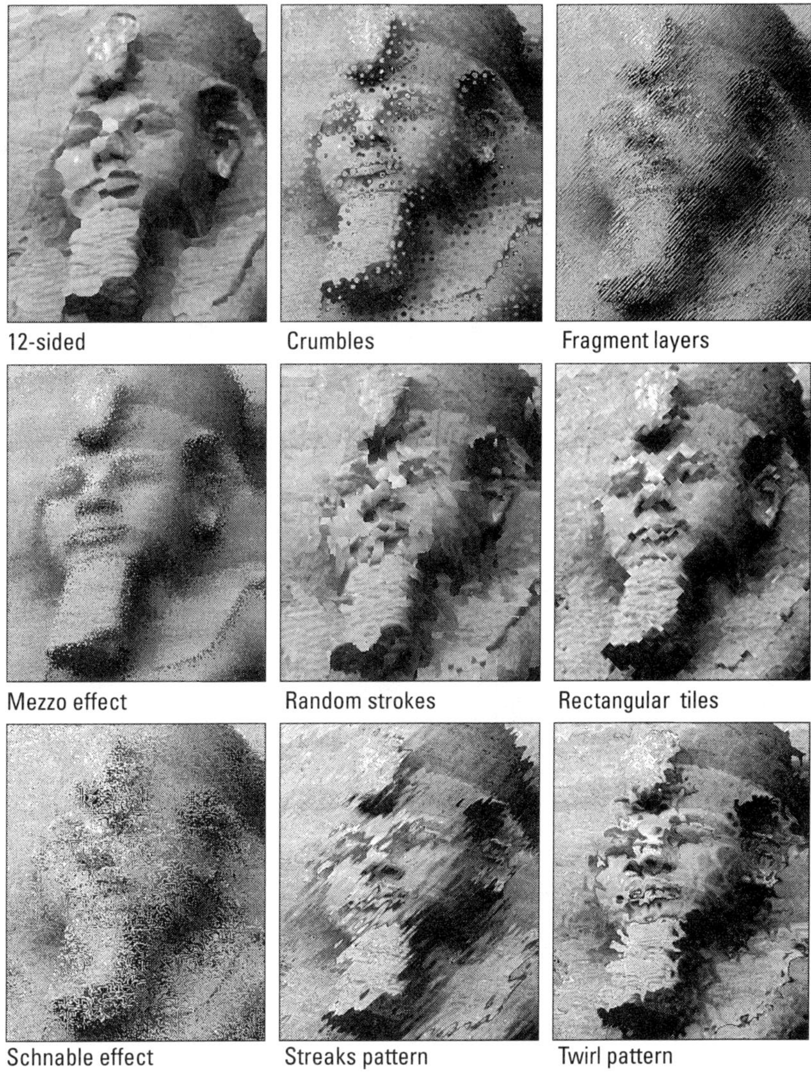

The stucco pattern is only one of an infinite number of textures you can create using filters. In fact, stucco is a great base texture on which to build. For example, to create the wavy texture that starts off the first row of Figure 13-38, I softened the stucco texture by applying the Gaussian Blur filter with a 0.3-pixel radius. I then applied the Ripple filter twice with the Large option selected and an Amount value of 100. That's all there was to it.

Figure 13-37: After creating a stucco texture with the Add Noise and Emboss filters (left), I applied the texture as a displacement map at 2 percent (middle) and 10 percent (right).

To create the second texture in the figure, I applied the Crystallize filter at its default Cell Size value of 10. Believe me, I could go on creating textures like this forever, and more importantly, so could you. The images in the second and third columns of the Figure 13-38 show the results of applying the textures with the Displace filter at 2 percent and 10 percent respectively.

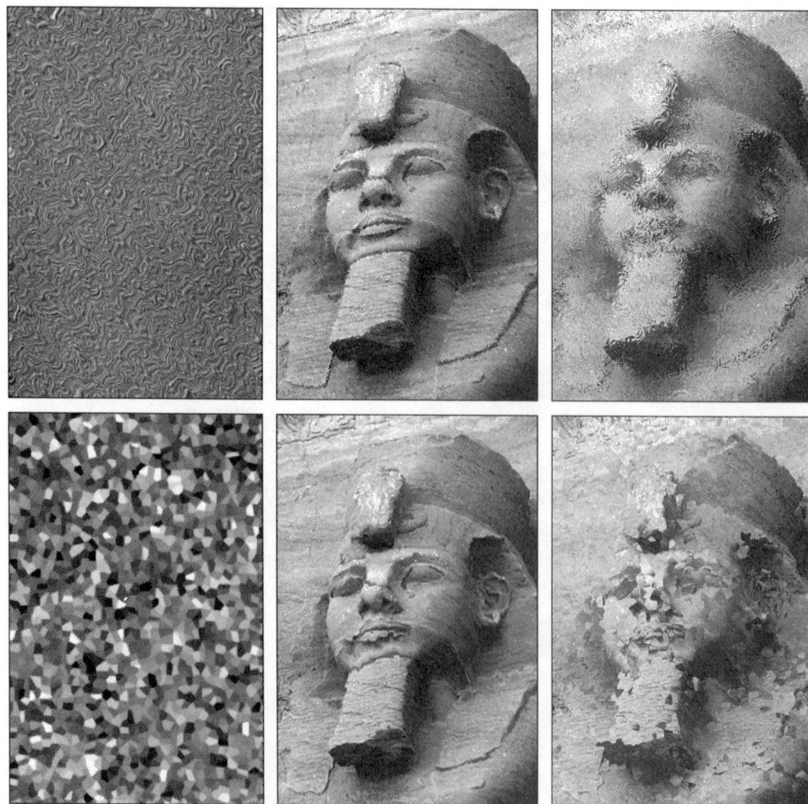

Figure 13-38: After creating two textures with the Add Noise, Emboss, and Ripple filters (first column), I applied the textures as displacement maps at 2 percent (middle) and 10 percent (right).

In the final analysis, any pattern you design for use with the rubber stamp tool is equally applicable for use with the Displace filter. Furthermore, of the two options — rubber stamp and Displace — the latter is more likely to yield the kind of textured effects that will leave your audience begging, pleading, and scraping for more.

Displacing an image onto itself

I throw this technique in just for laughs. Personally, I can't get enough of *Dr. Strangelove*. That's why I call this the *Make My Day at the Atomic Café* effect. Warning: This effect features simulated melting Egyptian carvings. If you find them unnerving, you have a very soft stomach.

I discovered this effect playing around with an old profile image of Richard Nixon, and I'm here to tell you, his face melted off good. Real good. That Bob Hope nose of his went sailing off his head. Unfortunately, I'm afraid Mr. Nixon might not see the bucketloads of humor in these images — which I flatly refuse to turn over to the DA's office, incidentally. So rather than get my behind sued clean off, the pharaoh will have to do.

The Make My Day at the Atomic Café effect involves nothing more the using an image as its own displacement map. First, make sure that the image you want to distort is saved to disk in the native Photoshop format. Then choose Filter ⇨ Distort ⇨ Displace, specify the desired settings, and select the version of the image saved to disk. Figure 13-39 shows three applications of this effect, once applied at 10 percent exclusively horizontally, the next at 10 percent vertically, and the last at 10 percent in both directions.

Figure 13-39: See Egypt, have a blast. Here I applied the pharaoh image as a displacement map onto itself at 10 percent horizontally (left), 10 percent vertically (middle), and 10 percent in both directions.

As a slight variation, save the image in its original form. Then choose Image ⇨ Map ⇨ Invert (Command-I) and save the inverted image to disk under a different name. Open the original image and use the Displace filter to apply the inverted image as a displacement map. Figure 13-40 shows some results.

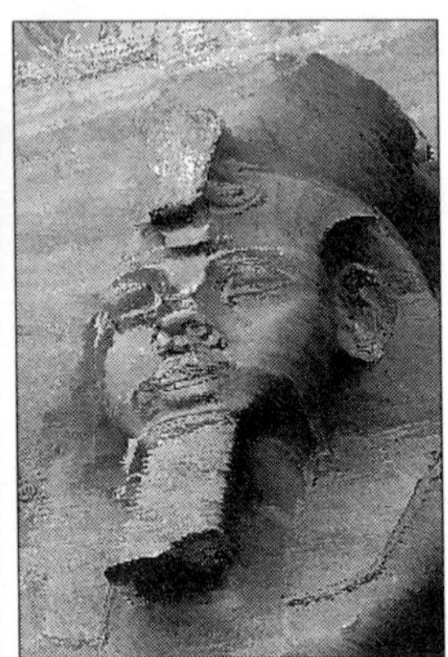

Figure 13-40: The results of applying an inverted version of the pharaoh as a displacement map onto the original image at 10 percent horizontally (left), 10 percent vertically (middle), and 10 percent in both directions.

If you really want to blow an image apart, apply Horizontal Scale and Vertical Scale values of 50 percent or greater. The first row of Figure 13-41 shows a series of 50 percent applications of the Displace filter. I took the liberty of sharpening each image to heighten the effect. In the second row, I applied the filter to floating selections and changed the translucency of each filtered image to 10 percent. In this way, I retained the detail of the original image while still managing to impart a smidgen of sandblasting.

Figure 13-41: The results of displacing the pharaoh image with itself at 50 percent horizontally, 50 percent vertically, and 50 percent in both directions (top row), followed by the same effects applied to highly translucent floating selections (bottom row).

Summary

- The Custom filter multiplies the brightness values of pixels by the corresponding numbers in the matrix, adds them up, divides the sum by the Scale value, and adds the Offset value to compute the new brightness value for a single pixel.
- As long as the sum of the matrix values divided by the Scale value is equal to 1, the Custom filter maintains the original color balance of an image.
- A positive central matrix value surrounded by negative values results in a sharpening effect; a positive CMV surrounded by positive values results in blurring; and a negative CMV surrounded by positive values results in edge-detection.
- Use the Offset value to compensate for overly dark or overly light custom effects.
- Non-symmetrical matrix values in which positive and negative numbers are arranged on opposite sides of the CMV result in embossing effects.
- The Displace filter works by moving colors in a selection according to the brightness values in a separate image saved to disk. This image is called a displacement map.
- If a displacement map features a single color channel, black regions in the dmap move colors down and to the right, and white regions move colors up and to the left. If a dmap contains more than one color channel, the first channel moves colors horizontally; the second channel moves them vertically.
- Use gradient dmaps to distort an image. Use repeating patterns such as those in the Displacement Maps folder to add texture to an image.
- Apply an image as a displacement map onto itself to melt the faces off those you love to hate.

PART V

The Wonderful World of Color

Chapter 14:
Defining Colors

Chapter 15:
Coloring Selections

Chapter 16:
Mapping and Adjusting Colors

Chapter 17:
Manipulating Channels

Color is the most essential ingredient in any image. After all, what good are precise retouching techniques and awesome special effects if the image appears overly dark or washed out when printed? Even if you work primarily in the grayscale mode, it's important to balance the amount of brightness and contrast in an image to retain the subtle nuances and painstaking detail that you spent so much time to develop.

These chapters, then, are about color, from gray values to the fully saturated hues in the rainbow. I show you how colors work, how to define colors, how to apply them, how to edit colors in an image, and how to manipulate the contents of individual color channels. By time you finish reading this section, you may not know enough to earn a Ph.D. in color theory, but you'll be able to create some spectacularly colorful images that will make those doctoral students drool.

If you already know how Photoshop's color controls work and you're experienced in color theory — that is, you understand the RGB, CMYK, and HSB color models — you probably can skip the majority of Chapter 14. Even experienced users, however, will do well to read the discussion of the Lab mode, Photoshop 2.5's new color model based on CIE color space.

This section really takes off in Chapters 16 and 17, which demonstrate ways to correct the colors in an image so that they more accurately represent real life. You also learn how to distort colors to achieve still more special effects. If you want to get a feel for some of the ideas and effects I cover in these chapters, take a quick look at the full-color images in the color plates section. Each color plate is numbered according to the chapter that discusses the image. In this way, the color plates serve as a sort of visual index to topics covered in the book.

Defining Colors

CHAPTER 14

In This Chapter

- How to use the color controls in the toolbox
- How to select and define colors in the Color Picker dialog box
- In-depth examinations of the RGB, HSB, CMYK, and Lab color models
- How and why to reduce a full-color image to 256 colors
- How to create grayscale and black-and-white images
- Introductions to the Trumatch and Pantone color standards
- How to use the Colors palette and eyedropper tool

Selecting and Editing Colors

Every once in a while, the state of Macintosh graphics technology reminds me of television in the early 1950s. Only the upper echelon of Photoshop artists can afford to work exclusively in the wonderful world of color. The rest of us print or view most of our images in black and white.

But regardless of who you are, color is a prime concern. Even gray values, after all, are colors. Many folks have problems accepting this premise — I guess we're all so used to separating the worlds of grays and other colors in our minds that never the twain shall meet — but the fact is, gray values are just variations on what Noah Webster used to call, "The sensation resulting from stimulation of the retina of the eye by light waves of certain lengths." (Give the guy a few drinks and he'd spout off 19 more definitions, not including the meanings of the transitive verb.) Just as black and white represent a subset of gray, gray is a subset of color. In fact, you'll find that using Photoshop involves an awful lot of navigating through these and other colorful subsets.

Specifying colors

First off, Photoshop 2.5 provides four color controls in the toolbox, as shown in Figure 14-1. These icons work as follows:

- **Foreground color**: The foreground color icon indicates the color you apply when you use the type, paint bucket, line, pencil, airbrush, or paintbrush tool, or if you Option-drag with the smudge tool. The foreground color also begins any gradation created with the gradient tool. You can apply the foreground color to a selection by choosing Edit ➪ Fill or Edit ➪ Stroke or by pressing Option-Delete. To change the foreground color, click on the foreground color icon to display the Color Picker dialog box or click in an open image window with the eyedropper tool.
- **Background color:** The active background color indicates the color you apply with the eraser tool. The background color also ends any gradation created with the gradient tool. You can apply the background color to a selection by pressing the Delete key. To change the background color, click on the background color icon to display the Color Picker dialog box or Option-click in an open image window with the eyedropper tool.
- **Switch colors:** Click on this icon to exchange the foreground and background colors.
- **Default colors:** Click on this icon to make the foreground color black and the background color white, according to their factory default settings.

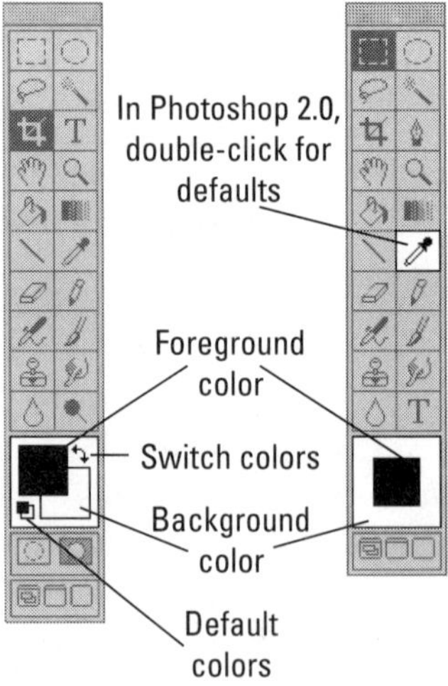

Figure 14-1: The color controls provided with Photoshop 2.5 (left) and 2.0 (right).

Photoshop 2.0 lacks the switch colors and default colors icons. However, it offers an equivalent for the latter. To change the foreground color to black and the background color to white, just double-click on the eyedropper tool icon in the toolbox.

Using the Color Picker

When you click on the foreground or background color icon, Photoshop displays the Color Picker dialog box. (This step assumes that Photoshop is the active option in the Color Picker pop-up menu in the General Preferences dialog box. If you select the Apple option, the generic Apple Color Picker appears, as described in the "HSB and HSL" section later in this chapter.) Figure 14-2 labels the wealth of elements and options in the Color Picker dialog box, which work as follows:

- **Color slider:** Use the *color slider* to home in on the color you want to select. Drag up or down on either of the *slider triangles* to select a color from a particular 8-bit range. The colors represented inside the slider correspond to the selected radio button. For example, if you select the H (Hue) radio button, which is the default setting, the slider colors represent the full 8-bit range of hues. If you select S (Saturation), the slider shows the current hue at full saturation at the top of the slider, down to no saturation — or gray — at the bottom of the slider. If you select B (Brightness), the slider shows the 8-bit range of brightness values, from solid color at the top of the slider to absolute black at the bottom. You also can select R (Red), G (Green) or B (Blue), in which case the top of the slider shows you what the current color looks like when subjected to full-intensity red, green, or blue (respectively) and the bottom of the slider shows every bit of red, green, or blue subtracted.

For a proper introduction to the HSB and RGB color models, including definitions of specific terms such as hue, saturation, and brightness, read the "Working in Different Color Models" section later in this chapter.

- **Color field:** The *color field* shows a 16-bit range of variations on the current slider color. Click inside it to move the *color selection marker* and thereby select a new color. The field graphs colors against the two remaining attributes *not* represented by the color slider. For example, if you select the H (Hue) radio button, the field graphs colors according to brightness vertically and saturation horizontally, as demonstrated in the first example of Figure 14-3. The other examples show what happens to the color field when you select the S (Saturation) and B (Brightness) radio buttons.

  Likewise, Figure 14-4 shows how the field graphs colors when you select the R (Red), G (Green), and B (Blue) radio buttons. Obviously, it would help a heck of a lot to see these images in color, but you probably wouldn't have been able to afford this big, fat book if we had printed it in full color. Therefore, I recommend that you experiment with the Color Picker inside your version of Photoshop or refer to Color Plate 14-1 to see how the dialog box looks when the H (Hue), S (Saturation), and B (Brightness) options are selected.

Slider and field always work together to represent the entire 16-million color range. The slider displays 256 colors, and the field displays 65,000 variations on the slider color; 256 times 65,000 is 16 million. Therefore, no matter which radio button you select, you have access to the same colors. Just your means of accessing them changes.

- **Current color:** The color currently selected from the color field appears in the top rectangle immediately to the right of the color slider. Click on the OK button or press Return to make this the current foreground or background color (depending on which color control icon in the toolbox you clicked to display the Color Picker dialog box in the first place).
- **Previous color:** The bottom rectangle just to the right of the color slider shows how the foreground or background color — whichever one you are in the process of editing — looked before you displayed the Color Picker dialog box. Click on the Cancel button or press Command-period to leave this color intact.
- **Alert triangle:** The *alert triangle* appears when you select a bright color that Photoshop can't print using standard process colors. The box below the triangle shows the closest CMYK equivalent, which is invariably a duller version of the color. Click either on the triangle or box to bring the color into the printable range.

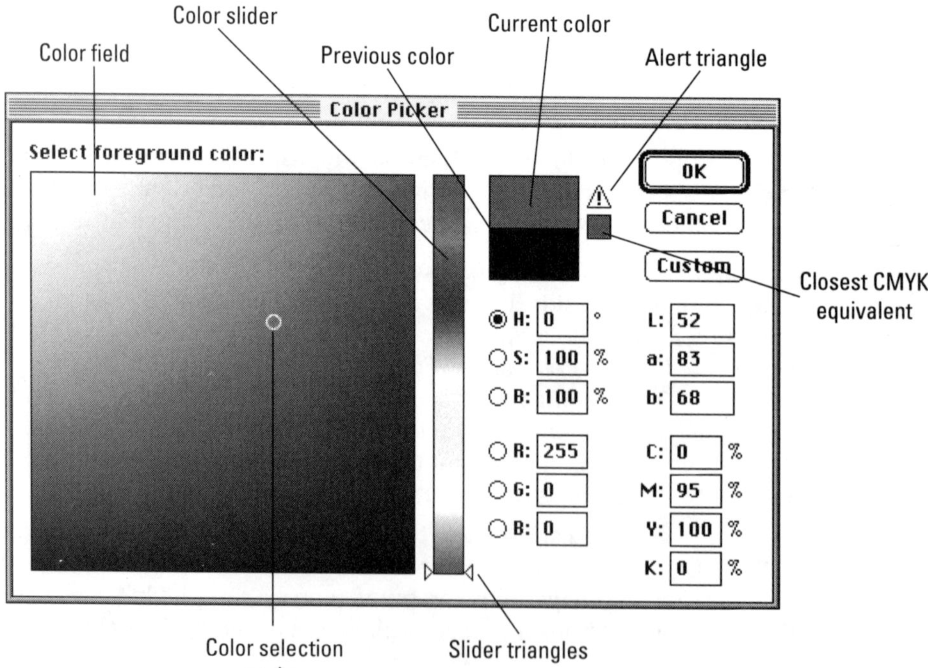

Figure 14-2: Use the elements and options in the Color Picker dialog box to specify a new foreground or background color from the 16-million-color range.

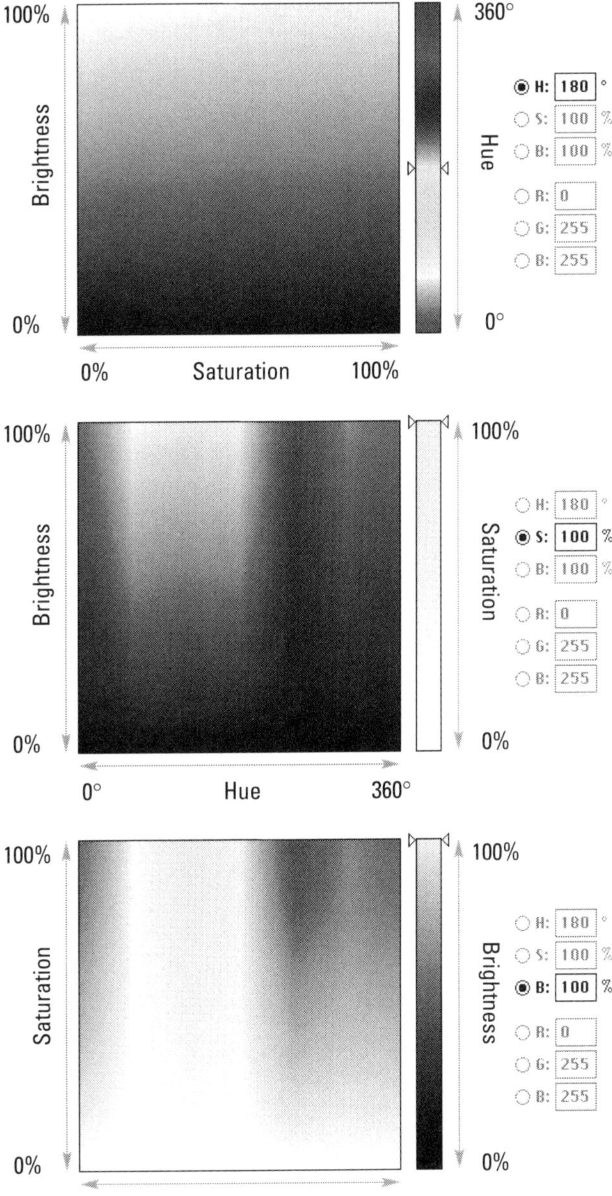

Figure 14-3: The color field graphs colors against the two attributes that are not represented in the slider. Here you can see how color is laid out when you select (top to bottom) the H (Hue), S (Saturation), and B (Brightness) radio buttons.

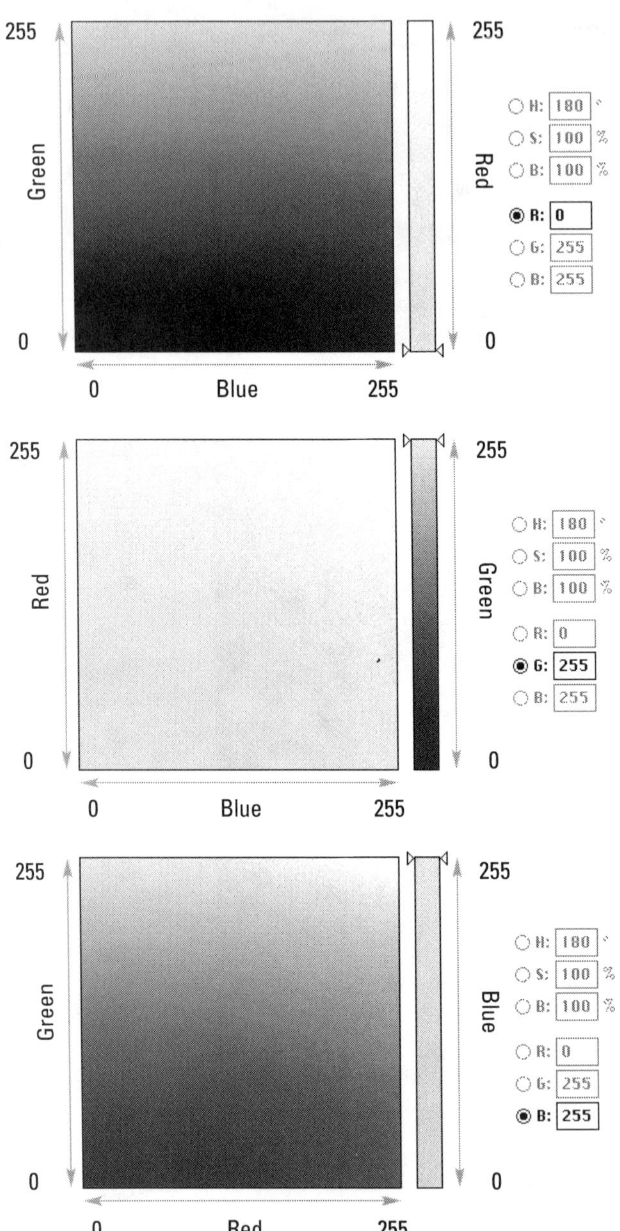

Figure 14-4: The results of selecting (top to bottom) the R (Red), G (Green), and B (Blue) radio buttons.

Entering numeric color values

In addition to selecting colors using the slider and color field, you can enter specific color values in the option boxes in the lower right region of the Color Picker dialog box. Novices and intermediates may find these options less satisfying to use than the slider and field. However, the options enable artists and print professionals to specify exact color values, whether to make controlled adjustments to a color already in use or to match a color used in another document. In Photoshop 2.5, these options fall into one of four camps:

- **HSB:** These options stand for hue, saturation, and brightness. Hue is measured on a 360-degree circle. Saturation and brightness are measured from 0 to 100 percent. These options permit access to more than 3 million color variations.
- **RGB:** You can change the amount of the primary colors red, green, and blue by specifying the brightness value of each color from 0 to 255. These options permit access to more than 16 million color variations.
- **Lab:** Exclusive to Photoshop 2.5, these options stand for *luminosity,* measured from 0 to 100 percent, and two arbitrary color axes, *a* and *b,* whose brightness values range from –128 to 127. These options permit access to more than 6 million color variations.
- **CMYK:** These options display the amount of cyan, magenta, yellow, and black ink required to print the current color. In fact, when you click on the alert triangle, these are the only values that don't change, because these are the values that make up the closest CMYK equivalent.

In my opinion, the numerical range of these options is extremely bewildering. For example, numerically speaking, the CMYK options enable you to create 100 million unique colors, whereas the RGB options permit the standard 16 million variations, and the Lab options permits a scant 6 million. Yet in point of fact, Lab is the largest color space, theoretically encompassing all colors from both CMYK and RGB. The printing standard CMYK provides by far the fewest colors, just the opposite of what you might expect. What gives? Misleading numerical ranges. How do these weird color models work? Keep reading and you'll find out.

Working in Different Color Modes

The four sets of option boxes inside the Color Picker dialog box represent *color models* — or, if you prefer, *color modes* (one less letter, no less meaning, perfect for you folks who are trying to cut down in life). Color models are different ways to define colors both on-screen and on the printed page.

Outside the Color Picker dialog box, you can work inside any one of these color models by choosing a command from the Modes menu. In doing so, you generally change the colors in your image by dumping a few hundred or even thousand colors that have no equivalents in the new color model. The only exception is Lab, which in theory encompasses every unique color your eyes can detect.

Rather than discuss the color models in the order in which they occur in the Modes menu, I cover them in logical order, starting with the most common and widely accepted color model, RGB. Also note that I don't discuss the duotone or multichannel modes. I already covered duotones in Chapter 7, "Printing Images," and I don't discuss the multichannel mode because it is not a color model. Rather, Mode ⇨ Multichannel enables you to separate an image into entirely independent channels which you then can swap around and splice back together to create special effects.

RGB

RGB is the color model of light. It comprises three *primary colors* — red, green, and blue — each of which can vary between 256 levels of intensity (called *brightness values,* as I've discussed in previous chapters). The RGB model is also called the *additive primary model,* because a color becomes lighter as you add higher levels of red, green, and blue light. All monitors, projection devices, and other items that transmit or filter light, including televisions, movie projectors, colored stage lights, and even stained glass, rely on the additive primary model.

Red, green, and blue light mix as follows:

- **Red and green:** Full-intensity red and green mix to form yellow. Subtract some red to make chartreuse; subtract some green to make orange. All these colors assume a complete lack of blue.
- **Green and blue:** Full-intensity green and blue with no red mix to form cyan. If you try hard enough, you can come up with 65,000 colors in the turquoise/jade/sky blue/sea green range.
- **Blue and red:** Full-intensity blue and red mix to form magenta. Subtract some blue to make rose; subtract some red to make purple. All these colors assume a complete lack of green.
- **Red, green, and blue:** Full-intensity red, green, and blue mix to form white, the absolute brightest color in the visible spectrum.
- **No light:** Low intensities of red, green, and blue plunge a color into blackness.

Insofar as image editing is concerned, the RGB color model is ideal for editing images on-screen because it provides access to the entire range of 24-bit screen colors. Furthermore, you can save an RGB image in any file format supported by Photoshop. As shown in Table 14-1, the only other color mode that is compatible with such a wide range of file formats is grayscale.

Table 14-1 File-Format Support for Photoshop 2.5's Color Models

	Bitmap	*Grayscale*	*Duotone*	*Indexed*	*RGB*	*Lab*	*CMYK*
EPS	yes	yes	yes	yes	yes	yes	yes
GIF	yes	yes	no	yes	yes	no	no
JPEG	no	yes	no	no	yes	no	yes
PCX	yes	yes	no	yes	yes	no	no
PICT	yes	yes	no	yes	yes	no	no
Scitex	no	yes	no	no	yes	no	yes
TIFF	yes	yes	no	yes	yes	yes	yes

Table 14-1 lists color models in the order they appear in the Modes menu. Again, I left out the multichannel mode because it is not a color model. The native Photoshop format, not listed in the table, supports all color models.

On the negative side, the RGB color model provides access to a wider range of colors than you can print. Therefore, if you are designing an image for full-color printing, you can expect to lose many of the brightest and most vivid colors in your image. The only way to entirely avoid such color loss is to scan your image and edit it in the CMYK mode, which can be an exceptionally slow proposition. The better solution is to scan your images to Photo CDs and edit them in the Lab mode, as explained in the upcoming "CIE's Lab" section.

HSB and HSL

In Photoshop 2.0, the Modes menu provides access to two color models dropped from Photoshop 2.5. The first is HSB — hue, saturation, brightness — the color model featured in the Color Picker dialog box. The second is HSL, which stands for hue, saturation, and luminosity. In either case, *hue* is pure color, the stuff rainbows are made of, measured on a 360-degree circle. Red is located at 0 degrees, yellow at 60 degrees, green at 120 degrees, cyan at 180 degrees (midway around the circle), blue at 240 degrees, and magenta at 300 degrees. It's basically a pie-shaped version of the RGB model at full-intensity.

If you want to see what the HSB color model looks like, choose Preference ➪ General (Command-K), select Apple from the Color Picker pop-up menu, and press Return. Then click on the foreground or background color icon in the toolbox to display the Apple Color Picker window shown in Figure 14-5. The perimeter of the color wheel shows each and every hue at full saturation. The center of the wheel represents lowest saturation. Use the scroll bar to change the brightness.

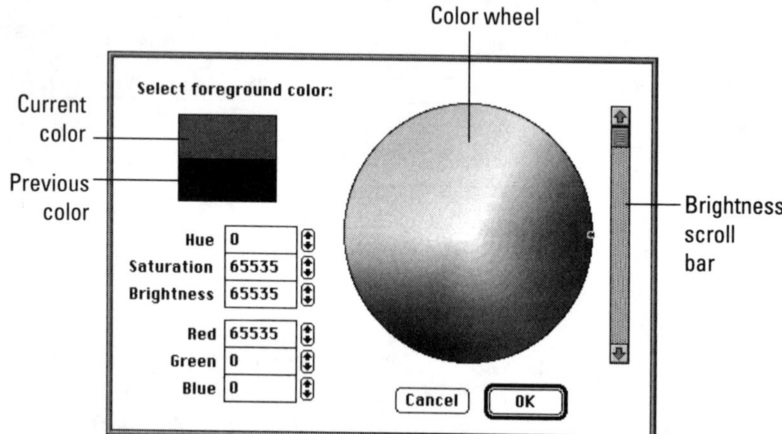

Figure 14-5: The Apple Color Picker dialog box graphically demonstrates the HSB color model.

Saturation represents the purity of the color. A zero saturation value equals gray. White, black, and any other colors you can express in a grayscale image have no saturation. Full saturation produces the purest version of a hue.

Brightness is the lightness or darkness of a color. A zero brightness value equals black. Full brightness combined with full saturation results in the most vivid version of any hue. *Luminosity* (also called *lightness*), which is the *L* in *HSL,* is slightly but significantly different than brightness. No luminosity still equals black, but full luminosity turns any hue or saturation value to white. Therefore, medium luminosity is required to produce the most vivid version of any hue.

HSB continues to hang on in the Color Picker dialog box, enabling you to define a color in the HSB model. In Photoshop 2.5.1, you can edit an RGB image in the HSL or HSB mode by choosing Filter ➪ Other ➪ HSL&HSB. A dialog box will appear, allowing you to switch from RGB to HSL or from RGB to HSB. You can then edit away, though Photoshop will not display the colors correctly. While each channel is converted to hue, saturation, and luminosity or brightness values, Photoshop continues to display the image in the RGB mode, making this ill-conceived option nearly useless. When you are finished, choose Filter ➪ Other ➪ HSL&HSB again and switch from HSL or HSB back to RGB.

CMYK

In nature, our eyes perceive pigments according to the *subtractive color model.* Sunlight contains every visible color found on earth. When sunlight is projected on an object, the object absorbs (subtracts) some of the light and reflects the rest. The reflected light is the color that you see. For example, a fire engine is bright red because it absorbs all non-red — meaning all blue and green — from the white-light spectrum.

Pigments on a sheet of paper work the same way. You can even mix pigments to create other colors. Suppose that you paint a red brush stroke, which absorbs green and blue light, over a blue brush stroke, which absorbs green and red light. You get a blackish mess that has only a modicum of blue and red light left, along with a smidgen of green because the colors weren't absolutely pure.

But wait — every child knows red and blue mix to form purple. So what gives? What gives is that what you learned in elementary school is only a rude approximation of the truth. Did you ever try mixing a vivid red with a canary yellow only to produce an ugly orange-brown gloop? The reason you didn't achieve the bright orange you wanted is obvious if you stop and think about it. The fact that red starts out darker than bright orange means you have to add a great deal of yellow before you arrive at orange. And even then, it had better be an incredibly bright lemon yellow, not some deep canary yellow that already has a lot of red in it.

Commercial subtractive primaries

The real subtractive primary colors used by commercial printers are for the most part very light. Cyan absorbs only red light, magenta absorbs only green light, and yellow absorbs only blue light. Unfortunately, on their own, these colors don't do a very good job of producing dark colors. In fact, at full intensities, cyan, magenta, and yellow all mixed together don't get much beyond a muddy brown. That's where black comes in. Black helps to accentuate shadows, deepen dark colors, and, of course, print real blacks.

In case you're wondering how colors mix in the CMYK model, it's basically the opposite of the RGB model. However, because pigments are not as pure as primary colors in the additive model, there are some differences:

- **Cyan and magenta:** Full-intensity cyan and magenta mix to form a deep blue with a little green in it. Subtract some cyan to make purple; subtract some magenta to make a dull medium blue. All these colors assume a complete lack of yellow.
- **Magenta and yellow:** Full-intensity magenta and yellow mix to form a brilliant red. Subtract some magenta to make vivid orange; subtract some yellow to make rose. All these colors assume a complete lack of cyan.

- **Yellow and cyan:** Full-intensity yellow and cyan mix to form a medium green with a surprising amount of blue in it. Subtract some yellow to make a deep teal; subtract some cyan to make chartreuse. All these colors assume a complete lack of magenta.
- **Cyan, magenta, and yellow:** Full-intensity cyan, magenta, and yellow mix to form a muddy brown.
- **Black:** Black pigmentation added to any other pigment darkens the color.
- **No pigment:** No pigmentation results in white (assuming that white is the color of the paper).

Editing in CMYK

If you're used to editing RGB images, editing in the CMYK mode can require some new approaches, especially when editing individual color channels. When you view a single color channel in the RGB mode, white indicates high-intensity color, and black indicates low-intensity color. It's just the opposite in CMYK. When you view an individual color channel, black means high-intensity color, and white means low-intensity color.

This doesn't mean that RGB and CMYK color channels look like inverted versions of each other. In fact, because the color theory is inverted, they look pretty much the same. But if you're trying to achieve the full-intensity colors mentioned in the preceding section, you should apply black to the individual color channels, not white as you would in the RGB mode.

CIE's Lab

Whereas the RGB mode is the color model of your luminescent computer screen and the CMYK mode is the color model of the reflective page, Lab — found only in Photoshop 2.5 — is independent of light or pigment. Perhaps you've already heard the bit about how in 1931, an international color organization called the *Commission Internationale d'Eclairage* (CIE) developed a color model that in theory contains every single color the human eye can see. (Gnats, iguanas, fruit bats, go find your own color models; humans, you have CIE. Mutants and aliens — maybe CIE, maybe not, too early to tell.) Then, in 1976, the significant birthday of our nation, the CIE celebrated by coming up with two additional color systems. One of those systems was Lab, and the other was shrouded in secrecy. Well, at least I don't know what the other one was.

The beauty of the Lab color model is that it fills in gaps in both the RGB and CMYK models. RGB, for example, provides an overabundance of colors in the blue-to-green range, but is stingy on yellows, oranges, and other colors in the green-to-red range. Meanwhile, the colors missing from CMYK are enough to fill the holes in Albert Hall. Lab gets everything just right.

Understanding Lab anatomy

The Lab mode features three color channels, one for luminosity and two others for color ranges known simply by the initials *a* and *b*. (The Greeks would have called them alpha and beta, if that's any help.) Upon hearing *luminosity*, you probably think, "Ah, just like HSL." Well, the truth is, Lab's luminosity is just like HSB's brightness. White indicates full-intensity color. Meanwhile, the *a* channel contains colors ranging from deep green (low brightness values) to gray (medium brightness values) to vivid pink (high brightness values). The *b* channel ranges from bright blue (low brightness values) to gray to burnt yellow (high brightness values). As in the RGB model, these colors mix together to produce lighter colors. Only the brightness values in the luminosity channel darken the colors. Therefore, you can think of Lab as a two-channel RGB with brightness thrown on top.

To get a glimpse of how it works, try the following simple experiment.

STEPS: Testing Out the Lab mode

Step 1. Create a new image in the Lab mode — say, 300 × 300 pixels.

Step 2. Option-drag from the center of the image with the elliptical marquee tool while pressing Shift to create a big circle. Then click on the default colors icon in the toolbox.

Step 3. Press Command-2 to go to the *a* channel. With the gradient tool set to create linear gradations (as explained in the next chapter), Shift-drag from the top to the bottom of the circle.

Step 4. Press Command-3 to go to the *b* channel. Shift-drag from left to right with the gradient tool to create a horizontal gradation.

Step 5. Press Command-0 to return to the composite display, which lets you view all channels at once. If you're using a 24-bit monitor, you should be looking at a circle of incredibly smooth color transitions.

Step 6. Just for laughs, compare this color circle to the one included in the Apple Color Picker dialog box. Press Command-K to bring up the General Preferences dialog box. Select Apple from the Color Picker pop-up menu (where's Peter Piper when you need him?) and press Return. Then click on the foreground color icon in the tool box. Drag the scroll box in the brightness scroll bar all the way up and check out the difference. You can see that although it appears slightly rotated, the Lab circle contains the same basic colors as in the hue/saturation circle, but far more of them. Or, at least, far more colors than are discernible to your eye, and that's what ultimately counts.

Using Lab

Because it's device independent, you can use the Lab mode to edit any image. Editing in the Lab mode is as fast as editing in the RGB mode and several times faster than editing in the CMYK mode. If you plan on printing your image to color separations, you may want to experiment with using the Lab mode instead of RGB, because Lab ensures that no colors are altered when you convert the image to CMYK, except to change colors that fall outside the CMYK range. In fact, any time you convert an image from RGB to CMYK, Photoshop automatically converts the image to the Lab mode as an intermediate step.

If you work with Photo CDs often, open the scans directly from the Photo CD format (as opposed to the PICT format) as Lab images. Kodak's proprietary YCC color model is nearly identical to Lab, so you can expect an absolute minimum of data loss; some people claim there is no loss whatsoever.

Indexed colors

In previous chapters, I mentioned that Photoshop automatically dithers your images to the bit depth of your monitor. Therefore, you can create 24-bit images regardless of the screen you use. However, if you specifically want to create an 8-bit or less-colorful image, you can choose Mode ⇨ Indexed Color to round off all the colors to a finite palette, known as a *color lookup table (CLUT*).

The Indexed Color command is by far the best way to convert 24-bit images to 8-bit images. Photoshop 2.0 offers another, *much* less useful method, which is to save the image as a PICT document and select the 8 Bits/Pixel radio button in the PICT File Options dialog box. Thank golly, that option is no longer available in Photoshop 2.5 except when you save grayscale images, which are already limited to 8-bits per pixel. If you ever used or considered using the 8 Bits/Pixel option when saving a full-color image, stop right now, cease and desist, never do it again — in seven words, swear off this evil option for good. Start your new life off right by using the Indexed Color command.

Using the Indexed Color command

To index the colors in an image, choose Mode ⇨ Indexed Color. (It's called *indexing*, incidentally, because you're reining in colors that used to roam free about the spectrum into a rigid, inflexible, maniacally oppressive CLUT. Will you ever be able to look another color in the face?) Photoshop displays the Indexed Color dialog box shown in Figure 14-6, which offers these tempting options:

- **Resolution:** Select one of these radio buttons to specify the number of colors you want to retain in your image. If the image already contains fewer than 256 colors, Photoshop computes this number and automatically enters it into the Other option box. If the Other option box is empty, you probably will want to select the default 8 Bits/Pixel option (not to be confused with its evil twin in the Photoshop 2.0 PICT File Options dialog box).

- **Palette:** These options determine how Photoshop computes the colors in the CLUT. If the image already contains fewer than 256 colors, select Exact to transfer every color found in the image to the CLUT. The next option is labeled *System* if the 8 Bits/Pixel option is selected; otherwise, it is labeled *Uniform*. Either way, Photoshop computes a CLUT based on a uniform sampling of colors from the RGB spectrum. (I discuss this option in more detail later in this chapter.) The Adaptive option selects the most frequently used colors in the image, which typically delivers the best possible result. Finally, you can select Custom to load a CLUT palette from disk or Previous to use the last CLUT created by the Indexed Color command. This last option is dimmed unless you have previously employed the command during the current session.
- **Dither:** Use the Dither options to specify how Photoshop distributes CLUT colors throughout the indexed image. If you select None, Photoshop maps each color in the image to its closest equivalent in the CLUT, pixel for pixel. This option is useful only if you selected Exact from the Palette options or if you want to perform further editing on an image that requires uninterrupted expanses of color. The Pattern option is available only if you selected System from the Palette options — but even then, avoid it like the plague, because it dithers colors in a geometric pattern, as shown in the lower right example in Figure 14-7. The final option, Diffusion, dithers colors randomly to create a naturalistic effect, as shown in the lower left example in Figure 14-7. Nine out of ten times, this is the option you'll want to use.

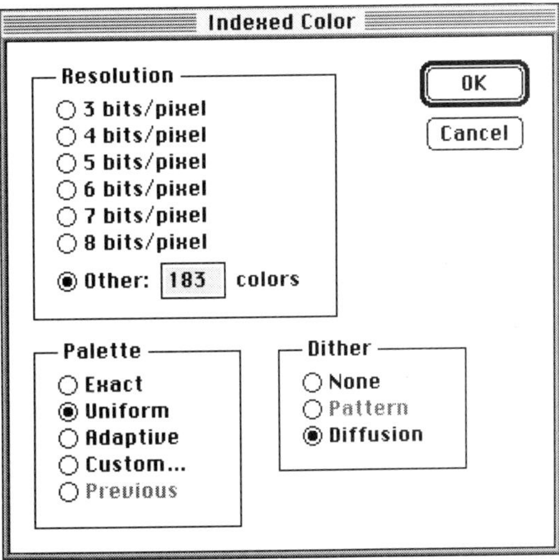

Figure 14-6: The Indexed Color options let you specify how many colors you want to retain in your image, how Photoshop computes the color lookup table, and the way in which colors are distributed throughout the image.

Figure 14-7: The results of converting an image (upper left) to the System CLUT palette subject to each of the three Dither options: (clockwise from upper right) None, Pattern, and Diffusion.

For some reason, Photoshop doesn't let you index Lab or CMYK images. If the Indexed Color command is dimmed, choose Mode ⇨ RGB to convert the image to the RGB mode and then choose Mode ⇨ Indexed Color.

Some of Photoshop's functions, including the gradient tool, all the edit tools, and the commands under the Filter menu, refuse to work in the indexed color mode. Others, like feathering and the paintbrush and airbrush tools, are a big disappointment. If you plan on editing an 8-bit image much in Photoshop, convert it to the RGB mode, edit it as desired, and then switch back to the indexed color mode when you're finished.

Creating images for the screen

Many people make the mistake of using the Indexed Color command to make an image smaller on disk. Certainly, an 8-bit indexed image is smaller than its 24-bit counterpart in RAM. However, this savings doesn't necessarily translate to disk. For example, the JPEG format almost always compresses a 24-bit image to a smaller size on disk than the same image indexed to 8-bit and saved in some other format. (As shown back in Table 14-1, JPEG doesn't support indexed images.) Furthermore, JPEG sacrifices considerably less information than does the Indexed Color command.

Therefore, the only reason to index an image is to prepare it for display on an 8-bit monitor. Suppose that you created a repeating pattern that you want to apply to the Finder desktop using a utility such as Thought I Could's Wallpaper. You figure that you may want to show off by distributing it to other users over a bulletin board, so the pattern should be 8-bit compatible. This means you need to adhere to the Macintosh system software's 8-bit CLUT palette. You can simply copy the pattern from Photoshop and paste it into Wallpaper, but if you do, the system software automatically dithers the image using the hideous Pattern motif. To prevent this from happening, choose the Indexed Color command, select 8 Bits/Pixel from the Resolution options, and select System from the Palette options to use the system software's CLUT palette. Finally, select Diffusion from the Dither options to achieve the most satisfying effect. After indexing the image, you can copy it and paste it into Wallpaper with no dire effects.

Mind you, Wallpaper represents just one of many ways to customize your system using images from Photoshop. You also can use Photoshop to create custom icons, replace the image in the Puzzle desk accessory, and even edit cursors, dialog boxes, splash screens, and a whole mess of other on-screen items using a customization utility such as ResEdit. In all cases, you should first index the image to the system's CLUT palette in Photoshop.

Editing indexed colors

If you're creating images to be displayed in an 8-bit application other than the Finder, such as a presentation program like Microsoft PowerPoint or Aldus Persuasion, you're better off selecting Adaptive from the Palette radio buttons in the Indexed Color dialog box. This setup permits Photoshop to pick the most popular colors from the 24-bit version of the image instead of constraining it to the system palette. But even the Adaptive option doesn't get things 100 percent right. On occasion, Photoshop selects some colors that look noticeably off base.

To replace all occurrences of one color in an indexed image with a different color, choose Mode ⇨ Color Table. The ensuing Color Table dialog box, shown in Figure 14-8, enables you to selectively edit the contents of the CLUT. To edit any color, click on it to display the Color Picker dialog box, select a different color, and click on the OK button to return to the Color Table dialog box. Then click on the OK button to close the Color Table dialog box and change every pixel colored in the old color to the new color.

The Color Table dialog box also enables you to open and save CLUTs and select predefined CLUTs from the Table pop-up menu. What the Color Table dialog box doesn't let you do is identify a color from the image. For example, if you're trying to fix a color in your image, you can't display the Color Table dialog box, click on the color in the image, and have the dialog box show you the corresponding color in the CLUT. The only way to be sure you're editing the correct color — and be forewarned, this is a royal pain in the behind — is to slog through the following steps, which begin before you choose Mode ⇨ Color Table.

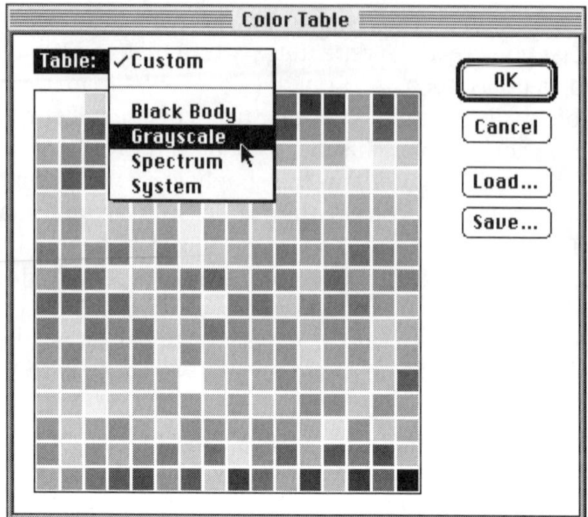

Figure 14-8: Use the Color Table command to edit colors in the color lookup table.

STEPS: Editing a Specific CLUT Color

Step 1. Use the eyedropper tool to click on the offending color in the image, making it the foreground color.

Step 2. Click on the foreground color icon to display the specs for the color in the Color Picker dialog box. Write down the RGB values on a handy piece of paper, the palm of your hand, a bald friend's scalp, or whatever. (Don't edit the color inside the Color Picker dialog box at this time. If you do, you just change the color without changing any pixel in the image associated with that color.) Press Command-period to escape the dialog box.

Step 3. Choose Mode ⇨ Color Table. Now here's the fun part: Click on a color that looks like it might be the right one. After the Color Picker appears, compare the color's RGB numbers to those you wrote down. If they match, boy, did you ever luck out. Go ahead and edit the color as desired. If the RGB values don't match, press Command-period to return to the Color Table dialog box and try again. And again. And again.

To create a *color ramp* — that is, a gradual color progression — in the CLUT, drag rather than click on the colors in the palette to select multiple colors at a time. Photoshop then displays the Color Picker dialog box, enabling you to edit the first color in the ramp. After you select the desired color and press Return, the Color Picker reappears, this time asking you to edit the last color in the ramp. After you specify this color, Photoshop automatically creates the colors between the first and last colors in the ramp in even RGB increments.

Grayscale

Grayscale is possibly my favorite color mode. It frees you from all the hassles and expense of working with color and provides access to every bit of Photoshop's power and functionality. Anyone who says you can't do just as much with grayscale as you can with color missed out on *Citizen Kane, L'Aventura, To Kill a Mockingbird,* and *Raging Bull.* You can print grayscale images to any laser printer, reproduce them in any publication, and edit them on nearly any machine. Besides, they remind you of old movies and they look great in a hefty book like this one. What could be better?

Other than extolling its virtues, however, there isn't a whole lot to say about grayscale. You can convert an image to the grayscale mode regardless of its current mode, and you can convert from grayscale to any other mode just as easily. In fact, choosing Mode ⇨ Grayscale is a necessary step in converting a color image to a duotone or black-and-white bitmap.

When you convert an image from one of the color modes to the grayscale mode, Photoshop normally weights the values of each color channel in a way that retains the apparent brightness of the overall image. For example, when you convert an image from RGB, Photoshop weights red more heavily than blue when computing dark values because red is a darker-looking color than blue (much as that might seem contrary to popular belief). However, if you choose Mode ⇨ Grayscale while viewing a single color channel, Photoshop retains all brightness values in that channel only and abandons the data in the other channels. This technique can be an especially useful for rescuing a grayscale image from a bad RGB scan.

If you use Photoshop 2.5, you should be aware of a little item that might throw off your gray value calculations. By default, Version 2.5 figures in dot gain when calculating the lightness and darkness of grayscale images. (For an introduction to dot gain, see the "Printer calibration" section of Chapter 7.)

Suppose that you click on the foreground color icon and change the B (Brightness) value in the Color Picker dialog box to 50 percent. Later, after applying the 50 percent gray to the current image, you move your cursor over some of the medium gray pixels while the Info palette is displayed. You notice that the Info palette interprets the pixels to be 56 percent gray, 6 percentage points darker than the color you specified; Photoshop automatically darkens the colors in your image to reflect how they will print subject to the dot gain specified in the Printing Inks setup dialog box.

At this point, I need to insert two bits of information to avoid (or perhaps enhance) confusion. First, as long as the S (Saturation) value is 0, the B (Brightness) value is the only Color Picker option you need to worry about when editing grayscale images. Second, although the B (Brightness) value measures luminosity, ranging from 0 percent for black to 100 percent for white, the K value in the Info dialog box measures ink coverage, thus reversing the figures to 100 percent for black and 0 percent for white. Ignoring dot gain for a moment, this means that a 50 percent brightness translates to 50 percent ink coverage, a 40 percent brightness translates to 60 percent ink coverage, a 30 percent brightness translates to 70 percent ink coverage, and so on.

In theory, automatic dot gain compensation is a good idea, but in practice, it frequently gets in the way. For example, in creating the displacement map gradations in the last chapter, I had a heck of a time trying to achieve a medium gray that didn't slightly move pixels in the affected image. The culprit was dot gain.

To turn this option off so that what you ask for is what you get — at least inside Photoshop — choose File ⇨ Preferences ⇨ Printing Inks Setup and deselect the Use Dot Gain for Grayscale Images check box. Then when you ask for a 50 percent gray, you get it.

In Version 2.5.1, the Use Dot Gain for Grayscale Images check box is turned off by default.

Black and white (bitmap)

Choose Mode ⇨ Bitmap to convert a grayscale image to exclusively black and white pixels. This may sound like a pretty boring option, but it can prove useful for gaining complete control over the printing of grayscale images. After all, output devices such as laser printers and imagesetters render grayscale images as series of tiny dots. Using the Bitmap command, you can specify the size, shape, and angle of those dots.

When you choose Mode ⇨ Bitmap, Photoshop displays the Bitmap dialog box, shown in Figure 14-9. Here you specify the resolution of the black-and-white image and select a conversion process. The options work as follows:

- **Output:** Specify the resolution of the black-and-white file. If you want control over every single pixel available to your printer, raise this value to match your printer's resolution. As a rule of thumb, try setting the Output value somewhere between 200 to 250 percent of the Input value.
- **50% Threshold:** Select this option to make every pixel that is darker than 50 percent gray black and every pixel that is 50 percent gray or lighter white. Unless you are working toward some special effect — for example, overlaying a black-

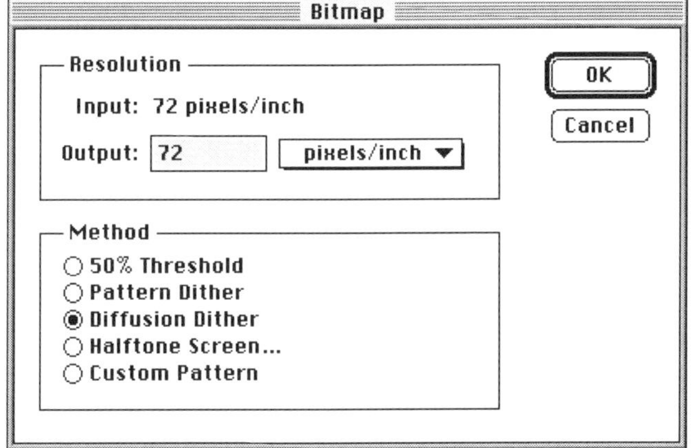

Figure 14-9: The Bitmap dialog box converts images from grayscale to black and white.

and-white version of an image over the original grayscale image — this option most likely isn't for you. (And if you're working toward a special effect, Image ⇨ Map ⇨ Threshold is the better alternative.)

- **Pattern Dither:** This option dithers an image using that worthless geometric pattern I discussed in the "Indexed colors" section. Not only are the images produced by this option ugly, as demonstrated in the left example in Figure 14-10, but the space between dots has a tendency to fill in, especially when you output to a laser printer.
- **Diffusion Dither:** Select this option to create a mezzotint-like effect, as demonstrated in the second example in Figure 14-10. Again, because this option converts an image into thousands of stray pixels, you can expect your image to darken dramatically when output to a low-resolution laser printer and when reproduced. Be sure to lighten the image with something like the Levels command, as described in the "Making Custom Brightness Adjustments" section of Chapter 16, before selecting this option.

Figure 14-10: The results of selecting the Pattern Dither option (left) and the Diffusion Dither option (right).

- **Halftone Screen:** When you select this option and press Return, Photoshop displays the Halftone Screen dialog box shown in Figure 14-11, which is nearly an exact duplicate of the one you access by clicking on the Screen button in the Page Setup dialog box. Enter the number of halftone cells per inch in the Frequency option box and the angle of the cells in the Angle option box. Then select a cell shape from the Shape pop-up menu. Figure 14-12 shows examples of four cell shapes, each with a frequency of 20 lpi (lines per inch). (The image appears reduced in the figure; therefore, the halftone frequency appears higher.)

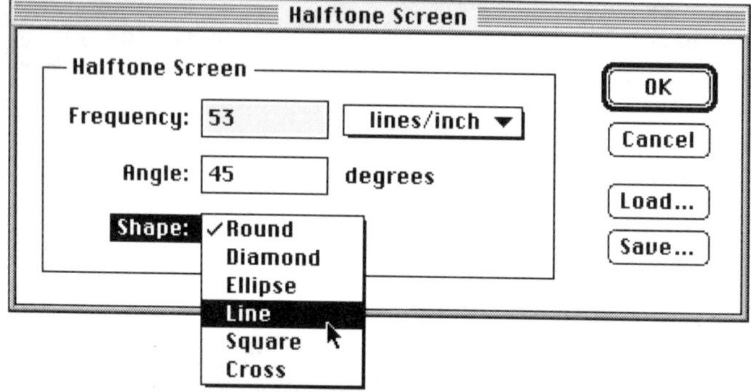

Figure 14-11: This dialog box appears when you select the Halftone Screen option in the Bitmap dialog box.

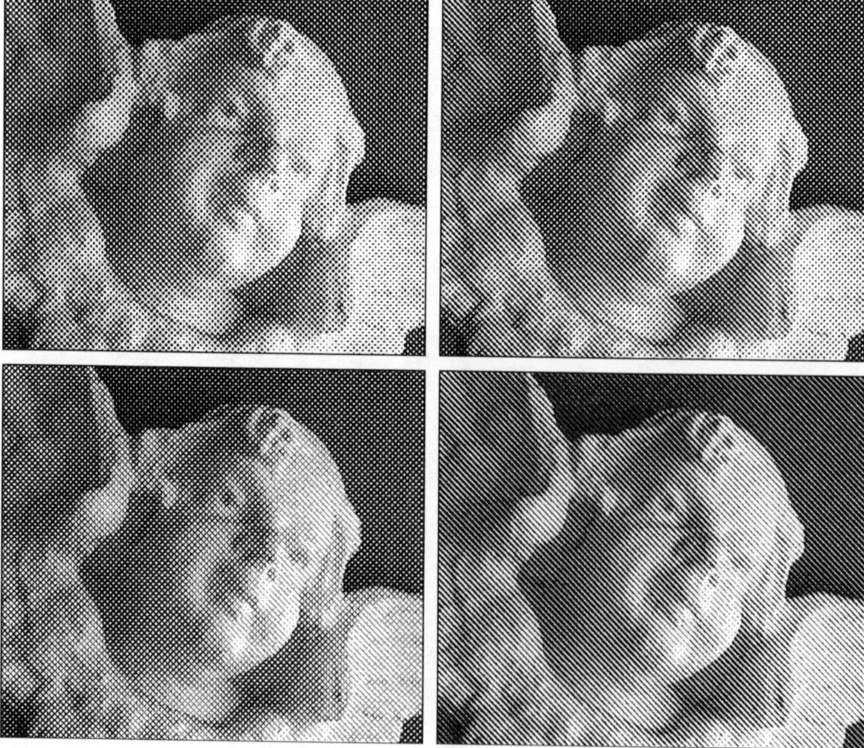

Figure 14-12: Four examples of halftone cell shapes, including (clockwise from upper left) Round, Diamond, Line, and Cross.

- **Custom Pattern:** If you specified a repeating pattern by choosing Edit ⇨ Define Pattern, you can use it as a custom halftoning pattern. Figure 14-13 shows two custom examples, one created using the filter pattern featured back in the first example of Figure 13-38, and the other created using the Twirl pattern file in the Displacement Maps folder. But the killer image appears in Figure 14-14. It might be hard to tell what's going on this example because it combines an image inside an image. But if you look closely, you can see a bunch of tiny Lenins from the seamless repeating pattern exercise in Chapter 10 that ended with Figure 10-20. Granted, the Lenin pattern competes with the original image to the extent that you can barely distinguish any of the cherub's features. But what the hey, it's worth a chuckle or two.

Photoshop lets you edit individual pixels in the so-called bitmap mode, but that's about the extent of it. After you go to black-and-white, you can't perform any serious editing and, worse, you can't expect to return to the grayscale mode. So be sure to finish your image editing before choosing Mode ⇨ Bitmap. More importantly, be sure to save your image before converting it to black and white. Frankly, saving is a good idea when performing any color conversion.

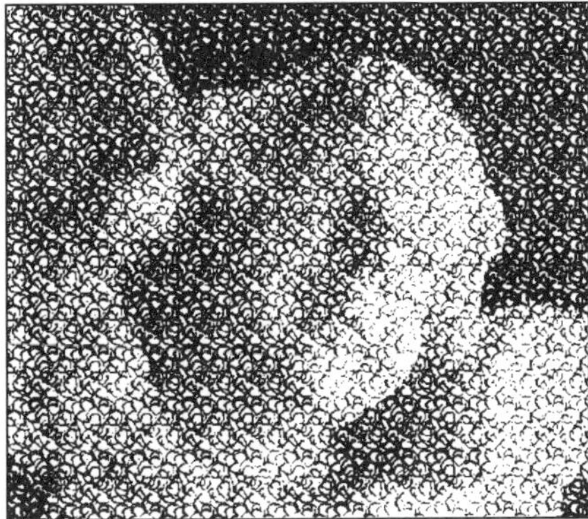

Figure 14-13: Two examples of employing repeating patterns as custom halftoning patterns. The patterns include the Ripple filter texture from the previous chapter (above) and the Twirl pattern image in the Displacement Maps folder (below).

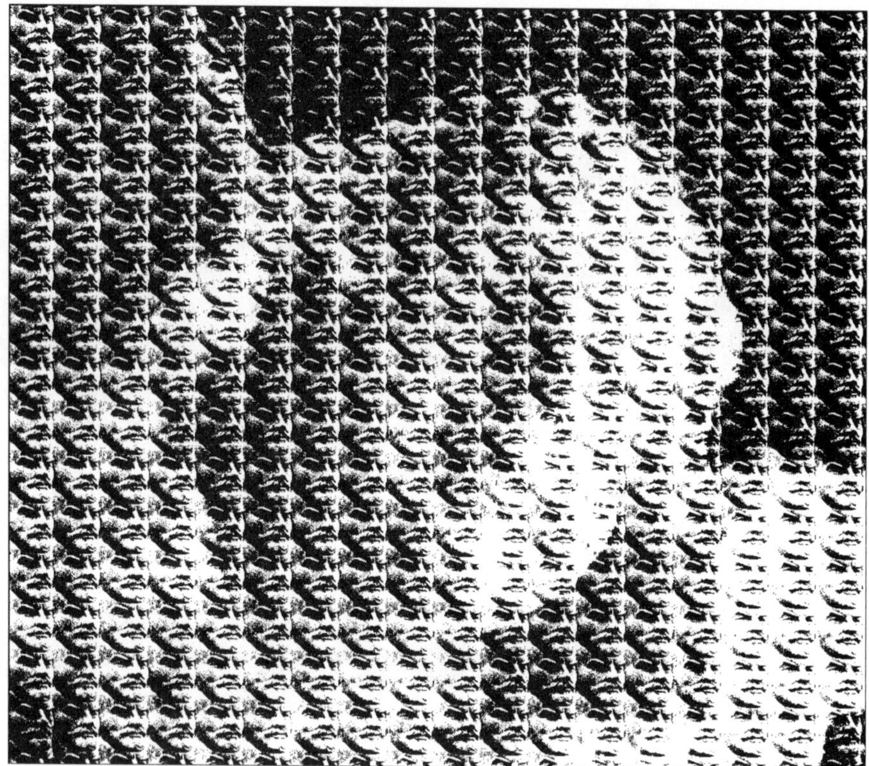

Figure 14-14: A black-and-white cherub composed entirely of itsy, bitsy little Lenin faces.

Using Photoshop's Other Color Selection Methods

In addition to the Color Picker dialog box, Photoshop provides a handful of additional techniques for selecting colors. The sections that finish out this chapter explain how to use the Custom Colors dialog box, the Colors palette (and its comparatively simplistic equivalent in Photoshop 2.0), and the eyedropper tool. None of this information is terribly exciting, but it will enable you to work more efficiently and more conveniently.

Predefined colors

If you click on the Custom button inside the Color Picker dialog box, Photoshop displays the Custom Colors dialog box shown in Figure 14-15. In this dialog box, you can select from a variety of predefined colors by choosing the color family from the Book pop-up menu, moving the slider triangles up and down the color slider to specify a general range of colors, and ultimately selecting a color from the color list on the left. If you own the swatch book for a color family, you can locate a specific color by entering its number into the Find # option box.

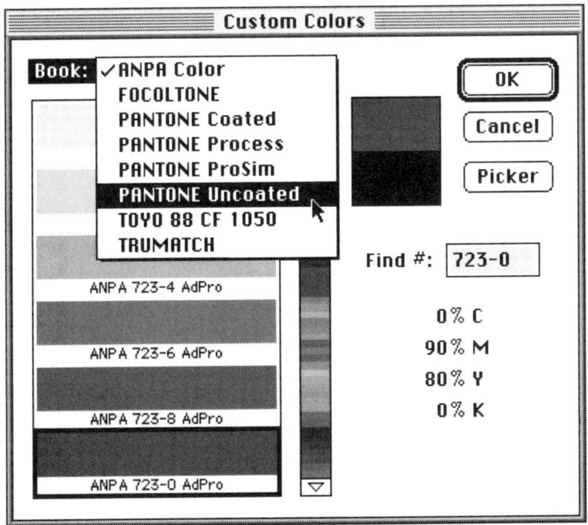

Figure 14-15: The Custom Colors dialog box enables you to select predefined colors from brand-name libraries.

The color families represented in the Book pop-up menu fall into five brands: ANPA (now NAA), Focoltone, Pantone, Toyo, and Trumatch, all of which get a big kick out of capitalizing their names in dialog boxes. I honestly think one of these companies would stand out better if its name *weren't* capitalized. Anyway, at the risk of offending a few of these companies, you're likely to find certain brands more useful than others. The following sections briefly introduce the brands in order of their impact on the American market — forgive me for being ethnocentric in this regard — from smallest impact to greatest.

The number-one use for predefined colors in Photoshop is in the creation of duotones, tritones, and quadtones (described in Chapter 7.) You can also use predefined colors to match the colors in a logo or some other important element in an image to a commercial standard.

Focoltone and Toyo

Both Focoltone and Toyo fall into the negligible impact category. Both are foreign color standards with followings abroad. Focoltone is an English company that used to have a branch office in Kansas; it recently up and left the United States, having made very little impression in this market. Toyo is very popular in the Japanese market but has next to no subscribers outside Japan.

Newspaper Association of America

ANPA — *American Newspaper Publishers Association* — recently changed its name to NAA, which stands for *Newspaper Association of America,* and updated its color catalog. NAA provides a small sampling of 33 *process colors* (mixes of cyan, magenta, yellow, and black ink) plus 5 *spot colors* (colors produced by printing a single ink). The idea behind the NAA colors is to isolate the color combinations that reproduce most successfully on inexpensive newsprint and to provide advertisers with a solid range of colors from which to choose without allowing the color choices to get out of hand. You can purchase a Pocket Tint Chart from NAA for $175. Members pay only $100.

Trumatch

Trumatch remains my personal favorite process-color standard. Designed entirely using a desktop system and created especially with desktop publishers in mind, the Trumatch Colorfinder swatchbook features more than 2,000 process colors, organized according to hue, saturation, and brightness. Each hue is broken down into 40 tints and shades. Tints are created by reducing the saturation in 15 percent increments; shades are created by adding black ink in 6 percent increments. The result is a guide that shows you exactly which colors you can attain using a desktop system. If you're wondering what a CMYK blend will look like when printed, you need look no farther than the Trumatch Colorfinder.

As if the Colorfinder weren't enough, Trumatch provides the ColorPrinter Software utility, which automatically prints the entire 2,000-color library to any PostScript-compatible output device. The utility integrates EfiColor and PostScript Level 2, thereby enabling design firms and commercial printers to test out the entire range of capabilities available to their hardware. Companies can provide select clients with swatches of colors created on their own printers, guaranteeing that what you see is darn well what you'll get.

The Colorfinder swatchbook retails for $85; the ColorPrinter Software costs $98. Together, swatchbook and utility sell for $133. Support for Trumatch is built into Illustrator, FreeHand, PageMaker, QuarkXPress, Cachet, as well as CorelDRAW and Micrografx Designer in the Windows environment.

Pantone

I've been hard on Pantone over the years, and for good reason. Prior to Trumatch, Pantone had a virtual monopoly on the desktop market, and the company acted like it. It was unresponsive to criticism, condescending to service bureaus and desktop designers alike, and slow to improve its product. Since Trumatch came along, however, Pantone has acted like a different company. In fact, I am beginning to warm up to it.

On the heels of Trumatch, Pantone released a 3,006-color Process Color System Guide (labeled *Pantone Process* in the Book pop-up menu) priced at $75, $10 less than the Trumatch Colorfinder. Pantone also produces the foremost spot color swatchbook, the Color Formula Guide 1000, and the Process Color Imaging Guide, which enables you to quickly figure out whether you can closely match a Pantone spot color using a process-color blend or whether you ought to just give it up and stick with the spot color. Pantone spot colors are ideal for creating duotones, discussed in Chapter 7, "Printing Images." Furthermore, Pantone is supported by every computer application that aspires to the color prepress market. As long as the company retains the old competitive spirit, you can most likely expect Pantone to remain the primary color printing standard for years to come.

The Colors palette

Another means of selecting colors in Photoshop 2.5 is to use the Colors palette, shown in Figure 14-16. The less capable Colors palette from Version 2.0 appears in Figure 14-17. If you're willing to sacrifice on-screen real estate for the convenience of being able to define colors on the spot, without having to call up the Color Picker dialog box, the Colors palette is a useful tool indeed.

To display the palette, choose Window ⇨ Colors. You then can use the elements and options inside the palette as follows:

- **Foreground color/background color:** Click on the foreground or background color icon in the Colors palette to specify the color that you want to edit. If you click on the foreground or background color icon when it is already highlighted — as indicated by a double-line frame — Photoshop 2.5 displays the Color Picker dialog box. In Photoshop 2.0, you specify the color you want to edit by selecting Fore or Back from the second pop-up menu (hidden by the mode pop-up menu in Figure 14-17).

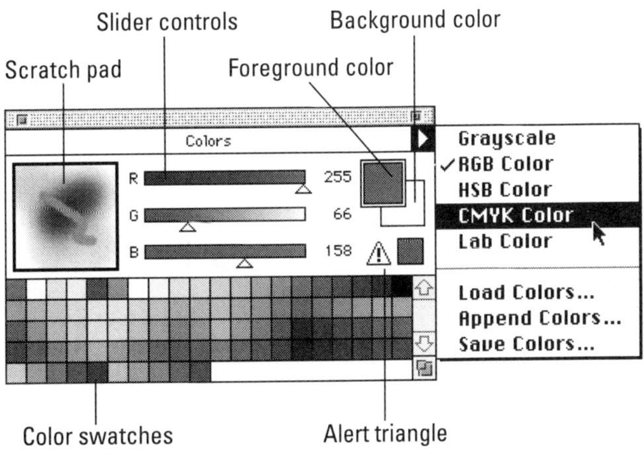

Figure 14-16: The Photoshop 2.5 Colors palette enables you to edit colors without having to display the Color Picker dialog box.

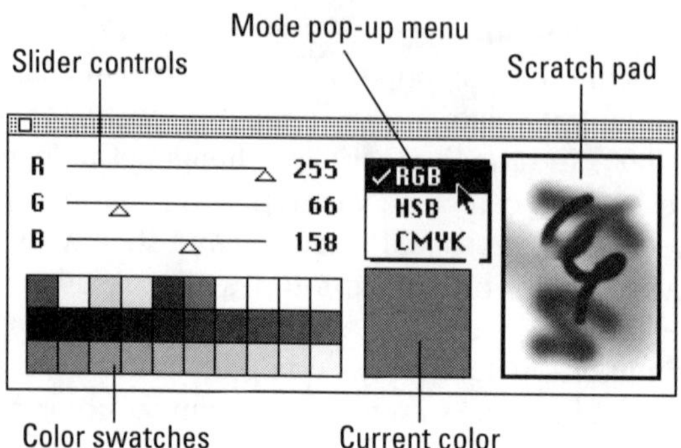

Figure 14-17: The Colors palette from Photoshop 2.0 offers fewer options than the one provided in Version 2.5, but is functional enough to get by.

- **Slider bars:** Drag the triangles in the slider controls to edit the highlighted color. By default, the sliders represent the red, green, and blue primary colors. You can change the slider bars by choosing a different color model from the palette menu (or from the mode pop-up menu in Photoshop 2.0).

To view the slider controls in color in Photoshop 2.5, drag the Dynamic Slider plug-in module into the Plug-ins folder at the Finder desktop. Then relaunch the Photoshop application.

- **Alert triangle:** Photoshop displays the alert triangle when a color falls outside the printable CMYK range. Click on the triangle to select the closest CMYK equivalent.
- **Color swatches:** The color swatches enable you to collect colors for future use, sort of like a favorite color reservoir. To select a color from the reservoir, click on it. To add the current color to the reservoir, Option-click on an existing color swatch to replace it or click in an empty portion of the reservoir. In either case, your cursor temporarily changes to a paint bucket. To delete a color in Photoshop 2.5, Command-click on a color swatch. Your cursor changes to a pair of scissors.
- **Scratch pad:** The scratch pad enables you to mix colors outside of the image window. You can paint and edit inside the scratch pad just as you paint and edit inside the image window. To sample a color from the mix, click on it with the eyedropper tool. To erase the scratch pad, drag inside it with the eraser tool.

The eyedropper tool

The eyedropper tool provides the most convenient and most straightforward means of selecting colors in Photoshop. It's so straightforward, in fact, that it's hardly worth explaining. But very quickly, here's how it works:

- **Selecting a foreground color:** To select a new foreground color, click on the desired color inside any open image window with the eyedropper tool. The eyedropper tool is the only tool that allows you to click in a background window without bringing it to the foreground. (You also can Option-click with the rubber stamp tool without switching windows.)
- **Selecting a background color:** To select a new background color, Option-click on the desired color with the eyedropper tool.
- **Skating over the color spectrum:** You can animate the foreground color control box by dragging with the eyedropper tool in the image window. As soon as you achieve the desired color, release your mouse button. To animate the background color icon, Option-drag with the eyedropper tool. The icon color changes as you move the eyedropper tool.
- **Sampling multiple pixels:** Normally, the eyedropper tool selects the color from the single pixel on which you click. However, if you prefer to average the colors of several neighboring pixels, double-click on the eyedropper icon in the toolbox in Photoshop 2.5 and select a different option from the Sample Size pop-up menu. In Photoshop 2.0, these options are found in the Eyedropper pop-up menu in the General Preferences dialog box.

To temporarily access the eyedropper tool when using the type, paint bucket, gradient, line, pencil, airbrush, or paintbrush tool, press the Option key. The eyedropper cursor remains in force for as long as the Option key is down. You can select only a foreground color while Option-clicking with any of these tools. To select a background color, you must select the eyedropper tool and then Option-click in an image window.

Summary

- The color slider and color field change to reflect the selected radio button in the Color Picker dialog box.
- You can save RGB and grayscale images in any file format supported by Photoshop. However, you can save Lab images only in the native, EPS, and TIFF formats. You can save CMYK images in those formats and the JPEG and Scitex CT formats.
- The Lab color model encompasses all colors found in the RGB and CMYK models.
- Use the Indexed Color command to prepare images for display at the Finder desktop or on less capable computer systems. The command reduces the bit depth of the image to 8-bit or less.
- When editing colors in the grayscale mode, set the S (Saturation) option in the Color Picker dialog box to 0 and rely exclusively on the B (Brightness) option.
- To accurately view gray values in the grayscale mode, choose File ⇨ Preferences ⇨ Printing Inks Setup and deselect the Use Dot Gain for Grayscale Images check box.
- You can use a repeating pattern as a custom halftoning pattern when you convert a grayscale image to a black-and-white painting by choosing Mode ⇨ Bitmap.
- Trumatch and Pantone are the foremost means for defining custom colors in desktop publishing.
- The Colors palette enables you to edit and assemble colors without having to constantly display and close the Color Picker dialog box.
- Use the eyedropper tool to select colors from any open image window.

Coloring Selections

15 CHAPTER

In This Chapter

- Applying color with the paint bucket tool, Fill command, or Delete key
- Using the Gradient Tool Options dialog box
- Using the gradient tool in combination with different brush modes
- Drawing gradient selection outlines in the quick mask mode
- Attaching arrowheads to any stroke
- Mixing floating selections with underlying images using overlay modes
- Using the options in the Composite Controls dialog box

Filling Portions of an Image

Now that you know how to define colors, it's high time you learn how to apply colors to an image. Certainly, I already covered a few ways to apply colors. You can drag with the pencil, paintbrush, or airbrush tool or Option-drag with the smudge tool to apply the foreground color to an image. Similarly, the eraser tool paints in the background color. But if you want to apply color more generously — for example, to color or tint an entire selected region of an image — you're in the market for one of Photoshop's automated coloring functions.

Photoshop provides two categories of coloring functions. In this chapter, I discuss the first category, which includes tools and commands that apply color to a selection or mix the colors in a floating selection with the colors in the image below. In the next chapter, I take on the commands in the Image ⇨ Map and Image ⇨ Adjust submenus, which alter the existing colors in an image. This second category of functions lets you make an image lighter or darker, change the amount of contrast, invert colors as in a photographic negative, and perform a whole bunch of other operations that are essential when you edit color and grayscale images alike. But alas, before you learn how to alter existing colors in an image, you need to know how to apply them in the first place, which I explain in the following pages.

Filling an area with color

You can fill an area of an image with color in three ways:

- **The paint bucket tool:** You can apply the foreground color or a repeating pattern to a similarly colored region in an image by clicking in the image window with the paint bucket tool (also known as the fill tool).
- **The Fill command:** Select the portion of the image that you want to color and then fill the entire selection with the foreground color or a repeating pattern by choosing Edit ➪ Fill.
- **Delete-key techniques:** Select a portion of the image and fill the selection with the background color by pressing the Delete key. To fill the selection with the foreground color, press Option-Delete.

The following sections discuss each of these options in depth.

The paint bucket tool

Unlike remedial paint bucket tools in other painting programs, which apply paint exclusively within outlined areas or areas of solid color — thereby exhibiting all the subtlety of dumping paint out of a bucket — the Photoshop paint bucket tool offers several useful adjustment options. To explore them, double-click on the paint bucket icon in the toolbox to display the Paint Bucket Options dialog box, shown in Figure 15-1.

Figure 15-1: The Paint Bucket Options dialog box governs the performance of the paint bucket tool.

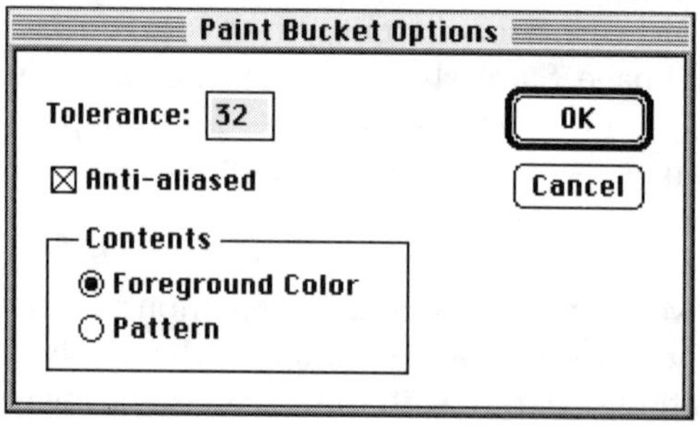

The first two options, Tolerance and Anti-aliased, work exactly like their counterparts in the Magic Wand Options dialog box, which I explained at length in the "Magic wand tolerance" section of Chapter 9. Just in case you need a refresher, here's how these and the other options work:

- **Tolerance:** Applying color with the paint bucket tool is a three-step process. Immediately after you click on a pixel with the tool, Photoshop reads the brightness value of that pixel from each color channel. Next, Photoshop calculates a tolerance range according to the value you enter in the Tolerance option box (you can enter any value from 0 to 255). It adds the Tolerance value to the brightness value of the pixel on which you click with the paint bucket tool to determine the top of the range; it subtracts the Tolerance value from the brightness value of the pixel to determine the bottom of the range. For example, if the pixel's brightness value is 100 and the Tolerance value is 32, the top of the range is 132 and the bottom is 68. After establishing a tolerance range, Photoshop applies the foreground color to any pixel that both falls inside the tolerance range and is contiguous to the pixel on which you clicked. A large Tolerance value causes the paint bucket to affect a greater number of pixels than a small Tolerance value. Figure 15-2 shows the result of clicking on the same pixel three times, each time using a lower Tolerance value.
- **Anti-aliased:** Select this option to soften the effect of the paint bucket tool. As demonstrated in the top example of Figure 15-3, Photoshop creates a border of translucent color between the filled pixels and their unaffected neighbors. If you don't want to soften the transition, deselect the Anti-aliased check box. Photoshop then fills only those pixels that fall inside the tolerance range, as demonstrated in the bottom example of the figure.
- **Contents:** You can either apply the foreground color or a repeating pattern created using Edit ⇨ Define Pattern. This option is available only in Photoshop 2.5.

In Photoshop 2.5, you can further adjust the performance of the paint bucket by manipulating options in the Brushes palette. Drag the Opacity slider or press a number key to change the translucency of a color applied with the paint bucket. Select an option from the brush mode pop-up menu to specify how and when color is applied. For example, if you select Darken, the paint bucket tool affects a pixel in the image only if the foreground color is darker than that pixel. If you select Color, the paint bucket colorizes the image without changing the brightness value of any pixel. For an in-depth look at brush modes, read the "Overlaying Floating Selections" section later in this chapter.

To limit the area affected by the paint bucket, select a portion of the image before using the tool. As when you use any other tool, the region outside the selection outline is protected from the paint bucket.

Figure 15-2: The results of applying the paint bucket tool to the exact same pixel after setting the Tolerance value to 32 (top), 16 (middle), and 8 (bottom). In each case, the foreground color is white.

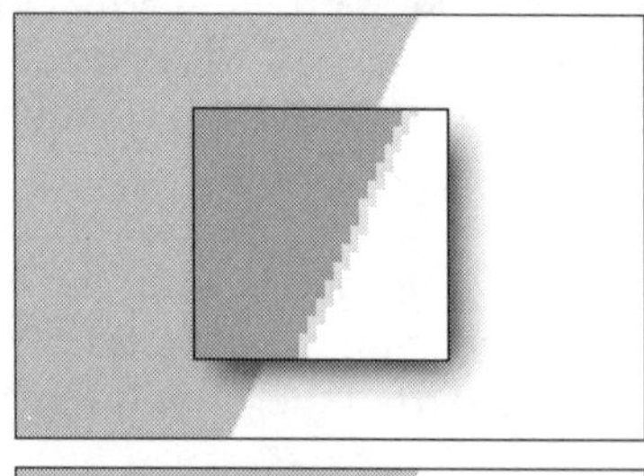

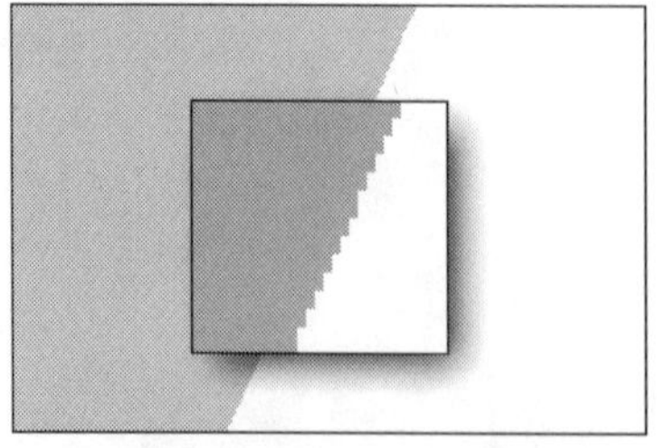

Figure 15-3: The results of selecting (top) and deselecting (bottom) the Anti-aliased check box prior to using the paint bucket tool. The inset rectangles show magnified pixels.

The Fill command

The one problem with the paint bucket tool is its lack of precision. Though undeniably convenient, the paint bucket suffers the exact same limitations as the magic wand. The effects of the Tolerance value are so difficult to predict that you typically have to click with the tool, choose Edit ⇨ Undo when you don't like the result, adjust the Tolerance value, and reclick with the tool several times more before you fill the image as desired. For my part, I've almost given up using the paint bucket for any purpose other than filling same-colored areas. On my machine, the Tolerance option is nearly always set to 0 and Anti-alias is always off, which puts me right back in the all-the-subtlety-of-dumping-paint-out-of-a-bucket camp. (For an exception to this, see the upcoming "Creating special fill effects" section.)

A better option is to select the area that you want to fill and choose Edit ⇨ Fill. In this way, you can define the exact area of the image you want to color using the entire range of Photoshop's selection tools — including the path tools and quick mask mode — instead of limiting yourself to the equivalent of the magic wand. For example, instead of putting your faith in the paint bucket tool's Anti-aliased option, you can draw a selection outline that features hard edges in one area, antialiased edges elsewhere, and feathered edges in between.

When you choose the Fill command, Photoshop displays the Fill dialog box shown in Figure 15-4. In this dialog box, you can specify whether you want to fill the selection with the foreground color, a repeating pattern, the saved version of the image, or the snapshot, by selecting an option from the Use pop-up menu. In addition, you can apply a translucent color or pattern by entering a value into the Opacity option box and you can choose a brush mode option from the Mode pop-up menu. In addition to its inherent precision, the Fill command maintains all the functionality of the paint bucket tool.

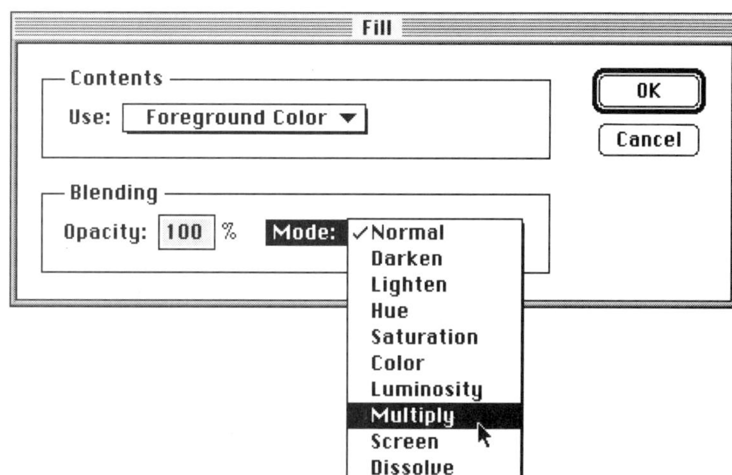

Figure 15-4: The Fill dialog box improves on the Contents options in the Paint Bucket Options dialog box and adds the functionality of the Opacity slider and brush mode pop-up menu from the Brushes palette.

How to fill paths

Photoshop 2.5 provides a variation on Edit ⇨ Fill that lets you fill paths created using the pen tool without first converting them to selections. After drawing a few paths and saving them (by choosing Save Path from the Paths palette menu), choose the Fill Path command. Photoshop displays a slight variation of the Fill dialog box from Figure 15-4, the only difference being the inclusion of the Anti-aliased check box. If you select the check box, Photoshop softens the outline of the filled area.

If one path falls inside another, Photoshop leaves the intersection of the two paths unfilled. (The Reverse Subpath command, incidentally, has no effect on the filling of a path.) Suppose that you draw two round paths, one fully inside the other. If you save the paths and then choose the Fill Path command, Photoshop fills only the area between the two paths, resulting in a letter *O*.

If the Fill Path command fills only part or none of the path, it is very likely because the path falls outside the selection outline. Choose Select ⇨ None (Command-D) to deselect the image and then choose the Fill Path command again.

If you select one or more paths with the arrow tool, the Fill Path command changes to Fill Subpaths, enabling you to fill the selected paths only.

Delete-key techniques

Of all the fill techniques, the Delete key is by far the most convenient and, in most respects, every bit as capable as the others. The key's only failing is that it can't fill a selection with a repeating pattern. But because you'll rarely *want* to fill a selection with a repeating pattern, you can rely on the Delete key for the overwhelming majority of your fill needs.

Here's how to get a ton of functionality out of the Delete key:

- **Background color:** To fill a selection with solid background color, press Delete. The selection outline remains intact. Keep in mind that this technique works only when the selection is *not* floating. If you float the selection and then press Delete, you delete the selection entirely. (Try selecting an area, choosing Select ⇨ Float, and pressing Delete to see what I mean.)
- **Foreground color:** To fill a selection with solid foreground color, press Option-Delete. You can fill floating and nonfloating selections alike by pressing Option-Delete.
- **Translucent color:** To fill a selection with a translucent coating of foreground color, choose Select ⇨ Float (Command-J) to float the selection. Then press

Option-Delete and press a number key to change the setting of the Opacity slider bar in the Brushes palette. In Photoshop 2.0, press Option-arrow key to float the selection and nudge it a pixel, press Option-Delete, and then choose Edit ➪ Paste Controls and enter a new value into the Opacity option box.

- **Accessing brush modes:** To mix foreground color and original image using brush modes, float the selection, press Option-Delete, and select a brush mode from the pop-up menu on the left side of the Brushes palette. In Photoshop 2.0, you can access brush modes inside the Paste Controls dialog box.

Creating special fill effects

So far, I've come up with two astounding generalizations: the paint bucket tool is mostly useless; and you can fill anything with the Delete key. Well, just to prove you shouldn't believe everything I say, the following steps explain how to create an effect that you can perform only with the paint bucket tool. Doubtless, it's the only such example you'll ever discover using Photoshop — after all, the paint bucket *is* mostly useless and you *can* fill anything with the Delete key — but I'm man enough to eat my rules just this once.

The steps explain how to create an antique photographic frame effect like the one shown in Figure 15-5. I first used the effect back in Figure 9-27, in case you're in an historical mood.

STEPS: Creating an Antique Photographic Frame

Step 1. Use the rectangular marquee tool to select the portion of the image that you want to frame. Make sure that the image extends at least 20 pixels outside the boundaries of the selection outline.

Step 2. Choose Select ➪ Feather and specify a hefty Radius value — somewhere in the neighborhood of 6 to 12 pixels.

Step 3. Choose Select ➪ Inverse to exchange the selected and deselected portions of the image.

Step 4. Press the Delete key to fill the selected area with white. (If white is not the background color, click on the default colors icon in the toolbox to make it so.)

Step 5. Double-click on the paint bucket tool icon in the toolbox to display the Paint Bucket Options dialog box. Enter 50 in the Tolerance option box, deselect the Anti-aliased check box, and press Return to confirm your changes.

Step 6. Click inside the feathered selection to fill it with black (or whatever other foreground color you prefer). The result is a an image fading into white and then into black, like a faded slide or photograph, as shown in Figure 15-5.

Figure 15-5: I created this antique frame effect by filling a feathered selection with the paint bucket tool.

Figure 15-6 shows a variation on this effect that you can create only in Photoshop 2.5. Rather than setting the Tolerance value to 50, raise it to something in the neighborhood of 80. Then, after selecting the paint bucket tool, select the Dissolve option from the brush mode pop-up menu in the Brushes palette. When you click inside the feathered selection with the paint bucket tool, you create a frame of random pixels, as illustrated in the figure.

Figure 15-6: Select Dissolve from the Brushes palette pop-up menu to achieve a speckled frame effect.

Applying Gradient Fills

Ever seen *Sid and Nancy*? It's this movie about Sid Vicious of the Sex Pistols. You know, the English punk band. No, really, it's a great movie, even if you don't like the Sex Pistols. Come on, with lyrics like, "God save the queen, she ain't no human being," what's not to like? But the point is, in one scene in the movie, Sid and Johnny Rotten (a fellow band member) climb onto the hood of a car that has this yappy poodle in it and kick in the windshield. (At least I think that's how it goes. I only saw the movie once and it was a long time ago, so I'm a little vague on the details. But really, it's a great picture.) Anyway, Sid and Johnny stand for a moment, staring down at what they've done, considering the damage. (Don't worry, the poodle's fine — it continues yapping away to prove it.) Then Sid and Johnny turn to each other and shout in unison, "Boring!" It's one of those classic movie moments that makes you feel tingly and weepy all over.

Sometimes I feel like Sid. I'm not going to spike my hair or anything, but, well, even Photoshop has its share of dull moments. I mean, filling selections? Boring! No doubt, you were mesmerized by my entertaining text blended cleverly with comprehensive coverage, but in the background I was lamenting my misspent youth. Face it, nowhere in the recipe for image-editing fun is there mention of a paint bucket, a Fill command, or a Delete key.

However, the recipe *does* call for a gradient tool, one of the most fun-filled, action-packed tools in the Photoshop ensemble. If you're like most folks, you've used the tool a couple of times to create gradient backgrounds, but that's about the extent of it. All I can say to that is, b-b-b-baby, you ain't seen nothing yet. (There I go mixing my rock genres. Can you see Bachman Turner Overdrive and the Sex Pistols together? Me neither. KC and the Sunshine Band, maybe, but BTO, never.)

The gradient tool

First, the basics. A *gradation* (also called a *gradient fill*) is a progression of colors that fade gradually into one another, as demonstrated in Figure 15-7. The foreground color represents the first color in the gradation; the background color is the final color in the gradation. Photoshop automatically generates the hundred or so colors in between to create a smooth transition.

You create gradations using the *gradient tool* (just to the right of the paint bucket in the toolbox). Unlike the paint bucket tool, which fills areas of similar color whether or not they are selected, the gradient tool fills the confines of a selection. If you don't select a portion of your image, Photoshop applies the gradation to the entire image.

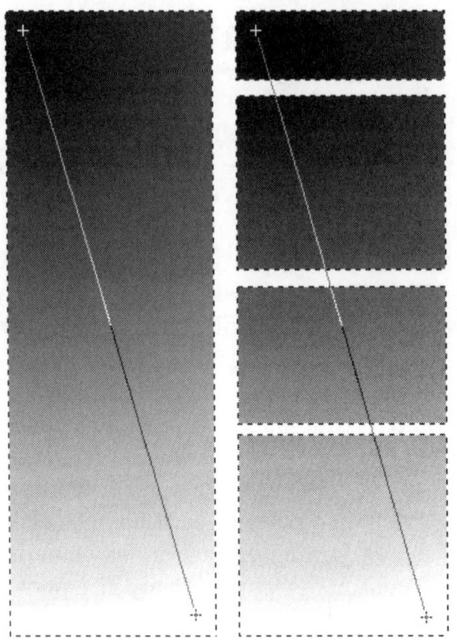

Figure 15-7: Dragging with the gradient tool within a single selection (left) and across multiple selections (right).

To use the gradient tool, drag inside the selection, as shown in the left example of Figure 15-7. The point at which you begin dragging (upper left corner in the figure) defines the location of the foreground color in the gradation. The point at which you release (lower right corner) defines the location of the background color. If multiple portions of the image are selected, the gradation fills all selections continuously, as demonstrated by the right example of Figure 15-7.

In Photoshop 2.0, the gradient tool is called the *blend tool.* Likewise, the Gradient Tool Options dialog box goes by the name *Blend Tool Options.* But other than the fact that Version 2.5's gradient tool can take advantage of a few more brush mode settings, the tools are identical.

Gradient tool options

To master the gradient tool, you have to fully understand how to modify its performance. Double-click on the gradient tool icon in the toolbox to display the Gradient Tool Options dialog box, shown in Figure 15-8. This dialog box allows you to specify the colors in a gradation as well as the arrangement of those colors by using the following options:

- **Style:** The three Style radio buttons — labeled *Color Space* in Photoshop 2.0 — determine how Photoshop selects colors in a gradation. Think of the foreground and background colors as points in the HSB color wheel featured in the Apple

Color Picker dialog box, as illustrated in Figure 15-9. When you select the Normal radio button (RGB/CMYK in Version 2.0), Photoshop selects colors in a beeline from the foreground color to the background color within the HSB color wheel. Such gradations typically travel through colors of low saturation near the middle of the wheel. To maintain a high level of saturation, pick the Clockwise Spectrum option (HSB-CW in Version 2.0), which selects colors in a clockwise direction around the color wheel, or Counterclockwise Spectrum (HSB-CCW), which selects colors in a counterclockwise direction. Figure 15-9 illustrates all these options. Color Plate 15-1 shows three gradations created using cyan as the foreground color and red as the background color. The only difference between the gradations is the setting of the Style options.

The Style options have no effect on grayscale gradations, nor do they influence gradations between any color and black, white, or any other shade of gray. To ensure the fastest gradations under these conditions, select the Normal radio button (RGB/CYMK in Photoshop 2.0).

- **Type:** Select Linear or Radial to specify the variety of gradation you want to create. A *linear gradation* progresses in linear bands of color in a straight line between the beginning and end of your drag, like the gradation shown in Figure 15-7. A *radial gradation* progresses outward from a central point in concentric circles, as shown in Figures 15-10 and 15-11. The point at which you begin dragging defines the center of the gradation; the point at which you release defines the outermost circle. (Incidentally, I created the radial gradations in Figures 15-10 and 15-11 using white as the foreground color and black as the background color.)
- **Midpoint Skew:** This option determines the location of the halfway point in the gradation. The default value of 50 percent sets the halfway point smack dab in the middle of your drag. If you lower the value, Photoshop arranges most of the colors in the gradation close to the beginning of your drag. This arrangement creates a gradation that progresses quickly at first and more slowly toward the end. If you raise the Midpoint Skew value above 50 percent, Photoshop arranges

Figure 15-8: These options enable you to adjust the appearance of a gradation drawn with the gradient tool.

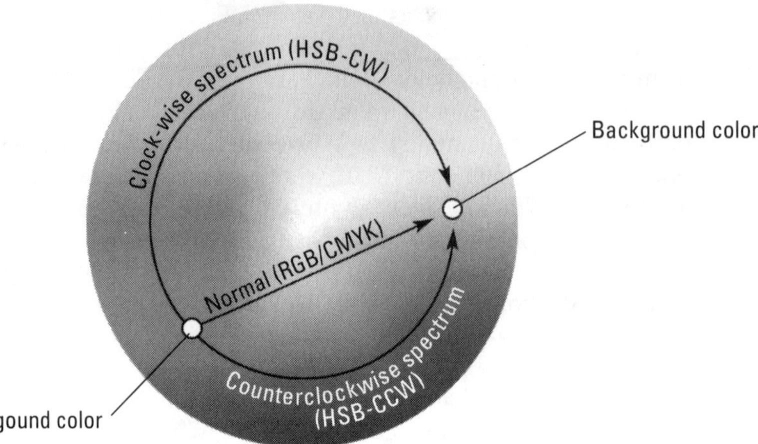

Figure 15-9: The Style options determine the direction in which a gradation processes with respect to the HSB color wheel. To see how each of these progressions looks in color, see Color Plate 15-1.

most of the colors toward the end of your drag, resulting in a gradation that progresses slowly at first and more quickly toward the end. Figure 15-10 shows four radial gradations subjected to different Midpoint Skew values, ranging from the minimum to maximum allowed values.

- **Radial Offset:** This option is applicable exclusively to radial gradations. It defines the size of the central circle of foreground color as a percentage of the size of the entire gradation. A value of 0 percent results in a dab of foreground color in the center of the gradation; a value of 99 percent results in a huge circle of foreground color with a thin band of other colors around its perimeter. Figure 15-11 shows four examples of radial gradations subject to different Radial Offset values. Note that the foreground color is white and the background color is black.

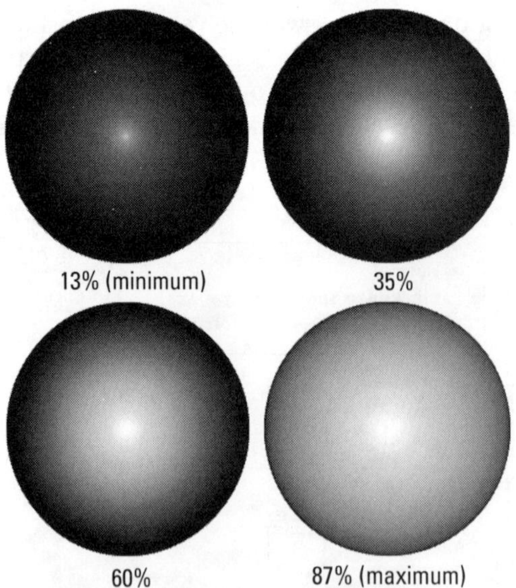

Figure 15-10: Four white-to-black radial gradations subject to different Midpoint Skew values.

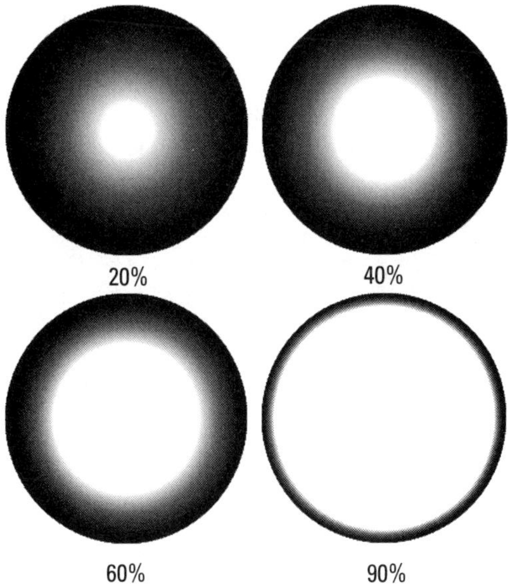

Figure 15-11: Four examples of Radial Offset values. In each case, the Midpoint Skew value was 50 percent.

How to eliminate banding

Each linear or radial band of color in a gradation is distinct from the band that precedes it and the band that follows it. As a result, you may encounter an effect known as *banding* during the printing process, which simply means that you can clearly distinguish the transition between two or more bands of color.

Strictly speaking, banding is a function of an improperly calibrated output device. Because the difference between any two side-by-side color bands in a Photoshop gradation can't vary by more than a single percentage point — less than your eye can differentiate — the problem *has* to be the fault of the printer. No doubt, you'll run across typesetter operators and commercial printers who will do their best to convince you that the fault is Photoshop's, but the math says they're wrong.

Still, why fight when you can take minimal precautions to eliminate banding in advance? The Add Noise filter randomizes pixels in a selection. Therefore, when you apply Filter ⇨ Noise ⇨ Add Noise to a gradation, it mixes the bands of color, in effect making your artwork both idiot- and environment-proof. The first column in Figure 15-12 shows linear and radial gradations. In the second column, I applied the Add Noise filter three times in a row to both gradations. To make the effect as subtle as possible — you don't want the noise to be obvious — I specified an Amount value of 8 and selected the Uniform radio button inside the Add Noise dialog box. Multiple repetitions of a subtle noise effect is preferable to a single application of a more radical effect.

If noise isn't enough or if the noise appears a little too obvious, you can further mix the colors in a gradation by applying a directional blur filter. To blur a linear gradation, apply the Motion Blur filter in the direction of the gradation. In the top right example of Figure 15-12, I applied Filter ⇨ Blur ⇨ Motion Blur with an Angle value of 90 degrees (straight up and down) and a Distance value of 3 pixels.

Figure 15-12: The results of applying noise (middle column) and directional blur effects (right column) to linear and radial gradations.

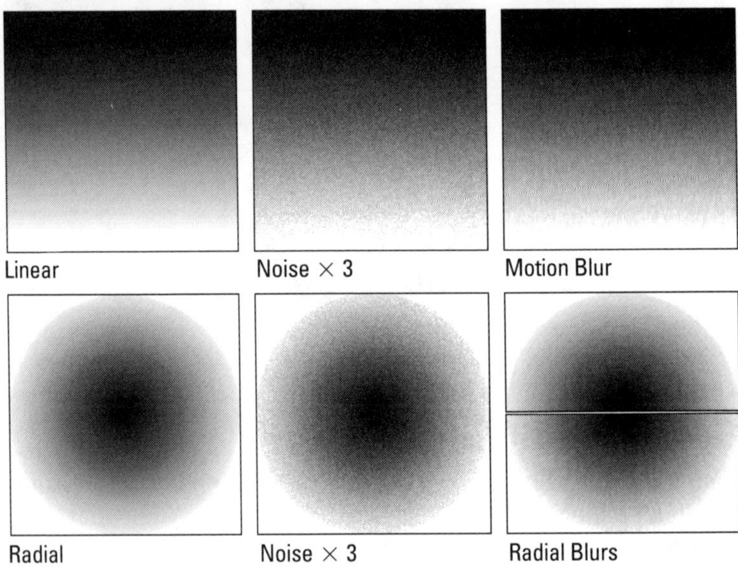

To blur a radial gradation, apply the Radial Blur filter. To mix the noise around the center of the gradation, select the Spin option in the Radial Blur dialog box. To blend color in the bands, select the Zoom option. The lower right example in Figure 15-12 is divided into two halves. To create the top half, I applied the Spin option with an Amount value of 10; to create the bottom half, I applied Zoom with an Amount value of 20.

To further de-emphasize color bands in a horizontal linear gradation, you can apply the Wind filter. Color Plate 15-2 shows the three gradation styles from Color Plate 15-1 subject to the Add Noise, Wind, and Motion Blur filters. In each case, I applied the Add Noise filter three times (just as in Figure 15-12), the Blast option in the Wind dialog box twice (once in each direction), and the Motion Blur filter in a horizontal direction at 10 pixels.

Gradations and brush modes

Like the paint bucket tool, the gradient tool in Photoshop 2.5 is sensitive to the settings of the Opacity slider bar and the brush mode pop-up menu in the Brushes palette. (In Photoshop 2.0, the Opacity option and a limited supply of mode settings are located in the Blend Tool Options dialog box.) When the Opacity value is less than 100 percent, Photoshop coats the selection with a translucent coat of colors. The brush modes determine when and how the application applies colors.

Randomized gradations

For a comprehensive description of the brush mode options, skip to the "Overlaying Floating Selections" section later in this chapter. In the meantime, the following steps describe how to use one brush mode option, Dissolve, in combination with a radial gradation to create an effect not unlike a supernova. (At least, it looks like a supernova to me — not that I've ever seen one up close, mind you.) Figures 15-13 through 15-15 show the nova in progress. In addition to allowing you to experiment with a brush mode setting, the steps offer some general insight into creating radial gradations. Because the Dissolve option is available only in Photoshop 2.5, Version 2.0 users can skip to the next section.

STEPS: Creating a Gradient Supernova

Step 1. Create a new image window — say, 500 × 500 pixels. A grayscale image is fine for this exercise.

Step 2. Click with the pencil tool at the apparent center of the image. Don't worry if it's not the exact center. This point is merely intended to serve as a guide. If a single point is not large enough for you to easily identify, draw a small cross.

Step 3. Option-drag from the point with the elliptical marquee tool to draw the marquee outward from the center. Before releasing the mouse button, press and hold the Shift key to constrain the marquee to a circle. Draw a marquee that fills about ¾ of the window.

Step 4. Choose Image ⇨ Map ⇨ Invert (Command-I) to fill the marquee with black and make the center point white.

Step 5. Choose Select ⇨ None (Command-D) to deselect the circle. Then Option-drag again from the center point with the elliptical marquee tool, again pressing Shift to constrain the shape to a circle, to create a marquee roughly 20 pixels larger than the black circle.

Step 6. Command-drag from the center point with the elliptical marquee tool and press and hold both Shift and Option midway into the drag to create a marquee roughly 20 pixels smaller than the black circle. The result is a doughnut-shaped selection — a large circle with a smaller circular hole — as shown in Figure 15-13.

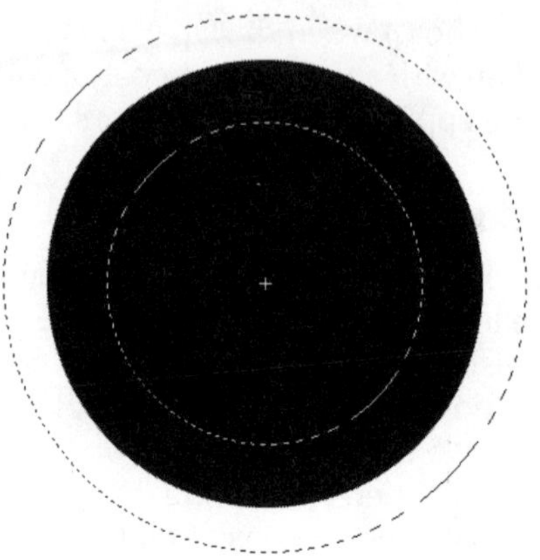

Figure 15-13: The result of creating a black circle and two circular marquees, all centered about a single point.

Step 7. Choose Select ⇨ Feather and enter 10 for the Radius value. Then press Return to feather the section outline.

Step 8. Click on the default colors icon in the toolbox and then click on the switch colors icon to make the foreground color white and the background color black.

Step 9. Double-click on the gradient tool icon. Select the Radial option and set the Radial Offset value to 60 percent to increase the size of the central circle of foreground color to roughly the same size as the center marquee.

Step 10. Select Dissolve from the brush mode pop-up menu on the left side of the Brushes palette.

Step 11. Drag from the center point in the image window to anywhere along the outer rim of the largest marquee. The result is the fuzzy gradation shown in Figure 15-14.

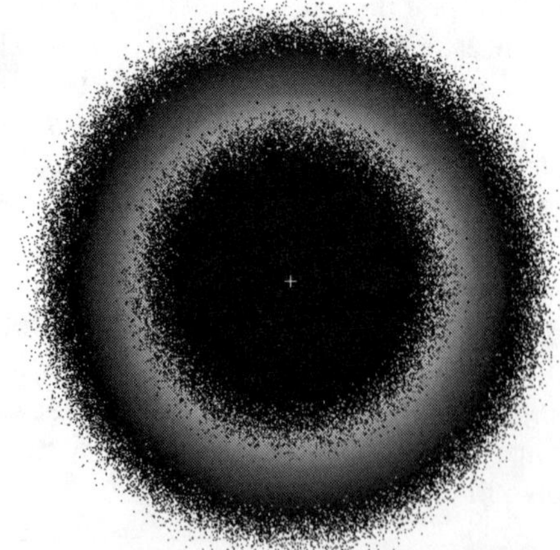

Figure 15-14: The Dissolve brush mode option randomizes the pixels around the feathered edges of the selection outlines.

Step 12. Choose Select ⇨ None (Command-D) to deselect the image. Then choose Image ⇨ Map ⇨ Invert (Command-I) to invert the entire image.

Step 13. Click on the default colors icon to restore black and white as foreground and background colors respectively. Then use the eraser tool to erase the center point. The finished supernova appears in Figure 15-15.

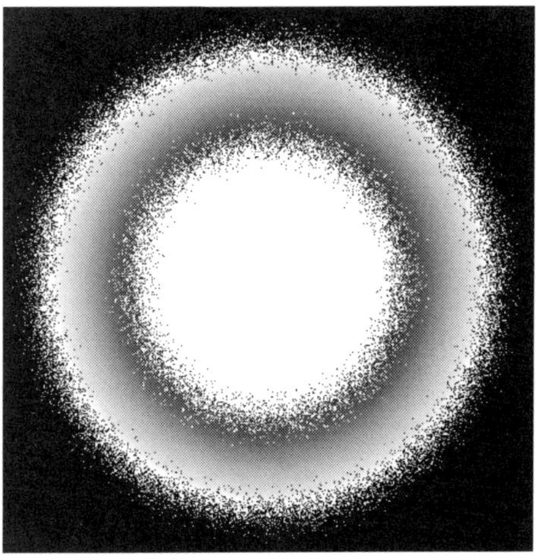

Figure 15-15: By inverting the image from the previous figure and erasing the center point, you achieve the effect of an expanding series of progressively lighter rings dissolving into the black void of space, an image better known to its friends as a supernova.

Amorphous gradient bubbles

Kai Krause, of Kai's Power Tools fame (discussed briefly back in the "Third-Party Filtering Tools" section of Chapter 12), came up with a way to mix radial gradations with the Lighten brush mode option to create soft bubbles like those shown in Figure 15-16. I call this the Larva Effect (talk about gall — naming other people's effects) because the darn thing looks like a goopy larva tail.

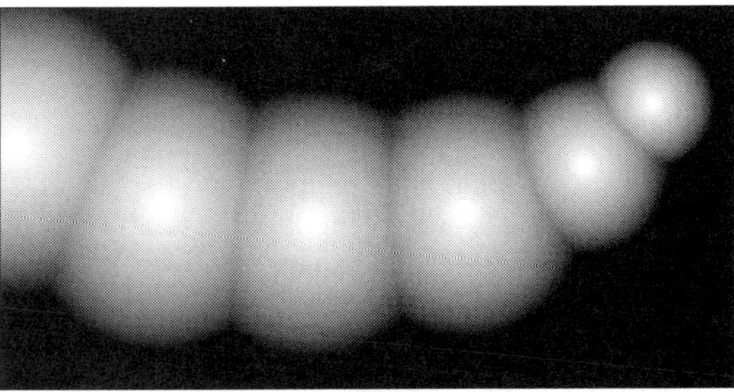

Figure 15-16: I painted this larva tail by filling the image with black, selecting Lighten from the brush mode pop-up menu, and creating six radial gradations from white to black with the gradient tool.

If you want to create this effect, click on the default colors icon and then click on the switch colors icon in the toolbox to make white the foreground color and black the background color. Next, double-click on the eraser tool icon to erase the entire screen to black. Set the gradient tool to create radial gradations and select Lighten from the brush mode pop-up menu. (In Photoshop 2.0, select the Lighten Only radio button in the Blend Tool Options dialog box.) Then drag with the tool in the image window to create one radial gradation after another. The Lighten option instructs Photoshop to apply a color to a pixel only if the color is lighter than the pixel's existing color. As a result, you only paint over part of a neighboring gradation when you create a new one, resulting in adjoining gradient bubbles like those shown in Figure 15-16.

To make the bubbles of larva flesh appear to emerge from a gradient pool, set the gradient tool to draw linear gradations and then drag upward from somewhere near the bottom of the image. The linear gradation starts out white at the bottom of the window and slowly fades to black, partially submerging the larva in gooey, glowing sludge. In Figure 15-17, I also dragged with the gradient tool from the top of the image to create a sort of larva cavern. Far out!

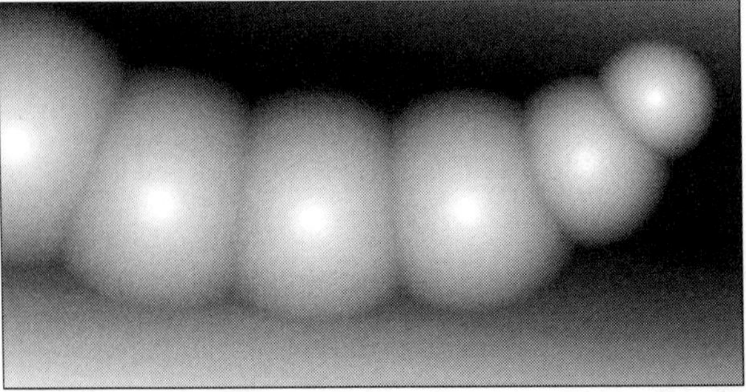

Figure 15-17: To create the larva cavern, I added two linear gradations, one beginning in the upper right corner of the image and the other beginning in the lower left corner.

Sharpened amorphous bubbles

The problem with the Larva Effect is that it results in amorphous blobs that look great on-screen but offer too little contrast for most printing situations. Luckily, you can add definition to the blobs using the Unsharp Mask filter with a Radius value of 2.0 or higher.

For example, Figure 15-18 shows the results of applying Unsharp Mask with an Amount value of 500 percent, a Radius of 2.0, and a Threshold of 0. The high Radius value helps the filter find the extremely soft edges in the image. (A lower Radius value would just heighten the contrast between individual pixels, creating a grainy effect — if any effect whatsoever.) I applied the filter once to achieve the top example in the figure. I applied the filter a second time to create the bottom example.

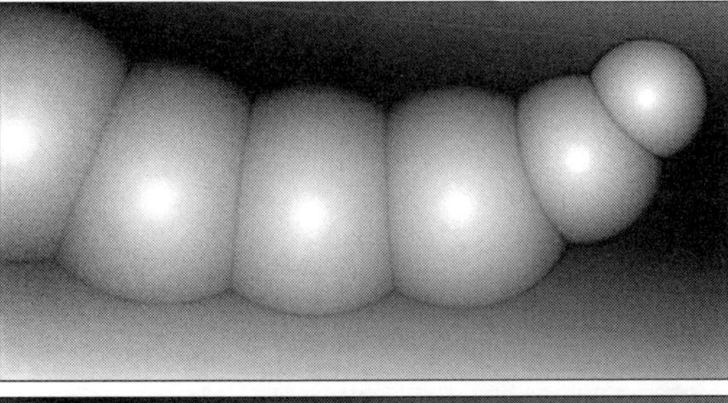

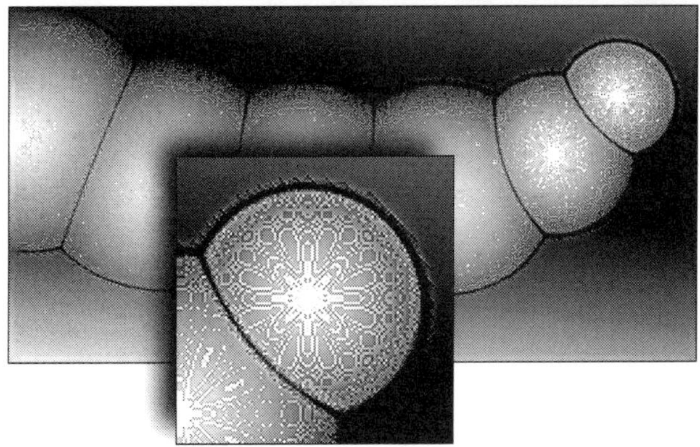

Figure 15-18: I sharpened the edges of the larva by applying the Unsharp Mask filter with a 2.0 Radius value once (top) and twice (bottom). Snowflake patterns begin to emerge with the second application of the filter (magnified inset).

As demonstrated in the magnified inset in Figure 15-18, crystalline snowflake patterns begin to emerge with the second application of Unsharp Mask. There's no doubt that the snowflakes are cool, doubly so because I stumbled on them completely by accident. However, if you would rather skip the snowflakes and further reinforce the edges, you're better off applying higher Radius values from the get-go. The top example in Figure 15-19 shows the result of applying the Unsharp Mask filter with a Radius value of 10.0; the bottom example shows the result of a 20.0 Radius value applied twice. What was once a larva tail is now a bony dinosaur tail.

If you're more interested in snowflakes than in sharpening, try applying an edge-detection effect with the Custom filter, as explained in the "Edge-detection" section of Chapter 13. Figure 15-20 shows some interesting crystals along with the Custom matrix values I used to create them. Welcome to the brave new world of op art, folks.

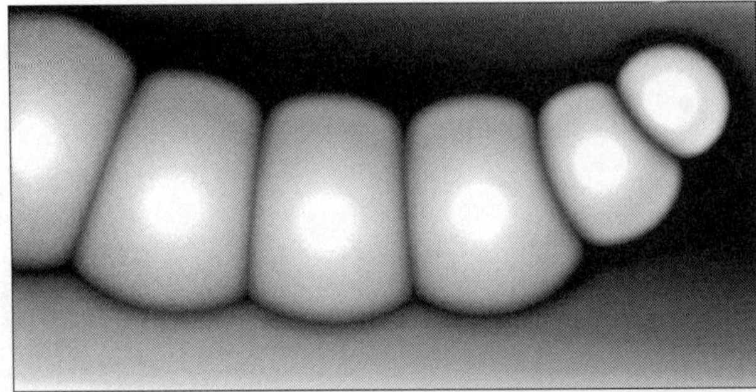

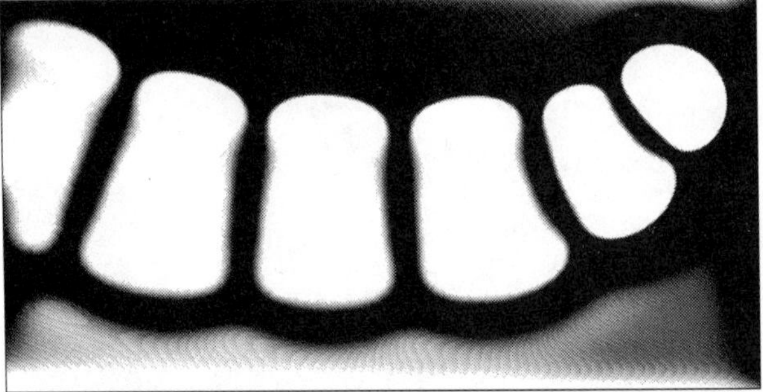

Figure 15-19: The results of applying Unsharp Mask once with a 10.0 radius (top) and twice with a 20.0 radius (bottom).

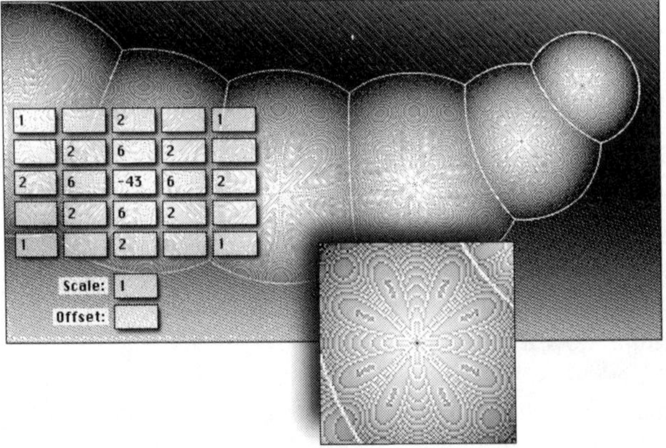

Figure 15-20: I filtered this image by entering some pretty extreme edge-detection values into the Custom dialog box (inset lower left). Edge-detection snowflakes (magnified inset) tend to be more spectacular than their Unsharp Mask equivalents.

Gradations as masks

If you think the Feather command is a hot tool for creating softened selection outlines, wait until you get a load of gradations in the quick mask mode. There's simply no better way to create fading effects than selecting an image with the gradient tool.

Fading an image

Consider the Moses set against a white background in Figure 15-21. He's familiar, he's got a beard that just won't quit, and he's got muscles bulging out of every corner of his body, including his neck, for heaven's sake. Now suppose you decide that maybe Moses could be even more impressive if he were to fade into view. You're in luck, because that is one of the easiest effects to pull off in Photoshop.

Figure 15-21: The star of Chapter 12 set against a plain white background.

Switch to the quick mask mode by clicking on the quick mask icon in the toolbox. (In Photoshop 2.0, choose Mode ⇨ New Channel.) Then use the gradient tool to draw a linear gradation from black to white. The white portion of the gradation represents the portion of the image that you want to select. I wanted to select and delete the bottom portion of Moses, so I drew the gradation from top to bottom, as shown in the first example of Figure 15-22.

Banding is typically even more noticeable when using a gradation as a selection outline. Therefore, to eliminate the banding effect, apply the Add Noise filter at a low setting several times. To create the right example in Figure 15-22, I applied Add Noise six times using an Amount value of 8 and the Uniform distribution option.

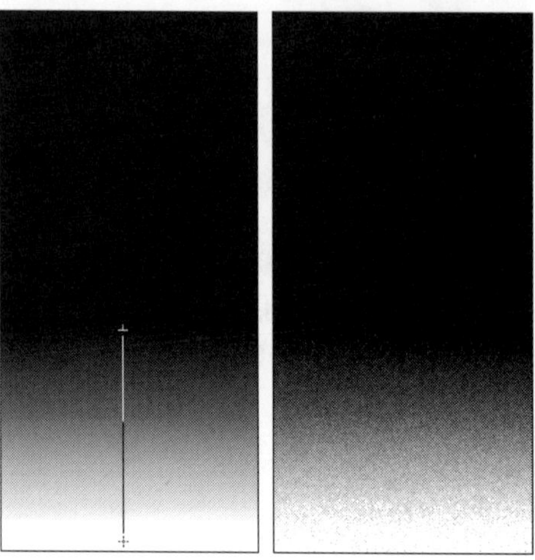

Figure 15-22: After drawing a linear gradation in the quick mask mode from top to bottom (left), I applied the Add Noise filter six times to mix up the colors a bit (right). Both images are shown narrower than their actual size.

To apply the gradation as a selection, return to the marching ants mode by clicking on the marching ants icon in the toolbox. (In Photoshop 2.0, press Command-0 or Command-1 — depending on whether the image is color or grayscale — to return to the main image channel. Then choose Select ⇨ Load Selection.) With white as the background color, press Delete to fill the selected portion of the image with white, creating a fading effect. In Figure 15-23, I combined a faded Moses with a traditional gradient background created in the marching ants mode.

Figure 15-23: The result of selecting the bottom portion of the image with a gradation and pressing Delete to fill it with white. I also added a gradient background to make the image more powerful.

Applying special effects gradually

You also can use gradations in the quick mask mode to taper the outcomes of filters and other automated special effects. For example, I wanted to apply a filter around the edges of the banner image that appears in Figure 15-24. I began by switching to the quick mask mode, choosing Select ⇨ All (Command-A), and pressing Option-Delete to fill the entire mask with black. Then I double-clicked on the gradient tool icon in the toolbox and selected the Linear radio button.

After closing the Gradient Tool Options dialog box, I selected Lighten from the brush mode pop-up menu in the Brushes palette. I clicked on the switch colors icon in the toolbox to make the foreground color white and the background color black. I then dragged with the gradient tool from each of the four edges of the image inward to create a series of short gradations that trace the boundaries of the banner, as shown in Figure 15-25. The white areas of the figure represent the portions of the image that I wanted to select.

After taking the above steps, I switched back to the marching ants mode and applied the desired effect, which in this case was the Color Halftone filter from the Filter ⇨ Stylize submenu. The result appears in Figure 15-26.

Figure 15-24: I wanted to highlight the background around the banner by applying a gradual filtering effect.

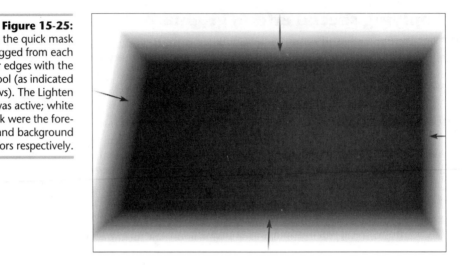

Figure 15-25: Inside the quick mask mode, I dragged from each of the four edges with the gradient tool (as indicated by the arrows). The Lighten brush mode was active; white and black were the foreground and background colors respectively.

Figure 15-26: After switching back to the marching ants mode, I chose Filter ⇨ Stylize ⇨ Color Halftone to create the halftoning effect shown here.

Applying Strokes and Arrowheads

In the "Using the Stroke Path command" section of Chapter 9, I discussed how to use one of the paint or edit tools to trace along a path created with the pen tool. The following sections discuss the more mundane aspects of stroking, namely how to apply a border around a selection outline and create arrowheads.

Stroking a selection outline

Stroking is useful for creating frames and outlines. Generally speaking, you can stroke an image in Photoshop in three ways:

- **Using the Stroke command:** Select the portion of the image that you want to stroke and choose Edit ⇨ Stroke to display the Stroke dialog box shown in Figure 15-27. Enter the thickness of the stroke in pixels into the Width option box. Select a Location radio button to specify the position of the stroke with respect to the selection outline. The Stroke dialog box also includes Opacity and Mode options that are just like those in the Fill dialog box.

When in doubt, select Inside from the Location radio buttons. This step ensures that the stroke is entirely inside the selection outline in case you decide to move the selection. If you select Center or Outside, Photoshop applies part or all of the stroke to the deselected area around the selection outline.

- **Using the Border command:** Select a portion of the image and choose Select ⇨ Border to retain only the outline of the selection. Specify the size of the border by entering a value in pixels into the Width option box and press Return. To fill the border with the background color, press Delete. To fill the border with the foreground color, press Option-Delete. To apply a repeating pattern to the border, choose Edit ⇨ Fill and select the Pattern radio button. You can even apply a filter command or special effect.
- **Framing the image:** Okay, so this is a throwaway, but it's pretty useful just the same. To create an outline around the entire image, change the background color to the color that you want to apply to the outline. Then choose Image ⇨ Canvas Size and add twice the desired border thickness to the Width and Height options in pixels. For example, to create a 1-pixel border, add 2 pixels to the Width value (1 for the left side and 1 for the right) and 2 pixels to the Height value (1 for the top edge and 1 for the bottom). When you press Return, Photoshop enlarges the canvas size according to your specifications and fills the new pixels around the perimeter of the image with the background color. Simplicity at its best.

Figure 15-27: Use the options in the Stroke dialog box to specify the thickness of a stroke and its location with respect to the selection outline.

Applying arrowheads

The one function missing from all the operations in the previous list is applying arrowheads. The fact is, in Photoshop, you can only apply arrowheads to straight lines drawn with the line tool. To create an arrowhead, double-click on the line tool icon in the toolbox to display the Line Tool Options dialog box shown in Figure 15-28. Enter a value into the Width option box to specify the thickness of the line — better known as the line's *weight* — and then use the Arrowheads options as follows:

- **At Start:** Select this check box to append an arrowhead to the beginning of a line drawn with the line tool.
- **At End:** Select this check box to append an arrowhead to the end of a line. (Like you needed me to tell you *that.*)
- **Width:** Enter the width of the arrowhead in pixels into this option box. The width of the arrowhead is completely independent of line weight.
- **Length:** Enter the length of the arrowhead, measured from the base of the arrowhead to its tip, into this option box. Again, length is measured in pixels and is independent of line weight.
- **Concavity:** You can specify the shape of the arrowhead by entering a value between negative and positive 50 percent into the Concavity option box. Figure 15-29 shows examples of a few Concavity settings applied to an arrowhead 50 pixels wide and 100 pixels long.

Applying arrowheads to straight lines is a simple matter. Double-click on the line tool icon, select a few choice options, and draw a line with the line tool. Applying an arrowhead to a stroked selection outline is a little trickier, but still possible. The following steps explain the process.

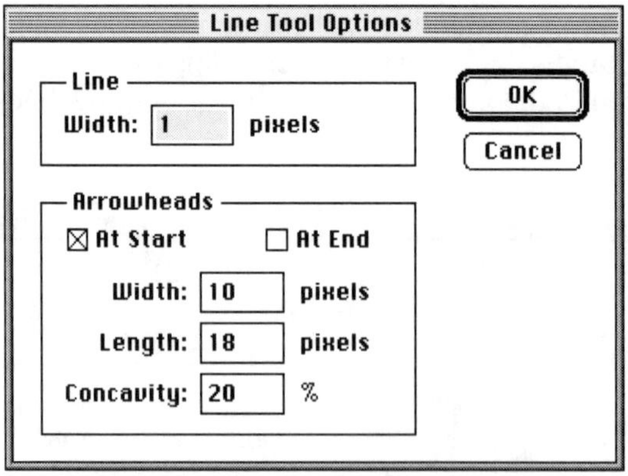

Figure 15-28: The Line Tool Options dialog box is the only place in Photoshop from which you can access arrowheads.

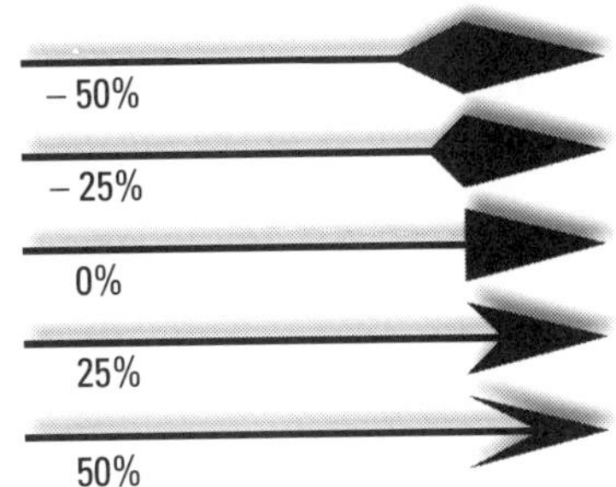

Figure 15-29: Examples of a 50 × 100-pixel arrowhead subject to five different Concavity values.

STEPS: Adding an Arrowhead to a Free-form Stroke

Step 1. You revert your image later in these steps, so save your image to disk now by choosing File ⇨ Save.

Step 2. Draw any selection outline you desire and stroke it by choosing Edit ⇨ Stroke and applying whatever settings strike your fancy. Remember the value you enter into the Width option. In Figure 15-30, I applied a 2-point stroke to a circular marquee.

Step 3. Choose Select ⇨ None (Command-D) to deselect all portions of the image.

Step 4. Select the eraser tool and Option-click anywhere in the image window to instruct Photoshop to load the saved image into memory. When the progress window disappears, Option-drag to revert the portions of the stroke at which you want to add arrowheads. I wanted to add arrowheads around the lions' tongues, so I Option-dragged around each tongue as demonstrated in Figure 15-30.

Figure 15-30: Stroke a selection, deselect it, and Option-drag with the eraser tool to create gaps in the stroke for the arrowheads.

Step 5. Double-click on the line tool icon. Enter the line weight that you used when stroking the selection outline (Step 2) into the Width option box. Select the At Start check box and deselect the At End check box if necessary. Then specify the width, length, and concavity of the arrowhead as desired and press Return.

Step 6. Zoom in on the point in the image at which you want to add the arrowhead. Draw a very short line exactly the length of the arrowhead at the tip of the stroke, as demonstrated in Figure 15-31. This step may take some practice to accomplish. Make sure to start the line a few pixels away from the end of the stroke, because the tip of the arrowhead is narrower than the line weight. If you mess up the first time, choose Edit ➪ Undo (Command-Z) and try again.

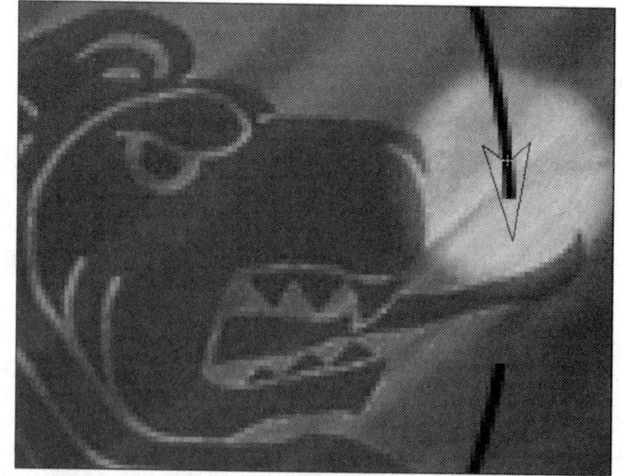

Figure 15-31: Draw a line no longer than the arrowhead with the line tool to append the arrowhead to the end of the stroke. This view size of the image is magnified 400 percent.

That's all there is to it. From there on, you just keep attaching as many arrowheads as you like. In Figure 15-32, I attached four arrowheads to the circular stroke, one above and one below each of the two tongues. Notice that I also reverted the area of the stroke that overlapped the lions' manes. I then created a circular feather marquee inside the circular stroke and drew six large arrowheads inside the selection mask. Finally, I inversed the selection and applied the Tiles and Radial Blur filters.

Figure 15-32: The finished image contains four arrowheads at the end of freeform strokes as well as six additional arrows inside a feathered selection.

Overlaying Floating Selections

So far in this book, I've discussed ways to edit text, apply filters, and color images using floating selections. But I have yet to explain exactly how Photoshop's overlay functions work. The remainder of this chapter explains how to mix floating selections with underlying images using Edit ⇨ Composite Controls (or in the case of Photoshop 2.0, Edit ⇨ Paste Controls), which takes you straight to central headquarters for overlaying operations.

For a review of the methods you can use to float and defloat selections in Photoshop, see the "Floating a selection" section of Chapter 9.

After you establish a floating selection, you can mix the colors in the selection with the colors in the image below by choosing Edit ⇨ Composite Controls (or Edit ⇨ Paste Controls in Photoshop 2.0). Photoshop displays the Composite Controls or Paste Controls dialog box, both shown in Figure 15-33.

Although not the most useful tip in this book — in fact, it's conceivably the *least* useful — I suppose it's worth mentioning that you can paste an image from the Clipboard and immediately display the Composite or Paste Controls dialog box in one operation. To do so, press Command-Option-V (or press the Option key when choosing Edit ⇨ Paste). The problem with this technique, and the reason I never use it, is that it prevents you from adjusting the placement of the pasted image and performing other preparatory operations, such as hiding the marching ants, before bringing up the dialog box. I prefer to assign a keyboard equivalent to Edit ⇨ Composite Controls and bring up the dialog box when I like for pasted and non pasted floating selections alike.

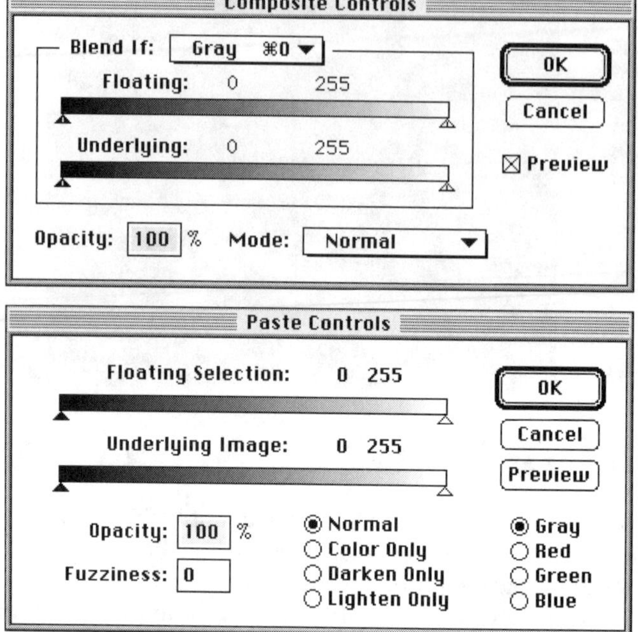

Figure 15-33: Photoshop 2.5 (top) and 2.0 (bottom) each provide a dialog box of options for mixing the colors in a floating selection with the colors in the image below.

As shown in Figure 15-33, each dialog box offers six groups of options:

- **Opacity:** The Opacity option box enables you to specify the translucency of the floating selection. A 100 percent setting makes the selection fully opaque; anything less makes the selection translucent. The lowest permissible value is 1 percent. This option works identically to the Opacity slider bar in the Brushes palette and can be changed in 10 percent increments in Photoshop 2.5 by pressing a number key on the keyboard.
- **Overlay modes:** Photoshop 2.5 provides access to 12 overlay modes in the Mode pop-up menu; Photoshop 2.0 provides four modes that you access by clicking on the Normal, Color, Darken Only, or Lighten Only radio buttons. Again, in Version 2.5, these options work just like their counterparts in the Brushes palette.
- **Color exclusion sliders:** The two slider bars let you exclude ranges of colors (according to brightness values) in the floating selection or underlying image. When you exclude colors in the floating selection, they disappear from view. When you exclude colors from the underlying image, those colors cannot be covered and are therefore visible regardless of the colors in the floating selection.
- **Fuzziness:** The slider bar settings can result in harsh transitions between included and excluded colors. To soften the transition, enter a brightness value range into the Fuzziness option box in Photoshop 2.0 or split the slider triangles in Photoshop 2.5 by dragging them while pressing the Option key.

- **Color channel options:** Select a color channel from the Blend If pop-up menu (or the Gray, Red, Green, and Blue radio buttons in Photoshop 2.0) to apply the effects of the color exclusion slider bars to one color channel independently of the others. When the Gray option is active, as it is by default, your changes affect all color channels equally. The Opacity value and overlay mode affect all channels regardless of the selected color channel.
- **Preview:** In Photoshop 2.0, click the Preview button to update the image window to correspond to the new settings without leaving the dialog box. In Photoshop 2.5, select the Preview check box to continually update the image every time you adjust a setting.

Some of these items are far too complicated to explain in a bulleted list. To find out more about any item other than the Opacity option box and the Preview check box or button — both of which fall under the category of 'nuff said — read the following sections. Each section is titled identically to its counterpart in the list.

In Photoshop 2.5, you can restore all options in the Composite Controls dialog box to their original settings by Option-clicking on the Reset button (the Cancel button changes to Reset when you press the Option key) or by simply pressing Command-Option-period.

Overlay modes

Photoshop 2.5 allows you to access *overlay modes,* the equivalent of brush modes for floating selections, in two ways. After selecting a selection tool from the toolbox or any of the tools from the Paths palette, you can select an option from the pop-up menu on the left side of the Brushes palette. (If you select some other tool, you affect the performance of that tool rather than the floating selection.) Or you can choose Edit ⇨ Composite Controls and select an option from the Mode pop-up menu, shown in Figure 15-34.

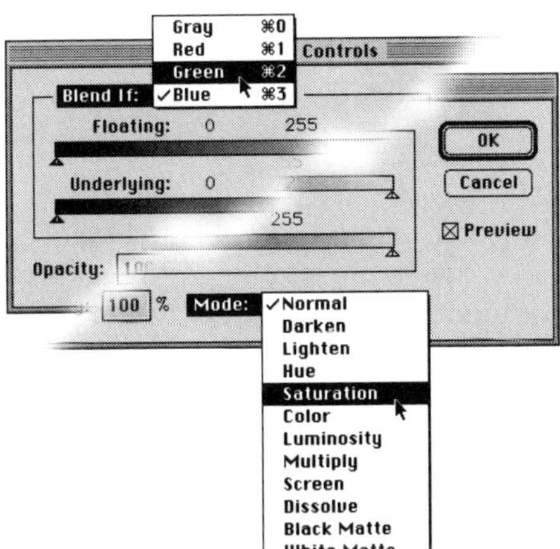

Figure 15-34: The two sets of pop-up menu options available in the Composite Controls dialog box.

Either way, Photoshop provides 12 overlay mode options:

- **Normal:** Select this option to view every pixel in the floating selection normally — subject, of course, to the settings of other options in the Composite Controls dialog box — regardless of the colors of the underlying image. Figure 15-35 shows the banner image floating in front of a stucco texture subject to the Normal overlay mode.
- **Darken:** When you select this option, Photoshop applies colors in the floating selection only if they are darker than the corresponding pixels in the underlying image. Keep in mind that Photoshop compares the brightness levels of pixels in an RGB, CMYK, or Lab image on a channel-by-channel basis. So although the red component of a pixel in the floating selection may be darker than the red component of the corresponding pixel in the underlying image, the green and blue components may be lighter. In this case, Photoshop assigns the red component of the floating pixel, but not the green and blue components, thereby subtracting some red and making the pixel slightly more turquoise. Compare the predictable grayscale example of the Darken overlay mode in Figure 15-36 to its more challenging color counterpart in Color Plate 15-3.
- **Lighten:** If you select this option, Photoshop applies colors in the floating selection only if they are lighter than the corresponding pixels in the underlying image. Again, Photoshop compares the brightness levels in all channels of a full-color image. Examples of the Lighten overlay mode appear in Figure 15-37 and Color Plate 15-3.

Figure 15-35: A floating selection (the banner image) subject to the Normal overlay mode.

- **Hue:** Remember the HSL (hue, saturation, and luminosity) color model from the last chapter? Well, the Hue mode and the following three overlay modes make use of the HSL color model to mix colors between floating selection and underlying image. When you select Hue, Photoshop retains the hue values from the floating selection and mixes them with the saturation and luminosity values from the underlying image. An example of this mode appears in the top middle image in Color Plate 15-3.

Figure 15-36: The same floating selection subject to the Darken overlay mode. Only those pixels in the selection that are darker than the pixels in the underlying stucco texture remain visible.

Figure 15-37: Our friend the floating selection subject to the Lighten overlay mode. Only those pixels in the selection that are lighter than the pixels in the underlying stucco texture remain visible.

I don't include grayscale figures for the Hue, Saturation, Color, and Luminosity overlay modes for the simple reason that those modes produce no effect on grayscale images. Actually, I shouldn't say *no* effect. In fact, they produce the exact same effect as the Normal option. After all, grayscale images don't include hue or saturation values; they only have luminosity.

- **Saturation:** When you select this option, Photoshop retains the saturation values from the floating selection and mixes them with the hue and luminosity values from the underlying image. An example of this mode appears in the center image in Color Plate 15-3.
- **Color:** This option combines hue and saturation. Therefore, when you select this option, Photoshop retains both the hue and saturation values from the floating selection and mixes them with the luminosity values from the underlying image. An example of the Color mode appears in the bottom middle image in Color Plate 15-3.
- **Luminosity:** When you select this option — is that phrase beginning to sound familiar? — Photoshop retains the luminosity values from the floating selection

and mixes them with the hue and saturation values from the underlying image. An example of this mode appears in the upper right image in Color Plate 15-3.

- **Multiply:** Finally, the end of the same-thing-only-slightly-different HSL overlay modes. On to the infinitely more entertaining Multiply and Screen modes. To understand these guys, you have to use a little imagination. So here goes. Imagine that the floating selection and the underlying image are both photos on transparent slides. The Multiply mode produces the same effect as holding those slides up to the light, one slide in front of the other. Because the light has to travel through two slides, the outcome is invariably a darker image that contains elements from both images. But unlike the Darken option, which ignores certain primary color components, Multiply mixes all colors evenly. Examples of the Multiply overlay mode appear in Figure 15-38 and Color Plate 15-3.
- **Screen:** Still have those transparent slides from the Multiply analogy? Well, throw them away; we don't need them anymore. Instead, imagine the floating selection and underlying image as two film negatives. If you were to fuse them together and develop a paper positive (standard photograph) from the two, you'd get the same effect as the Screen mode. So this time, instead of creating a darker image, as you do with Multiply, you create a lighter image, as demonstrated in Figure 15-39 and Color Plate 15-3.

Figure 15-38: The Multiply overlay mode produces the same effect as holding two overlapping transparencies up to the light; it always results in a darker image.

Figure 15-39: The Screen mode produces the same effect as developing two film negatives onto a paper positive; it always results in a lighter image.

- **Dissolve:** This option and the remaining two in the list are not represented in Color Plate 15-3 because they specifically affect feathered or softened edges. If the floating selection is entirely opaque with hard edges, none of these options has any effect. If the selection is antialiased, the effects are generally too subtle to be of much use. The Dissolve option randomizes the pixels in the feathered portion of a floating selection, as shown in the top example of Figure 15-40. It also randomizes pixels of hard- or soft-edged selections when the Opacity value is set below 100 percent, as witnessed by the second example.
- **Black Matte:** These next two options are special-use overlay modes. You'll almost never need them, but they are occasionally useful. For example, consider the top example in Figure 15-41. In this example, I set down a feathered selection against a black background. If I float it again and set it against the stucco background, I get a black ring around the image, as demonstrated in the top half of the second example in the figure. To eliminate the black ring, I selected the Black Matte option.
- **White Matte:** In the top example in Figure 15-42, I set the feathered selection onto a white background. When I later tried to apply the selection to the stucco texture, I got a white ring, as you can see in the top half of the bottom example. To eliminate the ring, I selected the White Matte option.

Figure 15-40: The Dissolve option applied to an opaque floating selection with heavily feathered edges (top) and to a second selection set to 40 percent opacity (bottom).

Figure 15-41: If you drop a feathered selection onto a black background (top) and try to reuse it, you get a black ring (upper half, bottom example). Luckily, you can eliminate this ring in Photoshop 2.5 by selecting the Black Matte overlay mode (lower half, bottom example).

Figure 15-42: Conversely, if you drop a feathered selection onto a white background (top) and try to reuse it, you get a white ring (upper half, bottom example), which you can eliminate by selecting the White Matte overlay mode (lower half, bottom example).

Color exclusion sliders

Drag the triangles along the Floating slider bar to abandon those pixels in the floating selection whose colors fall within a specified range of brightness values. You can abandon dark pixels by dragging the left slider triangle or light pixels by dragging the right slider triangle. Figure 15-43 shows examples of each. To create the top example, I dragged the left slider bar until the value immediately to the right of the *Floating* label read 50, thereby deleting pixels whose brightness values were 50 or less. To create the bottom example, I dragged the right slider triangle until the second value read 180, deleting pixels with brightness values of 180 or higher.

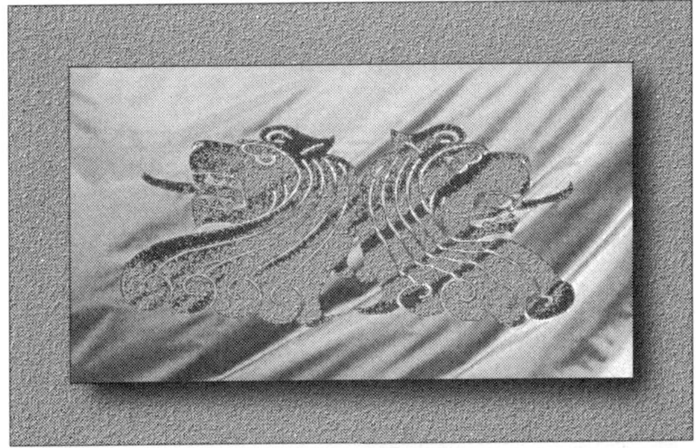

Figure 15-43: The results of moving the left Floating slider triangle to 50 (top) and the right Floating slider triangle to 180 (bottom).

Drag the triangles along the Underlying slider bar in order to force pixels in the underlying image to show through if they fall within a specified brightness range. To force dark pixels in the underlying image to show through, drag the left slider triangle; to force light pixels to show through, drag the right slider triangle.

To achieve the effect in the top example in Figure 15-44, I dragged the left slider triangle until the value immediately to the right of the *Underlying* label read 120, forcing the pixels in the stucco pattern that had brightness values of 120 or lower to show through. In the second example, I dragged the right slider triangle until the second value read 180, uncovering pixels at the bright end of the spectrum.

Figure 15-44: The results of moving the left Underlying slider triangle to 120 (top) and the right Underlying slider triangle to 180 (bottom).

Fuzziness

The problem with abandoning and forcing colors with the slider bars is that you achieve some pretty harsh color transitions. Both Figures 15-43 and 15-44 bear witness to this fact. Talk about your jagged edges! Luckily, you can soften the color transitions by abandoning and forcing pixels gradually over a *fuzziness range.*

In Photoshop 2.0, you specify a fuzziness range by entering a brightness value between 1 and 255 into the Fuzziness option box. Pixels fade away or fade into view over the course of this range. In other words, pixels at one end of the range are transparent; pixels at the other end are opaque; and pixels in between are translucent. This value applies equally to both of the Floating values and both of the Underlying values.

Photoshop 2.5 provides an even better solution. Rather than applying a single fuzziness range to all slider values, you can apply a different range to each value independently. To do so, Option-drag one of the slider triangles in the Composite Controls dialog box. The triangle splits into two halves, and the corresponding value above the slider bar splits into two values separated by a slash, as demonstrated in Figure 15-45.

The left triangle half represents the beginning of the fuzziness range — that is, the brightness values at which the pixels begin to fade into or away from view. The right half represents the end of the range — that is, the point at which the pixels are fully visible or invisible.

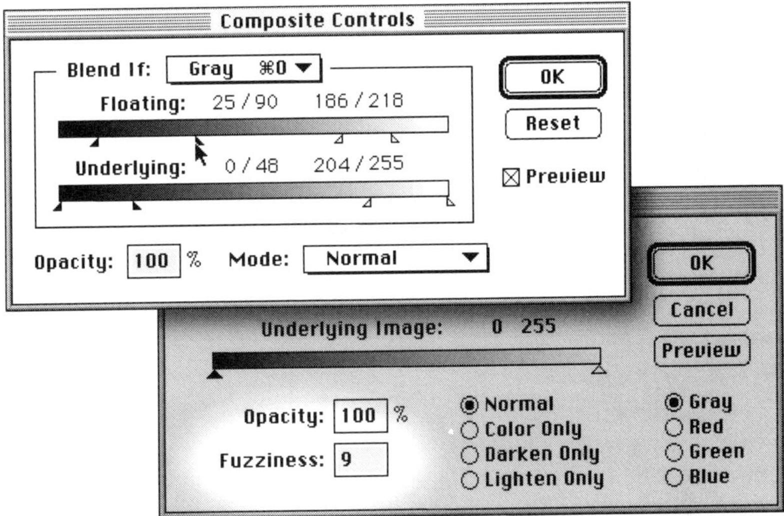

Figure 15-45: Option-drag a slider triangle to split it in half, thereby specifying a fuzziness range in Photoshop 2.5.

Figures 15-46 and 15-47 show softened versions of the effects from Figures 15-43 and 15-44. In the top example of Figure 15-46, for example, I adjusted the range of the left Floating slider triangle so that the value immediately to the right of the *Floating* label read 30/70. The result is a much smoother effect than achieved in the top example in Figure 15-43. In the bottom example of Figure 15-46, I changed the range of the right Floating slider triangle so the second value read 120/230.

In Figure 15-47, I applied fuzziness ranges with the Underlying slider. In fact, both examples in the figure are the result of applying the same value, 120/180, to opposite Underlying slider triangles. In the top example, all brightness values under 120 gradually extending to values up to 180 show through the floating selection. In the second example, all brightness values above 180 gradually extending down to 120 show through. The resulting two images look very much like sand art. (The next thing you know, I'll be showing you how to create string art and black velvet Elvises.)

Figure 15-46: The results of adjusting the fuzziness range of the left Floating slider triangle to 30/70 (top) and that of the right Floating slider triangle to 120/230 (bottom).

Figure 15-47: The results of adjusting the fuzziness range of both the left (top) and right (bottom) Underlying slider triangles to 120/180.

Color channel options

The options in the Blend If pop-up menu (and their radio-button equivalents in the lower right corner of Photoshop 2.0's Paste Controls dialog box) are applicable exclusively to the settings you apply using the Floating and Underlying slider bars. When you work with a grayscale image, the Blend If pop-up menu offers one option only — Black — meaning that you can write this option off in grayscale. However, when you work in the RGB, CMYK, or Lab mode, the Composite Controls dialog box enables you to abandon and force ranges of pixels independently within each color channel.

To do so, select a color channel from the Blend If pop-up menu (or from the Paste Controls radio buttons). Then set the slider triangles as desired. Each time you select a different Blend If option, the slider triangles retract to the positions at which you last set them for that color channel. Color Plate 15-4 demonstrates the effect of manipulating the Floating and Underlying slider triangles independently for the red, green, and blue color channels.

Summary

- To limit the area affected by the paint bucket tool, apply the tool inside the confines of a selection outline.
- Press Delete to fill a selection with the background color. Press Option-Delete to fill it with the foreground color.
- If you float a selection before pressing Option-Delete, you can easily make the color translucent by pressing a number key.
- Use the Style options inside the Gradient Tool Options dialog box to specify the way Photoshop selects colors for a gradation. These options have no effect on grayscale gradations.
- You can eliminate banding in a gradation by applying the Add Noise filter in combination with the Motion Blur and Radial Blur commands.
- You can paint amorphous bubbles and planes with the gradient tool by filling the image window with black, setting the brush mode to Lighten, and creating gradations from white to black.
- When sharpening gradations, set the Radius value inside the Unsharp Mask dialog box to 2.0 or higher. You also can use the Unsharp Mask and Custom filters to derive crystal structures from radial gradations.
- In the quick mask mode, you can apply gradations to create soft transitions between selected and deselected regions of an image.
- The Select ⇨ Border command can be a more versatile solution for stroking a selection outline than Edit ⇨ Stroke because it allows you to stroke with the background color, a repeating pattern, or a filter.
- Use the line tool to add arrowheads to the end of strokes.
- The Hue, Saturation, Color, and Luminosity overlay modes are applicable exclusively to full-color images.
- The Multiply and Screen overlay modes let you combine images as if they were photographic transparencies.
- In Photoshop 2.5, Option-drag the slider triangles in the Composite Controls dialog box to soften the exclusion of colors in the floating selection or the forcing of colors in the underlying image.

Mapping and Adjusting Colors

16 CHAPTER

In This Chapter

- Using commands in the Image ⇨ Map submenu
- Using Threshold and Posterize in combination with the High Pass filter
- Rotating colors in an image around the color wheel using the Hue/Saturation command
- Editing selective saturation levels within an image
- Colorizing grayscale images
- Using the Levels and Curves commands
- Boosting brightness and contrast levels
- Drawing arbitrary color maps that lead to psychedelic effects

Mapping Colors

Color mapping is just a fancy name for shuffling colors around. For example, to map Color A to Color B simply means to take all the A-colored pixels and convert them to B-colored pixels. Although many painting programs require you to map colors one color at a time, Photoshop provides several commands that enable you to map entire ranges of colors based on their hues, saturation levels, and, most frequently, brightness values.

Color effects and corrections

Why would you want to change colors around? For one reason, to achieve special effects. You know those psychedelic videos that show some guy's hair turning blue while his face turns purple and the palms of his hands glow a sort of cornflower yellow? Although not the most attractive effect by modern standards — you may be able to harvest more tasteful results if you put your shoulder to the color wheel — psychedelia qualifies as color mapping for the simple reason that each color shifts incrementally to a new color.

Another reason to use color mapping is to enhance the appearance of a scanned image. In this case, you're not creating special effects, just making straightforward color adjustments, known in the biz as *color corrections.* Scans are never perfect, no matter how much money you spend on a scanning device or a service bureau. They can always benefit from tweaking and subtle adjustments, if not outright overhauls, in the color department.

Keep in mind, however, that Photoshop can't make something from nothing. In creating the illusion of more and better colors, every color-adjustment operation that you perform actually takes some small amount of color *away* from the image. Invariably, two pixels that were two different colors before you started change to the same color. The image may look 10 times better, but it will in fact be less colorful than when you started.

It's important to keep this principle in mind because it demonstrates that color mapping is a balancing act. The first nine operations you perform may make an image look progressively better, but the tenth may send it into decline. There's no magic formula, unfortunately. The amount of color mapping you need to apply varies from image to image. For the moment, the only advice I can offer is that you use moderation, know when to stop, and — as always — save your image to disk before launching into the color mapping process.

This whole bit about how color mapping sucks color out of an image to produce the illusion of a more colorful image probably sounds strange on the face of it. But if you think about it, it has to be true. Photoshop maps colors by applying one or more complex equations to a pixel and then rounding off the results of those equations to the nearest brightness value, hue, what have you. Because entire communities of pixels in an image are very close in color — say, only a brightness value or two apart — the equations frequently convert two slightly different colors to the same color. By contrast, the equations never, *ever* change a single color into two different colors. So when it comes to color correction, colors don't procreate, they die like flies for the good cause, the illusion of better color.

Photoshop's color correction functions fall into three categories: those that produce immediate and useful effects, such as Invert and Threshold; those that require significantly more work but are nonetheless designed to be understood by novices, such as the Brightness/Contrast and Variations commands; and those that are still more complicated but provide better control and better functionality, such as Levels and Curves.

This chapter contains no information about the second category of commands for the simple reason that they are inadequate and ultimately a big waste of time. I know because I spent my first year with Photoshop relying exclusively on Brightness/Contrast and Color Balance, all the while wondering why I never achieved the effects I wanted. Then one happy day, after spending about a half an hour learning Levels and

Curves, the quality of my images skyrocketed and the amount of time I spent on them plummeted. So wouldn't you just rather learn it right in the first place? (I hope so, because you're stuck with it.) To this end, I discuss the supposedly more complicated and indisputably more capable high-end commands as if they were the only ones available.

Color mapping commands

Before we get into all the high-end gunk, however, I'll take a moment to explain the first category of commands, all of which happen to reside in the Image ⇨ Map submenu. These commands produce immediate effects that are either difficult to duplicate or not worth attempting with the more full-featured commands.

If you use Photoshop 2.0, one command under the Image ⇨ Map submenu that I won't be discussing at this time is the Arbitrary command, which enables you to map colors to other colors in any manner you desire to create truly wild effects. In Photoshop 2.5, the capabilities of this command have been transferred to Image ⇨ Adjust ⇨ Curves. For more information, read the "Making Custom Brightness Adjustments" section near the end of this chapter.

Invert

When you choose Image ⇨ Map ⇨ Invert (Command-I), Photoshop converts every color in your image to its exact opposite, just as in a photographic negative. As demonstrated in Figure 16-1 and in the upper left example of Color Plate 16-1, black becomes white, white becomes black, fire becomes water, good becomes evil, Imelda Marcos goes barefoot, and the brightness value of every primary color component changes to 255 minus the original brightness value. The only color that doesn't change is medium gray, because it is its own opposite. (Ooh, I saw a movie like that once.) If you were to float a selection, apply the Invert command, and change the opacity to 50 percent, every pixel in the selection would appear medium gray.

Figure 16-1: An image before the advent of the Invert command (left) and after (right).

Image ➪ Map ➪ Invert is just about the only color mapping command that retains every single drop of color in an image. (The Hue/Saturation command also retains colors under specific conditions.) If you apply the Invert command twice in a row, you arrive at your original image.

Equalize

Equalize is possibly the smartest and at the same time least useful of the Image ➪ Map pack. When you invoke this command, Photoshop searches for the lightest and darkest color values in a selection. Then it maps the lightest color to white, maps the darkest color to black, and distributes the remaining colors to other brightness levels in an effort to evenly distribute pixels over the entire brightness spectrum.

If no portion of the image is selected when you choose Image ➪ Map ➪ Equalize (Command-E), Photoshop automatically maps out the entire image across the brightness spectrum, as shown in the upper right example of Figure 16-2. However, if you select a portion of the image before choosing the Equalize command, Photoshop displays a dialog box containing the following two radio buttons:

- **Selected Area Only:** Select this option to apply the equalize filter strictly within the confines of the selection. The lightest pixel in the selection becomes white, the darkest pixel becomes black, and so on.
- **Entire Image Based on Area:** If you select the second radio button, which is the default setting, Photoshop applies the Equalize command to the entire image based on the lightest and darkest colors in the selection. All colors in the image that are lighter than the lightest color in the selection become white, and all colors darker than the darkest color in the selection become black.

The bottom two examples in Figure 16-2 (as well as the upper right example in Color Plate 16-1) show the effects of selecting different parts of the image when the Entire Image Based on Area option is in force. In the left example, I selected a very dark portion of the image, which resulted in over-lightening of the entire image. In the right example, I selected an area with both light and dark values, which boosted the amount of contrast between highlights and shadows in the image.

The problem with the Equalize command is that it relies too heavily on automation to be of much use as a color correction tool. Certainly, you can create some interesting special effects. But if you want to adjust the tonal balance in a scanned image, the Levels and Curves commands are far more useful.

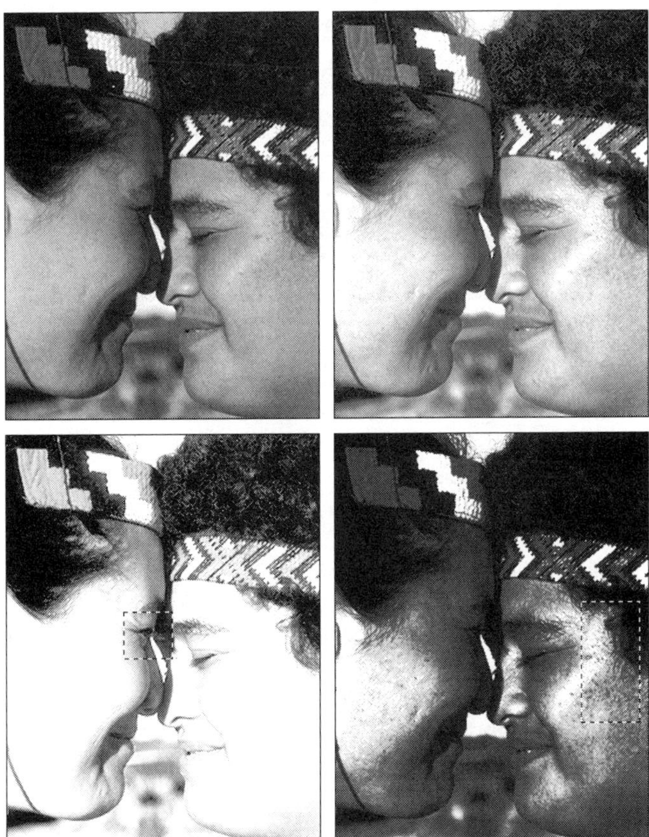

Figure 16-2: An image before (top left) and after (top right) applying the Equalize command when no portion of the image is selected. You also can use the brightness values in a selected region as the basis for equalizing an entire image (bottom left and right).

Threshold

I touched on the Threshold command a couple of times in previous chapters. As you may recall, Threshold converts all colors to either black or white based on their brightness values. When you choose Image ⇨ Map ⇨ Threshold (Command-T), Photoshop displays the Threshold dialog box shown in Figure 16-3. The dialog box offers a single option box and a slider bar, either of which you can use to specify the medium brightness value in the image. Photoshop changes any color lighter than the value in the Threshold option box to white and any color darker than the value to black.

Situated directly above the slider bar is a graph of the colors in the selection (or in the entire image if no portion of the image is selected). The width of the graph represents all 256 possible brightness values, starting at black on the left and progressing through white on the right. The height of each vertical line in the graph demonstrates the number of pixels in the image currently associated with that brightness value. Such a graph is called a *histogram.* (You can see a more detailed version of the graph in the Histogram and Levels dialog boxes.)

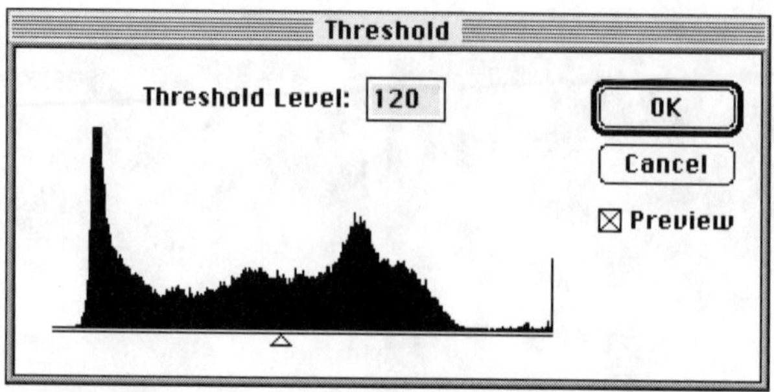

Figure 16-3: The histogram in the Threshold dialog box shows the distribution of brightness values in the selection.

Generally speaking, you achieve the best effects if you change an equal number of pixels to black as you change to white (and vice versa). So rather than moving the slider bar to 128, which is the medium brightness value, move it to the point at which the area of the vertical lines to the left of the slider triangle looks roughly equivalent to the area of the vertical lines to the right of the slider triangle.

The upper right example in Figure 16-4 shows the result of applying the Threshold command with a Threshold Level value of 120 (as in Figure 16-3). Although this value more or less evenly distributes black and white pixels, I lost a lot of detail in the dark areas.

As you may recall from my discussion in “Using the High Pass filter” section of Chapter 12, you can use Filter ⇨ Other ⇨ High Pass in advance of the Threshold command to retain areas of contrast. For example, in the lower left image in Figure 16-4, I applied the High Pass filter with a radius of 10.0 pixels, followed by the Threshold command with a value of 124. In the lower right example, I applied High Pass with a radius of 3.0 pixels and then applied Threshold with a value of 126.

Higher High Pass radiuses combined with higher Threshold values result in more detail, which is the good news, as well as more random artifacts, which can detract from an image. So it’s a mixed bag. Isn’t everything? If you’re looking for a real life application of the Threshold command, Figure 16-5 shows all the effects from Figure 16-5 applied to floating selections set to 15 percent opacity. In each example, the translucent selection helps to add contrast and reinforce details in the original image. (Color Plate 16-1 offers a color version of the lower right example in Figure 16-5.)

Posterize

The Posterize command is Threshold's rich cousin. Whereas Threshold boils down an image into two colors only, Posterize can retain as many colors as you like. However, you can't control how colors are mapped, as you can when you use Threshold. The Posterize dialog box provides no histogram or slider bar. Instead, Posterize automatically divides the full range of 256 brightness values into a specified number of equal increments.

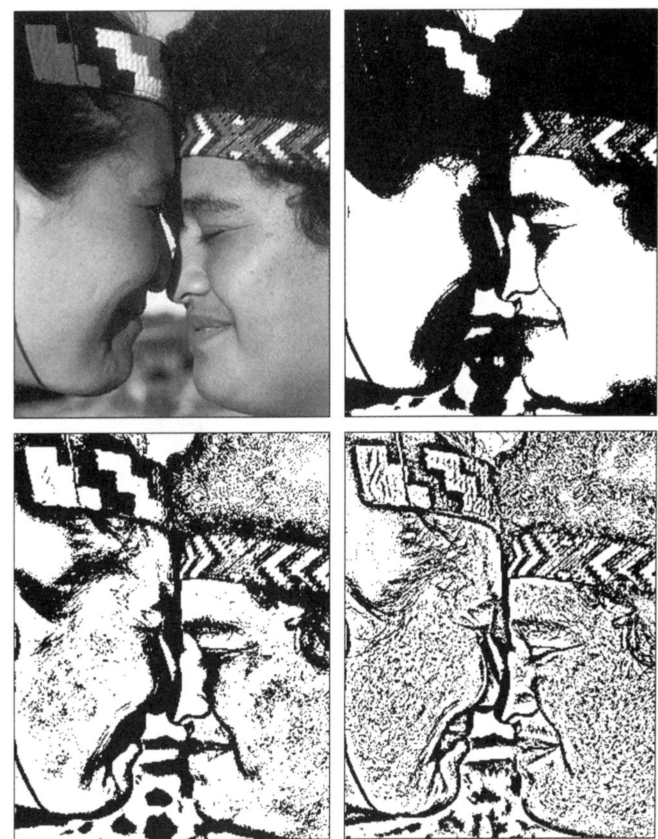

Figure 16-4: An image before applying the Threshold command (top left) and after (top right). You can retain more detail in the image by applying the High Pass filter before applying Threshold (bottom left and right).

Figure 16-5: The Threshold and High Pass operations from Figure 16-4 applied to floating selections set to 15 percent opacity, thus permitting the underlying original to show through.

To use this command, choose Image ⇨ Map ⇨ Posterize (or press Command-J in Photoshop 2.0) and enter a value into the Levels option box. The Levels value represents the number of brightness values the Posterize command retains. Higher values result in subtle color adjustments; lower values produce more dramatic effects. The upper right example in Figure 16-6 shows an image subject to a Levels value of 8. If you want to see the effect in color, the lower left example in Color Plate 16-1 shows an image subject to a Levels value of 16.

By now, you may be thinking, "By golly, if Posterize is so similar to Threshold, I wonder how it works when applied after the High Pass filter?" Well, if you *were* thinking that, you're in luck, because this is exactly the purpose of the two bottom examples in Figure 16-6. As in Figure 16-4, I applied the High Pass filter with Radius values of 10.0 and 3.0 respectively to the left and right examples. I then applied the Posterize filter with the same Levels value as before (8) to achieve some unusual, high-contrast effects.

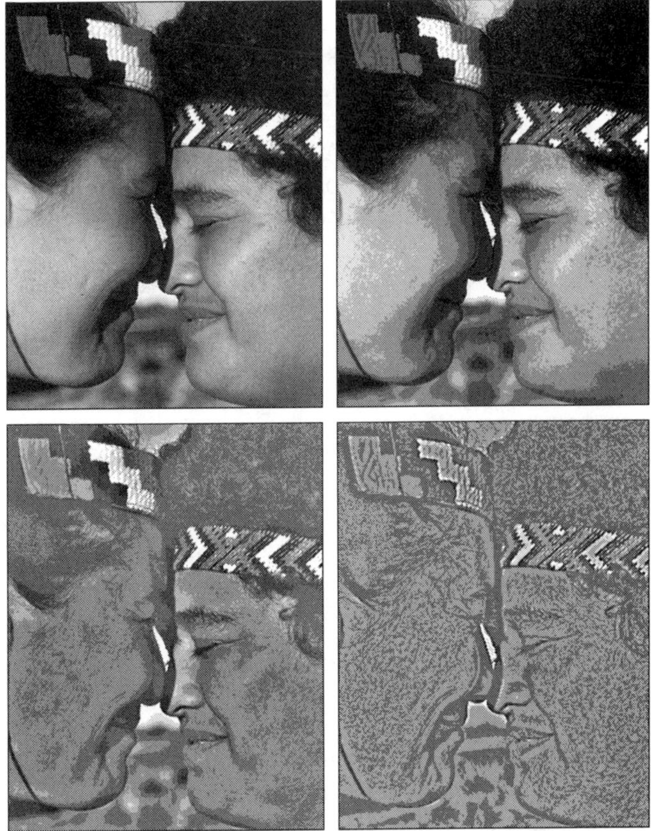

Figure 16-6: An image before (top left) and after (top right) applying the Posterize command with a Levels value of 8. As you can when using the Threshold command, you can retain detail in an image by applying the High Pass filter before applying Posterize (bottom left and right).

Hue Shifting and Colorizing

We now move slightly down the command hierarchy, from the Image ⇨ Map submenu to the Image ⇨ Adjust submenu. In fact, the remainder of this chapter covers three commands in this submenu to the exclusion of all others: Hue/Saturation (Command-U), Levels (Command-L), and Curves (Command-M), in that order.

Using the Hue/Saturation command

The Hue/Saturation command provides two functions. First, it enables you to adjust colors in an image according to their hues and saturation levels. You can apply the changes to individual color channels or affect all colors equally across the spectrum. And second, the command lets you colorize images by applying new hue and saturation values while retaining the core brightness information from the original image.

This command is perfect for colorizing grayscale images. I know, I know, Woody Allen wouldn't approve, but with some effort, you can make Ted Turner green with envy. Just scan him and change the Hue value to 140 degrees. (It's a joke, son.)

When you choose Image ⇨ Adjust ⇨ Hue/Saturation (Command-U), Photoshop displays the Hue/Saturation dialog box, shown in Figure 16-7. (The Hue/Saturation dialog box in Photoshop 2.0 looks slightly different but provides the same options.)

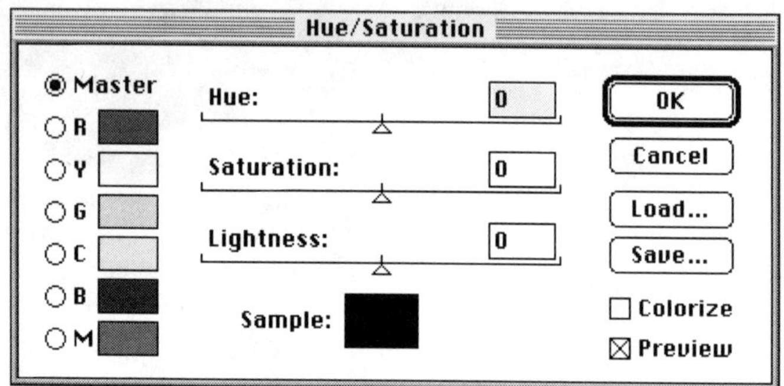

Figure 16-7: The Hue/Saturation dialog box enables you to adjust the hues and saturation values in a color image or colorize a grayscale image.

Before I explain how to use this dialog box to produce specific effects, let me briefly introduce the options:

- **Master:** Select the Master option to adjust all colors in an image to the same degree. If you prefer to adjust some colors in the image differently than others, select one of the color radio buttons along the left side of the dialog box. In the RGB and CMYK modes, the dialog box offers the R (Red), Y (Yellow), G (Green), C (Cyan), B (Blue), and M (Magenta) options, as shown in Figure 16-7. In the Lab mode, two radio buttons bite the dust, leaving Y (Yellow), G (Green), B (Blue), and M (Magenta), each of which represents an extreme end of the *a* or *b* spectrum. You can specify different slider bar settings for every one of the color ranges. For example, you might select R (Red) and move the Hue slider triangle to +50 and then select Y (Yellow) and move the Hue triangle to –30. All radio buttons are dimmed when you select the Colorize check box.
- **Hue:** The Hue slider bar measures colors on the 360-degree color circle, familiar from the Apple Color Picker dialog box. When Master is selected, you can adjust the Hue value from negative to positive 180 degrees. When one of the other color radio buttons is active in the RGB or CMYK mode, the Hue value can vary from negative to positive 60 degrees, because each of the colors is 60 degrees from either of its neighbors in the color wheel. (Red is 60 degrees from yellow, which is 60 degrees from green, and so on.)

When a color radio button is active in the Lab mode, the Hue value can vary from negative to positive 90 degrees, thanks to Lab's specialized color organization. Regardless of mode, letters appear at either end of the Hue slider when any option except Master is selected. The letters indicate the effect of moving the slider triangle in either direction. For example, if you select R (Red), the letters *M* and *Y* flank the slider, indicating that a negative value maps red pixels toward magenta, while a positive value maps red pixels toward yellow.

- **Saturation:** Normally, the Saturation value can vary from negative to positive 100. The only exception occurs when the Colorize check box is active, in which case saturation becomes an absolute value. In other words, you can't subtract saturation from a colorized image; therefore, the range becomes 0 to 100.

Photoshop precedes positive values in the Hue, Saturation, and Lightness option boxes with plus signs (+) to show that you are adding to the current color attributes of the pixels. When you select Colorize, the plus signs disappear from all but the Lightness value because hue and saturation become absolute values that you apply to pixels rather than adding or subtracting to existing pixel colors.

- **Lightness:** You can darken or lighten an image by varying the Lightness value from negative to positive 100. However, because this value invariably changes *all* brightness levels in an image to an equal extent — whether or not Colorize is selected — it permanently dulls highlights and shadows. Therefore, you'll most likely want to avoid this option like the plague and rely instead on the Levels or Curves command to edit brightness and contrast.
- **Sample:** This color swatch serves as a guidepost. Really, it's pretty redundant, because you can monitor the effects that your settings have on an image by selecting the Preview check box. But if you want to see the impact of your settings on one color in particular, you can isolate it by clicking on that color in the image window with the eyedropper cursor. (The cursor automatically changes to an eyedropper when you move it outside the Hue/Saturation dialog box and into the image window.)
- **Load/Save:** As in all the best color correction dialog boxes (including Levels and Curves, naturally), you can load and save settings to disk in case you want to reapply the options to other images. These options are especially useful if you find a magic combination of color-correction settings that accounts for most of the color mistakes produced by your scanner.
- **Colorize:** Select this check box to apply a single hue and a single saturation level to the entire selection, regardless of how it was previously colored. All brightness levels remain intact, though you can adjust them incrementally using the Lightness slider bar (a practice that I do *not* recommend, as I mentioned earlier).

- **Preview:** In Photoshop 2.0, click on the Preview button to update the image window in keeping with the new settings without leaving the dialog box. In Photoshop 2.5, select the Preview check box to continually update the image every time you adjust a setting.

In Photoshop 2.5, you can restore the options in the Hue/Saturation, Levels, and Curves dialog boxes to their original settings by Option-clicking on the Reset button (the Cancel button changes to Reset when you press the Option key) or by simply pressing Command-Option-period.

If the Hue/Saturation command is dimmed, you're probably in the wrong color mode. The command is not applicable to grayscale images. You must first convert the image to the RGB, CMYK, or Lab mode before applying the command.

Adjusting hue and saturation

All right, now that you know how the options work, it's time to give them a whirl. One caveat before I launch into things: grayscale figures won't help you one whit in understanding the Hue/Saturation options, so I refer you a few times to three color plates. You may want to take a moment to slap a Post-it note in the general area of Color Plates 16-2, 16-3, and 16-4 before you begin reading so you can easily flip back and forth between text and color plates.

Changing hues

When the Colorize check box is inactive, the Hue slider bar shifts colors in an image around the color wheel. It's as if the pixels were playing a colorful game of musical chairs, except that none of the chairs disappear. If you select the Master radio button and enter a value of +60 degrees, for example, all pixels stand up, march one sixth of the way around the color wheel, and sit down, assuming the colors of their new chairs. A pixel that was red becomes yellow, a pixel that was yellow becomes green, and so on. The top row of Color Plate 16-2 shows the result of applying various Hue values to a single image. Note that, in each case, all colors in the image change to an equal degree.

As long as you select only the Master option and edit only the Hue value, Photoshop retains all colors in an image. In other words, after shifting the hues in an image +60 degrees, you can later choose Hue/Saturation and shift the hues –60 degrees to restore the original colors.

If you select any radio button other than Master, the musical chairs metaphor breaks down a little. All pixels that correspond to the color you select move to the exclusion of other pixels in the image. The pixels that move must, well, sit on the non-moving pixels' laps, meaning that you sacrifice colors in the image.

For example, I edited the images in the second row of Color Plate 16-2 by applying Hue values while the R (Red) radio button only was selected. (In other words, I didn't apply Hue changes in combination with any other radio button.) All pixels that included some amount of red shifted to new hues according to the amount of red the pixels contained; all non-red pixels remained unchanged. Despite the fact that the Hue values in each column of the color plate are identical, the colors in the faces changed less dramatically when R (Red) was selected than when I used the Master option. This occurs because most of the pixels in the face contain some amount of yellow, which is excluded from the R (Red) hue adjustments.

Changing saturation levels

When I was a little kid, I used to love watching my grandmother's television because she kept the Color knob cranked at all times. The images appeared to leap off the screen, like maybe they were radioactive or something. Way cool. Well, the Saturation option works just like that Color knob. I don't recommend that you follow my grandmother's example and send the saturation for every image through the roof, but it can prove helpful for enhancing or downplaying the colors in an image. If the image looks washed out, try adding saturation; if colors leap off the screen so that everybody in the image looks like they're wearing neon makeup, subtract saturation.

Just as the Saturation option works like the Color knob on a TV set, the Hue value serves the same purpose as the Tint knob and the Lightness value works like the Brightness knob.

The top row of Color Plate 16-3 shows the results of applying Saturation values when the Master option is selected. As you can see, all colors in the image fade or fortify equally. However, by applying the Saturation values to specific color options only, you can selectively fade and fortify colors, as demonstrated in the second row of the color plate.

For example, the lower left image in Color Plate 16-3 shows the result of selecting each color radio button except R (Red) in turn and lowering the Saturation to –100, which translates to no saturation whatsoever, or all grays. All that's left are grays and reds, producing an effect that looks like traditional paint applied to a black-and-white photo. In the lower right image, I lowered the Saturation for R (Red) to –100 and raised the saturation of all other colors to +50, thus eliminating the image's strongest color and enhancing the remaining weaker colors.

Colorizing images

When you select the Colorize check box, the rules change. The pixels, instead of walking around a circle of musical chairs, all get up and go sit in the same chair. Every pixel in the selection receives the same hue and the same level of saturation. Only the brightness values remain intact to ensure the that image remains recognizable.

The top row of Color Plate 16-4 shows the results of shifting the hues in an image in two different directions around the color wheel. In each case, the Colorize option is inactive. The second row shows similar colors applied separately to the faces and background of the image using the Colorize option. The colors look approximately the same within each column in the color plate. However, the Hue values are different in the shifted images than those in the colorized images because the shifted colors are based on flesh tones in the orange (25 degree) range as well as a variety of other colors in the original image, while all of the colorized colors are based on absolute 0 degree, which is red.

In most cases, you'll only want to colorize grayscale images or bad color scans, because colorizing ruins the original color composition of an image. You probably also will want to lower the Saturation value to somewhere in the neighborhood of 50 to 75 degrees. All the colors in the second-row images in Color Plate 16-4 are the result of entering Saturation values of 60 degrees.

To touch up areas in a colorized image, change the foreground color to match the Hue and Saturation values that you used in the Hue/Saturation dialog box. The B (Brightness) value in the Color Picker dialog box should be 100 percent. Select the paintbrush tool and change the brush mode in the Brushes palette to Color (or Color Only in Photoshop 2.0's Paint Brush Options dialog box). Then paint away.

Making Custom Brightness Adjustments

Photoshop provides two high-end commands for adjusting the brightness levels in an image. The Levels command is ideal for most color corrections, enabling you to adjust the darkest values, lightest values, and midrange colors for the entire selection or independently within each color channel. The Curves command is great for creating special effects and correcting images that are beyond the help of the Levels command. Using the Curves command, you can map every brightness value in every color channel to an entirely different brightness value.

The Levels command

When you choose Image ➪ Adjust ➪ Levels (Command-L), Photoshop displays the Levels dialog box shown in Figure 16-8. The dialog box offers a histogram, as explained in the "Threshold" section earlier in this chapter, as well as two sets of slider bars with corresponding options boxes and a few automated eyedropper options in the lower right corner. You can compress and expand the range of brightness values in an image by manipulating the Input Levels options and then map those brightness values to new brightness values by adjusting the Output Levels options.

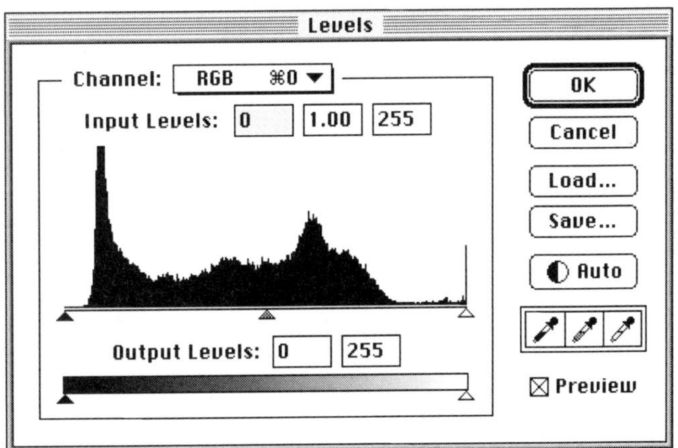

Figure 16-8: Use the Levels dialog box to map brightness values in the image (Input Levels) to new brightness values (Output Levels).

The options in the Levels dialog box work as follows:

- **Channel:** Select the color channel that you want to edit from this pop-up menu. You can apply different Input Levels and Output Levels values to each color channel. However, the options along the right side of the dialog box affect all colors in the selected portion of an image regardless of which Channel option is active.
- **Input Levels:** Use these options to select the darkest and lightest colors in the selected portion of an image, which is useful when the selection is washed out, offering insufficient shadows or highlights. The Input Levels option boxes correspond to the slider bar immediately below the histogram. You map pixels to black (or the darkest Output Levels value) by entering a number from 0 to 255 into the first option box or by dragging the black slider triangle. For example, if you raise the value to 55, all colors with brightness values of 55 or less in the original image become black, darkening the image as shown in the first example of Figure 16-9.

You can map pixels at the opposite end of the brightness scale to white (or the lightest Output Levels value) by entering a number from 0 to 255 into the last option box or by dragging the white slider triangle. If you lower the value to 200, all colors with brightness values of 200 or greater become white, lightening the image as shown in the second example of Figure 16-9. In the last example of the figure, I raised the first value and lowered the last value, thereby increasing the amount of contrast in the image.

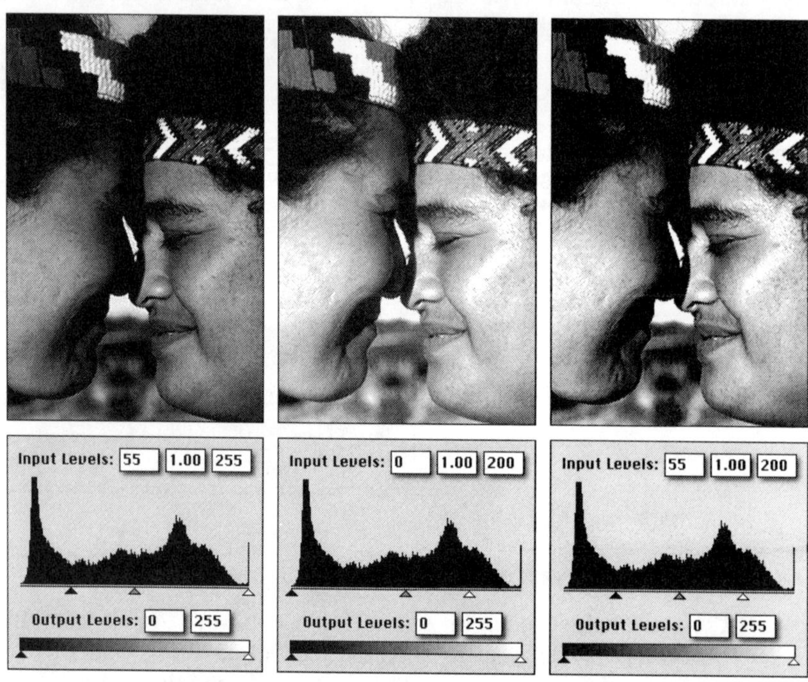

Figure 16-9: The results of raising the first Input Levels value to 55 (left), lowering the last value to 200 (middle), and combining the two (right).

- **Gamma:** The middle Input Levels option box and the corresponding gray triangle in the slider bar (shown highlighted in Figure 16-10) represent the *gamma* value, which is the brightness level of the medium gray value in the image. The gamma value can range from 0.10 to 9.99, 1.00 being dead-on medium gray. Any change to the gamma value has the effect of decreasing the amount of contrast in the image by lightening or darkening grays without changing shadows and highlights. Increase the gamma value or drag the gray slider triangle to the left to lighten the medium grays (also called *midtones*), as in the first and second examples of Figure 6-11. Lower the gamma value or drag the gray triangle to the right to darken the medium grays, as in the last example in the figure.

Incidentally, I achieved the spotlight effect that I use to highlight portions of dialog boxes throughout this book — including the one in Figure 16-10 — by using the Levels command. First, I selected the area that I wanted to highlight with the elliptical marquee tool and applied feathering with a radius of 6 or 8. I then inversed the selection (by choosing Select ⇨ Inverse) to select the portion of the image that I wanted to lie in the shadows. I next chose the Levels command and lowered the second Output Levels value to 200 to create the shadows and slightly raised the gamma value to decrease the contrast.

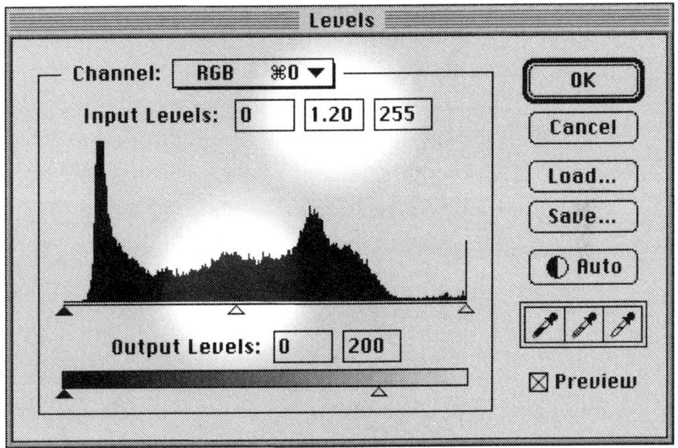

Figure 16-10: I highlighted the gamma options by selecting everything but the highlighted areas and applying the values shown above.

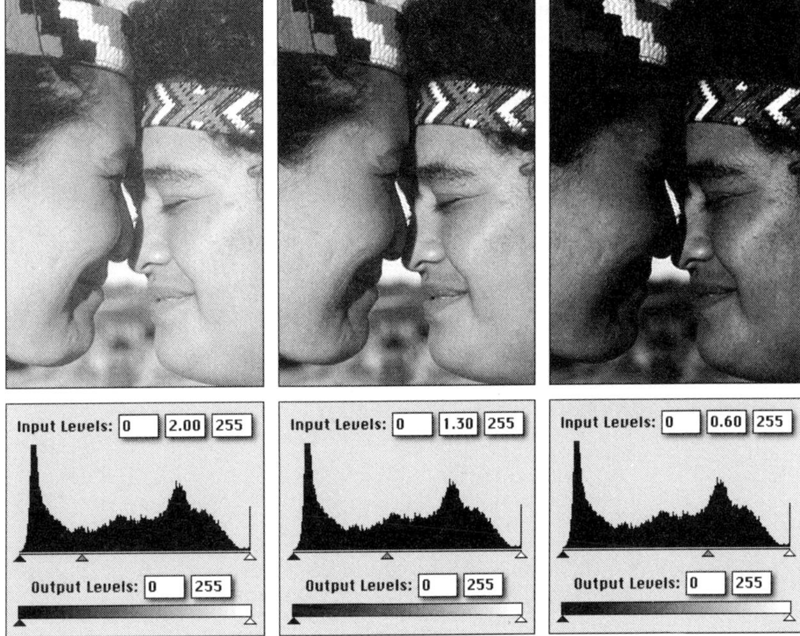

Figure 16-11: The results of raising (left and middle) and lowering (right) the gamma value to lighten and darken the midtones in an image.

- **Output Levels:** Use these options to curtail the range of brightness levels in an image by lightening the darkest pixels and darkening the lightest pixels. You adjust the brightness of the darkest pixels — those that correspond to the black Input Levels slider triangle — by entering a number from 0 to 255 into the first option box or by dragging the black slider triangle. For example, if you raise the value to 55, no color can be darker than that brightness level (roughly 80 percent black), which lightens the image as shown in the first example of Figure 16-12. You adjust the brightness of the lightest pixels — those that correspond to the white Input Levels slider triangle — by entering a number from 0 to 255 into the second option box or by dragging the white slider triangle. If you lower the value to 200, no color can be lighter than that brightness level (roughly 20 percent black), darkening the image as shown in the second example of Figure 16-12. In the last example of the figure, I raised the first value and lowered the second value, thereby dramatically decreasing the amount of contrast in the image.

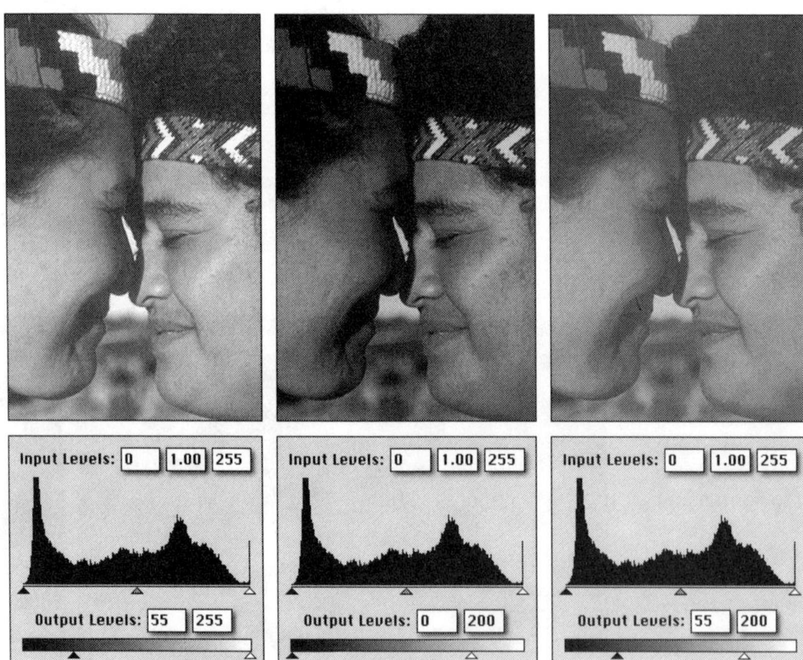

Figure 16-12: The results of raising the first Output Levels value to 55 (left), lowering the second value to 200 (middle), and combining the two (right).

- **Load/Save:** You can load and save settings to disk using these buttons.
- **Auto:** Click on the Auto button (which in Photoshop 2.0 shows the half-black/half-white circle only) to automatically map the darkest pixel in your selection to black and the lightest pixel to white. Photoshop actually darkens and lightens the image by an extra half a percent to account for the fact that the darkest and lightest pixels may be anomalies. To enter a percentage of your own, Option-click on the Auto button (the button name changes to Options) to display the Auto Range Options dialog box shown in Figure 16-13. Enter higher values to increase the number of pixels mapped to black and white; decrease the values to lessen the effect. The first two examples in Figure 16-14 compare the effect of the default 0.50 percent values to higher values of 5.00 percent.

Figure 16-13: Option-click on the Auto button to change the extent to which Photoshop closes the range of black and white pixels.

Figure 16-14: The default effect of the Auto button (left), the effect of the Auto button after raising the Clip values (middle), and the effect of the Equalize filter (right).

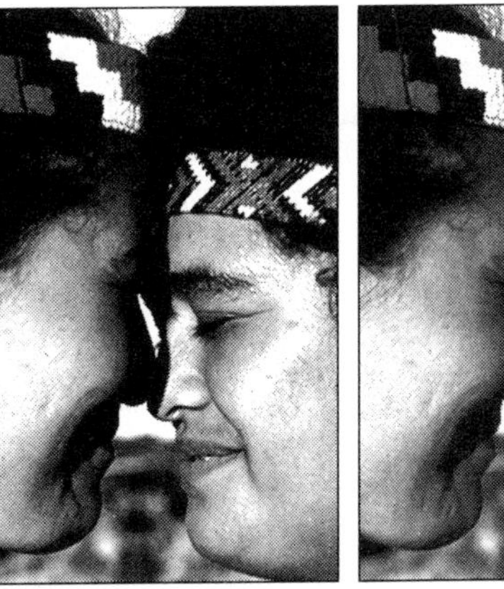

0.50% Clips   5.00% Clips   Equalize

For comparative purposes, the last image in the figure demonstrates the effect of the Equalize command applied to the entire image. Both functions automatically color correct an image. However, unlike Equalize, the Auto button makes no attempt to evenly distribute brightness values.

- **Eyedroppers:** Select one of the eyedropper tools in the Levels dialog box and click on a pixel in the image window to automatically adjust the color of that pixel. If you click on a pixel with the black eyedropper tool (the first of the three), Photoshop maps the color of the pixel and all darker colors to black. If you click on a pixel with the white eyedropper tool (last of the three), Photoshop maps it and all lighter colors to white. Use the gray eyedropper tool (middle, not included with Photoshop 2.0) to change the exact color on which you click to medium gray and adjust all other colors in accordance. For example, if you click on a white pixel, all white pixels change to medium gray and all other pixels change to even darker colors.

One way to use the eyedropper tools is to color correct scans without a lot of messing around. Include a neutral swatch of gray with the photograph you want to scan. (If you own a Pantone swatch book, Cool Gray 5 or 6 is your best bet.) After opening the scan in Photoshop, choose the Levels command, select the gray eyedropper tool, and click on the neutral gray swatch in the image window. This technique won't perform miracles, but it will help you to more evenly distribute lights and darks in the image. You then can fine-tune the image using the Input Levels and Output Levels options.

- **Preview:** Select this option to preview the effects of your settings in the image window.

When the Preview check box is inactive — yes, you read that right, *in*active — you can preview the exact pixels that will turn to black or white in the image window by Option-dragging the black or white triangle in the Input Levels slider bar.

The Curves command

If you want to be able to map any brightness value in an image to absolutely any other brightness value — no holds barred, as they say at the drive-in movies — you want the Curves command. When you choose Image ⇨ Adjust ⇨ Curves (Command-M), Photoshop displays the Curves dialog box, shown in Figure 16-15, which must be the most functional collection of color correction options on the planet.

Quickly, here's how the options work:

- **Channel:** Surely you know how this option works by now. You select the color channel that you want to edit from this pop-up menu. You can apply different mapping functions to different channels by drawing in the graph below the pop-up menu. But, as is always the case, the options along the right side of the dialog box affect all colors in the selected portion of an image regardless of which Channel option is active.

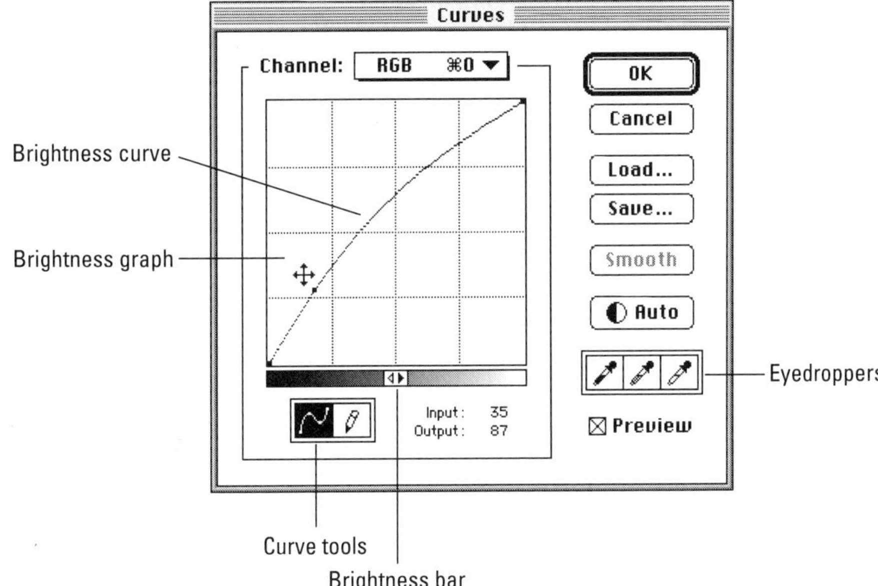

Figure 16-15: The Curves dialog box lets you distribute brightness values by drawing curves on a graph.

- **Brightness graph:** The *brightness graph* is where you map brightness values in the original image to new brightness values. The horizontal axis of the graph represents input levels; the vertical axis represents output levels. The *brightness curve* charts the relationship between input and output levels. The lower left corner is the origin of the graph (the point at which both input and output values are 0). Move right in the graph for higher input values, up for higher output values. Because the brightness graph is the core of this dialog box, upcoming sections explain it in more detail.
- **Brightness bar:** The *brightness bar* shows the direction of light and dark values in the graph. By default, colors are measured in terms of brightness values, in which case the colors in the brightness bar proceed from black to white (reading left to right), as demonstrated in the left example of Figure 16-16. Therefore, higher values produce lighter colors. However, if you click on the brightness bar, white and black switch places, as shown in the second example of the figure. The result is that Photoshop measures the colors in terms of ink coverage, from 0 percent of the primary color to 100 percent of the primary color. Higher values now produce darker colors. If you click on the brightness bar in the process of drawing a curve, the curve automatically flips so as to retain any changes you made, as the figure illustrates.

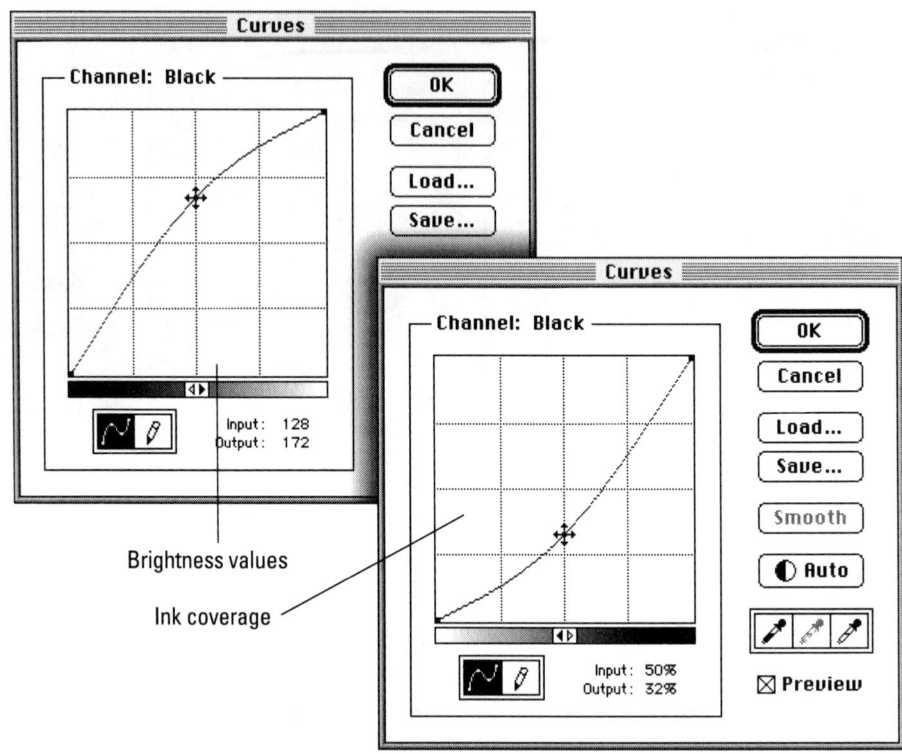

Figure 16-16: Click on the brightness bar to change the way in which the graph measures color: by brightness values (left) or by ink coverage (right).

- **Curve tools:** Use the curve tools to draw the curve inside the brightness graph. Click in the graph with the point tool (on the left, selected by default) to add a point to the curve. Drag a point to move it. To delete a point, drag it outside the boundaries of the graph. The pencil tool (on the right) enables you to draw free-form curves simply by dragging inside the graph, as shown in Figure 16-17. You can perform the same function in Photoshop 2.0 by using the pencil tool in the Arbitrary dialog box (accessed by choosing Image ⇨ Map ⇨ Arbitrary).

You can draw straight lines with the pencil tool by clicking at one location in the graph and Shift-clicking at a different point, just as you can when using the real pencil tool in the image window.

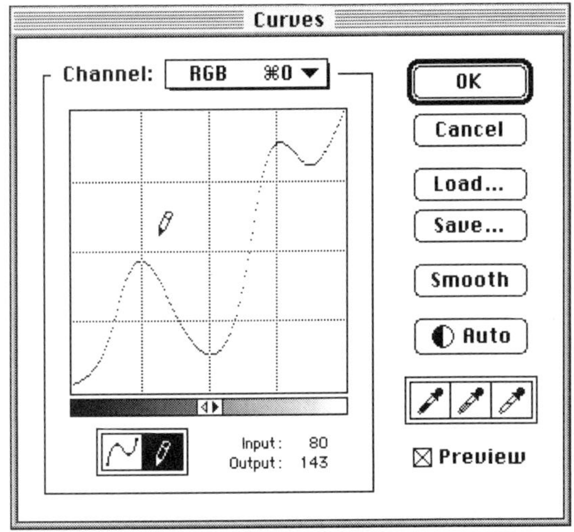

Figure 16-17: Use the pencil tool (available by choosing Image ⇨ Map ⇨ Arbitrary in Photoshop 2.0) to draw free-form lines in the brightness graph.

- **Input/Output numbers:** The input and output numbers monitor the location of your cursor in the graph according to brightness values or ink coverage, depending on the setting of the brightness bar.
- **Load/Save:** Use these buttons to load and save settings to disk.
- **Smooth:** Click on the Smooth button to smooth out curves drawn with the pencil tool. Doing so leads to smoother color transitions in the image window. This button is dimmed except when you use the pencil tool.
- **Auto:** Click on this button to automatically map the darkest pixel in your selection to black and the lightest pixel to white. Photoshop throws in some additional darkening and lightening according to the Clip percentages, which you can edit by Option-clicking on the button.
- **Eyedroppers:** Photoshop actually permits you to use a fourth eyedropper from the Curves dialog box. If you don't select any eyedropper tool (or you click in the graph to deselect the current eyedropper) and move the cursor out of the dialog box into the image window, you get the standard eyedropper cursor. Click on a pixel in the image to locate the brightness value of that pixel in the graph. A circle appears in the graph, and the input and output numbers list the value for as long as you hold down the mouse button, as shown in the first example in Figure 16-18.

The other eyedroppers work as they do in the Levels dialog box, mapping pixels to black, medium gray, or white. For example, the second image in Figure 16-18 shows the white eyedropper tool clicking on a light pixel, thereby mapping that value to white, as shown in highlighted portion of the graph below the image. You can further adjust the brightness value of that pixel by dragging the corresponding point in the graph, as demonstrated in the last example of the figure.

- **Preview:** Select this option to preview your settings in the image window.

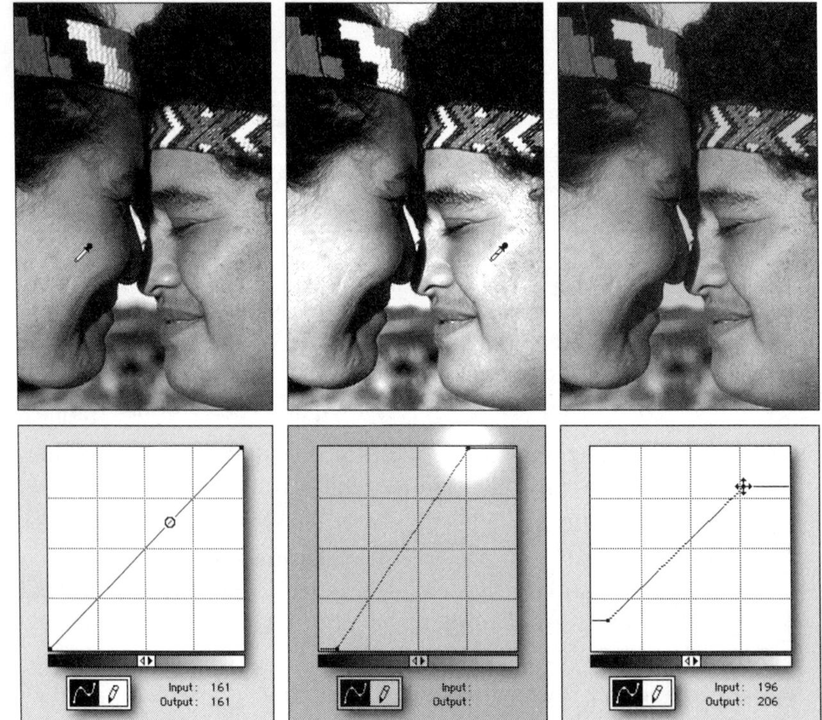

Figure 16-18: Use the standard eyedropper cursor to locate a color in the brightness graph (left). Click with one of the eyedropper tools from the Curves dialog box to map the color of that pixel in the graph (middle). You then can edit the location of the point in the graph by dragging it (right).

Continuous curves

All discussions in the few remaining pages of this chapter assume that the brightness bar is set to edit brightness values (in which case, the gradation in the bar lightens from left to right). If you set the bar to edit ink coverage (the bar darkens from left to right), you can still achieve the effects I describe, but you must drag in the opposite direction. For example, if I tell you to lighten colors by dragging upward, you drag downward. In a backward world live the ink coverage people.

When you first enter the Curves dialog box, the brightness curve appears as a straight line strung between two points, as shown in the first example of Figure 16-19, mapping every input level from white (the lower left point) to black (the upper right point) to an identical output level. If you want to perform seamless color corrections, the point tool is your best bet because it enables you to edit the levels in the brightness graph while maintaining a continuous curve.

To lighten the colors in the selected portion of the image, click near the middle of the curve with the point tool to create a new point and then drag the point upward, as demonstrated in the second example of Figure 16-19. To darken the image, drag the point downward, as in the third example.

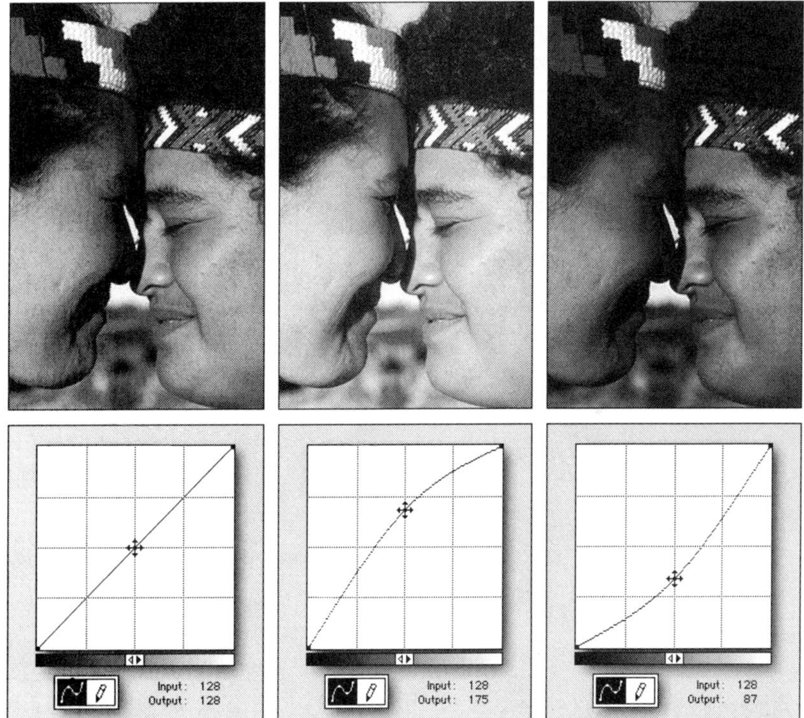

Figure 16-19: Create a single point in the curve with the point tool (left) and then drag it upward (middle) or downward (right) to lighten or darken the image evenly.

Create two points in the curve to boost or lessen the contrast between colors in the image. In the first example of Figure 16-20, I created one point very near the white point in the curve and another point very close to the black point. I then dragged down on the left-hand point and up on the right-hand point to make the dark pixels darker and the light pixels lighter, which translates to higher contrast.

In the second example of the figure, I did just the opposite, dragging up on the left-hand point to lighten the dark pixels and down on the right-hand point to darken the light pixels. As you can see in the second image, this option lessens the contrast between colors, making the image more gray.

In the last example in Figure 16-20, I bolstered the contrast with a vengeance by dragging the right-hand point down and to the left. This has the effect of springing the right half of the curve farther upward, thus increasing the brightness of the light pixels in the image.

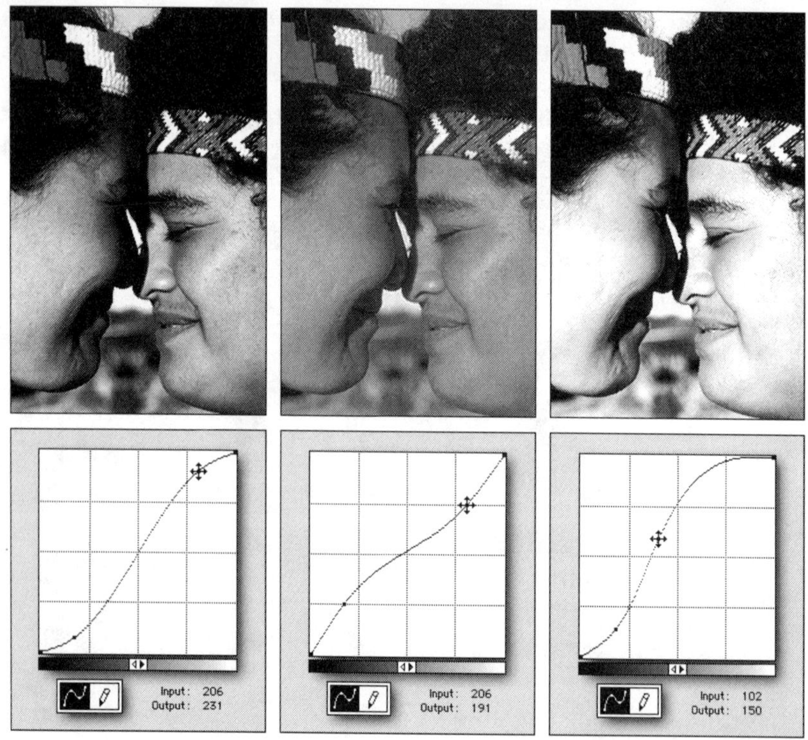

Figure 16-20: Create two points in the curve to change the appearance of contrast in an image, whether by increasing it mildly (left), decreasing it (middle), or boosting it dramatically (right).

Arbitrary curves

You can create some mind-numbing color variations by adjusting the brightness curve arbitrarily, mapping light pixels to dark, dark pixels to light, and in-between pixels all over the place. In the first example of Figure 16-21, I used the point tool to achieve an arbitrary curve. By dragging the left-hand point severely upward and the right-hand point severely downward, I caused dark and light pixels alike to soar across the spectrum.

If you're interested in something a little more subtle, try applying an arbitrary curve to a single channel in a color image. Color Plate 16-5, for example, shows an image subject to relatively basic color manipulations in the red and green channels, followed by an arbitrary adjustment to the blue channel.

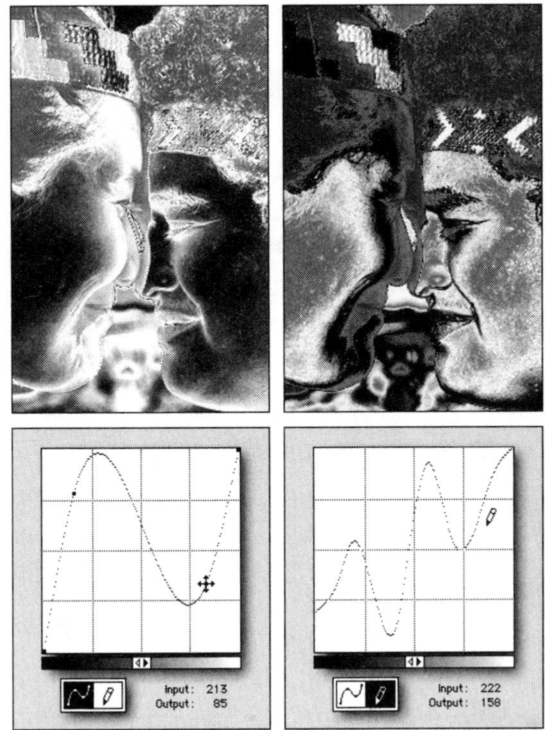

Figure 16-21: Arbitrary brightness curves created using the point tool (left) and the pencil tool (right).

Although you can certainly achieve arbitrary effects using the point tool, the pencil tool is more versatile and less inhibiting. As shown in the second example of Figure 16-21, I created an effect that would alarm Carlos Castaneda just by zigzagging my way across the graph and clicking on the Smooth button.

In fact, the Smooth button is an integral part of using the pencil tool. Try this little experiment: draw a bunch of completely random lines and squiggles with the pencil tool in the brightness graph. As shown in the first example of Figure 16-22, your efforts will most likely yield an unspeakably hideous and utterly unrecognizable effect.

Next, click on the Smooth button. Photoshop automatically connects all portions of the curve, miraculously smoothing out the color-mapping effect and rescuing some semblance of your image, as shown in the second example of the figure. If the effect is still too radical, you can continue to smooth it out by clicking additional times on the Smooth button. I clicked on the button twice more to create the right image in Figure 16-22. Eventually, the Smooth button restores the curve to a straight line.

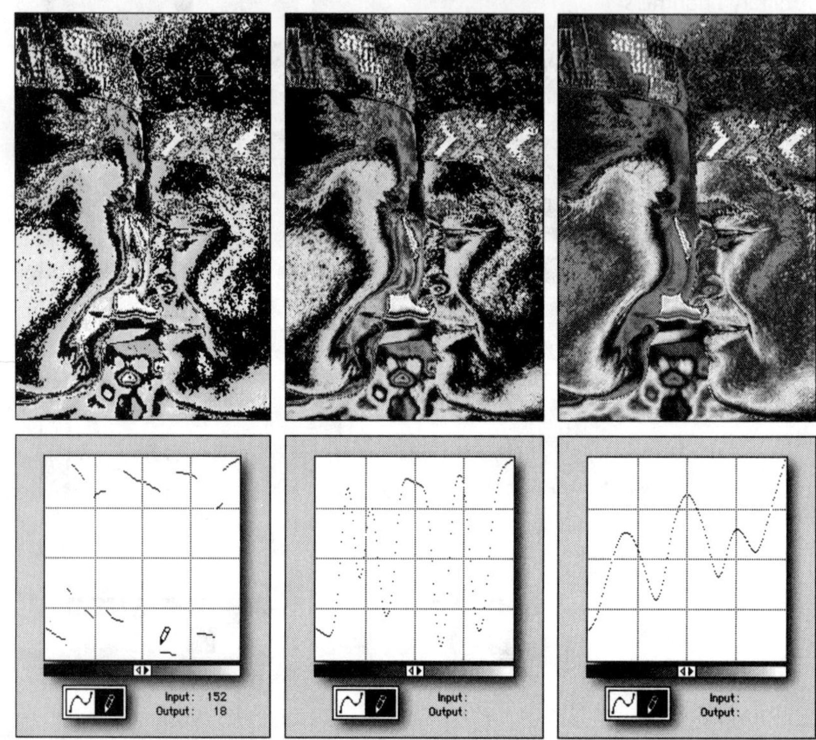

Figure 16-22: After drawing a series of completely random lines with the pencil tool (left), I clicked on the Smooth button once to connect the lines into a frenetic curve (middle) and then twice more to even out the curve, thus preserving more of the original image (right).

Summary

- Color mapping is useful for creating special effects and correcting and balancing colors in an image.
- The Invert command and hue changes applied to all colors from the Hue/Saturation dialog box are the only color-mapping functions that do not destroy so much as a single color in an image.
- The Equalize command automatically redistributes colors in an entire image according to the colors in a selected portion of the image. This Photoshop command is the only one that can affect pixels outside a selection.
- The Hue/Saturation command lets you rotate colors in an image around the color wheel, an effect called *color shifting.*
- To reset all options in the Hue/Saturation, Levels, and Curves dialog boxes, press Command-Option-period.
- If you were to attempt color mapping on a television, you would change the hue with the Tint knob, manipulate saturation levels with the Color knob, and edit lightness values with the Brightness knob.
- The Colorize option in the Hue/Saturation dialog box applies an absolute hue and saturation level to an image while retaining the image's original brightness values.
- The Levels and Curves commands work by changing brightness levels inside one or more color channels in an image.
- Use the Auto button and eyedropper tool to apply automated color corrections to an image.
- Draw a curve in the brightness graph in the Curves dialog box to map any brightness value in an image to any other brightness value.
- The Smooth button smooths out curves drawn with the pencil tool, regardless of how erratic they are.

Manipulating Channels

17 CHAPTER

In This Chapter

- Viewing the contents of independent color channels within a full-color image
- Using channel editing commands in the Mode menu and the Channels palette menu
- Improving the appearance of poorly scanned images
- Editing channels to achieve special effects
- Working with each command in the Image ⇨ Calculate submenu
- Using the Duplicate command to clone images and selection outlines between open documents
- Applying channel operations to achieve unique effects

Editing Color Channels

One of the most remarkable features that currently distinguishes Photoshop from other full-color painting programs is its ability to edit individual color channels. In fact, as I write this, only two competing programs — Fractal Design ColorStudio 1.5 and Caere's Image Assistant 1.1 — provide anything close to this capability, and neither approaches Photoshop's range of channel editing options. Simply put, if you haven't edited a channel, you're missing out on one of Photoshop's most unique and powerful functions.

I mentioned channels several times in previous chapters, but just so you're clear on what the heck I'm talking about, a *channel* is a distinct plane of primary color in a full-color image. For example, an RGB image comprises three channels, one each for the red, green, and blue primary colors. Channels frequently correspond to the structure of an input or output device. If you scanned an RGB image, chances are each channel corresponds to a pass of the red, green, or blue scanner sensor over the original photograph or artwork. When you print a CMYK image, each channel corresponds to a different sheet of film.

Photoshop devotes 8 bits of data to each pixel in each channel, thus permitting 256 brightness values, from 0 (black) to 255 (white). You can add channels above and beyond those required to represent a color image for the purpose of storing masks, as described in the "Using a mask channel" section of Chapter 9.

Photoshop 2.0 and 2.5 provide very similar channel editing functions. However, you access these functions differently. In Photoshop 2.0, you edit channels using commands in the lower half of the Mode menu, as shown in the left example of Figure 17-1. To edit channels in Version 2.5, choose Window ⇨ Show Channels to display the floating Channels palette (right example of Figure 17-1). Photoshop 2.5 provides a few convenience functions that are missing from its predecessor, but you can get the job done using either version of the program.

Figure 17-1: The channel options provided by Photoshop 2.0 (left) and 2.5 (right).

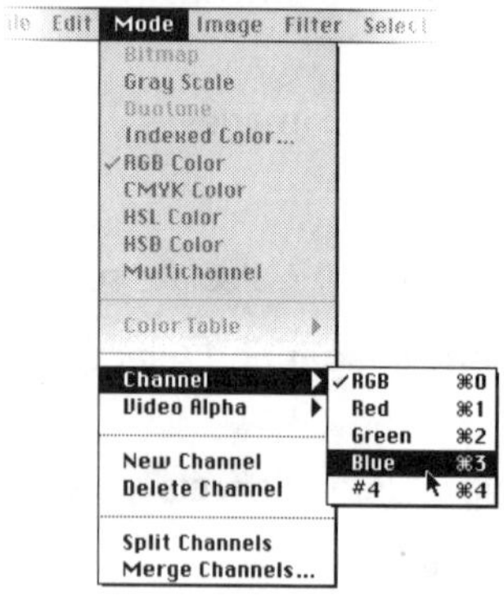

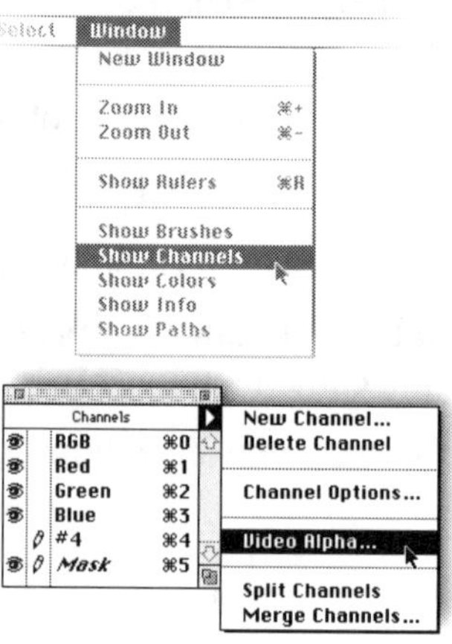

How to view channels

To view a different channel in an image in Photoshop 2.0, choose a command from the Mode ⇨ Channel submenu. In Version 2.5, click on a channel name in the Channels palette.

When you work with a full-color image in the RGB, CMYK, or Lab modes, Photoshop provides access to a *composite view,* which displays all colors in an image at once, and a handful of independent primary color channels. The composite channel is listed first and is displayed by default. This is the channel in which you will do (and have done) the majority of your image editing. To return to the composite view at any time, press Command-0.

When you work in a color mode that permits 8 bits or less of data — whether the image is grayscale, duotone, indexed, or black-and-white (bitmap) — Photoshop provides only one channel to represent the entire image. You can, of course, add mask channels, but they do not affect the appearance of the image on-screen or when it is printed.

In addition to the composite view, the RGB and Lab modes provide three independent color channels; the CMYK mode provides four. Each of these channels contains 8 bits of data, just like a grayscale image. In fact, for all practical purposes, each channel *is* a grayscale image. The only difference is that Photoshop interprets the channel as a plane of primary color in the final full-color composite.

Press Command plus a number key to switch between color channels. Command-1 always takes you to the red (RGB), cyan (CMYK), or luminosity (Lab) channel; Command-2 takes you to the green, magenta, or *a* channel; and Command-3 takes you to the blue, yellow, or *b* channel. In the CMYK mode, Command-4 displays the black channel. Other Command-key equivalents — up to Command-9 — take you to mask channels.

RGB channels

Feeling a little skeptical? Need some examples? Fair enough. Color Plate 17-1 shows the yellow-orange dome of the United States Capitol building set against a deep blue evening sky. These colors — yellow-orange and deep blue — are very nearly opposites. Therefore, you can expect to see a lot of variation between the images in the independent color channels.

Figure 17-2 compares a grayscale composite of this same image (created by choosing Mode ⇨ Grayscale) with the contents of the red, green, and blue color channels from the original color image. The green channel is more or less in keeping with the grayscale composite because it is the neutral channel in this image (that is, no element in Color Plate 17-1 is predominantly green). But the red and blue channels differ significantly. The pixels in the red channel are lightest on the Capitol dome because the dome contains a high concentration of red. The pixels in the blue channel are lightest in the sky because — you guessed it — the sky is blue.

Notice how the channels in Figure 17-2 make interesting grayscale images in and of themselves? The blue channel, for example, looks like a photo of the Capitol on a cloudy day, when the picture actually was shot at night.

When converting a color image to grayscale, you have the option of calculating a grayscale composite or simply retaining the image exactly as it appears in one of the channels. To create a grayscale composite, choose Mode ⇨ Grayscale when viewing all colors in the image in the composite view, as usual. To retain a single channel only, switch to that channel and then choose Mode ⇨ Grayscale. Instead of the usual `Discard color information?` message, Photoshop displays the message `Discard other channels?` If you click on the OK button, Photoshop chucks the other channels into the electronic abyss.

Figure 17-2: A grayscale composite of the image from Color Plate 17-1 followed by the contents of the red, green, and blue color channels.

Grayscale composite

Red

Green

Blue

CMYK channels

In the name of fair and unbiased coverage, Figures 17-3 through 17-5 show the channels from the image after it was converted to other color modes. In Figure 17-3, I converted the image to the CMYK mode and examined its channels. Here, the predominant colors are cyan (the sky) and yellow (the dome). Because this color mode relies on pigments rather than light, as explained in the "CMYK" section of Chapter 14, dark areas in the channels represent high color intensity. For that reason, the sky in the cyan channel is dark, whereas it is light in the blue channel shown in Figure 17-2.

Lab channels

In Figure 17-4, I converted the image in Color Plate 17-1 to the Lab mode. The image in the luminosity channel looks a lot like the grayscale composite because it contains the lightness and darkness values for the image. Because the *b* channel maps the yellows and blues in the image, it contains the highest degree of contrast. Meanwhile, the *a* channel, which maps colors from green to magenta, is almost uniformly gray. The only remarkable greens occur in the statue at the top of the dome and in the bright area inside the rotunda.

You can achieve some entertaining effects by applying commands from the Image ⇨ Map and Image ⇨ Adjust submenus to the *a* and *b* color channels. For example, if I reverse the brightness values in the *b* channel in Figure 17-4 by choosing Image ⇨ Map ⇨ Invert, the building turns bright blue and the sky changes to a moody orange-brown. If I apply Image ⇨ Map ⇨ Equalize to the *a* channel, the sky lights up with brilliant blue and purple sparks, and the Capitol becomes deep emerald. Holy Photoshop!

Figure 17-3: The contents of the cyan, magenta, yellow, and black channels from the image shown in Color Plate 17-1.

Cyan

Magenta

Yellow

Black

Figure 17-4: The grayscale composite followed by the contents of the luminosity channel and the *a* and *b* color channels after converting the image shown in Color Plate 17-1 to the Lab mode.

Grayscale composite

Luminosity

a (black is green, white is magenta)

b (black is blue, white is yellow)

HSB channels

Photoshop 2.0 lacks the Lab mode, but makes up for it in part by providing the HSB mode, dropped from Photoshop 2.5 (as explained in the "HSB and HSL" section of Chapter 14). Figure 17-5 shows the result of choosing Mode ⇨ HSB Color and switching between the hue, saturation, and brightness channels. In the hue channel, dark areas indicate the warm colors (red, orange, and yellow), while the light areas indicate cooler colors (blue and purple). As you can with Lab's *a* and *b* channels, you can apply the color mapping commands to achieve special color effects. If I invert the hue channel, for example, the Capitol building changes to a hot pink, and the sky clouds over with vivid green.

Figure 17-5: The grayscale composite followed by the contents of the hue, saturation, and brightness channels after converting the image in Color Plate 17-1 to the HSB mode in Photoshop 2.0.

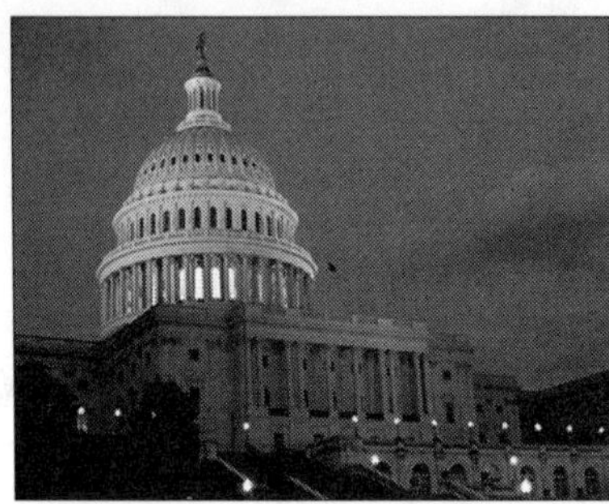

Grayscale composite

Hue

Saturation

Brightness

In the saturation channel, light areas represent high saturation levels; dark areas represent low saturation levels — that is, grays. Like the luminosity channel in the Lab color mode, HSB's brightness channel maps out the lightness and darkness values of the image.

Photoshop 2.0's HSB mode and HSL mode (not shown) lack composite views, meaning that you can't correctly view the colors in the image in either of these modes. Therefore, after editing the HSB or HSL channels, switch back to the RGB or CMYK mode to confirm your changes.

Other channel functions

One function provided by Photoshop 2.5 that Version 2.0 lacks is the ability to view and apply edits to multiple channels at a time. You do this by clicking in the left two columns of the Channels palette to alternately hide and display icons. The eyeball icon indicates visible channels; the pencil icon indicates the channels you can edit. For a detailed description of these options, read the "Viewing mask and image" section of Chapter 9.

In addition to viewing and editing channels using any of the techniques discussed in the previous chapters of this book, you can choose commands from Photoshop 2.0's Modes menu or Version 2.5's Channels palette menu. These commands work as follows:

- **New Channel:** Choose this command to add a mask channel to the current image. In Photoshop 2.5, the Channel Options dialog box appears, enabling you to name the channel. You also can specify the color and translucency Photoshop applies to the channel when you view it with other channels. I explain how these options work in the "Changing the red coating" section of Chapter 9. An image can contain no more than 16 channels.
- **Delete Channel:** To delete a channel from an image, click on the channel and choose this command. You can delete only one channel at a time. The Delete Channel command is dimmed when the composite view is active or when more than one pencil icon appears in the second column.
- **Channel Options:** Choose this command, offered in Photoshop 2.5 only, or double-click on the channel name in the palette's scrolling list to change the name, color, and translucency settings of a mask channel, as described in the "Viewing mask and image" section of Chapter 9. The Channel Options command is dimmed when the composite view or any of the color channels is active. It is applicable to mask channels only.
- **Video Alpha:** If you own a bona fide 32-bit video board such as TrueVision's NuVista+ or RasterOps' ProVideo32, you can copy a mask channel to the board's built-in 8-bit alpha channel (introduced in the "Video card technology" section of Chapter 3). This *video mask* determines the translucency of the Photoshop image when you lay the image over live video. Black areas in the mask result in opaque image pixels; gray areas result in translucent pixels over video; and white areas result in unobscured video. After you specify the mask channel you want to copy to the board's alpha channel, Photoshop 2.5 displays a small TV icon in front of the channel name, as shown in Figure 17-6.

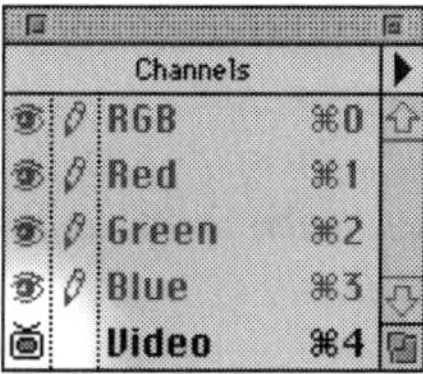

Figure 17-6: A TV icon appears in front of a channel copied to a 32-bit video board's alpha channel.

- **Split Channels:** When you choose this command, Photoshop splits off each channel in an image to its own independent grayscale image window. As demonstrated in Figure 17-7, Photoshop automatically appends the channel color to the end of the window name. The Split Channels command is useful as a first step in redistributing channels in an image prior to choosing Merge Channels (as demonstrated later in this chapter).

Figure 17-7: When you choose the Split Channels command, Photoshop relocates each channel to an independent image window.

- **Merge Channels:** Choose this command to merge several images into a single multichannel image. The images you want to merge must be open, they must be grayscale, and they must be of absolutely equal size — the same number of pixels horizontally and vertically. When you choose Merge Channels, Photoshop displays the Merge Channels dialog box, shown in Figure 17-8. It then assigns a color mode for the new image based on the number of open grayscale images that contain the same number of pixels as the foreground image.

  You can override Photoshop's choice by selecting a different option from the Mode pop-up menu. (Generally, you won't want to change the value in the Channels option box because doing so causes Photoshop to automatically select Multichannel from the Mode pop-up menu. I explain multichannel images in the upcoming "Using multichannel techniques" section.) After you press Return or click on the OK button, Photoshop displays a second dialog box. In this dialog box, you can specify which grayscale image goes with which channel by choosing options from pop-up menus, as demonstrated in the second example in Figure 17-8. When working from an image split with the Split Channels command, Photoshop automatically organizes each window into a pop-up menu according to the color appended to the window's name. For example, Photoshop associates the window *Capitol Dome.Red* with the Red pop-up menu.

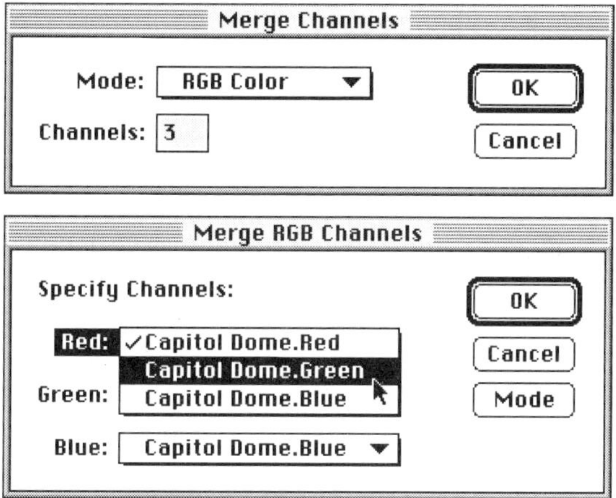

Figure 17-8: The two dialog boxes that appear after you choose Merge Channels enable you to select a color mode for the merged image (top) and to associate images with color channels (bottom).

Color channel effects

Now that you know how to navigate among channels and apply commands, allow me to suggest a few reasons for doing so. The most pragmatic applications for channel effects involve the restoration of bad color scans. If you use a color scanner, know someone who uses a color scanner, or just have a bunch of color scans lying around, you can be sure that some of them look like dog meat. (Nothing against dog meat, mind you. I'm sure Purina has some very lovely dog meat scans in their advertising archives.) With Photoshop's help, you can turn those scans into filet mignon — or at the very least, into an acceptable Sunday roast.

Improving the appearance of color scans

The following are a few channel editing techniques you can use to improve the appearance of poorly scanned full-color images. Keep in mind that these techniques don't work miracles, but they can retrieve an image from the brink of absolute ugliness into the realm of tolerability.

In all cases, it's a good idea to first choose Window ⇨ New Window to maintain a composite view. You then can see how applying a change to a single channel affects the full-color image. Be sure to drag the composite view off to an empty portion of your screen so that you can see what you're doing.

- **Aligning channels:** Sometimes, a scan still looks out of focus even after you sharpen the heck out of it. If, on closer inspection, you can see slight shadows or halos around colored areas, one of the color channels probably is out of alignment. To remedy the problem, switch to the color channel that corresponds to the color of the halos. Then choose Select ⇨ All (Command-A) and use the arrow keys to nudge the contents of the channel into alignment. Use the separate composite view (created by choosing Window ⇨ New Window) to monitor your changes.

- **Channel focusing:** If all channels seem to be in alignment (or, at least, as aligned as they're going to get), one of your channels may be poorly focused. Use the Command-key equivalents to search for the responsible channel. When and if you find it, use the Unsharp Mask filter to sharpen it as desired.
- **Bad channels:** In your color channel tour, if you discover that a channel is not so much poorly focused as simply rotten to the core — complete with harsh transitions, jagged edges, and random brightness variations — you may be able to improve the appearance of the channel by overlaying the other channels on top of it. Suppose that the red channel is awful, but the green and blue channels are in fairly decent shape. First, save your image to disk in case this technique does more to harm the image than help it. Then switch to the green channel (Command-2), select the entire image (Command-A), and copy it (Command-C). Switch back to the red channel, paste the contents of the Clipboard (Command-V), and change the opacity of the floating selection to somewhere in the neighborhood of 30 to 50 percent. Next, switch to the blue channel (Command-3) and repeat the process. The colors in the composite view will change slightly or dramatically depending on the range of colors in your image. But if you can live with the color changes, the appearance of the image will improve dramatically.

Using multichannel techniques

The one channel function I have so far ignored is Mode ⇨ Multichannel. When you choose this command, Photoshop changes your image so that channels no longer have a specific relationship to one another. They don't blend to create a full-color image; instead, they exist independently within the confines of a single image. The multichannel mode is generally a intermediary step for converting between different color modes without recalculating the contents of the channels.

For example, normally when you convert between the RGB and CMYK modes, Photoshop maps RGB colors to the CMYK color model, changing the contents of each channel as demonstrated back in Figures 17-2 and 17-3. But suppose, just as an experiment, that you want to bypass the color mapping and instead transfer the exact contents of the red channel to the cyan channel, the contents of the green channel to the magenta channel, and so on. You convert from RGB to the multichannel mode and then from multichannel to CMYK as described in the following steps.

STEPS: Using the Multichannel Mode as an Intermediary Step

Step 1. Open an RGB image. If the image is already open, make sure that it is saved to disk.

Step 2. Choose Mode ⇨ Multichannel to eliminate any relationship between the formerly red, green, and blue color channels.

Step 3. Choose the New Channel command from the Channels palette menu (or Mode ⇨ New Channel in Photoshop 2.0) to add a mask channel to the image. When the Channel Options dialog box appears in Photoshop 2.5, press Return to accept the default settings. This empty channel will serve as the black channel in the CMYK image. (Photoshop won't let you convert from the multichannel mode to CMYK with less than four channels.)

Step 4. Choose Mode ⇨ CMYK. The image looks washed out and a tad bit dark compared to its original RGB counterpart, but the overall color scheme of the image remains more or less intact. This result is because the red, green, and blue color channels each have a respective opposite in the cyan, magenta, and yellow channels.

Step 5. The one problem with the image is that it lacks any information in the black channel. So although it may look OK on-screen, it will lose much of its definition when printed. To fill in the black channel, convert the image to the RGB mode and then convert it back to the CMYK mode. Photoshop automatically adds an image to the black channel in keeping with your specifications in the Separation Setup dialog box (as described in the "How to prepare CMYK conversions" section of Chapter 7).

Replacing and swapping color channels

If you truly want to abuse the colors in an RGB or CMYK image, there's nothing like replacing one color channel with another to produce spectacular effects. Color Plate 17-2 shows a few examples applied to an RGB image. In the upper left example, I copied the image in the blue channel (Command-3, Command-A, Command-C) and pasted it into the red channel (Command-1, Command-V). The result was a green Capitol against a purple sky. To achieve the upper right example (starting again from the original RGB image), I copied the green channel and pasted it into the blue channel. The result this time was a pink building against a deep jade sky. To create a lemon yellow Capitol against a backdrop of bright blue, shown in the lower left corner of Color Plate 17-2, I copied the red channel and pasted it into the green channel.

Instead of copying and pasting, you can transfer images between channels without upsetting the contents of the Clipboard by using Image ⇨ Calculate ⇨ Duplicate. I discuss this and other commands under the Image ⇨ Calculate submenu in the upcoming "Calculate commands" section of this chapter.

You can create equally amusing effects by swapping the contents of color channels. For example, in the lower right example of Color Plate 17-2, I swapped the contents of the red and blue channels to create a blue Capitol against an orange-brown sky (very similar to the effect of inverting the *b* channel in the Lab mode, as I suggested in the "Lab channels" section of this chapter). To accomplish this, I chose the Split Channels command from the Channels palette menu (Mode ➪ Split Channels in Version 2.0). I then chose the Merge Channels command and accepted the default settings in the Merge Channels dialog box. When the Merge RGB Channels dialog box appeared, I selected the blue channel from the Red pop-up menu and the red channel from the Blue pop-up menu.

When experimenting, it's a good idea to keep the original contents of each color channel close at hand just in case you don't like the results. I recommend using the New Channel command to create a mask channel for each color channel in the image and then copying the contents of each channel to one of the mask channels. For example, when editing an RGB image, create three mask channels, one each for duplicates of the red, green, and blue channels, for a total of six channels in the image. You then can replace channels with impunity, knowing that you have backups if you need them.

Using Channel Operation Commands

I devote the remainder of this chapter to the commands in the Image ➪ Calculate submenu. Known as *channel operations,* these commands represent some of the most powerful functions in Photoshop. They allow you to duplicate images between channels, mix images in different channels or windows, and convert images to selection outlines. They're among the most complex of Photoshop's features, but they likewise provide a tremendous range of functions you won't find in any other painting program.

Source and destination options

Channel operations work by transferring a specified image, called the *source,* to a specified channel, called the *destination.* One of the most straightforward examples is Image ➪ Calculate ➪ Duplicate. This command clones the contents of one channel and transfers them to another.

When you choose Image ➪ Calculate ➪ Duplicate, Photoshop displays the Duplicate dialog box shown in Figure 17-9. The dialog box contains a series of pop-up menus that are staples of all channel operation dialog boxes:

- **Source Document:** Select the image that is the source for the channel operation from this pop-up menu. When indicating a source, the Document pop-up menu contains the name of the foreground image, followed by all other images that are both open and exactly the same size as the foreground image. You cannot apply a channel operation to a closed image or to an image that contains a different number of pixels than the foreground image.
- **Source Channel:** When specifying a source, the Channel pop-up menu lists all channels included in the image selected from the Document pop-up menu. Both composite views and individual color and mask channels are included. If a portion of the image is selected, the pop-up menu offers a Selection option, which lets you duplicate the selection to a different channel. The selection becomes a grayscale image, just like a selection viewed in the quick mask mode.
- **Destination Document:** When specifying a destination image, the Document pop-up menu lists the foreground image plus all open images of identical size. It also offers a New option, which lets you create an entirely new image window the same size as the foreground image. Because it is such a common choice, New is the default destination for channel operations.
- **Destination Channel:** This pop-up menu lists all channels in the specified destination image plus two other options, New and Selection. (If you select New from the Document pop-up menu in the Destination box, New and Selection are the only options in the Channel pop-up menu.) Select New to add a new channel to a new or existing image. Select the Selection option to convert the source image to a selection outline, just as if you had transferred the image to the quick mask mode.

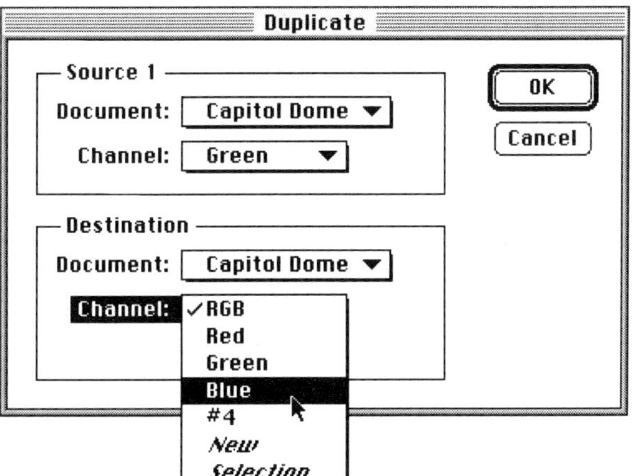

Figure 17-9: All channel operation dialog boxes contain one or more sets of Document and Channel pop-up menus.

Calculate commands

The Image ⇨ Calculate submenu contains 11 commands. The following list contains brief explanations of each. A few of these commands — Darker, Lighter, Multiply, and Screen — correspond directly to brush and overlay modes discussed in Chapters 8 and 15. The Blend command serves the same function as floating a translucent selection over an underlying image. The other commands are entirely new and are therefore detailed in later sections.

- **Add:** This command combines two source images by adding the brightness value of a pixel in the first image to the brightness value of the corresponding pixel in the second image. It then divides the sum by the Scale value and adds the Offset value. For more information, see the upcoming "Add and Subtract" section.
- **Blend:** This command combines two source images exactly as if the first were a translucent floating selection and the second were the underlying image. For example, you can use this command to expedite the process of mixing color channels described in the last item of the "Improving the appearance of color scans" section earlier in this chapter. The percentage value entered into the Weight option box works just like the setting of the Opacity slider bar in the Brushes palette.
- **Composite:** This command combines two images according to a third image in a mask channel. Where the mask is white, the first source image shows through. Where the mask is black, the second image shows through. See the "Composite" section for a demonstration.
- **Constant:** This command fills a channel with a brightness value between 0 (black) and 255 (white). You specify a brightness value; that value in essence serves as the source image. Photoshop applies the specified brightness value to the entire destination channel. This command can be useful for creating a uniform translucent selection.
- **Darker:** This command works just like the Darken option in the brush mode pop-up menu in the Brushes palette. It combines two source images by comparing a pixel in the first image to its counterpart in the second image and then transferring the darker of the two to the destination image.
- **Difference:** This command combines two source images by subtracting the brightness value of a pixel in the second image from the brightness value of the corresponding pixel in the first image. If the result is a positive value, it becomes the brightness value of the pixel in the destination image. If the result is a negative value, Photoshop makes the value positive and applies it to the destination image. See the "Difference" section for more information.
- **Duplicate:** Like any good Duplicate command, this one clones the contents of a source image and transfers it to a specified destination, all without affecting the contents of the Clipboard.

- **Lighter:** This command works just like the Lighten option in the brush mode pop-up menu in the Brushes palette. It combines two source images by comparing a pixel in the first image to its counterpart in the second image and then transferring the lighter of the two to the destination image.
- **Multiply:** Like the Multiply overlay mode described in the "Overlay modes" section of Chapter 15, this command mixes the brightness values in the first source image with those in the second source to achieve a destination image that is uniformly darker. It's as if both source images were transparencies, and you laid one on top of the other on a light table.
- **Screen:** Like the Screen overlay mode, this command mixes the brightness values in the first source image with those in the second source to achieve a destination image that is uniformly lighter. It's as if both source images were photographic negatives fused together and used to develop a paper positive.
- **Subtract:** This command combines two source images by subtracting the brightness value of a pixel in the second image from the brightness value of the corresponding pixel in the first image. It then divides the difference by the Scale value and adds the Offset value. For more information, see the upcoming "Add and Subtract" section.

Duplicate

If you learn to use only one command from the Image ⇨ Calculate submenu, let it be Duplicate. Relatively easy to use, this command enables you to duplicate absolutely any channel or selection outline from absolutely any open image. Here are just a few applications:

- **Creating variations on a theme:** Suppose you want to create several variations on a single image, like Andy Wharhol's Marilyn Monroe series. Open an image, choose Image ⇨ Calculate ⇨ Duplicate, and edit away on your first variation. When it comes time to work on the second variation, bring the original image to the foreground and again choose the Duplicate command. As you work, the original image remains on-screen as a visual reference.
- **Replacing color channels:** Remember those wild color channel effects from Color Plate 17-2? Well, instead of laboriously copying the contents of one channel and pasting them into another, as described in the "Replacing and swapping color channels" section, I could simply use the Duplicate command to clone the contents of one channel and transfer them to a different channel inside the same image. Inside the Duplicate dialog box, I would select the same image from both of the Destination pop-up menus but select different colors from the Channel pop-up menus. Figure 17-9, for example, displays the options required to produce the upper right example shown in Color Plate 17-2.

- **Backing up a selection:** Here's another blast from the past. In the "Saving selections" section of Chapter 9, I explained how to save particularly complicated selection outlines for later use. The Duplicate command provides yet another way to accomplish this task. It enables you to transfer a selection outline to a mask channel inside the same image or some other open image of identical size. To copy a selection outline from the marching ants mode, select the Selection option from the first Channel pop-up menu in the Duplicate dialog box. If you're in the quick mask mode, select the Mask option from the pop-up menu. Then copy the selection to the desired destination.

Add and Subtract

The Add and Subtract commands work a bit like the Custom filter discussed in Chapter 13. However, instead of multiplying brightness values by matrix numbers and calculating a sum, as the Custom filter does, these commands add and subtract the brightness values of pixels in different channels.

The Add command adds the brightness value of each pixel in the first source image to that of its corresponding pixel in the second source image. The Subtract command takes the brightness value of each pixel in the first source image and subtracts the brightness value of its corresponding pixel in a second source image. Either command then divides the sum or difference by the Scale value (from 1.000 to 2.000) and adds the Offset value (from negative to positive 255).

If equations will help, here's the equation for the Add command:

Destination brightness value = (Source 1 + Source 2) ÷ Scale + Offset

And here's the equation for the Subtract command:

Destination brightness value = (Source 1 – Source 2) ÷ Scale + Offset

But if you are sick of equations, the real deal is this: The Add command results in a destination image that is lighter than either source; the Subtract command results in a destination image that is darker than either source. If you want to darken the image further, raise the Scale value. To darken each pixel in the destination by a constant amount, which is useful when applying the Add command, enter a negative Offset value. If you want to lighten each pixel, as when applying the Subtract command, enter a positive Offset value.

Applying the Add command

The best way to demonstrate how these commands work is to offer an example. To create the effects shown in Figures 17-12 and 17-13, I began with the two images shown in Figure 17-10. The first image, Capitol Gray, is merely a grayscale composite of the image from Color Plate 17-1. To create the second image, Capitol Blur, I duplicated the yellow channel from the CMYK version of the color image (see Figure 17-3), because it does a good job of separating building and sky. I then applied the Minimum filter to enlarge the dark regions of the image by a radius of 3 pixels and applied the Gaussian Blur filter with a radius of 6.0 pixels. I next chose Image ➪ Adjust ➪ Levels (Command-L) and changed the lighter of the two Output Levels values to 140, thus uniformly darkening the image. (The Add and Subtract commands work best when neither source image contains large areas of white.) Finally, I drew in some clouds and lightning bolts with the airbrush and smudge tools.

Figure 17-10: The two source images used to create the effects shown in Figures 17-12 and 17-13.

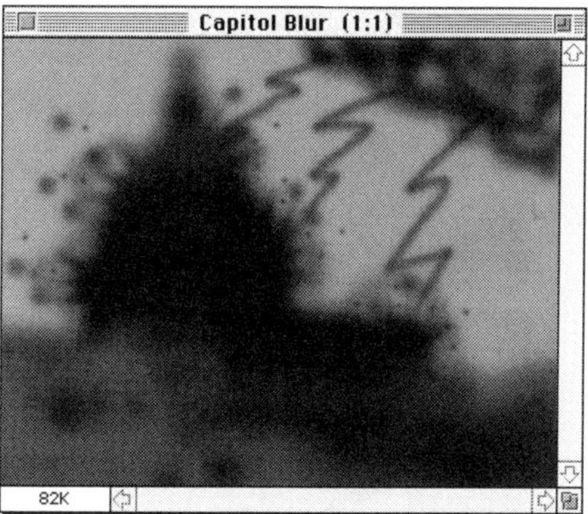

I next chose Image ➪ Calculate ➪ Add and selected Capitol Gray and Capitol Blur as the two source images, as shown in Figure 17-11. I accepted the default Scale and Offset values of 1 and 0 respectively to achieve the first example in Figure 17-12. Because the skies in both of the source images were medium gray, they added up to white in the destination image. The black areas in the second source image helped prevent the colors inside the building from becoming overly light.

Figure 17-11: The Add dialog box set to create the first example in Figure 17-12.

Figure 17-12: Two applications of the Add command on the source images from Figure 17-10, one subject to Scale and Offset values of 1 and 0 (top) and the other subject to values of 1.2 and –60 (bottom).

Unfortunately, the image I created was a bit washed out. To improve the quality and detail of the image, I reapplied the Add command, this time entering a Scale value of 1.2 to slightly downplay the brightness values and an Offset value of –60 to darken the colors uniformly. The result of this operation is the more satisfactory image shown in the second example of Figure 17-12.

Applying the Subtract command

To create the first example in Figure 17-13, I applied the Subtract command to the Capitol Gray and Capitol Blur source images, once again changing the Scale value to 1 and the Offset value to 0. This time, the sky turns pitch black because I subtracted the medium gray of the Capitol Blur image from the medium gray of the Capitol Gray image, leaving no brightness value at all. The building, however, remains a sparkling white because most of that area in the Capitol Blur image is black. Subtracting black from a color is like subtracting 0 from a number — it leaves the value unchanged.

Figure 17-13: Two applications of the Subtract command on the source images from Figure 17-10, one subject to Scale and Offset values of 1 and 0 (top) and the other subject to values of 1.2 and 60 (bottom).

The image seemed overly dark, so I lightened it by raising the Scale and Offset values. To create the second image in Figure 17-13, I upped the Scale value to 1.2, just as in the second Add example, and changed the Offset value to 60, thus adding 60 points of brightness value to each pixel. This second image is more likely to survive reproduction with all detail intact.

Difference

Like Subtract, the Difference command subtracts the brightness values in the second source from those in the first source. However, instead of treating negative values as black, as the Subtract command does, or allowing you to compensate for overly dark colors with the Scale and Offset options, Difference changes all calculations to positive values.

If the brightness value of a pixel in the first source is 20 and the brightness value of the corresponding pixel in the second source is 65, the Difference filter performs the following equation: 20 – 65 = –35. It then takes the *absolute value* of –35 (or, in layman's terms, hacks off the minus sign) to achieve a brightness value of 35. Pretty easy stuff, huh?

Any divergence between the Subtract and Difference commands becomes more noticeable on repeated applications. The top row of Figure 17-14, for example, shows the effect of applying the Subtract command (left) versus the Difference command (right). As before, I applied these commands to the Capitol Gray and Capitol Blur images from Figure 17-10.

As far as perceptible differences between the two images are concerned, the pixels that make up the bushes in the lower left corner of each image and those of the clouds along each image's right side are on the rebound in the Difference example. In effect, they became so dark that they are again lightening up. But that's about the extent of it.

Figure 17-14: Repeated applications of the Subtract (left column) and Difference (right column) commands.

In the second row of Figure 17-14, I applied the Subtract and Filter images a second time. Using the top left example in the figure as the first source and the Capitol Blur image as the second source, I achieved two very different results. When calculating the colors of the pixels in the sky, the Difference command apparently encountered sufficiently low negative values that removing the minus signs left the sky ablaze with light. Everything dark is light again.

Just for fun, the top examples in Color Plate 17-3 feature full-color versions of the bottom two images in Figure 17-14. In each case, I used the full-color Capitol Dome image from Color Plate 17-1 instead of the Capital Gray image as the first source and used the grayscale Capitol Blur as the second source. As if that weren't enough fun already, the bottom examples in Color Plate 17-3 show the same images after swapping the red and blue color channels in each. Trying to create images like these without resorting to channel operations is like trying to fly the Enterprise without computerized camera tracking and a blue screen. It simply can't be done.

Composite

The Composite dialog box, shown in Figure 17-15, looks pretty scary. The addition of the options in the Mask box is enough to send most folks scrambling for the manual. But in reality, this command is pretty straightforward. It works exactly as if you were to use a mask to select the first source image, copy the selected region, and paste it in front of the second source image.

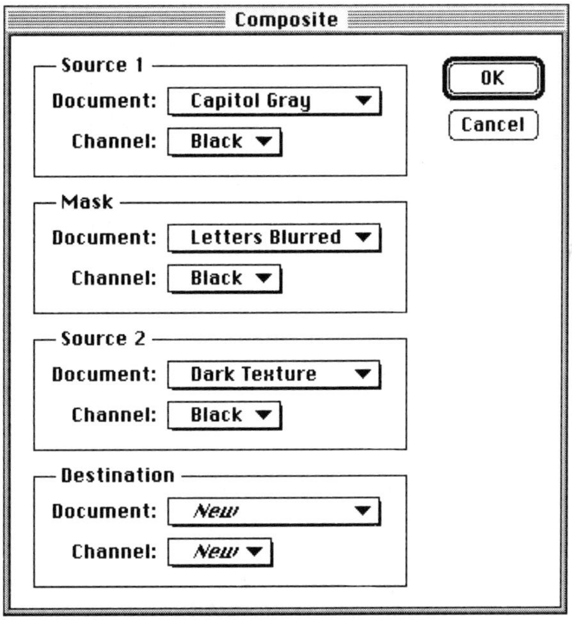

Figure 17-15: The Composite dialog box lets you combine two source images according to a selection mask.

Composite
Source 1
Document: Capitol Gray
Channel: Black
Mask
Document: Letters Blurred
Channel: Black
Source 2
Document: Dark Texture
Channel: Black
Destination
Document: *New*
Channel: *New*
OK
Cancel

Still not sure what I'm talking about? Here's a bit more information to clarify matters. The grayscale image you choose from the Document pop-up menu in the Mask section of the dialog box functions as a standard selection mask. White areas represent selected areas, black areas represent deselected areas, and gray areas represent partial selections. The first source image (called the *foreground image* in Photoshop 2.0) shows through the white regions of the mask, and the second source image (or *background image*) shows through the black regions of the mask. First and second source blend together in the gray areas.

The Channel option in the Mask box offers a Selection option. You can use a selection outline to contain the first source image, just as if you had selected the image normally. Then why not merely select the image normally and be done with it? Well, it's just a different means to achieve the same effect. If you take the time to become familiar with this method, you may find it more flexible and more convenient than standard copy-and-paste techniques. After all, the Composite command doesn't upset the contents of the Clipboard, and you can make all your adjustments from inside a single dialog box.

Again, the best way to understand the Composite command is to see it in action. To create the images in Figures 17-17 and 17-18, I used the Capitol Gray image from Figure 17-10 along with the three images shown in Figure 17-16. The two top images — Letters and Letters Blurred — serve as masks at one time or another. (I created the Letters Blurred image, incidentally, by applying the Minimum filter with a radius of 3 pixels to the Letters image and then applying Gaussian Blur with a radius of 4.0 pixels. The bottom image, Dark Texture, is a variation on the standard stucco texture that I described back in the "How to create patterns" section of Chapter 10. I darkened the texture by applying the Levels command and lowering the second Output Levels value to 100.)

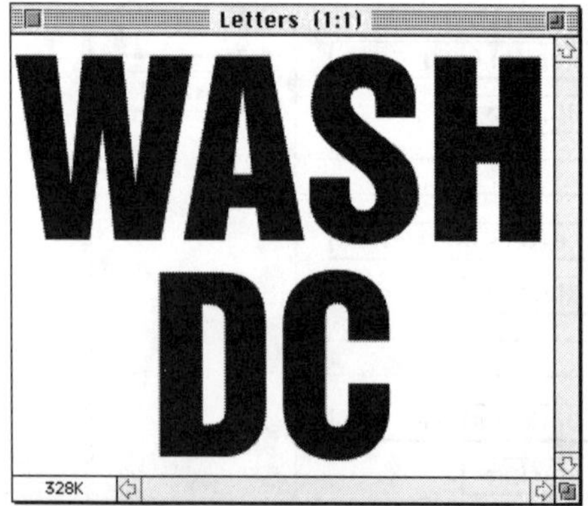

Figure 17-16: Together with the Capitol Gray image from Figure 17-10, I used these images to create Figures 17-17 and 17-18.

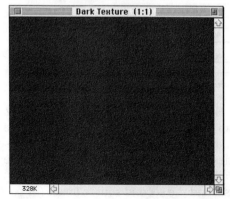

After choosing the Composite command, I specified Capitol Gray as the first source image, Letters Blurred as the mask, and Dark Texture as the second source, as shown back in Figure 17-15. The result is the first image in Figure 17-17. Notice that the stucco texture correlates to the black areas of the mask and the Capitol Gray image correlates to the white areas.

Figure 17-17: The results of applying the Capitol Gray image to the Dark Texture image using the Letters Blurred mask (top) and then applying that image to the Capitol Gray image using Letters as the mask (bottom).

To display the Capitol Gray image inside hard-edged character outlines, as in the second example of Figure 17-17, I reapplied the Composite command using the top image from the figure as the first source, the Letters image as the mask, and Capitol Gray as the second source. This time, Capitol Gray correlates to the black areas in the mask.

The letters in the second image in Figure 17-17 are interesting to look at, but difficult to read. I remedied this by lightening the letters independently of the rest of the image. To accomplish this, I first inverted the characters in the Letters image by choosing Image ➪ Map ➪ Invert. Then I darkened the characters by choosing Image ➪ Adjust ➪ Levels and changing the second Output Levels value to 80. The result appears in the first image in Figure 17-18.

Finally, I chose Image ➪ Calculate ➪ Screen and selected the second image from Figure 17-17 as the first source and the altered Letters image as the second source. The second image in Figure 17-18 shows the result.

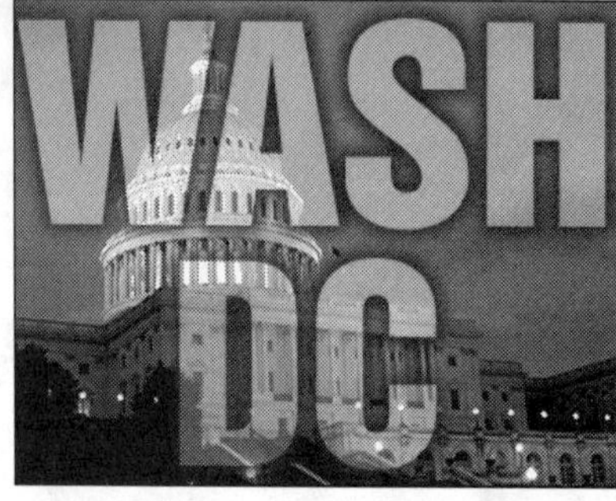

Figure 17-18: After inverting and darkening the Letters image (top), I used the Screen command to combine the letters with the second image from Figure 17-17 (bottom).

More channel madness

Are you a closet channels-head? Well, there's more information out there in the form of *Kai's Power Tips* (from Kai Krause). If you subscribe to America Online or know someone who does, you can find some remarkable applications for channel operations. While on-line, press Command-K to access America Online's key word function. Then enter *KPT* and press Return, which takes you to the HSC Software window. Double-click on the Kai's Power Tips icon and you're raring to go. Tips 1, 2, 16, 17, and 18 contain information about using Calculate commands, and you'll find many other useful nuggets as well.

As I write this, most tips haven't been updated since late 1992. But don't let that worry you. Old or not, KPT is about the best Photoshop resource out there. Short of this book, of course. I mean, come on, nothing's as good as this book. Right?

Summary

- Channels fall into three camps: planes of color in a full-color image; mask channels for editing selection outlines; and video alpha channels for masking an image overlaid onto live video.
- The composite view in a RGB, CMYK, or Lab image shows all colors in an image simultaneously.
- Grayscale images, duotones, black-and-white bitmaps, and images with indexed color contain only one color channel apiece.
- You can view a channel independently by pressing Command plus a number key. Command-1 takes you to the first channel, Command-2 takes you to the second, and so on. Press Command-0 to return to the composite view when working in the RGB, CMYK, or Lab mode.
- Use the Split Channels and Merge Channels commands to rearrange color channels in an image to produce special effects.
- Sometimes, a poor full-color scan is the fault of a single color channel. You can remedy the appearance of a channel by nudging it with the arrow keys, applying the Unsharp Mask filter, or blending the two remaining color channels.
- All channel operations under the Image ⇨ Calculate submenu except Constant and Duplicate work by combining two source images and sending the result to a destination image. Duplicate clones one source image to a destination, and Constant fills the destination image with a brightness value.
- You can apply channel operations only to images that are open and exactly equal in size.
- Use the Duplicate command to duplicate an image or to transfer data between different open image windows without upsetting the contents of the Clipboard.
- The Composite command enables you to combine images using a mask, much like selecting a portion of one image, copying it, and pasting it into another.

Part VI

Appendixes

Appendix A:
Photograph Credits

Appendix B:
Products and Vendors

Photograph Credits

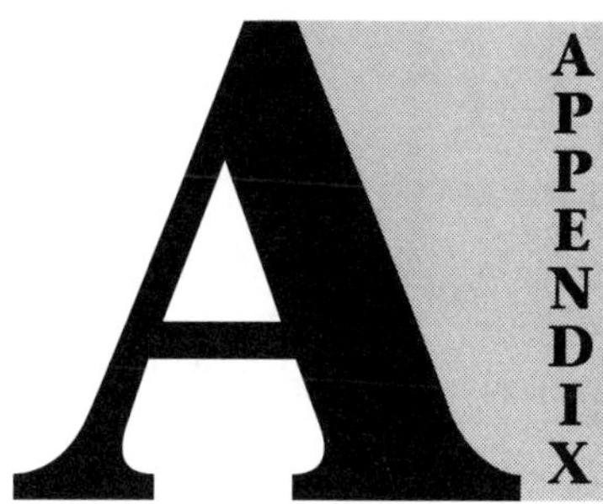

The images used in this book came from all kinds of sources. The following list cites the figure(s) or color plate in which a photograph appears. Following the figure number is the name of the photographer and the company from which the photo was licensed. In each case, the photographer holds the copyright. If the photograph comes from a CD collection, the product name appears in italics along with or instead of a photographer's name, and the company holds the copyright. If no company is listed, the photo was licensed from the photographer directly.

To all who contributed their photography, my heartfelt thanks.

Images	*Photographer/Product*	*Company*
Figures 2-13 through 2-15, 2-17, and 2-18	Russell McDougal	
Figure 2-23	Denise McClelland	
Figure 3-9	*PhotoDisc, Volume V*	21st Century Media
Figures 4-2, 4-4, 4-5, and 4-8 through 4-10	*PhotoDisc, Volume I*	21st Century Media
Figures 5-1 and 5-22	*Photo CD Snapshots*	Eastman Kodak
Figures 5-9 and 5-21	*Sampler One*	ColorBytes
Figures 5-24, 5-25, 5-27, and 5-28	Denise McClelland	
Figures 6-4 and 6-6	Denise McClelland	
Figures 6-3 and 6-7	Denise McClelland	
Figure 6-10	*PhotoDisc, Volume II*	21st Century Media
Figure 6-11, left	*Sampler One*	ColorBytes
Figure 6-11, right	Bob Barber, *Sampler One*	ColorBytes
Figure 6-13, upper left	Dennis Hallinan	FPG International
Figure 6-13, upper right	Jim Stuart	AllStock
Figure 6-13, lower left	David Joel	Tony Stone Worldwide

Images	*Photographer/Product*	*Company*
Figure 6-13, lower right	Mug Shots	The Stock Market
Figure 6-14, left		The Bettmann Archive
Figure 6-14, right		Bettmann-UPI
Color Plate 6-1	Russell McDougal	
Color Plates 6-2 and 6-3 (elements)	*PhotoDisc, Volume I*	21st Century Media
Color Plate 6-4	Denise McClelland	
Color Plate 6-5	*PhotoDisc, Volume II*	21st Century Media
Color Plate 6-6	Dan Norris, *Sampler One*	Color Bytes
Color Plate 6-7, upper left	Jon Eisberq	FPG International
Color Plate 6-7, upper right	Michael Ian Shopenn	AllStock
Color Plate 6-7, lower left	Phil Borges	Tony Stone Worldwide
Color Plate 6-7, lower right	Gerald Zanetti	The Stock Market
Color Plate 6-8, left	Blake Sell	Reuters
Color Plate 6-8, right	Phelan Ebenhack	Reuters
Color Plate 6-9, top	Mike Powell	AllSport
Color Plate 6-9, bottom	David Cannon	AllSport
Figure 7-4	Denise McClelland	
Figure 7-13	Mark Collen	
Color Plate 7-1	Mark Collen	
Figures 8-6 through 8-8, 8-26, and 8-27	Russell McDougal	
Figures 9-4, 9-6, 9-10, 9-12 through 9-14, 9-23 through 9-36, 9-46, and 9-48 through 9-56	*PhotoDisc, Volume IV*	21st Century Media
Figures 9-7 through 9-9	Russell McDougal	
Figures 9-15 and 9-42 through 9-44	*PhotoDisc, Volume IV*	21st Century Media
Figures 9-16 through 9-20	*PhotoDisc, Volume IV*	21st Century Media
Figure 9-22 (background)	*PhotoDisc, Volume IV*	21st Century Media
Figures 9-37 through 9-40	Russell McDougal	
Figures 9-60 through 9-63		The Bettmann Archive

Images	*Photographer/Product*	*Company*
Figures 10-2 through 10-5, 10-12, and 10-21	Denise McClelland	
Figures 10-6 and 10-7	Russell McDougal	
Figures 10-8 through 10-11, and 10-17 through 10-20	Michael Probst	Reuters
Figure 10-16, top	*Wraptures*	Form and Function
Figure 10-16, bottom	*Folio 1*	D'pix
Figure 11-2, 11-11 through 11-16, and 11-20 through 11-22	Carlye Calvin, *Sampler One*	ColorBytes
Figures 12-1, 12-2, 12-5 through 12-7, 12-9 through 12-16, 12-19 through 12-21, 12-25 through 12-27, 12-29, 12-30, 12-39, 12-41, 12-42, 12-44 through 12-48, 12-50 through 12-53, 12-56, 12-62, 12-63, and 12-77 through 12-80	*PhotoDisc, Volume V*	21st Century Media
Figures 12-17, 12-18, 12-31 through 12-37, and 12-43	*PhotoDisc, Volume V*	21st Century Media
Figure 12-54	Mark Collen	
Color Plates 12-1 and 12-2	*PhotoDisc, Volume V*	21st Century Media
Color Plate 12-3	Mark Collen	
Figures 13-3 through 13-31 and 13-33 through 13-41	*PhotoDisc, Volume V*	21st Century Media
Color Plates 13-1 and 13-2	*PhotoDisc, Volume V*	21st Century Media
Figures 14-7, and 14-12 through 14-14	Denise McClelland	
Figures 15-2, 15-5, 15-6, 15-24, 15-26, 15-30 through 15-32, 15-35 through 15-44, 15-46, and 15-47	Russell McDougal	
Figures 15-21 and 15-23	*PhotoDisc, Volume V*	21st Century Media
Color Plates 15-3 and 15-4	Russell McDougal	

Images	*Photographer/Product*	*Company*
Figures 16-1, 16-2, 16-4 through 16-6, 16-9, 16-11, 16-12, 16-14, and 16-18 through 16-22	*PhotoDisc, Volume V*	21st Century Media
Colors Plates 16-1 through 16-5	*PhotoDisc, Volume V*	21st Century Media
Figures 17-2 through 17-5, 17-10, 17-12 through 17-14, and 17-16 through 17-18	Carlye Calvin, *Sampler One*	ColorBytes
Colors Plates 17-1 through 17-3	Carlye Calvin, *Sampler One*	ColorBytes

Products and Vendors

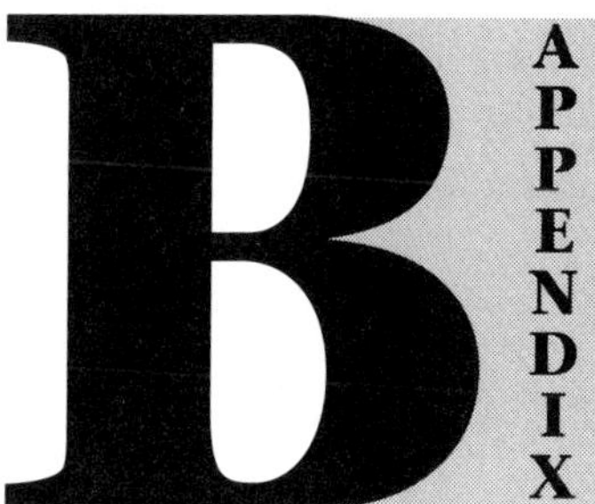

The following is a list of all the products mentioned in this book, along with vendors, prices, and phone numbers. This list is in no way intended to serve as a recommendation for any of these products; it is provided merely as a reference so you can find out more information on your own.

I've also taken the liberty of including a few products that I did not mention in the book. Some arrived on my desk after the book was finished. Nonetheless, these products relate directly to Photoshop or to some peripheral Photoshop concern, such as Photo CD, scanning, or printing.

Product	*Vendor*	*List price*	*Phone*
Alias Sketch	Alias Research	$995	416/362-9181
The Allsport Library	Allsport USA	NA	310/395-2955
Arcus flatbed scanner	Agfa	$3,950	508/658-5600
ArtZ drawing tablet	Wacom	$449	201/265-4226
Cachet	Electronics for Imaging	$595	415/286-8600
Canvas	Deneba	$399	305/596-5644
CD Stock (all four-disks)	3M	$650	612/628-6295
CD Stock (individual disks)	AllStock	$195	206/622-6262
	FPG International	$195	212/777-4210
	The Stock Market	$195	212/684-7878
	Tony Stone Worldwide	$195	312/787-7880
CD-ROM Toolkit	FWB	$79	415/474-8055
Charger DSP board	DayStar Digital	$949	404/967-2077
Charger Pro DSP board	DayStar Digital	$1,599	404/967-2077
CIS 3515 slide scanner	Barneyscan	$4,495	510/562-2480
ColorFinder	Trumatch	$85	212/351-2360
Color It	Timeworks	$300	708/559-1300

Product	Vendor	List price	Phone
ColorPrinter Software	Trumatch	$98	212/351-2360
ColorServer PDS/30	Lapis Technologies	$499	510/748-1600
ColorStudio	Fractal Design	$795	408/688-8800
ComputerEyes/Pro	Digital Vision	$400	617/329-5400
Dimensions	Adobe Systems	$199	415/961-4400
DrawingPad drawing tablet	CalComp	$395	714/821-2000
EfiColor for Photoshop	Electronics for Imaging	$199	415/286-8600
ElectricImage Animation System	Electric Image	$7,495	818/577-1627
Folio 1 Media Kit	D'pix	$300	415/664-4010
Folio 1 Print Pro CD	D'pix	$500	614/299-7192
FreeHand	Aldus	$595	206/628-2320
Gallery Effects: Classic Art 1	Aldus	$199	206/628-2320
Gallery Effects: Classic Art 2	Aldus	$99	206/628-2320
Illustrator	Adobe Systems	$595	415/961-4400
Image Assistant	Caere	$495	408/395-7000
Image Magic DSP board	Newer Technology	$995	316/685-4904
Image Magic+ DSP board	Newer Technology	$1,295	316/685-4904
Kai's Power Tools	HSC Software	$149	310/392-8441
LeafScan 35 slide scanner	Leaf Systems	$9,995	508/460-8300
Lightning Effects DSP board	Spectral Innovations	$695	408/955-0366
MacDraw Pro	Claris	$399	408/987-7000
MacPaint	Claris	$199	408/987-7000
MacRenderMan	Pixar	$695	510/236-4000
MacroMind Director	Macromedia	$1,195	415/252-2000
MacVision Color Digitizer	Koala Acquisitions	$799	408/776-8181
MediaMaker	Macromedia	$695	415/252-2000
MultiSpin 74 CD-ROM drive	NEC Technologies	$615	708/860-9500
NuMedia multimedia board	Spectral Innovations	$1,295	408/955-0366
NuVista+	TrueVision	$3,595	317/841-0332
Ofoto	Light Source	$395	415/461-8000

Product	Vendor	List price	Phone
PageMaker	Aldus	$895	206/628-2320
Paint Alchemy	Xaos Tools	$99	415/558-9831
Painter	Fractal Design	$399	408/688-8800
PassPort Producer	PassPort Designs	$495	415/726-0280
Persuasion	Aldus	$495	206/628-2320
Photo CD Access	Eastman Kodak	$40	716/724-4000
PhotoDisc Starter Disk	21st Century Media	$69	206/441-9355
PhotoDisc, Vols. III, IV-VII	21st Century Media	$395 each	206/441-9355
PhotoDisc, Volume III	21st Century Media	$295	206/441-9355
PhotoEdge	Eastman Kodak	$139	716/724-4000
Photoshop	Adobe Systems	$895	415/961-4400
PhotoSpeed*	SuperMac Technology	$3,999	408/773-4498
Photostyler	Aldus	$795	206/628-2320
PicturePress	Storm Technology	$199	415/691-6600
PicturePro	Ventura	$795	619/673-0172
Picture Publisher	Micrografx	$495	214/234-1769
Pocket Tint Chart	NAA	$175	703/648-1000
PowerPoint	Microsoft	$495	206/882-8080
Premier	Adobe Systems	$495	415/961-4400
PressLink media service	PressLink	NA	305/376-3818
Process Color Imaging Guide	Pantone	$75	201/935-5500
Process Color System Guide	Pantone	$75	201/935-5500
ProColorServer 24x PDS/30	Lapis Technologies	$699	510/748-1600
ProVideo32	RasterOps	$1,995	408/562-4200
QuarkXPress	Quark	$895	303/894-8888
Ray Dream Designer	Ray Dream	$895	415/960-0765
Remedy font	Emigre	$95	916/451-4344
Renaissance	Eastman Kodak	$695	716/724-4000
Sampler One	ColorBytes	$399	303/989-9205
SD-510 drawing tablet	Wacom	$695	201/265-4226
Shoebox	Eastman Kodak	$395	716/724-4000

Product	*Vendor*	*List price*	*Phone*
ShowPlace	Pixar	$695	510/236-4000
Sketcher	Fractal Design	$149	408/688-8800
SuperATM	Adobe Systems	$149	415/961-4400
SuperMatch 20-T monitor	SuperMac Technology	$2,999	408/773-4498
Swivel 3D Professional	Macromedia	$695	415/252-2000
Thunder/24 video board	SuperMac Technology	$2,999	408/773-4498
ThunderStorm DSP board	SuperMac Technology	$999	408/773-4498
TXM-3401E1 CD-ROM drive	Toshiba	$895	714/583-3111
Typestry	Pixar	$299	510/236-4000
UC630 flatbed scanner	Umax Technologies	$1,995	408/982-0771
VideoSpigot (NuBus)	SuperMac Technology	$449	408/773-4498
Wraptures One and Two	Form and Function	$129 each	415/664-4010

* PhotoSpeed includes everything you need to make the most of Photoshop and Kodak's Photo CD technology, including a Toshiba multi-session CD-ROM drive; software from Kodak, HSC Software, and Storm Technology; an accelerated 24-bit video board; and stock images from ColorBytes and 21st Century Media.

Index

• Numeric •

3-D graphic, 20
30-pin SIMMs, 80
32-bit addressing, 80
64-pin SIMMs, 80
72-pin SIMMs, 80

• A •

a and b color channels, 620
a channel, 527
About Photoshop command, 90
About Plug-in submenu, 397
About The Finder command, 52
About This command, 81
About This Macintosh command, 46
absolute full screen, 99
  shortcuts, 112–114
absolute value, 636
Acquire submenu, 131, 143, 153, 171
active matrix screens, 67
active window, 35
  resizing, 35
Adaptive Discrete Cosine Transform (or ADCT), 144
Add command, 630, 632–635
  applications, 632–634
  equation, 632
Add Noise command, 433
Add Noise dialog box, 430
  options, 430–431
Add Noise filter, 432, 557
adding/subtracting selections, 270–271
additive primary model, 522
Adobe Illustrator, 138
Adobe Photoshop folder, 77
Adobe Photoshop Installer, 78
Adobe Type Library, 374
Adobe Type Manager (ATM), 55, 58-60, 370
  See also ATM
  font cache, 59
Adobe Type Manager control panel, 58
AeQ (Appearance Equivalence), 176
Agence France-Presse image libraries, 190
Agfa Arcus scanners, 170
airbrush
  cursor, 97
  tool, 94, 229
Aladdin's StuffIt, 72
Alarm Clock, 31
Aldus FreeHand, EPS format, 138
Aldus Gallery Effects, 396
  folders, 77
Aldus PageMaker, 19
Aldus Photostyler, 13
alert box, 38
alert triangle, 518
algorithm, 502
alias, 34
Alias icon, 34
aligned cloning, 343
aligning channels, 625
All (Command-A) command, 390
Allsport image library, 190
alpha channels, 84, 137
alphabet, Macintosh, 27
America Online, 189, 398, 640
Amiga, 135
Andromeda Software folder, 77
Angle option box, 417
ANPA (now NAA), 539
Anti-alias PostScript option, 120
Anti-aliased
  check box, 266, 550
  option, 267
  PICT dialog box, 153
antialiasing, 138, 265, 283
Antique Photographic Frame, 551–552
Append Brushes command, 245

Apple
discontinued models, 67
Color Picker, 517
menu, 31, 33, 46, 51, 81, 90, 397
items folder, 35
option, 517
Photo Access, 183
Application icon, 34
application
memory, 44
RAM, 43–44
applications
Clipboards, 53–54
memory size requirements
Minimum size value, 45
Suggested size value, 44
multiple, managing, 48–51
starting, 43
switching, 53–55
switching between, 48
Applications menu, 33, 48
arbitrary curves, 612–615
arc, in path, 93
architectural plans, 18
arrow tool, 290, 303–305
clone a path, 304
drag a Bézier control handle, 304
drag a segment directly, 304
drag selected points, 303
selecting points, 303
arrowheads
adding to lines, 232
applying, 568–575
free-form stroke, 571–572
Arrowheads options, 570
art, poster, 18
artwork
impressionistic-type, 17
realistic, 17
(ASCII) American Standard Code for
Inform, 139
ascenders, 374
aspect ratio, 264
ATM 3.0
On or Off, 59
options, 59
Preserve, 59
printer fonts, 58
ATM 3.5, 60
author, to contact, 9
Auto Erase check box, 361
automated outline style, 377
automatic dot gain, 534
Avalon Development Group, 14
AV machines, 69, 158, 469–470

• B •

B (Brightness) value, 534
b channel, 527
Background
color icon, 98, 516
icon, 8
option, 203
Printing option
off when spooling, 201
backgrounds
application, 48
color, 98, 516
delete key, 516
painting, 361
elements, eliminating, 347–352
image, 637
printing, 50–51
processing, 50
selecting image elements from, 411–412
window, 48
backlight text, feathering, 385–386
bad channels, 626
balloon help feature, 33
banding, 557, 565
eliminate, 557–559
BBS (bulletin-board service), 189
Beep When Done option, 121
Bettmann Archive image library, 2, 190
Bézier control handles, 291, 304
Bézier paths, 291
bicubic, 118
bicubic interpolation, 118
bilinear, 118
bilinear interpolation, 118
binary counting system, 26
Binary encoding option, 139
bit, 15
bit depths, 84
Bitmap command, 534

Bitmap dialog box, 534
  options, 534–537
bitmaps, 14, 15
  image, 14, 53, 125
  type, 370–372
  vs objects, 14–15
bits, 26
Black and white (bitmap), convert grayscale to b/w, 534–539
blemishes, touching up, 345–347
Blend command, 630
Blend If pop-up menu, 585
blistered effect, 454
block filters, 438–439
Blur Center box, 422
Blur command, 416
blur cursor, 97
Blur filters, 402
Blur More command,402, 416
Blur submenu, 435
blur tool, 230
blur/sharpen tool, 94
blurring
  directional, 493
  effect, 485
  symetrical values, 481
  with edge-detection, 481
BMP (Windows Bitmap) format, 136
book
  chapter topics, 3–6
  conventions, 6–9
  icons, 8–9
  organization, 2–6
  user level, 2
Book pop-up menu, 538
Border option, 204
brightness, 524
  adjustments, 600–615
  bar, 607
  curve, 607
  graph , 607
  value transitions, 502–512
  values, 198, 478, 522
  values/shades, 198
brochures, drawing programs, 18
brush mode pop-up menu, 441
brush modes, 256–260
Brush Options, 240
Brush Options dialog box, 244
  Angle, 242
  Diameter, 241
  Hardness, 241
  Roundness, 242
  Spacing, 241
brush pressure, size disparity, 255–260
brushes
  adjusting angle, 243
  custom, 244–249
  new, 240
  shape/opacity, 239–255
Brushes palette, 237, 239–251
  cloning, 343
  finger painting, 237
  pressure, 237
buffer, 52
bulletin-board service (BBS), 189
burn cursor, 97
burn tool, 231
business graphics, 18
button, 38
Byte Order option, 147
bytes, 26

• C •

cache, 59
Caere's Image Assistant 1.1, 617
CalComp, 252
Calculate commands, 630–631
Calculate submenu, 628
Calculator, 31
Calibration Bars check box, 204
Calibration folder, 77
cameras, digital, 180
Cancel (Command-period) button, 40
Cancel button, 38
cancel cursor, 95
canvas, 162
  size, changing, 162
Canvas Size command, 162
Canvas Size dialog box, 162
Caps Lock key, 96
  cross-hair cursor, 347
  cursor, 239

Caption option, 204
capturing, Macintosh, 20
Caution icon, 8
CD-ROM Toolkit, 182
CD-ROM XA (Extended Architecture), 182
CD-ROMs
  drive, 168
    multisession, 182
    single session, 182
  images, 180–188
  memory/disk space, 26
  Photo CD images, 149–150
  standard, 182
central processing unit (CPU), 25
Centris, 69, 158, 469–470
changes, selectively undoing, 360–365
channel focusing, 626
channel operations, 628
  commands, 628–640
  dialog boxes, 629
Channel option, 638
Channel Options command, 623
channels, 617
  bad, 626
  CMYK, 620
  editing color, 617–628
  HSB, 622–625
  hue, 622
  Lab, 620
  manipulating, 617–641
  RGB, 619
  saturation, 622
  viewing, 618–622
Channels palette, 269, 618
Channels palette menu, 623
Character Masks, 380–392
character outlines, 380–381
  path tools, 390–391
characters
  converting to paths, 389–391
  customizing, 371
  Macintosh alphabet, 27
charge-coupled device (CCD), 180
check boxes, 38
choke, 427
choose vs select, 6–7
Chooser desk accessories, 51
  Scrapbook, 54
Chooser dialog box, 201
Chooser extensions, 32
Chooser window, 51
chroma keying, 137
chrominance signal, 179
CIE (Commission Internationale de l'Eclairage), 148
Claris, 143
click mouse, 28
click with a tool, 28
Clipboard, 32
  applications, 53–54
  transfer contents to Scrapbook, 54
  using, 52
Clipboard command, 116
clock speed
  CPU, 66
clone, 94, 278
Clone (Aligned) option, 342–343
Clone (Non-Aligned) option, 342–343
clone path cursor, 96
cloning
  aligned/non-aligned, 343
  from duplicate, 345
  from separate window, 342
  image elements, 341–352
  process, 342–345
  recloning, avoiding, 345
close box, 35
close path cursor, 96
closed path, 291
CMV, for central matrix value, 476
CMYK (cyan-magenta-yellow-black), 132
  editing in, 526
  channels, 620
  color mode, 83
  color model, 525–526
    colors mix, 525–526
  color separations
    printing, 213–214
  conversions, preparing, 217–218
CMYK color value option, 521
CMYK Color command, 141
collapse box, 101
color channels
  a and b, 620
  editing, 526, 617–628
  effects, 625
  options, 585–586

replacing, 627–641
swapping, 627–632
Color Formula Guide 1000, 541
Color Halftone filter, 567
color image to grayscale,, 619
color lookup table (CLUT), 120, 528
animation, 120
editing specific, 532–533
color mapping, 587–594
commands, 589
color modes, 132–135, 521–537
CMYK (cyan-magenta-yellow-black), 132
Lab (luminosity a & b), 132
RBG (red-green-blue), 132
color models, 521
color options, scanners, 168–169
Color Picker dialog box, 97, 117, 203, 221–222, 516–518
options, 517–518
Color Picker option, 117
Color Picker pop-up menu, 517
Color Table dialog box, 531
color trapping, 219–220
ColorBytes, 2, 185
ColorBytes gears image, 390
Colorfinder, 540
Colorize check box, 598, 600
ColorPrinter Software utility, 540
colors, 5
balance, 478
background, 516
bleeding, 179
controls, 92
corrections, 588
defining, 515
editing indexed, 531–539
editing specific CLUT, 532–533
effects, 587–589
exclusion sliders, 581–582
field, 517
gradual transition, 93
indexed, 528–533
mix, 525
mapping/adjusting, 587–615
moving, 499
numeric values, 521–522
pickers, 117
printers, 197
predefined, 538–541
ramp, 532
scans, improving, 625–626
scanned transparency, 170
selecting/editing, 515–521
selection marker, 517
selection methods, 538–544
separations, 116, 199
creating, 212–219
printing CMTK, 213–214
slider, 517
specifying, 516–517
trap, 219–220
Colors palette, 538, 541–542
options/elements, 541–542
Column option, 132
Column Size option box, 132
column width, 132
Command key, 35, 378
selection outlines, 270
command names, 7
Command plus a number key to switch between channels, 619
Command-dragging, type tool, 378–379
Command-Option-dragging, move selection, 280
Command-Shift-drag, selection outlines, 271
commands
About Photoshop, 90
About The Finder, 52
About This, 81
About This Macintosh, 46
Add, 632–635
Add command, 630
Add Noise, 433
All (Command-A), 390
Append Brushes, 245
Bitmap, 534
Blend, 630
Blur, 416
Blur More, 402, 416
Calculate, 630–631
Canvas Size, 162
channel operation, 628–640
Channel Options, 623
Clipboard, 116
CMYK Color, 141
color mapping, 589–595

Composite, 630, 637–639
Composite Controls, 573
Constant, 630
Control Panels, 31
Copy (Command-C), 27, 52, 54
Crop, 164
Curves (Command-M), 606–615
Custom, 476–478, 482
Cut (Command-X), 52, 390
Darker, 630
De-Interlace, 178
Decompress EPS, 140
Define Brush, 244
Define Pattern, 352
Defringe, 282
Delete Channel, 623
Deselect (Command-D), 270
Despeckle, 435
Difference, 630, 635–637
Displace, 500
Distort, 437
Duotone, 220
Duplicate, 630, 631–632
ellipsis (...), 37
Empty Trash, 34
Equalize, 590
Feather, 266, 405, 565
Fill, 546, 549
Fill Path, 550
Filter menu, 437
Find Edges, 410
Float (Command-J), 279
Function Keys, 115
General (Command-K), 115–122
Get Info, 44–46
Grow (Command-G), 271
Hide Edges (Command-H), 269, 378
Horizontal, 307
Hue/Saturation, 595–598
Image Size, 127, 159
Indexed Color, 528–530
Inverse, 270
Invert (Command-I), 589
Levels (Command-L), 601–606
Lighter, 631
Make Alias, 35
Make Path, 119, 389
Median, 436
Merge Channels, 624
Monitor Setup, 116
Motion Blur, 420
Multichannel, 152, 626
Multiply, 631
New (Command-N), 130
New Channel, 623, 628
New Folder (Command-N), 34, 41
New Window, 104
None (Command-D), 396
Open (Command-O), 39, 43, 130
Open As, 133
Page Setup, 127
Paste (Command-V), 42, 52–53, 130
Paste Controls, 371
PICT Resource, 155
Pinch, 445
Place, 139
Plug-ins, 115
Posterize, 593–598
Preferences, 115–116
previewing filter, 397
Print (Command-P), 200, 210
Printing Inks Setup, 116
Put Away, 34
Revert, 361
Save (Command-S), 41, 134, 400
Save As, 41, 134
Scratch Disks (Virtual Memory), 116
Screen, 631
Select-All (Command-A), 354
Separation Setup, 116, 217
Separation Tables, 116
Sharpen Edges, 402, 409
Show Brushes, 239
Show Info, 278
Similar, 271
Spherize, 446
Split Channels, 624
Storm JPEG Compress, 156
Stylize, 437
Subtract, 631–635
Take Snapshot, 363
Threshold (Command-T), 410, 591
transformation, 444
Trap, 219
TWAIN Select Source, 175

Undo (Command-Z), 163, 178, 253, 274, 346, 361, 373
Units, 116
Video Alpha, 623
Wind, 420
Zoom In (Command-plus), 104
Zoom Out (Command-minus), 104
commercial
image collections, 184
printer, 196
subtractive primaries, 525–526
Commission Internationale d'Eclairage (CIE)
Lab, 526–528
Commodore Amiga, 135
common I-beam cursor, 95
component video output, 179
Composite command, 630, 637–639
Composite Controls command, 573
Composite Controls dialog box, 583
options, 574–575
Composite dialog box, 637
composites, 198
image, 141
printing, 199–212
view, 618
compression
files, 72–73
formats
JPEG, 143–146, 155–158
schemes, 134
LZW (Lempel-Ziv-Welch), 136
RLE (Run-Length Encoding), 136
CompuServe, 136, 189
computer program, 13
ComputerEyes/Pro, 177
computers, 23–28
brains, 24–27
powering up, 30
sensory organs, 27–29
shopping for, 67–70
Comstock, 189
concentric pond ripples, 451
conical gradation, 447
Constant command, 630
Constrain Proportions check box, 154
Constrained Aspect Ratio check box, 264
constructing a drawing, 16
Contents radio button, 549
continuous curves, 610–612
continuous-tone images, 146, 219
Control key, 105
control panel devices (cdevs), 31
control panels, 31
Control Panels command, 31
conventions, book, 6–9
convert point
cursor, 95
tool, 290
cooperative multitasking, 42
Copy (Command-C) command, 27, 52, 54
copyright holder
editing photos, 352
corner handles, 93, 162
corner poin, 292
handles, 301
corners in paths, 93
Corrective filters, 394
CPU, 25
chips, 66
clock speed, 66
Intel chips, 66
Motorola CPU chips, 66
program requirements, 66
rating, 70
creator code, 152
credits, photography, 645–648
Crop command, 164
crop cursor, 95
crop marks, 204
Crop Marks check box, 204
crop marquee, rotating, 163–164
crop tool, 93, 162–163
cropping, 160–165
cropping a selection, 164–165
cross cursor, 95
cross-platform formats, 135–137
Cross-Reference icon, 9
crosshair cursor, 97
Caps Lock key, 347
crosshair pickup, 96
Crystal Halo effect, 438–439
Crystallize filter, 438
cumulative compression scheme, 146
cursors, 27, 94–105
airbrush, 97

blur, 97
burn, 97
cancel, 95
clone path, 96
close path, 96
common I-beam, 95
convert point, 95
crop, 95
cross, 95
crosshair, 97
crosshair pickup, 96
dodge, 97
eraser, 96
eyedropper, 96
gavel, 95
hand, 96
insert point, 95
lasso, 95
left-pointing arrow, 95
line/gradient, 96
magic eraser, 96
marquee, 95
move path, 96
paint bucket, 96
paintbrush, 97
pen, 95
pencil, 96
remove point, 95
right-pointing arrow, 95
scissors, 95, 162
select path, 96
shape by function, 27–28
Sharpen, 97
smudge, 97
stamp, 97
stamp pickup, 97
type, 95
wand, 95
watch, 97
zoom in, 96
zoom limit, 96
zoom out, 96

curved segment, 292
curves
arbitrary, 612–615
continuous, 610–612
Curves (Command-M) command, 606–615
Curves dialog box, 606
options, 606–610
cusp point, 292
cusps
creating, 298–302
smooth point, 299–300
custom brightness adjustments, 600–615
Custom button, 538
Custom Colors dialog box, 538
Custom command, 476–478, 482
Custom dialog box, 476, 478, 484
custom effects, 475–481
Custom filter, 476–478
advice, 478
embossing, 497
Custom values, applying, 481–497
Cut (Command-X) command, 52, 390

• D •

dark effects, lightening, 488–489
Darker command, 630
data
interleaving, 182
retrieving from disk, 54
DCS (Desktop Color Separation) format, 140–141
De-Interlace command, 178
De-Interlace dialog box, 178
deactivate window, 35
Decompress EPS command, 140
Default colors icon, 516
default
colors, 98
screen settings, 208
unit of measure, changing, 132
Define Brush command, 244
Define Pattern command, 352
defloat a selection, 281
Defringe command, 282
deinterlacing, 177–178
Delete Channel command, 623
Delete key, 98
background color, 516
techniques, 546
fill color, 550–554

descenders, 374
Deselect (Command-D) command, 270
Desk accessories (DAs), 31
  Alarm Clock, 31
  Calculator, 31
  key caps, 31
  Scrapbook, 31
Desktop (Command-D) button, 40
Despeckle command, 435
Despeckle filter, 436
destination, 628
Destination Channel pop-up menu, 629
Destination Document pop-up menu, 629
destination options, 628
Destructive filters, 395, 437–464
dialog box elements
  folder bar, 39
  scrolling list, 39–40
dialog box options
  alert box, 38
  button, 38
  check boxes, 38
  option box, 37
  pop-up menus, 38
  radio button, 37
dialog boxes, 37–42
  navigating, 39–42
Difference command, 630, 635–637
Difference filter, 636
diffuses, 423
diffusion dither, 120
digital
  cameras, 176, 180
    storage devices, 180
  film, 62
  imagery, 3–4
  space
    managing, 46
    measuring, 26–27
digital-signal processor (DSP), 155
digitized photograph, 168
dimmed buttons, 53
dipping, 237
directional
  blurring, 417–423
    filters, 417, 493
  sharpening, 494–495
  smudging, 420
directory windows, 35
  closing all, 35
disk icon, 34
disk space, 25
  memory, 26
  required, 66
disks
  ejecting, 34
  floppy, 25
  photos, shooting to, 176–180
  scratch, 82–83
  space, 25
Displace command, 500
Displace dialog box, 503–506
  options, 503–506
  texture effects, 506–509
Displace filter, 498
displacement
  direction, 500–501
  maps, 498
    colors, 498–499
    using, 506–512
  theory, 500–503
Displacement Maps folder, 354, 506
Display CMYK Composites option, 119
Display Color Channels in Color option, 120
Display Using System Palette option, 120
displays, video, 66–81
Dissipated filter, 400–401
Dissolve option, 391
Distance option box, 417
Distance value, 417
Distort command, 437
Distort submenu, 395
Distortion filters, 444–465
  rules, 444–445
Distortion plug-in module, 398
distributing the effect, sharpening, 405–407
Dither options, 531
dithering, 70, 85
dmap, 498
document icon, 34
documents, 34
  EPS, saving, 139–140
  raw, saving, 152–153
  selecting, key entry, 39

dodge cursor, 97
dodge tool, 231
dodge/burn tool, 94
dot gain, 216
dots per inch (dpi), 128, 196
double-click
  rubber stamp icon, 363
  zoom tool, 93
  with mouse, 28
Double-secret About Box, 90
down arrow key, 40
download, 189
Draft option, filters, 423
drag, 93
  mouse, 28
drawing, 16–17
  applications, 19
  curved segments, 296–297
  straight-sided polygon, 294–295
  programs, 15
    logos, 18
    when to use, 18–21
Drive button, 41
Drivers, 32
drives
  optical, 25
  removable hard, 25
drop shadows
  creating, 387–389
  feathered, 388–389
  hard-edged, 387
drop-launching programs, 43
duotone, 199, 220
  creating, 220–222
  printing, 220–223
  reproducing, 222–223
Duotone command, 220
Duotone Options dialog box, 220–221
Duplicate command, 630–632
  applications, 631–632
Duplicate dialog box, 629
duplication techniques, 339–365
dye-sublimation, 197
dynamic data, 61
Dynamic Sliders module, 77

• E •

Easter Eggs, 90
Eastman Kodak, 148
Easy Install dialog box, 75
edges, 402
  recognizing, 407–408
Edit menu, 42, 52, 130, 244, 373
edit tools, 227–239
  blur, 230
  dodge, 231
  images, 227–260
  sharpen, 230
  smudge, 230
edition file, 35
Edition file icon, 35
effects
  Antique Photographic Frame, 551–552
  blistered, 454
  Blurring, 485
  color, 587–589
  color channel, 625
  concentric pond ripples, 451
  Crystal Halo, 438–439
  custom, 475–481
  darkening light, 490
  embossing, 495–500
  gradient Supernova, 559–561
  homemade, 475–512
  iridescent, 415
  Larva, 561
  lightening dark, 488–489
  Make My Day at the Atomic Café, 509
  Non-1 variations, 488–492
  parallel ripples and waves, 453–457
  sharpened amorphous bubbles, 562–563
  Sharpening, 482–485
  softeneng, 405
  symmetrical, 481–488
  texture, 506–509
EFI's Cachet, 18
Eject (Command-E) button, 40
electronic typography, 55

elements
  cloning image, 341–352
  eliminating background, 347–352
  removing from images, 285–286
elliptical marquee, 93
elliptical marquee tool, 262
  Shift key, 263
Emboss dialog box, 440
  options, 440–442
Emboss filter, 236, 398, 440–442
embossing effect, 495–500
Empty Trash command, 34
emulsion, 204
Emulsion Down option, 204
Encoding option, 139
End key, 36, 40
environmental preference settings, 115
EPS (Encapsulated PostScript), 138
EPS dialog box options, 139–140
EPS document, saving, 139–140
EPS illustration, 138–139
EPS Rasterizer dialog box, 138
Equalize command, 590
eraser cursor, 96
eraser tool, 94, 361
executable program, 34
exiting folders, 40
Export Clipboard option, 121
Export submenu, 143
Exposure slider bar, 247
extended keyboard, 36
external video boards, 85–86
eyedropper cursor, 96, 378
Eyedropper option, 118
eyedropper tools, 94, 542–544, 606
  Option-click, 516

• F •

Facet filter, 438
factory default settings, 114
  restoring, 115
Fade-out option box, 248
Fade-out options, 248
Fade-out value, 249
fading/spacing, 249
feather, 264
Feather command, 266, 405, 565
Feather dialog boxes, 405
Feather Radius option box, 283
Feather Radius value, 283
feathering, 265, 283
  backlight text, 385–386
  effects, 384–386
  outward from a selection, 427–431
fields, 177

File Format pop-up menu, 133, 151
file formats, 134
  compression schemes, 134
  image, 134
  native, 135
File menu, 43, 114, 130–134
File Size check box, 127
File Size option, 159
file-swapping option, 141
files
  decompressing, 72–73
  deleting, 34
  download, 189
  Finder, 31
  object-oriented PICT, 153
  opening, 40
  Photoshop Prefs, 115
  rescuing, 34
  support, 32
  System, 31
  TIFF, 148
  virtual memory, 81
Fill command, 546, 549
Fill dialog box, 549
fill effects, creating special, 551–553
Fill Path command, 550
film recorder, 197
Filmstrip document, 141
  changing size, 142
  editing, 142
Filmstrip format, 20, 141, 143
Filter menu, 394, 396
Filter menu commands, 437

filtering
effects, dissipating, 398
techniques, 396–402
filters
Add Noise, 432, 557
basics, 393–401
block, 438–439
Blur, 402
blurring, preset, 416–417
Color Halftone, 567
Corrective, 394
create textures, 354
Crystallize, 438
Custom, 476–478
Despeckle, 436
Destructive, 395
destructive, 437–464
Difference, 636
directional blurring, 417
Displace, 498
Dissipated filter, 400–401
distortion, 444–465
Emboss, 398, 440–442
external, 396
Facet, 438
Gaussian Blur, 413–416
High Pass, 409–412
Maximum, 427
Median, 436
Minimum, 427
Mosaic, 438
Motion Blur, 417–418
noise removal, 435
Option key, 397
Pinch, 446–447
Pointillize, 434, 438
Polar Coordinates, 398
preset blurring, 416–417
previewing, 397–398
Radial Blur, 447, 558
Ripple, 453–457
Sharpen Edges, 402
sharpening, 409–413
Spherize, 446–447
Twirl, 447–450
Unsharp, 408
Unsharp Mask, 170, 402–409, 425, 435, 562
Wave, 453–457
Wind, 418–420, 425, 558
Zigzag, 451
Filters menu, 79
Find (Command-F) command, 77
Find Again (Command-G) command, 77
Find # option box, 539
Find Edges command, 410
Finder desktop, 31–36, 173
Alias icon, 34
Apple menu, 33
Application icon, 34
Applications menu, 33
directory window, 35
Disk icon, 34
Document icon, 34
Edition file, 35
folder, 34
Hard drive icon, 33
Help menu, 33
menu bar, 32
run programs, 43–44
System Folder icon, 34
Trash icon, 34
Finger Painting check box, 237
fit-in-window view, 102
flatbed scanners, 170
Flip submenu, 307
Float (Command-J) command, 279
floating, clone a selection, 279
floating palette elements
collapse box, 101
palette menu, 101
palette options, 100
floating palettes, 92, 100–102
floating selections, 281
overlaying, 573–586
Floating slider bar, 581
floppy, 25
floppy disk, 25
See also disks, floppy
mounted, 34
Focoltone color standards, 539
folder bar, 39

Folder icon, 34
folders, 34
  Adobe Photoshop, 77
  Aldus Gallery Effects, 77
  Andromeda Software, 77
  Apple Menu Items, 35
  Calibration, 77
  Displacement Maps, 354, 506
  exiting, 40
  Kai's Power Tools, 77
  opening, 40
  Optional Extensions, 77
  parent, 39
  Plug-ins, 77, 115, 354, 396
  selecting, key entry, 39
  Separation Sources, 77
  System, 29–36
  Third Party Filters, 77
font metrics, 60
fonts, 55
  multiple master, 60
  PostScript printer, 57–60
  PostScript screen, 55–57
  TrueType, 60–61
  using, 55–61
Force Quit button, 76
force quit installation, 76
foreground application, 48
foreground color, 97
  switched, 383
foreground color icon, 97, 516
foreground image, 637
Foreign File Access, 183
formats
  cross-platform, 135–137
  documents, 34
  Filmstrip, 141
formatting type, 374–376
Fractal Design, 14
Fractal Design ColorStudio 1.5, 617
Fractal Design Painter, 255
Fractal Design's ColorStudio, 13
fragmentation of memory, 46–48
fragmented memory, 46–48
frame, loading into image window, 177
free-form
  outlines, 265–266
  polygons, creating, 232
From Saved option, 363
From Snapshot option, 363
full intensity, 398
full screen
  with menu bar, 99
  without menu bar, 99
full-color, 169
  scanner, 169
  video board, 84
Function Key Preferences dialog box, 108, 114
function key shortcuts, establishing, 108–109
Function Keys command, 115
functions
  undo, 360–361
fuzziness, 582–586
fuzziness range, 582
FWB's CD-ROM Toolkit, 184

• G •

gamma, 116
Gamma control panel, 214
gamma value, 602
Gaussian blur filter, 413–416
Gaussian distribution curve, 405
Gaussian radio button, 354
gavel cursor, 95
GCR (gray component replacement) option, 218
General (Command-K) command, 115–122
General environmental preferences, 116
General Preferences dialog box, 116, 517
geometric selection outlines, 263–265
geometric shape tools, 265
Get Info command, 44–46
GIF (Graphics Interchange Format), 136
gigabyte, 26
glass refraction, 506
gradations, 93, 553
  as masks, 565–568
  brush modes, 558–559
  randomized, 559–561
gradient, 93
  bubbles, 561–562
  fills, 553–567

lines, 249
Supernova effect, 559–561
tool, 93, 530, 553–558
tool options, 554–556
Gradient Tool Options dialog box, 554, 567
graphics, business, 18
gray value, 84
gray scale scan, 14
grayscale color model, 533–534
Grow (Command-G) command, 271
Gutter value, 132

• H •

hairs, retouching, 346
halftone cells, 197, 205–206
halftone screen, changing, 205–208
Halftone Screens dialog box, 206–207
Angle option, 207
Auto, 208
Frequency option, 207
ink, 207
Load/Save, 208
Shape, 207
Use Accurate screens, 207
Use Printer's Default Screens, 208
Use Same Shape for All Inks, 207
halftoning, 205
halos, removing, 282–288
HAM (Hold and Modify) format, 135
hand cursor, 96
hand tool, 93
accessing, 105
Hand tool icon, 102
hand-held scanner, 169–170
handles, 291
corner Point, 301
deleting from smooth points, 298
hard disk space, 66–67
hard drive, virtual memory, 82
Hard drive icon, 33
hard-wired memory, 25
hardware
issues, 65–67
requirements, 65–70
Photo CD, 182–188
Height pop-up menu, 132
Help menu, 33
Hide Edges (Command-H) command, 269, 378
hierarchical submenu, 37. *See also* submenus
High Pass filter, 409–412
highlights, option box contents, 37
Home key, 36, 40
homemade effects, 475–512
Horizontal command, 307
horizontal displacement, 500
HSB color model, 523–524
HSB color value option, 521
HSC Software window, 640
HSL color model, 523–524
hue channel, 622
Hue slider bar, 598
hue/saturation, adjusting, 598–600
Hue/Saturation command, 595–598
hues, 523
changing, 598–600
Huffman encoding, 139

• I •

icons, 33
Alias, 34
Application, 34
Background color, 98, 516
book, 8–9
default colors, 516
Disk, 34
Document, 34
Edition file, 35
Folder, 34
Foreground color, 97, 516
Hand tool, 102
Hard drive, 33
Kai's Power Tips (America Online), 640
LaserWriter, 51
Magic Wand, 267
Marquee tool, 264
Orientation icon, 202
Paint bucket, 546
shortcuts for, 112
Switch colors, 98, 516
System Folder, 34, 58

Tool, 92
Trash, 34
Zoom tool, 93
IFF (Interchange File Format) format, 135–136
illustration programs, 15
Illustrator EPS file, 20
image
collections, unlimited reproduction rights, 185–186
compression, QuickTime, 62
editor, 14
elements
busy background, 411–412
deleting, 347–352
file, 20
image file formats, 134–158
BMP (Windows Bitmap), 136
DCS (Desktop Color Separation) format, 140–141
Filmstrip format, 143
GIF (Graphics Interchange Format), 136
HAM (Hold and Modify) format, 135–136
IFF (Interchange File Format) format, 135–136
interapplication formats, 137–143
JPEG, 143–146
LZW (Lempel-Ziv-Welch), 136
MacPaint, 143
mainstream, 143–158
oddball, 148–153
PCX format, 136
Photo CD, 148–149
PICT (Macintosh Picture), 146–147
PIXAR workstations, 137
PixelPaint, 143
RLE (Run-Length Encoding), 136
Scitex CT (Continuous Tone), 137
TGA (Targa), 137
TIFF (Tag Image File Format), 147–148
image libraries
Agence France-Presse, 190
Allsport image library, 190
Bettmann Archive, 190
Reuters, 190
Image menu, 127, 159
image setter, 128
image size, 126
Image Size command, 127, 159
image window, 91, 177, 372
creating, 130, 130–134
manipulating type, 378–379
image window controls, 92
image window tools
airbrush tool, 94
blur/sharpen tool, 94
crop tool, 93
dodge/burn tool, 94
elliptical marquee, 93
eraser tool, 94
eyedropper tool, 94
gradient tool, 93
hand tool, 93
lasso, 93
line tool, 94
magic wand, 93
paintbrush tool, 94
paint bucket tool, 93
pen tool, 93
pencil tool, 94
rubber stamp tool, 94
smudge tool, 94
type tool, 93
zoom tool, 93
imageable area, 202
images, 14, 380
amount of sharpening, 403–404
animation, 19
bitmapped, 53
blurring, 413–416
CD-ROM, 180–188
cloning elements, 341–352
colorizing, 600–610
commercial collections, 184
composite, 141
converting color to grayscale, 533
creating, 383
creating for the screen, 530–531
creating new, 131–132
degradation, 157
displacing onto itself, 509–512
displacing pixels, 498–505
display, 84
editing, 227–260

editing application, 13
editing theory, 14–18
elements from busy background, 411–412
fading, 565–566
file formats, 134–158
filling portions, 545–552
fundamentals, 125–165
isolating comples, 272
measuring, 85
multiple-column, 132
number pixels, 126
on-line libraries, 189–193
on-screen size, 132
open/save, 130–134
opening existing, 133–134
original, 20
painting, 227–260
photograph credits, 645–648
pixels, 125
printed resolution, 127–128
printing, 195–223
printing composite, 200
printing versus screen display, 127–131
QuickTime, 62–64
reflecting in a spoon, 445–447
removing element, 285–286
removing halos, 282–288
repeating patterns from scanned, 356–360
resample, 158–160
resampling, 159–161
resized, reverting, 364
resizing, 158–159
resolution, 126
retouching, 4
reverting to last saved, 361–364
saving raw, 152
saving to disk, 134
scan line, 177
scanned
opening, 131
retouching, 345–347
scanning, 168–176
selecting, 380–381
selecting part, 380–392
sharpening, 402–409
size, 126
size during importing, 128
storing in memory, 363
touch up areas, 600
transfer between channels, 627
work, 125–130
zooming appearance, 425
imagesetter, 197
ImageStudio, 14
imaging system, 180
impressionistic-type artwork, 17
Include Halftone Screen option, 140
Include Transfer Function option, 140
Indexed Color command, 528–530
Indexed Color dialog box, 528
options, 528–530
indexed colors, editing, 531–539
indexing, 528
Industrial Light and Magic, 14
Info dialog box, 44, 534
Info palette, 264, 278
INITs, 31
ink-jet and thermal-wax printers, 197
inks, priortizing, 221
insert point cursor, 95
insert point tool, 290
installation, force quit, 76
Intel chips, PC, 66
interapplication formats, 137–143
EPS illustration, 138–139
interface, customizing, 114–122
interior point, 295
interlaced video, 178
Interleaved Order option, 152
interpolate, 117
interpolation
scanners, 170
Interpolation option, 117, 204
interpolations
softened, 118
softened with enhanced contrast, 118
Inverse command, 270
Invert (Command-I) command, 378, 589
iridescent effects, 415
ISO 9660 File Access, 183

• J •

Joint Photographic Experts Group(JPEG), 62, 155
- compressed images, 530
  - ompression scheme, 62
- compression format, 147–148
- EPS format, 140
  - format, 134, 143–146
- modules, 157
  - utility, 191

• K •

Kai's Power Tips icon, 640
Kai's Power Tools, 396
folder, 77
kerning, 378
key caps, 31
keyboard
- extended, 36
- mouse, 28
- scrolling, 105
- select documents, 39
- select folders, 39
- techniques, 27

keyboard equivalents, 27
keyboard shortcuts, 105–108
- absolute full screen mode, 112–114
- Command plus a number key, 619
- Command-D (Desktop), 40
- Command-down arrow, 40
- Command-E (Eject), 40
- Command-F (Filer), 396
- Command-I (Get Info), 44
- Command-N (New Folder), 41
- Command-N (New), 130
- Command-O (Open), 39, 40, 130
- Command-Option-Esc, 76
- Command-Option-F, 396
- Command-period, 50, 397
- Command-period (Cancel), 40
- Command-plus (Zoom-in), 104
- Command-S (Save), 41
- command-spacebar, 103
- Command-up arrow, 40
- Command-Y (Put Away), 34
- Option-click (Resize window), 35
- Option-drag, 263
- suggestions, 110–112

keyboard/mouse. *See* mouse/keyboard
keys
- Caps Lock, 96
- Command, 35, 378
- Control, 105
- Delete, 98
- down arrow, 40
- End, 36, 40
- Home, 36, 40
- Option, 34, 97
- Page Down, 36, 40
- Page Up, 36, 40
- Return, 40
- Tab, 38, 100
- up arrow, 40

keystroke aliases, 112
keyword search functions
- download thumbnail images, 190

kilobyte, 26
Knight-Ridder news service, 190
Knoll Software screen, 90
Kodak Photo CD, 62, 181–184
Kurta, 252

• L •

Lab, 132
- anatomy, 527
- channels, 620
- color mode, 83, 148
- olor model, 526–528
- using, 528

Lab Color option, 149
Lab color value option, 521
Lab mode, test, 527
Labels check box, 204
landscape setting, 202
Lapis Technologies, 86
Larger Print Area check box, 202
Largest Unused Block value, 46
Larva Effect, 561
laser printer, 196
Laserwriter dialog box
- Copies, 210
- Cover Page, 211
- Destination, 211

Encoding, 212
Pages, 211
paper, 202
Paper Source, 211
Print, 211
Print In, 211
Print Selected Area, 211
Reduce or Enlarge option, 202
LaserWriter dialog box options, 210–212
LaserWriter icon, 51
LaserWriter Options dialog box, 202
Background option, 203
Border option, 204
Caption option, 204
Emulsion Down option, 204
Interpolation, 204
Negative option, 204
orientation, 202
Printer Effects, 203
Registration Marks option, 204
Screens option, 203
Transfer option, 203
LaserWriter Page Setup dialog box, 202, 206, 209
LaserWriter SC series, 50
lasso, 93
lasso cursor, 95, 378
Lasso Options dialog box, 265
lasso tool, 262
Option key, 266
launching a program, 43
leading, 374
left-pointing arrow, 95
Lens Flare filter, 251
Lens Type options, 250
Levels (Command-L) command, 601–606
Levels dialog box, 601
options, 601–606
libraries, on-line image, 189–193
light effects, darkening, 490
Light Source, 18
Lighter command, 631
lightness, 524
limitcheck errors, 139
line spacing, 374
line tool, 94, 232–235
line/gradient cursor, 96
linear gradation, 555
lines
drawing perpendicular, 234–236
drawing straight, 232–235
fading/spacing, 249
pressure-sensitive tablets, 252
pressure-sensitive, undoing, 253
tapered, 248
lines per inch, or lpi, 207
list, scrolling through, 40
locked files, deleting, 34
logic board, 25
logos, 18
drawing programs, 18
lossless compression scheme, 136
lossy compression routines, 136
Lumena, 14
Luminence 19
Luminosity, 524
luminosity, 132, 521, 527
Luxo, Jr, 137
LZW (Lempel-Ziv-Welch), 136
LZW Compression option, 147

• M •

Mac icon, 30
Mac Plus, 66
Mac SE machine, 66
Macintosh alphabet, 27
Macintosh design scheme, 18
Macintosh screen, capturing, 20
MacPaint, 143
MacPaint format, 143
macro utility, 109
QuicKeys, 110
ResEdit, 109
sequences, 110
Tempo, 110
using, 109–115
MacroMind Director program, 73
Macworld page, 176
Macworld Photoshop 2.5 Bible, 2
magic eraser, 94
magic eraser cursor, 96
magic eraser tool, 362
magic wand, 93

Magic wand icon, 267
Magic Wand Options dialog box, 271
magic wand tolerance, 267–269
magic wand tool, 262
  clicking midtones maintains a higher range, 268
  creating a contiguous selection, 268
  selecting brightness ranges, 269
  selecting from a single channel, 269
mainstream formats, 143–158
Make Alias command, 35
Make My Day at the Atomic Café effect, 509
Make Path command, 119, 389
map, 209
marching ants, 93, 98, 262
marching ants mode, 98
marquee, 93, 262
marquee cursor, 95
Marquee tool icon, 264
mask channel, 275, 281
  selection to, 275–276
mask controls, 92
math, rendering, 17
matrix options, 490
matrix value (MV), 478
  changing, 496
  manipulating, 488–492
Maximum filter, 427
Median command, 436
Median filter, 436
megabyte (MB), 26
megahertz (MHz), measure clock speed, 66
memory, 25
  application, 44
  disk space, 26
  fragmentation, 46–48
  fragmented, 46–48
  program requirements, 79–83
  SIMMs (single in-line memory), 80
  uninterrupted, 47–48
  virtual, 81–83
memory size requirements
  Minimum size value, 45
  Preferred size value, 45
  Suggested size value, 44
menu bar, 32
menus, 37
Merge Channels command, 624
Merge Channels dialog box, 624
Microsoft Micrografx Picture Publisher, 13
midtones, 116, 602
Minimum dialog box, 427
Minimum filter, 427
Minimum size value, applications, 45
minutes:seconds:frames, 142
misregistration, 219
Mode pop-up menu, 132, 624
models, YCC color, 148
modes
  absolute full screen, 99
  brush, 256–260
  color, 132–135, 521–537
  marching ants, 98
  multichannel, 626–627
  Overlay, 575–579
  quick mask, 98
  standard, 98
  standard window, 98
Modes menu, 522, 623
moiré patterns, 128, 207
monitor calibration, 116, 214–216
monitor movement values, 278–280
monitor resolution, 87
Monitor Setup command, 116
Monitor Setup dialog box, 214
  Ambient light, 216
  Gamma, 215
  Monitor, 214
  Phosphors, 215
  White Point, 215
monitor standards, 129–130
monitors, zupgrading, 87
Monochrome (black and white), 168
Mosaic filters, 438
mosaic tiles, 125
motherboard, 25
Motion Blur command, 420
Motion Blur filter, 417–418
motion lines, smudge tool, 421
Motorola CPU chips, 66
mounted floppy disk, 34

mouse
  click, 28
  click on object, 28
  click with a tool, 28
  double-click, 28
  drag with a tool, 28
  keyboard, 28
  move, 28
  press and hold, 28
  quadruple-clicks, 28
  techniques, 27–28
  terminology, 28
  triple-clicks, 28
mouse button, perpendicular lines, 234
mouse/keyboard
  Command-dragging, 378–379
  Command-Option-drag, 379
  Command-Option-dragging, 280
  Command-Shift-drag, 271
  Option-arrowing, 279
  Option-click, 345, 346, 516
  Option-click and click, 346
  Option-drag, 263, 362
  Option-dragging, 279
  Shift-click, 264, 270
  Shift-drag, 378
move path cursor, 96
multi-session CD-ROM drive, 182
Multichannel command, 152, 626
Multichannel Mode, 626–627
multichannel techniques, using, 626–627
MultiFinder file, 42
multiple applications, 48–51
multiple channels, editing, 623
multiple master fonts, 60
multiple-column images, 132
Multiply command, 631
multitasking, 42

• N •

native formats, 34, 135
navigation buttons, 40–41
Nearest Neighbor interpolation, 118
Negative option, 204
negative value, Offset option box, 490
neighboring pixel (NP), 478
New (Command-N) command, 130
New Brush dialog box, 241
New Channel command, 623, 628
New dialog box, 131, 132, 138
New Folder command, 34, 41
New Window command, 104
news services, 190
Newspaper Association of America color standards, 540
noise, 430
  adding, 430–435
  chunky, 434–445
  factors, 430–437
  removal filters, 435
  removing, 435–437
  variations, 432
Noise submenu, 430
Non-1 variations, 488–492
non-aligned cloning, 343
Non-interleaved Order option, 152
non-PostScript printer, 60
None (Command-D) command, 396
Note icon, 8
NTSC (National Television Standards Committee), 178
NuBus adapter card, 85
NuBus boards, 177
NuBus slot, 158
NuBus video boards, 85
numeric color values, 521–522
NuVista+, 177

• O •

object-oriented, drawing programs, 15
object-oriented PICT file, 153
objects, 15
objects vs bitmaps, 14–15
OCR (optical character recognition), 168
oddball formats, 148–153
Offset option box, negative value, 490
Offset value, 476, 488, 490, 632
offsets, extreme, 490–493
Ofoto, 18, 175–177
  capabilities, 176
  Version 2.0, 175–177
OK button, 38

on-line image libraries, 189–193
on-screen image size, 132
one-pass scanners, 169
opacity brush, 239–255
Opacity option box, 549
Opacity slider bar, 247, 343, 398, 441
Open (Command-O) button, 40
Open (Command-O) command, 39, 43, 130
Open As command, 133
Open dialog box, 39, 133, 505
open-ended, 294
open/save, images, 130–134
opening, folders, 40
operating system, 29
Operations Tip icon, 8
opposite order
  quit applications, 48
optical drives, 25
optical size, 60
option box, 37
Option key, 34, 97
  filters, 397
  lasso tool, 266
  magic eraser tool, 362
option names, 7
Option-arrowing, clone a selection, 279
Option-click
  cloning, 345
  rubber stamp tool, 346
Option-clicking, 28
  blur/sharpen tool, 232
Option-drag, 263
  magic eraser tool, 362
Option-dragging, 279
  clone a selection, 279
  crop tool, 163
Optional Extensions folder, 77
options, 37
Options button, 38
options dialog box, 151–152
Orientation icon, 202
orientation option, 202
outline fonts, 55
Outline option, 376
output device, 196
Overlay modes, 575–579
Overprint Colors button, 222
Overprint Colors dialog box, 222

• P •

Page Down key, 36, 40
Page Setup command, 127
Page Setup options, 210
Page Up key, 36, 40
page-description language, 197
page-layout programs, 19
pages
  setting up, 202–205
  printing, 210
paint tool basics, 227–239
paint bucket cursor, 96
Paint bucket icon, 546
Paint Bucket Options dialog box, 546
  options, 546–547
paint bucket tool, 93, 546–547
paint tools, 229–230
  airbrush, 229
  paintbrush, 229
  pencil, 229
paintbrush cursors, 97
paintbrush tool, 27, 94, 229
painting
  background color, 361
  images, 227–260
  limitations, 16
  smudge tool, 236–240
painting programs, 14, 15–16
Palette menu, 101, 240
Palette options, 100
palettes
  Brushes, 239–246
  Channels, 269
  Channels palette, 618
  Colors, 538, 541–542
  floating, 100–102
  Info, 264, 278
Pantone, 539
Pantone color standard, 540–544
Pantone Process, 541
paper, 202
paper positives, 170
parallel ripples and waves, 453–457
parent folder, 39
passive matrix LCD screen, 67
Paste (Command-V) command, 42, 52–53, 130

Paste Controls command, 371
Paste Controls dialog box
 options, 574–575
Path Tolerance option, 119
path tools
 character outlines, 390-391
 draw a selection, 289
paths, 262, 288–290
 adding/deleting points, 305–306
 characters, converting from, 389–391
 converting to selection, 290
 fill with color, 550
 how work, 289–290
 reshaping existing, 302–307
Paths palette
 Arrow tool, 290
 convert point tool, 290
 insert point tool, 290
 pen tool, 93, 290
 saving, 290
 remove point tool, 290
 tools, 290–291
Paths palette menu, 389, 550
Paths palette tools, 290–291
Pattern (Aligned) option, 352, 389
Pattern (Non-aligned) option, 354
pattern options, 352–354
patterns
 applying repeating, 352–360
 continuous, 354–360
 creating, 354–360
 repeating, 20–21, 352–360
 repeating from scanned images, 356–360
 stucco, 507
PC
 Intel chips, 66
 Paintbrush, 136
PCX format, 136
PDS (processor direct slot)., 85–86
PDS boards, 177
PDS video board, 83
pen cursor, 95
pen tool, 93, 262, 290
 drawing curved segments, 296–297
 drawing with, 291–301
 reshaping existing paths, 302
 straight-sided polygon, 294–295
 test-driving, 294–295
pencil, 229
pencil cursor, 96
pencil tool, 94
 erasing, 361
perpendicular line
 drawing, 234–236
Personal LaserWriter LS, 50
Photo CD
 QuickTime, 62–64
 Slide Show Viewer utility, 63
 software requirements, 183–184
Photo CD format, 148–149
PhotoCD Options dialog box, 149
PhotoDisc, 2, 185
photograph
 digitized, 168
 scanned, 19
photograph credits, 645–648
photographs/computer images, 167–168
PhotoMac, 14
photos
 scanned, 17
 shooting to disks, 176–180
 touching up scanned, 345–347
 to disk, 176–180
Photoshop, 13
 bitmapped images, 53
 cursor shape, 27–28
 Deluxe on CD-ROM, 71
 disks, contents, 71–73
 explanation, 1–2
 inside, 89
 installing, 71–78
 scenarios, 19–21
 version 1, 71
 Version 2.5, 71–73
 when to use, 17–18
Photoshop 2.0
 blend tool, 554
 brush modes, 256
 channels, editing, 618
 color models, 523
 Custom brushes file, 244
 icon, 8
 image file format, 135
 installation, 78

Opacity/Pressure options, accessing, 248
paint tools, 229
Pressure option, 239
printer fonts, 57
rubber stamp tool, 344–363
select path cursor, 96
switch colors, 517
Photoshop 2.0/2.1
environmental preference settings, 115
Photoshop 2.5
Assorted brushes file, 244
brush modes, 256–259
channels, editing, 618
clone path cursor, 96
color models file format, 523
custom brushes, adjusting, 245–246
default colors icon, 98
Distortion plug-in module, 398
Dodge tool, 231
floating palettes, 100
gavel cursor, 95
gradient lines, 249
hidden splash screens, 90
image file format, 135
installation
fine-tuning, 76–77
Installer utility, 75
installing, 75–77
keystroke aliases, 112
pressure sensitive options, 254
printer fonts, 58
rubber stamp tool, 344–363
Separation Tables command, 116
switch colors icon, 98
Photoshop Deluxe Edition, 185
Photoshop desktop, 89–101
elements, 91–92
floating palettes, 92
Image window, 91
toolbox, 92
Photoshop Prefs file, 115
PICT (Macintosh Picture), 146–147
drawing, rendering, 153–154
elements, importing, 153–155
File Options dialog box, 528
resource, startup screens, 150
Resource command, 155
Resource option, 150
resources, lifting, 154–155
PicturePress
program, 155
Selective compression, 156
Thumbnails and captions, 157
utility, 156–157
Pinch command, 445
Pinch dialog box, 446
Pinch filter, 446–447
pix-map, 15
PIXAR workstations, 137
Pixel Resources, 143
PixelPaint format, 143
PixelPaint Professional 3.0, 143
pixels, 14, 17
displacing in image, 498–505
editing individual, 537
images, 125
lighten/darken, 94
number in image, 126
resolution, 16
pixels per inch, 126
Place command, 139
plate, 199
plug-in modules, 79
scanners, 171–177
plug-ins, 79
Plug-ins command, 115
Plug-ins folder, 77, 115, 354, 396
PlusTek's ScanPlus, 169
Pointillize filter, 434, 438
points, 55, 131, 290
adding/deleting, 305–306
converting, 306–307
defining, 292
Polar Coordinates filter, 398
polygons, drawing, 266
pop-up menus, 38
portrait setting, 202
positive values, 494
poster art, 18
Posterize command, 593–598
PostScript, 197
background printing, 50
fonts, 370
screen fonts, installing, 55–57

PowerBooks, 67
preference settings, 114
Preferences commands, 115–116
Preferences submenu, 114, 222, 396
Preferred size value, 45
Premier Filmstrip, 141–143
Premier program, 20
preset blurring filters, 416–417
PressLink, 189
Pressure slider bar, 236, 247
pressure-sensitive
  drawing table, tapered lines, 248
  lines, undo, 253
  options, 254
  tablets, lines, 252
preview box, 91
Preview button, 154
Preview option, 139
previewing commands, 397
primary colors, 522
Primary pop-up menu, 82
Print (Command-P) command, 200, 210
printable shades formula, 207
printed resolution
  determining, 127–128
printer calibration, 216–217
printer drivers, 200
Printer Effects check boxes, 203
Printer Effects option, 203
printer fonts, 55
  ATM 3.0, 58
  installing PostScript, 57–60
  Photoshop 2.0, 57
  Photoshop 2.5, 58
  System 6, 57
  System 7.0, 57
  System 7.1, 57
printer pixels, 196
printer port, 201
printer spooling, 198
printers, 196
  choosing, 200–201
printing
  CMYK color separations, 213–214
  composites, 199–212
  duotone, tritone, or quadtone, 222
  images, 195–223
  in background, 50–51
  non-PostScript printer, 60
  pages, 210–214
  printing, 220–223
  understanding terminology, 196–199
Printing Inks Setup command, 116
Printing Inks Setup dialog box, 216
Printing Links Setup dialog box options
  Dot Gain, 216
  Gray Balance, 217
  Ink Colors, 216
  Use Dot Gain for Grayscale Images, 217
printing vs screen display, 127–131
PrintMonitor program, 198
Pro Photo CD Mastering system, 188
Process Color Imaging Guide, 541
process colors, 540
processor, film, 197
product designs, 18
products, mentioned in book, 649–652
program, installing, 71–78
program requirements
  CPU, 66
  disk space, 66
  memory needs, 79–83
  RAM, 66
  software, 70–71
  video display, 66–70
programs
  page-layout, 19
  painting, 15–16
  PicturePress, 155
  PrintMonitor, 198
  QuickDraw, 70
  running from Finder desktop, 43
  SuperATM, 60–62
  TeachText, 77
  working with, 42–54
Progress window, 50
proof, 199
Proofing, 199
prospective monitor, 129
protected-mode multitasking, 42
publish and subscribe feature, 35
Put Away command, 34

• Q •

Quadra, 69, 158, 469–470
quadtone, 199, 220
  printing, 222
Quality option, 423
quantization matrix, 144
QuarkXPress, 19, 140–141
quick mask, 98
quick mask method, 399
quick mask mode, 98
  create text, 378
  Gaussian blur, 414
  softening edges, 428
QuickDraw, 198
QuickDraw program, 70
QuicKeys macro utility program, 110
QuickTime
  image compression, 62
  movie editing application, 141–143
  Photo CD, 62–64
  state of, 61–62
  still images, 62–64
  using, 61–64

• R •

Radial Blur dialog box, 422, 558
Radial Blur filter, 447, 558
radial gradation, 555
radio button, 37
Radius option box, 405, 413
RAM, 25, 30
  adding, 79–80
  allocating, 81
  application, 44
  assigning application, 43–44
  program requirements, 66
  uninterrupted, 47–48
  VRAM (video RAM), 84
random-access memory (RAM), 25
randomizing selections, 433
RasterOps MediaTime, 177
raw document, 151
  opening, 151–152
  saving, 152–153
raw materials, aquiring, 167–193
Raw Options dialog box
  Channels, 151
  File Creator, 152
  File Type, 152
  Guess, 151
  Header, 151, 152
  Height, 151
  Interleaved Order option, 152
  Non-interleaved Order, 152
  Retain Header When Saving, 151
  Save Image In, 152
  Swap, 151
  Width, 151
read-only memory (ROM), 25
realistic artwork, 17
recloning, avoiding, 345
rectangular marquee, 93
Rectangular Marquee Options dialog box, 264
rectangular marquee tool, 262, 352
rectangular tool, Shift key, 263
Red, green, and blue light mix, 522
Reduce or Enlarge option, 128, 202
Reduce or Enlarge option box, 159
Reduce or Enlarge value, 128
reference window, creating, 104
Registration Marks option, 204
removable media devices, 25
remove point cursor, 95
remove point tool, 290
renders (or rasterizes), 138
repeating patterns
  applying, 352–360
  scanned images, 356–360
resampling, 158–160
  images, 159–161
resampling/cropping methods, 158–165
ResEdit, 109
resizing, 158
  images, 159–160
  vs resampling, 158–160
resolution, 126
  monitor, 87
  pixel size, 16
  printed, 127–128
  resizing/resampling, 159

Resolution option, 128, 160
Resolution option box, 127, 159
resolution options, 16
Resolution value, 128, 160
resolutions, 170
resource forks, 155
resources, 31
Restore Windows option, 121
retouch hairs, 346
Return key, 40
Reuters, 2
Reuters image library, 190, 347
reversion, 360
reversion limitations, 364
reversion techniques, 339–365
Revert command, 361
Revert option in, 363
reverting, resized images, 364
RGB
  channels, 619
  color model, 522–523
  color value option, 521
  video, 84
ribbed structures, drawing, 235
right-pointing arrow, 95
Ripple dialog box, 453
  options, 453–457
Ripple filter, 453–457
RLE (Run-Length Encoding), 136
ROM, 25, 30
  chips, updating, 29
ROM software licensing, 29
ROM-based data, 29
root directory, 76
rotoscoping, 142
rubber stamp, 339
Rubber Stamp Options dialog box, 343
  settings, 340–341
rubber stamp tool, 94, 339–341
  reverting, 363
rubylith, 98
Ruler Units pop-up menu, 132
running a program, 43

• S •

S (Saturation) value, 534
S-Video output, 179
Saturation, 524
saturation channel, 622
saturation levels
  changing, 599
Saturation option, 599
Save (Command-S) command, 41, 134, 400
Save Alpha Channels option, 147
Save As command, 41, 134
Save dialog box, 41, 134
Save Preview Icons options, 121
saved images, reverting, 361–364
Scale option, 476, 488
Scale option box, 487
Scale value, 478
scan line, 177
scan line fields, 177
scanned
  image, repeating pattern, 356–360
  photo, touching up, 345–347
  photos, 17
  transparency, colors, 170
scanner, 168
  models, 169–170
scanner dialog box
  brightness and contrast, 172
  color mode, 171
scanner dialog box options, 171–172
  resolution, 171
  brightness and contrast, 172
  cropping boundary, 173
scanners
  color options, 168–169
  flatbed, 170
  Full-color, 169
  Grayscale, 168
  hand-held, 169–170
  interpolation, 170
  Monochrome (black and white), 168
  plug-in modules, 171–177
  sheet-fed, 169–170
  slide, 170
  slide or transparency, 170

scanning
  TWAIN, 174–175
  artifacts, 172
  images, 168–176
  software, 171–177
scissors cursor, 95, 162
Scitex CT (Continuous Tone) format, 137
Scitex image-processors, 137
Scrapbook, 31, 54
Scratch Disk Preferences dialog box, 82
scratch disks, 82–83
Scratch Disks (Virtual Memory) command, 116
scratch-and-doodle techniques, 142
screen, changing halftone, 205–208
Screen command, 631
screen fonts, 55
  installing, 55–57
    System 6, 56, 61
    System 7.0, 56, 61
    System 7.1, 56, 61
screen frequency, 206
Screen resolution, 129–132
screen sizes, 129–130
screen-capture utility, 155
Screens option, 203
scroll arrow, 36
scroll bars, 36
scroll box, 36
scrolling with keyboard, 105
scrolling list, 39–40
  using, 39–40
SCSI port, video input device, 177
Secondary pop-up menu, 82
secret features, 90
segments, 291
  defining, 292
  drawing curved, 296–297
  Shift-click, 292
select, 262
Select ⇨ All (Command-A) command, 354
Select menu, 269–271, 303
select path cursor, 96
select vs choose, 6–7
selection
  comverting path to, 290
  drawing with path tools, 289
  feathering outward from, 427–431
  mask channel, 275–276
  previewing, 278
  softening, 427–430
selection outlines, 262
  adding to, 270
  antialiasing, 283
  automated adjustments, 269–270
  changes, 269–272
  Command-Shift-drag, 271
  feathering, 283
  geometric, 263–265
  intersecting, 271
  moving, 280
  softening, 283–288
  stroking, 569
  subtracting, 270
  tools, 262
selection tools, 263–269
  adding/subtracting, 270–271
  antialiasing, 265
  constraining the aspect ratio, 264
  constraining to square or circle, 263
  drawing feathered selections, 264
  drawing out from the center, 263
  drawing polygons, 266
  feathering, 265
  selecting a single-pixel line, 264
  sizing the marquee numerically, 264
selections
  cloning, 278–279
  coloring, 545–586
  command to add to, 271–278
  floating, overlaying, 573–586
  monitor movemen values, 278–280
  move/duplicate, 277–283
  precision movements, 278
  randomizing, 433
  saving, 274–276
  work, 262–286
selective reversion functions, 361
Separation Setup command, 116, 217
Separation Setup dialog box, 217
  Black Generation, 218
  Black Ink Limit, 218
  Separation Type, 218
  Total Ink Limit, 218
  UCA Amount, 218

Separation Setup dialog box options, 218
Separation Sources folder, 77
Separation Tables command, 116
sequences, macro utility, 110
Service bureau, 196
shades, 198
Shadow option, 376
shaft of light, 407
Sharpen cursor, 97
Sharpen Edges command, 402, 409
Sharpen Edges filter, 402
sharpen tool, 230
sharpened amorphous bubbles effect, 562–563
sharpening
  directional, 494–495
  distributing the effect, 405–407
  specifying amount, 403–404
Sharpening effect, 482–485
sharpening filters
  preset, 409–413
sharpening, recognizing edges, 407–408
sheet-fed scanner, 169–170
Shift key
  blur/sharpen tools, 233
  draw straight lines, 232
  elliptical tool, 263
  perpendicular lines, 234
  rectangular tool, 263
  ribbed structures, 235
Shift-click
  segments, 292
  selection outline, 270
Shift-clicking to form polygons, 232
Shift-dragging, 28
Short Pantone Names option, 121
shortcuts, 27, 105–114
  absolute full screen mode, 112–114
  icons, 112
  suggestions, 110
Show Brushes command, 239
Show Info command, 278
Show Previews & Sliders check box, 397
side bearing, 374
Similar command, 271
SIMMs (single in-line memory modules, 80
single-session CD ROM drive, 182
size box, 35
Size pop-up menu, 374
Slide or transparency scanners, 170
slide scanner, 170
slider triangles, 517
Smooth button, 613
smooth point, 290, 292
  cusp, 299–300
smooth points, 297
  handles, deleting, 298
smudge cursor, 97
smudge tool, 94, 230
  motion lines, 421
  painting, 236–240
  smears colors, 236
smudging, directional, 420
snapshot, 363
  reverting from, 363
softening effects, 405
software
  issues, 70–71
  requirements, 65–70
  scanning, 171–177
  system, using, 29–36
software requirements, 183
source, 628
Source Channel pop-up menu, 629
Source Document pop-up menu, 629
source manager, TWAIN, 174–177
Source options, 628
space, measuring digital, 26–27
Spacing value, 249
sparkles/comets, creating, 250–252
special effects, 4–5
  See also effects
  creating, 551–553
  gradually, 567–586
  Photoshop, 18
Spherize command, 446
Spherize filter, 446
splash screens, 89
  hidden, 90
Split Channels command, 624
spooling, 198
spooling definition, 201
spot colors, 540
spread, 427
stamp cursor, 97
stamp pickup cursor, 97

standard bit depths, 84
standard mode, 98
standard window, 98
standard window mode, 98
start-up disk, 83
starting a program, 43
Startup Disk control panel, 30
startup screens, 150
static image window, 104
stock photo agencies, 186–193
Storm JPEG advantages, 156–157
Storm JPEG Compress command, 156
Storm JPEG Compress dialog box
  functions, 156–157
  options, 156–157
Storm JPEG compression, 155–158
Storm Technology, 155
straight line, drawing, 232–235
straight segment, 292
straight-sided polygon, drawing, 294–295
strokes, applying, 568–572
stucco pattern, 507
Style check boxes, 375
StyleWriter, 50
Stylize commands, 437
Stylize submenu, 398, 438
stylus, 252
submenus, 37
Subtract command, 631, 632–635
  applying, 635–641
  equation, 632
subtractive color model, 525
subtractive primaries, 525–526
suitcase, 56
SuperATM program, 60–62
SuperMatch monitor, 87
support files, 32
surface texture
  scanning, 20
switch colors icon, 98, 516
switching, 48
switching between applications, 48
symetrical values
  blurring with edge-detection, 481
  sharpening, 481–488
symmetrical effects, 481–488
SyQuest cartridges, 25, 82
System 6
  Drive button, 41
  Finder, limitations, 32
  fonts, installing, 56
  MultiFinder file, 42
  printer fonts, 57
  screen fonts, installing, 61
System 6.0.7
  Quick Time, 61
System 7
  Alias icon, 34
  Applications menu, 33
  background printing, 50–51
  balloon help feature, 33
  fonts, installing, 56, 61
  memory values, 45
  memory with Photoshop, 79
  multiple programs, 42
  program requirements, 70
  printer fonts, 57
  system files, optional, 32
System 7 icon, 9
System 7.1
  fonts, installing, 56, 61
  Memory Requirements, 44
  printer fonts, 57
system extensions, 31, 183–184
System file, 31
system file extensions
  Apple Photo Access, 183
  Foreign File Access, 183
  ISO 9660 File Access, 183
System Folder, 29–36
  Finder desktop, 31
  System file, 31
System Folder icon, 34, 58
system software, 29
  anatomy, 30–32
  Chooser extensions, 32
  control panel devices (cdevs), 31
  Desk accessories (DAs), 31
  drivers, 32
  elements, 36–42
  optional elements, 31–32
  organization, 29–32
  scrapbook, 54
  screen fonts, installing, 57
  support files, 32

system extensions, 31
using, 29–36
system software elements
dialog box, 37
dialog box options, 37–38
menus, 37
submenus, 37
System Software value, 46

• T •

Tab key, 38
hide toolbox, 100
Take Snapshot command, 363
tapered lines, 248
TeachText program, 77
Tempo macro utility program, 110
terminology, mouse, 28
text
characters, moving, 378
effects, 369–392
Feathering effects, 384–386
feathering to backlight, 385–386
TEXT code, 133
text-entry box, 373
text-only, 139
texture collections, 356
texture effects, 506–509
TGA (Targa) format, 137
The Hue/Saturation dialog box, 596
options, 596–598
Thermal-wax printers, 197
Thick-liquid Droplet, creating, 450
Third Party Filters folder, 77
Threshold (Command-T) command, 410, 591
Threshold value, 407
Thunder/24, 87
ThunderStorm, 158–159
TIFF (Tag Image File Format), 147–148
TIFF Options dialog box, 147
Tile radio button, 506
Time Arts, 14
time code, minutes:seconds:frames, 142
Tin Toy, 137
tints, 198
title bar, 35
To Background radio button, 249
toggle (switch), blur/sharpen tool, 232
tolerance, 268
Tolerance option box, 267
Tolerance value, 267
tool icons, 92
tool techniques, 232–239
toolbox, 92
Tab key to hide, 100
toolbox controls, 97–100
absolute full screen, 99
background color, 98
default colors, 98
foreground color, 97
full screen with menu bar, 99
marching ants, 98
quick mask, 98
standard window, 98
switch colors, 98
tools, 92–94
burn, 231
changing operation, 114
elliptical marquee, 262
eraser, 361
eyedropper, 542–544, 606
geometric shape, 265
gradient, 553–558
increase performance, 94
lasso, 262
magic eraser, 362
magic wand, 262
paint bucket, 546–547
Paths palette, 290–291
pen, 262
rectangular marquee, 262, 352
rubber stamp, 339–341, 363
selection, 263–269
selection outline, 262
type, 263, 372–380
zoom, 103–104
touch up areas, colorized image, 600
touching up blemishes, 345–347
Toyo color standards, 539
Traditional (72.27 points/inch) radio button, 131
traditional undo functions, 360–361
transfer curve, 209

transfer function, 209–210
  specifying, 209–210
Transfer Functions dialog box, 209, 221
  Ink controls, 210
  Load/Save, 210
  Override Printer's Default Functions, 210
  Percentage option boxes, 210
transfer graph, 209
Transfer option, 203
transformation commands, 444
transformation mode, 95
Transfunction Function dialog box
  transfer graph, 209
trap, color, 219–220
Trap command, 219
Trap dialog box, 219
Trash icon, 34
tritone, 220
  printing, 222
tritones (three inks), 199
TrueType fonts, 60–61, 370
TrueVision, 137
Trumatch, 539
Trumatch color standard, 540
TWAIN
  scanning, 174–175
  source manager, 174–177
TWAIN plug-in module, 173–175
TWAIN Select Source command, 175
Twirl dialog box, 448
Twirl filter, 447–450
twirling spirals, 447–450
type
  advantages in painting program, 371–372
  as a selection, 371
  basics, 369–379
  bitmapped, 370–372
  entering/editing, 373
  filling with image, 380
  formatting, 374–376
  manipulating in image window, 378–379
  painting program, 370
  painting raised, 383–392
type code, 133
  view/alter, 134
Type Dialog box, 378
Type pop-up menu, 220
type size, 55
type style, 55
type tool, 93, 263, 372–380
Type Tool dialog box, 53, 93, 95, 372, 373, 374
  Alignment, 376
  Anti-aliased, 376
  font, 374
  formatting options, 374–376
  Leading, 374
  Shadow, 376
  Size, 374
  Spacing, 374
  Style, 375

• U •

UCR (under color removal) option, 218
Umax, 171
under color addition, 218
Underlying slide, 583
Undo (Command-Z) command, 163, 178, 253, 274, 346, 361, 373
undo functions, 360–361
undoing
  changes selectively, 360–365
Uniform, 529
uninterrupted memory, 46
Units command, 116
unlimited reproduction rights, 185
Unsharp filter, 408
Unsharp Mask dialog box, 403
  options, 403
Unsharp Mask filter, 170, 402–409, 425, 435, 562
up-arrow key, 40
upload, 189
Use Diffusion Dither option, 120
Use Video LUT Animation option, 120
Using extreme offsets, 490–493
utilities, 31
  PicturePress, 156–157
  screen-capture, 155

• V •

values
  applying custom, 481–497
  blurring with edge-detection, 481
  numeric color, 521–522
  symmetrical, 481–488
variable-size font file, 60
vector-based, drawing programs, 15
vendors, products in book, 649–652
Ventura PicturePro, 13
Version 2.5.1, 7, 41, 42, 121, 133, 140, 150, 289, 363, 534
version numbers, 7–8
vertical displacement, 500
Video Alpha command, 623
video boards
  external, 85–86
  NuBus, 85
  PDS (processor direct slot), 85–86
video capabilities, 83–88
video capture, 177–179
video card, 83
  technology, 83–85
  upgrading, 87
video display
  program requirements, 66–81
video input device
  SCSI port, 177
video mask, 623
video source, 177, 178–182
Video Toaster, 135
video-input boards, 177
video-input device, 177–179
video-input devices, 177
VideoSpigot, 177
View menu, 35
view size, 102
  changes, 103
virtual memory, 81–83
  file, temporary, 66
  hard drive, 82
  operation, 81–82
  scratch disks, 82–83
  SyQuest cartridge, 82
  temporary file, 81
vocabulary, 6
VRAM (video RAM), 84

• W •

Wacom, 252
Wacom pressure-sensitive tablet, 20
wand cursor, 95
watch cursor, 97
Wave filter, 50, 453–457
Width and Height values, 160
Width option, 151
Wind command, 420
Wind dialog box, 418, 558
Wind filter, 418–420, 425, 558
window elements
  close box, 35
  extended keyboard, 36
  scroll arrow, 36
  scroll bars, 36
  scroll box, 36
  size box, 35
  title bar, 35
  zoom box, 35
Window menu, 278, 541
windows
  active, 35
    resizing, 35
  background, 48
  changing size, 104
  Chooser, 51
  deactivate, 35
  directory, 35
    closing all, 35
  image, 91
  image, 372
  inactive
    moving, 35
  parts, 35–36
  Progress, 50
  reference, creating, 104
  scrolling inside, 105–110
  static image, 104
Windows icon, 8
Windows NT (New Technology), 42
Wondrous Iridescent Effect, 415

• X •

XA drives, 182
Xaos Tools, 396
xerography, 142

• Y •

YCC color model, 148

• Z •

Zigzag dialog box, 451
  options, 451
Zigzag filter, 451
zoom box, 35
Zoom In (Command-plus) command, 104
zoom in cursor, 96
zoom limit cursor, 96
Zoom option, 558
Zoom Out (Command-minus) command, 104
zoom out cursor, 96
zoom ratio, 102, 129
zoom tool, 93
zoom tool icon, 93

Notes

Notes

Notes

Notes

Order Form

Order Center: (800) 762-2974 (8 a.m.-5 p.m., PST, weekdays) or (415) 312-0600

For Fastest Service: Photocopy This Order Form and FAX it to : (415) 358-1260

Quantity	ISBN	Title	Price	Total

Shipping & Handling Charges

Subtotal	U.S.	Canada & International	International Air Mail
Up to $20.00	Add $3.00	Add $4.00	Add $10.00
$20.01-40.00	$4.00	$5.00	$20.00
$40.01-60.00	$5.00	$6.00	$25.00
$60.01-80.00	$6.00	$8.00	$35.00
Over $80.00	$7.00	$10.00	$50.00

In U.S. and Canada, shipping is UPS ground or equivalent.
For Rush shipping call (800) 762-2974.

Subtotal ____________

CA residents add applicable sales tax ____________

IN residents add 5% sales tax ____________

Canadian residents add 7% GST tax ____________

Shipping ____________

TOTAL ____________

Ship to:

Name ____

Company ____

Address ____

City/State/Zip ____

Daytime Phone ____

Payment: ❑ Check to IDG Books (US Funds Only) ❑ Visa ❑ MasterCard ❑ American Express

Card # ____________________ Exp. ________ Signature ____________________

Please send this order form to: IDG Books, 155 Bovet Road, San Mateo, CA 94402.
Allow up to 3 weeks for delivery. Thank you!

BOBMW93

IDG BOOKS WORLDWIDE REGISTRATION CARD

RETURN THIS
REGISTRATION CARD
FOR FREE CATALOG

Title of this book: Macworld Photoshop 2.5 Bible

My overall rating of this book: ❑ Very good [1] ❑ Good [2] ❑ Satisfactory [3] ❑ Fair [4] ❑ Poor [5]

How I first heard about this book:

❑ Found in bookstore; name: [6] ❑ Book review: [7]

❑ Advertisement: [8] ❑ Catalog: [9]

❑ Word of mouth; heard about book from friend, co-worker, etc.: [10] ❑ Other: [11]

What I liked most about this book:

What I would change, add, delete, etc., in future editions of this book:

Other comments:

Number of computer books I purchase in a year: ❑ 1 [12] ❑ 2-5 [13] ❑ 6-10 [14] ❑ More than 10 [15]

I would characterize my computer skills as: ❑ Beginner [16] ❑ Intermediate [17] ❑ Advanced [18] ❑ Professional [19]

I use ❑ DOS [20] ❑ Windows [21] ❑ OS/2 [22] ❑ Unix [23] ❑ Macintosh [24] ❑ Other: [25] ______ (please specify)

I would be interested in new books on the following subjects:
(please check all that apply, and use the spaces provided to identify specific software)

❑ Word processing: [26] ❑ Spreadsheets: [27]

❑ Data bases: [28] ❑ Desktop publishing: [29]

❑ File Utilities: [30] ❑ Money management: [31]

❑ Networking: [32] ❑ Programming languages: [33]

❑ Other: [34]

I use a PC at (please check all that apply): ❑ home [35] ❑ work [36] ❑ school [37] ❑ other: [38] ______

The disks I prefer to use are ❑ 5.25 [39] ❑ 3.5 [40] ❑ other: [41] ______

I have a CD ROM: ❑ yes [42] ❑ no [43]

I plan to buy or upgrade computer hardware this year: ❑ yes [44] ❑ no [45]

I plan to buy or upgrade computer software this year: ❑ yes [46] ❑ no [47]

Name: Business title: [48] Type of Business: [49]

Address (❑ home [50] ❑ work [51]/Company name:)

Street/Suite#

City [52]/State [53]/Zipcode [54]: Country [55]

❑ **I liked this book!** You may quote me by name in future IDG Books Worldwide promotional materials.

My daytime phone number is ______

IDG BOOKS
THE WORLD OF COMPUTER KNOWLEDGE

❑ YES!

Please keep me informed about IDG's World of Computer Knowledge. Send me the latest IDG Books catalog.

NO POSTAGE NECESSARY IF MAILED IN THE UNITED STATES

BUSINESS REPLY MAIL

FIRST CLASS MAIL PERMIT NO. 2605 SAN MATEO, CALIFORNIA

IDG Books Worldwide
155 Bovet Road Suite 310
San Mateo CA 94402-9833